Framing Youth

Ten Myths
About the Next Generation

Mike A. Males

Common Courage Press   Monroe, Maine

Library of Congress Cataloging-in-Publication Data
Males, Mike A.
Framing youth : ten myths about the next generation / Mike A. Males.
p.   cm.
Includes bibliographical references and index.
ISBN 1-56751-149-X (cloth). -- ISBN 1-156751-148-1 (pbk.)
1. Teenagers--United States--Social conditions. 2. Youth--United States--Social
conditions. 3. Teenagers--United States--Public opinion. 4. Youth--United States--
Public opinion. 5. Conflict of generations--United States. 6. Social problems--
United States.
I. Title
HQ796.M2577 1998
305.235'0973--dc21   98-49506
CIP

Common Courage Press
P.O. Box 702
Monroe ME 04951

www.commoncouragepress.com

207-525-0900
Fax: 207-525-3068
E-mail: orders-info@commoncouragepress.com

Acknowledgments

This book is dedicated to my mother, Ruth Males, who taught me skepticism of things official and is definitely not the source of my hostility against grownups. (That happened when my skepticism of things official encountered the Oklahoma City public schools of the Fifties, then Vietnam.) Thanks especially to Robin Templeton of Pacific News Service and *The Beat Within*, and Lori Nelson of the National Conference for Communities and Justice, for reading the drafts and rendering tons of valuable commentary from their ironic acumen and practical work. No one except me can be blamed for what is to follow.

Mike A. Males
Irvine, California

mmales@earthlink.net

October 1998

Contents

Introduction

Myth:
Today's Youth Are America's Worst Generation Ever

Flanked by three past presidents and bipartisan luminaries in a bombed-out north Philadelphia neighborhood one fine April Sunday, President Clinton keynoted the official abandonment of America's impoverished youth.

Volunteers, not "more government," will be called on mentor the impoverished young to become "good citizens," Clinton said at the 1997 President's Summit for America's Future. Moderate Republican Colin Powell and liberal Democrat Bill Bradley, White House prospects both, echoed that private initiatives must help kids, not more taxes and Big Government.

Some might say that private initiative combined with vanishing government, the Washington-aided business and industrial flight which devastated the economy of north Philadelphia and left inner cities charred wastelands of silent factories and broken neighborhoods, had done quite enough already. As sociologist William Julius Wilson pointed out in *When Work Disappears*, half the inner city job loss and subsequent growth of severely impoverished, primarily black populations could be traced to private abandonment:

> In the twenty-year period from 1967 to 1987, Philadelphia lost 64 percent of its manufacturing jobs; Chicago lost 60 percent; New York City, 58 percent; Detroit, 51 percent. In absolute numbers, these percentages represent the loss of 160,000 jobs in Philadelphia, 326,000 in Chicago, 520,000—over half a million—in New York, and 108,000 in Detroit.[1]

"You've got to go to work or be in school, you've got to pay your taxes and—oh, yes—you have to serve your community to make it a better place," Clinton lectured from his stadium microphone to youths living amid the rubble.

The Big Government deplored by Clinton and Republicans was perking along fine, still the vital solution to the problems of Americans who count. Powell did not call for an end to the $250 billion defense budget or offer to rely on private donors to equip the next march on Baghdad. Clinton did not announce that the $400 billion Social Security and Medicare programs would be slashed and volunteers recruited to care for seniors. Bradley did not suggest cutting the yearly $200 billion in economically purposeless "big government" subsidies and tax breaks to business.[2]

All insinuated that the Aid to Families with Dependent Children program, costing about $20 billion per year and slated for shredding under bipartisan welfare reform, was a big cause of social malaise. Yet no one called for the nation's wealthiest 5 percent of homeowners to be "good citizens" by giving up their $30 billion in annual federal "welfare" subsidies doled out under home mortgage interest tax deductions.[3]

The assemblage did not visit the inner-city schools they recommended. Nor did they entreat lawmakers to force rich suburban districts to yield funds to their upgrading. Jonathan Kozol did both, citing the industry-abandoned city of Camden, New Jersey, a 10-minute drive across the Ben Franklin Bridge.

Camden is America's post-industrial national monument. Its devastation has to be seen to understand the particular cruelty that is post-Reagan America. Looming, vacant factories backdrop mile after mile of once-prosperous working-class blocks now chock-full of falling-down row houses. If Camden were a ghost town, abandoned, it would be tolerable. But the city of no jobs, no newspaper, no grocery store, no lodging save a burned-out hulk, is inhabited by 100,000 people— and growing. Average age by census count is 23, though the visitor could be excused for thinking from visual assessment it couldn't be more than 12.

Camden teachers told Kozol they did "not have books for half the students in their classes." Tiles fell from splotched ceilings. The high school had no lunchroom. The lab had no equipment. The typing room had no computers. In the nation's third richest state, spending on Camden students, 98 percent black and Latino, averaged half that of nearby suburban schools.[4]

Before departing the Volunteer Summit, Clinton and other dignitaries made it clear who they blamed for the lamentable social conditions of America's young:

> The president, First Lady Hillary Rodham Clinton, Vice President Al Gore and his wife Tipper, helped paint over black, green and red graffiti—including the names of local gangs—with tan paint.[5]

None of Clinton's 1997 Summiteers answered the question posed by Paul Goodman 40 years ago in *Growing Up Absurd* to a gubernatorial call for volunteers and programs to lure New York City's youth of 1955 away from gangs: "Does the governor seriously think he can offer a good community that warrants equal loyalty?"[6]

A Democratic president, Republican chieftains, a full spectrum of liberals, an academic and business establishment, allied in self-aggrandizement. "The forces of organized greed," Franklin Roosevelt lambasted their like back in an era when presidents exhorted the young to fight back.[7]

Not today. Imperious moral tone blared over the burned-out shell of inner Philadelphia and its shattered neighborhoods, boarded storefronts, vacant factories, vanished jobs, crumbling schools and segregation enforced more stringently by 1990s mercantilism than 1950s Bull-Connor cattle prods. Even Kozol, relentlessly optimistic since Jim Crow days that America's goodness would finally overcome its "savage inequalities," sounds weary: "I have never lived through a time as cold as this in the United States," he concluded in *Amazing Grace*. "I don't know what can change this."[8] What, then, is there to be hopeful about as America approaches the new millennium?

Plenty, it turns out. But not due to the attitudes or policies of those at the upper ends of America's age and power scales.

The Superpredators Are...White Adults?

When America's elders screw up big time, expect them to trash the younger generation with a vengeance. Such happened during the Depression, after a decade of economic and personal indulgence combined with puritanical Prohibition rhetoric wrecked American economy and society. Such is happening in the 1990s, largely for the same reasons. Today, national leaders skilfully meld racism and fear of the young into a potent political crusade that menaces the fabric of American society in new and complex ways.

Americans are becoming aware that we are evolving toward a nation without a racial majority in the next half-century. No other industrial culture has faced this challenge. The initial phase involves abject lying about the young, the leading edge of the diverse tomorrow. But that is not the whole story. The rapidly deteriorating behavior of American grownups (particularly aging Baby Boomers) in both personal and social realms has led to a crisis of adulthood in which youth is the target of displaced anxiety and fury.

"For the past decade," historians Neil Howe and Bill Strauss wrote in *13th Gen: Abort, Retry, Ignore, Fail?*,

> 13ers ["Generation Xers"] have been bombarded with study after story after column about how bad they supposedly are. Americans in their teens and twenties, we are told, are consumed with violence, selfishness, greed, bad work habits, and civic apathy. Turn on the TV, and it's hard to see a bad-news-for-America story—from crime to welfare to consumerism—in which young bodies and faces don't show up prominently in the footage.[9]

Howe and Strauss's excellent 1993 cultural history provides pages of vitriol by elder America on the young people *it raised*—including many statements which are not just pejorative excess, but bizarrely shallow. Do Allan Bloom and his followers seriously regard the snobby name-calling against the younger generation in *The Closing of the American Mind* an example of seasoned intellect? Can it be that columnist Ellen Goodman and fellow liberals, whose 40–50-something generation set rocketing records for lavish personal consumption, really puzzle over where their kids get consumerist values? Do the mass of professors and teachers blasting the stupidity of today's students realize Baby Boom kids sported lower test scores? Did former New York Mayor David Dinkins and the legions of grownups who wonder "who taught our children to hate so thoroughly and mercilessly" ever visit a hospital emergency room to appraise the numbers of battered kids and drug-addicted parents of the over-30 generation?

No, indeed. From the most august of authorities and media, we routinely hear cliched lies such as the following: yesterday's kids ran in halls and shoplifted; today's kids gun and slaughter. The press headlines recent school shootings in Pearl, West Paducah, Jonesboro, Edinboro, Springfield, which killed a total of 11 youths over an eight-month period. None of the anguished commentary on these school tragedies mentioned that is the average number of children murdered by their parents in *two days* of domestic violence in the United States. In a society in which Simi Valley, Daly City, Riverside (California), Weston (West Virginia), Kerrville (Texas)—a few examples of many communities where multiple killings of children (totalling 16 dead in these cases) by parents recently occurred—were as well-known to the public and deplored by officials as Jonesboro or Springfield, what we call "youth violence" would be better understood. We are further from that understanding in 1998 than ever.

True, the average teenager of the mid-1990s is 0.00025 times more likely to commit murder than the average teen of the 1950s. A small proportion of young people display worse rates of violence, primarily murder and robbery. Most of these are directly traceable to rapidly deteriorating urban conditions. Homicide has risen among a fraction of impoverished youth living in inner-city moonscapes, but not middle- or upper-class kids. Today, 1,999 of 2,000 youths will not commit murder at any time during their adolescence. Normally, a society would characterize its young people by the vast majority who are not murderous.

If we did, there would be generous things to say. As a group, today's American youth are less criminal than those of the 1970s or 1980s. The decline in serious youth crime has occurred while major crime among their parents, the 30–40-agers, has risen sharply. By a wide variety of measures, kids today act more maturely than kids of the past and more responsibly than adults today.

In the mid-1990s, 12–19 year-olds comprise:

- 14 percent of the population ages 12 and older (according to the Bureau of the Census).

They account for:

- 18 percent of the nation's violent crime, and
- 15 percent of murders (estimates from Department of Justice crime clearance and conviction rates);

- 9 percent of violent deaths,
- 14 percent of gun deaths,
- 15 percent of murder victims,
- 7 percent of suicides, and
- 2 percent of drug deaths (according to the National Center for Health Statistics);

- 14 percent of highway deaths and
- 9 percent of drunken driving deaths (according to the National Highway Traffic Safety Administration); and

- 12 percent of births (only 4 percent when both the mother and father are under age 20), and

- 15 percent of HIV infections (practically none if both partners are under age 20) (according to the NCHS and Centers for Disease Control).

Table 1

Who's showing California's biggest crime increase?
White adults over age 30.

Felony crime increase, 1980–97:

Rate, violent crime	age 10–19	20–29	30+
White	+6%	+47%	+148%
Latino	-12	+20	+75
Black	-16	-5	+56
Asian	+58	+61	+137
Total	-2	+33	+111

Rate, all felonies	age 10–19	20–29	30+
White	-42%	+23%	+138%
Latino	-18	+12	+62
Black	-27	-19	+63
Asian	+51	+84	+118
Total	-27	+13	+102

Rate is per 100,000 population ages 10–19, 20–29, and 30–69, by race.
Source: California Department of Justice, Crime & Deliquency in California, 1980, 1997 update.

In short, teenagers do not account for a high percentage of America's social problems. Teens' share of problem-causing does not even exceed their share of the 12-and-older population in most cases. Conversely, what experts and the media aren't saying about the deteriorating behaviors of adults is even more incredible. If that sounds exactly the opposite of what the press and authorities proclaim, well, get ready for the rest of this book.

Table 1 shows why officials might be reluctant to discuss what groups are displaying the largest, most astonishing crime increases. (California crime figures are cited because, unlike national figures, they are the nation's most completely and consistently tabulated over the last two decades and because they separate Euro-whites from Latinos. Where they are comparable, California trends appear to be a couple of years ahead of, but otherwise similar to, national crime trends). The truth, abundantly obvious from official crime reports over the last one to two decades, is that it is not minority teenagers, but adults over the age of 30—*white* adults, most specifically—who consistently display the largest increases in serious (felony) violent, property, and drug-related crime rates.

Note that it isn't even close. Youths display decreases in felonies, 20-agers small increases, and over-30-agers large increases—with whites over 30 showing by far the largest rise. The pattern of these trends is consistent for felony violent crime (shown above), property crime, and drug offenses regardless of what years are con-

Table 2

California's secret: serious crime plummeting among nonwhite youths, exploding among older white grownups

Change in California felony arrest rates:

	White adults over age 30	Nonwhite youths
1997 vs 1976	+160%	-32%
1997 vs 1980	+138	-32
1997 vs 1985	+74	+5
1997 vs 1990	+21	-28

Rate is per 100,000 Euro-whites ages 30–69 and per 100,000 black, Asian and Latino youths ages 10–17. Felony arrests include all violent, property, drug and other felonies. The year 1976 is the first for which consistent statistics by age and race are available and which is not confounded by 1975's drug law reforms changing marijuana possession to a misdemeanor.
Source: see Table 1.

strasted (ie, comparing 1997 with 1975 or with 1985, etc.). Nor are we talking small numbers. There were 72,000 more annual felony arrests among California whites over age 30 in 1997 than in 1980, versus 19,000 FEWER among teenagers.

Yet not a single major criminologist seems to have noticed. Examining California's extremes—the poorest population everyone *thinks* is causing rising crime (nonwhite and Latino youths) versus the richest population no one thinks of as crime-prone (white adults over age 30)—reveals trends both consistent and suprising (Table 2).

The upshot is too startling to immediately comprehend: In the late 1970s, whites over age 30 comprised 40 percent of California's population and 7 percent of its felony arrests; in the late 1990s, 37 percent of the population but one-fifth of felony arrests. In what must be a criminological first, aging whites accounted for a larger share of California's felony crime increase (40 percent) than they contributed to its population increase (30 percent). In two decades, the proneness of over-30 whites to serious criminality *tripled* compared to that of younger age groups and non-whites!

What does this mean? About six impossible things before breakfast, the first of which is: for 20 years, *crime trends have been dramatically and diametrically the opposite of what California officials and the media have been saying*. Except for a rise from 1985 to 1990, serious crime trends among nonwhite teenagers have been on the decline for 20 years—but major crimes among white adults have been surging steadily upward. Nonwhite adults show lesser increases in felony rates than white adults (up 38 percent from 1976 to 1997), and white youths show the largest decreases of all (down 53 percent over the last 20 years).

Similar trends are going on nationwide. The FBI lists eight serious felonies (murder, rape, robbery, aggravated assault, burglary, larceny/theft, motor vehicle theft, and arson) as "index crimes." These have been tabulated reasonably consistently for the last three decades. The FBI's annual *Uniform Crime Reports* provides two measures of these serious crimes: offenses known to police, and arrests. The first measure tells how much crime is reported. The second tells how many persons were arrested by age for each offense. Examining the two measures together allows us to factor out whether crime is really increasing or police are just making more arrests to solve ("clear") reported crimes (see Chapter 1 for method).

Using these two measures of crime, it is evident that the rate of serious offenses committed by youths—that is, index crimes divided by the youth population ages 13–17—has *declined* by 5 to 10 percent over the last two decades. However, the index crime rate of their parents, age 30–49, has *risen* by 30 percent. It is hard to believe such dramatic trends could have gone unnoticed among experts whose job it is to monitor crime statistics—and who have had 20 years to get used to the new and astonishing developments.

Why the silence, then? The first reason may simply be genuine disbelief. That America's most affluent, aging population should show the largest rise in serious offenses fits no known theory of crime. So much of modern criminology, as it has for decades, consists of defining and studying crime as a young-male problem[10] that authorities may be adrift when confronted with graying misdeed.

I presented the above figures (in the form of a "news story" the media ought to be running, headlined, "Rising crime by white grownups, not minority teens, drives California's serious crime wave") to the May 1998 Children Now conference in Los Angeles. The theme of the conference was negative media images of youth of color, documented by a new Children Now survey showing kids of all races felt black, Latino, and Asian kids were depicted as criminals "doing bad things."[11] Engaged in earnest soul-searching over media unfairness to minority youths were top reporters from the *Washington Post, Dateline NBC*, CNN, MTV, Associated Press, *Time, Fox News, Los Angeles Times*, ABC News, CBS News, and *TV Guide*.

Well, I suggested in my 15 seconds of panel time, the media might try this novel strategy: tell the truth. The facts provide ample basis for refashioning a stunningly positive image of black and brown kids showing healthy crime declines even as privileged white elders are running amok. Oddly, none of the Big Media representatives at the conference seemed the slightest bit interested in *examining real crime reports* and *telling the truth about kids*. Perhaps they thought I was making a bizarre joke or pulling a lies-and-damned-lies crime statistics shenanigan such as equating parking tickets with drive-bys. What I suspect is that Big Media and other luminaries have so much invested in hyping youths as the American terror that their idea of image-busting was a few more profiles on Hmong teenage violinists or Rastafarian female center fielders.

Second, of course, any statistic may not show what it appears to show. Perhaps it is not a real violence increase, but growing attention to domestic violence, including new laws mandating arrests of offenders, that produced the skyrocketing rate of arrests of over-30 adults for violent crime. Even if true, this development would be unsettling. It would show that homes are much more violent than previously thought. It would show that adults do not "age out" of violence-prone younger years so much as they take their fury indoors. Since domestic violence represents the chief violent crime (including murder) threat to children under age 13 and to women of all ages, the surge in arrests should indicate that household, not street, violence is our biggest menace. Whatever the explanation, authorities' refusal even to talk about the sharp increase in adult violence arrests remains deeply puzzling.

Further, the concomitant leap in property and drug felonies among over-30 adults, particularly whites, indicates that something more is afoot than simply better enforcement. This age group is becoming more criminal in lots of ways. There is no way to avoid the fact that it is adult behavior, particularly among the 30- and 40-age Baby Boomers, that has deteriorated sharply, endangering children and disrupting families and communities. This deterioration has occurred without economic decline to explain it.

However, beyond the growth in aging adults' rising, record levels of drug abuse and criminality lies the politics of the crime debate. The only issue of interest is this: who would benefit from talking about rising adult crime, particularly white-adult crime? No prominent entity would. The art of successful politicking of wedge issues requires blaming vexing national problems on unpopular groups *outside* of the constituencies candidates wish to flatter. By definition, no major political interest would be crazy enough to blame the cohort most known for Big Voting—over-30 adults, whites, "soccer moms"—for the worsening state of what this same cohort calls the Big Issue—crime.

White Hot Fear

Still and all, why is there an attack on young people today, and why is it so hard to redirect? "Today's young people are scapegoated by an adult generation that is abandoning them," declares Lori Nelson, youth and education director for Los Angeles's National Conference on Communities and Justice. "Race is a big reason. The kids people are scared of are kids of color."[12]

Fear of racial transition appears a powerful factor. The Census Bureau reports that 80 percent of America's adults over age 40 are whites of European origin (Euro-white). Thirty-five percent of children and youths under age 18 are nonwhite or of Hispanic (Latino) origin, a proportion that has doubled since 1970.[13] In most of America's big cities, white elders govern nonwhite kids. In California, two-thirds of the elders are Euro-white; three-fifths of the youths are nonwhite or Latino. As California and the cities are, so America is becoming.

In growing multi-racial and -ethnic areas, outspoken fear of young people mixes with unspoken fear of racial transition. "Whites are scared," reports Stanford professor Dale Maharidge of his interviews and study for his moderate book on "California's eruptions," *The Coming White Minority*. "The depth of white fear is underestimated and misunderstood by progressive thinkers and the media." Maharidge points to research showing that when the minority share of the population reaches one-third, most whites express negative opinions and desires to escape.[14] That proportion has been exceeded among American youth, harbingers of the multi-racial future. Figuratively as well as actually, then, aging whites and more prosperous minorities who identify with them are "moving out" of children's "neighborhoods."

Thus, one aspect of aging America's hostility toward its young derives from reflexive racial and ethnic discomfort: the kids don't look like the parents. It is no accident that political authorities, scholars, and the media now ascribe to adolescents the same prejudices once hurled at nonwhites—violent, hypersexed, irrational, volatile, dangerous.

Second, racial fear is building at a time when racism is impolitic to openly express. The increase in (white) adult crime is most inconvenient for politically-adept interests courting that dominant constituency, and so it has been swept aside in an obsessive focus on violent crime by inner-city youth. But trumpeting that violent crime increased only among minority, not Euro-white, teens would insult major Democratic voting blocs. Thus, New Democrats led by President Clinton have developed racialist code words such as "youth violence" and "teen pregnancy," which are modernized versions of the 1960s "law'n'order" and pre-'60s "Negro question" ("nigger-baiting," or "niggering," in plain stump talk) employed by traditional southern politicians.[15] The function of modern crypto-racism is more refined than that of its cruder past: to simultaneously flatter majority constituencies, avoid antagonizing key minority groups, and avail aging America's fears of the rising population of nonwhite youth. Because racial coding cannot be admitted today, it is hidden behind a false image of an entire generation out of control, from meanstreet to megamall.

For the crassest of political reasons, then, an utterly unreal symbol of American crime has emerged: the violent teenager, white, black, brown, threatening inner-city and affluent suburb alike. The most intensive headline and feature stories target the wealthy killer kid who, by definition, hales from an adoring family and went bad strictly from surrender to his personal darkside. The twisted affirmative-action remedy for media demonizing of dark-skinned kids was not accurate reporting of the adult-created reality of violence and abandonment inflicted on the young, but to demonize more white kids.

The Clinton regime is not unique among American presidencies in its propensity to lie, but it is singular in its willingness to warp statistics and studies wholesale to lend a liberal-sounding, scientific veneer to its lying. For moderates and liberals, "racism" is officially deplored with a formulaic clubbiness codified in the President's Initiative on Race, in which older African Americans recount the brutality of Sheriff Clark apartheid and shake their heads as rainbow coalitions of '90s students lament high school lunchroom segregation. In such a climate, carefully scrutinizing why black and Latino youth homicide rose in the 1980s would raise socioeconomic issues of the sort candidate handlers rate as fearful and loathesome on the '90s campaign trail. And so, by popular default, "moral values" became the winner.

Third, while the race-transition argument has been cited by a growing number of progressives to explain California's and America's astonishing hostility toward the young (following Maharidge, former *Sacramento Bee* editor Peter Schrag buttresses it in his 1998 work, *Paradise Lost*[16]), it explains only a part of the older generation's fear. Like Cub Scouts around a nighttime forest campfire terrifying themselves with embellished slasher tales, latter-day grownup America delights in horror stories about suburban stone-killer kids. *Within* white, black, and Latino populations, there is growing anger and disowning of youth by elder. Wealth differences are paramount. In every group, kids are poorer than older adults, and the affluence gap between young and old is mushrooming. Growing numbers of well-off minority middle-agers join their white golfing buddies in fear of youths, from gang shootouts downtown headlined on News at 11 to the suburban devil-worshipping killers festooning *People*.

Crumbling Adulthood

Politicians and interest groups have caught hold of public anxieties and bent them to profit. The attack by the Clinton administration, the Republican Congress, and major media and institutions against America's young people marks the most anti-youth period in American history. Fear of the young is enthusiastically embraced by modern economic and political interests busy dismantling the public sector, promoting unprecedented concentration of wealth, and building an enclave/prison society to manage the inevitable conflict such inequality creates. Practically nothing that today's top officials and the media declare about teenagers is true. The magnitude of the falsehood is in direct proportion to how stridently and often it is repeated.

Are teenagers "ruining America"? The fairest summary of "kids of the 1990s" I could muster would be the following:

- Despite being worse off economically on average, the *average* youth today is better behaved than the *average* youth of 25 years ago and the *average* adult of today.

- Because of being *much* worse off economically, the *most troubled 1 percent* of youth today are *more* troubled than the *most troubled 1 percent* of youths 25 years ago— but not as bad off as today's most troubled adults. It takes a lot of killer kids to equal one Timothy McVeigh, thousands of 'hoodsful of teenage robbers to do the damage of a single S&L looter.

Before making my case for the above convolution, let me say that "today's most troubled adults" should mean those in positions of government, institutional, and corporate leadership whose selfish, shortsighted policies have exploited younger and poorer people to the point that this powerful country's future is in severe jeopardy. More skilled polemicists than I have covered that point well. My purpose is to show that even using conventional measures of "troubled"—violent crime, criminal arrest, drug abuse, alcohol abuse, suicide, AIDS, other risky behavior—what popular authorities and news media say about kids today just ain't so. Not even nearly so.

The unadmitted reality of youth and adult behavior is bad for the immediate needs of politicians and their institutional support networks, but it is a hopeful one for the future of America's larger, noble experiment. Despite being poorer, despite suffering the most violent, addicted, and disarrayed parent generation in knowable history, today's children and teenagers are holding up remarkably well. Notwithstanding the drumbeat of fear organized by varied enterprises and spread in the media, adolescents display declining rates of crime, drug abuse, alcohol abuse, and suicidal behaviors. The elders should be doing so well.

It is an adult generation at loose ends that spreads false fear and slander against the young. The attack on youth has grown ever more shrill as interests compete for support in the cold, penurious '90s of tightened pursestrings and slashed sympathies. Liberal moralism flowed in part from the fund-raising and political difficulties liberal groups weathered in the hostile 1980s and '90s. Well-intentioned youth services justified overstatement on the grounds that modern funders would not turn loose of bucks unless grantees could present evidence of a serious teenage menace. To survive in a hardening climate, sex education, drug and alcohol abuse prevention, gun control, media reform, mental health, and other progressive services wildly hyped youth misbehaviors. Only we, programmers intoned, stand between your wealthy fundee's pleasant suburb-ville and the legions of gnashing superpredators downtown.

More led to more, and today, there appears no limit to the extremity of untruths that the most august of authorities will proclaim in pursuit of attention, funding, and poll points. In the most abysmal example, leading crime experts fan anti-youth phobia with predictions of a "coming crime storm" by rising hordes of "adolescent superpredators" in the new millennium. The regression by top criminologists to long-debunked "demographic" theories (that crime is caused by the composition of the population) represents academic laziness at its worst. And not incidentally, charging that certain race/ethnic/age groups are just naturally crime-prone serves to insulate crime policies from criticism. Today, the demographic scapegoat is the Adolescent. Standard crime and census reports clearly show the presence of more teenagers in the population has nothing to do with violent, property, drug, or any other kind of crime. It is aging Baby Boomers, not adolescents or young adults, who drive today's crime numbers.

In 1980, the FBI reported 450,000 Americans ages 30–49 arrested for serious violent, property, or drug crimes. In 1996, 1.5 million. Adults age 30–49 accounted for nearly three-fourths of the nation's crime rise. Both violent and property felony rates have risen among the parent-age group, indicating a rapid increase in criminality among these adults even as crime among other groups has declined.

What is causing an increased crime rate—made up of dumb stuff, like aggravated assault, burglary, and car theft—in a privileged, aging population? It turns out that the increase in major crimes committed by adults closely tracks skyrocketing drug abuse among aging Baby Boomers. Among 30- and 40-agers, the number of hospital emergency cases involving drug overdose rose from 60,000 in 1980 to over 200,000 in 1995. Heroin and cocaine cases soared from 10,000 to 100,000. Other measures of drug abuse also mushroomed in this age group.

Unlike the increase in homicide and robbery among the poorest fraction of the teenage population from a mid-'80s trough to an early-'90s peak, the increase in 30–40-ager crime and drug woes is larger, more broadly-based, and more persistent. It has occurred among all races over the last 25 years. Paradoxically, it has accompanied *rising* middle-aged wealth. While the cyclical teenage homicide and robbery increases appear socioeconomic in origin, the sustained Baby Boom crime boom appears to result from rising drug abuse. This, in turn, creates more family instability and, in further turn, leads to negative views of kids among adults unwilling to face their own misbehaviors.

It does not take Sherlock Holmes to deduce that parents involved in drugs and crime are more likely to have trouble parenting. Normal family functions become more difficult. Conflicts routinely settled in healthy households produce spousal warfare and parent-child alienation. Divorce and separation explode; modern marriages last only seven years, on average. Kids seem more trouble to raise.

As parenting competence, and American adulthood itself, declined, parents' movements of the 1980s and '90s arose to demand that government and private interests step in to manage their kids. "Often," wrote a veteran California Appeals Court judge of the avalanche of youths shoveled into institutional management, the child "was a minor nuisance some inadequate parent was trying to fob off on the court...He usually just did not get along with his parents and, when one met the parents, this was often completely understandable."[17] The director of Montana's state juvenile prison had a remedy: "In most cases, we should leave the kid home and send the parents to Pine Hills."[18]

Woes of low-income parents and families, increasingly isolated in abandoned inner cities and depopulating rural areas, continued to be ignored. But more affluent, politically-connected Baby Boom parents got attention. Government and private enterprise were happy to intervene when kid and progenitor did not get along.

Beginning in the mid-1970s, kid-fixing services erupted to meet the market. They were of two kinds. Prison gates opened wide in the 1980s to receive tens of thousands more poorer teens, three-fourths of them nonwhite. Confinement of minority youths in prisons increased by 80 percent in the last decade. Imprisonment of Euro-white youth did not rise.[19]

At the same time, mental health and other treatment centers raked in huge profits therapizing hundreds of thousands more health-insured children of the affluent, nearly all white.[20] The *annual* growth rate in private youth correctional facilities "has been a staggering 45 percent over the last decade," *Youth Today* reported in May 1998. Youth treatment is now a $25 billion per year business with "a record of steady profit growth:"

> The wave of tough anti-drug laws and the public's lock-'em-up attitude for juvenile offenders is now sweeping along for-profits that focus on young people. Equitable Securities Research, in what it terms a "very conservative" forecast, looks for a six percent annual growth rate for juvenile residential programs and an eight percent rate for non-residential programs. That would mean 93,000 youths locked up by 2004, up from about 52,000 in 1995. By 2004, more than 107,000 teens are likely to be in for-profit non-residential programs, compared with 51,000 in 1995.[21]

Yet, as will be documented in later chapters, teenage drug abuse, suicide, crime, and other maladies have generally been declining over the last 25 years. Serious problems are concentrated in a shrinking, not growing, proportion of the youth population. No matter. At a 20-year construction and maintenance investment of $1.5 million per bed, private treatment facilities will have enormous interest in planting a steady drumbeat of bad news in the pliant media about "rising" teenage woes to ensure a steady flow of clientele. Just as the psychiatric industry hawked a "teenage suicide epidemic" in the 1980s to fill empty beds in its overbuilt private hospitals (see Chapter 7), today's teen-fixing entrepreneurs can be counted on to generate maximum hysteria.

Thus, there are political and profit-driven reasons for drug and alcohol abuse, law enforcement, political, and media authorities to trumpet a succession of unprecedented "teenage" behavior crises. All of these combine with psychological solace. Authorities who morally condemned the sins of poorer parents for their bad kids benignly excused, and serviced, the failings of more affluent parents. It was not parents', or adults', values and behaviors, but demons lurking in "popular culture" and "drugs" corrupting a teenage generation just naturally eager to embrace any and every evil. If every kid was bad, parents by definition were not to blame. "Blaming drugs for kids' troubles also worked within the family just as demonizing individuals' drug use worked in wider society," wrote drug-war chronicler Dan Baum: "it obviated concern for 'root causes' and let parents take their own behavior off the hook."[22] Not just parents, but an entire parent generation, had a lot of behaviors to take off the hook.

The rising cascade of bad news about teenagers tracked growing disarray of Baby Boomers, a generation also becoming the nation's wealthiest. A chunk of this wealth accumulated from the lavish public subsidies of Baby Boomers combined with their refusal to support their children. An aging, self-preoccupied America was in no mood to share its time or lucre with the young—not personally following divorce and family breakup, not privately through providing job opportunity, not publicly through taxes. Rationales for abandonment abounded: today's kids are so rotten that they don't deserve our hard-earned money, so dissolute that resources invested in them would be wasted anyway. Statistics of disownment abound and are cited throughout this book, evidencing how little today's adults value kids compared to the way our parents valued us. A typical one, lamented by Kozol: in 1970, New York City employed 400 school physicians; today, fewer than two dozen.[23]

What "kids these days" need, adult respondents to a 1997 Public Agenda poll declared, is stern values sermons and tough discipline. Faithful to the public ire they helped inflame, experts and the media combed the country for sensational teenage murder, drunken driving crash, heroin overdose, welfare mother, devil cult, just plain badness. Most in media demand are evil young wastoids, preferably white and suburban, from "good families" to prove that all kids everywhere fit the "satanic" label applied by *Toughlove*'s rotten-parent emeriti Phyllis and David York. More common, worse adult incidents and trends are ignored or downplayed. Today's result is a weird climate in which authorities, liberal and conservative, refuse to discuss the most obvious implications of their most obvious studies and clearest statistics.

Major institutions from the conservative American Medical Association to the liberal Carnegie Corporation jumped in front of the public mood. They assembled blue-ribbon panels to issue a stream of reports (actually, recyclings of the same report) depicting a peace-loving, healthy adult society besieged by barbaric brats. Drastic measures were proposed, many enacted. Nighttime and daytime curfews so strict that (as endorsed by President Clinton) teenagers could legally be in public only a couple of hours on most days. Mass drug-testing, forced strip-searches of students, and draconian punishments for runaways and curfew violators evidence grownups' anti-youth frenzy. California's 1998 governor's race kicked off with the top Democrat candidate demanding random drug-testing of students, his chief challenger backing capital punishment for 14-year-olds, and the leading Democrat for lieutenant governor on record favoring execution of 13-year-olds. (What's left for Republicans—random executions of fifth graders?)

Left Meets Right

The response by liberals to the attacks of Clinton and the Right has ranged from ineffective to disastrous. When conservatives and New Democrats attack youth, liberals respond not with fundamental challenges to repressive assumptions, but with traditional arguments designed to advance their own agendas. The emergence of the Cultural Left, which leftist theorist Richard Rorty points out has "collaborated with the Right in making cultural issues central to public debate," amiably pillow-fights with Bill Bennett's Virtuecrats over TV violence, consumerism, and pop culture sins. "It is as if," Rorty added in *Achieving Our Country*,

> sometime around 1980, the children of the people who made it through the Great Depression and into the suburbs had decided to pull up the drawbridge behind them. They decided that although social mobility had been appropriate for their parents, it was not to be allowed for the next generation. These suburbanites seem to see nothing wrong with belonging to a hereditary caste and have initiated what Robert Reich (in his book *The Work of Nations*) calls "the secession of the successful."[24]

The Cultural Left's war against sin has abetted this secession, a double calamity for the young. On the one hand, the Cultural Left rarely talks about tangible realities such as child abuse, rape of young girls, parents abusing drugs, parents damaging their kids' health with passive smoke, or the menaces to kids caused by grownups' rising crime and addiction. In fact, the Cultural Left talks less and less about youth poverty and socioeconomic attrition. Instead, the secondary symptoms of powerlessness and poverty, such as drinking or gun possession, have been elevated into *primary causes* of malaise. Like the Right, the Cultural Left claims that personal morality is the problem, teenagers' natural depravity the base chemistry, evil pop culture the catalyst. Endless, moral tongue-clucking that a bare butt on *NYPD Blue*, a candy ad, corporate "messages," or an explicit website deprave kids to violate sacred Baby-Boomer values emanates from both ends of the political spectrum.

The conservative fear lobby paints a dire statistical picture of hordes of black and Latino "adolescent superpredators" born of ghetto teenage moms. Liberals smartly respond with anecdotes to prove that white, suburban kids are just as criminal. Conservatives hype a "drug crisis" among teenagers. Liberals rejoin that teenage alcohol disaster is worse. The Right blames teenage miscreancy on immoral kids seduced by internet porn, Tupac Shakur, and Marilyn Manson. The Liberal/Left blames stupid kids enthralled by Joe Camel, Channel One, and media-fed consumerism. The Right warns of a teen AIDS plague created by *Our Bodies, Ourselves*, the Left about teen alcoholics spawned by a Budweiser bullfrog. Conservatives hawk censorship, purity lectures, and prison. Liberals push censorship, purity lectures, and behavior education (see Chapter 8).

The Leftist stance fit into Rightist campaigns that emphasized "personal morality" (for certain people) over social equality. When race and poverty were taken off the table, "values" and "responsibility" became the issues. The result was that the two most important influences on teenage behavior—family and socioeconomics—were buried in an avalanche of punitive moralizing. As the more sophisticatedly exploitative Clinton era unfolded, any semblance of perspective winged into the sunset.

Interests seeking profit, funding, and popularity pumped ever-scarier prevarications about terrible teens. The self-reporting survey, the weakest, most easily manipulated of social science tools, was deified, replacing more reliable statistical measures. Pump those numbers up! In truth, teenage suicide rates are low, so rephrase the question to whether they ever *thought* of killing themselves. In fact, teenage heroin and cocaine use is practically nil, so ask if they *know* anyone who *ever* used a hard drug. In fact, the teenage drunk driving toll is minuscule compared to adults', so recalculate it as a function of some absurd index such as *miles driven drunk*. Hell, just make something up: All teenagers lead secret lives of debauchery! 135,000 bring guns to school every day! All kids snort smack! Two-thirds of fifth graders approve of rape! Sixty percent of high schoolers are suicidal! Your kids have sex in your bed! Your child will kill you!

The eruption of rash statements such as the above, using numbers to give scientific veneer, splashed in the press and political arenas to create pressure for funding. Mark Twain had a handle on such proprietary statistics in his 1901 anti-colonialism essay, "To the Person Sitting in Darkness:"

> He presented the facts—some of the facts—and showed these confiding people what the facts meant. He did it statistically, which is a good way. He used the formula: twice 2 are 14, and 2 from 9 leaves 35. Figures are effective; figures will convince the elect.

Some of the weirder figures on teenagers tossed out by the most luminous of expert in the most august of forum are just that chimerical. To believe proprietary statistics purveyors is to wonder why every teenager in America isn't dead twice over.

In a Gresham's Law by which bad information drives out good, ridiculous proprietary numerology has all but eliminated the most carefully gathered and explicitly defined statistics (the latter of whose limitations and errors are much better understood). Today, it is all but impossible to induce a leading authority to examine teenage *and adult* death, birth, or crime statistics in the *complete context* of what they show and *don't* show. It is much more profitable to bellow about the phony Top Ten School Problems of Today (drug abuse, alcohol abuse, pregnancy, suicide, rape, robbery, assault, etc.) versus the Top Ten School Problems of 1940 (talking, gum-chewing, making noise, running in halls, getting out of line, wearing improper clothing, not putting paper in wastebaskets). I defy anyone to produce the "study" behind these statements, which are treated as gospel from "Dear Abby" to *Congressional Record*. There is no study. It was made up.[25] Who cares?

In the cold '90s in which hysteria, not humanitarianism, generates bucks and acclaim, humane groups joined the shouting. Funds flowed—for a while. But now the bill for two decades of unfounded shrieking about adolescents has come due. Washington and the public are fed up with young people and their intractable evil. An angry electorate and political system has thrown up its hands and declared the next generation hopeless, not worthy of investment in anything except sermons and cagings. The Clinton/Republican litany of convenience holds that liberal solutions were tried, so earnestly, and just didn't work.

As of this writing, in August 1998, the low point is low indeed. The scholar-and-statistics brandishing Clinton presidency legitimized official, scholarly, and media falsification of adolescent issues. Making things up. Maintaining silence on the growing mass of inconvenient information that did not advance immediate political or monetary profit. Public emotings about "caring for kids" after polls, focus groups, and professional handler strategies pinpointed how craftily to exploit them. It is no accident that a New Democrat, far more effectively than Reagan or Bush, finally destroyed Roosevelt's future-directed policies of power disbursement and replaced them with regressive measures of concentrated wealth and police control. "When it comes to corporate welfare or policing powers, Clinton, like Reagan, adores big government and only derides its role in helping the poor," Alexander Cockburn understates.[26] Clinton's capitulation to popular Republicanism is so complete that even the most courageous thrust of his presidency—universal health care—has disintegrated to endorsement of the Patient Access to Responsible Care (or "Bill of Rights") Act of 1998. This Republican-whooped "I've-got-mine" travesty, even conservative professor James Pinkerton laments, will "make health care more of a perk" by rewarding the already insured with better coverage while pricing the poor and young who can't afford insurance "out of the market."[27]

When crime, public health, education, and other standard sources are examined, popular statements about teenagers not only evaporate, they turn out to be outrageously false. Dismayingly, it doesn't make any difference. The shame of academia, institutions, and the media is that few of prominent status challenge official lies about young people. The institutions charged with questioning authority in a democracy could weakly justify their past acquiescences by lack of good information. Today's luminaries, however, refuse to examine the wealth of information available.

Many of today's adults seem to *want* young people to feel hopeless and self-hating. A May 1998 poll by *USA Today*'s tabloid *USA Weekend* of a quarter-million teenagers in grades 6–12 reaffirms how trapped the media are in their own concocted image of the miserable '90s wastrel.[28] The poll's questions and youths' responses are as follows:

- "In general, how do you feel about yourself?" GOOD, 93 percent; BAD, 7 percent (VERY BAD, 1 percent).

- "Do you consider yourself healthy?" YES, 89 percent.

- "About how often do you have a conversation with one of your parents that lasts longer than 15 minutes?" A FEW TIMES A MONTH to EVERY DAY, 83 percent; ALMOST NEVER, 17 percent.

- "Do you have an adult you can confide in, inside or outside the family?" YES, 80 percent.

- "How pressured do you feel to do the following...?" NOT AT ALL: drink alcohol, 77 percent; smoke, 77 percent; take illegal drugs, 84 percent; have sex, 72 percent; look a certain way, 45 percent.

- "How much influence does each of the following have on your life?" A LOT: parents, 70 percent; religion, 34 percent; teacher, 25 percent; girlfriend/boyfriend, 24 percent; other kids, 21 percent; celebrities, 21 percent; TV shows, 8 percent; advertising, 4 percent.

- "Which do you think describe you...?" Kind, 78 percent; honest, 75 percent; good sense of humor, 69 percent; smart, 66 percent; self-confident, 65 percent; creative, 63 percent; good at sports, 53 percent; not influenced by others, 53 percent; attractive, 40 percent; tough, 40 percent; popular, 32 percent; rich, 10 percent.

Note that the eight most-claimed teenage traits are those of personal achievement while the four least-claimed are of dubious, and/or outside-awarded, distinction. Boasting or not, kids are proud of themselves. Even when the poll deliberately tried to elicit negative responses, such as by the following questions...

- "Two million teens suffer from severe depression, according to one estimate. Do you ever feel really depressed?"

- "Have any of your friends ever tried to commit suicide, or discussed it?"

...only 16 percent of the youths reporting feeling depressed "often." Even though youths may be aware of the grapevine news on hundreds of students in school, only one-third had ever heard of a peer who discussed or tried suicide. When asked directly "which of the following would make you feel better about yourself," teens did volunteer some shortcomings: half wanted better grades, a third wanted to look better and to get along better with their parents. Imagine in all cases what 40-age adults, given sodium pentathol, might answer to the above questions.

USA Weekend would have to bend its poll results completely out of shape to present a negative image of youths. Warp it did. Here is how it headlined the findings: "Teens tackle their identity crisis...teens are riddled with self-doubt about everything from their looks to their relationships with adults...Looks are key...Teens find lots of imperfections...Depression is common...Families aren't communicating..." Ironically, the most abruptly negative response about grownups was to the question, "do you think adults generally value your opinions?" Thirty-six percent said "no." I'd like to know if that percentage shot up after they saw how the newspaper relentlessly negativized their positive poll responses.

Pop media, luminous expert symposium, all the same. At the State of the World Forum in San Francisco in November 1997, I ask my fellow "Global Portrayal of Youth" panelists if young people are vilified in their home countries as they are in the United States. Represented are Mexico, Peru, Slovenia, United Kingdom, Singapore, South Africa, Russia, Thailand, China, Australia, Nigeria, and Pakistan. They look puzzled. The young man from Slovenia takes the microphone: "We do not see in our press or official discourse at home the kind of negative statements about young people that we see in America's." The man from UK seconds that view. The rest of the panelists nod. Two hours later, they will be treated to yet another dismality, as the Forum's All-American roundtable on drugs winds up its session with a sensationally idiotic denigration of teenage drinking and marijuana use—just before a glitterati dinner at the luxurious Nob Hill digs in which booze flows like Niagara. Pompously billed as the international conference that will accomplish "paradigm shifts" in international thinking about youth, the State of the World's U.S. participants vie to peddle their own wares with misleading claims and and stale programmatic solutions.

New Calvinist "Messages"

What has emerged from the jockeying of interest groups is an abysmally upside-down notion of "prevention" which seeks to blame virtually all major social and health problems on young people. Since, as noted, youths actually cause very few of society's serious problems, an unreal world in which adults don't exist has been constructed.

A 1995 study by the American Medical Association warns that one in 12 drunken driving instances involves a person under age 21 (uh…who're involved in the other eleven-twelfths?). The 1994 Surgeon General's report blamed smoking entirely on the character flaws of young people. The Carnegie Council on Adolescent Development blamed bad adult health on time bombs set by bad youth habits. Expert America agrees: the dark force that walks among us is Youth Culture. Even when obliged to admit the existence of widespread drug, drinking, smoking, violence, and crime among adults, the claim is that "prevention" policies must impose draconian restrictions on young people to forestall them from setting off a new cycle. Adults who smoke or take drugs are hopelessly habituated, says former cabinet secretary and current drug-war general Joseph Califano Jr. So leave the grownups alone and take drastic steps to nip any and all wrongheaded teenage habits in the bud.[29]

This prevention theory might be called New Calvinism. Instead of infant damnation, "teenage damnation" preaches that adults exist simply as embodiments of the worst courses they locked onto in adolescence. A convenient enabler for party-on adults, no question. But this youth-obsessed concept of "prevention" has such serious flaws it is no wonder nations with more successful health strategies don't go near it:

It is *cruel*. The policy of clamp-down-on-teens while going-easy-on-grownups effectively "writes off" the suffering caused by addiction in the adult generation. As will be shown in subsequent chapters, kids who grow up in families with addicted parents risk severe health damage, violent abuse, and fatality.

It is *self-defeating*. Addiction does not "begin with teenagers." It is a circular process from parent generation to youth generation. As documented in later chapters, kids who grow up in families and communities where adults abuse drugs, alcohol, and tobacco are many times more likely to abuse these substances in adolescence and adulthood than youths in communities where addiction is low.

It is *derelict*. This concept of prevention challenges the very notion of adulthood itself. It defines "adult" not by the responsibility to be mature, but by the *privi-*

lege to engage in immature behavior. Child raising is no longer seen as the art of set-ting good example, but of "monitoring" and "referral."

It is *arrogant*. The condescending, superior tone of prevention programmers toward youths, especially toward teens trapped in addicted and abusive families, leads to the absurd notion that "prevention" consists of "sending messages." The 1994 Surgeon General report's petulant complaint that some teenagers (the report made it sound like all) *still* take up smoking despite the "messages" health officials send betrays a common prejudice: that programmers' golden words should magically reform a youth away from years of day-to-day exposure to unhealthy adult behaviors that officials, for political gain, pretend do not exist.

This is a crock. Adult behaviors set the standards for society. It is adults who decide how, when, where, and at what price products may be used. Adults govern how products will be produced, sold, taxed, and regulated. Adults impose their smoking, drinking, drug habits, and rewards and consequences thereof upon chil-dren and youths in their homes. For adults to blame young people and their sup-posed attraction to media debauchery for the persistence of bad habits in society belies the maturity and responsibility adults claim to represent.

But for the above reasons, teen-obsessed policy is also *popular*. Alcohol control policies that assessed individual capacities to drink safely would curb the drinking rights of many prominent adults (legislators, to be blunt), but a policy based solely on preventing persons under age 21 from drinking does not threaten adult habits. This dereliction of adulthood is manifested by the variety of interest groups which now reap solace and profit from the Clinton message of exonerating grownups and demonizing kids. Not surprisingly, the worst punishments have fallen on poor, most-ly nonwhite youths who were the conservative targets in the first place.

And so, America of the 1990s is an extraordinarily difficult society to grow up in. Consult this morning's (May 31, 1998) paper. President Clinton, moralizing on school prayer, implores that "children" should be "spiritually grounded" because they are exposed to "images of immorality." Many of those images derived from the grotesquely immoral behavior of Clinton and legions of cronies in a White House that aspires to no higher grounding than poll-driven popularity. Republican Senator Christopher Bond of Missouri declares that "illegal drugs are a terrible influence on our young people," failing to mention that Republicans' own elected legislative chief, House Speaker Newt Gingrich, was a prominent illegal-drug user and adulter-er.[30] California Governor Pete Wilson, who personally benefitted from free univer-sity education in the 1960s, raised college tuitions through the roof in the '90s to avoid taxing his wealthier constituents. The nation's sternest welfare-reformist, anti-single-mom crusader is California (formerly Wisconsin) social services director Eloise Anderson, herself a former single welfare mother. As columnist Molly Ivins pointed out, a parade of 1996 GOP presidential aspirants condemned single mothers as the killers of civilization, excepting their own former wives whom they made sin-gle mothers.[31]

Flip on the radio to hear high-toned morals-doctor Laura Schlessinger holler, "How could you do that?!" and demand rigidly disciplined civility from dissolute America. She who derides callers as "moral slime, bimbos, bums, jerks, manipula-tors, idiots, scum, sluts, whores and bitches." She of divorce, angrily estranged from her own mother and sister, so hostile to her family she calls herself an "orphan."[32] Spin the dial and arrive at right-wing black radio host Larry Elder, denouncing affirmative action, dismissing racism, browbeating poor kids who stumble in school as losers, kicking single mothers. He who checked the "race" box on his own college application in order to win admission to Brown University under affirmative action guidelines in 1970 despite his own below-par grades. He who himself is bitterly divorced.[33] On TV, there is Geraldo, whipping up the audience to a rage against teenage mothers, labeling a 14-year-old girl in big screen letters: "WANTS TO BE A SEXUAL SLUT JUST LIKE HER SISTER." He of super-slutdom who, in a 1989 *Playboy* interview, bragged of having boffed "thousands of women, literally thousands." He whose 1991 autobiography did not admit that his own unsafe sex produced a son, which he admitted only after it was disclosed in a *People* profile.[34] *Rolling Stone* founder/publisher Jan Wenner waxes piously sarcastic against teenage drinking and sex. He whose once-reasonably-honest, now-money-glam-worshipping rag sloshes with liquor, cigarette, lavish fashion, and nude starlet grabbers. Gary Hart concubine Donna Rice rails hysterically against internet porn seducing children. Rich, celebrated, indignantly defended as a right, Baby Boom hypocrisy never ends. The parent generation message is not lost on teens: self-discipline counts for nothing; stridently voiced values and morals to be imposed on others is everything.

The young are held up as symbols of all that has gone wrong with America even in exemplary liberal works. Boston University sociology professor Charles Derber's *The Wilding of America* adroitly details how the looting of the economy by the wealthy, corporate, and politically powerful contributes to the "ungluing of society" far more than sensational street crimes. Derber focuses most of his appropriately broad-brush attack on the greedy and amoral government-business skulduggeries of the Reagan and post-Reagan eras. He cites rising community and family disintegration. When it comes to the sins of the old, his attack is on individual villains and villainies, of which there are plenty. But young people are attacked in their entirety as a *demographic group* (that is, a group defined by race, age, sex, or ethnicity). Derber cites anecdotes and the typical kinds of bile elders of every era express toward juniors to paint a picture of faceless, violent, indifferent, materialistic, television-hooked young.[35] The biases routinely expressed against youth as a group would be offensive if, say, "blacks" or "women" were substituted for "youths" or "adolescents" in the sentences of many modern liberal commentaries.

Today's angry barrage against adolescents appears unique to the United States. Other societies, even our aging peer countries, don't seem enraged and terrified of their kids. In this volume, Europeans, Canadians, Australians, and Japanese will be lauded for the humanity of their nations' social insurance systems, the higher standards their governments enforce in health and welfare, their more enlightened views of youth, their more relaxed perspective on vice, their low crime and behavior problems. European health and social policy focuses not on age but on harmful behavior. The U.S. has much to learn from Europe's social policies, even though powerful movements in those nations, apparently envious of America's copious poverty, murder, and prisons, would dismantle their entitlement and employment systems.

But we have much to un-learn from Europe as well. European nations tend to be monocultures. Their borders are drawn to promote ethnic and religious homogeneity. A hundred million or so dead this century testifies to how badly Europeans handle ethnic disparities. The multicultural United States faces a more difficult domestic challenge than other Western societies. That challenge is presaged in multi-ethnic states such as Hawai'i, California, and New Mexico, and in most urban centers led by New York and Los Angeles.

At present, America's grownups in the Clinton era are not up to the challenge. Moralizing, coded fears and harmonious platitudes cover policies of division and repression. By every measure, public and private, today's wealthier adults are not giving today's youths the same chance to succeed as the poorer parents and grandparents of previous generations afforded us. Children and adolescents of the new millennium are raised by the most self-fixated adult generation in known history, one which seems unwilling to fulfill either its parenting or public policy obligations toward the young. It is adults whose crises are troubling and inexplicable.

The hopeful news is that 1990s children and adolescents are behaving far better than we have a right to expect. The next generation shows signs of stability and strength reflected in surprising statistics. And so this book is essentially just one repeating chapter. Whether the issue is violence, crime, suicide and self destruction, drugs, smoking, drinking, risk, or attitude, the sequence is the same. Teenagers are universally denigrated when, in reality, they are behaving well amid severe stresses.

Indeed, the 1997 Public Agenda poll's sermonizing adult hostility against children and teenagers included an tragicomic comeuppance. The teenagers surveyed revealed considerable warmth toward the very adults who castigated them en masse. Adolescents responding to the poll judged their elders as individuals rather than as faceless demographic stereotypes. They liked most of us. But at some point, if this society is to survive, their tolerance for the 1990s Raw Deal must wear thin.

Growing Up in a State of Extremes

By conventional logic, America's most extreme state should have been burned to its ungrounded foundations by adolescent superpredator mobs. California's teenage population is rising faster than in any other state—up half a million since 1990 with another million and a half, lurking in grade school, on the way. The reversal of fortunes among California youth has been more cataclysmic than that of teens elsewhere even as adults remain richer than their national counterparts.

In the last quarter century, California's young have fallen from among the nation's richest to its among its poorest. Poverty doubled among youths, exceeding 25 percent by 1997.[36] Per-pupil funding of schools plummeted from among the top five states in 1965 to among the bottom 15 in 1998. Today, the state consistently has the most crowded classrooms and fewest teachers and school personnel per student of any state. University tuition rose from free in the Sixties to $4,000-plus in the '90s. Cities have lost hundreds of thousands of industrial jobs.

The economic and social disaster that has befallen California youths and young families is set against the sunny fortunes of its aging Euro-whites and prospering nonwhites. Poverty has declined among Californians over 40. Median household incomes top $50,000 per year. Seventy percent own their own homes (and nearly all younger people's, too).

Baby Boomers are the apex of California affluence. Yet average tax rates have fallen by one-quarter, with special windfalls accruing to wealthy senior homeowners. Lush communities of opulence grace coastal and hilltop retreats, sprouting gates, guards, and surveillance. "Welcome to post-liberal Los Angeles," writes urban historian Mike Davis, "where the defense of luxury lifestyles is translated into a proliferation of new repressions in space and movement...the militarization of city life."[37]

Yet what has transpired among California's diverse populations in the last 25 years is so unbelievable that a whole new social theory may evolve to explain it. Reactionary to Marxist, conventional logic holds that extremes of violence, personal degradation, rage, anomie, poisonous apathy, and every other malaise *should be* pushing California's young to new depths of debauchery. Meanwhile, middle-agers *should be* basking in tiptop granola health and serenity. In standard determinism, scholars and media portray California exactly as orthodoxy says it should be: the Golden State of grownups versus the Gundown State of adolescents.

Eminently logical—except that's not what is going on at all.

Consider a mega-metropolis of 10 million, fountainhead of super-lethal permutations of heroin, cocaine, speed, and pharmaceuticals. One million teens age 10–19 live in this sprawling conurbation. Imagine now its drug overdose death toll for an entire year: adults, 562; teens, zero.

That would be real Los Angeles County, 1994.

Imagine a mega-state of 32 million that accounts for one-fourth of the nation's heroin deaths. Three million teens, 750,000 in families with annual incomes of less than $15,000, inhabit it. Imagine now its heroin overdose toll for a year: adults, 528; teenagers, zero.

That would be California, 1994.

A state whose adult drug abuse toll tripled from the 1970s to the 1990s—but whose teenage drug death toll fell by 90 percent. Where an exhaustive report would find a record 36,000 emergency hospitalizations for cocaine and heroin abuse in 1995—fewer than 2 percent of whom were teenagers.

Imagine that in this state, teenage suicide and self-destructive deaths—drug overdoses, gunshot accidents, hangings, drownings, car wrecks, other self-dispatch—declined by 50 percent in the last two decades.

Whose teenage population increased by half a million and youth poverty doubled from 1975 to 1997. But where 80,000 *fewer* teenagers were arrested every year in the mid-'90s than in the mid-'70s. Where teenage felonies were down 35 percent. Teenage misdemeanors down 23 percent. Teenage drug offenses down 35 percent. Even an august crime commission appointed by the Republican governor would scratch its head over the youth crime decline, burying that finding in its final report so as not to disturb the lucrative political issue of "youth crime."

Whose murder decreases among teenagers from 1990 to 1997 read as follows: Euro-whites, down 49 percent. Blacks, down 70 percent. Latinos, down 50 percent. Asians and Native Americans, down 52 percent. Especially strong teenage murder declines occurred in Los Angeles, where no coherent city law enforcement strategy could have caused it: 251 youth homicides in 1990, 75 in 1997.

Imagine how much interest these utterly unbelievable statistics generated among academic scholars, agency officials, politicians, or the news media (who, Mark Twain might say, worship "some of the facts"). That would be zero as well.

The Writing on the Wall

Once a month or so, I take the Blue Line urban train from Long Beach to downtown Los Angeles. The train smoothly whisks through the city's ripped backsides: silent industrial yards and dilapidated stucco blocks of Artesia, Compton, Watts, Firestone, Florence, Slauson, 18th Street, into the diseased and bustling Garment District.

After a few trips you, too, may find yourself monitoring the pitched battles between Southcentral's fleetfooted black, brown, "Asian/other" (and a few white) graffitists and taggers versus the plodding pastel paintover patrols. Graffiti first appears below the railway bridge on the cement banks of the Los Angeles River, a story in itself. Writes University of California, Irvine, doctoral graffitologist Faye Docuyanan:

> The history of the L.A. River is a particularly poignant example of the relationship between the proliferation of graffiti in urban environments and an abandonment of the public sphere in favor of more predictable and seemingly secure spaces such as "fortified enclaves" and "normalized" gated communities.[38]

In 1930, the renowned Olmsted and Bartholomew urban design firm recommended that the L.A. River connect "a unified system of beaches, parks, playgrounds, and mountain reserves" through the heart of the expanding city, designed to serve lower income working-class families.[39] Instead, at the behest of the Southern Pacific Railroad and allied cut-and-fill octopi, the river was paved from source to mouth to facilitate private development. The city shut out poor communities and created an immense canvas for their later retaliation.

On the train, I join the ghosts of Olmsted and Bartholomew in irony at the sight of the shaded, accented, wildstyle flourishes and murals adorning miles of river wall. Public displays along freeway and train vistas extend for blocks. Factories, vacant and broken-windowed, are enameled story above story. Scrawly three-letter tags appear on impossibly angular freeway bridges, defacing 50-foot razor-wire-defended signs no mortal could scale or depend. Graffiti galleries flank the river, where cavernous vaults of cement are enameled two to three stories high. These are not for public view, but trade admiration. Parked beside the Blue Line route, I see heavily spraypainted freight cars, descendents of Southern Pacific rolling stock, ready to spread L.A. tagger messages from sea to shining sea.

Reversing the trends of larger society, the police enforcers of beige are hopelessly outflanked and outcanned. Caltrans says it spends $3 million per year to erase graffiti from its freeway walls, train stations, and signs, 20 times more than a decade ago. Yet colorful murals and ugly curlicue tags abound, mile after mile. Even the brightly lit Firestone station's barricades are graffiti-blanketed, pastel-painted-over, then re-enameled.

Consider this blaze of energy amid what William Julius Wilson's *When Work Disappears* tells about the psychology of chronic inner-city unemployment.[40] "None of the other industrialized democracies has allowed its city centers to deteriorate as has the United States," Wilson writes. Where industries have shut down and unemployment is widespread, "lack of self-efficacy" takes over. Jobless adults, in the shadow of abandoned factories, spend lost days and months in which "they are unable to recall anything worth mentioning." Men loiter in unlimited time, talking aimlessly, drinking on corners, trapped in "emotional depression," surrendering to futility and paralyzing apathy. Where predatory manufacturing industries depart, predatory intoxicant industries (legal worse than illicit) infiltrate.

Yet selves are gloriously efficating in southcentral L.A. The eruption of adolescent spraycan exuberance annoys, infuriates, challenges at visceral range. "We paint trains even though they don't run," rues graffitist theoretician William Upski Wimsatt in *Bomb the Suburbs*.[41] Someone, thousands of ones, give up comfortable blunt and malt-liquor lounging to venture out for nights of creative wallwork. They wage what Mayor Richard Riordan calls "a constant assault on the psyches of Angelinos."[42]

Apropos, the angriest, most bitingly articulate rejoinders I've ever received were to my 1994 *Coast Weekly* editorial, "In Defense of Graffiti:"

> Whatever taggers' good, bad, or ugly intentions, spray-paint vandalism serves to remind us of a vital point: we alleged adults don't *deserve* to bask complacently in pretty vistas as we motor and stroll through a nation whose children's future we have unconscionably wrecked.
>
> ...So taggers, just as Washington and Sacramento target your young age groups for yet more legislated attrition, do America's future a favor by targeting your lost and avaricious elders for graffiti-canings right where it hurts us most—smack in our material souls. Colorize Winnebagos. Decorate country clubs. Claim fortress architecture as a challenge (it was built to keep your kind out—forever). Prioritize upscale Prop-13-happy suburbs for a field night. Enamel the Capitol.
>
> Just maybe, as we wrathfully behold your superficial sprayings, a few of us old folks might start thinking about how our devastating intergenerational economic and social vandalism has uglified the lives of millions to come.[43]

The reactions of the Winnebago, suburban, fortress, country-clubbing, and capitol folks whose environs I volunteered to bear the burden of intergenerational redress can be imagined. Said a Monterey property owners' association letter-writer in a more thoughtful response: "I doubt that the kids who are applying graffiti" are doing so "to punish the over-40 group for being irresponsible and selfish."[44]

Unbeknownst to me at the time, some are. Reported the *Bay Guardian*'s A. Clay Thompson in 1998...

> Grease and Solid...are graffiti writers, armed with spray paint, and they are on a continuing mission—a battle against the new San Francisco, a sanitized city purged of grimy homeless lowlife and housing project problem children.

> For Grease and Solid, graffiti is direct action against gentrification, part
> of a campaign not on any politician's agenda: to curb property values by keep-
> ing the city seedy.[45]

...so the poorer young can afford to live in the new Boutique City by the Bay, 1998, average house price $271,000, in the post-Proposition-13 world. "I hope my graffiti annoys yuppies," Grease, age 20, said. "If we all get pushed out of this city (due to gentrification), I'll still come back and write graffiti. Just for retaliation. Just to leave a piece of me here." Adds colleague Light:

> I'm more or less pissed at the world, the government, laws. The laws aren't
> there to treat people fairly—they're totally biased racially, economically. You
> have to be rich to have a real voice. Graffiti is a choice to have an impact.
> Rich people have huge advertisemements and billboards. We have walls.

Good for their psyche assault. It is apathy in the young we should fear. The biggest failing of adolescents, Franklin Roosevelt told the jobless young in 1936, is that they lose idealism, are not rebellious enough. Kids need adults and adults need kids. Yet we are disinheriting them, and we are doing it with our eyes wide open.

"Young people," writes Luis Rodríguez in *La Vida Loca*, "can only satisfy their needs through collective strength—against the police, who hold the power of life and death, against poverty, against idleness, against their impotence in society."[46]

The sheer volume of graffiti, more than the dramatic artism of its pieces, inspires awe. This is energy, power. More than cops and curfews can contain. I feel nervous in cities where there's no graffiti, nothing to gauge what the indigent young are about. Outrage at the smug lies of the privileged old, amazement at the frenetic energy of the disowned young, are why this book was written.

A Note on Presentation

There seem to me five banes of 1990s public discussion of youth (and probably many other) issues that I attempt to avoid:

- **The Gut-Grabbing Neverland Anecdote.** Rush Limbaugh's got stories, Jim Hightower's got stories. Anecdotes and cases give a human face to cold statistics. "Jimmy" (non-existent eight-year-old heroin addict), Becky Bell (teenage abortion death), Polly Klaas (murder provoked Three Strikes), Willie Horton, Jonesboro, and Ryan White all stimulat-ed larger debate and action good, bad, and disastrous. But whether an anecdote is true, and whether it illustrates a general problem or an exceptional case is crucial when considering whether to enact sweeping new laws and policies. In order to inflate the importance of news sto-ries, extremely rare cases (such as school shootings or teenage heroin deaths) are irresponsibly depicted as "alarming new trends." In this book, anecdotes are used to illustrate general cases, not rare exceptions.

- **The Dangling Statistic.** Liberals and rightists uniformly pick and choose only the few statistics which buttress their case and ignore the avalanche that refute it. Proprietary statistics, many simply manufactured, are a '90s epidemic evidencing how little today's interests care what conditions and behaviors really affect kids. In this book, I attempt to present complete statistics and major studies that bracket the issue discussed.

- **The Secondary Source.** By now, any Ph.D. has said just about anything, "experts" quote whatever the quoter wants, and studies can be found to buttress any cockamamie notion. I attempt to cite primary sources (original statistics) rather than what someone said about original statistics. This is the most fun part. Lots of kings are wearing barrels.

- **The Great Unread.** Both liberals and conservatives cite sound bites from studies pleasing to their agendas—but which they never read. Lots of studies, when examined, do not show what they claim to show or even claim what they are claimed to show. Studies of tobacco advertising and other media effects, and all "blue ribbon" reports, are particularly egregious, yet they are universally cited by interests who have never even read them. It is impossible to fully apprise every study cited, but I attempt to read and evaluate the major studies on opposing sides of the points discussed and to present the flaws therein.

- **False Egalitarianism.** The Right claims racism is dead; any impoverished minority kid can succeed on equal terms with a more affluent white kid today. Liberals claim advantaged white kids cause just as much murder, pregnancy, and drug abuse as poorer nonwhite kids. Baloney and baloney. Socioeconomics is a crucial determinant of behavior (and official response to behavior), and it remains intimately intertwined with race. Conservatives' lionizing of against-the-odds successes of individual minority youths does not relieve larger society of its obligation to take much stronger actions to compensate for racism. Liberals' demonizing of white kids with Gut-Grabbing Anecdotes does not make up for demonizing minority kids with Dangling Statistics. It is flatly untrue that most nonwhite youth have opportunity even remotely approaching that of most white youth. It is flatly untrue that white teenagers suffer even nearly as much homicide, violent crime, or AIDS as nonwhite youth. These two facts are interrelated. I attempt to treat race and economic inequality bluntly rather than fitting them to false egalitarian agendas.

Finally, a note about racial/ethnic references: America is undergoing a period of realignment in racial terminology, good for society but hell on communicating the topic. No terminology seems right. Referring to African Americans, Latinos, Asians, and Native Americans collectively as "nonwhites" is objectionable because it combines disparate groups into a word denoting what they aren't. "People of color" is awkward to use in many sentences, does not wear well in repitition, and seems to me little more than a rephrasing of the old term of segregation, "colored people." "Minority" no longer means anything in most cities and in California, where all races/ethnicities are minorities. Listing each race/ethnicity seperately each time is cumbersome. Since there are many circumstances in this book in which people of color/nonwhites as a group endure conditions and present characteristics different from those of whites as a group (and since, unfortunately, statistics are gathered most reliably by racial categorization), some use of collective references is needed. I use the term "nonwhite," and where it applies, "minority," since these are at least accurate and simple with regard to who is being talked about. Finally, consistently hyphenating every racial/ethnic reference (Asian-American, Latino-American, European-American, etc., to parallel African-American), gets old quick, and so I use the simpler terms denoting color (black, white) or ethnicity (Latino, Asian). I apologize to readers in advance who may find those terms inappropriate, and suggestions are welcome.

1 Myth: Teens Are Violent Thugs

Back when we were kids, the standard grownup head-shaker goes, it was a little running in the hall, talking out of turn, and neighborhood pranks. Then every year, the kids got a little worse and a little worse, and bam...now it's homeroom crack carnage and schoolyard shoot-outs.

"KIDS Without a Conscience," bellowed *People*. "Wild in the Streets!" screamed *Newsweek*. "Teenage Wolf Packs!" shrieked *U.S. News & World Report*. "Mayhem!" shouted the *Los Angeles Times*. "Teenage Time Bombs!" chorused *Time* and *U.S. News*.

Today's crime isn't just the dark-skinned indigents any more...look at *Rolling Stone*, *People*, CNN, *New York Times Sunday Magazine*. Upscale white kids in stoned slut death demise. Today's innocent, trusting adults aren't prepared to accept that "good kids" are "a figment of their parents' imagination," warns *Rolling Stone* crime expert Randall Sullivan. Unlike the halcyon days of yore, no place is safe; ferocity is everywhere, RAND Corporation's Peter Greenwood laments.[1]

Pounding on the younger generation brings all political stripes together. A Democratic president and GOP congressman declare youths to be our scariest population and unite to execute 16-year-olds through tougher juvenile crime legislation. Republican House pitbull Bill McCollum of Florida introduces the modestly titled "Juvenile Superpredator Incapacitation Act." In California, Republican Governor Pete Wilson leads an ace: frying 14-year-olds; Democratic House Speaker Cruz Bustamente trumps it with capital punishment for seventh graders.[2] California Republican and Democratic chieftains unite behind a $900 million prison bond issue in the 1996 election, half of it earmarked for youth lockup.

More teenage boys, more crime, declares the liberal Brookings Institution's "crime doctor" John DiIulio. Period. Northeastern University's College of Criminal Justice dean, James Alan Fox, brands teenagers as "temporary sociopaths—impulsive and immature."[3] Famed UCLA criminologist James Q. Wilson declares the mere existence of young people in quantity *causes* "crime, addiction, and welfare dependency."[4] Former Republican drug czar William Bennett and New Democrat DiIulio warn of a growing "population of teenagers with higher incidence of serious drug use, more access to powerful firearms, and fewer moral restraints than any such group in American history."[5] Children's magazine publisher Dan Dailey disgorges the scariest ultimate: wait'll internet-savvy teenagers Go Nuclear.[6] (Update Tom Lehrer's classic '60s nuke proliferation satire, "Who's Next?": "We'll try to remain serene and calm...When ADOLESCENTS get The Bomb.")

Wolf packs on crack would display noble moral restraint compared to the prestigious lynch mob raging from scholar, agency, and media podia.

Superpredators Marching Down Maple Street

From Criminology 1 to the anti-crime echelon, the dogma is simple: adolescents equal villainy. Just abolish the word "crime" and substitute "teenager," as in "the coming teenager wave."

Unlike murkier notions of crime, this "demographic theory" is easy to test. The census tells us the number of teenagers. Crime reports tell us how much violent crime there is by three different measures. It took me an hour to plot population and crime trends by year for the last few decades. When I saw the results (Figure 1), I realized why criminologists avoid putting their pet theory to the test.

In 1977, the proportion of teen males ages 15–19 peaked at 5.03 percent of America's population. Then the teen-male share fell by one-third, bottoming out at 3.42 percent in 1992. So we can use these two years as high and low brackets.

According to traditional crime theory, fewer teenage boys should have been followed by a dramatic reduction in crime. Table 1 shows the serious ("index," or felony violent and property) crimes tabulated by the FBI for 1977 and 1992.

There were not fewer, but 3.5 million more reports of serious crimes in the country in 1992 than in 1977—including 900,000 more violent crimes, 2.5 million more property felonies, and half a million more drug offenses. While the numbers of teenage males plunged by nearly two million, crime, especially violent and drug offense, grew rapidly.

Who, then, is and is not boosting America's arrest surges? See if you can separate the fall guys from the true culprits (Tables 2 and 3). If you can't spot whose crime has increased the most, you, too, can be a quotable '90s crime expert.

Figure 1

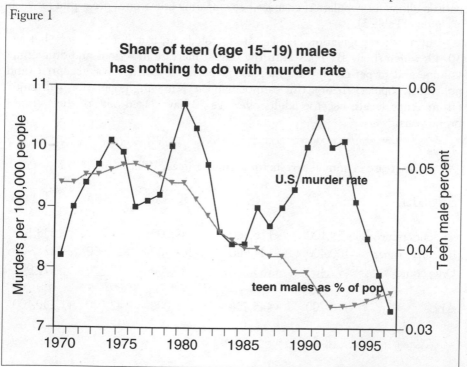

Table 1

The teen population fell, but America's serious crime rose:

Index crimes*	Violent	Property	Drug	All index	Male teens as pct of pop
1977	1,029,580	9,955,580	598,873	10,984,500	5.03%
1992	1,932,370	12,505,900	1,099,907	14,438,200	3.42%
Volume Change	+902,790	+2,550,320	+501,034	+3,453,700	-1,854,000
Rate Change	+59%	+7%	+56%	+11%	-17%

*Crimes reported to police. Violent crimes are murder, rape, robbery, and aggravated assault. Property crimes are burglary, larceny, motor vehicle theft, and arson. Index crimes are violent plus property crimes. Rates are calculated and compared based on national populations for 1977 and 1992.
Source: FBI, *Uniform Crime Reports*, 1977, 1992. Washington, DC: U.S. Department of Justice. Bureau of the Census, *Statistical Abstract of the United States, 1997*. Washington, DC: U.S. Department of Commerce.

Time's up. In the last two decades, the volume of serious teenage violent and drug crime declined. But crime rose for all other age groups, most staggeringly among the 30–49 age group. However, Table 2's comparison is not fair, since the teenage population declined, the 20-age and senior populations remained stable, and the Baby Boomers in the 30–49 class showed the largest increase. A fairer comparison allows for population changes by comparing crime rates per capita for each age group (Table 3).

Even when population changes are factored out, it is not teenagers, but age 30–49, which shows BY FAR both the largest increase in serious and drug crime volume and in per-capita rate increase. According to the most accepted (and politically popular) theory, this cannot happen. An aging population will enjoy falling crime levels, because adults over age 30 have "aged out" of their crime-prone years.

Table 2

Increase in annual arrests for serious crimes, 1992 minus 1977:

Arrests for:	age 13–19	20–29	30–49	50+	Total
Violent crimes	+59,100	+116,500	+149,200	+7,200	+338,100
Property crimes	-100,400	+144,000	+361,900	+19,600	+ 421,900
Drug crimes	-77,400	+185,200	+346,900	+15,900	+470,000
ALL	-118,700	+445,700	+858,000	+42,700	+1,230,100

Sources and definitions: See Table 1.

Table 3

Change in per-capita annual arrest rates by age, 1992 versus 1977:

Arrests for:	age 13–19	20–29	30–49	50+	Total
Violent crimes	+69%	+63%	+69%	+30%	+54%
Property crimes	+4	+27	+88	+25	+6
Drug crimes	-18	+59	+307	+255	+50
ALL	+18	+60	+160	+51	+38

Sources and definitions: See Table 1.

To be fair, some inside the Beltway did notice this two-decade explosion in serious adult offense, a bit belatedly. After noting that violent crime arrest rates had risen among youths and young adults from 1986 to 1996, the November 1997 "Juvenile Justice Bulletin," issued by the U.S. Department of Justice's Office of Juvenile Justice and Delinquency Prevention, revealed the following in footnotes on pages four and six:

> The largest increase in violent crime arrests in the adult population was for persons in their thirties (up 64%)...For juveniles and young adults, the property crime arrest rate changed little between 1980 and 1996, while the arrest rates for persons in their thirties and forties increased an average of nearly 50% (emphasis mine).

Uh...isn't this kinda important? A big violent and property crime surge among the old parental units? A 30–40 something could well be Dad or Mom to the 10–14 or 15–17 year-old frightening the establishment. But the nation's most august criminologists resolutely decreed that over-30 types had "aged out of their crime-prone years" and could not possibly be committing more offenses. Case closed.

Thus was born the Big Lie of America's crime non-debate. It surfaced in the 1990s in an avalanche of cloned conventionalities:

> While the crime rate is dropping for adults, it is soaring for teens.
> —*Time*, 15 January 1996, p. 15

> Crime may be down, but juvenile crime is way up.
> —Jonathan Alter, *Newsweek*, 28 April 1997, p 30

> Juvenile offenses have soared since the mid-1980s, while adult violent-crime rates have remained fairly steady.
> —*U.S. News & World Report*, 25 March 1996, p. 29

Where did the Big Media get these whoppers? From the experts—those devout crusaders against "moral poverty":

Except for [juvenile] homicide, things have been getting better for over a decade.
                —James Q. Wilson Ph.D., *Commentary*, September 1994, p. 25

At a time when overall crime rates are dropping, youth crime rates, especially for crimes of violence, have been soaring.
                —John DiIulio Ph.D., *Chicago Tribune*, 16 December 1995

There are actually two crime trends in America—one for the young, one for the mature—which are moving in opposite directions and balancing off in the statistics.
                —James Alan Fox Ph.D., *Los Angeles Times*, 29 October 1995, p. B5

While overall crime rates have remained fairly steady in recent years, the arrest rates for juveniles accused of violent crimes has risen dramatically.
                —FBI, U.S. Department of Justice, in *Juvenile Crime*, 1997, pp. 12–13

In the last three and one-half years, the crime rate is down, but violence among young people under eighteen is up.
                —President Clinton, Albuquerque, New Mexico, 11 June 1996

Everyone was saying it, everyone was lying. The press was exercising its First Amendment freedoms by incessantly repeating the worst official untruths.

Lies and Statistics

This is how authorities fabricated the claim about teenage violence: First, experts took the declining trends in *reported crime* from police agency reports or from household interviews in the *National Crime Victimization Survey* and announced: "Overall, crime is down—" Then, they took the rising teenage violent crime *arrest* figures from *Uniform Crime Reports* and declared: "—but teenage violence is soaring." They then mashed the two incompatible halves of the sentence together.

As will be shown, there is no measure (or honest combination of measures) for which the statement, "crime is down, but youth violence is up" can be made. If arrests are used, both teen and adult crime are up. If crimes reported to police and crimes cleared are used, both teen and adult crime are down. If victims' surveys are used, no conclusion can be drawn, since the handling of age groups and crimes is inconsistent. Since crime authorities are well aware of what these measures show and don't show, they have perpetrated fraud.

Before we investigate this high-level hoax, note the flyspeck of truth in the crime debate cowlot: from 1984 to 1993, the homicide rate among persons under age 25 doubled at the same time it was declining among adults over age 30. Thus, Fox, quoted above, insinuated that our entire violence increase is caused young persons. To wit: young, dark-skinned persons.

However, murder is a very rare crime even among violent criminals. At its peak in 1993, the number of juvenile murder arrests equaled just 2.7 percent of all juvenile violent crime arrests, 0.16% of total juvenile arrests, and one in 5,000 of the population ages 13–17. While murder is the most serious crime, it is not an index of violence in the general youth population. Further, its impact is highly localized. In California and in the major cities whose statistics I examined, murder is rarer among youths today than in the 1970s—with the major exception of inner-city nonwhite males. Most of what was termed "white" youth homicide turned out to be Latino, not Euro. As will be shown, this homicide surge was not and is not a race- or age-based, but a socioeconomic, phenomenon born of rising inner-city unemployment and drug marketing chaos in the late 1980s—conditions from which older adults and whites of all ages were largely exempt.

A much better (though still flawed) measure of violence in the general population is felony violent crime, which is 100 times more common than murder. It is here that official untruths are the most incredible. To understand the cynicism with which the myth, "adult crime is down while juvenile violence is soaring," is concocted, it is necessary to analyze the basic measures of crime the U.S. Bureau of Justice Statistics provides:

- The *National Crime Victimization Survey* (NCVS) of approximately 100,000 residents over age twelve in 50,000 households, surveyed every year since 1973 with regard to their victimizations.

- Law enforcement agencies' annual records of crimes reported and of arrests made. These latter two measures have been reported by the FBI annually in *Uniform Crime Reports* (UCR) since the 1930s and are available with reasonable reliability from around 1965 to the present.

Each of these measures has a few strengths and giant weaknesses, and they do not combine well. The first, the NCVS, does not interview subjects under age 13, so violence against children is untallied. Nor, its authors rue, does it interview murder victims. It suffers from the weaknesses of self-reporting surveys: respondents can have difficulty recalling when or by what age of offender a crime was committed, or what is meant by a crime. Respondents are asked to estimate the ages of offenders in broad categories, such as "12 to 20" or "30 and older." Survey revisions make it difficult to compare NCVS reports after 1992 with those before. Overall, the NCV survey is useful for ballparking citizens' victimizations that are not reported to police. But it is useless for calculating trends by age of criminal.

Records of law enforcement agencies collected by the FBI also are problematic in that they provide no clue as to who committed the majority of crimes for which no arrest results, and they vastly overstate the contribution of youths to the nation's crime volume. Only a fraction of crimes are reported to police, only a fraction of these are "cleared" (result in an arrest), and in some fraction of these the cops bust the wrong guy. These fractions add up. Ages of arrestees are reported well but can be used to estimate crime trends by age group only if it is assumed that the ages of the inept or unlucky who get arrested are pretty much like the ages of wily or lucky who got away.

Kids tend to be arrested in groups. Teens are more likely than adults to commit crimes in groups and police are more likely to round up a gaggle of kids at the scene whether or not they had anything to do with the blood on the pavement. Conversely, adult miscreants are much better at not getting caught and remain free to commit more crime. The upshot is that criminal for criminal, adult offenders commit more crimes against more victims. Further, adult criminals are much more deadly than their teen counterparts because they are much more likely to kill or injure their victims.

Thus, youths are over-arrested compared to the numbers of crimes they commit, which inflates their arrest statistics. In 1996, the FBI reported that youths comprised 19 percent of all violent crime arrestees but accounted for only 13 percent of the violent crimes that were solved (or "cleared") by an arrest. The same was true for property crimes: youths comprised 35 percent of those arrested but committed only 24 percent of property crimes. Youths are particularly likely to be over-arrested for murder: 15 percent of those handcuffed for homicide are youths, but only 8 percent of all murders are committed by youths. (Pause and absorb that: the killer youths panicking Congress and the White House commit just 8 percent of the nation's homicides).

Thus, while youths comprise a high proportion of arrestees for serious offenses, they account for a much lower proportion of the nation's total crime volume. *Crime volume* is important. When apprehended, an adult criminal who commits 40 robberies and a youth who commits one hallway shakedown both show up in police records as one adult arrest and one youth arrest, though the former's "crime volume" (number of crimes solved by his arrest) is 40 times that of the latter.

Using the total number of solved plus unsolved crimes reported to police, and the percent of crimes solved by arrest of a youth, we can estimate the crime volume for which youths account. To calculate crime volume by age, apportion the crimes reported to police each year which are unsolved to each age group based on that age group's proportion of total crimes solved by an arrest. This assumption is biased against youths because we would expect adult criminals to be more experienced at not getting caught; hence their greater numbers of victims per offender. Even with this flaw, "crime volume" may be the best available measure of crime, especially with regard to changes over time. Table 4 shows the change in the per-capita crime volume by age.

In 1980, there were 11.6 serious ("index") violent and property youth crimes committed per 100 youths ages 10–17. In 1996, that number was 9.8—a decline of 15 percent. (This doesn't mean 9.8 in every 100 youths is a criminal, because one criminal typically accounts for several crimes). The 30–49 age group distinguishes itself once again, this time as the only age group whose crime volume has risen faster than its population. By 1996, the volume of crime per American age 30–39 was approaching that per juvenile age 10–17. This is a stunning development, since the poverty rate among youths (the best predictor of likelihood of arrest), 20 percent and rising in 1996, is double that of 30-agers (9 percent and stable).

Frosting the cake of confusion, victim-survey tallies lead to maddeningly different conclusions than law enforcement figures. Thus, authorities can assert anything they want to about crime at any time—and they do. Time to terrorize the

Table 4

Serious crime rising among adults over 30, down among teens

Total index crime volume per 100 persons of each age, 1996 versus 1980:

	age 10–17	18–29	30–39	40–49	50+
1980	11.6	18.0	6.3	3.4	1.3
1996	9.8	16.1	8.8	4.3	0.9
Change	-15%	-11%	+36%	+20%	-29%

Sources: See Table 1.

public into building a block of new prisons? Hype arrest figures in the *Uniform Crime Reports*, which (see above) have risen sharply. Time to pat yourself on the back for lassoing the bad guys? Trot out the victimization surveys, which show that crime in the U.S. hasn't changed much in the last quarter century; in fact, 1996 would be the least violent year since the survey began.

Officials' subterfuge in mixing and matching crime measures to suit prevaricative ends is the foundation of the academic malpractice used to assemble the 1990s version of the Demographic Scapegoat Theory. As discussed below, this theory holds that social ills are to be blamed on whatever group in the population politicians designate as the most undesirable in any given era.

The Demographic Fallacy

The political assault weapon of the pop-criminologists throughout the last century has been the demographic theory of crime, which might be better termed the "demographic fallacy." The demographic fallacy holds that crime goes up or down depending on the *composition of the population*—that is, whether larger or smaller numbers of certain biologically defective groups are present. Which group gets blamed for causing crime depends on who is hated most at the moment: non-white race, immigrant status, minority religion, and young age are the most enduring demographic scapegoats.

In the late 1800s and early 1900s, leading Western social scientists claimed that the presence of nonwhites and certain immigrants in the population caused more violence. "Scientific testing" by top authorities reported that violence and shiftiness were innate to black people, Chinese, Mexicans, Jews, eastern or southern European immigrants, and "atavistic" types. The last were throwbacks to primitive humans, identifiable by physical traits whose pictorial renderings just happened to look like a Klan karicaturist's sketch of an African. In every era, Harvard zoologist Stephen Jay Gould's *The Mismeasure of Man* documents, social scientists' demographic finger-pointing just happened to aim at the groups against whom political authorities were (and are) fanning public fears.[7]

The 1990s recrudescence of the demographic fallacy now holds that more teenagers and young adults in the population causes more crime and social ills. The language used by authorities who promote demographic fallacies never changes. Leading social scientists in 1998 deploy the same terms that their forebears used in 1898: inferior chemistry renders the disliked group *innately* "hot blooded," impulsive, trigger-happy, coldly savage, sexually dissolute, indifferent to the consequences of their acts, and attracted to base influences.

A frank, searing analysis and refutation of the demographic fallacy is found in the writings of Frantz Fanon, a Martinique psychiatrist and social theorist. His classic 1963 treatise, *The Wretched of the Earth*, described classical French bigotries regarding the colonized Algerians:

> *The Algerian frequently kills other men…The Algerian kills savagely…The Algerian kills for no reason…*The Algerian is strongly marked by mental debility…His actions are always impulsive and aggressive…The Algerians rob each other, cut each other up, and kill each other…The motives of a murder…may arise out of a gesture, an allusion, an ambiguous statement, a…disappointing triviality [emphasis in original].[8]

So American political and social science authorities describe today's U.S. teenagers:

> Children as young as 13 are shooting other young people for a bicycle or a leather jacket, setting fire to homeless men and women, participating in gang rapes (Governor's Commission on Youth Violence, New York, June 1994).

Or consider this, written by Pacific News Service editor Richard Rodríguez under a blaring headline, "The Coming Mayhem," in the Sunday *Los Angeles Times* opinion section:

> James Q. Wilson, for example, predicts that the growing population of teenage boys will mean an increase in murders, rapes, and muggings. A new type of criminal is emerging…Remorseless, vacant-eyed, sullen—and very young…We are entering a Stephen King novel. We are entering an America where adults are afraid of children. Where children rule the streets. Where adults cower at the approaching tiny figure on the sidewalk ahead.[9]

Authorities assert that criminal populations are innately inferior: "the biologically limited possibilities of the native," reports Fanon tongue in cheek, is a "fact" established by the finest European psychiatry:

> …his predatory instinct is well known; his intense aggressivity is visible to the naked eye…We find him incapable of self-discipline…a congenital impulsive…aggressive and generally homicidal.[10]

Today, by a similar process, American "social scientists argue that teenage aggression is natural:"[11]

> Teenagers are the most crime-prone group…in the view of Northeastern University criminologist James Alan Fox, "temporary sociopaths—impulsive and immature."[12]

> Like his former teacher, UCLA's James Q. Wilson—another popular intellectual in Washington—[top criminologist John] DiIulio comes from the school of research that says crime is largely driven by demographics. More male teenagers, more crime. Period.[13]

A century of research convincingly debunked racist theories of crime by showing that high crime rates adhere to low-income, transitional inner-city neighborhoods, not the succession of racial groups (Irish, Italian, Chinese, black, Latino) who inhabited them.[14] Yet without missing a beat, the new "age theory" of crime invoked the same language and the same paternalistic remedies as the old "race theory." In fact, champions of the 1990s "age theory" readily admit it is really a "race theory." Fox and DiIulio apply it only to inner-city minority males who, DiIulio declares, grow up "jobless, Godless, and fatherless." Although these and other mainstream crime experts use the term "youth violence," in practice (and often in direct reference) they focus on black and Latino youths. In the policy realm, 95 percent of the gang members toward whom the president's anti-crime package is aimed are minorities. A visit to a modern youth prison demonstrates that the new "age theory" is caging blacks and Latinos even more efficiently than the old "race theories" did.

Yet where Fanon concluded a half-century ago that the violence of Algerians was not due to biology but was a "direct product of the colonial situation," modern American crime authorities ignore social conditions and remain stuck in myths of innate teenage (particularly nonwhite teenage) biology. The value of Fanon's more honest analysis was that it correctly predicted the eventual unity of Algerians to expel the French, while America's doctrine-shackled experts shuffle in a state of consistent misprediction about crime.

Why Bring Up Race?

Many moderates and liberals understandably shudder at citing negative statistics on racial matters because they might—probably will—be warped to feed the new Bell-Curve racism advanced by popular rightist social thinkers such as Charles Murray. Many conservatives also dismiss race, and race-sensitive strategies such as affirmative action, arguing that society has become reasonably "color blind." Many others are just sick of the topic after four tumultuous decades and apparently nothing further to gain.

Unfortunately, ignoring race means turning a blind eye to how present "nonracist" anti-youth policies are filling prisons and destitute neighborhoods with young nonwhite men. Facing that means talking about race. And, as will be shown, there is a huge irony to the 1990s race question, an 800-pound white elephant, you might say, rampaging in the crimeyard.

Do the various "demographic scapegoats," that have been fingered through the ages really display unusually high violence and crime levels? In nearly all cases, as Fanon unsentimentally pointed out, they do—by a wide margin. The homicide rate among nonwhite populations has always exceeded that of whites; nonwhite youths have murder rates a dozen times higher than those of white youths. Progressive groups are correct to fear that these statistics can be twisted by reactionary interests to resurrect long-refuted claims that violence is innate to certain racial groups.

To prove their campaign is not racist, the increasingly mainstream conservative law enforcement juggernaut is perfectly willing to bring the hammer down on white kids. This creates a harsher social landscape in which poorer youths, especially nonwhites, suffer the most. In keeping with this need to appear nonracist, moderates and liberals have concocted "false egalitarian" arguments which are both nonsensical and dangerous. Some liberals have claimed that white kids "commit just as much crime," that violent crime among white youth has risen faster than among black youth, and that "the suburbs are getting just as perilous as the inner city." A senseless tactic, since scaring the suburbs into believing thugs are at their door has been a major success playing into police- and prison-happy policy.

The worst aspect of liberals' denial of race and class issues in youth behavior is that it is wrong. They allow conservatives such as DiIulio and Bennett to express righteous disbelief that leftists can make an issue of the fact that black men are more likely to go to prison than Euro-white men. Black men commit more serious crime! Bennett and DiIulio use statistics to deny institutional racism exists: look at the vast, undisputed differences in the black and Euro-white homicide rates, they say. Wouldn't police be even more racist, they needle, if they left black murderers on the street to kill and maim more black people?

Liberals once had a correct response to this rhetoric: institutional racism has a lot to do with why blacks are more likely to commit violent crimes and to be arrested. The effects of racism began long before the trigger was pulled. William Julius Wilson has revealed the effects of the destruction of the inner-city industrial base. Mike Davis's analysis of the police war waged against L.A.'s black and brown youth in communities pounded by job loss and isolation has delineated the roots of urban violence. Davis noted that Los Angeles lost 200,000 industrial jobs in the postwar period, including one-fourth of the nation's job loss in the 1990s recession. Today,

> most researchers now accept that the increasing appeal of gang counterculture in the 1980s was a direct result of the catastrophic collapse of urban employment opportunities for minority males during the 1970s. Blue-collar jobs no longer reincorporate teenage gang members into family and community life.[15]

But these were not seen by mainstream liberals as profitable arguments to make in the Reagan or 1990s eras. Rather than emphasizing the impact of economic issues on race, most liberals found it more politic to claim that youth violence rested in the intersection of bad teenage culture and guns, a mass juvenile attitude problem accumulating a body count, and to quietly ignore race and poverty altogether.

But statistics do not support the oft-made claims in the media, or by such experts as the Rand Corporation's Peter Greenwood and liberal juvenile justice author Ed Humes, that murder has risen among all classes of youth. Those states which split statistics by ethnicity show that most (60 percent in 1995, national figures show) of what is called "white" teenage homicide is actually Latino. California's crime statistics going back to 1975 show that Euro-white teenagers' murder arrest rates are low, stable, and declined by 20 to 30 percent from the mid-1970s to the mid-1990s.

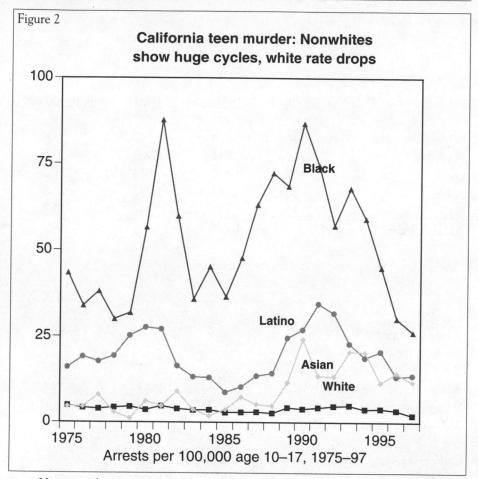

Figure 2

California teen murder: Nonwhites show huge cycles, white rate drops

Arrests per 100,000 age 10–17, 1975–97

However, large increases in homicide arrest were found among Asian, black, and Latino youths from the mid-1980s to the early 1990s. The latter two groups show very high peaks in 1980 and 1990, followed by sharp declines. National figures for rate of homicide arrest and for risk of death by homicide, though less complete, both confirm Euro-white teens' low numbers and stable trends. Trends in California murder arrest rates (Figure 2) show that nonwhites account for the entire increase inflaming the media and politicians. It is important to repeat that the increases in murder and robbery among nonwhite youths in the 1980s were temporary upward trends within a greater, 20-year crime *decline* among youths of all races—a point no major authority has admitted.

Nationally, African-American teens are 14 times more likely, and Latino youth 7.5 times more likely, to be murdered than are Euro-white teens. California accounts for one in six teen murders. Its arrest rates show that even after seven years of sharp decline, black teens in 1997 were 11.5 times, and Latino teens six times, more likely to be arrested for murder than Euro-whites. California teenagers, particularly whites, are more likely to be murdered than their national counterparts. The most recent figures as of this writing in all cases are shown in Table 5.

Table 5

Poorer youth have much higher murder rates

U.S. teenage homicide deaths, by race/ethnicity, 1995

	age 13–17	18–19	Total	Rate/100,000
White (European)	344	296	640	3.6
Black	968	941	1,909	50.4
Latino	464	410	874	27.0
Asian	46	41	87	12.8
Native American	35	12	47	24.7
ALL (including unknown)	1,875	1,726	3,601	14.1

California teenage homicide deaths, by race/ethnicity, 1996

	age 13–17	18–19	Total	Rate/100,000
White (European)	34	27	61	4.3
Black	56	76	132	52.5
Latino	177	160	337	29.3
Asian	18	14	32	9.6
Native American	0	0	0	0
ALL (including unknown)	285	277	562	17.6

California teenage homicide arrests, by race/ethnicity, 1997

	age 13–17	18–19	Total	Rate/100,000
White (European)	33	49	82	3.9
Black	78	88	166	44.9
Latino	191	206	397	23.0
Asian	51	37	88	16.3
ALL (including unknown)	353	380	733	15.5

Source: National Center for Health Statistics (1998). U.S. Mortality Detail File, 1995; California Criminal Justice Statistics Center (1998), *Crime & Delinquency in California 1997* update.

Viewed benignly, media and expert preoccupation with murderous white teenagers reflects a conscientious desire not to inflame racial antagonisms. Or, perhaps the suburban nature of most editors and academics makes them focus on the suburban murders they care most about. Either way, rather than generate an accurate picture and seek to understand the conditions that create violence, the strongly anti-youth image used depicts kids of all races as latent brutalizers prone to murder.

Benign or elitist, the problem with false egalitarianism is that key factors such as socioeconomic class and histories of discrimination are sidestepped. It is true that poorer people are more likely than richer ones to be arrested (as we deploy police to make arrests in poorer communities) for violent crimes (as our laws define a violent crime). It is true that blacks are poorer than whites and are subject to greater dislocation and community instability that predicts higher rates of crime. It follows that blacks will be arrested for violence more often than whites.

It does not follow that blacks are innately violent and whites innately pacific. In fact, more affluent, suburban blacks often display violent crime rates lower than those of similarly affluent whites. Modern social scientists, a few popularized exceptions notwithstanding, accept that race is not the defining factor in violence or other behavior. Yet, by ignoring the pivotal role of socioeconomic status, today's "youths-are-violent" demographic fallacy amounts to a coded recycling of the century-old assertion that nonwhite races are inherently violent. If violence is *innate* to youth, and socioeconomics is not a factor, then why are black and Latino rates so much higher than for whites?

The "teenage theory" of crime, when examined, is as fallacious as the "nonwhite race theory"—in fact, these wind up being the same theory. It is true that U.S. teenagers are arrested more for violent crimes than persons over 40. It does not follow that teenagers are innately more violent.

If teenagers are naturally savage, we would expect them to be so everywhere. Yet in Europe, Canada, Australia, and Japan, homicide peaks at low levels around age 25–34. In other Western nations, 40-year-olds are more likely to be involved in homicide than 19-year-olds. In fact, U.S. *senior citizens* are three times more likely to commit murder than are European teens and young adults.

California and Canada, the Western nation whose youth poverty level is closest to the U.S.'s, have about the same numbers of people (33 million and 30 million in 1997, respectively). Yet their patterns of homicide arrest and homicide death are very different (Table 6).

As the raw numbers for 1996 show, Canadian and California white (Euro) teenagers display virtually the same *structure* of murder by age. Of the five race/ethnicity groups displayed above (lumping Canadian teens as one ethnicity), those with the lowest poverty levels (California Euro-white, and Canadian) display the lowest murder arrest levels, particularly at young ages. California black middle agers (40–69) display murder rates twice as high as California white teenagers and three times higher than Canadian teenagers. This argues strongly that popular theories used to explain high teenage murder levels (innate teenage trigger-happiness, impulsiveness, media violence, gun availability, raging hormones, etc.) are dubious because they do not apply to whites.

But as the murder arrest *rates* show, there is something particularly violent about the United States irrespective of poverty and regardless of age. At *every age level*, despite similar incomes, California Euro-whites have homicide levels double, and gun murder rates triple, those of Canadians (who are 87 percent European white). California whites over age 40 are much wealthier than their Canadian counterparts but have a twice the rate of murder arrest. (In preliminary figures for 1997, however,

Table 6

California murder arrests by race versus. Canada, 1996, 1997

Age of murderers	California					Canada
	All	White	Latino	Black	Asian	
10–19	802	110	396	200	96	108
20–29	1,017	161	490	290	76	179
30–39	427	138	153	109	27	137
40+	289	128	71	64	26	117
TOTAL	2,535	537	1,110	663	225	541

Murder arrests per 100,000 population, 1996

Age of murderers	All	White	Latino	Black	Asian	Canada
10–19	17.0	5.3	22.9	54.1	17.8	2.7
20–29	21.0	7.8	26.6	80.6	13.6	4.2
30–39	7.1	4.5	8.1	26.5	4.2	2.6
40+	2.8	2.0	3.3	9.6	2.3	1.1
TOTAL	9.8	3.9	14.6	36.7	7.6	2.3

Murder arrests per 100,000 population, 1997 (age detail limited)

Age of murderers	All	White	Latino	Black	Asian	Canada
Youths age 12–17	335	27	188	72	48	54
Rate/100,000 pop	11.7	2.1	17.8	32.1	14.6	2.2
Adults age 18–69	1,761	361	794	504	102	527
Rate/100,000 pop	7.9	3.0	19.2	33.4	4.2	2.6
Youth poverty rates	24%	13%	40%	45%	25%	13%

Source: California Law Enforcement Information Center; Statistics Canada.

California's white-youth murder rate declined to the same as Canada's; this may be a one-year anomaly). It is here that factors such as America's gun proliferation and cultural attitudes favoring violence may exert influences that affect all age groups, not just adolescents. For example, in 1996, Canada suffered 200 gun murders (one for every 150,000 citizens) compared to 14,000 in the U.S. (one per 19,000 citizens).

"There are more than 30 times more firearms in the United States than in Canada," reports Statistics Canada: 222 million in the U.S. (including 76 million handguns) versus 7.4 million in Canada (1.2 million of them tightly-restricted handguns).[16] That is, for every 100 Americans, there are 84 guns, including 29 handguns; for every 100 Canadians, 25 guns, including four handguns. With personal armament, Yanks are eight times more murderous than Maple Leafers; unarmed, twice as homicide-prone.

When Squeegees Are Outlawed...

By luck, I got to visit Toronto for three days on the American Bar Association tab in early August 1998. I know that Toronto has four million people and suffers a murder a week, thereabouts. I picture a manicured, affluent, homogenous metropolis patrolled by mounties who cordially shoo little towheads away from drunken hockeymen. I am 90 percent wrong. Long hours of streetcar riding and walking reveal a city of astonishing diversity, inner neighborhoods dilapidated but vital. Thousands mill the streets—the Caribana festival is drumming for 700,000 visitors. Black, Asian, and ethnic European and Latin neighborhoods ring the downtown. I realize that these are the kinds of neighborhoods which, in States cities, have collapsed in bombed-out devastation. Canada's social policies—evident in the national government funded health insurance, the massive streetcar and subway network, the housing subsidies, the small numbers of homeless, the intact vitality of even the shabbiest districts—so far are staving off the urban destruction wrought by the industrial abandonment which has hit Canada as well.

I flag down a mountie at Yongue and Dundas streets as the multi-hued crowds gather for Caribana. He clops to a halt. Does Toronto have a youth curfew? The officer looks puzzled. What age of youth, sir? Sixteen. Oh, no, sixteen, they come and go as they like, all hours. Well, thirteen, then. Consultation ensues. Several Toronto police tell me that if they see a genuine child in public after midnight with no adult in sight, they take him/her home under the "child in need of protection" ordinance, or, if home is not the place, to a shelter not affiliated with jail or police. And what is the drinking age in Ontario? I ask. Nineteen, the police reply. Over in Ottawa, eighteen. I see many teenagers in bars and liquor stores. There are no age-warning signs, and carding is a discreet rarity rather than the Big Deal common to States alcohol sellers.

The police, without exception, tell me the city, which allows teenagers to drink alcohol and to roam the streets at all hours as if they were adults, is quite safe. There are gangs, but they mainly attack each other. Certain districts get rowdy now and then. Why the low violence toll? "Not as many guns here," one officer said crisply. "Practically no one has a pistol, except by special dispensation. Hard to come by—even for us." He opens his jacket to show me he isn't packing iron, though other police I see later in the evening have full holsters.

Toronto's vexing youth problem, profiled in the local papers and vigorously debated in government forums, seems to be "squeegee kids." As in New York, a red stoplight in many areas means a windshield assault-wash by street kids armed with soap buckets and squeegees. The lengthy Sunday *Toronto Star* profile of "Squeegees" reads like an alternative weekly in the States. The sympathetic feature details Squeegee culture, where kids brutalized by violent homes and system failures eke out marginal livings soaping windshields (with detergent donated by a local rental car agency) and dodging incessant political-police harassment. A curmudgeonly ad campaign urging city saviors to "just put them on a one-way bus to Buffalo," New York, brought indignant response from the city's largest paper. The ad campaign "was not only mean, but stupid, for then the people of Buffalo would have our kids to squeegee their windshields. And who would be left to do ours?"[17]

Postal

Of Los Angeles County's 300 postal zip codes, three reported six juvenile murders each in 1996. Those 18 juvenile murders were more than occurred in the nine urban counties *combined* of the San Francisco Bay Area (population 6.5 million) *plus* two dozen other California counties (population 3 million). More than Minnesota, Iowa, North and South Dakota, Idaho, and Montana put together.

Two populous urban counties, San Mateo and Sonoma (combined population 1.1 million), had zero youth murders in 1996. Marin County (population 250,000) hasn't had a juvenile murder arrest in more than a decade. California's arrest imbalance is typical. Three-fourths of New York's state prison inmates come from seven New York City neighborhoods, six of which are all-minority; 97 percent of the city's imprisoned youths are black or Latino.[18]

When just three central L.A. zip codes account for more youth homicides than counties holding one-third of California's population, it is clear that Fox's claim that all teenagers are "temporary sociopaths" is absurd. Efforts by the media and juvenile crime authors such as Ed Humes to depict youth violence as random, terrorizing pastoral town, suburb, and central city alike, are ludicrous.

Ludicrous and, ultimately, damaging. Los Angeles County's 250,000 Euro-white teens comprised one-fourth of the youth population—but just 13 of 331 youth homicide arrestees in 1996–97. Crime among Euro-white kids, including murder and violence, has declined. This means the practical result of punitive, "color blind," anti-youth crackdowns is exactly what can be seen in the yards at Chino and others urban youth prisons: a sea of black and brown faces.

In truth, race is not the culprit, even statistically. When considered in terms of their poverty rates, nonwhites are no more likely to commit violent crimes than are whites. I recently compared violent crime levels in California's poorest major urban county (Fresno) with its richest (Ventura). Fresno County's poverty rates consistently are two to three times higher than those of Ventura County's across all population groups. And Fresnans' violent crime levels consistently are twice as high as those of Venturans for all racial and ethnic groups, both sexes, and all age groups from children to senior citizens.

The question, then, is not why "teenagers" or "nonwhites" have higher crime rates, but why poorer groups regardless of age or race do. One answer is biased definitions of crime, such as cocaine sentencing laws that lock up poorer nonwhites for crack twice as long as wealthier whites busted for powder cocaine. But even for crimes enforced more or less equitably, such as murder, rates can vary 100-fold between poorer areas (such as inner Washington, DC) and wealthier populations a 10-minute drive away (such as Georgetown).

A great debate in criminology is whether poverty causes crime. To me, the debate confuses psychological (individual) with sociological (population group) issues. Do poverty and inequality cause any individual to be a criminal? NO. Most poor people are not criminals. Does poverty raise the crime and arrest rate for population groups? YES. Poverty is a serious stressor, tipping larger segments of poorer than richer populations toward crime. Like nonwhite race, poverty is a "signal" to police promoting greater suspicion and likelihood of arrest.

Murder levels tend to grade along a continuum of economics, not race or age. In most cities, the highest rates are found among inner-city blacks, followed by inner-city Latinos and inner-city whites. Suburban blacks and whites display the lowest rates.

Is poverty a perfect predictor of crime? NO. Asians and Latinos have lower rates of crime, and blacks and Euro-whites higher, than their poverty levels alone would predict. Further, *when poverty rates are held constant, teenagers are actually LESS likely to commit violent crime than are adults in their 20s and 30s.* Poverty is simply the best, by far, of many incomplete factors that account for differences in arrest rates.

Conservatives such as Bennett and New Democrats such as DiIulio call socioeconomic theories of crime a "liberal fallacy." Americans, they argue, "suffered lawfully through the Great Depression."[19] Abolutely false, even by the authorities Bennett and DiIulio cite. As David Rubenstein (whom they quote) observes, murder rates were stunningly high in early years of the Depression (see below). They declined by 40 percent from 1933 to 1938, and property crime similarly fell, as the economy improved. Rubenstein argues that unemployment is a better predictor of crime rate than poverty alone. His thesis finds modern support in sociologist William Julius Wilson's studies of inner-city joblessness.

When socioeconomic status is factored out, teenagers are no more violent than adults. Thus, their presence in large numbers does not cause crime. Unlike the press, which worshipfully circulates the demographic scapegoat claim at every turn, let us unravel the basic for it.

Baby Boomers: Criminals of the Century?

Proponents of the age theory of crime rest their claims on two facts:

(a) Men age 15–24 have higher arrest rates for violent crime than older or younger age groups;

(b) For the period 1930 to 1970, the proportion of men age 15–24 in the population tracked the U.S. homicide rate.

If you extended Figure 1 backwards in time to 1925 or so, you would see that prior to 1975, homicide rates indeed tracked the proportion of males ages 15–24 in the population. That is, murders peaked in the early 1930s along with the share of young men in the population; murder rates then declined to a mid-1950s trough along with a declining proportion of young men and rose again in the 1960s as the young-male population grew. With the same illogic of those who misinterpret any correlation as proving causation, modern criminologists left to right insisted that age demographics is the most important cause of crime.

Let us look at the pattern more closely. The previous peak in murder was in 1931–34, at levels similar to those of modern decades. If we reflect a moment, we might think of something going on at that time (other than more teenage males) to cause high homicide rates. And not just homicide—even the more incomplete urban arrest tabulations of the 1930s indicate rates of robbery and rape exceeded urban violence rates of the 1990s. If we look at the ages of the 30,000 murderers tabulated by the FBI for 1931–34 and surrounding years, we notice that the rise in murder was driven by increases among offenders over age 25, who accounted for seven in 10 homicides. So the peak in Depression-era homicide had nothing to do with the presence of more young men.

Now look at the homicide peak in the late 1960s and early 1970s, which coincided with the increase in the teen population. This time, checking crime reports, we find the teenage murder and violent crime rate doubled from the early 1960s to the early 1970s. But the teenage rise was accompanied by hefty increases among persons in their 20s (homicide up 60 percent, violent crime 120 percent), their 30s (homicide up 50 percent, violent crime up 65 percent), and 40s (homicide up 35 percent, violent crime up 55 percent).

So the increase in the youth population in the 1960s was not the cause of rising violence, but coincided with more crime by all age groups. As will be seen in Chapter 3, America's 1960s' increase in crime and addiction began among grownups, fueled by an eruption of barbiturate drug abuse among 30- and 40-year-olds that constituted that era's most alarming drug crisis. Many of the same experts, such as UCLA's much-quoted James Q. Wilson, who ignored that pattern in the Sixties, also ignored it in the Eighties and Nineties.

Let us move ahead to the modern era. Since 1974, murder and violent crime trends have changed to a new pattern characterized by sharp, short cycles. The small peak in 1980 occurred not just among teenagers, but among all ages under 50 as well. It also coincided with a period in which the proportion of males ages 15–19 in the population had been *declining* for five years. After another trough in 1984–85, homicide rose to another peak in 1991. This increase in murder occurred only among teenagers and young adults, but the violent crime rise occurred among all age groups—including senior citizens. Again, this sharp rise in violence occurred during a period in which the teenage and young adult population was *decreasing* rapidly (refer to Figure 1 and Tables 1–3 and 9).

A fundamental statistical technique, mathematical correlation analysis, combines annual trends over the entire 1970–97 period to produce a measure showing the relationship between the proportion of young men in the population and violent crime/homicide rates. A correlation of +1.00 indicates a perfect positive correlation (when the young-male proportion rises, violent crime rises, and vice versa); -1.00 a perfect negative correlation (when the young-male proportion rises, violent crime falls, and vice versa); a correlation of 0 suggests no relationship. No matter what measure of crime is used—victimization reports, police reports, arrest records—the correlation between the proportion of young males ages 15–19 (or 15–24) in the population and the nation's violent crime and homicide rate over the last 25 years is *negative*. The reason is that rising rates of crime among aging Baby Boomers have overwhelmed youth trends. It is 30–40-agers, not teenagers, who are driving America's crime and violence trends.

James Q. Wilson admitted he was caught "flatfooted" by the counter-trends. Fox argued, "who could have foreseen" the crack cocaine and gang violence cycles of the 1980s?[20] Those mired in the theory that "demography is destiny" are destined not to foresee crucial factors leading to changes in violent crime trends—or recognize them even long after they have occurred.

The demographic theory of crime has never made much sense. In the modern era, it is imbecilic. Flipping a coin produces more accurate crime prediction. But that isn't the point. Media-quotable crime experts who disingenuously perpetuate exactly those conclusions that the best crime data demonstrate are utterly wrong achieve their popularity by inflaming public prejudices, not by being right.

Top reporters are so locked into the demographic fallacy that *New York Times* crime specialist Fox Butterfield couldn't sort out which ways teenagers affect crime. In a 1997 article, he quoted crime experts declaring that declining teen populations caused property crime trends to go south as violent crime went north, neither of which (had anyone bothered to graph them) coincided with adolescent population changes.[21] *Los Angeles Times* crime specialist and author Miles Corwin (in his 1994 book, *Killing Season*) likewise cited the proportion of young males as the big factor in swings in Los Angeles's murder rates. The cold figures show that L.A. homicides rose rapidly in the late 1980s as the young-male population plummeted, then reversed and declined sharply in the 1990s as the young-male population started rising. Note to crime reporters: the fact that experts are lying shamelessly is big news.

The Theory of Critical Mass versus Critical Thinking

Demographic fallacies and scapegoating, past and present, are rooted in bigotry, not science. What the much-quoted Wilson, Fox, and DiIulio hold in common is unrestrained ephebiphobia (fear of adolescents)—or more accurately, kourophobia (fear of the adult *stereotype* of adolescents, from the Greek word "kouros," or adolescent image). An obscure aside by demographer Norman Ryder regarding the increase in youth population after the 1950s Baby Boom achieved stardom in modern texts:

> There is a perennial invasion of barbarians who must somehow be civilized and turned into contributors to the fulfillment of the various functions requisite to societal survival...The increase in the magnitude of the socialization task in the United States during the past decades was completely outside the bounds of previous experience.[22]

Crime authorities gush that this statement is "perceptive," "insightful," and "provocative." It is idiotic. Persons under age 20, at the Baby Boom's barbarian apex in 1969, comprised 39 percent of the U.S. population and declined quickly thereafter, compared to an *average* of 40 to 45 percent during the early 1900s and over 50 percent prior to 1870. The burden on American adults for socializing children in the 1960s was considerably lighter than borne by grownups of the past.

In many respects, James Q. Wilson is the godfather of modern crime policy, quoted in hushed tones by rightists such as Bennett, governors such as Pete Wilson, and liberals such as author Ed Humes. Bennett, arguing that poverty has nothing to do with crime, favorably cites the lead chapter, "Crime amidst plenty: The paradox of the Sixties," of Wilson's famous 1975 treatise *Thinking About Crime*. This chapter arrives at Wilson's own much-quoted kourophobia, stemming from his conclusions regarding the growth of crime and drug abuse that took place as the Baby Boom youth population grew rapidly in the 1960s:

> A 'critical mass' of young persons...creates an explosive increase in the amount of crime, addiction, and welfare dependency.[23]

Garbage, as proven by Wilson's own analysis. I recommend a reading of his famous book and chapter to understand how muddled modern crime policy flowed from Wilson's doctrinaire thinking and its misapplication.

Surprisingly, Wilson's only real explanation for the increase in crime during the 1960s was a distinctly leftist one:

> The United States made tremendous strides in providing jobs during the 1960s, but adults benefited more than young people. During a decade when the unemployment rate generally declined, the unemployment rate for persons sixteen to nineteen years of age actually increased, so that whereas the young made up only one sixth of the unemployed in 1961, they accounted for more than one-quarter of it by 1971...As the Bureau of Labor Statistics was later to write, "In 1963, the relative position of teenagers began to deteriorate markedly." Whereas before their unemployment was never more than two or three times greater than that of adults, after 1963 it was at least four times greater, and by 1968 was better than five times greater.[24]

Which teenagers of the 1960s suffered the most? What a surprise: "The increase in teenage and young adult unemployment was particularly sharp among nonwhites...almost one-third of all the young nonwhites in the labor force" were jobless. And nonwhites, indeed, were the group in which teenage crime increased most dramatically. So Wilson had solid grounds for concluding in standard liberal fashion that "crime amidst plenty" does not result from violence by the plentified haves, but from social disadvantage: many of those left out of society's prosperity, mostly unemployed inner-citians, can be expected to turn to anti-social entrepreneurship to survive.

Wilson's "Crime amidst plenty" essay also cited a number of studies that explicitly rejected the right-wing notion that demographics drive crime. For example, analyses concluded that "the increase in the murder rate during the 1960s was more than ten times greater than what one would have expected from the changing age structure of the population alone." Further, "only 13.4 percent of the increase in arrests for robbery between 1950 and 1965 could be accounted for by the increase in the number of persons between the ages of ten and twenty-four."

So, Wilson and his evidence reported, the best scholarship showed more young people was *not* the reason for more crime. But Wilson then turned around and declared that more young people was indeed the reason for more crime. Worse than that: he argued that the huge, unexplained surplus in 1960s crime was caused not just by more young people, but by the "exponential effect" of a "critical mass" of more young people. Further, "heroin addiction is an example" of how too many young people create a mass-anti-social climate, Wilson said, adding misrepresentation of 1960s drug woes to his addled crime analysis. The problem: the statistics he cited from FBI and drug reports showed '60s crises were not caused solely by young people, exponentially or otherwise.

Had Wilson moved his gaze rightward on the malaise charts, away from the youth columns and toward the adult ones, he would have noticed that homicide, crime, and drug abuse (as well as other ills such as divorce and sexually transmitted diseases) grew among all age groups under age 50 during the 1960s (see above). That era's most serious and deadly drug epidemic was barbiturate addiction among the 30–40-age group, the parents of Sixties kids. In California, the epicenter of the barbiturate and heroin quakes, four-fifths of the heroin deaths and 95 percent of the barbiturate deaths involved persons over age 25 in 1966, the year the deadly drug scourge erupted. The 1960s crime and dope epidemics could not be explained by more young people because they tended to be centered in *older age groups*.

So Wilson, against his own evidence, popularized a faulty notion that more teenagers means more drugs and violence. His bad science has been cloned in greater absurdity in the 1980s and through the 1990s—eras in which rising crime and drug abuse occurred as teenage populations were *declining*.

Now, consider excitable crime scholar James Alan Fox's youth-bashing analysis:

> Teenagers are "temporary sociopaths, impulsive and immature...A 45-year-old with a gun in his hand, though he may be a better shot, is not as likely to use that gun as a 14-year-old. Fourteen-year-olds tend to be trigger happy...They'll pull that trigger if someone looks at them the wrong way. They'll pull that trigger if someone swears at them. They'll pull that trigger without thinking about the consequences."[25]

More hotheaded-expert rubbish. FBI arrest statistics, available for combined age groups (13–14, 40–44, and 45–49 in this case), show the rate for homicide among "trigger happy" 13–14 year-olds (around 350 arrests every year out of a population of 7.5 million) is almost exactly the same as for "mature" 40-agers (1,750 annual arrests in a population of 37.5 million). Statistics on such rare crimes cannot plausibly be used to tell us what the millions in any age group "tend to..." be like.

When poverty rates, number of victims per arrestee, and other factors social scientists are supposed to rule out before issuing broad allegations about an entire group's proclivities are held constant, people in their 40s are more murderous than younger teenagers. Given the small number of shootings along with evidence that guns are readily available to anyone regardless of age, it appears that younger teenagers are not intrinsically interested in acquiring one in order to gratuitously shoot someone for looks or swearing. As will be analyzed later, public schools stuffed with thousands of adolescents are among the safest places from homicide in society—far safer than environments dominated by adults.

The Word From the Elite Homeboys Gang

In the early 1990s, criminologists such as DiIulio, Wilson, and Fox issued their dire warnings about "adolescent superpredators" and the "coming crime storm" forecast by the growing teenage population. Said DiIulio of his wildly quotable notion of the "adolescent superpredator":

> Nationally, there are about 40 million children under the age of 10, the largest number in decades. By simple math, in a decade today's 4- to 7-year-olds will become 14- to 17-year-olds. By 2005, the number of males in this age group will have risen about 25 percent overall and 50 percent for blacks...On the horizon, therefore, are tens of thousands of severely morally impoverished juvenile superpredators...So long as their youthful energies hold out, they will do what comes "naturally": murder, rape, rob, assault, burglarize, deal deadly drugs and get high.[26]

Impeccable logic. "By simple math," a larger population, such as Chicago's, will harbor more criminals than a smaller one, such as Cucamonga's. The same alarm could be raised about more 34–37-year-olds who, as shown, account for more of America's growth in violent crime over the last decade than do 14–17-year-olds. DiIulio's prediction ignores what we know about adolescent crime: it tends to involve fewer victims, and less chance of injury, than violence committed by adults. The teenage superpredator mob with its massive numbers of victims is not in evidence.

DiIulio's forecast of "30,000 more murderers, rapists, and muggers on the streets" by 2005 seems a bit of a yawner in a nation that had already seen a "crime storm" jump of nearly *one million* annual violent crime arrests in the previous two decades—driven by over-30-agers! The 30- and 40-age increase in violent felonies was so trivial, in fact, that top criminologists still haven't admitted it happened. But count on the press to be utterly mesmerized by shock-quotes about adolescents: DiIulio's and Fox's Fourteen-Agers-of-the-Apocalypse was greeted with horror headlines, such as those beginning this chapter.

DiIulio's essay accuses the young of "moral poverty." What is striking in the high moral tone he and his colleagues adopt is how much their own attitudes resemble the superpredator mentality. With more candor than Clinton officials muster, DiIulio at least admits that millions of children grow up in "abusive, violence-ridden" homes subjected to severe brutality by adults. "I have never seen a kid who criminally violated others in a heinous way who was not also terribly sinned against," he told *Sojourners* magazine. "What a society does to its children, its children will do to society," he said, quoting the Roman proverb.[27]

Yet DiIulio does not consider adult violence against children a "crime epidemic" worthy of a national crusade. He does not denounce the beatings and murders of children as *evils in their own right*, as violent crime every bit as worthy of society's concern as that which street youths perpetrate. Experts and media articles, writes child advocate Lucia Hodgson, "assiduously calculate future rates of crimes children will commit based on current trends, but rarely calculate future rates of circumstances children will endure such as childhood poverty and violent treatment at the hands of adults."[28]

DiIulio's concern over adult violence against children is limited to the fact that abused kids might turn into the "young offenders [who] are committing more homicides, robberies, and other crimes against adults." Like the superpredator he denounces, his moral horizon is confined to what affects him and his homies. But if the DiIulio Gang and its Elite Homeboys don't care about the violently abused child, why should the abused child care about DiIulio's cherished society?

DiIulio and Fox make it clear their main fear is not just of more kids, but of more black kids. Fox, one of the most lavishly quoted experts and top consultant for the Bureau of Justice Statistics, explicitly modeled (that is, blamed) crime trends on the percentage of the population that is nonwhite and ages 14–21, along with the consumer price index. Using this model, Fox, in *Forecasting Crime* in 1978, predicted that the nation's violent crime rate would decline from 1981 to a low in 1992, then rise. He further predicted that property crime would level off through 1985, then rise rapidly.

It is difficult to imagine a prediction that turned out to be more monumentally wrong. In fact, violent crime rose sharply from the early 1980s to a *peak* in 1991–92, then fell; property crime fell sharply from 1980 to 1985, rose to 1991, then fell sharply. Fox was not alone—other top criminologists such as Alfred Blumstein, who similarly relied on youth-bashing demographic models, also proved poor prognosticators.[29] It is no sin to fail to predict such an unpredictable phenomenon as crime; my own notions that more poverty = more crime also need refinement. The sin is that these same prominent criminologists learned nothing from their mistakes. They continue to insist today that young age means more crime, stepping up their emotional pitch as anti-youth politics became politically saleable.

Because of his penchant for ear-grabbing terminology validating popular prejudices, DiIulio has been coronated by the press as the nation's leading "crime doctor" ministering to Republicans and Democrats alike. Imagine how his panic message plays in Washington, where the capitol enclave dissolves a few blocks away into bombed-out slums inhabited by the urban black majority, whose children suffer poverty rates (economic, not moral) 25 times higher and homicide rates 35 times higher than the children of the whites who dominate the governing aristocracy.

Underachieving Predators

When crime trends are broken down by gender, race, state and locality, type of crime, and era, a clear pattern emerges: rates in violent crime among youth are closely tied to trends and rates in violent crime among adults around them. As noted in the previous section, most "youth violence"—whether committed singly or in groups—directly involves adults as co-offenders, victimizers, and victims. Surprisingly, recent *trends*, especially in California, show adult crime rising faster than youth crime, but similarities between teen and adult crime *rates* remain dominant.

White teens commit crime like white adults, black teens commit crime like black adults, and crime trends and rates for black youths and black grownups are dramatically different from those of white youths and white adults. Adolescent girls commit crime like adult women, adolescent boys like adult men, and each sex's patterns are different from the other's. Los Angeles urban youths commit crime like Los Angeles urban adults, Los Angeles suburban youths commit crime like Los Angeles suburban adults, and the urban and suburban twain do not meet.

On an individual level, the same adult-youth violence patterns also apply. Children of violent parents and violent adult communities are many times more violent than children from more pacific households and adult communities. Effective intervention to lower crime rates depends on focusing on adult behaviors and socio-economic situations, not on getting tough on youths and their supposedly inherent immorality. At the home and street level, it is doubtful that there exists any distinct entity which can be defined and addressed as "youth crime."

So one was created. In unveiling his Anti-Gang and Youth Violence Act of 1997, President Clinton lent full endorsement to the age theory of crime: "We've got about six years to turn this juvenile crime thing around, or our country is going to be living with chaos." Attorney General Janet Reno echoed that only with tough law enforcement and prevention aimed at juveniles, especially gangs, can we defeat the "destiny" of youth to be violent.

With get-tough intervention, Los Angeles has been there, done that, and failed to conquer. L.A.'s infamous "Operation Hammer" of the late 1980s enforced vigorous curfew, anti-gang, and other status laws (laws aimed only at juveniles) against thousands of minority youths. L.A. urban archeologist Mike Davis (in *City of Quartz*, which in 1990 prophesied the tumult of 1992) chronicled the 1987 Los Angeles police raids:

> This so-called Gang Related Active Trafficker Suppression program (GRATS) targeted "drug neighborhoods" for raids by 200-300 police under orders to "stop and interrogate anyone who they suspect is a gang member, basing their assumptions on their dress or their use of gang hand signals." Thus, on the flimsy "probable cause" of red shoelaces or high-five handshakes, the taskforces in February and March mounted nine sweeps, impounded five hundred cars, and made nearly fifteen hundred arrests…As the HAMMER mercilessly pounded away at Southcentral's mean streets, it became increasingly apparent that its principal catch consisted of drunks, delinquent motorists and teenage curfew violators (offenders only by virtue of the selective application of curfews to non-Anglo neighborhoods). By 1990, the combined forces of the LAPD and the Sheriff's (implementing their own street saturation strategy) had picked up as many as 50,000 suspects…In some highly touted sweeps, moreover, as many as 90 percent of detained suspects have been released without charges.[30]

These police assault tactics were followed by massive increases in violence and, after Rodney King, a Big One. Now these same types of measures are recycled in the mid-'90s as new strategies to reduce youth crime.

Using "Children Killing Children" as Posterboys for the Clampdown

FBI figures report that approximately 250 youths under age 18 were murdered by other youths in 1996. "Children killing children" and "killer kids" have received intensive publicity. What has received virtually no publicity is that those same 1996 FBI figures show that 750 youths under age 18 were murdered by adults.

The U.S. Office of Juvenile Justice and Delinquency Prevention (OJJDP) reported in 1996 that three-fourths of all murder victims under age 18—including 90 percent of all murdered children and 70 percent of all murdered teens ages 12–17—were killed by adults, not by other juveniles.[31] The U.S. Advisory Board on Child Abuse and Neglect reported 2,000 to 3,000 children and youths murdered every year by their parents,[32] six to nine times the toll of "children killing children" and two to three times more than the 1,000 adults killed by youths every year. Although children certainly do victimize other children, child abuse overwhelmingly involves adult offenders. Studies of child abuse and of sexual abuse victimization consistently have found that abusers' average age is over 30, while the age of the victims averages seven to 10.[33]

Further, the FBI attributed 850 murders in 1996 to "juvenile gangs." This, too, is misleading in two important ways. First, juveniles and adults are separable only in the press's and experts' fantasy constructs, not in the real world. OJJDP found that two-thirds of group crimes involving youths also involve adult offenders.[34] Second, the notion of a "juvenile gang" is passé, if it ever made sense. Though the president and other authorities call them "youth gangs," the evidence is that adults are dominant players.

"Age is becoming less of a defining characteristic," veteran gang researcher Malcolm Klein of the University of Southern California reports. "Nowadays, a surprising number of gang members are in their mid- and late twenties, some in their thirties, and a few in their forties. They're hanging on longer and longer."[35]

> Although some writers and officials decry the 8- and 10-year-old gang member, they haven't been in the business long enough to realize that we heard the same reports twenty and forty years ago...[These claims are] more important to media hyping than to criminological description of gang activity.
>
> On the other hand, it is clear that the upper age range has expanded dramatically. Both the crack and homicide studies among gangs in Los Angeles reveal the same change: the average offender in both cases was almost 20 years old, and the upper limits went into the forties. San Francisco, Honolulu, and Chicago all report similar patterns.[36]

Older gang members suffer from long-term unemployment and other "underclass" stresses, Klein points out, and therefore are "more likely to engage their companions in criminal pursuits, such as drug sales."

A January 1998 report by Orange County, California, District Attorney found *adults ages 22 and older* comprised both the largest (57 percent) and the fastest-growing (up 64 percent since 1993) gang membership category. Youths under age 15 comprised just 1 percent of the county's estimated (probably overestimated) 24,000 gang "members."[37] By odd coincidence, the Orange County Latino activist organization Los Amigos reported, the police estimate of the number of "gang members" at affluent San Clemente High School equaled the number of Latino students enrolled.

But adult behavior remains a taboo topic. Headlining "children killing children" is the latest official ploy to pretend to care for America's young while advancing political anti-youth agendas. The agonizing by President Clinton and the media over the gunning of three West Paducah, Kentucky, students by a 14-year-old in December 1997 stands in stark contrast to the silence surrounding tragedies of adults murdering children. A few days after the Kentucky murders, for example, the following story appeared in the inside news pages:

> Weston, W.Va., December 11 (AP)—When a fire roared through a house in this Appalachian town last month, all the adults made it out alive and then watched and wailed as firefighters found five little bodies inside.
>
> Now, two of the parents and a stepfather who initially said the children were playing with matches have been charged with setting the fire themselves with gasoline to collect on a homeowner's insurance policy.

The adults face charges of murder by arson. No official agonizing or claims that such incomprehensible crimes are a statement on the morals of parents today.

Similarly, when two students were arrested for shooting and killing four classmates and a teacher in an ambush outside a Jonesboro, Arkansas, middle school in late March 1998, the press and politicians once again headlined its singular incomprehensibility. Front-page, multi-page, lead-story features full of photos illustrating the scene and victims were understandable.[38] Such commando-style slaughter is incomprehensible.

But so were the murders of three children, ages two, three, and seven, that led to the arrest that same day of a suburban California mother:

> Daly City, Calif. (AP)—A mother used duct tape to suffocate her three little girls in their pajamas, then climbed in bed with them and took an overdose of prescription drugs in what police said was a phony suicide gesture.
>
> ..."In 29 years, I've seen a lot of evil. Nothing like this," said Lt. Steven Lowe. "She bound their hands and their faces with duct tape. She did them one at a time. She took them into the bedroom, suffocated them and came back and got the next one."[39]

This tiny, four-inch story, no photos, appeared on page 19 of the *LA Times*, California's biggest newspaper.

Probably the incident most fueling the "moral meltdown" charge hurled at the younger generation was the callousness of the Lacey Township, New Jersey, high school senior who had a baby at the prom, dumped the infant in the bathroom trash, and partied on. She made the cover of *People*. Oddly, the same meltdown charge was not affixed to all 29-year-olds after Chicago parents that age cut up their 16-month-old (couldn't stand her crying, prosecutor said) and fed her to rats.[40] Just postage-stamp-sized newspaper briefs were all that this crime received.

Such incongruities illustrate "our completely irrational attitudes toward violence," writes child advocate Lucia Hodgson, "emphasizing that which almost never occurs, and ignoring that which forms the experiential fabric of our children's lives."[41] In 1997–98, school murders occurred at about four per month. Parents murdering children at home clocked in at a half-dozen per *day*.

I was in Louisville, Kentucky, at a conference the week after the student murders in West Paducah. "While the nation's eyes shed tears for the three teen-age
girls gunned down at school in Paducah," the alternative paper, *LEO*, reported,
"nine local residents turned up dead in an uncommonly gruesome week of homicides and discoveries of homicide victims."[42] Two were children.

It was a record toll, capping Louisville's most murderous year since 1971. Eight
were from domestic violence or neighbor killings, and nearly all involved drug
abuse. "That is the kind of violence we see the most," said a police officer with
whom I rode on patrol in the city's devastated neighborhoods and grim public housing projects around downtown. "Families, friends, neighbors."

Putting violence in context, four months earlier, the U.S. Bureau of Justice
Statistics reported on "Violence-Related Injuries Treated in Hospital Emergency
Departments."[43] The Bureau estimated that 1.4 million ER treatments resulted from
violence in 1994. Of these, the place the injury occurred was known for 860,000:

> 410,000 (48 percent), home
> 246,000 (29 percent), workplace
> 128,000 (15 percent), street
> 55,000 (6 percent), school
> 20,000 (2 percent), recreation areas.

Families accounted for triple the violence of streets and eight times the brutality of schools. Workplaces were also astonishingly disagreeable. Compared to the
relative numbers of people who use them, a person was more likely to be injured in a
violent attack at a recreation area than a school.

Offender age was reported for 900,000 cases:

> Adult men (over age 20), 67 percent
> Teen males (age 12–19), 15 percent
> Adult women, 11 percent
> Teen females, 4 percent
> Teen or adult, 3 percent.

For all the talk about parent-teen conflict, spouses, partners, friends, acquain-
tances, and other relatives each accounted for much more violence. Of the 52,000
parent-child incidents, parents were the assailants in four times more attacks than
were children—which is probably a low estimate. (How many violent parents take
their beaten kids to ER?) Hospital records indicate that domestic violence was far
less likely to be reported, even voluntarily on the National Crime Victimization
Survey, than crime committed by strangers.

Debunking the teenager-as-root-of-savagery thesis, two well-designed studies
reported in *Science* found that violent abuse in childhood is a powerful predictor of
violent crime careers in teenhood and adulthood.[44] The National Center on Child
Abuse and Neglect reported 245,000 confirmed cases of violent abuse and 126,000
of sexual abuse in 1995.[45] The National Institute of Justice studied 900 individuals
with court determinations of abuse in childhood and 670 with no court records of
abuse.[46] The abused sample was 38 percent more likely to be arrested for a violent

crime, committed 1.7 times more crimes per arrestee, began criminal behavior at an earlier age, and was nearly twice as likely to be chronic offenders (five or more arrests). Add these factors up: about 70 percent of the violent crime volume appears to be committed by persons violently abused as children. This is a conservative finding, since at least some of those with no court records of abuse also may have been abused.

A 1996 California Legislative Analyst's report found:

> In 1994, there were 664,000 reports of child abuse/neglect and about 90,000 children in foster care in California. Between 1987–88 and 1994–95, the number of children served by the Child Welfare Services (CWS) system, after controlling for changes in population, increased 27 percent.[47]

By uncanny coincidence, that is just about the same percentage that juvenile violent crime increased in California during the period. And the number of substantiated child abuse cases is about equal to the number of juveniles arrested every year.

Since President Clinton took office in January 1993, more than two million children have been substantiated (investigation-confirmed) victims of physical injuries and sexual violence inflicted by parents or caretakers.

The president has not given a single major address or proposed any major initiative on the subject.

Adult and Teen Rage killings: Different or the Same?

After a 15-year-old student opened fire on a Springfield, Oregon, school cafeteria in late May, killing two students and wounding 21, the Lane County sheriff had the following observations regarding the massive arsenal, including "very sophisticated" bombs, found in the boy's home:

> When you take it [the quantity and sophistication of the weaponry] and hook it up with a 15-year-old, I don't think "remarkable" is an overstatement. It absolutely is unbelievable to those of us who seem to think rationally and understand what society is all about and how it operates.[48]

Unfortunately, the massacre by a 15-year-old taught us a lot about how society operates. The five school "rage killings" (murders resulting from random expressions of rage rather than simply anger at particular victims or utilitarian motives) closely resembled public slaughters by adults. Rage killings differ from other murderous public shootouts, such as the 1997 North Hollywood bank robbery, in that revenge and anger at personal insult, not calculated monetary gain or political sabotage, seem the only motive.

Adult rage killings are regular, if unevenly reported, events. A few days after the West Paducah, Kentucky, student murders in December 1997, a 41-year-old Orange, California, state employee raked a Caltrans yard full of maintenance yard workers with AK-47 fire, killing four. The next day, a Milwaukee, Wisconsin, postal worker, age 37, shot three in a "fatal rampage" at work.

Four days before an Edinboro, Pennsylvania, 14-year-old fatally shot a teacher at a school dance in April 1998, a 51-year-old Inglewood, California, Agriculture

Department employee sprayed 13 bullets from a semiautomatic handgun at co-workers, killing two. Two days later, a 40-year-old Huntington Beach aerospace worker murdered five and then himself in "one of the largest murder-suicide tolls in recent Los Angeles County history."

The day before the Springfield student murders in May 1998, a 30-year-old Tampa, Florida, man shot and killed three police officers investigating the shooting death of his four-year-old son. The day after, a 35-year-old Arleta, California, mother was arrested for murdering her two children and burying them in the national forest.

Only hours before nationwide headlines announced in August 1998 that a Chicago seven- and eight-year-old were arrested for allegedly bashing the skull of 11-year-old Ryan Harris for her bicycle ("a case certain to inflame passions over the punishment of juvenile offenders," the L.A. Times reported), a suburban Los Angeles father gunned down his three kids and wife to zero national (and only scant local) notice. A routine domestic slaughter certain to inflame no passions outside of a small circle of friends.[49]

Then, in early September 1998, came ultimate proof of the self-promotional exploitation of kid-violence by political and media luminaries. New evidence in the Chicago case indicated Ryan was murdered by an adult rapist, not by the two grade schoolers as previously thought.[50] The young black girl's murder was played up by authorities and the media not out of concern for her tragedy, but only for the political mileage it contained. That mileage, and whether the case is exhaustively followed and headlined or reduced to a few sporadic squibs (or nothing), is directly proportional to how young her killer turns out to be.

Rage killings by teenagers closely resemble those by adults. All involve males, none poor, nearly all white, nearly all wielding guns (or, more rarely, bombs), nearly all motivated by generalized rage. In the Pearl, Mississippi, and Springfield, Oregon, cases, murders of family members preceded the school gunnings—as in a large share of adult rage killings. Co-workers and co-students are usually victimized. The motivators, teenage and adult, are eerily similar: extreme reactions to rejection by girlfriends/wives or peers, or to dismissal from work or suspension from school. The killers are middle-class or more affluent. Drugs or alcohol almost never seem to be involved. Police often find large caches of weaponry, including bombs, indicating that months or years of planning preceded the triggering event.

Youths involved in rage killings, especially the Jonesboro and Springfield boys, acted much like adult rampagers in extensive planning and arsenal accumulation. As will be discussed in Chapter 7, junior high youths are as cognitively capable as adults of the kind of plotting and sophisticated weapons assembly required to carry out large-scale killings. Bizarrely, violence experts reacting to school shootings seemed determined to ignore the evidence at hand. After the Springfield shooting, a public health luminary from the University of Southern California Medical School's violence intervention program told newscasters in fluent epidemiobabble that the school shootings represented a "new disease" borne by adolescents, all of whom by definition have "poor impulse control," whom "we" expose to media violence and to whom "we" give guns. Thus, to "eradicate" the "epidemic," "we" should just stop infecting disease-prone teens with these pathogens to which adults are

implied to be immune. Public health concepts indeed have much to offer in addressing violence compared to standard criminal justice strategy, but only if practitioners'
thinking rises above simplistic stereotype.

A note to experts who are paid to provide thoughtful perspective, not alarmist
foolishness: get a grip. The "teenage" rage-killing disease is a scarce subform of the
already unusual "adult" disease. School shootings are *extremely rare* events. Twenty
million students attend middle and high schools; six students in five schools perpetrated the gun mayhem. The vast majority of teenagers, exposed to violent media
and guns and their own supposed impulsiveness, *do not* shoot up schools.

Schools are, in fact, among society's safest places from murder, as will be
shown next.

School Killings: The Photo-Op

After the Springfield school killings, Clinton made his most exploitative pitch
for punitive juvenile justice legislation, none of which would have done anything
more to deter student shootings than the much-touted juvenile curfews or juvenile
gun-control measures he championed earlier. Clinton blamed:

> a changing culture that desensitizes our children to violence, where most
> teenagers have seen hundreds or even thousands of murders on television and
> in movies and in video games before they graduate from high school, where
> too many young people seem unable or unwilling to take responsibility for
> their actions, where all too often everyday conflicts are resolved not with
> words but with weapons, which, even when illegal to possess by children, are
> all too easy to get.[51]

An astonishing lack of introspection for a president who, only a few weeks earlier,
had threatened Iraq with the "severest consequences" (military attack) for failing
to comply with United Nations inspection resolutions. The last time America's
conflict with Iraq had been resolved "not with words but with weapons," the Gulf
War, a quarter million died—including at least 46,000 children under age five, a
Harvard University Medical School team found.[52] Clinton's example to young
people of presidential readiness to yet again deploy weapons of mass destruction to
settle grownup differences evidenced a leader "desensitized" to war's violence.
Fortunately, Russian president Boris Yeltsin, a staunch American ally who warned
that Clinton's bellicosity "could lead to world war," intervened with a negotiation
strategy the White House, in dire need of a foreign crusade to divert attention from
Oval Office sex scandals, found unsatisfying.[53] The distinctions between the mind-
sets of heavily armed urban gangs and heavily armed adult governments are not
immediately evident.

Clinton's liberal/conservative buzzwords ("culture," "responsibility," ad nause-
am) defied clear reality revealed in the aftermaths of the school killings. News
scenes showed hundreds of teenagers in tears, shock, and revulsion. Their sensitivi-
ties were working fine despite exposure to fictional TV and video-game blood, evidencing no trouble distinguishing that from the real blood in their cafeterias and
schoolyards. The masses of grieving students are the representatives of the next gen-

eration, not the half-dozen isolated gunners Clinton held up as typical of "young people." On the other hand, the president is most definitely representative of an adult generation that refuses to take responsibility for the violent part of American culture typified by militarism, adult rage killings, household violence, and a grownup citizenry eight to 100 times more likely to murder with guns than adults in other Western nations.

Clinton continued to swing for the cheap seats. Highlighted by the White House's nationwide crusade for uniforms, curfews, drug tests, and unprecedented kid-shackles, he and the media depicted "the rising tide of school violence" as symptomatic of a blank-eyed generation of teens in drugged, hedonistic carnage. The president seized on the school murders as "an insistent, angry wake-up call" to face "rising" school brutality.[54] A president genuinely concerned for child safety would be outraged at violence against kids wherever it occurred, which is overwhelmingly in families. But Clinton seems only concerned for kids victimized by other kids. There was little pretense to the political momentum presidential handlers rushed to grab.

The president called a "school safety conference" to vent yet more hysteria at one of America's safest major institutions and to advocate for more police officers in school hallways. "Although Clinton repeatedly said that school safety should not be a partisan issue, the safety conference October 15 will come just weeks before the midterm congressional elections, allowing Democrats to press an issue that they see as a vote-winner," the LA Times reported after interviewing unnamed advisors.[55] On so many issues, from the silence on the real epidemics of household drugs and violence to the loud pieties underlying crass political profiteering from schoolyard bullets, it is difficult to see the Clinton White House as anything other than a product of icy handlerology.

Maligning Schools

In this age of image, anecdote, and message, the human refutation to Clinton's scare campaign targeting youth came just four days after his latest "school safety" speech to teachers in New Orleans, deploring "terrible" kids who infest schools with their "small acts of aggression" and "constant back talk." On July 24, a 41-year-old blasted into a tourist-packed capitol building in Washington with a handgun, killing two guards and seriously wounding a tourist. A sickening confirmation of every antagonist's criticism of Clinton's compulsive maundering on youth. Remove "age" and it is impossible to distinguish the 40-ager's rampage from a school shooting. The gunman had been kicked out of the house by his dad because he massacred cats and apparently had paranoid fears of government. Imagine the outraged reaction if Clinton had identified the bullet-spraying madman with the victims he was shooting at as products of one common culture of "adult violence"! That a Capitol building staffed with the finest security in the country could not prevent a determined gunman from killing, that rage gunners know no age or institution and are tragically isolated from their horrified peers, is a powerful irony lost in politicians' self-serving rush to popularize themselves by slamming kids and demanding more cops in schools.

Obediently, the media exploded with reports asserting public schools were the habitat of random slaughter. In the summer of 1996, Paramount Pictures released the movie "187," supposedly a "teacher's reality" of rape, rumbles, and wanton killings infecting city schools. The title referred to the California penal code section for homicide. The screenplay author, former teacher Scott Yagemann, asserted that, "Ninety percent of what you see in '187' either happened to me or to other teachers."[56] He didn't say which 10 percent was made up. The movie's promos screamed: "Every day, 160,000 students stay home because they are afraid to go to school."

The film's fictional hero, disillusioned black educator Trevor Garfield, was lauded by conservative pundit George Will as the modern warrior against "the slow-motion riot that is life in an inner-city high school:"

> The youth culture that "187" captures is primitively tribal but also intensely individualistic. Its dominating spirit is a prickly, lethal cultivation of pride by people with virtually nothing in their past, present, or future to justify it...Decorated by tattoos, observing the elaborate gang-bangers' protocols, they radiate a barely-leashed menace that makes teaching and learning impossible by bringing the chaos of the street into the classroom...a foreign country composed of young people, especially young men, in America's wilder urban neighborhoods.[57]

Like DiIulio, Will displays the same primitively tribal attitude he attributes to gangster kids. Ghetto youth have nothing to be proud of, Will sniffs. But he effuses compassion for Garfield, "a doomed ambassador" from polite society to inner-city culture, who "is driven to derangement by the stress of unrelieved menace and anarchy." (Yagemann calls his film a "cautionary tale about a good man who is destroyed by his environment.") Will and Yagemann readily comprehend that white-collar heroes can be corrupted by evil conditions. But they muster no similar understanding that the youths they pillory also might be affected by that same environment, which (like Garfield) they did not create but (unlike the temporary ambassador) they have survived day after day for years.

If only 160,000 of America's 54 million students (3 in 1,000) fail to attend school out of fear, that would make schools one of the least fearsome environments young people negotiate. Other teachers disputed Yagemann's dirist claims. "Let me tell you something," Cypress, California, teacher Lou Cohan wrote. "Movies like '187' do not portray in any real sense what is going on in our public schools today:"

> I have finally realized why the public is so down on teachers, students, and public education in general. They've seen so many of these movies, going back to Rock Hudson raping and murdering students in "Pretty Maids All in a Row" and continuing through such recent gems as "The Substitute," "The Principal," "High School High," "Lean on Me," and "Dangerous Minds," that they think all public schools are like the ones they see on the silver screen. Meaning, the students are all illiterate, foul-mouthed, undisciplined, armed-to-the-teeth, multi-tattooed gang members bent on murdering teachers before going on to destroy Western civilization as we know it, and the teachers (with few exceptions), if they aren't cowardly jerks or burned-out cynics, are all child-molesting murderers with MAC-10s in their briefcases just itching for an excuse to send Johnny to that principal's office up in the sky. No won-

der the public is screaming for vouchers, refusing to provide adequate funding and…calling for total dismantling of our system.[58]

True Crime Stories—by the Numbers

How murderous are public schools, including the inner-city ones ruled by the lethal tribes Yagemann and Will postulate? Let's take "187" up on its title and take a hard look at school homicide in Los Angeles.

The numbers: L.A. County's 9.4 million residents contributed a total of 5,000 murders to the national toll during the most recently tabulated three years (1995–97). Some 800,000 students ages 12 to 18 attend Los Angeles schools every day, 180 days per year. Eighty percent are nonwhite, mostly Latino and black. Allegedly, tens of thousands are gang members. Allegedly, some thousands bring guns to school every day. Factually, L.A. schools are the most crowded of any in the nation.

Add these together and you have the ingredients in a conservative-liberal recipe for what should be mass gunplay. By statistical odds alone (that is, if a teenage student merely had the *same* odds of killing someone that any other Los Angeles resident did during 180 eight-hour days), we would expect 50 to 100 student-perpetrated murders in L.A. public schools in the last three years.

How many occurred? There were seven homicides on or around L.A. school campuses (including off-campus and nighttime school activities) in the last three years—*none* involving student killers. As of this writing in September 1998, the last Los Angeles student murder of a student at school was in spring 1995. It did not involve a gun.

Similarly, Orange County's 2.5 million people have suffered a total of 1,500 homicides over the last decade. Its public schools are attended by 200,000 mostly-nonwhite youth daily. Yet the county recorded its only school-related murder in law enforcement memory (confirmed by a media check) back in 1987—a nine year-old abducted while walking home from school and killed by an unknown assailant. New York City public schools, in a city of seven million, have not had a murder since 1992.

What officials and the media could have pointed out but didn't was that in a few seconds, a Kentucky private school student killed more kids at school than have been murdered in all L.A., Orange County, and New York City public schools (combined student population three million) in the last *five years*. Note that officials and the press have heaped lavish praise upon the city of Boston, home to 40,000 teenagers, which has had only two youth gun homicides since July 1995.[59] Los Angeles and Orange county public schools, with a teenage population 10 times higher and no youth homicides of any kind during the same period, make Boston look murderous. Southern California schools need a new PR firm.

The lack of homicide in public schools extends beyond the nation's two largest urban areas. The California Department of Education posted its "California Safe Schools Assessment" of the hundreds of state schools with more than 1,000 students through 1996–97.[60] It showed low rates of school crime compared to elsewhere. In a state with 5.5 million students enrolled in public schools, there were zero school murders in 1995–96 and zero in 1996–97—compared to 6,700 in other locales. For every 1,000 students, there were three assaults/batteries, one weapons case, three robberies, and five other property crimes. The average victim of a shakedown or other theft was relieved of four dollars. School offenses are almost certainly under-reported—just like those in larger society.

School crime was down statewide. Contrary to Hillary's (*It Takes a Village*) and President Bill's fervent odes to the miracles of school uniforms as proven by the Long Beach success, the survey showed Long Beach Unified Schools had no greater decline in crime (or lower crime rates) than other Los Angeles County or California schools which did not require uniforms. (I recently stopped by a number of Long Beach schools, and I found the uniform policy most subtle. I would swear most students were togged in the attire of their choice.)

Nor is California's safe-schools record unique. In 1996, the Centers for Disease Control released a study showing the rarity of school violent deaths.[61] Its authors combed law enforcement, school, and coroner records for homicides that occurred in or around a school, or at a school event, in the 1992–93 and 1993–94 school years. The study found 85 persons murdered at school in the two-year study period, of which 50 involved killers who were students. School homicide and suicide are "rare events," CDC authors admitted, a finding the press didn't care to headline.

Let's put this in perspective. There are approximately 20 million youths ages 12–18 who attend junior (middle) and senior high schools daily, 180 days per year. This would mean that a student would have to attend school every day for 1.5 million years (perfect attendance since the late Pleistocene) to run an even risk of being murdered. Now consider the New Urban Legend that 100,000-plus students bring guns to school every day. In 180 school days, this would amount to 18 million "student-gun-days" (to coin a 1990s epidemiologism). Thus, a student would have to bring a gun to school every day for 2,000 years before the odds would favor its use in a murder.

Of America's 25,000 annual homicides, two dozen involve public school students killing someone at school. For murder, at least, our public schools sport a safety record that is phenomenally good. For other types of violence, schools appear somewhat less risky than other social institutions as well.

A 1998 Department of Education survey of a sample of 1,200 schools (Table 7) found that only one in five middle and high schools reported *even one serious crime* such as a rape or a robbery during the 1996–97 school year (elementary schools reported virtually none).[62] Forty-three percent reported *no* serious crimes.

The study calculated that for every 100,000 high school students, there were 18 rapes and sexual assaults, 46 fights with a weapon, 38 robberies, and 800 fistfights in a year's time. Like the officials who tabulate adult crime, principals and disciplinarians are not aware of all the crime that occurs in their schools. Nonetheless, the most serious crimes should get attention, and the numbers are strikingly low.

Using this sample, the Department projected 11,000 fights in which weapons were used, 4,000 rapes, and 7,000 robberies in schools nationwide. How does that stack up against the rest of society? In 1996, the FBI reported that approximately 1.7 million felony assaults, rapes, and robberies were reported to police. If the above sur-

Table 7

Despite official scare campaign, the violent crime rate is low in public schools

Violent incidents per 100,000 students, 1996–97 school year:

	All	Elementary	Middle	Senior
Murder	*	*	*	*
Rape/sexual assault	10	3	17	18
Assault/fight with weapon	26	7	49	46
Robbery	17	2	28	38
Assault/fight, no weapon	444	96	872	808

*None reported.

Source: National Center for Education Statistics (1998). Principal/school disciplinarian survey on school violence. Washington, DC: U.S. Department of Education. Survey of 1,234 public schools.

vey is accurate, public schools attended by 20 million middle and senior high students 180 days per year accounted for just 1.3 percent of these offenses. (Auburn University's Arthur Wilke, using methods similar to mine above, calculated that students were "100 times safer in school" than at home or on the streets.)[63] Few institutions with equivalent numbers of adults could boast such a safety record.

Certainly not workplaces. The Bureau of Justice Statistics' July 1998 report, *Workplace Violence*, analyzed data from 95,000 individuals in its victimization survey for 1992 through 1996.[64] It found that two million people are violently victimized at work, including 1,000 murders, 51,000 rapes and sexual assaults, and 84,000 robberies, every year. Clearly, workplaces make schools look like love-ins. Further, "those who committed workplace violence were predominantly male, white, and older than 21," the Bureau of Justice Statistics found. Just as adults commit some of the violence in schools, about one-tenth of the workplace violence is committed by youths. A president, a press, an academia interested in a conscientious approach toward violence would point out that America is a violent society where it lives, works, and learns—youths are simply one small part.

The administration's own best evidence indicates that public schools may be one institution that has *not* experienced a rise in violence. Said DOE study author Edith McArthur:

> The numbers seem pretty flat. I'm a parent, too, and you get even one of these horrible shootings and it's scary. But it's such a rare event that they didn't show up at all in our study, and as a statistician, I'd have to say there's no data showing any increase.

The only long-term survey of school violence, the University of Michigan's annual Monitoring the Future poll of 2,500 high school seniors, found that fewer reported being threatened or injured with a weapon in school in the most recent,

1996, survey than in the first one taken in 1976.[65] (This is the same survey with figures on student drug use that are eagerly headlined. For those who, like me, are skeptical of self-reporting surveys, it should be noted that the Monitoring the Future school violence cycles generally track those of violence arrests among white and black youth.)

The National School Safety Center, which tracks deaths from shootings in public schools (both suicide and homicide, and both student and adult-perpetrated), reported a declining pattern. In 1992–93, there were 55 such killings and suicides nationwide. In 1997–98, 40 killings and suicides, nearly all in inner-city schools. The killers are not average students, center director Ronald Stephens said. "Typically, the perpetrators have had a history of problems."[66]

Often, they are not even students. For example, the Justice Policy Institute pointed out, the school murder figures include all homicides that occur at schools, around schools, and at school events, whether or not the killers are students or adults. On May 29, 1998, a 26-year-old speech diagnostician was shot and killed in her Fort Lauderdale, Florida, high school parking lot by her jealous 34-year-old man-friend, who then shot himself. A similar adult murder/suicide occurred in February at New Jersey's Hoboken High School. These two incidents alone, both involving adults killing adults, accounted for 10 percent of the 40 gun deaths in public schools during 1997–98. Other, similar incidents in 1996 and 1997 involved a 16-year-old Norwalk, California, student murdered at school by her 21-year-old non-student paramour and an armored truck driver killed in an organized-crime robbery at a Los Angeles grade school. These statistically skewing events and perspectives were omitted or buried in press and political reactions to the recent student killings.

Even as the media was shrieking that "violence has become commonplace in almost all levels, types, and sizes of school" (USA Today) and "arguments used to be settled with fists" but "now, however, guns, knives, and other weapons meet even the slightest provocation" (Wall Street Journal),[67] Phi Delta Kappan magazine's 1995 survey found that only 2 percent of the nation's teachers felt "not very safe" or "not safe at all" at school; more than three-fourths felt "very safe."[68]

In late 1997, the Los Angeles Times randomly polled 1,300 parents, 1,100 teachers, 1,500 other adults, and 545 students ages 12–17 on California school issues.[69] Asked about violence, 83 percent of the students reported they had never been in a fight or had a weapon pulled on them at school; 14 percent had been in a fight; 2 percent had a weapon pulled on them; 1 percent had been in a fight involving a weapon. Only 3 percent of the teachers rated "crime/gangs/violence/drugs" as "the most important problem facing public schools today" (the most-cited problems were inadequate parenting, budget cuts, and large class size). Ninety-one percent of the students and 92 percent of the teachers felt "safe" (most of these felt "very safe") at school; only 2 percent of either felt "very unsafe." So much for "187's" claimed "reality."

Symptomatic of inflammatory media and politician claims on public attitudes, one-fifth of the non-teacher adults surveyed by the Times rated "crime/gangs/violence/drugs" as a top school problem—six to 10 times more than the teachers and students who attend school every day! As the Center for Media and Public Affairs survey found, real homicides dropped by 13 percent from 1990 to 1995, but coverage of murders by ABC, CBS, and NBC evening news leaped 240 percent in that time[70]—heavily tilted toward violence by the young. So much for the media's integrity in general.

Los Angeles Unified School District police figures, posted on the California Criminal Justice Statistics Center website, also dispute the "rising tide of school violence" image fostered by the president and press. From the 1990–91 to the 1996–97 school year, student enrollment increased from 790,000 to 850,000. Yet over the six-year period, school robberies fell by 22 percent, assault and battery dropped 23 percent, property crimes fell by 34 percent, assaults involving deadly weapons declined by half, weapons-related offenses fell by 65 percent, and sex offenses declined by 80 percent. Only drug offenses rose, and these due largely to expanded definitions of "chemical substances." For those offenses which are comparable to statutory crimes, L.A. schools, serving nearly one-tenth of the county's population, accounted for well below one-half of 1 percent of the county's reported crime.

But police reports, school surveys, and the Department of Education's finding that "the incidence of crime in schools has not grown significantly over the last two decades" did not meet politicians' needs. Instead, Clinton and the Republicans waxed horrific. "The threat of violence hangs over children's heads and closes their minds to learning," the president said. "We cannot let violence, guns, and drugs stand between our children and the education they need." Republican Senator Jeff Sessions of Alabama called for stepped-up expulsions. In a particularly idiotic synaptic misfire, Virginia Governor James Gilmore (R) proposed cutting nighttime athletic events to forestall "the shocking pattern of violence that is terrorizing our nation's schools."[71] So much for the president's and other politicians' integrity.

That any violence in schools is troubling does not justify the wholesale loss of perspective by the media and, especially, political leaders. Documenting that public schools full of dark-skinned teenagers are far safer from murder than even upscale suburban homes is not the sort of point that gets politicians elected, academic scholars top billing in breathless news stories, or Hollywood producers in a celluloid froth. The remarkable lack of school killing must be depressing news, judging from the failure of authorities to acknowledge it. At this point, it is impossible to imagine a major news outlet or academic authority, let alone prominent politicians, with the honest serenity to take the Justice Policy Institute's advice:

> The public discourse could tremendously benefit from the presentation of broader perspectives on juvenile killings. To provide greater context to such cases, the media should at least explain: that school killings are not on the increase; that such killings make up a small minority of all killings of and by juveniles; that the specific communities in which these killings occurred generally experience very few killings by juveniles; that children are 3 times more likely to be killed by adults than by other juveniles; and that there is no trend toward younger and younger juvenile killings. These data are readily available and would tremendously benefit the public's understanding of youth crime.[72]

Mild in the Streets

If there is a locale where crime statistics are meaningful, it is California. The state's excellent Criminal Justice Statistics Center has assembled consistent, virtually complete crime reports in massive detail since 1977. Call their Sacramento warren and crime-tomes will be forklifted into your den. If these don't have the specific numeral you want, an e-mail to their information specialists will have it in your fax inbox by sundown.

For all the work and money put into gathering California crime statistics, it seems that experts on crime like James Q. Wilson should actually look at them. I did, and here in brief is what I found:

- From the 1970s to the 1990s, teenage felony and misdemeanor arrests *plummeted*. During that same period, California's teenage population evolved from solidly Euro-white to a much poorer Latino, Asian, and black majority.

- In that same period, serious crime of *every* type among 30–49-year-olds, a population dominated by increasingly wealthy Euro-whites, *exploded*.

- Result: a stunning transformation. In 1978, a California high school freshman was *three times more likely* to be arrested for a felony than his 40-year-old parent. By 1996, high schooler and parent had virtually *equal* felony arrest odds.[73]

I later discovered that the governor-appointed California Task Force to Review Juvenile Crime and the Juvenile Justice Response's September 1996 *Final Report* reached the same conclusion. In the report's most ignored sentences:

> The arrest statistics are not reflective of the concern expressed about juvenile crime. In fact, the data showed a *marked decline in both the number of total juvenile arrests and arrest rates* since the early 1970s (page 20, emphasis mine).

Indeed there was. The trends in California teenage index crime rates (Figure 3) and in youth arrest rates by race, comparing the most recent three-year period of the 1990s (1995–97) with the corresponding three-year period of the mid-1970s are shown in Table 8.

Who would have guessed it? Crime DOWN BIG TIME among California youth? Black and Latino included? (Asian crime rose, but from a very low initial level. Note that even after increases, Asian youth remain less arrest-prone than any other group in 1997). Property, drug, misdemeanor, and felony crime has plummeted? Violent crime only marginally higher?

Talk about keeping the truth out of the papers—California's authorities and the media have done themselves proud.

I read the Task Force's report's passage and the above figures to silence in an address to the annual assemblage of California prosecutors, police, and prison officials at last summer's conference on youth crime. The state had the same number of Euro-white and 1 million more dark-skinned teenagers in 1997 than in 1975—and far less youth crime. No one disputed the numbers.

"There is no juvenile crime wave," declared University of San Diego Law School professor and Children's Advocacy Institute director Robert Fellmeth, the

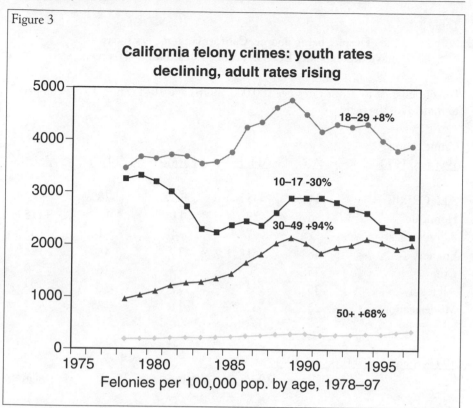

Figure 3

California felony crimes: youth rates declining, adult rates rising

18–29 +8%

10–17 -30%

30–49 +94%

50+ +68%

Felonies per 100,000 pop. by age, 1978–97

only crime expert I've encountered who actually *looked at the crime statistics*. "Earth to media and professional pundits: It does not exist."

> Department of Justice arrest data are unambiguous: juvenile crime was low in the 1960s and hit its zenith in the 1968 to 1979 period. It has declined fairly steadily since—for 17 continuous years—and steeply in the last five years…The entire picture is a better guide for law and policy than the anomalies picked out for dramatic value. They tell a story of youth who are generally and increasingly law-abiding.[74]

This, it seems, is why the True Crime story isn't being told: Of California's ethnic crazy-quilt, the groups showing *the biggest increases in violent, property, drug and other felony crimes by far are Euro-whites over age 30* and, second, Asians over age 30.

Exactly the state's most privileged country-clubbers. Granted, white and Asian adults' crime levels were pretty low in the 1970s. For Asians, they still are. But for middle-aged whites, serious crime rates have risen so rapidly that they now approach those of Latinos, despite the fact that average incomes among white adults are double those of Latinos.

The July 1998 report by California's prison statisticians is dully presented but revolutionary in information content. For the first time, a big majority—56 percent—of 1997's freshman class of prison inmates are over age 30.[75] More than

Table 8

Despite being poorer, California teenagers today
have dramatically LOWER crime rates than 1970s teens

Percent change in arrest rates per 100,000 youths age 10–17, mid-1990s compared to mid-1970s, by race

Crime change 1990s vs. 1970s	All	White	Latino	Black	Asian
ALL CRIME	-34%	-45%	-18%	-28%	+9%
Homicide	+6	-29	-11	-12	+118
All violent	+11	+7	+4	-1	+55
Property	-48	-61	-33	-48	+22
Drug	-35	-50	+9	-16	-9
All felony	-35	-53	-17	-30	+28
Misdemeanor	-23	-32	-11	-3	+17

1997 crime rate/100,000 age 10–17	All	White	Latino	Black	Asian
ALL CRIME	7,229	5,632	8,223	14,892	4,944
Homicide	9.2	2.0	13.6	26.2	11.7
All violent	549	290	625	1,911	373
Property	1,082	721	1,209	2,624	1,007
Drug	693	581	836	1,253	278
All felony	2,163	1,364	2,506	5,764	1,678
Misdemeanor	4,030	3,509	4,295	7,661	2,697
Status	1,036	758	1,421	1,467	569

Note: Violent crimes are homicide, rape, robbery, and aggravated assault. Property crimes are burglary, larceny, motor vehicle theft, and arson. Drug offenses include felony and misdemeanor sale and possession. Status refers to laws applying only to youths, such as curfew, truancy, running away, etc. Years compared are 1995–97 versus 1975–77.
Source: California Criminal Justice Statistics Center, Department of Justice.

26,000 people over 30 were outfitted for orange suits in 1997, representing a state liability of more than $2 billion to confine for their terms—as much as the state spends on the entire, 180,000-student University of California system! Of these adult cons, the largest contingent was white, a dozen-fold increase in two decades. When California's criminal justice system stirs itself to commit 10,000 aging whites to the Best Western Iron Hotel, these must be some true bad-asses.

(I use California as an example, but try this exercise for any state: examine the official crime statistics *for all age groups* over the last 15 years to see if they have anything to do with what politicians, experts, and the media have been hollering. Iowa, to pick one I had a chance to examine, had the same pattern as California. From 1985 to 1994, Iowa's violent crime rates rose 50 percent more rapidly among 30–40-agers than among teenagers.)

But, again, the Middle-Aged White Superpredator did not fit the needs of Governor Pete Wilson (Republican), Attorney General Dan Lungren (Republican), Senator Diane Feinstein (Democrat), Lieutenant Governor Gray Davis (Democrat), or other political aspirants. In fact, party leaders teamed up to push a $900 million prison bond issue in the 1996 election, *half* of it earmarked to cage more juveniles—a population which accounted for just 15 percent of the state's felony arrests and 8 percent of its crime increase in the last decade.[76]

No standard theory of crime, including mine, can explain why today's California kids are less crime-prone (though I'll try in the final chapter). Pick your own favorite explanation, radical to racist: more poverty, more criminally-inclined adults, more chaotic families, a greater share of black and Latino kids, more violent media, more guns. All the supposed causal factors had been going up while kid crime had been going down. Given the hassle of having to reconsider cherished notions, crime authorities ignored and falsified the statistical information.

Obsessive focus on the five-year rise in violent crime among a small segment of the youth population from 1987 through 1993 was trumpeted as the Four Horsemen marching from ghetto to suburb. The puzzle was that by all leading social indicators, kids should be superpredating en masse the way the media incessantly depicts a tiny fraction of their number. But they weren't and they aren't.

Needed: A New Sheriff

Today's debate over violent crime is driven by sensational anecdotes, mangled statistics, and long-discredited notions of the causes of crime more appropriate to 1898 than 1998. In the face of clear trends and developments suggesting dramatic new patterns in American violence that demand new and imaginative analysis, criminologists and officials have responded with Model-T crime theory.

Recent research and crime statistics show that far more violence occurs within families, and adults over age 30 are much more violently inclined, than traditional criminologists have acknowledged. Over-30 adults do not "age out" of "crime-prone" years so much as they "take it indoors." The California Legislative Analysts' report on perpetrators of child abuse is typical: average age of abuser: 31; 85 percent are parents or stepparents, and 7 percent are other relatives. Even though there were more than 100,000 substantiated cases of violent and sexual abuses of California children, only about 11,000 arrests were made in 1994. If child abuse had the same rate of arrests as for other violent crimes, the violence arrest rates of Californians over age 30 (already skyrocketing) would rise by another 50 percent.

For women and for children under age 13, who together comprise three-fifths of America's population, domestic violence is the chief crime threatening physical safety and life itself. From a child's point of view, streets, playgrounds, alleys, and schools are safer places to be than at home with parents. Yet to traditional criminologists and politicians, domestic violence (other than when spectacular events

Table 9

Teen male population rises, crime falls

Index crimes*	Violent	Property	Drug	All index	Male teens as pct of pop
1992	1,932,400	12,505,900	1,099,900	14,438,200	3.46%
1997	1,602,200	11,337,800	1,576,500	12,939,900	3.67%
Volume change	-330,200	-1,168,100	+476,600	-1,498,300	+996,000
Rate change	-21%	-14%	+38%	-15%	+11%

*Source and definitions: FBI, web posting, May 17, 1998, estimate from 9,582 police agencies for 1997; see also table 1. Drug offenses available only through 1996.

intrude, especially those involving celebrities) is not "real" crime.

One reason for the official silence is that while youth violence increases have occurred among increasingly impoverished inner-city populations, adult violence surges have been spread among all races and income groups and are more baffling. Thus, the racial issue is once again evident: the increase in minority youth violence is easier to deplore than the even greater rise in violence among more affluent, mostly white, adults.

Further, the demographic "age theory" provides authorities with a ready-made excuse insulating them from accountability for the strategies they employ against violent crime. If crime goes up, it is blamed on the rising youth population; if it goes down, officials laud themselves for defeating demographic destiny.

Thus, king malarkey endures no matter how obviously unclothed. In the early 1990s, the invasion of murderous savages—our own kids—began (refer back to Tables 1 and 2). From 1992 to 1997, the numbers and proportion of teenage males rose ominously, adding 1 million first-wave "temporary sociopaths" to the population. By DiIulio/Wilson/Fox mathematics, tens of thousands more superpredators should be prowling the streets "to do what comes naturally: murder, rape, rob, assault, burglarize, deal deadly drugs, and get high."[77] Criminologists hatched omens and battened hatches. Table 9 shows what the FBI reported actually happened.

One million *more* teen boys. One and one-half million *fewer* serious crimes. After three more years of shrieking about rising crime, the media belatedly noticed the decline and polled the experts: Why is crime down? Why, wondrous police work, brilliant official salvos against "juvenile crime," plus "an aging population," according to the lies from Attorney General Janet Reno, White House senior policy advisor Ralph Emanuel, Carnegie Mellon University crime expert Alfred Blumstein, and other top authorities.[78]

2 Myth: Teens Need More Policing

Monrovia, California, was an ideal symbol for Clinton Campaign '96. The quaint city of 40,000 in the affluent foothills east of Pasadena had instituted a "zero tolerance for juvenile crime" policy. Its crown jewel was the nation's first daytime curfew aimed at youths, called an anti-truancy ordinance even though truancy was already outlawed by state statutes. Mandatory school uniforms and other controls on kids included principal's interviews with students' out-of-town prom dates. Monrovia's Safe City/Safe Campus task force had recommended tougher policies (including the curfew, implemented in October 1994) because:

> In 1994, the City and School District began to notice some disturbing trends. There were between 75 and 100 truant students every day. Many of these truants were suspected of contributing to an increase in daytime criminal activity. In a ninety-day period, guns were discovered three times on campus. Local gangs had begun to hang around the schools to recruit and pressure students…Police responses to school campuses were increasing.[1]

Puzzling. In the first nine months of 1994 that the task force found so worrisome, police records show Monrovia had dramatically *lower* levels of all types of crime than the same months of 1993. Crimes reported to police had dropped 20 percent, theft and larceny were down 12 percent, burglary was down 23 percent, violent crime had declined 42 percent. Juvenile arrests had fallen by 22 percent. Only 18 juvenile arrests for any sort of offense had taken place during school hours in the previous 10-month school year. No juvenile had been arrested for murder in three years. Monrovia, in short, enjoyed one of America's lowest youth crime problems as well as one in sharp decline.

Nevertheless, in October 1994, the curfew took effect. Through July 1997, police records show that 800 youths were handed citations of $135 each. Parents had one hour to pick up their kids from the police or face custodial charges of $62 per hour.

City and news reports were glowing. "Small Town Success," cheered a *Los Angeles Times* feature.[2] (Ironically, as the press wildly touted the presidentially-endorsed youth curfews of 1996, on other pages the press was lamenting the shameful legacy of another presidentially-endorsed curfew: that of March 24, 1942, against Japanese-Americans in California and other western states. At the time the press cheered for the "rigid new curfew" on "Japs" as well, articles in the California and national press displayed by the Museum of San Francisco showed.)[3]

"Curfews work!" everyone agreed. Monrovia school officials reported a 57 percent decline in school dropout. Monrovia police reported that after the curfew was adopted, burglaries during school hours dropped 54 percent, theft was down 48 percent, and auto rip-off had plunged 55 percent. The Monrovia numbers acquired messianic quality, spreading from community to community in a nation eager to adopt this seemingly no-cost no-hassle (to anyone important) crime-busting notion.

Only one problem: Monrovia officials would later admit much of the good news was not true.

It's doubtful that this detail would have made much difference to preachers of the get-tough-on-juveniles religion. Its Chief Preacher, President Clinton, visited the shrine in July 1996. "We have about six years to get ahead of this juvenile crime and drug problem that will be almost unbearable, unmanageable, and painful," he told Monrovians, invoking the standard fear of coming hordes of young. "You have proof that it can be done, and it will get done." The *Times* news story, an unabashed advertisement, declared that the president, teachers, parents, and good kids were all for the curfew. The only ones against it were "students who brag about their poor attendance the way some people boast about their children."[4]

There were other dissenters, however. The Home School Legal Defense Association filed suit on behalf of several Monrovia parents angry that their kids, tutored in Christian homes to avoid the evils of public education, had been stopped dozens of times for curfew violations.[5] The association cast about for a reputable scholar to analyze crime and curfew data. Unable to find one, they contacted me. Boxes filled with Monrovia police reports and statements arrived.

Such a curfew presents clear ethical problems. Law enforcement was effecting house (or school) arrest on youths who had committed no criminal offense. If the 1990s legal precept is that the mere presence of juveniles in a public place represents such a threat that all must be curfewed, then there is no limit to the restrictions that can be imposed.

The Color of Curfew

The first question was who was getting curfewed. Monrovia, like most California cities of any size, is stratified. The uphill, northern part is affluent and nearly all white; family incomes top $50,000. The southern part is mostly Latino and black; one-third of the kids live in poverty. The high school sits in the middle. After school, masses of white kids drive north and masses of dark kids walk south. As a practical matter, youths who walk are more likely to be arrested for curfew than youths who drive, making curfews inherently biased against poorer teens.

Prior to the 1980s, most of Monrovia's 2,500 teens were white; now, 55 percent are nonwhite. I found that black and Latino youths were slapped with 70 percent of the curfew citations, a rate nearly double that of whites. Even more troubling, nonwhites were 40 percent more likely than whites to be curfewed even after each racial group's overall crime rate was factored out. After the curfew took effect, more than half of all offenses committed by nonwhite youths were curfew violations. That is, the curfew doubled the black and Latino youth "crime rate."

Zero Tolerance or Denial?

But did it cut crime? The police data I was provided for January 1, 1992, through July 31, 1997, neatly fell into 33 months before and 33 months after the curfew took effect, allowing direct comparison. Few times have I beheld a pattern that LESS resembled a juvenile crime decline than Monrovia's after its school-day curfew (Table 1).

After adopting the curfew, Monrovia experienced a 53 percent increase in juveniles arrested for non-curfew crimes during the school months in which the curfew was enforced. In contrast, during the summer months of July and August, when the curfew was not enforced, juvenile crime declined by 12 percent. Adult crime showed only modest changes over the period.

"If every community in America woke up tomorrow and decided to organize themselves the way you have here, the difference would be breathtaking," Clinton told Monrovians. Breathtaking is the word. Each year after enforcing its curfew, Monrovia suffered quantum leaps in youth crime that tracked greater curfew enforcement (Table 1).

In a January 1998 deposition in the Home School case, the Monrovia Police Department admitted the figures they had provided to the media regarding the curfew and juvenile crime had been unreliable. Mistakes were made entering data into computer spreadsheets, their statistician said.[6] This admission did not make the news, nor did the police ruefully call the White House to 'fess up.

Au contraire. In response to our initial study, Monrovia police chief J.J. Santoro called us liars ("That's a lie and you know it!" he yelled at study co-author Dan Macallair of the Justice Policy Institute on the *Today Show*) and "hired guns." Perhaps hired water pistols: I received a whopping $440 from the conservative Home School Legal Defense Association and $25 from the American Civil Liberties Union of West Virginia for presenting a deposition and testimony regarding the effects of curfews in California counties and cities, including Monrovia and San Jose, that I had undertaken the previous year for my doctoral dissertation.

New figures, Chief Santoro thundered, showed that after the curfew took effect, Monrovia displayed a 29 percent reduction in daytime burglaries (a bit less than the 54 percent originally claimed) and a jaw dropping 92 percent decline in bicycle thefts! In more tempered comments, Chief Santoro declared that arrests were irrelevant; what mattered was the trend in overall Part I crimes reported to police. Part I crimes—the so-called "index" offenses used by police agencies as a consistent measure of overall crime—consist of the Big Four violent crimes (murder, rape, robbery, and aggravated assault) plus the Big Four property crimes (burglary, grand larceny, motor vehicle theft, and arson).

Reported crime is a lousy measure, as noted in the last chapter, since it provides no age breakdown. It's lousier still for Monrovia, whose crime clearance figures indicate that around 90 percent of reported offenses are committed by adults, making it hard to sift out whether the curfew had any effect on the 10 percent committed by youths. No one knows who stole those 17 bicycles in Monrovia in 1993, or the one in 1996 (a 92 percent decline!). They could have been purloined by truant fourth graders, the CIA-Contra crack ring, or the ghost of Vittorio DeSica. But,

Table 1

Youth crime rose during Monrovia's school curfew period but fell during non-curfewed summer months

Monrovia curfew citations and youth crime

School Year	Curfew citations	Non-curfew crimes*	Total
1992–93	0	203	203
1993–94	0	148	148
1994–95	140	180	320
1995–96	246	296	542
1996–97	405	348	760
Before curfew, 33 months			
1/92 to 9/94	0	371	371
After curfew, 33 months			
11/94 to 7/97	789	728	1,517
Rate change*		+80%	

Summer	Curfew citations	Non-curfew crimes*	Total
July–Aug 1992	0	27	27
July–Aug 1993	0	42	42
July–Aug 1994	0	30	30
July–Aug 1995	0	23	23
July–Aug 1996	2	30	32
Before curfew, 33 months			
1/92 to 9/94	0	99	99
After curfew, 33 months			
11/94 to 7/97	2	105	107
Rate change*		-12%	

*includes violent, property, drug, and other felonies and misdemeanors. Rate is based on population ages 12–17 (youth) and 18–69 (adult).

Source: Monrovia Police Department. *Monthly Report*, January 1992–July 1997.

since Monrovia is held up nationwide as an example of curfew success, let us examine proponents' claims at face value.

The city of Monrovia hired its own Paladin, RAND Corporation research scientist Stephen Klein, to shoot down the critics. Klein's two-page study claimed that "there was a 29 percent reduction in the Part I crime rate" during school hours in

Table 2

**Overall crime in Monrovia declined more rapidly during
periods when the curfew was *not* enforced**

Index (serious) crimes* reported to police:

School year*	Curfew hours School year	Non-curfew hours* School year	Summer	Non-curfew Total	Grand Total
1992–93	na	na	408	na	2,322
1993–94	410	1,205	362	1,567	1,977
curfew adopted, 10/94					
1994–95	391	1,045	296	1,341	1,732
1995–96	380	882	279	1,161	1,541
1996–97	293	792	206	998	1,291
Change, 1996–97 vs. 1993–94	-29%	-34%	-43%	-36%	-35%

*Index crimes are burglary, felony theft, motor vehicle theft, arson, murder, rape, robbery, and aggravated assault. "Curfew hours" include those reported crimes which police estimate occurred during school hours, Monday through Friday, September 1 through June 30. "Non-curfew hours" shows crime occuring during other school-year hours from September 1 though June 30 and during the summer (the August before and the July after bracketing each school year), when the curfew is not in effect. "Total" refers to all school-year and non-curfew hours combined.
Sources: Monrovia Police Department, *Monthly Report*, and "Crime During School Hours"; California Criminal Justice Profiles, Los Angeles County, 1993–96.

the 1996–97 school year (the latest period available) compared to the 1993–94 school year (the last before the curfew took effect). "In contrast, there was only a 22 percent reduction in Part I [index] crimes during non-school hours between these periods," Klein stated. By simple subtraction, he concluded, "these data suggest the program reduced Part I crimes in Monrovia by about 7 percent (i.e., 29 percent - 22 percent = 7 percent)."

In addition to being unfettered by such routine statistical accoutrements as time-series analysis and significance testing, Klein's study got the basic numbers wrong. Even using police figures, the decline in crime was considerably larger during periods in which the curfew was not enforced than when it was. Monrovia police statistics show crimes reported to police and crimes estimated to have occurred during curfew (school) hours. All other crimes would have occurred during non-curfew hours. Curfew hours occur during school days; non-curfew hours are divided into those during the school year (evenings, weekends, holidays) and those in the summer (July and August). The results are shown in Table 2.

It is not clear how Klein came to the conclusion that "there was only a 22 percent reduction in Part I crimes during non-school hours." The fact was that the decrease in reported index offenses in Monrovia was considerably larger in the summer months (down 43 percent) and during the hours of the school year when the curfew was not in effect (down 34 percent). *Overall, crime declined much more during periods in which juveniles were free to be in public (down 36 percent) than during the curfew hours (down 29 percent)*. In particular, the decline in property crimes, the offenses most likely to be committed by juveniles) was substantially stronger in the non-curfew hours of the school year and summer months than during the curfew hours. Further, note from Table 2 that Monrovia's crime decline from 1992–93 to 1993–94, before the curfew took effect, was larger than in any year after the curfew's adoption.

Crediting a single law with a city's crime decline is simplistic; crime is down everywhere. So, finally, our study compared Monrovia's crime patterns before and after the curfew's adoption with those of its 11 neighboring, northeastern Los Angeles cities which had levels of curfew enforcement ranging from moderately vigorous to zero. The analysis showed Monrovia had no unusual decline in crime compared to its neighbors, except for an impressive 56 percent decrease in aggravated assault. However, police records show Monrovia youths commit only 3 to 5 percent of the city's aggravated assaults; this offense primarily stems from domestic violence. It is highly unlikely that a curfew prohibiting youths from being outdoors would have caused a huge decline in a crime committed, overwhelmingly, by adults indoors.

More to the point, for the five crimes youths are most likely to commit (listed in order), Monrovia ranked 6th of 12 cities in reduction in arson, tied for 3rd in robbery reduction, 8th in motor vehicle theft decline, tied for 4th in burglary decrease, and first in theft decline. If the curfew caused or contributed to the decrease in reported thefts, it is not clear why it had no effect on the other four crimes that are more likely to be committed by juveniles. Overall, Monrovia's experience in youth-indicated crime is average for the region.

Thus, whether measured by juvenile arrests or by reported offenses, Monrovia's curfew did not reduce crime. When numbers were refigured, they showed that juveniles accounted for only one to two crimes per month during school hours prior to the curfew, and three to four after school hours. Compare that small youth crime toll to the average of 30 curfew citations per month. Recalculation of the school dropout rate produced similar results. Before the curfew, Monrovia had a low rate of dropout just as it did afterward. The law had no discernible effect. Not only was the curfew a proverbial cannon aimed at a mosquito, it had badly misfired.

"Please, please keep it up," Clinton implored in 1996. During the 1996–97 school year, Monrovia police indeed intensified the curfew blizzard to a record 405 citations. Juvenile crime increased yet again. By 1997, nonwhite kids were 70 percent more likely to be cited for curfew than white youths compared to each racial group's contribution to the city's crime.

The irony, Los Angeles' National Conference for Communities and Justice youth and education director Lori Nelson, a Monrovia parent, told me, is that the city also provides stellar positive programs for young people. In the summer, any Monrovia youth can hop a bus for a free ride to recreation centers where a variety of free, high-quality programs abound. The summer, let liberal hearts bleed, is exactly when youth crime declined. The law'n'order school year—when the discipline should have produced a drop—was when youth crime rose drastically.

The White House didn't examine readily available police records showing the dubious results and large racial disparities in Monrovia's curfew enforcement before the president ringingly endorsed the law. Its bad effects were readily apparent well before the president visited in July 1996.

It's doubtful those facts, even had he known them, would have made much difference to a president campaigning for get-tough measures, one who argued do-good government spending was not the answer to youth malaise. Clinton didn't travel to Monrovia to whoop it up for a summer recreation program.

Leave Those Kids Alone

California's increase in curfew arrests was huge—up 400 percent during the 1990s. Yet study of their effect was astonishingly sparse. An internet search turned up only 25 recent citations. Most covered constitutional issues, or a single jurisdiction, or anecdotes, or (mostly) polemics. But given that all three branches of government and adulthood in general don't give a rip about fundamental fairness, rights, or freedoms for adolescents, let's cut to the only issue anyone cares about: do curfews reduce juvenile crime? Or is Monrovia's experience—loudly asserted success disproven by careful analysis—apply to curfews in general?

Recently, the U.S. Conference of Mayors surveyed the nation's 1,010 cities with populations of more than 30,000 asking, in effect, if law enforcement authorities would be pleased to take credit for any recent reductions in juvenile crime. Surprisingly, only one-third, or 347, of the cities responded to this invitation to self-praise. Not surprisingly, 88 percent of those responding claimed their curfew enforcement was responsible for reducing youth crime. None, however, documented any decrease. The survey "did not include a statistical analysis of the effect curfews have had on crime."[7]

However, the Los Angeles Police Department did attempt a statistical analysis in two 1998 reports on its 10 PM curfew.[8] The first, in February, concluded that its Enhanced Curfew Enforcement Effort "*has not* significantly decreased" juvenile victimization or crime. The second, in July, announced that it "*has* impacted" juvenile victimization and crime (emphasis in both originals). Despite their opposite conclusions, the two reports made identical recommendations: the curfew should continue to be enforced because it is "an effective tool." This suggests the LAPD's view of the curfew is not based on whether it works.

Taken together, the two reports make interesting reading. In the first six-month period examined, May to October 1997, officers wrote 4,810 curfew citations—a 90 percent increase over the previous six months, the report said. More than 800 officers put in 3,600 officer-hours, supplemented by more than 1,000 volunteer hours and 101 special curfew task forces. It was a major effort. But evaluation of it found that "the Enhanced Curfew Enforcement Effort...has not significantly decreased the number of minors who become crime victims or the total number of violent crimes committed."

In the second six-month period, October to April 1998, 3,341 curfew tickets were issued, "a 69 percent decrease" from the previous period. Only 650 officers put in 2,500 officer hours, volunteers contributed another 600 hours, and 87 task forces participated—all major declines from the previous six months. Yet evalua-tion of this period found that "the curfew enforcement effort has impacted the number of minors who became crime victims and the total number of violent crimes committed."

Taken together and at face value, the reports seem to find that the fewer cita-tions, the fewer officer and volunteer hours, and the fewer task forces dedicated to enforcing the curfew, the better. The LAPD's arrest figures over the last eight years show that whether police were writing 82 curfew citations (1990), 500 (1993), or 11,500 (1997), the trends in youth crime appear to track the trends in adult crime almost exactly, weakening the argument that curfews have a positive impact. Finally, though blacks and Latinos comprise 70 percent of the city's youth popula-tion, they received 87 percent of the curfew citations—2.5 times the rate of Asians and whites.

The LAPD's inconsistent studies do not employ baseline data before the cur-few effort, nor do they use adult arrests or other jurisdictions without curfews as points of comparison. Juvenile victimizations resulting from domestic violence are lumped in with those from street violence, and the vast majority of "violent crime reports" involve adults, factors which argue that the reports only peripherally assess curfew effects. But at least the LAPD made a stab at evaluation.

The nearest to a study that appears to exist is an April 1996 report by the Office of Juvenile Justice and Delinquency Prevention on "comprehensive, com-munity-based curfew programs" in seven cities.[9] The report concluded that "infor-mation by communities where curfews have been implemented indicates that comprehensive, community-based curfew programs are helping to reduce juvenile delinquency and victimization." However, the report does not present any analysis necessary to support that conclusion. For some cities, selected juvenile victimiza-tions are cited; for others, selected juvenile arrests; for others, selected crimes (such as burglaries or vehicle theft) reported to police. No complete assessments of crime are presented. No controlled comparisons are made with cities that did not enforce curfews. Clearly, for any jurisdiction and year, some crimes and some victimizations will increase and others will decrease due to natural variation alone. The OJJDP report is not a study but an invitation to police to selectively claim credit for whatever crimes go down while avoiding mention of those that increased.

In short, no systematic studies are evident. Given the enthusiasm for curfews, why no serious analysis? Curfews are not that hard to study. Juvenile crime is exhaustively tabulated.

At the behest of the Center on Juvenile and Criminal Justice in San Francisco, I analyzed whether state and local curfew arrests had any effect on youth crime in California, tabulating curfew and crime arrests statewide since 1980, for each of the state's 24 major counties (population 22 million). I looked at Los Angeles and Orange counties' cities of over 100,000 population, 21 in all. I looked at specific, celebrated cases such as Monrovia and San Jose.

The result: curfews do not reduce youth crime. Monrovia is a failure in point. Los Angeles is dubious. San Jose's curfew also is a misfire.

Consider the tale of two Sans, Jose and Francisco, 50 miles apart, cities of similar populations (800,000). San Jose received intensive publicity for its anti-gang initiatives in the early 1990s. The city won a landmark 1997 California Supreme Court decision upholding a 1993 injunction that barred 38 police-suspected Latino gang members from "standing, sitting, walking, driving, gathering or appearing anywhere in public view" with each other in a four-block neighborhood known as Rocksprings. Those subject to the injunction did not have to be convicted of any crimes, only identified by police as "gang members" according to dress, tattoos, hand signs, etc.[10]

In contrast, San Francisco police ceased enforcement of curfews in the 1990s. In the 1995 election, voters solidly defeated reimposing the curfew, the result of a successful opposition campaign by the Youth Uprising Coalition formed by high school students.

The two cities' diametrically opposed approaches to curfew enforcement are shown in Table 3, along with juvenile crime trends before and after San Jose's curfew crackdown. Although crime rates have always been higher in San Francisco than in suburban San Jose regardless of curfew enforcement, crime trends over the last decade do not favor San Jose. Even radical increases in curfew arrests did not reduce San Jose's juvenile crime rates, either felony or total—in fact, they rose. Conversely, even complete abandonment of curfew enforcement did not lead to a youth crime wave in San Francisco; rates were stable or falling.

If, as curfew defenders insist (when convenient), crimes reported to police are a better index, note from Table 3 that San Francisco's decline in reported crime over the relevant period (early 1990s to mid 1990s) is more impressive than San Jose's. This is especially true if new figures for January-June 1998 are included: compared to the first half of 1997, major (index) crime declined another 11 percent in San Francisco, but increased 2 percent in San Jose.

Boston provides a different contrast. The city is widely praised for practically eliminating juvenile homicide.[11] From 1990 through mid-1995, there were an average of 10 juveniles murdered by guns every year. Since July 1995, there have been (as of this writing) only two youths gunned down in the city.

Whatever caused Boston's "miracle," it was not the usual palliatives. The city has no youth curfew, no strict enforcement of status laws (laws such as curfew or truancy that apply to youths but not adults), no general policy of get-tough measures. Boston's approach has been to concentrate probation department resources on a relatively small number of serious offenders, both youth and adult. Only those convicted of serious offenses are subjected to curfew.

San Francisco again provides an interesting contrast. San Francisco has 200,000 more people, 10,000 more youths ages 10–17, and an unquestionably larger gang presence than Boston. While Boston is situated in a relatively bullet-free zone (150 firearms homicides per year in the state of Massachusetts), San Francisco is a wing of the Gundown State (2,700 California gun murders per year, triple Massachusetts' per-person bulletings).

Yet San Francisco experienced only an average of three youth gunshot murders per year during 1990–94; in 1995, one, in 1996, two. In terms of youths arrested for

Table 3

San Jose curfew arrests skyrocket, San Francisco's plummet

	San Francisco	San Jose
Curfew arrest rates*		
1987–89	843	0
1990–94	29	4
1995–97	2	585
Youth felony arrest rate*		
1987–89	4,975	1,533
1990–94	4,899	2,422
1995–97	4,933	2,650
Youth total arrest rate*		
1987–89	11,448	6,308
1990–94	9,699	7,570
1995–97	8,866	7,983
Crimes reported to police*		
1987–89	8,991	5,099
1990–94	9,721	4,870
1995–97	7,511	4,034
1998 (Jan–June)	5,924	3,568

*Arrest rate is per 100,000 age 10–17. "Total arrests" excludes curfew and status offenses. "Crimes reported to police" are FBI index offenses per 100,000 population of all ages; rates for 1998 are for January–June divided by half of each city's 1996 population to produce an annualized rate.
Source: Criminal Justice Statistics Center, California Department of Justice (1986–98).

murder, San Francisco's annual numbers for 1990 through 1997 are flabbergasting: 13, 18, 17, 34, 14, 8, 3, 1. A 90 percent-plus decline! The City by the Polluted Bay (West Coast) "miracle" cannot be credited to tough law enforcement. San Francisco recorded just one juvenile status crime arrest in the last five years. It is noted for law enforcement liberality, a sheriff and county attorney who defend medical marijuana laws against federal and state agents, and an electorate which rejected a tougher teenage curfew law. Boston's and San Francisco's "miracles" lend no support to get-tough ideology. San Francisco's experience is particularly emphatic: even zero-curfew enforcement does not lead to Youth Gone Wild. Maybe just the opposite.

Weird Science

In June 1998, the Justice Policy Institute released our curfew study, which had been reviewed by several criminologists and accepted for publication in *Western*

Criminology Review.[12] I thought the press would shrug, as it had at what I thought were my much more dramatic findings on youth crime, drugs, and pregnancy.

All hell broke loose. Something about curfews in the psyche of America of 1998 hit raw nerves coast to coast. For three days, it was CNN, NPR, ABC, *USA Today*, *Christian Science Monitor*, *Today Show*, Ollie North on line 1, ACLU on call waiting. The mayor of San Diego branded us biased. The police in San Jose, where the *Mercury-News* headlined the study, vowed to show their curfew indeed did work.

Mayors, police, and California prosecutors issued statements declaring that since our study used juvenile arrests as its chief measure, it was suspect. Arrests, law enforcement officials and prosecutors declared, are a poor measure of juvenile crime.

Wrong, but first…huh?

Hadn't law enforcement been shouting for the entire decade that the increase in juvenile *arrests* proved juvenile crime was rising? Take back all those sensational stories, reporters. Hadn't Attorney General Dan Lungren recently declared that the statewide decline in juvenile *arrests* proved curfews were working? No dissent from police and prosecutors about that.

A better measure, officers declared, was crimes reported to police. Here we go again—the mix'n'match. As noted in the last section, crimes reported to police tell us nothing about the age of whoever committed them. But okay. We re-ran our curfew analysis using "crimes reported to police" rather than "arrests" as the measure. The results: curfews have no effect on reported crimes, either. Except for one: arson—the index crime juveniles are the most likely to commit. The more curfew arrests, the *more* arson. Not good, unless you assume burning down almost any California building beautifies the state. Further, the major city/county showing the state's biggest decline in reported crime was none other than San Francisco, which boldly lets its juveniles roam in public at all hours.

The angry emotionality of the curfew furor was troubling. What is it about American adults of the late 1990s that yearns to sweep all juveniles off the street, daytime and nighttime—a curfew policy no other Western nation has adopted, except in times of war or revolution? As with American's fervor for executing youths, why are we so far out of step with our sister nations—in fact, nearly all other societies on earth?

Testifying in July 1998 on behalf of the American Civil Liberties Union against the Charleston, West Virginia, youth curfew, I see yet another example of the indignant demand by flawed adults for absolute teenage purity. Lawyers for the city and neighborhood intervenors obnoxiously question the three teenage witnesses who describe how the 10 p.m.–6 a.m. curfew would pointlessly curtail the nighttime volunteer, cultural, and entertainment activities—rights adults take for granted—of thousands of responsible youths. This sweeping restriction was intended to confront what statistics showed, and everyone agreed, was the quiet city's minimal teenage crime problem. Have the teenage plaintiffs ever consumed alcohol? Have they ever been at parties where alcohol was consumed? Do they have peers who use drugs? Do they consider their violations of underage drinking laws an example of the maturity to conduct themselves in public at night?

Earlier, Charleston's police chief defended the curfew. No one asked whether he had ever consumed alcohol, driven after drinking, or broken any laws—and whether any admitted indiscretions in his life did not demonstrate his immaturity to enforce a curfew ordinance (which included discretion to override parents' decisions to allow their kids in public at night). One of the chief lawyers grilling the teen plaintiffs was not known as a teetotaler ("he's drunk a lot at ——," a popular downtown bar, another lawyer told me). I was glad to see anger building among the teenage witnesses as lawyers probed every detail of any of their honestly admitted behaviors, knowing the judge would never allow such questions of grownups. Finally, 17-year-old Katelyn Kimmons snapped that, yes, she had seen her friends drive after drinking, "but I've seen more adults drive when they were even more intoxicated, and that's just as dangerous."[13] I'm delighted to see what happens when teenagers threaten to bring up how adults act: No more questions, your honor.

The U.S. on Executions: Allied with Saddam

The United States, practically alone among the world's nations, has decided that kids are old enough to face capital punishment.

In 1989, the U.S. Supreme Court upheld capital punishment of 16- and 17-year-olds. Evidencing how America has hardened in recent decades, the dissenters from the 1989 Court decision were four senior justices (three since retired) appointed by Presidents Eisenhower, Johnson, Nixon, and Ford. The Court majority justified its decision as founded in the "common law tradition" of America: "at least 281 offenders under the age of 18 have been executed in this country and at least 126 under the age of 17."[14] Funny the Court didn't uphold the traditions of lynching, wife-beating, and slave-rape while they were at it.

Since 1979, fourteen juvenile executions have occurred worldwide. The enlightened democracies of Pakistan, Rwanda, Barbados, and Bangladesh accounted for five. The U.S., nine.[15]

In 1991, the United Nations Convention on the Rights of the Child finalized its proposed document. Article 37 requires each government to "protect children from torture or other cruel, inhuman, or degrading treatment or punishment," including "capital punishment or life imprisonment for offenses committed by persons below the age of 18."[16] This document has been ratified by every nation, including the above-mentioned Pakistan, Rwanda, Barbados, and Bangladesh. However, it proved too radical for three: Iran, Iraq, and our very own.

In April 1998, a detailed report ratified by the U.N. Commission on Human Rights condemned the United States' death penalty for "arbitrariness. Race, ethnic origin, and economic status appear to be key determinants of who will and who will not receive a sentence of death."[17] The report and Commission were especially critical of U.S. laws allowing execution for crimes committed as juveniles, which also violate the International Covenant on Human and Political Rights. Only four other nations—Iran, Pakistan, Saudi Arabia, and Yemen—still permit execution of juveniles, the report said.

This alone should give Americans pause—what makes our hostility toward children so intense that we stand alongside a handful of fundamentalist religious states and outside the opinion of the rest of the world? Objections to the report were not limited to conservatives such as Senator Jesse Helms (R-North Carolina) who backed our policy and threatened to withhold payment of U.S. dues to the U.N. The Clinton-appointed U.S. ambassador replied that the death penalty reflected "the will of the people." These reactions constituted a guilty plea to the U.N. Commission's charge that Americans subject our law to a standard of popularity rather than of inviolable human rights.

The Clinton administration supports execution of 16- and 17-year-olds, as does the Republican Congress. The Supreme Court majority thought that was fine. Supreme Court rulings have found states to be justified in banishing juveniles en masse from legal rights to vote, drive, or drink because of age, yet permitted states to subject juveniles to "individualized tests" in order to put them to death. That is, kids are only seen as individual persons when we want to lock them up or kill them.

In 1989, fourteen juveniles were on death row in the U.S. This, Court dissenters wrote, was how states conducted their "individualized tests:"

> A recent diagnostic evaluation of all 14 juveniles on death row in 4 states is instructive. Seven of the adolescents sentenced to die were psychotic when evaluated, or had been so diagnosed in early childhood; 4 others had histories consistent with diagnoses of severe mood disorders; and the remaining 3 experienced periodic paranoid episodes, during which they would assault perceived enemies. Eight had suffered severe head injuries during childhood and 9 suffered from neurological abnormalities. Psychoeducational testing showed that only 2 of these death row inmates had IQ scores above 90 (that is, in the normal range)—and both individuals suffered from psychiatric disorders—while 10 offenders showed impaired abstract reasoning on at least some tests. All but 2 of the adolescents had been physically abused, and 5 sexually abused. Within the families of these children, violence, alcoholism, drug abuse, and psychiatric disorders were commonplace.[18]

Quit whining, get-tough folks might say. Capital punishment's rough on grownups, too. During the 1992 campaign, Clinton rushed back to Arkansas to ratify the execution of a man so delusional that he asked that the dessert from his last meal be saved so he could eat it after returning from the death chamber.[19]

Clinton would go further, treating juveniles not just equally, but more harshly than, adults. The crazily draconian Violent and Repeat Juvenile Offender Act (S.10 and its companion bill, H.R.3 by number) which passed the House in 1997 and has Clinton's general endorsement, encourages sentencing juveniles to adult jails; allows runaways, truants and other status offenders to be jailed for up to two weeks before trial (including up to 24 hours with adult cellmates); appropriates $250 million to ensure that many agencies from colleges to Job Corps to employers can obtain juvenile offense records; and mandates expulsion from school for up to six months for possession of drugs, alcohol, or nicotine. Note that these standards, particularly the latter, are far harsher than imposed on adults. Congress and the Clinton regime do not suspend or expel their own personnel who fail drug tests, drink and drive, or even engage in sex with teenage pages. Youth Today's editorial on S.10 rightly noted that even imperial England under King George III permitted petitions to the monarch on behalf of youths for protection against "assault on common sense, decency, and human rights."[20]

In response, some have argued for preserving the juvenile justice system and preventing execution of juveniles on the grounds that youths are incapable of reason, planning, or understanding the consequences of their acts. This does not seem to be true. Decades of psychological study consistently show that even young adolescents make decisions in much the same way adults do.[21] Indeed, the findings of the great Swiss psychologist Jean Piaget that children achieve the adult stages of "autonomous morality" beginning around age 11 and "formal operational thinking" from ages 11 to 15 have generally been upheld by later research. Newer studies indicate younger children are capable of much more complex thought than Piaget's pioneering studies found.[22]

Psychological researchers such as the University of Nebraska's Gary Melton and the University of Virginia's Lois Weithorn[23] argue that adolescents deserve more legal rights because they are fully capable of adult rationality. In a dozen years of working with kids, I got plenty of lessons in the ability of adolescents to think abstractly, design complex plans, and foresee future consequences. Around age 12–14, teenagers become more interested in the outside world, politics, arguing about morality, weighing adults' behaviors and judgments. Mexico's "quinceañera," introducing youth to adulthood at age 15, makes sense in terms of human cognitive and moral development.

So if adolescents think like adults, why not accept Clinton/conservative schemes to try 16- or 14-year-olds, or even younger kids, as adults and subject them to adult penalties for the same criminal acts? The reason for not abolishing juvenile courts and imposing adult (let alone harsher-than-adult) standards on juveniles revolves around the principle of the assignment of responsibility, which in turn demonstrates the hostility embodied in America's "child-when-convenient, adult-when-convenient" policies toward adolescents. If society demands full adult accountability from youths for their acts, then society is obligated to provide youths with the full adult freedom necessary to control their acts. This is not simply a moral obligation, but a practical one. Thirteen-, 14- or 16-year-olds are not allowed the rights under law to decide where they live, who they associate with, who they will be supervised by, what adults they may be coerced or punished by for failure to obey, who they will contract with, what business they conduct, what activities will occupy their day, or even where they legally can be.

The principle of balancing rights and responsibilities means that a society that denies adult rights to youths when they act properly is without moral standing to punish them as adults when they act improperly. The principle is founded in the concept that accountability goes hand in hand with freedom to control one's life.

The U.S. has gone in the opposite direction. As the nation has become more angrily insistent that youths be held absolutely accountable for criminal (and noncriminal) misbehavior, it has systematically stripped away even the minimal rights of young people to control their lives. U.S. Supreme Court decisions upholding these inconsistencies reflect the increasing grownup immaturity of the 1980s and 1990s. The Court stated flatly that American adults bear no obligation to act in a consistent or principled manner toward the young. On nothing more than momentary adult whim, 17-year-olds may be reduced to "children" unable to decide if they may be in public, obtain an abortion, view internet sites without censorship, or drink a lite beer. Adults need not choose between competing principles, responsibly accepting the logical consequences of whichever status adolescents are assigned, the Court states. We can have it both ways. The only right worth respecting is the convenience of grownup society and institutions.

The Breadth of Debate

Paul Campos, University of Colorado law professor and constitutional authority, bizarrely claimed that recent cases in which Colorado schools suspended students for possessing lemon drops or lunchbox apple corers are proof that children have too many rights.[24] The old days, when administrators had arbitrary discretion to punish, even unfairly, were better than today's codified "draconian rules" and "zero tolerance" under which one student's sip of wine at home or on a trip to France is punished as severely as another's drunken rampage at the Christmas formal, Campos wrote. It is curious to argue that school officials who toss kids out of school for possessing lemon drops should be given *more* arbitrary authority. You see, there is a middle ground, the sort which adults expect of our justice systems which somehow, without being arbitrary or draconian, manage to differentiate between an overdue library book and a Uzi massacre. This middle ground is called mature appraisal and judicious response, as distinguished from histrionic zero-tolerance idiocy.

America's viciousness toward children—real, pre-puberty children—is coming to resemble that toward adolescents, as the 1997 Public Agenda poll (in which adults condemned the morals and values of tots as young as five) discussed in the final chapter shows. So it is not surprising that there is growing sentiment for strapping fifth graders in the death chamber. Texas State Representative Jim Pitts introduced legislation to try 10-year-olds as adults and permit executions of 11-year-olds. "As witnessed in Jonesboro," Pitts declared, "...current juvenile laws could not have anticipated violent crimes being committed by children this young."

More lunacy. Table 4 shows the murder arrest rate, murder victimization rate, and felony violent crime rates of children under age 13 for the last three decades, beginning with the first year (1964) for which children's crime statistics became available. Note that compared to their parents' generation, children of the 1960s and '70s, children of the 1990s are less murderous. Other than the elderly, children 12 and younger are the only age group which is less homicidal than they were in the 1960s. Today, fewer than three in 1 million children ages 8–12 are arrested for murder every year, hardly a trigger-tyke wave. So once again, Pitts and every crime expert in the nation has it completely wrong and with no excuse—the facts in *Uniform Crime Reports* can be found in every middling-sized library, including in Texas.

The Beauty of Anecdotes: Statistics Just Get in the Way

In September 1997, the Office of Juvenile Justice and Delinquency Prevention issued a study by data analysts Jeffrey Butts and Howard Snyder entitled, "The Youngest Delinquents." The study found that youths under age 15 accounted for 10 percent of all juvenile homicide arrests in 1996, the same as in 1980. The study concluded that "today's serious and violent juvenile offenders are not significantly

Table 4			
Murder by children is rarer now than 30 years ago...			
but more kids are killed by adults			
Time	Murder arrest rate*	Violent crime rate*	Murder death rate*
1964–69	0.29	29.4	1.1
1970–74	0.40	40.2	1.3
1975–79	0.32	38.7	1.6
1980–84	0.22	38.1	1.9
1985–89	0.22	42.1	2.1
1990–96	0.28	59.2	2.2
Percent change,			
1990s vs. 1970s -35%		+47%	+67%

*Murder and violent crime rate is per 100,000 age 8–12; murder death rate is per 100,000 age 0–12.
Source: FBI, *Uniform Crime Reports*, 1964–96; National Center for Health Statistics, U.S. Mortality Detail File.

younger than those of 10 or 15 years ago. Yet many juvenile justice professionals, as well as the public would assert the opposite." Why?

Butts and Snyder pointed out that current understaffing means that the average judge, prosecutor, or probation officer's caseload has doubled since 1970, so that professionals physically see more delinquents than in the past. Further, "justice professionals tend to accumulate memories of exceptional cases. Every 12-year-old killer is remembered, even though such cases are few in number." Finally, the media headline crime (especially juvenile crime) more than in the past. "The growing publicity about these cases may suggest to the public that they are occurring more frequently, even if juvenile crime trends indicate otherwise."[25] Like other Unwelcome Findings Debunking the Moral Panic, this study was ignored.

Note also that children are much more likely to be murdered today than children of the Sixties. For victims in the 12-and-younger age group, 92 percent of the murderers are adults, nearly all of these parents, the Office of Juvenile Justice and Delinquency Prevention reported in yet another ignored finding.

Note third that children's arrest rates for violent crimes other than murder have risen substantially—up 47 percent since 1970. This increase is only half as large as that displayed by adults old enough to be their parents. So children today are actually *less violent in relation to their parents* than they were 20 and 30 years ago. Children today are much less homicidal, absolutely and especially in relation to their parents, than in the past. So not only do popular crime experts have it completely wrong, they have it perversely backwards—kids aren't murdering more today, but they are getting killed more today, mostly by adults. On the issue of youth crime, getting things backwards seems to be a prerequisite for being popular.

Finally, California provides the fascinatingly exaggerated trend. Since 1980, murder by children has plunged 35 percent and children's other violence has remained stable. *Children are the only age group in the state to show no increase in violent crime.* Not only that, children's violent crime is *less* serious today than two decades ago (in 1980, 47 percent of children arrested for violence were charged with felonies; in 1996, 37 percent). In 1978–82, the first five years the state tabulated complete statistics on child crime, there were 23 children ages 12 and younger arrested for homicide. In the most recent five years, 1992–96, in a child population (ages 8–12) one million larger, there were 22 murder arrests—a per-child decrease of 25 percent.

So in a state in which the child population has risen rapidly, become more nonwhite, become more impoverished, and suffered more violent adults, children are less savage than ever. It took me less than an hour to assemble these figures from easily-found, easily-read state crime reports. Yet after three Richmond, California, boys ages six, eight, and eight almost beat a baby to death in 1995, the media and authorities went berserk, screaming that "kids today are more violent at younger ages." Three years later, the Richmond case is *still* cited, proving how extremely rare such child murderousness is. The media are acting deplorably, as expected. But why isn't it possible to prosecute California's crime experts for malpractice—or at least enforce a reasonable Three Lies and You're Out?

Maybe cigarettes will clarify these bizarre hypocrisies: the first juvenile sternly denied a last cigarette by the warden before being executed because he's too young to smoke; the first adult prosecuted for illegally giving a minor a cigarette after having legal sex with her (see Chapter 6 for the contradictions of the statutory rape debate). Maybe such tragicomedies will make a laughingstock of increasingly strident, muddled assertions from courts and institutions of society's right to demand "super-adult" responsibility from youths at the same time it reduces them to "infantile" status with regard to rights.

Senescent Super Prevaricators

Suddenly, on August 10, 1996, the officials shrieking about "skyrocketing teenage violence" only days earlier reversed field and started grabbing credit for "reducing youth crime." Attorney General Janet Reno emceed the halo-donnings. The nation was being rescued from "demography is destiny," as she termed it, by aggressive anti-crime policies. "I was wrong," James Alan Fox acknowledged sunnily. In fact, he told *USA Today,* "I never meant there would a bloodbath."[26] Of course not. Fox's calm and scientific nomenclature, such as "the young and the ruthless," "coming teenage crime storm," and "temporary sociopath," would never lend such inference. Just "trying to get attention," he grinned.

Having fabricated the superpredator monster in the basement of bad crime science, crime luminaries now congratulated themselves for snatching us from its superpredatory jaws. Nothing had changed about the inner-city conditions feeding high rates of crime; the post-1970 violence cycle was just declining from its latest peak. But officially, the adolescent horror was now in retreat, shackled by a righteous onslaught of curfew, uniform, drug-test, zero tolerance, and adult-tough sen-

Table 5

Murder arrests plummet among L.A. youths of color...why?

	All	Male	Female	White	Latino	Black	Asian
1990	251	241	10	3	100	107	41
1991	220	215	5	1	146	70	3
1992	208	196	12	3	151	47	7
1993	164	162	2	2	91	68	3
1994	114	109	5	4	56	51	3
1995	148	139	9	10	88	42	8
1996	90	85	5	3	53	27	7
1997	75	73	2	4	46	17	8

Source: Criminal Justice Statistics Center, California Department of Justice (1998).

tencing. Killer-kid snarling was replaced by the gentle sounds of self back-patting.

The about-face was particularly amusing in California, where arrests of teenagers for murder and other violent crime had been declining for six years before a single major official so acknowledged. From 1990 to 1996, while politicians and experts howled about exploding teen carnage, the homicide rate among youth plummeted by 53 percent.

In a '96 twinkling, Keystone Kalifornia politicians, officials, and academicians switched to credit their pet solutions for bridling evil youth. The media failed to perceive the drollery. The "miracle" was reported in breathless hero-worship. If the high-level scrambling was funny to witness on a national and state basis, it was downright ludicrous in Los Angeles.

The L.A. Police Department had been in utter disarray, from Rodney King to Mayday 1992 to acrimonious chief changes, internal dissension, quarrels with the City Council, Mark Fuhrman-style racist-cop scandals, and declining patrol and arrest efficiency. Yet homicides among Los Angeles (city) teens dropped dramatically, from 251 in 1990 to 75 in 1997. Adult homicide arrests also fell, from 800 to 368. The murder plummet in America's most gang-involved city is something to see (Table 5). Notice that for whites of both sexes, females of all colors, and Asians after 1990, L.A.'s teen murder scourge barely existed. Just another of those complexities scholars and the media never got around to mentioning.

So what caused the large murder decline among black and Latino youth? Not even the LAPD tried to take credit until very recently, after New York's and Boston's police public relations machines showed how easy credit-grabbing is. Gang researcher and University of Southern California social scientist Malcolm Klein observes:

> During the post-riot period in 1992, Crip and Blood [gang] factions continued a truce process [begun in 1991] that, according to LAPD statistics, seemed to be correlated with a reduction in gang violence (including homicides).[27]

But under no circumstances could any authority give credit to young and minority groups themselves for the crime decline. In fact, Mike Davis points out, the police took a dim view of gangs' successes, facilitated by Jesse Jackson and local church leaders, in reaching the formal truce in April 1992 between formerly warring Crips and Bloods of Southcentral Los Angeles's bloodiest Watts, Compton, Avalon, and Hoover war zones:

> Organizers of Southcentral's year-old gang truce—which even the police con-
> cede has saved hundreds of lives—have faced relentless harassment from the
> LAPD and Sheriff's Department. A cause celebre, which speaks volumes
> about the real logic of the so-called war on gangs, is the case of DeWayne
> Holmes, the truce's key architect, who is now serving seven years in prison on
> a trumped up ten-dollar robbery charge.[28]

Holmes was arrested only days after the truce was signed on a minor, weeks-old warrant in what witnesses called "a straight-up frame" and given a near-maximum sentence. Since L.A. cops couldn't plausibly grab credit for the decline in violence (the only real question was whether law enforcement was fomenting more of it) in the post-riot political climate, the decrease was simply denied.

Soon the press's pressure to bestow glory on the get-tough cops, "community policing," truancy citations, and crime experts became impossible to resist. By 1997, L.A. police were in full auto-congratulation mode, crediting their new truancy enforcement for a burglary decline which had begun years earlier and occurred in nearly every city no matter what police had done.

The youth crime scare was a hoax in the first place. Both felony and misde-meanor arrests among youths had been dropping dramatically for two decades—not just in volume, but in per-capita rate. There were only two exceptions. One was a sharp rise in homicide and robbery arrests among minority teenagers in the late 1980s, a cyclical upswing which quickly reversed in the 1990s. The second was a post-1992 surge in marijuana possession arrests coinciding with President Clinton's re-ignition of the punitive side of the War on Drugs (see Chapter 3).

The two-decade drop in youth crime began long before the get-tough measures of the 1980s took effect. In truth, the curfew sweeps and prison-happy sentencing of the late 1980s coincided with the increases in crime now deplored. That set of facts did not mesh with politicians' needs. So in 1998, California Governor Pete Wilson took the next logical step in the youth crime debate—unabashed fabrication.

After a year or so of self-lauding for "declining youth crime," Governor Wilson and other Republicans decided truth be damned; it was time to get back to the win-ning strategy of fear-mongering, using minority teenagers as a scapegoat. On February 3, 1998, the governor issued a "Fact Sheet" which set a new low in sophis-ticated, systematic falsification of crime statistics:

> Crime in California has declined for four straight years, thanks to tough new
> laws such as "Three Strikes and You're Out" and "10–20-Life"…But one area
> has lagged behind: juvenile and gang-related crime.[29]

The opposite was true. As clearly shown in California crime reports, juvenile violent crime had been declining for six years. Youth violence, led by a huge fall in

Table 6

Youths serve terms just as long as adults for the same crimes

Average months in confinement, California prisoners released in 1996

Offense	Adult	Total	Youth Court	Youth, sentenced by Adult Court
All	22.6 mos	26.4	26.1	30.9
Number	57,520	2,278	2,150	126
Murder	55.0	70.6	72.4	54.9
Number	772	107	96	11
Rape	66.2	55.3	55.5	53.0
Robbery	36.0	29.3	29.6	27.7
Assault	28.1	28.8	28.4	33.5
Burglary	24.1	18.7	18.6	23.5
Theft	15.7	16.5	16.3	20.4
Auto theft	17.0	17.2	17.0	22.1
Sex offenses	42.1	42.0	42.2	34.9
Drugs	19.3	20.4	20.0	26.4

Source: California Department of Corrections and California Youth Authority, 1997.

murder, had declined faster than for any other age since 1990. The only age group to show an increase in violent crime was adults over age 30, a group heavily sentenced under "Three Strikes" and other reforms.

The "Fact Sheet" selectively compared adult and juvenile homicide and robbery trends over the last two decades (which made youths look worse). But it omitted the most common violent crime, aggravated assault, and failed to compare overall violent crime trends (which would make adults look worse). The "Fact Sheet" cited the decline in the California Crime Index (crimes reported to police) from 1996 to 1997 as evidence of a "dramatic" decline in crime. It then scoured the *arrest* statistics (a measure incompatible with Crime Index statistics) to find any year or crime for which juvenile numbers rose, without comparing them to adult arrest statistics.

Wilson also claimed that "juveniles face far lighter penalties from the criminal justice system" than adults. Like most of the privileges politicians complain that youth receive, the claim that juveniles get mere wrist-slappings for major crimes is dubious. Note the 1996 comparison of youth and adult sentences from the California Youth Authority (Table 6). This is not a picture of juvenile courts tapping kids' wrists. On average, youths spend more time imprisoned than adults do for murder, assault, theft, auto theft, drugs, and all offenses together; adults lodge in the iron hotel longer for rape, robbery, burglary, and sex offenses. When only juvenile sentences are examined, youth courts impose longer sentences for violent crime while adult courts hand out longer terms for property and drug offenses.

That youth courts are issuing tougher sentences at all is surprising. Those transferred from juvenile to adult courts typically are those charged with the most brutal crimes. Further, that youths' sentences should be close to—in some cases, exceeding—adults' sentences is also astonishing, given that adults typically have longer criminal records and have committed worse crimes involving more victims. For example, the average adult arrested for murder had 1.1 victims, the average youth murderer 0.6 (concepts that sound absurd when averaged, I realize).[30] An adult robber is about 50 percent more likely to injure his victim than a juvenile robber is, victim surveys report.[31]

It could be argued that youths are less likely to be imprisoned in the first place. Youths comprise 15 percent of felony arrestees and around 10 percent of felony crime, but only 4 percent of prisoners released. However, this argument may be misleading. Youths are less likely to be imprisoned because they are more likely to be first-time offenders, who are seldom imprisoned regardless of age. For homicide, youths constitute around the same share of those imprisoned compared to the share of murders they commit (18 percent of arrestees, 10 percent of murders, 12 percent of prisoners released). Yet juveniles serve considerably longer average sentences for homicide than adults do—especially if sentenced by youth courts.

In sum, Governor Wilson's "Fact Sheet" represented the kind of careful deception that can only be accomplished with knowledgeable intent. Kids of the '90s would have the right to wonder: are adult leaders pathologically unable to tell the truth?

Liberal Drive-Bys and Three-Strikes Gaffes

And why the weak responses from liberals to Wilson's claims? Liberals have been reluctant to point out that crime is skyrocketing among adults over age 30 because this lends support to conservatives' push for "Three Strikes" laws, which mandate imprisonment of 25 years to life for certain career offenders. Liberals claim that money is wasted imprisoning older persons under Three Strikes because older offenders would be unlikely to commit more crimes.[32]

The Washington, DC-based Campaign for an Effective Crime Policy, argues against Three Strikes in a 1995 report using the thoroughly wrong thesis that "demographics show that overall crime rates tend to rise and fall with the number of males in the crime-prone 15–24 year-old age group:"

> Most jurisdictions concentrate on incapacitating [imprisoning] habitual convicted offenders, who are identified only late in their careers when the amount of crime they commit is on the decline. Thus, states imprison many offenders at a time when they would commit relatively few crimes.
>
> For example, arrest rates for robbery show that these offenders are at the peak of their criminal careers at the age of 18–19, and that rates of robbery by the age of 24 are half the peak rate. However, an offender convicted

of robbery is twice as likely to go to prison at the age of 23 than at the age of 19.[33]

The sources for the Center's misstatements, with which the report is replete, are references dated 1986 and 1978. Statistics from this decade, and a broader perspective which includes violent crimes such as aggravated assault and other domestic violence, lends an entirely different picture.

The most idiotic anti-Three Strikes extreme was voiced by critic Harry Shorstein, State Attorney for Florida's Fourth Judicial Circuit:

> 'Three strikes and you're out' is very popular. But most violent crime is committed by people between 14 and 19. If you sentence a 25-year-old to life in prison, it will cost the state between half a million and a million dollars—and he was almost certainly at the end of his criminal career. If you take a 15-year-old off the street for a year, you prevent more crime than you would by sentencing a 25-year-old to life in prison.[34]

Though *Parade Magazine* reported Shorstein's "expert" statement worshipfully, it is absolute trash. Persons under age 20 accounted for about one-fifth of violent crimes; persons over age 25, around 60 percent, FBI and court records show.[35] Some 8.5 million persons ages 25 and older were arrested in 1996, 17 times more than 15-year-olds. Like conservatives, liberal analysis fails to include domestic violence committed by older ages as "crime" and thus inadvertently creates the impression that youths are the entire violent crime problem.

Thus, the liberal argument seems to be: imprison 18-year-olds, not 24-year-olds. Although the demographic theories underlying this thinking were never true, they are especially wrong in the 1990s. Let us review crime statistics for 1997 from California, the leading Three Strikes state:

1997 arrests	Felony	Misdemeanor	Total
Age <20	129,064	228,184	357,248
Age 20–24	92,425	162,337	254,762
Age 25–29	84,546	146,245	230,791
Age 20–29	176,971	308,582	485,553
Age 30–39	153,147	273,005	426,152
Age 40+	88,368	223,425	311,793

Californians over age 25 account for 61 percent of the state's arrests and (given FBI findings that adult arrestees commit about twice as many crimes per offender as juvenile ones) a still larger proportion of its crime volume. Evidently, no one likes these particular facts.

Conservatives don't cite them because they show that four years of "Three Strikes" has not been effective in reducing crime by the older offenders most heavily sentenced under the law. Of the 4,300 Californians sentenced under Three Strikes' 25-years-to-life mandate from its initiation in March 1994 through June 1998, four-fifths were over age 30 (average age 36). For the 35,000 "Second Strike" offenders receiving doubled sentences under the law, two-thirds were over age 30 (average age

33). Given all the geezer-felons being forcibly removed from the population by this new get-tough law, how come the over-30 set remains California's fastest-growing criminal population—and why are the lightly-sentenced under-25 criminals becoming scarcer? Tough questions, and so conservatives ignore them.

Conversely, a lot of crime is committed by older offenders, a point liberal critics of Three Strikes would prefer to avoid. These over-30 convicts can't simply be presumed safe because of their age and released, as the Three Strikes critics quoted above imply. Their long-term drug addictions guarantee more serious crimes, including violence against children and families. So critics of Three Strikes have had no incentive to talk about the aging crime problem, either.

The conservative attack on youths is bad enough. But the liberals and leftists, who embrace conservative assumptions and sloppy statistics regarding juvenile crime even as they attempt to dispute conservative policies, are doing serious damage as well.

Los Angeles author Ed Humes passionately pleads for preserving the juvenile courts in the face of the conservative/Clinton blitzkrieg to force kids into the adult system. Yet, while Humes likes certain teenagers, he betrays an unrelenting animosity toward adolescents as a group. "Fear of our own children," he writes in his 1996 study of the L.A. juvenile justice system, *No Matter How Loud I Shout*,[36] "is a fear well grounded in fact,"

> as juvenile crime, particularly violent crime, has ripped through the cities and suburbs of America like a new and deadly virus. The figures are staggering: a 175 percent increase in juvenile murder rates since the 1970s, with similar boosts in juvenile crime of all kinds. Just in the last five years, violent offenses by children—murder, rape, assault, robbery—have risen 68 percent.
>
> The growth of juvenile violent crime rates in recent years (up 68 percent between 1988 and 1992, and 165 percent since 1985) far (exceeds) violent crime increases by adults.

Humes' statistics are patently false, as will be shown. In Los Angeles County, he writes:

> ...children are killing children, violently, inhumanly, forcing one another to duck bullets, spraying whole crowds in order to take out a single intended victim, transforming urban American teenagers into the psychological equivalent of war orphans.

He reports two cases of "children killing children." One involved adults shooting a youth, the other a teenage murder suspect found to have been wrongly accused.

After reducing issues of race and poverty (in Los Angeles!) to a couple of footnotes, Humes invokes the popular legend of the Killer White Girl epidemic:

> Carla James...is the leading edge of two new and disturbing trends...a still-small but rapidly growing group of girls who commit violent crimes, once the exclusive domain of boys. And she is part of a growing legion of kids whose criminal roots cannot be traced to any sort of abuse or deprivation, children who have potential, privilege, and solid families, yet take a turn toward darkness simply out of personal choice, who have the insight and

ability to reflect about the immorality of what they are doing, then do it anyway.

Fewer than 2 percent of L.A.'s violence arrests today are juvenile girls, making trend analysis meaningless—and in any case, increases among girls are less than among adult women (see Chapter 8). Crime and vital statistics records clearly show there was no violence or homicide increase among white youth in L.A. in recent decades. Of 125,000 white teenage girls in L.A. County, fewer than 100 are arrested in a year for violent crimes, including one or two for murder. The supposed youth sympathizer Humes picked the one girl in 50,000 as illustrating some kind of trend!

And..."a growing legion" whose violence "cannot be traced to any sort of abuse"? "Aggression and violent behavior are experienced and learned *primarily* in the home," concluded the California Task Force on juvenile crime that Humes (except for this quote) quotes extensively (emphasis mine). Cases of family violence in California have been growing rapidly, another point he fails to make.[37]

The point is: Humes claims he is defending the juvenile justice system. Yet what would an intelligent reader conclude after absorbing Humes' two most gripping points: (a) juvenile crime is handled by the juvenile justice system, and (b) juvenile savagery has exploded, while adult crime has stayed low? That conservatives are right: Abolish juvenile courts and slam the evil kids into the adult system. After all, by Humes' own evidence, the adult court works, the juvenile court fails.

My criticism and Humes' reply led to a recent L.A. *Times Magazine* exchange:

> "Ed Humes' moving piece on juvenile justice ('Rage Against the Machine,' Nov. 23) fails to perceive that his own rhetoric has contributed to the anti-youth punitiveness he deplores. Examples: Humes' acclaimed 1996 book, *No Matter How Loud I Shout*, declared that 'juvenile crime, particularly violent crime, has ripped through the cities and suburbs of America like a new and deadly virus.' False: state crime figures show L.A. juvenile violent crime rates are no higher, and overall youth crime rates are much LOWER, today than 20 years ago. Contrary to Humes' portrayal, it is ADULTS' violent, property, and drug crime rates that have risen rapidly. Had Humes debunked rather than perpetuated today's wildly hyped 'teen crime' scare, his commendable plea for compassion would be strengthened."
>
> —Mike Males, Irvine

> Humes responds: "Males quotes a line from my book about juvenile crime in America, then attempts to rebut it with L.A. statistics alone, an invalid comparison. As of 1995, when I completed my research, juvenile crime in Los Angeles and the nation was on the rise. (Since I wrote my book, juvenile crime has indeed declined somewhat). A May 1995 Justice Department report states: 'The proportion of violent crimes committed by juveniles is disproportionately high compared with their share of the U.S. population, and the number of these crimes is growing.'
>
> "I agree with Males' central point: that juveniles have too often been unfairly demonized and punished far too harshly in our war on crime—a main theme of my book."[38]

Amazing.

Humes wrote a massively acclaimed, award-winning, influential book from inside the Los Angeles juvenile justice system. He portrayed youth crime as exploding, confronting authorities with massively increasing, unheard-of challenges. His own florid prose demonizes kids as an *entire generation* of urban slaughterers, "a virus," violent, inhumane, many of whom willfully choose evil. He applies no like descriptions to adults, even when the most violent of child abuses are evident. His claims are based not on his review of easily-available, original statistics, but on quoted secondary sources—a fatal mistake when teenagers are the topic—and then only selectively.

That is why Humes has no clue that "as of 1995," Los Angeles juvenile crime was not "on the rise," but had already *declined* rapidly for five years. I'm not talking ripples. From 1990 to 1994, the last year of statistics available when Humes finished his research, L.A. County's juvenile (10–17) population rose by 25,000. Yet:

- L.A. juvenile violent crimes were DOWN 2,500.
- Juvenile murders were DOWN 175.
- Juvenile property crime was DOWN 4,500.
- Juvenile felonies were DOWN 7,700.
- Juvenile misdemeanors were DOWN 5,000.
- All juvenile crime was DOWN 12,500.

At the highest level of statistical certitude, that is known as DECREASING JUVENILE CRIME.

Moreover, L.A.'s 1990s teenage crime plummet was part of a larger 20-YEAR DECLINE in youth crime. Here are Los Angeles's actual 20-year trends in youth crime rates, comparing the most stable measure available: five-year arrest averages divided by corresponding youth populations for the mid-1990s (1993 through 1997, the latest five years available) versus the mid-1970s (1973–77, the earliest):

- All crime (equals felony+misdemeanor+status), down 43 percent
- Felony crime, down 44 percent
- Misdemeanor crime, down 37 percent
- Violent crime, down 8 percent
- Homicide, up 13 percent
- Property crime, down 50 percent
- Drug/alcohol offenses, down 62 percent
- Status crime, down 53 percent.

Only homicide, the most serious but also the rarest offense, is up, and not nearly as terrifyingly as Humes and other commentators would have us believe. All other crime among L.A. youth has fallen steadily and dramatically over the past two decades.

The youth crime decline kissed not just Los Angeles, not just California, but the nation as a whole. Kids as a whole are less criminally-inclined today than their parents' generation. Such was not supposed to occur in a youth population becoming darker in shade and poorer, nor the reverse in an elder generation becoming richer and smugger.

Now, what does this pattern suggest? Two guesses. First, a tiny fraction of L.A. kids is more dangerous than ever, reflected in the small homicide rise. But the large majority of youth is *less* criminally inclined than in the past. We don't have a "youth crime problem." We have a highly-concentrated problem among a small sliver of youths—the ones Humes acknowledges are "neglected, abused, discarded children." Thus, "fear of our children" is *not* justified—children's fear of adults is, however, more than ever.

Now, it seems logical that Humes, a staunch defender of the juvenile justice system, would be eager to cite statistics such as the above to debunk the official scare campaign. Rapidly-declining youth crime in the face of rising youth poverty and adult criminality surely adds up to a powerful testament to the success of both young people and the juvenile justice system he champions.

Given his access to the system's innards, Humes could have written a revolutionary book. He blew it. His anti-youth emotionalities were so strong that they sabotaged what could have been his most effective argument and led him to ape official fictions that juvenile crime is skyrocketing. What reaction did liberal juvenile-justice defender Humes expect, then, to his fearsome imagery of kids everywhere going berserk for no reason? Other than a more terrified public and politicians ready to fry seventh graders?

Ironically, the rise in adult drug and alcohol abuse, strongly connected to crime, suggests that adult courts should be made more like juvenile ones are supposed to be—not the other way around. Courts set up to assess individual problems, family situations, and service/punishment tailorings seem more appropriate to the addiction problems plaguing aging Californians than more imprisonment.

More Gunnings

Pop cliché holds that guns are the teenage fight-finishers of the '90s. President Clinton and liberal lobbies sell us the hooey that while a teenage fistfight of past decades was just that, today someone routinely gets a gun and slaughters. Casting any semblance of truth aside, the Education Fund to End Handgun Violence blames "the rashness of youth" for the "fact" (actually, the lie) that "there is nothing unusual about a child being shot in school."[39] It is extremely unusual. The Department of Education survey estimated 201,000 fights at school annually, 11,000 involving weapons. There were 19 murders. So around 1 in 200 youths gets into a fight at school annually, and roughly 1 in 10,000 of these fights ends with a gun killing. I would call an event that happens to 1 in two million people in a year's time unusual, but I was raised on the New Math.

The most complete, recent tabulation by the National Center for Health Statistics provides ages of deceased for 5,200 handgun deaths in 1995. It shows that a youth age 13–17 has *lower* odds of dying by a handgun (312 deaths) than an adult ages 43–47 (379). As for whether murder now ends more teenage fights than in the past, the answer—no, although there was a temporary, 1980s surge among poorer youth that has now abated—is one to give more pause. Table 7 shows California statistics, using the first year the state tabulated crimes by race (1975) to the peak homicide year (1991).

Table 7

Are guns the teenage "fight-finishers" today?
Less so for whites, no more so for nonwhites

California teenage murders, murder rates, and murders as proportion of all assaults, 1975 (first year reported), 1991 (peak year), and 1997 (most recent year)

	Assaults	Murders	Murders as pct of assaults	Murder rate
White non-Latino				
1975	10,613	101	0.94%	4.9%
1991	10,195	63	0.61	3.8
1997	11,842	27	0.23	1.6
Change, 1975–91			-34%	-22%
Change, 1975–97			-75%	-67%
Latino, Black, Asian				
1975	11,235	247	2.15%	21.5%
1991	11,916	633	5.04	34.3
1997	14,011	308	2.20	14.4
Change, 1975–91			+134%	+59%
Change, 1975–97			+2%	-33%

Source: California Department of Justice, *Crime & Delinquency in California*, 1991, 1975 (1975 figures adjusted to reflect complete statewide reports).

Table 7 shows that both the murder rate and the likelihood that an assault (misdemeanor plus felony) will end in murder declined substantially for white, non-Latino youth at the same time both rose sharply for nonwhite youths to a peak in 1991. In 1991, the murder arrest rate for nonwhite youths was nine times higher than for whites. Where the ratio of murders to assaults was 1 in 20 for nonwhites, it was 1 in 164 for Euro-whites. From 1991 to 1997, the murder-versus-assault ratio declined sharply, to 1 in 45 for nonwhites and 1 in 440 for whites—at, and well below, respectively, 1975 levels.

What the anti-handgun groups are saying, in reality, is that minorities, not youths, are guilty of "rashness." Liberals have chosen a disastrously wrong forum to confront juvenile homicide. The issue is not whether guns kill people (the liberal position) or people kill people (gun lobby homily). It is whether the conditions of nonwhite youth in this country create circumstances and enterprises in which gun violence is heightened.

Actually, there is no argument between liberals and conservatives on juvenile gun control. Even the National Rifle Association, no doubt in recognition of its great diversionary value, endorses it. The rule seems to be that whenever liberals

Table 8

**Youths have higher homicide, lower suicide, and
lower overall gun death rates than grownups**

U.S. gun deaths, 1995

	Suicide/accident		Homicide		Total	
	Number	Rate*	Number	Rate*	Number	Rate*
Age 0–12	141	0.3	221	0.4	362	0.7
Age 13–17	1,100	5.9	1,562	8.4	2,662	14.3
Age 18+	18,888	9.7	13,799	7.1	32,687	16.8

*Rate is per 100,000 by age. "Suicide/accident" includes deaths undetermined as to intent.
Source: National Center for Health Statistics. Mortality Detail File (1995).

and conservatives agree on a youth policy, it is the most misguided course of action possible, guaranteed to hassle a lot of innocent young people while doing nothing to corral the few dangerous ones.

The liberal Justice Policy Institute (JPI) lent a calming perspective to the hysteria following highly publicized juvenile murders by pointing out the youth homicide is not sweeping the nation, but is highly concentrated in a few urban centers. After the Jonesboro massacre, the JPI released findings that 93.4 percent of the nation's counties experienced one or no youth murders in 1995, up from 92 percent in 1994. That is, just 200 of America's 3,000 counties account for nearly all youth homicide. The spectacular school murders headlined in the press are "idiosyncratic events rather than evidence of a trend," JPI declared.[40] Too bad we don't have crime experts or a president who can bring themselves to put it that way.

The JPI argued that "stronger gun control" should be passed so that "kids like the ones in Jonesboro, Arkansas; West Paducah, Kentucky; and Pearl, Mississippi, no longer had access to guns." If this means controls on adult access to guns as well, this is a good suggestion; if it means only more restrictions on kids, it is pointless. Kid gun control we already have—remember all the platitudes about protecting kids that accompanied the 1994 federal ban on gun possession by youths? Imagine what the rhetoric would be if the feds had *permitted* youths to acquire guns and a Jonesboro occurred.

That the U.S. is "the Western world's capital for child gun deaths" is common knowledge; why the reluctance to admit it is also the capital for adult gun deaths? In 1996, the most recent year statistics are available by age, there were 38,000 deaths from guns in the United States (1995's figures by age are shown in Table 8). Of these, 3,000, or 8 percent were youths under age 18. Five out of six gun deaths involve persons over 21. Juveniles are a very small part of America's very large gun problem. Let us pause for the breathtaking lifetaking statistics on gun slaughter Americana:

Firearms murders by adults per year, mid-1990s:

	Raw totals by country	Ratio, per-capita rate of U.S. adults' gun murder rate to other nations'
Japan	60	130 to 1
United Kingdom	50	65 to 1
Australia	70	15 to 1
Canada	200	8 to 1
United States	15,000	—

American grownups are eight to 100 times more likely to murder with guns than grownups in other Western nations, including our closest Anglo peers. If only U.S. Euro-white murder rates are compared, America's murder surplus still is five times higher than that of other Western nations' residents.

Further, of America's young people who die from gunshots, more than *half are killed by adults* in murders and accidental or undetermined shootings. FBI figures show that while "kids killing kids" (under age 18) account for 3 percent of U.S. murders, adults killing kids account for 9 percent. These points need to be made every time the statement about the U.S.'s child gun murder rate is made. They never are. Neither liberal nor conservative agendas would profit by doing so.

As to whether gun laws prevent youths from getting guns, death statistics suggest otherwise (Table 9). In 1994, the last year before the federal juvenile gun ban took effect, 29 states had laws banning gun possession by juveniles (under 18 or 21), while 21 states permitted youths to have guns.

Table 9

States which outlaw juvenile gun possession do not have fewer gun deaths

Gunshot death rates

	Suicide/accident		Homicide		Total	
	12–17	Adult	12 17	Adult	12–17	Adult
States which ban youths youths from having guns						
Rate/100,000 pop	6.4	10.2	6.3	6.7	12.7	16.9
Ratio, youth/adult		0.625		0.949		0.754
States which allow youths to own/possess guns						
Rate/100,000 pop	8.8	13.6	4.9	5.9	13.7	19.5
Ratio, youth/adult		0.651		0.821		0.703

Source: National Center for Health Statistics. Mortality Detail File (1994); Office of Juvenile Justice and Delinquency Prevention (1996). *Juvenile Victims and Offenders.*

States have varying gun death rates for varying reasons—bigger cities, more hunting, etc. These factors should be reflected in the adult firearms death rate. Thus, we would expect laws which ban juvenile gun possession to reduce the rates of youthful gunshot death relative to adults'. This is not the case. States which ban "kids and guns" have slightly lower youth firearms suicide/accident rates, considerably higher youth gun murder rates, and higher total youth gun-death rates relative to adult rates.

Thus, laws singling out youths for gun prohibition do not appear to work. The reasons are immediately clear. First, there are 220 million guns loose in America. The notion that adults can freely own firearms but youths can somehow be "denied access to guns" is ludicrous.

Second, how youths use guns is directly related to adult practices. How many teenagers die from guns has little to do with laws but everything to do with how many adults so die. I lived in Montana for 14 years. Hunting is popular and guns proliferate. The state of 800,000 people allowed youths to own and possess firearms, and many youths I knew stored guns and ammunition in their rooms or closets. Montana has perhaps one or two youth and 15 to 20 adult gun homicides every year. In contrast, Washington, DC, has 550,000 people and prohibits all gun ownership or possession by persons under age 21. The city, with half as many teenagers as Montana, typically has *two to three dozen* youth and 300 adult firearms murders per year.

An April 1998 *New York Times*/*CBS News* poll of 1,048 teens ages 13–17 found nearly 40 percent (a projected 7.5 million) live in homes where guns are present. Fifteen percent (3 million) personally own guns. In regions, such as the South, where more adults own guns, more teens own guns, the poll found.[41] It is not the fact of youth "access" to firearms or the laws governing such access that is the issue, but how American culture (that is, adults) regards and uses firearms. This can be shown not just anecdotally, but mathematically. For the 50 states, the correlation between the teenage gun death rate and the adult gun death rate is extremely precise (0.81 for suicides/accidents, 0.82 for homicides, 0.83 for all gun deaths). The maximum correlation possible is 1.00; correlations of more than 0.60 generally are considered powerful. Ones as high as 0.80 are rare in most social science research, indicating in this case probabilities of less than one in a million of occurrence by mere chance.

Third, let us look at California's socioeconomic patterns in youthful firearms death, as measured by race. The state's first figures on gun mortality by race became available in 1985 and span the decade of major increase (Table 10). If media and gun availability were to blame for adolescent firearms deaths, as liberal and public health lobbies insist, how did the media-fed and guns-awash white kids escape the carnage? Not just that, but how did they experience a *lower* gun fatality rate today than back in the peaceable mid-'80s? Once again, today's guns-and-kids discourse as framed by progressives depends on suppressing the salient issues of racism and poverty.

In 1996, the California Department of Health Services released a study of juvenile homicide. It found that in the peak years of 1991–92, there were 1,335 gunshot deaths and 2,321 non-fatal gunshot wounds among Californians ages

Table 10

California gun deaths, all causes, age 10–17

	White (non-Latino)	Non-white/Latino
1985–86	182	230
1993–94 (peak)	169	764
1995–96	156	651
Rate change*	-21%	+122%

Sources: California Center for Health Statistics (gun deaths by accident, suicide, homicide, and undetermined), and California Department of Finance (population). Based on annual populations age 10–17 of whites, 1.50 million in 1985–86, 1.62 million in 1995–96; non-white/Latino, 1.61 million in 1985–86, 2.05 million in 1995–96.

16–20. (Note that this includes 19 and 20 year-olds and a different year, which is why the figures are different from those above). Of these, whites comprised 131 dead and 151 wounded—less than 8 percent. The firearms casualty toll was *25 times higher* among black than among white teens.

While white kids were more in danger of being murdered by mom or dad than other races, only one white youth homicide was attributed to "gang members," compared to 129 among Latino, black, and Asian youths.[42] The latter may involve greater eagerness on the part of law enforcement to attribute nonwhite violence to gang members. Still, the vastly different bullet tolls and murderer characteristics suggest that white and nonwhite youths experience such divergent risks that the terms "kids and guns" and "youth violence" are completely meaningless. If curfews to "protect youths" were based on the real dangers to them, nonwhite kids would be forbidden to go outdoors and white kids forbidden to go home.

Finally, America's high adult firearms death rates, especially for murder (and doubly especially for murder of kids by adults), suggest there is no greater reason to ban teenagers from having guns than to ban adults from having guns. The above complications are crucial points that gun-control and "smart gun" lobbies are going to have to analyze and incorporate if they are ever to advance public safety rather than just emotional exhortation. Liberal campaigns singling out juveniles for gun control are misdirected, ineffective, exacerbate fear and negativism toward youths, and get in the way of the larger, more difficult necessity to address America's death-affair with firearms as a society-wide problem whose main perpetrators are grownups.

The last was the point made by Children's Defense Fund director Marion Wright Edelman at the 1998 conference in Los Angeles.[43] At first I thought Edelman was going to confine her speech to indulging the innocuous-and-futile liberal call for "getting guns away from children." But Edelman's larger denunciation was of America's entire "culture of guns, culture of violence" that begins with children subjected to brutality in their own homes: "spouses violent against spouses, parents violent against children." Thirty-five thousand American adults shoot each other, themselves, and kids to death every year. Selective shock and outrage that 3,000 kids do likewise is industrial-strength phony.

Uncontrolled Uncontrols

In a 1992 order against the Blythe Street Gang, the Los Angeles City Attorney's office proposed "gang-free zones" in which friends, even brothers, would be forbidden from associating with one another; certain clothes and jewelry would be banned; 500 yet-to-be-named individuals would be prohibited from referring to gangs in any way or discussing anything whatsoever while riding in cars; all such individuals would be forbidden to wait for a bus, stay in any public place for more than five minutes, or engage in a wide variety of lawful activities on their own property and in their own homes; children would not be allowed to climb trees or fences; razors, baseball bats, flashlights, even screwdrivers would be contraband; and 500 unnamed individuals would be required to carry special papers to prove their everyday activities are lawful.[44] Conviction of an offense would not be necessary to invoke these controls; mere police designation of gang affiliation would suffice.

"Suppression programs have shown no evidence of success," Malcolm Klein concludes from 35 years of research. "Uncontrolled forces will determine gang growth and decline:"

> Failure to share both social power and social responsibility yields a surfeit of social ills. Street gangs are one of these...an amalgam of racism, of urban underclass poverty, of minority and youth cultures, of fatalism in the face of rampant deprivation, of political insensitivity, and the gross ignorance of inner-city (and inner-town) America on the part of most of us who don't have to survive there.[45]

Inner-city "minority and youth cultures" have grown up in response to, are shaped by, and are bent on surviving the larger factors Klein cites. They are reasonable responses by urban youth to their environments and brutal policings, however irrational they may appear to the privileged who critique from afar. Until racism, poverty, and gross ignorance by those in power are changed, America's urban young for their own survival will remain beyond larger society's control.

3 Myth: Teens Are Druggie Wastoids

Local school and law enforcement officials suspected a major drug network operating out of fashionable Union High School in Redondo Beach, California. Two sheriff's deputies chosen because they looked young began posing as students in September 1995. The undercover agents waved $20 bills in front of youths suspected of dealing. Some they approached five or more times. After three months of daily solicitings, the two deputies made 17 arrests. Their culprits included 14-year-olds, a special education student, and one youth new to the school who said he was having trouble making friends. Few actually provided dope to the deputies. Most were busted simply for taking the money in an "implied agreement" to provide drugs. When the handcuffed suspects were led out of the school, reporters alerted by authorities were waiting, cameras and recorders whirring. The students were expelled in quick hearings in which the school district's attorney also represented the undercover deputies.

The big drug problem in the 1,700-student school turned out to be "relatively light," the sheriff's department later admitted. Loquacious before the cameras at the bust, deputies didn't want to talk later about how many students actually wound up being charged. This was not a new tactic. Since the 1980s, Los Angeles-area police have a history of boosting arrest statistics by deploying youthful-looking undercover cops to infiltrate high schools, especially targeting special education students for entrapment in drug-selling, American Civil Liberties attorneys reported.[1] Upscale Redondo Beach may have been targeted to get more white-kid arrests to offset recent public charges that drug enforcement targeted nonwhites.

After Faye Docuyanan, a University of California, Irvine, social ecologist, and I wrote on the Redondo bust for *The Progressive* (May 1996), I got letters from around the country where schools had conducted similar drug raids. A reader provided reports of an "ongoing effort" by Springfield, Ohio, deputies "to do random, unannounced searches at as many high schools as possible:"

> Drug sniffing dogs made a surprise visit to Tecumseh and Northwestern high schools Wednesday, but their noses failed to find drugs.
> ...The Greene County Sheriff's K-9 unit assisted in the search at (Greenon High) school, which did not yield any drugs. Clark County Sheriff Gene Kelly said deputies also searched Shawnee High School on Monday but found no drugs.[2]

In Newport-Costa Mesa, California, police and school district chiefs declared they had a major "drug problem." They brought in marijuana-trained sheriff's dogs for a series of unannounced sniff-searches in 1994. No drugs. In a system with 8,000 junior and senior high students, only 10 lockers were nosed as ones where dope might ever have been stored.[3]

Vernonia, Oregon, officials declared a major drug crisis, with "startling and progressive" drug abuse fomenting "students in a state of rebellion." They randomly tested 500 athletes in four years at a cost of $30,000. Three tested positive. The Supreme Court was so impressed with such evidence of what Justice Anthony Kennedy called "a nationwide drug problem in the schools" that it ruled in favor of schools' rights to mandate tests for student athletes.[4]

Using drugs as the pretext, "schoolchildren everywhere were written out of the Fourth Amendment" by the Supreme Court in 1985, drug-war chronicler Dan Baum wrote. "School officials could now frisk students, turn out their pockets, cut locks off their lockers, invade their privacy at will without obtaining a search warrant, and call the police with their findings."[5] In 1997, the Court ruled that school officials' invasive "strip searches" of youths on the merest (or no) suspicion do not violate students' "clearly established" right to freedom from "unreasonable searches."[6] The Court rulings showed readiness to hold that simply being a young person constitutes probable cause to suspect wrongdoing.

Drastic times demand tough responses. Everyone "knows" the public schools and their students are "full of drugs."

So where are all the little stoners and their stashes?

Where are the vomit-crusted teenage bodies? Newly released Drug Abuse Warning Network figures showed that in Los Angeles County, 1,100 people died from any kind of drug-related cause (overdose, suicide, car wreck, anything) in 1995. Seven were teenagers.

Where are the shaking needle-pocked teen o.d.'s? California's Public Statistics Institute released two exhaustive analyses of hospital emergency data in 1996 and 1997. They showed that youths ages 17 and younger comprised just over 1 percent of the state's 35,000 heroin and cocaine admissions in 1995, a proportion that was low and declining over the previous decade.

Where is the "exploding" teenage drug crisis and heroin "epidemic" drug czar Barry McCaffrey and every drug-war authority claims? The federal Drug Abuse Warning Network released its 1995 survey of 141 coroners in major metropolises, reporting a record 9,000 deaths from drug-related causes. Of these, 96 were under age 18, and 143 ages 18–19.[7]

Across the nation, figures on drug overdoses, hospitalizations, and addiction treatment agree on two stark developments. America's drug problem has indeed grown to crisis proportions. But teenagers have not made up any significant part of it in two decades.

No side in the drug war debate wants to grapple with those facts. It's lying time again.

In Denial

Said President Clinton: "Drug use is down all across America, but unfortunately it is still rising among young people."[8]

Said White House Drug Policy chief Barry McCaffrey: "Overall drug use in America has fallen by half in 15 years. However, drugs are a sustained threat to our young people."[9]

Said Chuck Thomas of the Marijuana Policy Project, a group which argues that it would be good policy to legalize marijuana for adults but enforce stronger prohibitions on teenagers: "Kids should not use marijuana at all, period."[10]

Said top drug policy surveyor Lloyd Johnston of the University of Michigan: "This generation doesn't know about the dangers of drugs the way the last one did."[11]

Said Joseph Califano Jr., chairman of the National Center on Addiction and Substance Abuse: "The high school years are likely to be the toughest for American teens in avoiding drug, alcohol and cigarette abuse and addiction."[12]

Said George Foster, the Drug Enforcement Administration's New England chief of the reason for the resurgence in heroin: "A lack of memory on the part of youth."[13]

Bald-faced prevarications by leading experts, from hardest-line drug warriors to the most liberal of pot-legalizers. All know well that this generation of American teenagers is extraordinarily unlikely to abuse drugs. All further know that drug abuse has exploded among American adults, posing dangers to young people far in excess of the moderate use of milder drugs that typifies modern adolescents. All know that today's kids, far from being ignorant, have seen more heroin abuse among their parents than any previous generation.

And all tacitly seem to agree that their political agendas, no matter how divergent, require suppression of these facts and vilification of American youth.

Stoked

In January 1988, California Lieutenant Governor Gray Davis proposed random drug testing of all students. In one sentence he stuffed three '90s platitudes: "zero tolerance no nonsense tough love."[14] Of course, a student could refuse to surrender the required bodily sample for testing. In that case, the parent would be told of the student's refusal. But this raises a question: would the parent be sober enough to notice? A November 1997 Los Angeles Times series, "Orphans of Addiction," reported that one in five parents are alcoholics or drug addicts.[15]

Evidence of a large and growing adult drug abuse crisis was abundant:

- Since 1980, the number of adults in their 30s and 40s hauled in to hospital emergency rooms for overdoing cocaine or heroin rose 2,500 percent, reaching 100,000 in 1996.[16] In contrast, only 1,000 teenagers nationwide suffered heroin or cocaine emergencies in 1996—up from 500 in 1980.[17]

- The 1995 Drug Abuse Warning Network survey of urban coroners (the one that reported 240 drug-related deaths among teens) also reported the toll among their 30- and 40-age parents: 6,000.

- In 1970, teenagers and young adults under age 25 comprised 44 percent of California's heroin deaths. In 1996, 3 percent.[18]

- From 1980 to the 1990s, the proportion of teenagers in drug abuse treatment nationwide declined by 70 percent. Every age group under 25 declined sharply. Every age group over 25 rose rapidly.[19]

- The federal Drug Abuse Warning Network's most recent surveys of hospital emergency rooms and coroners found that teenagers comprise a small fraction of America's drug problem (Table 1).

The teenage drug crisis is a myth. It was concocted and maintained for political convenience. This does not mean no teenagers abuse drugs. It means that as a social or health issue, teenage drug abuse of the '90s is infinitesimal, on the scale of Orthodox Jewish alcoholism.

The straight-faced McCaffrey fib that Baby Boomers' drug days are over and done with, that adults today are fine except for nagging guilt by parents "who may be ambivalent about their own past drug use and inadvertently send mixed messages to kids,"[20] actually endangers kids in profound ways.

Buried in the August 1996 National Household Survey on Drug Abuse was the following truth well known to those of any expertise in the drug abuse field:

> Cocaine-related emergency room visits have increased from 5,000 in 1981 to 29,000 in 1985 (the peak year for past month cocaine prevalence in the NHSDA) to 142,000 in 1995. Heroin-related emergency room visits have increased from 12,000 in 1979 to 76,000 in 1995.
>
> ...The NHSDA (National Household Survey on Drug Abuse) continues to show the aging of the drug using population...The proportion of drug users that are age 35 and older continues to increase (from 10 percent in 1979 to 35 percent in 1995). Data from the Drug Abuse Warning Network (DAWN) on drug-related hospital emergency department episodes also show the impact of the aging cohort of drug users. In 1979, 12 percent of the patients with cocaine episodes were age 35 and older. By 1985 the proportion was 19, and by 1995 it was 43.[21]

Devastating commentary on the failure of the War on Drugs' decade-long, $100-plus billion,[22] 12-million-arrest crusade: a 500 percent increase in serious abuse of the most dangerous illegal drugs—among adults.

Hospital emergencies, the above report found, involve the "aging cohort, composed primarily of those in the baby boom" who are "heavy users"—not "occasional users or those who use only marijuana."[23] In contrast, teenage drug abuse rates were too low to even show up on federal charts of trends by age.[24]

Federal hospital emergency room surveys show that adults' three worst drugs of abuse are alcohol in combination with drugs, cocaine, and heroin. In contrast, the Big Three showing up most often in teenagers' relatively small number of drug emergency mishaps are not recreational drugs but: acetaminophen (Tylenol), aspirin, and ibuprofen (Advil). These three common pain remedies accounted for twice as many teenage hospital emergency cases as marijuana, LSD, cocaine (including crack), heroin, methamphetamine, alcohol mixed with drugs, and PCP ("angel dust") *put together*.[25]

Table 1

Baby Boomers, not teens, are America's drug crisis

Illicit drugs causing injury and death, 1995–96

Age	Drug emergency cases*		Drug deaths**	
12–17	4,609	3.7%	96	1.0%
18–25	20,846	16.9%	823	9.0
26–34	43,908	35.5%	2,190	23.9
35–44	na	na	3,701	40.4
45–54	na	na	1,653	18.0
55+	na	na	707	7.7
35–older	54,312	43.9%	6,061	66.1
Total	124,023		9,216	

*Marijuana, heroin, cocaine, and speed/methamphetamine-related (national), January–June 1996.
**All drug-related deaths, 41 major metropolitan areas, 1995.
Sources: Substance Abuse and Mental Health Administration (1997). *Drug Abuse Warning Network Annual Medical Examiner Data* and *Mid-year Preliminary Estimates from the 1996 Drug Abuse Warning Network*. Rockville, MD: Department of Health and Human Services.

Prescription drugs also show up as six of the top 15 drugs found in teenage hospital ER visits. And no wonder. The American Psychiatric Association found that prescription of psychotropic drugs such as Ritalin to children and adolescents rose from 1.1 million prescriptions in 1985 to 3.7 million in 1994. Increased diagnoses for Attention Deficit Hyperactivity Disorder (ADHD) were the reason. "Much more information is needed," the study authors laconically concluded.[26]

Peter Breggin, MD, and Ginger Breggin, veterans in the war against psychiatric drugging of children, bring the astonishing truth about childhood and adolescent drug abuse a full circle in *The War against Children of Color*:

> As a result of the efforts of the psycho-pharmaceutical complex, including the drug companies and the federal mental health establishment, many millions of children will be psychiatrically diagnosed and medicated in the future. Prozac, with its stimulant qualities, will probably prove itself able to space out and suppress children in much the same fashion as Ritalin. We fear it will soon rival Ritalin as a widely-used agent for the biomedical suppression of children, especially older ones.
>
> …Most children labeled DBD [diagnosed with Disruptive Behavior Disorder], including ADHD, are in fact suffering from…conflict and stress due largely to the adult world around them.[27]

Drug Abuse Warning Network surveys show that fluoxetine (Prozac) already is found in more than 1,000 hospital emergency room treatments of persons under 18 for drug overdose every year, more than heroin and crystal methamphetamine put together.[28] The Breggins' work points to another, more sinister motive for the rampant official lying about "teens and pot" or "teens and heroin" than simply crass politicking: diversion of attention from the more destructive pharmaceutical drugging of "difficult" kids, including federal initiatives to promote biomedication as the solution to social problems such as inner-city violence.

Brainstopping

The rampant disavowal of America's serious drug malaise among grownups and hyperventilating over a much smaller teenage problem goes beyond simple psychology; that is, that Baby Boomers sublimating their own behavior defects onto their kids. There is that, but America's hate-affair with its adolescents surrounding drugs and alcohol has an additional bizarre twist: it is precisely because teenagers in fairly large numbers use drugs *without suffering harm* that they are condemned so angrily.

Teens age 12–17 comprise 11 percent of the total teen-adult population and 16 percent of the illicit drug users. But teens comprise less than 4 percent of the drug emergency cases (the best immediate measure of drug abuse) and 1 percent of the drug-related deaths—including not just overdoses, but other drug-caused casualties such as car wrecks, drownings, suicides, etc.

How can three to four million 1990s teenagers use drugs but, unlike their elders, avoid winding up in hospital emergency or the morgue?

The reason is not that teenagers are invulnerable to drug abuse mishap. Back in 1970, 600 California teenagers and young adults under age 25 died from drugs—one third of the state's total. Today, in the 1996 California of super-lethal forms of heroin, speed, and cocaine, 120 persons under age 25 died from drugs—less than 5 percent of California's toll. This despite the fact that California's teen and young adult population is larger today. Based on a per capita analysis, a California teen of 1996 is an astonishing 90 percent less likely to die from drugs than a California teen of 25 years ago.

The reason today's teens are not dying in rising hordes from drugs contradicts every stereotype of the reckless adolescent. Even Peter Gorman, editor of the marijuana-friendly *High Times*, invokes the image: "When you're 17 you just smoke anything you can get your hands on...Of course we would prefer that they not get high until they're adults, but they're always the most insane, wild group."[29]

Image aside, the relative teenage drug safety is no mystery. Today's teenagers handle drugs more responsibly than today's adults.

Today's generation is hardly one of stoners. If surveys are accurate, half the 12–17-year-olds never used an illegal drug even once during junior-senior high years. Of the half that did, only one-third try a drug as often as once a year. Of that one-sixth, only half use a drug as often as once a month. Of that 9 percent who use a drug once a month or more, four-fifths patronize only marijuana.

Only tiny fractions used heroin (0.3 percent), cocaine (1.4 percent, including crack, 0.4 percent), speed or methamphetamine (1.5 percent), PCP (0.7 percent), or any drug requiring a needle (0.1 percent) even once in the previous year. The number of youths who use hard drugs on a regular basis is too small to reliably guess.[30]

Table 2

Teens use drugs more moderately than adults

Teens age 12–17 as percent of all drug users (teen and adult) who used drugs in the following frequencies in 1995:

Teenage share who:	At least once	1–12 times	50+ times
Used any illicit drug	16.1%	n.a.	n.a.
Used marijuana	17.7	20.3%	16.7%
Used cocaine	10.0	10.8	8.4
Used alcohol	5.6	9.7	2.2

Source: Substance Abuse and Mental Health Services Administration (1996). *National Household Survey on Drug Abuse: Population Estimates 1995*. Rockville, MD: U.S. Department of Health and Human Services.

Every reliable measure shows that compared to adults, modern adolescents use milder drugs. Teens take drugs in lower quantities. Teens use drugs less frequently. Teens use drugs in less risky settings. Teens are less likely to mix drugs with each other and with alcohol. Teens are particularly unlikely to drive after using alcohol or drugs. That is why teenagers don't have serious problems with drugs or alcohol— at least, not nearly as serious as the problems of American adults.

Using 1995 as the most recent year for which consistent figures are available, notice how the teenage drug-use pattern is less risky than the adult pattern (Table 2). While teens comprise one-sixth of the population who used drugs at least once, they comprise only 8 percent of those who frequently (more than 50 times per year) use cocaine and 2 percent of those who frequently use alcohol.

Practical statistics reinforce this point. Teenagers who use illicit drugs are only one-third as likely as adult users to wind up in emergency treatment or dead. A teen who uses speed, cocaine, or heroin is just one-third, one-sixth, and one-tenth as likely, respectively, to become an overdose casualty than an adult who uses these same drugs (Table 3). The risk of drug use by adults escalates rapidly each year after age 25. Marijuana appears to be the only drug which adults can use as safely as teens—around three hospital emergencies per 1,000 tokers per year, and nearly all of these result from mixing pot with harder stuff such as alcohol. (Alternatively, and of even more critical policy importance, perhaps adult drug use is drastically under-reported in surveys).

For those drug liberalizers who emphasize responsible use (and public health advocates who endorse "harm reduction"), the teenage pattern exemplifies it more than the adult pattern. It is not surprising that teens should comprise such a small fraction of drug-related hospital emergencies and deaths (Tables 1 and 3).

The above analysis reaches unusual conclusions because, instead of pulling out this or that breathless statistic out of this or that selective measure as drug-war interests commonly do, it puts teen numbers in the context of adult numbers across a variety of measures. But what if the measures producing the numbers are faulty?

Table 3

**Drug user for user, teens are much less likely than adults
to die or wind up in an ER**

Percent of drug users who suffered death or hospitalization
from overdose in 1995, by drug and age group

	Teens	Adults 25+
Heroin	0.3%	32.4%
Cocaine	0.6	6.4
Speed/methampetamine	0.5	1.4
Marijuana/hallucinogens	0.3	0.3

Sources: Drug use, see Table 2. Drug overdose morbidity and mortality is from SAMSHA, *Preliminary Estimates from the DAWN 1995* and *DAWN Annual Medical Examiner Data 1995*, adjusted to reflect national drug death statistics using National Center for Health Statistics, U.S. Mortality Detail File (1995).

The above surveys and statistics are the ones everyone uses, so if they're wrong, everyone's positions have to be re-thought. Coroner statistics on drug-related deaths clearly are the most accurate, given the completeness of death registration and the toxicology tests to detect thousands of drugs that modern forensic science employs. On the other hand, I have severe doubts about the reliability of behaviors reported on self-reporting surveys.

The point is that the most reliable statistics, drug deaths, are those that show teenage risk extremely low. Conversely, the least reliable and most easily inflatable statistics, self-reported drug use, form the major public impression that teenage drug use is high and rising. So if the numbers are wrong, a lot more rethinking of traditional drug-war notions would have to be undertaken than the counter-analysis I present.

Do Americans accurately report their criminal drug use to surveyors sponsored by agencies of the government? Four decades of research indicates self-reported surveys of behaviors can be inaccurate. The recent, acclaimed "state-of-the-art" *Sex in America* survey turned out to underestimate abortion by 50 percent compared to clinical records.

Americans may deny socially disapproved conduct to drug surveys as well, especially given the draconian penalties users risk. Adults' clinically verified deaths, injuries, and hospitalizations for drug abuse are far higher than their self-reported claims of use would predict. McCaffrey's analysis of survey reports concluded that Americans consume 50 billion alcoholic drinks per year, yet a General Accounting Office analysis of alcohol tax records found the total closer to 100 billion.[31] Similarly, while self-reporting surveys report smoking rates down 25 percent since 1970, the U.S. cigarette sales volume declined by only 10 percent per capita in that period. Since alcohol taxes are probably underpaid and cigarette sales underreported, it is evident that American adults drink and smoke much more than we admit.

The one unassailable point is that drug warriors have not been willing to explore the full implications of the statistics they cite in limited and biased form. It takes no deep thought to figure why. No adult agenda, personal or political, crackdown or liberalize, is served by pointing out that today's adolescents handle drugs and alcohol better than adults do. Even to make such an assertion is to invite hysterical wrath from anti-drug groups.

Pro-Drug-War interests popularize their strategies by setting up images of wise parents against imperiled teens, upright adult society battling corrupting "youth culture." "The fight against drugs must be waged and won at kitchen tables all across America," Clinton intones, calling on parents to fight popular media images promoting drug use.[32]

Along came former Health, Education and Welfare Secretary Joseph Califano with another obfuscatory survey, asking parents if they thought their kids would ever use an illegal drug. When half said yes, Califano fumed that parents were abetting the teenage drug "mess" and intimated that it was because so many had smoked pot in their youths.[33] ("What kind of dumb-ass question was that?" one parent told me. "If I said I thought my kid would never use drugs, he'd scream that I was in denial.")

"Denial!" was exactly the scream of an April 1998 Partnership for a Drug-Free America survey, which claimed Baby Boom parents "many of whom have 'been there, done that,' are surprisingly and ironically out of step with the reality of drugs in their children's lives."[34] Got 'em coming and going. Califano and the Partnership were careful not to ask, and Clinton was careful not to mention, the problem of parents' *current* drug use—and, of course, no one mentioned those embarrassing stats on pharmaceuticals. The popularity- and grant-grubbing value of their anti-youth crusade would be shattered by admitting that there are many more kids with drug-addicted parents than there are parents with drug-addicted kids.

Drug reformers and marijuana legalizers face a more difficult dilemma. The political climate is hostile to the notion of freer use of illegal drugs except in limited situations, such as marijuana therapy for the terminally ill. Admitting the U.S. is in the throes of the most serious drug abuse crisis in known history does not seem a good strategy to promote a more tolerant stance. Liberal reformers seem to believe their only hope for success lies in downplaying the larger crisis and instead pinning drug woes on an unpopular adolescent age group widely portrayed as in need of more controls. Thus, those seeking liberalization of drug laws have joined the anti-drug warriors in evading adult drug abuse and hyping the anti-youth crusade. Let us adults smoke weed, reformers say, but get mean with teens.

Reformers' construction of an artificial world in which "adult drug/alcohol use" is neatly separable from "teenage drug/alcohol use" requires ignoring all kinds of realities. An irony of drug surveys is the revelation that teenagers often use drugs and alcohol *with* adults.

The detailed supplement to the 1995 Monitoring the Future survey contains a bit of information neither drug warriors nor reformers care to ponder (Table 4). Other drugs (and, unfortunately, cigarettes) were not surveyed. Notice that these are not just high school seniors partying with adults over age 21, but with the untrustworthy over-30 set. Intergenerational highs don't fit into the comfortable agenda of the drug debate.

Table 4

Kids drink and use drugs WITH adults

Percent of high school seniors who used drugs/alchohol in the
past year in settings where adults over age 30 were present

Beer/wine coolers	60.5%
Marijuana	32.7
Methamphetamine	35.5
Cocaine	32.9
Narcotics (illegal)	40.5

Source: Johnston, LD; Bachman, JG; O'Malley, PM (1997). *Questionnaire Responses from the Nation's High School Seniors.* Monitoring the Future Survey. Ann Arbor: University of Michigan, Institute for Social Research, pp 49–80.

Insane Clown Posse

That today's absurd, vicious attack on adolescent pot smokers serves a range of political agendas makes it no less reprehensible. It continues an American tradition of vilifying entire classes of easily-blamed people for drug woes. The newest round of anti-drug hysteria is occurring at the very time science has most clearly established that drug abusing individuals harbor fundamentally different (and treatable) characteristics than individuals who use drugs moderately. It is not age, but proneness to addiction that determines who can use drugs more or less safely.

The reason such reasonable stances are not taken, and such lunatic twistings of data and science common to all sides now dominate the drug debate, involves yet another weird American moral precept. Americans of all stripes so angrily attack teenage drug use not because youths suffer some unique vulnerability to abuse, but because *teenagers engage in widespread drug use without suffering serious consequences*.

Anyone who works for any time in drug and alcohol abuse prevention, as I did, will discover that the vilest of profanities is "responsible use." There is no such thing as responsible use of drugs (or alcohol), say-noers moralize. Liberals tack on "by teenagers" in the same pious tone. Department of Health and Human Services Secretary Donna Shalala is typical in singling out "casual marijuana use, single-time marijuana use" for special condemnation[35] even though, by definition, these are the least likely to cause problems.

Absolutist stances, especially when directed only at certain groups, are counter to the most effective public health approach aimed at limiting problems of drug use, often referred to as "harm reduction." Harm reduction seeks to maximize healthy behavior not by demanding absolute purity by all people at all times, but by recognizing that all humans sometimes take risks, and some humans take large risks.

The Netherlands' spectacularly successful reforms under its 1976 Opium Act are fine examples of harm reduction.[36] The reformed Dutch law decriminalized marijuana possession in small amounts, provided for heroin needle exchanges, and led to concentration of police and treatment measures on the small numbers of serious addicts. These reforms were followed by reductions in drug deaths of 60 percent in the last 20 years. In the last decade, while America's drug death toll rocketed upward by 50 percent, Dutch drug deaths fell by 40 percent, with especially sharp declines among young people.[37]

Because it is solidly successful in reducing the toll of drug abuse, Dutch policy is furiously attacked by drug-war proponents, particularly the U.S. A 1995 editorial in the English medical journal *The Lancet* drew fire when it endorsed the Dutch reforms because "cannabis per se is not a hazard to society but driving it further underground is."[38] In a letter of response, Dr. Herbert Kleber of Califano's National Center on Addiction and Substance Abuse sought to blame the Dutch marijuana law for every real and imagined woe short of dike failure. Kleber charged "the Dutch murder rate is higher than that of the USA."[39] According to World Health Organization statistics, the Netherlands' homicide rate is one-eighth that of the U.S.[40]

Califano followed with an absurd tirade against European Union officials for supporting Dutch drug liberalization, published in the *International Herald Tribune* on October 18, 1996. It was meticulously (and effortlessly) picked apart by University of California, Santa Cruz, sociologist Craig Reinarman in the *International Journal of Drug Policy*.[41] "In the 1970s, the United States de facto decriminalized marijuana," Califano declared de falso, producing "a soaring increase in the use of marijuana, particularly among the young." But California Criminal Justice statistics show that in my state alone, there were more than 600,000 people arrested for marijuana during the 1970s (half charged with felonies); one-third of those arrested were youths. That is not decriminalization. Califano also claimed that the Dutch "Justice Ministry acknowledges a steady increase in drug-related crime during the past decade." Califano cited no source for this statement. When Reinarman provided a copy of Califano's article to the Justice Ministry and asked for comments on his claims, the Ministry's scientist responded: "This man is insane."

"Harm reduction" on the Dutch model may work, but it challenges conventional morality which holds that bad behavior must result in suffering. If a person uses drugs in defiance of moral values set forth by authority, that person should incur misery. The precept behind laws punishing mere use of certain drugs is that if the chemical itself does not cause suffering, the state must cause it. Even if punishment serves no public health goals, or sabotages them, it upholds moral standards.

Dan Baum's excellent *Smoke and Mirrors* and Franklin Zimring and Gordon Hawkins' cogent *The Search for Rational Drug Control* showed how such contradictory absolutisms became a disaster when incorporated into public policy. The Drug War's architect was President Bush's first czar, William Bennett, a nicotine addict who availed costly treatment to end his habit. In 1989, Bennett drafted the National Drug Control Strategy, begetting a stubborn and moralistic denial that became the drug war's credo.

Bennett's doctrine defined drug "use itself," particularly its challenge to moral authority, as the crisis. Preventing drug abuse and addiction was of little interest; in fact, abusers were seen as useful. Drug addicts are "a mess," the strategy declared, and make "the worst possible advertisement for drug use." Addicts' debilitations were the result of their immoral choices. Leave them on display and let society see the consequences of sin.

However, folks who get high on occasion and have the temerity to enjoy it, even to lead productive lives, serve as "a highly contagious" example to non-users, the Strategy stressed. So "experimental first use, 'casual' use" were defined as "the essence" of "the worst epidemic of illegal drug use in (our) history...far more severe, in fact, than any ever experienced by an industrial nation."

It never has been a policy of the War on Drugs to reduce drug abuse. Eight of the nine goals presented in the Strategy focused only on reducing drug use. "Fewer drug overdose deaths in the United States or fewer babies born drug addicted are not among the quantified objectives of the national drug control policy as presented in the National Drug Control Strategy," Zimring and Hawkins noted.[42]

Bennett's only goal was to prevent all use of certain street drugs by anyone anywhere anytime. The only measures of success were pounds of drugs seized by authorities, bodies arrested and imprisoned, and most crucially, percentages of Americans who reported to surveys that they used these selected drugs.

Ironically, both teenage and adult drug use had been declining on their own for several years before the drug war's advent in the mid-'80s. At the height of the crack epidemic, 96 percent of high school seniors had never even tried it. Teenage and adult drug deaths were at their lowest point in 1985 in two decades.

The embryonic drug war's political needs, however, required revving up the drug scare. Then-Education Secretary Bennett claimed in his 1986 *Schools Without Drugs* that among teenagers, "use of some of the most harmful drugs is increasing" and that "because of drugs, children are failing, suffering and dying. We have to get tough, and we have to do it now."[43] Over the next few years, in the Bennett and post-Bennett era, authorities proudly waved the same surveys Bennett had earlier denied. They claimed declines in drug use (which began years before the drug war) were proof of their success.

Donkey Bong

Bennett's policy sought to punish the drug users causing the least problem with "tough and coherently punitive anti-drug measures." It left drug addicts causing the worst problems on display as public testimonies to the evils of dope. It does not take Jeremiah to prophesy that Bennett's policy would (a) deter moderate drug users from indulging (or at least, telling surveys that they did), and (b) push marginal cases and addicts over the edge by handling drug addiction as a moral failing deserving of society's cold shoulder. In short, it was the recipe that would perpetuate exactly the reduction in self-reported drug use combined with the explosion in drug abuse that statistics indicate took place.

It was also the recipe for the pogrom against adolescents by Clinton, whose regime embraced police/prison solutions to drug abuse even more drastic than Reagan's and Bush's. In the Clinton era, arrests (particularly of youths) for possession of small amounts of marijuana rocketed to heights unheard-of during Bennett's reign.

At the peak of the Republican War on Drugs in 1989, 1.3 million Americans were arrested for drugs. In 1996 (which may not turn out to be the Clinton peak), 1.6 million. The drug arrest rate of youths actually declined by 9 percent during the

Table 5

The Drug War increasingly targets kids,
the least of the drug problem

Drug arrest numbers and rates per 100,000 adults and youths, 1980–96

| | Raw numbers | | Rates per 100,000 | |
	Youth	Adult	Youth	Adult
1980	110,000	471,000	463.3	289.3
1985	94,000	729,000	440.7	415.9
1989*	111,000	1,217,000	533.1	663.7
1992	88,000	1,011,000	424.1	535.4
1996	221,000	1,355,000	976.6	690.6
Change				
1980–92	-22,000	+540,000	-8.5%	+85.1%
1989–96	+133,000	+344,000	+130.3%	+29.0%

*Peak arrest year, Republican War on Drugs; 1996 is most recent year of data.
Youth is 12–17, adults 18+.
Source: FBI (1980–96). *Uniform Crime Reports.*

Reagan-Bush years as it skyrocketed (up 85 percent) for adults (Table 5). Further, the growth in arrests under the GOP War on Drugs primarily consisted of felonies— dealers and larger possessors, not casual tokers.

Whether or not one approves of arrests as a way to deal with drug problems, the law enforcement thrust during the Republican Drug War did reflect the real growth in abuse of illegal drugs among adults shown in hospital emergency and death statistics (Table 6).

For all the moralistic bluster of Nicorette-chomping Bennett and his fellow virtuists, the GOP War on Drugs at least targeted a real problem, albeit in a destructive way. Drug abuse and deaths soared among adults during their arrest-happy years. Among youths, the rather small problem did not get better.

After the Republican bust-pinnacle in 1989, arrests were down considerably until the Clinton surge began after 1993. The Clinton War on Drugs takes the Republican neglect-addicts/imprison-users philosophy to a worse extreme: get tough on kids, go easy on grownups. Because youths don't have much of a drug problem, that means focusing on smaller marijuana offenses and ignoring larger grownup heroin and cocaine disasters.

The new explosion in drug arrests during the Clinton presidency was of a different sort than preoccupied Bush and Bennett. The FBI's 1996 *Uniform Crime Report* points out:

Table 6

Adults, particularly over-30 adults, display rising drug addiction

Drug-related hospital emergencies* and overdose deaths

	Hospital emergencies*				Overdose deaths**	
	Youths	Adults			Teens	Adults
1980	3,100	29,500		1980	261	5,761
1985	4,200	66,200		1985	227	6,789
1989	5,900	166,500		1989	318	8,857
1992	4,869	186,974		1992	251	10,301
1996	8,800	231,300		1995	221	12,512

*Heroin, cocaine, and marijuana. Youth is age 12–17, adult 18+.

**Overdose deaths are for all drugs. Teen is age 10–19, adult 20+.

Sources: SAMSA, *Historical Estimates from DAWN 1978–94*, and *Preliminary Estimates from the 1996 DAWN*; National Center for Health Statistics, *Vital Statistics of the United States* (annual through 1992) and U.S. Mortality Detail File (1995)

When examining 1995 versus 1990, the number of juvenile arrests for drug violations has increased at a faster rate than that of adults. During this period, juvenile drug arrests increased 132 percent, versus a 28 percent increase for adults. This overall increase in juvenile drug arrests was influenced by a 278-percent rise in marijuana arrests.[44]

Clinton's strategy employed the Bennett philosophy, but now targeted youths. The FBI reports that compared to 1990, heroin and cocaine arrests (nearly all of adults) are up only slightly. However, adult *abuses* of cocaine and heroin soared during that period—112,000 hospital cases in 1990, 190,000 in 1996. That is four times the total for marijuana. As noted, nearly all marijuana episodes that land users in the hospital also involve harder drugs.

Thus, the Clinton policy disconnected drug policing from serious drug abuse and bent it to an anti-youth (which means an anti-marijuana) agenda. As might be surmised, an anti-youth agenda is also an anti-minority agenda. The FBI reports that marijuana arrests among nonwhites have risen 50 percent faster than among whites.

In California, marijuana possession arrests increased four times faster than all arrests for felony drug sale. Youths comprised one-seventh of California's over-10 population and accounted for just 6 percent of its drug arrests in 1992. Yet youths suffered one-third of the increase in drug cuffings from 1992 to 1996.

This sharp shift in law enforcement priorities away from drug felonies (mostly for hard drugs) involving adults to marijuana possession by youths did not occur because adult problems with hard drugs declined. To the contrary. Detailed reports by the Public Statistics Institute of California analyzing hospital emergency room data showed a 40 percent increase in adults admitted for cocaine and heroin abuse

Table 7

California drug arrests in the "bust kids" era

	1992	1997	Change
Number of adult arrests	214,440	253,766	+39,326
Marijuana possession	8.3%	11.6%	+65.4%
Other drug possession	32.1	31.4	+15.8
Total misdemeanors	40.4	43.0	+26.0
Marijuana sale	6.2%	4.8%	-8.4%
Other drug sale	53.4	52.2	+15.7
Total felonies	59.6	57.0	+13.2
Number of youth arrests	14,553	26,498	+11,945
Marijuana possession	32.9%	51.9%	+187.3%
Other drug possession	14.6	16.1	+100.8
Total misdemeanors	47.5	68.0	+160.7
Marijuana sale	11.4%	8.7%	+39.0%
Other drug sale	41.0	23.4	+3.9
Total felonies	52.4	32.0	+11.2

Source: California Criminal Justice Statistics Center (1992, 1998), Criminal Justice Profiles.

from 1992 to 1995—especially in the 30–49 age group. In 1995, 35,000 hospital emergency treatments (98.8 percent of them adults) for heroin[45] and cocaine[46] abuse cost half a billion dollars, up from 25,000 admissions costing $300 million four years earlier. Marijuana abuse remained an infinitesimal fraction of the state's problem.

The shift in California arrest policy (Table 7) to target youths and marijuana was not based on rational response to the state's drug problem, then, but on national changes in drug war politics. California's switch resulted in disproportionate arrests of youths despite a low and declining youth drug problem. Especially hard-hit were black and Hispanic youth and, to a lesser extent, white youths and black adults. The policy change favored white and Asian adults with fewer arrests despite high and rising drug problems. This is not simply an anti-youth, but an anti-nonwhite and anti-poor drug enforcement strategy. And an anti-common-sense one, profoundly misdirected when it comes to meeting the true drug crisis.

Under Clinton, more than Reagan, Bush, or Nixon, the target of massive test-ing, arrest, re-education, moral condemnation, and punishment is the occasional teenage marijuana smoker. Exactly the age group and drug least to blame for America's drug woes. Due to the political needs of New Democrats and the Republicans fast catching on to kid-bashing politics, then, America is pursuing the most punitively irrational anti-drug strategy in its history.

Gateway Ganja?

Okay, but even if kids don't have big troubles with drugs right now, aren't today's teenage pot smokers tomorrow's smack addicts? Isn't prevention of the adult problems described above the reason to nip teenage toking in the bud?

It takes no gift for calculus to look backwards in time: the drugged-out 40-agers of the mid-90s were teen- and 20-agers in the '70s. So when I give talks to pro-drug-war groups, their response is: see, proves our point. Those potheads of the Sixties are now the heroin- and pipe-heads of 1990s. So we gotta crack down on even the mer-est teenage nibbling at "gateway drugs" such as pot or beer to prevent future adult addictions of the kind Sixties weed-freaks bequeathed themselves as strung-out mid-dle-agers of the '90s.

That is not what Sixties weed-freaks bequeathed at all.

In fact, that kind of misimpression flows from the two great drug fallacies Americans embrace: one drug is the same as another, and use equals abuse.

First, the notion of mass teenage drug use in the Sixties is a myth. In the late '60s, the usual official and media hysteria claimed a "teenage drug epidemic" cen-tered in high schools. Estimates claimed up to 70 percent of kids were stoned.

Time found a 12-year-old junkie and bellowed, "Kids and Heroin: The New Epidemic." (It could have run the same story verbatim for every new smack-scare since). "Heroin, long considered the affliction of the criminal, the derelict, the debauched, is increasingly attacking America's children," *Time* claimed in 1970. "Experts" predict that the number of teenage addicts in New York "may mushroom fantastically to 100,000 or more this summer…Many experts believe that disaster looms large…Something frightening is sweeping into the corridors and onto the pavements of America's playgrounds."[47]

Of course, nothing of the sort was happening. When the University of Michigan's Institute for Social Research surveyed 2,200 male high school seniors (the age and gender most likely to toke) in 1969, it found 80 percent had never tried pot *even once*. Only 1 percent smoked every day. No other drugs even made a blip. "There certainly was not a widespread 'epidemic' of illegal drug use among these high school students as the popular press has suggested," chief surveyor Lloyd Johnston concluded.[48]

A Burns-Roper Poll of 1,000 college students in 1970 similarly found only a quarter had ever burned any hemp. Only about one in eight had smoked pot more than once.[49]

In 1972, the National Commission on Marihuana and Drug Abuse's surveys reported that 86 percent of 12–17 year-olds had *never* tried pot, 95 percent had *never* used LSD, and 99 percent *never* tried cocaine or heroin. Only 18 percent had used an illegal drug even once in their lives.[50] (Neither *Time* nor the major press, which had raged about the teen epidemic, reported on the Commission's findings).

Second and equally convincing is the experience of today's Fifties kids, now 50–64 years old. This group would have graduated from high school in the 1950s and early '60s, when conventional wisdom held that "reefer" was unheard-of except among beatniks, "skid road bums" and "colored people." Yet this youthfully abstemious age group has a serious 1990s drug problem. The Drug Abuse Warning Network reports some 10,000 hospital emergency visits for cocaine and heroin and 1,000 drug-related deaths among 50- and 60-agers annually in the mid-'90s, both representing large increases. Since 1980, drug arrests have quadrupled in this age group.

Today's 30–50-year-olds' terrible drug woes are not due to their widespread doping in high school in the Sixties and early '70s. What the experiences of Fifties and Sixties youths demonstrate is that relatively low rates of drug use during adolescence do not prevent drug abuse from developing later in life.

Third, there is simple math. The 1996 National Household Survey estimates that 68.5 million Americans have used marijuana. But only 3 million are regular users of hard drugs. This is the highest possible estimate, since it results from adding all monthly users of heroin, cocaine (including crack), speed (including crystal methamphetamine), PCP, and other hard drugs without subtracting those who use more than one drug or those who are recreational users but not addicts.

So even under the worst possible assumptions—that EVERY hard-drug abuser started out with marijuana, that marijuana CAUSED the user to progress to harder drugs, and that ALL persons who use one hard drug per month are abusers—95 percent of those who smoked pot do not abuse hard drugs. Eighty-five percent of past pot smokers no longer even use marijuana.

Fourth, there is extensive research. Long-term studies of hundreds of youths by UCLA[51] and UC Berkeley[52] psychological teams found that those who used marijuana or other hallucinogens in moderation are very unlikely to become hard-drug or long-term drug abusers. In a finding that drew enraged reaction from drug-war interests, Berkeley researchers found that "adolescents who engaged in some drug experimentation (primarily with marijuana) were the best-adjusted" psychologically, better oo than drug abusers or abstainers. Moderate use of alcohol or marijuana "is not the type of drug use that will create problems as the teenager matures into adulthood," UCLA's study found.

The Lindesmith Center's exhaustive 1997 research review, *Marijuana Myths, Marijuana Facts*, reveals there is no evidence that teenage or young adult pot smoking is a gateway, or in any way causes, the use of harder drugs. Lindesmith sociologist Lynn Zimmer and pharmacologist/physician John Morgan marshal 50 to over 100 scientific studies in each chapter to debunk the worst myths of marijuana. "Over and over, we discovered that governmental officials, journalists, and even many 'drug experts' had misinterpreted, misrepresented, or distorted the scientific evidence," they conclude.[53] Seventy million Americans who have known this drug at the roach level are evidence that except for a tiny fraction, marijuana is a harmless, smoke-it-or-leave-it drug.

Pointedly, nowhere does these authors' exhaustive research review show that marijuana is more harmful for teenagers than for adults. They report scientific consensus on point after point:

- Few adolescents harbor serious, multi-drug abuse problems. Those who do are likely to be poor, disturbed, and from unhealthy families before they used drugs (page 35).

- Most teenage marijuana use is occasional and experimental (page 144).

- Marijuana is far more likely to be the last than the "gateway," drug for teenagers (page 34).

- "Most young people who try marijuana are normal and well-adjusted." If anything, "teens who used marijuana occasionally were better adjusted socially and psychologically, than non-marijuana using teens" (page 83).

- Marijuana does not lead teenagers to abuse cocaine or harder drugs. In fact, it almost never does (page 37).

- "Marijuana use makes no significant (negative) contribution to high school students' academic performance" (page 64).

- There is "no long-term memory deficit related directly to marijuana use by adolescents" (page 79).

- "There is no convincing scientific evidence that marijuana causes psychological damage or mental illness in either teenagers or adults" (page 80).

- There is "no systematic clinical data showing delayed sexual maturation in adolescents who use marijuana" (page 96).

- There is no long-term damage to chromosomes, body organs, brain function, or memory, nor greater likelihood of accidents, caused by marijuana smoking (entire book). Even damage to lungs appears minimal; abnormalities show up only in heavy smokers and may be related to cigarette smoking (pages 112-16).

- "Marijuana does not cause crime" among either juveniles or adults. Criminal tendencies pre-date marijuana use (pages 90-91).

- Despite claims of radically more potent pot today, there is "no change from 1975 to the present in students' ranking of the intensity or duration of the 'high' they get from marijuana" (page 140).

- No evidence is presented that marijuana use harms teenagers in any unique way. Where adults and youths are contrasted, teens turn out to be slightly less at risk. "Older brains are generally less resilient in response to drugs than younger ones" so that "the same dose" of drugs "produces more dramatic effects in adults than in youths" (page 140). Further, persons who begin using marijuana as adults rather than as teens "are prone to having panic reactions" (page 84).

- August commissions in several nations conclude that laws criminalizing marijuana use foster disrespect for the law among young people (pages 152-55).

- Dutch-style decriminalization does not lead to more pot smoking by teenagers; just the opposite. Dutch teens use marijuana less than American teens do (page 48).

In the Lindesmith authors' comprehensive review of research on pot, they argue passionately and articulately for setting public policy according to the consensus of scientific findings, not popular claims, political biases, or cultural myths. They present no evidence that marijuana represents any unique threat to adolescents or any research justification for extreme anti-youth statements by drug-war combatants.

Yet these authors declare: "Using psychoactive drugs is an activity for adults, not children." (One Lindesmith official's statement, reported in *Drug Sense Weekly* in September 1998, declared to college students that "people your age should not use drugs or alcohol"—fine, but such advice applies equally to the age group of the older adult giving it, and it's time Lindesmith stated that). The use of the word "children" to describe all ages from toddler to college-ager muddies the question. If we are talking about third graders, marijuana use is so rare that it isn't a public issue. If we are talking about 16-year-olds, we would expect some evidence that there is some difference between adults and adolescents to justify permission for the former and prohibition for the latter. Absent that, the ritualistic condemnation of teenage pot smoking by drug reformers (who accept adult pot smoking) is an example of the same unscientific, moralistic thinking they accuse drug warriors of perpetrating.

Junk Reporting

In 1996, the Partnership for a Drug-Free America whipped up a kids-on-heroin scare out of thin air in what it frankly admitted was a fund-raising strategy[54]—yet the latest in its series of propaganda campaigns thoroughly disconnected from reality. Earlier Partnership ads misrepresented the flatliner encephalograph of a coma patient as "the brain waves of a marijuana smoker." In 1989, the Partnership claimed 15 million Americans used cocaine, and five million needed medical help. When *Scientific American* called to inquire where such wildly inflated numbers came from, Partnership officials had no clue.[55]

No matter. The press was always up for a "new teenage drug scare" and had displayed no ethics of its own in cooking them up. In 1970, as noted, *Time* concocted an "adolescent heroin epidemic." In 1980, a *Washington Post* reporter won a Pulitzer prize for fabricating the story of "Jimmy," a black eight-year-old heroin addict, as the symbol of the new child scourge. A citywide search launched by an anxious Mayor Marion Berry (!) not only failed to find that second grade junkie, it unearthed no other grade school trainspotters, either.[56]

The short-memoried ever-obedient media of 1996 scoured the country coast to coast in search of kids on smack. Eventually, in late 1997, the press would find Plano, Texas, where a dozen teens and young adults died from heroin in two years. Reporters had never covered the thousands of adult heroin deaths (and the lack of youthful heroin demise) in their own cities—apparently because General McCaffrey hadn't authorized them to. Yet they flocked from all points to the Dallas suburb to clarion that "Generation X" was dying en masse from smack. The *Los Angeles Times*

story tossed aside all perspective, failing to point out that the teenage heroin toll in
Plano (population 200,000) was more than double the toll in the entire L.A. metropolitan region (population 16 million).[57]

But in 1996, when the Partnership needed the ink and bucks, pickings were
thin. Blaring articles rehashed little more than breathless quotes and a few celebrity
tragedies of a kind no newer than Hendrix, Joplin, and Holiday. *Newsweek's*
"HEROIN ALERT: Rockers, Models, and the New Drug Crisis—Are Teens at
Risk?" answered the last question...no, "no disaster in the making:"

> The statistics on teen drug use are...easy to overstate. Although the statistics
> say teen drug use jumped 33 percent between 1994 and 1995, only 10.9 per-
> cent of teens used any kind of drug in 1994. That means the current total is
> about 13.3 percent...marijuana remains the overwhelming drug of choice
> among young people...cocaine or heroin use is relatively rare.

Nevertheless, there was a good seven pages to be spent overstating it, with jux-
taposed charts of eighth-grade marijuana use with unrelated ones of heroin overdoses, berating pop culture, claiming that "kids emulate pop stars" and "parents have a
right to be scared." But when it came time to get down to the needle point,
Newsweek reported that "most heroin users today are still old-timers." Even veteran
drug warrior Lloyd Johnston wouldn't play along with the manufactured crisis:
"Obviously [heroin] is not a runaway drug among teens."[58]

To anti-drug interests' chagrin, practically no teenagers actually use heroin
(0.3% in the largest surveys). The allergy medication Benadryl was implicated in far
more teen hospitalizations and deaths (still practically none) than killer junk. No
problem. Kleber and Califano's professionals decided in 1997 to ask kids if they
knew *anyone* who *ever used* either heroin, cocaine, *or* LSD. Success! Fifty-six percent! The press headlined the "poll conducted for a respected drug abuse organization" showing a "sharp rise in drug use among youngsters...a sharp increase in heroin use."[59]

How do the experts explain why today's clean-living grownups spawned such a
crop of stoner punks? Here the authoritative idiocy becomes too much to bear. "A
drumbeat of pro-drug messages in the media," said Kleber. Califano's and Kleber's
own efforts to craft absurdly overhyped surveys making teen hard-drug use appear
normative, the habit of the Everyteen, are themselves contributors to the "drumbeat." The media-drug claim also overlooks the $2 billion in anti-drug ads the
Partnership for a Drug-Free America has broadcast in the last eight years—"the
nation's third biggest ad campaign after AT&T and McDonald's."[60]

Ignoring 400,000 drug emergency episodes among adults and 35,000 pharma-
ceutical-drug emergencies among teenagers, former drug czar Lee Brown went
berserk in 1995 over 4,300 teen marijuana cases. "Marijuana is a very dangerous
drug that can well cause you to fight for your health and your life in a hospital emergency room," Brown lied.[61] Fortunately for his media strategy, no one in the
Washington press corps bothered to open the federal reports to discover that a staggering 96 percent of hospital emergencies involving marijuana also involve harder
drugs such as cocaine, heroin, alcohol, and Tylenol. Pot by itself sends practically
no one, teen or grownup, to the ER.[62] Since big pharmaceutical companies such as

Bristol Meyers-Squibb, Merck & Company, and Proctor & Gamble pour hundreds of thousands of dollars into the Partnership (and heavily sponsored *ABC News*'s March 1997 month-long beratement of teens and drugs),[63] guess how likely it is that the public will learn the Big Three teenage drugs of abuse are over-the-counter pain-killers.

God Damn the Veterinarian

Yet fear of teens clouds even mild reforms, such as physician-prescribed marijuana for "seriously-ill Californians" (in the words of Proposition 215).

Judge James Gray, the conservative Orange County Superior Court jurist whose criticism of the War on Drugs made him a hero to reformers until he waffled abysmally in his 1998 campaign, is getting shellacked in a debate with Sheriff Brad Gates and his DARE patrol. Granted, it's a tough audience, the Orange County Grand Jury Association, getting shellacked itself on scotch and martinis during lunch at a posh Anaheim restaurant. The titanic debate is over Proposition 215, California's mild move to legalize marijuana smoking by the "seriously ill."

Gray is affable and unprepared for the raft of compost Gates and a DARE high schooler can hurl at such an innocuous proposal. The sheriff and posse tick off reefer madnesses—super-potent pot causing brain damage, zombied students, wasted young lives, stoned teenage murder and suicide. All to be brought one giant step closer if AIDS and glaucoma sufferers are allowed to blaze up. The sheriff is launching into how the initiative will unleash suburban housewives to glom onto legal marijuana prescriptions from veterinarians, mommies seeding backyard blunt plantations to medicate junior's teenage angst.

I have a Hunter Thompson headache. In my head Steppenwolf growls, "God damn...GOD DAMN THE VETERINARIAN!" The just-say-no crowd is showing the colors, lacerating Gray's confused manifesto for drug tolerance with emotional anecdotes. We hear of a promising UCLA student who smoked pot one time and now lives behind a dumpster. What would pot legalizers say to parents of dead stoners?

Gray asks for a show of hands on how many would prohibit alcohol, his one good point. No hands. No one, not even the sheriff and DARE crowd, opt to criminalize California's leading killer drug, which many are downing in 86-proof form right at lunch. "Alcohol is a different issue," Gates murmurs. It surely is. Frank Fitzpatrick, the Orange County Coroner's chief toxicologist, sees about 150 corpses per year delivered to his slab because of some kind of drug. Yet, "we almost never see marijuana implicated in deaths," he told me. "We almost never see any teenagers dead from drugs, either." However, county records show 400 Orange Countians died and 18,000 were injured in booze-besotted traffic crackups in the last five years.

The blind fear of marijuana once derived from its purported favor among black musicians and in Mexican dens. As drug historian David F. Musto reported in *Scientific American*, America's periodic anti-drug scares involved officials promoting and exploiting the "linkage between a drug and a feared or rejected group within society."[64] Marijuana is now scary because it is the drug of the terrifying teenager.

Adolescents comprise only 16 percent of the pot smokers in the country, and only 13 percent of those who use it as much as once a week. In fact, one of Califano's few useful poll findings is that one-third of the parents of teenagers have friends who smoke pot.[65] Yet officials portray pot solely as a teenage drug. Medical marijuana measures mess with that image, which is one reason drug warriors loathe such laws.

Gates' chief point is that permitting terminally-ill patients to smoke pot would "be sending absolutely the wrong message to kids."[66] Drug czar McCaffrey whips up a phobia against young people and pot which transcends cannabis itself.

Silence is Acceptance

The most puzzling development is not the Drug War's misdirection, but that of reformers. The drug-war line issued by General McCaffrey and his predecessor czars for the previous five years is that drug abuse by adults was declining, which it was not and is not. Drug war interests bent on jailing millions and "tearing up the Constitution" never had much use for addiction numbers, hospitalization figures, or drug and crime statistics, Baum points out.[67] Today, neither side has any use for an honest assessment.

After professors Zimring and Hawkins deliver a devastating critique of the failure of national drug policies, they prioritize the same goal as McCaffrey: stop all teenagers from using drugs, ever. Baum's clear-headed journalistic chronicle of 30 years of drug policy failure fails to incorporate the most striking feature of America's new drug landscape—skyrocketing addiction by aging Baby Boomers and its underlying impacts both on kids and policy. Lindesmith Center's excellent marijuana research compendium incorporates the same denial: marijuana use is acceptable for older adults but absolutely wrong for teenagers and young adults. Once again, though purportedly coming from radically different vantages and promoting very different strategies, hard-liner and pot-legalizer wind up with the same dreary conclusion that ignores the most obvious realities and perpetuates the most pointlessly punishing policies.

For reformers, this approach is a fleeting, self-defeating expediency. The War on Drugs in the Clinton era, to an even greater extent than in Republican years, is driven by fear of teenagers. If liberal reformers continue to endorse the War's distorted image of "youth" as the symbol of drug menace, rising repression is guaranteed.

Marijuana prohibition "is a new form of tyranny by the old over the young," a noted scholar once said. "You have the adult with a cocktail in one hand and a cigarette in the other saying, 'you cannot' to the child. This is untenable." Use of intoxicating substances should be legal for anyone over age 16, she said.[68] The hypocrisy Margaret Mead deplored in 1969 has doubled in the '90s: today, both marijuana prohibition and legalization represent tyranny of the old over the young.

Instead of exposing ripe drug-war lunacies, many marijuana legalizers and reformers have jumped aboard the anti-teen bandwagon in order to win legal bonghood for grownups. Those 1990s drug reformers who push a continued prohibitionist stance against teenagers while claiming prohibitionist measures are harmful sound less humanitarian than simply self-serving. Baby Boom hypocrisy rears its ugly head: let us dudes party on, but jail our kids if they even think of doing likewise.

Richard Evans, board member of the National Organization for the Reform of Marijuana Laws (NORML), gives the same message to youths that McCaffrey does: "Kids don't drive cars, they don't sign contracts, and they don't do drugs."[69] Uh...kids drive cars at 15 or 16, they can sign many contracts before age 18 and all contracts after that age. In a supreme irony discussed in Chapter 6, adults can have sex legally with 16-year-old "kids" in most states. Drug liberalizers would legalize drugs only for those over 21, ratifying the same age-based hypocrisies that define a teen as a child, or as an adult, when convenient for adults.

As Baum's *Smoke and Mirrors* records, drug reformers have a dismal history of self-destructive tactics. Reformers seem not to comprehend the intense terror of teenagers that disarrayed modern parents have spread and politicians have availed, and which drug legalizers themselves now contribute to. Marijuana, harmless for 99 percent of the population, has acquired pointless apocalyptic symbolism to warring grownups frightened of and furious with their kids. As such, marijuana decriminalization, a difficult goal to win in any case, will not occur until Americans' irrational fear and loathing of adolescents abates. The better approach is to flatly declare that some people are addiction prone and should never use drugs (or alcohol) regardless of age, others can safely use drugs in moderation, few are the occasions when drug use is appropriate even for low-risk persons, and individual characteristics, not age, race, or other demographic class, are the defining criteria.

There are vastly more important issues being crowded out by the spliff tiff. Teenage marijuana use, even under worst-case assumptions, has only minuscule odds of leading to adult drug abuse. But parents' drug abuse repeatedly has been shown to be a crucial factor in drug and alcohol abuse, and other serious problems, among youths.[70] A 1998 U.S. Bureau of Justice Statistics study of 6,000 inmates in 400 jails nationwide found that 60 percent had booze or dope problems and 40 percent had parents who abused alcohol or drugs.[71]

I worked for years with families and saw the immense toll of parents' drug and alcohol abuse on kids. In 1995 and 1996, to official and media shrugs, national child abuse panels reported 2,000 to 3,000 kids murdered and half a million injured every year in violence inflicted by their parents. The California Legislative Analyst's 1996 report listed the most common, and typically related, problems among parents who abuse their kids: alcohol abuse, unemployment, drug abuse, marital problems, and income problems, in that order.[72] Stingier public assistance and treatment unavailability add up to more kids shoved back into homes where parents crave bottle, pipe, and syringe.

Many addicted parents are poor, unable to exercise William Bennett's privilege to obtain extravagant treatment at a "therapeutic resort."[73] "The majority of children I work with have parents who abuse alcohol and/or drugs," wrote San Francisco social worker Nicole Hamilton of abused kids placed in foster care. "Due to current welfare policies, the children most likely will return to these homes."[74]

Buried under the medical-marijuana and kids-and-pot tumult is the plight of several million children raised by drug- and alcohol-addicted parents. A rare exception, a grim *Los Angeles Times* series on Dependency Court hearings on child abuse and neglect in Orange County, reported the human face of what studies show:

> Drugs are numbingly pervasive. In four out of five cases, the mother or
> father is a drug user. Dozens of little girls are named Crystal after the rock
> form of methamphetamine. Hungry kids with mouths full of rotting teeth
> who learned young that food, shelter, and clothing take a back seat to mom's
> habit. One toddler is called Pea Bee Cola, street slang for pure blown cocaine.
>
> The files show children's lives disintegrating before the court stepped
> in. In one pile, more than half the children had four or more abuse reports,
> three had more than 10, and one family had 17 calls reporting abuse before
> the mother abandoned her 9-year-old daughter and her two sons, age 7 and 2,
> in a motel.
>
> …"You go through the calendar on a daily basis and the number of
> cases that include the word 'methamphetamine' is staggering," says (Judge
> Richard) Toohey.[75]

Yes, the drug war is going to be won across the kitchen tables of America, in conversations started by little girls named Crystal.

Treatment services for the poor are sparse and "the government treatment
bureaucracy is manifestly ineffective," former federal drug policy analyst John P.
Walters said. The Reagan years brought cutbacks in treatment funding; Bush and
Clinton raised it modestly; '90s Contract-with-America Congresses cut it back
again. Small increases are "pointless," said one California urban alcoholism services
official. "We should either double the investment in drug treatment or stop talking
about it." Studies by UCLA's Drug Abuse Research Center found demand for gov-
ernment-funded treatment in Los Angeles was four times the available capacity.[76]
Kern County, California, which has 600,000 people and one of the state's highest
poverty rates, has just 50 publicly-funded residential treatment center beds.

Clinton's first drug czar, Lee Brown, came to office with an astoundingly sensible view on just that topic. Said Brown of his first plan in 1993:

> The principal drug problem lies with hard-core drug users—those
> heaviest users who use drugs at least once a week. Hard-core drug use
> has not been reduced by past anti-drug efforts, especially in our inner
> cities and among the disadvantaged.
>
> …We'll look at what we do in health reform, the educational sys-
> tem, economic development, particularly in developing more jobs, and
> what we do in terms of decent housing. If we can address those issues—
> that's what is pushing the hard-core drug user in my estimation—then
> we'll make a difference.[77]

Even Bennett agreed with placing more emphasis on drug addicts. The only
thing that didn't agree was the political lucre at stake in the Clinton-GOP shadow
boxing over "family values." After the Democratic drubbing at the hands of
Republican moralists in the 1994 election, Brown was demoted to the anti-teen-pot
crusade. He left office in January 1996 disappointed that none of the root-cause
issues had been addressed.[78]

His replacement, Barry McCaffrey, is the most retrograde drug czar yet, making
even Bennett look benign. Only one-fifth of the national drug control budget is
now assigned to treatment; the General Accounting Office reports that the bulk

goes to law enforcement.[79] Welfare reforms negotiated by Clinton and Republicans denied addicts treatment services far more modest than former drug czar Bennett thought necessary to rescue himself from killer nicotine. Changes to Supplemental Security Income (SSI) programs cut all drug and alcohol addicts from benefits, or even money for treatment, as of January 1, 1997. Thirty-three thousand were cut off in California alone, having a devastating impact not only on them but their families as well.[80] What a good idea. With any luck at all, no more than 10,000 might be parents.

Flashback

The most profound danger of the drug war is not just today's rise in drug abuse that it provoked or did nothing about. It is also what may happen in the near future among the millions of youths raised in families where parents and other adults abuse drugs. Normally, kids act like the adult family and society that raises them. When Califano and McCaffrey claim that teenage drug use leads to adult drug abuse, they ignore the even greater link between adult drug and alcohol addictions and teenage abuses.

Drug policies and reforms which downplay the effects of letting kids grow up for a dozen years with alcoholic and drug-abusing parents, then wax hysterical when the kid smokes a jay, are not just hypocritically inhumane. They ultimately are self-defeating.

It is here that a troubling chapter of California and American drug history provides a warning. Beginning in the late 1950s, physicians began prescribing new drugs known as barbiturates—Seconal, Demerol, Nembutal, etc.—thought to be the miracle antidote to anxiety and insomnia. The "little yellow pill" turned out to be far more addictive and lethal than previously thought, especially when mixed with booze. Ten thousand Californians, Marilyn Monroe being the most famous, died from barbiturate overdoses in the 1960s and 1970s.

Contrary to culture-war claimants, there wasn't just one Sixties "drug scene." There was pot, acid, and mushrooms, whose aficionados for the most part are doing fine today. Then there were barbiturates, and a heroin epidemic spawned by the Vietnam War, that comprised the true Sixties "drug crisis." Barbiturate habits began among older age groups in the early and mid-1960s and spread to younger ones. By 1970, California had a genuine drug abuse disaster among young adults. Those young who, like their Fifties elders, patronized harder drugs with which society then had little experience suffered a staggering addiction and death toll.

The University of Wisconsin's Alfred McCoy provides a stunning summary of drug use in Vietnam in *Scribner's Encyclopedia of the Vietnam War.* Government surveys of returning troops found 30 to 40 percent used heroin regularly and one-fifth described themselves as "addicted." Many of the estimated one-fourth of enlisted men who previously used marijuana had switched to more easily concealed heroin (compact, no telltale smoke) after a vigorous anti-pot campaign by the Army, including arrests of up to 1,000 tokers per week. Then, alarmed at the extent of heroin abuse, the military instituted a screening program prohibiting those with dirty tests from boarding flights back home. Most found the tests easy to evade. Or, as an alternative, those who failed two tests were discharged and sent home without treatment or even detoxification.

Thus, the high command's multiple drug miscalculations became the gift that kept on giving, spawning a heroin epidemic stateside on top of the war toll in Southeast Asia. Perhaps no graph I have seen is so dramatic as the heroin scourge that hit California in the early and mid 1970s (Figure 1), as subtle as the Matterhorn sprouting in Kansas. But initial fears of a long-lasting American heroin plague proved premature, McCoy noted:

> At the start of the Vietnam heroin epidemic in 1970, there was great concern that veterans would return home with lasting heroin habits. But by 1974 it was clear that drug use in the war zone was largely a situational response to combat stress. The great majority of veterans who admitted to addiction in Vietnam did not continue to use the drug after they returned to the United States.[81]

Now, heroin is back with a vengeance among the 35–55 age group. Considerable long-term study indicates that many heroin and other drug addicts today are Vietnam combat veterans.[82] It is not clear what "situational" stresses today are causing the middle-aged relapse—indeed, officially it doesn't exist.

Whether initiated by wartime, pharmaceutical, or some other situational strain, today's middle-aged trainspotters are legacies of long-term hard-drug and multiple-drug problems radically different from the turn-on tune-in legacy. The legacy of hard-drug and multiple-drug use among a small fraction of Sixties young, following Sixties old, appears to be driving the new cycle of today's middle-aged drug carnage. The worst drug crises of the Sixties and Nineties, then, were barbiturates and heroin, fueled by the pharmaceutical industry and government war policy. The drug czar and Drug-Free Partnership, which are the government and pharmaceutical industry, have considerable self-interest in deflecting attention from their own disgraces and on to "personal responsibility" and "kids and marijuana."

Bill Clinton and Newt Gingrich, wrapped in yet another round of jockeying to exploit the teen-drug non-issue as the 1998 mid-term elections loom, are typical Sixties pot smokers—addicted to mid-life puritan hypocrisy, not dope. Gingrich, who as a youngster crusaded for pot-proliferation and smoked his politics diligently, laments today that "drug use among teens has skyrocketed…an unthinkable 70 percent" since 1992.[83] Then, Newt and other House leaders quietly squashed a measure by two Republican zealots to require drug testing of all House members and their staffs.[84] Why, drug testing is humiliating, an infringement of privacy, and likely to turn up some embarrassing positives to prove that Congress has lower drug standards than a high school club.

In July, Republicans and Democrats launched a $1 billion, five-year ad campaign "to send a signal to young people" and to "break the back of the drug culture," Gingrich announced in a platform shared with Clinton. The new ads contained nothing that hadn't been floated in the $2 billion in previous Partnership advertising salvo, which had been followed by rising drug abuse. The first of the "provocative anti-drug ads" which were "produced gratis by some of Madison Avenue's premier ad agencies" (the Associated Press's puff-piece gushed), targeted parents and

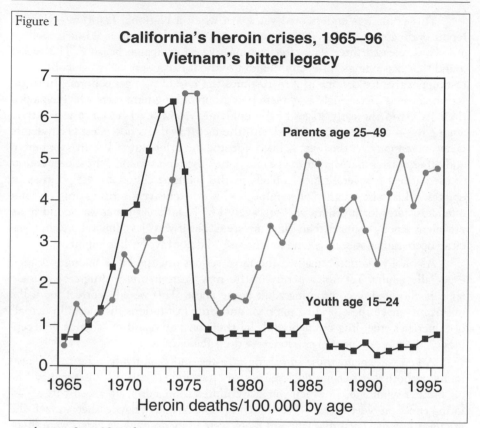

Figure 1

California's heroin crises, 1965–96
Vietnam's bitter legacy

Parents age 25–49

Youth age 15–24

Heroin deaths/100,000 by age

youth ages 9 to 18 and were set to run in 75 major newspapers and four major TV networks beginning July 9. One showed "a Winona Ryder look alike busting up an egg and her whole kitchen with a frying pan" to show how drugs wreck families[85] (the real Winona would have been in a nicotine fit).

Another pictured a suburban "soccer-mommy" declaring, "My kid doesn't smoke pot. He's either at school, soccer practice, piano lessons, or at a friend's house." Below was the kid, smirking, "I usually get stoned at school, after soccer practice, before piano lessons, or at my friend's house." Your standard four-times-a-day eighth grade pothead is depicted as clean cut, high-functioning, scholarly, artistic, and athletic. The 1997 Household Survey found such overachievers quite rare—only 3.6 percent of teens smoke pot even as often as once a week, and the fraction toking up daily is minuscule. Interestingly, that's about the same percentage as among the soccer-moms and -dads in the 30s and 40s age range, who have far worse problems with coke, heroin, and booze.

What the new infusion of $1 billion in public funds was being spent to do was provide a forum for politicians to aggrandize themselves, publicize McCaffrey's office and the Partnership's name, flack for local drug-war interests, and financially reward the media for its tame servitude. By sustaining a hullabaloo over the small fraction of today's 12–17 year-olds who smoke pot instead of facing the legacy of today's drug abuse among adults, the lessons of 1965 are ignored. It is adult abuse of hard drugs that is the issue in creating future crises, not "kids and pot."

This point was underscored yet again when a National Institute of Justice report of drug tests of 27,000 adult and 4,000 juvenile arrestees in 23 metropolitan areas was released three days after the massive ad campaign began.[86] The report found that depending on the city, "almost without exception, older age cohorts are testing positive for cocaine at 2 to 10 times the rate of younger cohorts." In truth, "cocaine use is increasingly a problem of a group of long term users who developed their habits in the early stages of the epidemic...Low levels of cocaine positives among the youth cohort, combined with the fact that the cohort's test positive rate is not increasing over time, imply lower cocaine initiation rates." Patterns for heroin and other opiates are "similar to cocaine data," the report found: "the oldest cohort of users (36+) is several times as likely as the youngest cohort to test positive for opiates." Likewise, methamphetamine is almost exclusively a rising drug of adult offenders; rates for juveniles are "relatively low." Only marijuana was found more prevalent among younger than older arrestees, but it was "levelling off and in some cities decreasing noticeably," and in any case "did not involve large numbers."

Alcohol addiction remained the most serious drug problem among arrestees, especially adults. Yet not a penny of the new Partnership or drug-czar crusade appears allocated to confronting adult booze abuse. This would—correct me if I'm mistaken—make these leading national anti-drug institutions the most "in denial" of America's true drug problem and, by their own standard of "silence is acceptance," the most influential condoners of drug abuse today.

Asked to explain these surprising arrestee and drug figures, the *L.A. Times* found authorities reversing field yet again: "Researchers call this discrepancy 'the big brother syndrome,' in which younger children shun a drug after seeing its devastating effect on older users."[87] Previously, up to a couple of days earlier, in fact, the drug-war line had been that ignorant teens were using drugs while elders were shunning them.

This is the umpteenth august report to find the same thing: drugs are a major factor in rising crime among adults over age 30 (especially whites), a phenomenon that still has not been admitted (refer to Chapter 1). Once again, officials' nonchalance over adult drug abuse kicked in: "Older cocaine users are aging out or dying out," said Jack Riley, National Institute of Justice drug expert, predicting lower crime rates. "Aging in to" rather than "aging out of" addiction has been the pattern of the last 20 years, as shown by the huge surges in serious over-30 crime, drug treatments, and family violence top officials still don't admit is happening.

Given the drug-war's delusions and evasions, we are lucky teenagers are doing as well as they are. Whether the astonishingly low rates of teenage drug abuse will continue seems to depend not on policy, but—indeed—on the skills of adolescents in learning from the woes of their elders.

Normies Rule

In "The American Freshmen: Twenty-Five Year Trends," UCLA reported that in the late 1960s, 13 percent of freshmen women lettered in a high school sport and 15 percent used sedatives. In the 1990s, 42 percent lettered in sports and only 2 percent took sedatives.[88]

Will the luck continue? Teenagers using milder drugs and fewer suffering tragedies?

In 1995, I and fellow doctoral student Faye Docuyanan interviewed four recovering teenage addicts in Anaheim for an article for *Orange County Weekly*.[89] The Touchstones Residential Adolescent Treatment home staff generously left us alone.

We had some interesting figures to ask them about. In the three worst years of the Sixties (1969-71), Orange County's drug death toll went like this: 252 adults, 40 teens. In the most recent three years (1992-94): 480 adults, one teen.

It's much easier to figure what didn't cause the massive decline in youthful drug abuse than what did. The decline was rapid in the late 1970s and early 1980s, when marijuana policy was more tolerant and drug programs were criticized for being "pharmacological" instead of demanding abstinence. The decline slowed in the 1980s and '90s. This timing would suggest that War on Drugs policing or programming played no role—at least, not a positive one.

Maybe the best ones to ask would have been teenagers who use drugs but aren't addicted, called "normies" by this group. But we wanted to start with the worst possibilities.

Possibility number one: is it because kids today don't use drugs? Perish that thought. "There's a lot of drugs around the schools," said Richard, 16. In junior high, mostly pot. Senior high, "you get into a bigger variety of drugs," added Jeff, 17. "Doing drugs on a daily basis. Pot. Tweakers (speed). Lots of crystal meth."

How many kids are using drugs? Four schools are represented. "Half," 15-year-old Julie estimates. "Probably 75 percent experiment with drugs. Half use them." They all nod.

Okay, so teenagers are using more drugs. Or maybe druggies hang out with druggies and think everyone is on something. Whichever. Three of the four say they have exaggerated their drug use on surveys given at school. "I don't take them (surveys) seriously," Dierdre, 17, said.

But still, in this county of 2.5 million souls, this land of deadlier forms of crack, smack, and meth...only one teenage drug death in three years?

The room falls silent. Some puzzled looks, an intense stare at the printout of figures on the table, and head-shaking.

"Weird," Richard said.

"That's hard to believe," Jeff said.

The teens at the group home report storied histories of selling and consuming pot, acid, speed, crystal meth, and plenty of alcohol. But none knew of any teens who died from drugs. Not, like, personally. "I should be dead," Richard said.

It is uncharted waters that teenagers navigate best. They quickly formulate new possibilities.

Possibility Two: Maybe the numbers are just plain wrong.

(I recite from my notes that toxicologist Frank Fitzpatrick of the Orange County Coroner's office told me he thinks "the figures are good. I don't think too many drug deaths are escaping detection." All suspected accident, homicide, and suicide victims are tested for alcohol, heroin, cocaine, and methamphetamine.

Where circumstances indicate, "we can test for thousands of different drugs." His examiners see lots of middle-aged o.d. Methamphetamine fatalities, in particular. But no teenagers. "I don't know why we're not seeing any teen overdose deaths," he said. "We don't seem to have a heavy drug abusing population among youths here").

The surprised kids propose Possibility Three: "Maybe it's because kids' parents or friends get them to the hospital quick, so they don't die as much now," Julie speculated. But she and the other students quickly reject that idea.

"People who are younger are scared of going to the emergency room," Dierdre said. "They won't take their friends to the hospital. They'll do anything to revive them on their own."

They recount the various ways to manage a friend who has overdosed, including giving them drugs to counteract drugs. They readily admit these home remedies may backfire.

Mental note: maybe that's why teenage hospital emergency numbers are so low. But…kids throwing overdosers in cold baths, administering amateur cures without professional attention, should mean lots more teenage deaths—if there really are lots of teenage overdoses.

Possibility Four: Maybe, they suggest, there aren't that many overdoses because kids don't use drugs as heavily as grownups do. "When I did drugs with adults, I just did a little bit at first. But they were slamming it," said Richard. "You mainline it like that, it goes right to the heart, right to the brain." Years of drug taking "wreck your body" and cause death in adulthood, Julie surmised.

Reminder to those who would legalize drugs for adults but push puritan prohibitions on teens: teens use drugs *with* adults. "Age doesn't mean much in the drug culture," Jeff shrugged.

So if it's a natural progression from light teenage toking to heavy middle-age slamming, why did Baby Boom kids have such a high death and injury toll while today's kids seem almost immune?

Possibility Five, a refinement of Possibility Four: "It must have something to do with the generations," Julie guessed. "Maybe our parents gave us some kind of genetic immunity or something."

Drug abuse appears to be widespread among parents of their peers, they said. Two of the four youths have addicted parents, and a third has close relatives who are alcoholics.

Adult behaviors influence teenage behaviors. "If a parent uses, the kid is almost always going to use," Julie said. But drug abuse is not a straight line from parent addict to kid addict—nor, in reverse, from teen pothead to adult crackhead. It is a circle in which adults and youths reinforce each other.

So why are kids using drugs more moderately now than their parents' generation did then, or does now?

Genetic immunity is discarded as biologically questionable. Takes a lot longer than just one generation to install, doesn't it?

Possibility Six: Perhaps it's awareness gained from their parents' bad experiences. "People have learned a lot since then about how to use drugs," Dierdre said. "It's more controlled now. I know a lot of people who are pretty responsible about using drugs."

"Normies," they call them—students who use drugs "recreationally, maybe once or twice a month." Normies "can control it—they don't have an addiction. They can quit when other things in life seem more important," she added. "My sister's a normie and I'm an addict," the girl who had most vigorously disputed genetic theories chipped in.

Lost amid the shrill "just say no," "you use, you lose" noise is the concept of the teenage "normie"—observing, learning from others' mistakes, moderating rather than abstaining. The Steppenwolf-Metallica tradition—a little grass, a little wine or beer now and then never hurt a normie. But stay clear of the coke, the smack, the speed, the Masters of Puppets walking around with tombstones in their eyes.

Standard epidemiology axioms argue that a "disease" does the most damage to a population which has high exposure to but low experience with it. Smallpox and the Aztecs. Barbiturates, heroin, and speed, and the middle-class novices of the 1950s and '60s. High death tolls eventually confer immunity, biological for some diseases, attitudinal for others. Maybe today's kids, the second "drug" generation, are more experienced with the "disease" of dope. Fewer use drugs, and those who do go for the milder ones: beer and marijuana.

Normie theory fits the known facts. Unless someone can explain where the young bodies are hidden, that seems the only way to reconcile the idea that adolescent drug use is fairly widespread while teenage drug deaths and injuries are rare. Still…

"History usually repeats itself," puzzled Dierdre. Kids tend to turn out like their parents. Logic teaches that the rampant drug abuse among middle-agers today should be leading kids to abuse drugs as well. "But in this case, it's not."

"The answer to this isn't going to come easy," said Jeff. "This is going to take a lot of people thinking about why."

In a society in which sheriffs warn that veterinarians will stoke the suburbs, presidents joust with heroin chic, and busting low-level pot possession is the drug-war's newest shopworn innovation, thinking is a tall order. If 17-year-olds whose lives were ruined by drugs and drinking can think about such questions so clearly, why do the experts remain addicted to notions that haven't advanced one baby step from demon rum and Reefer Madness?

Nearly 100,000 Baby Boomers have died from drug overdoses, and perhaps 50,000 more from drug-related mishaps. Twenty thousand Baby Boomers died from overdoses before age 25, a per-youngster rate double that suffered by youths and young adults of Generations X and (so far) Y. More sobering still: two-thirds of Baby Boom drug deaths occurred *after age 30*. (We really were right—you can't trust 'em.)

And we're not done yet. Wait'll society sees what Nazi-hippie 50-aged dope fiends we're planning for our next number.

If adults' concerns over youthful drug-taking represented sincere concern, the escalating drug carnage among aging Boomers would be frankly admitted and youths urged in positive tones to do better than their elders' sad examples. But that is not what is happening. Today's drug pogrom against the young is angry and punishing, accompanied by moralistic sermons against adolescents and rigid denial of adults' far worse levels of addiction.

"I know one thing," Dierdre said. "It's not a love-in out there."

Party On

> Narcotics police are an enormous, corrupt international bureaucracy and now
> fund a coterie of researchers who provide them with "scientific"
> support...fanatics who distort the legitimate research of others...The anti-
> marijuana campaign is a cancerous tissue of lies, undermining law enforce-
> ment, aggravating the drug problem, depriving the sick of needed help, and
> suckering well-intentioned conservatives and countless frightened parents.[90]

said America's conservative emeritus, William F. Buckley, quoted in *Drug Sense Weekly*.

At the very end of 1997, drug-war officials finally admitted what they had denied for several years: drug abuse was skyrocketing, not declining.

McCaffrey handed out the newest, 1996 Drug Abuse Warning Network (DAWN) survey to reporters at a December 30, 1997, press conference. It showed that since 1990, hospital emergency treatments for heroin had doubled. Cocaine ER cases had risen by 78 percent, and methamphetamine bad trips had tripled.

McCaffrey claimed the new figures showed the "success we are seeing" in that "the upward slope of drug abuse has indeed begun to be arrested."

UPWARD slope? Hadn't McCaffrey—and every other dope-war commandant and his pet rottweiler—been telling us drug problems were down?

McCaffrey modestly shared credit for the "slight" success with "parents, teachers, coaches, religious leaders and community coalitions" and (pat, pat) "the media." Just as Reagan's anti-drug warriors had warbled in 1988 over a couple of favorable surveys even as deaths were mounting, McCaffrey was announcing "Victory in Sight"—replacing "Urgent Crisis" in the alternating cycle of drug war whoppers. New boss same as the old boss.

And as usual, the pages of the new DAWN report reported a different message than McCaffrey proclaimed. It showed that hospital emergency drug cases were down because of fewer admissions for prescription and over-the-counter medications such as aspirin and ibuprofen. Funny, but I can't recall a single drug-czar, parent, teacher, religious leader, community coalition, or media crusade showing a Winona Ryder look-alike smashing up her kitchen because of Bufferin. Or ad urging parents to "talk to your kids about Tylenol."

But when it came to the drugs McCaffrey's war has attacked, the success was slight indeed. So slight that some might call it failure. Cases involving the big four illicits—cocaine, heroin, methamphetamine, and marijuana—rose from 272,200 in 1995 to 275,500 in 1996.

But that didn't tell the real story. The most recent six-month period recorded, July-December 1996, registered the sharpest increase in years. It displayed the highest levels ever of abuse of the four major illegal drugs (Table 8).

McCaffrey had a lot to be modest about. The July-December 1996 period represented by far the worst period on record for cases involving the four illegal drugs most targeted by the War on Drugs. Heroin, cocaine, and marijuana set new records (highs, if you will). In contrast, other drugs, mostly pharmaceuticals left alone by the drug war, declined.

Table 8

After a dozen years of Drug-War punishments and pieties, street drug abuse is at record-high level today

Hospital emergency cases, the "big four" street drugs
targeted by the War on Drugs versus all other drugs

				Jul–Dec 96 versus	
	Jul–Dec 95	Jan–Jun 96	Jul–Dec 96	Jul–Dec 95	Jan–Jun 96
Cocaine	63,782	65,501	76,700	+20.3%	+17.1%
Heroin	36,111	32,654	37,800	+4.7	+15.8
Marijuana	21,282	21,902	28,700	+34.9	+31.0
Meth[†]	6,413	3,966	6,800	+6.0	+71.5
Total, big four	127,588	124,023	150,000	+17.6	+20.9
All other drugs*	118,464	106,849	106,728	-10.0	-0.1

[†]Methampetamine.
*Mostly pharmaceuticals.
Source: Drug Abuse Warning Network, Mid-Year and Preliminary 1996 estimates.

Thus continues the decade-long record: whatever drug the drug war touches turns into an epidemic. Once again, lies would have to be told. The "success" lies in the fact that "the rate of increase appears to be slowing, officials said."[91]

McCaffrey can't be the first drug czar to rely on the abiding tameness of the Washington press corps. The *Los Angeles Times* story, typical of coverage, began: "In another sign of progress in the war on substance abuse, the number of drug-related visits to hospital emergency rooms across the country has fallen for the first time in the 1990s, federal health officials announced."

Since the Office of Drug Control Policy was established in 1989, drug abuse deaths and hospitalizations have skyrocketed. The only function of the office, from mid-ranking prevaricator William Bennett to four-star distortionist McCaffrey, is to enable the White House to squander tax dollars lying to the public. McCaffrey has taken lying to a level that can only be called surreal.

In July 1998, the general junketed to Amsterdam for the sole purpose of pronouncing Dutch drug reforms an "unmitigated disaster." He issued the whopper that because of decriminalized marijuana and heroin needle exchanges, "the murder rate in Holland is double that of the United States" and "the overall crime rate in Holland is probably 40 percent higher than the United States'. That's [because of] drugs."[92] Mind boggling. For the most recent comparable year, 1995, the United Nations' 1996 *Demographic Yearbook* reported 193 homicides in Holland versus 25,100 in the United States. America's per capita murder rate is eight times higher than The Netherlands'.

Let us assume McCaffrey's mistake was understandable. The general said he got the numbers from Interpol, the international crime statistics gathering agency—which, by the way, firmly warns at the beginning of each edition of *International Crime Statistics* against using its figures to compare different countries with different notions of defining and tabulating crimes. If he missed that prominent caveat, it might be expected that McCaffrey and staff didn't notice Interpol's footnote pointing out that Holland's statistics include "attempted murder" (that is, what we call "aggravated assault") in its homicide figures while the U.S. numbers separate out attempted murders from actual murders. Aggravated assaults are many times more common than actual murders. So that's why Holland's raw numbers looked larger.

The U.S. Bureau of Justice Statistics in its highly informative *International Crime Rates* found that when statistics are adjusted to be reasonably comparable, U.S. rates of violent crime (homicide, rape, and robbery) are four to seven times higher than in Europe. Rates for major property crimes (burglary, theft, and motor vehicle theft) are more than twice as high in the U.S. as in Holland. The Netherlands ranks near the bottom for violent crime and near the middle by European standards for property crime.[93]

Now that that's cleared up, back to the philosophical matter. McCaffrey claimed Holland's murder rate was double that of the U.S. because of Holland's liberal drug policy. In fact, as noted, the reverse is true: America's murder, violent, and property crime rates are several times higher than those of Holland. By his own logic ("that's drugs"), shouldn't America's crime glut be blamed on America's *illiberal* drug policy?

But McCaffrey's real concern was not homicide or crime or drug woes, but availing a forum for falsification. He further claimed Dutch drug-related deaths had dramatically increased since 1978. Another lie. WHO statistics showed Dutch drug overdose and poisoning deaths declined steadily from 92 in 1978 to 60 in 1994. During that same period, U.S. drug deaths doubled from 4,500 to nearly 9,000, reaching a per-person rate 10 times higher than Holland's. Fortunately, the Dutch government was outraged at McCaffrey's fabrications and called in the American ambassador to complain, leading McCaffrey to back off.[94] Again, after that clarification, we return to the philosophical question the general himself raised: if drug policy causes drug death, doesn't the Netherlands' drug-death *decline* prove its policy's merits, and doesn't the U.S.'s drug-death leap suggest McCaffrey's drug war is (to pull a phrase out of the air) an "unmitigated disaster"?

While McCaffrey backed off his more idiotic claims about Dutch crime, he bounced back with another invention in a syndicated column following his D-Day in reverse. "The percentage of Dutch 18-year-olds who tried pot rose from 15 percent to 34 percent from 1984 to 1992," he declared. "...By contrast, in 1992 teenage use of marijuana in the United States was estimated at 10.6 percent."[95]

Now this is a flat lie. McCaffrey may be hazy on the nuances of Interpol stats and most everything else, but he lives and breathes drug surveys. The Dutch figure he cites is contradicted by studies in that country,[96] the U.S. figure he cites appears in no major survey I can find, and McCaffrey knew the comparison was fraudulent on its face. The Youth Risk Behavior Surveillance and Monitoring the Future surveys of U.S. high school seniors in 1992 showed 33 to 40 percent had tried marijuana.[97] McCaffrey himself had only months earlier, for the opposite expediency, deplored U.S. teen marijuana use as "exploding." Dishonesty, L.A. *Times* columnist Robert Scheer pointed out, is a crucial strategy for officials who know "the war will never be won with honest statistics."[98]

The most appalling aspect is McCaffrey's and Califano's incessantly claimed mega-concerns about the welfare of "young people." Well, then, they ought to be damned impressed with the Dutch record on "young people" after nearly two decades' experience with drug reforms: 35 homicides and 12 drug/poisoning deaths in 1995 among 15–24 year-olds. The comparable U.S. figures: 7,323 and 640, per-capita rates 10 times higher than among Netherlands teens and young adults.

McCaffrey and Califano don't care about "young people." They and other drug warriors aren't interested in success in terms of reducing drug abuse; none of their goals include that result. McCaffrey's promotion of ever-more ineffective, counter-productive policies is not due to dark conspiracy so much as natural gravitation. Drug-war interests profit from high rates of drug malaise. Their very survival is threatened by genuine success such as indicated in The Netherlands' low numbers. The drug war vilifies the younger generation not because young people display high rates of drug abuse, but because they don't. It counts on the quietude of the media, whose own car has now been hooked up to the gravy train via a promised, billion-dollar anti-drug ad campaign. It counts on maddeningly foolish attitudes such as those the American public expressed toward the war on Vietnam and now the war on drugs—the battle is wrong, destructive, and pointless, but let's escalate until a few hundred thousand more casualties accrue.

4 Myth: Teens Are Drunken Killers

Instead of confronting the rampant falsehoods spread about teenagers by anti-drug warriors, liberal and leftist groups just as stridently rejoin: teens have even worse problems with alcohol and tobacco. In response to the corporate collusion between *ABC News* and the Partnership for a Drug-Free America to spend the month of March 1997 hyperventilating over teenagers and pot, a coalition of liberals and leftists urged more airtime for "the devastating impact of alcohol and tobacco use by teens."[1]

Making teenagers into national symbols of alcohol, nicotine, *and* drug abuse is dandy for buffing the morals images of leftist groups. It's rotten for the image of America's young people. Nor is it fair or true. The truth is that teenagers have fewer problems with tobacco, alcohol, *or* drugs than adults do.

Progressive groups such as Communications Works have a legitimate beef with the egregious failure of the Partnership for a Drug-Free America to include legal drugs in its campaign. The Partnership is not an anti-drug group. It was created to *protect* the hawkers of legal dope—the booze, tobacco, and pharmaceutical firms—from suffering profit loss due to anti-drug hysteria.

The Marin Institute reported that in 1991, the Partnership for a Drug-Free America received $150,000 each in donations from Philip Morris (Miller beer, Marlboro and Virginia Slims cigarettes), Anheuser-Busch (Budweiser, Michelob, Bud Light, Natural Light, Busch beers), and R.J. Reynolds (Winston, Salem, Camel cigarettes); $120,000 from Proctor & Gamble (Vicks, Pepto-Bismol, other pharmaceuticals); $110,000 from Bristol-Meyers Squibb (Bufferin, Comtrex, Excedrin); and $100,000 from American Brands (Jim Beam whisky), among others.[2]

The Partnership collected hundreds of thousands of dollars from whisky, beer, cigarette, and pharmaceutical industries, whose products are implicated in hundreds of thousands of deaths annually. After exposure, the Partnership decided it would no longer take booze and tobacco bucks.

Partnership president Tom Hedrick revealed the philosophy legal-drug interests bought with their baksheesh. Hedrick flatly labeled anyone who dared to implicate alcohol as a drug problem a "prohibitionist." Anyone who questioned the dangers of marijuana was a "legalizer." Mixing the alcohol and illegal drug issues was "too complicated," Hedrick told Amherst professor David Buchanan and University of California professor Lawrence Wallack.

(Alcohol and drugs are not too complicated for illegal drug users to mix themselves. The Drug Abuse Warning Network's 1995 survey of 145 urban coroners found 3,600 of the 9,200 drug-stuffed corpses also had booze in their bloodstreams.)[3]

Just keep that "message" simple, Hedrick told Wallack and Buchanan:

> The thought of reducing poverty, improving schools, strengthening families, and providing programs to enhance students' social and academic skills was both infeasible and misguided...The two most important things (to the Partnership) are to tell kids to "stay in school" and "stay off drugs."[4]

The Partnership spent $2 billion doing just that over the last decade. It now complains of rising heroin and drug epidemics among kids, worse than ever. Such thinking demands strong rebuttal. Instead, the left (see Chapter 8) has avoided the larger implications and joined the attack on adolescents.

Frequently quoted by liberal lobbies are an American Medical Association study which claimed that drunk driving occurs 14,000 times per hour, with drivers under the legal drinking age of 21 accounting for one-twelfth of the cases, and a 1994 study of youthful "binge" drinking by Harvard University's Henry Wechsler.[5]

The AMA study really shows how many adult drivers over age 21, who account for eleven-twelfths of drunk driving, abuse their privilege to drink. Drinker for drinker, adults are much more likely to cause drunken highway (and personal) tragedy than teenagers are. As will be shown, drunken adults kill a lot of kids as well. "It seems that when push comes to shove," writes author and youth advocate Lucia Hodgson, "despite all of our hand-wringing about children's welfare, we are much more concerned with adult privileges, such as unfettered profit and unfettered pleasure."[6]

As I am writing this, Adam Carolla, co-host of the nationally syndicated radio show *Loveline*, on in the background, is advising a 17-year-old caller outraged that his just-say-no parents have pot stashed in their closet. Of course the hypocrisy is troubling, Carolla says. But it's okay for adults to drink or smoke pot and at the same time tell their 17-year-old "children" to abstain. Co-host Dr. Drew Pinsky agrees, but demurs that parents' habits get picked up by their kids.[7] Later, they are hollering about underage drinking.

Loveline, MTV- and radio-syndicated and the brightest of the mushrooming crop of sexfotainment talk shows, features a comedian and physician. Both reflexively convert nearly every caller problem into a flaw inherent to young age. Naturally, the show gets a boatload of calls from adolescents with low self-esteem. What strikes me as the biggest thing lost on the co-hosts is that the teenagers are the ones calling—not the raft of grownups whose violence, addiction, sexual abuses, abandoning, and psychotic behaviors caused the problems prompting the agonized calls. With mint Clinton-era logic-of-convenience transferring the obligations of "personal responsibility" from old to young, the hosts place the onus on young people not to breed more psychopaths of the type that previously got to them, rather than admonishing older people to quit abusing younger ones. The hosts advocates sweeping government-mandated restraints on teenagers solely because of their age.

There is a predictable quality to '90s moralizing: the moralist's outrage isn't directed at defending virtue as a rule, but at his own brand of sin which purportedly is being repressed. Sure enough, it comes out: Carolla (who ceaselessly demands that mothers on welfare and crack addicts be forced to use the contraceptive Norplant) is furious that recent California laws doused his "right" to smoke cigarettes in restaurants and other public places—that is, his privilege to force unwilling nonsmokers, including children, pregnant women, the elderly, and asthmatics, to consume his nicotine fumes. Seven in ten Californians have told surveyors they do not want to be subjected to tobacco smoke in public places, but this has not deterred nicotine addicts from lighting up in mass personal indulgence over the years, which is why a law now bans their derelictions. On the show, Pinsky, a physician and "addiction medicine specialist" whose selective citations of addiction research do not include the stack showing bad effects from secondhand smoke (see Chapter 5), ridicules those concerned about the health effects of passive smoking.

Given the well-documented health damage caused to fetuses and children by parents' smoking, all smokers should be vasectomized or Norplanted as well under Carolla's regime—but don't bet on hearing that. Carolla's radio personage also brags about his frequent intoxicated public indiscretions. Evidently, his attitudes and behavior demonstrate the greater maturity of grownups to handle alcohol, tobacco, and other rights. This common philosophy, hardly unique to *Loveline*, goes a long way toward explaining America's tragic alcohol, drug, nicotine and violence toll, as statistics below demonstrate.

I have the 1996 California Highway Patrol report open. I am inspired by the radio commentary to reproduce the page on drunk driving injuries and deaths (Table 1). When adults rail against the unacceptable perils of teenage drinking, I ask them to find their own ages on the Highway Patrol alcohol casualty tabulation.

Sixteen-year-old drinkers have about the same number of drunken crashes as 53-year-old drinkers. Age 17 boozing is safer than age 47 indulgence. Bottoms up at 18 less perilous than tippling at 40. Nineteen safer than 28. Carolla, age 34, is 2.5 times the statistical menace of a 17-year-old. Pinsky, age 38, is a tad safer at merely double. In addition, the conservative doctor proudly admits being hell on wheels sober, burning rubber and tearing up the freeways. In its most recent report, the National Highway Traffic Safety Administration estimated that speeding kills 13,000 people (thousands of times more than the marijuana, LSD, and other hallucinogens the doctor warns against), injures three-quarters of a million people, and costs society $29 billion every year[8] (more even than the highest, most biased estimate of the cost of teenage mothers to society). And Carolla and Pinsky are indignant at the "denial" of others whose bad behaviors are munching up the hosts' hard-earned tax dollars.

One of the many inconvenient facts left out of the American Medical Association's splashy campaign against "underage drinking" entitled, "We've Got a Drinking Problem: Youth and Alcohol,"[9] is that a 45-year-old (the average age of doctors, a group with singularly high rates of addiction[10]) is considerably more likely to maim or kill in a drunken driving crash, and far more likely to overdose on alcohol, than a 17-year-old. This October, when I turn 48, I finally will be statistically safer from causing a drunken crash than a high school senior is. In another three years, President Clinton will be (statistically) less of a drunken motorway menace than the 16-year-old for whom he demands drug tests and "zero tolerance." Yet, an adult can troop into any licensed outlet and stagger out with enough Evercleer to pickle Godzilla. He (five-sixths of drunken killers and maimers are men) could do so even if he had 10 past drunken driving convictions as soon as he was off probation.

Table 1

Is your age safer with alcohol than 17-year-olds?
Ages of had-been-drinking drivers in fatal and injury collisions,
California, 1996

Age	Total	Fatal	Age	Total	Fatal	Age	Total	Fatal
0–14	19	0	34	634	26	54	157	3
15	39	4	35	620	28	55	130	4
16	138	6	36	622	27	56	115	4
17	263	16	37	545	21	57	119	9
18	494	16	38	589	33	58	84	3
19	642	28	39	508	10	59	86	6
20	660	36	40	517	20	60–64	354	16
21	851	48	41	511	22	65–69	265	11
22	862	48	42	420	23	70–74	159	12
23	828	31	43	400	15	75–79	110	3
24	768	35	44	350	17	80–84	45	2
25	819	32	45	363	19	85–89	7	0
26	778	31	46	321	9	90+	10	0
27	697	37	47	276	20			
28	667	32	48	252	10	**Unstated Ages:**		
29	623	31	49	268	15		701	7
30	602	20	50	204	8	**Total:**		
31	630	27	51	171	11		21,959	953
32	639	27	52	190	7			
33	674	20	53	163	7			

Source: California Highway Patrol (1997). *Annual Report of Fatal and Injury Motor Vehicle Traffic Collisions*. Sacramento, CA: Department of Justice, Table 5J.

He can drink a sixpack, or five shots of whisky, in two hours and drive home barely legal, knowing that California's lenient 0.08 percent blood-alcohol standard applied to adult drunk driving—which is stricter than most states' 0.10 percent—would not subject him to arrest. No matter that intoxicated adult drivers with blood alcohol levels within the legal limit kill 3,000 people on the motorways every year.

U.S. figures are less detailed but similar to California's (Table 2). Drivers ages 21–44 are more hazardous than 16–20 year-olds. Men as a group are 60 percent deadlier than teenagers.

Yet many high schools now mandate expulsion, revocation of extra-curricular privileges, and denial of a diploma if a high school senior with no history of drink-

Table 2

**Nationally as well, adults up to age 45 are
more dangerous with booze than teens are**

U.S. drunken driving crashes by age of intoxicated driver or pedestrian, 1996

Age	Drivers	Pedestrians	Total	Rate/100,000*
16–20	1,100	100	1,200	6.7
21–24	1,670	130	1,800	13.2
25–34	3,370	420	3,790	9.6
35–44	2,390	470	2,860	6.8
45–64	1,540	420	1,960	3.7
65+	350	130	480	1.6
Unstated	260	60	320	—
Men	8,820	na		10.8
Women	1,640	na		1.9
Total	10,680	1,730	12,410	6.2

*'Unstated' pro-rated to all groups. Over 65 is 65–84. Total is divided by population ages 16–84.
Source: National Highway Safety Administration (1997). *Traffic Safety Facts 1996*. Washington: U.S. Department of Transportation, Tables 3, 5.

ing problems gets caught taking a swallow of a lite beer (or even being at a gathering where someone else drank). This is on top of the fines, community service, and mandated counseling the law dishes out under "zero tolerance" and "zero-zero" and "not one drop" standards for underage drinking.

Highway safety officials have masked this greater adult drunk driving risk by switching the measure. Accidents per mile driven and per driver are often cited. Accidents per mile driven is an absurd measure of drunk driving. Since what it actually means is "accidents per mile driven drunk," such a measure would rate a driver who drove drunk 1,000 miles per year and had 100 wrecks as safer than one who drove drunk one mile per year and had one wreck. Accidents per licensed driver is also inadequate. A 1990 California Department of Transportation study found that unlicensed drivers accounted for a whopping 40 percent of fatal, drunken driving, and other felony crashes.[11] In addition, one in seven drunken traffic deaths involve intoxicated pedestrians. Therefore, the total number of drivers (licensed and unlicensed) and pedestrians at risk for each age group is better estimated by the total population than just licensed drivers.

Greater teenage responsibility with alcohol is not the result of banning and punishing teenage drinking. Underage Prohibition is a joke. Teens age 17–18 drink as often as adults do: about 50 percent of teenagers in a given month,[12] the same as 30- and 40-agers.[13] As noted in Chapter 3, teen drinkers frequently party with adults over age 30.[14]

Table 3

Binge drinking is a far bigger problem among grownups than teens

Percent reporting "binge" drinking in past month:

	1985	1990	1992	1994	1996
Age 12–17	21.9	15.4	10.0	8.3	7.2
Age 18–25	34.4	29.5	29.9	33.6	32.0
Age 26–34	27.5	21.1	22.8	24.0	22.8
Age 35+	12.9	8.0	9.0	11.8	11.3

Source: Substance Abuse and Mental Health Services Administration (1997). *National Household Survey on Drug Abuse 1996*. Preliminary estimates. Rockville, MD: U.S. Department of Health and Human Services, Table 121B.

Wechsler's survey of 17,000 college students in 1993 found that what he called "binge drinking"—downing five or more (men) or four or more (women) drinks on one occasion in the previous two weeks—is prevalent among young people. In the previous month, 44 percent of college students qualified as binge drinkers. By the same standard, 32 percent of college students were binge drinkers in high school. Interestingly, high school and college binge drinkers usually were not the same people. Six in 10 binge drinkers either did so in college or high school, but not both.

Yet teenagers are far less likely to suffer serious consequences from alcohol use, such as drunken driving injury or death, or overdose fatality, than are grownups—at least, up to age 50. Wechsler found binge drinking rates similar among students ages 18–20 as among 21 to 23. Yet the statistics indicate older bingers are twice as likely to overdose or to get into a bad drunk-driving wreck than younger ones.

Wechsler's responses were from a mailed survey, which means that those more interested in the subject of drinking might have been more likely to respond. There are also serious questions about the reliability of self-reports to any survey, including the more scientifically administered National Household Survey on Drug Abuse. The 1996 Household Survey found binge drinking among youths lower, and declining faster, than among grownups (Table 3). This is, of course, why no interest groups cite it.

Maybe the Partnership for a Drug-Free America should keep on evading the alcohol issue. Teenage trends seem healthier for the drugs it ignores. But as with illegal drugs, it's adults who are having trouble giving up the party pounding.

That may be a big reason why drunken adults kill more people. And themselves. Every year, nationwide, around a dozen young people in their teens or early 20s die from alcohol overdose (Table 4). Press sensation is guaranteed. However, among persons over 25, 150 to 200 die from binge drinking every year. We don't hear about those.

To the press, Wechsler indulges in the classic 1990s non-sequitur: "The number of adult drinkers has declined, but the number of binge drinkers in college has stayed really strongly the same."[15] This mixes incompatible "alcohol use" with

Table 4

Adults are more at risk of alcohol overdose and drug-alcohol excesses

Annual U.S. alcohol overdose deaths and drug-alcohol deaths (1995)

Ages	Drug/alcohol combination	Alcohol o.d.	Rate/100,000
12–17	13	4	0.1
18–19	52	7	0.9
20–25	248	14	1.2
26–34	937	43	2.6
35–54	2,161	187	3.2
55–older	188	63	0.8
Total	3,613	318	

Source: National Center for Health Statistics (1997). U.S. Mortality Detail File (electronic), 1995; SAMSHA (1997). *Drug Abuse Warning Network Annual Medical Examiner Data 1995.* Rockville, MD: U.S. Department of Health and Human Serivces.

"binge drinking" surveys. The same surveys Wechsler cites also show that the number of teenage and college-age drinkers has declined. They also show (Table 3) that adult binge drinking has stayed the same or risen.

Figures showing teenage moderation, or challenging conventional notions, are not cited by anyone. For example, the 1995 Monitoring the Future survey reports that four- fifths of high school seniors (the heaviest-drinking age in high school) do not get drunk even as often as once every two months. Half do not get drunk at all. Fewer than one in 10 gets drunk as often as once a week. In fact, two-thirds have been drunk fewer than a half dozen times in their entire lives. High school seniors were more likely to drink with people over 30 than on dates (excluding those dating people over 30). They were six times more likely to drink at home than at school.[16]

More important than how people *say* they drink, cold-slab statistics show *a 40-year-old is three to four times more likely to die from alcohol overdose than an 18-year-old.* The higher adult risk is worsened by mixing booze with drugs (Table 4). This high death toll persists even though lots of overdrinking grownups are saved in hospital emergency rooms. Of the approximately 150,000 Americans treated in hospital emergency rooms for overdosing on alcohol combined with drugs every year:

- 3 percent are under age 18
- 18 percent are 18–25
- 36 percent are 26–34
- 31 percent are 35–44
- 9 percent are 45–54
- 3 percent are 55 or older.

The number of alcohol/drug emergencies in 1996 was triple that of 1980. So Dr. Wechsler is not being candid in his insinuation that adult alcohol abuse has declined—though that is certainly the preferred political stance.

So we are back to the same mystery seen for drugs. Teenagers drink as frequently as adults do. They apparently drink as heavily per occasion as adults do. (Of course, five drinks spaced over five hours have entirely different effects than five drinks slammed in five minutes, but the stereotype is that teenagers would be more likely to binge in the latter fashion.) Teenagers are less experienced with alcohol and less likely to know their personal limits. They are less experienced drivers. They are thought to have poorer judgment. All of these risk factors should add up to the teenage alcohol carnage everyone thinks is going on. Except that it isn't.

Why, then, are both the drinking individual and larger society *much* safer with a glass of booze in the hand of a 17-year-old than in the hand of a 40-year-old?

The reason for the greater teenage safety with alcohol is that teenagers appear to practice more responsible drinking. Teenagers are less likely to drive after drinking. Adolescents drink milder beverages—beer (6.4 percent ethanol by content), lite beer (1.5 percent), and wine coolers (5 to 6 percent). For 20 years I have heard alcohol program types wail in horrified tones: "3.2 [percent] beer is the alcoholic drink of choice among teenagers!" Would they feel better if kids drank more Jim Beam and Cutty (43 percent ethanol content), like their elders?

Excuses can be made for the higher adult drinking risk. It may be argued that teenagers "localize" their drinking in safer private settings because they are subject to arrest for public boozing. A youth who's had a few may flop on a basement couch to sleep it off. The need to hide drinking from parents may promote extra teenage caution. However, an adult may find himself in a bar at 2 a.m. and decide to chance the drive home.

But the conclusion from this logic would be to shift the focus away from teens and toward policing adults, such as requiring "zero tolerance" for adult drinking and driving or banning public drinking by adults altogether. Not a chance. Saving some of the 15,000 lives (including the hundreds of kids) killed by drunken grownup drivers every year is clearly not worth the inconvenience, if I read correctly the thundering silence of the press, legislators, and president.

In any case, it's the adult drinking carnage that liberal drug and media reform lobbies concerned about the public health and safety menace of the alcohol industry (see Chapter 8) should be pounding the podium about. Put down the scotches first.

Using "Teenage Drinking" to Deny the Adult Problem

As with drugs and crime, quick and painless solutions are sought. The National Highway Traffic Safety Administration estimates that "minimum drinking age laws have saved 16,513 lives since 1975." This would be astonishing if it weren't absurd. This number is equivalent to the elimination of 14 years of alcohol-related fatalities among 18–20 year-olds at 1996 levels, based in turn on drastic exaggeration of the 1987 Insurance Institute for Highway Safety study it is supposedly based on.[17] Further, the NHTSA ignored Rutgers University studies indicating that the only accomplishment achieved by raising drinking ages from 18 or

19 to 21 was shifting a few fatalities from the 18–20 to the 21–24 age group.[18] In fact, the Insurance Institute based its estimate of "lives saved" by the 21 drinking age on *comparing* crashes involving 18–20 year-olds with those involving 21–24 year-olds. So if the latter group was adversely affected, it would make the former group appear safer in comparison. Overall, wrote Rutgers economists Peter Asch and David Levy after extensive analysis, the "minimum legal drinking age is not a significant—or even a perceptible—factor in the fatality experience of all drivers or of young drivers."

The Insurance Institute study on which present claims about the effects of raising the drinking age to 21 are based is now a dozen years out of date. Reexamination of the effects of raising the drinking age, using data through 1995, substantiate Asch and Levy's findings that all that was accomplished by setting a higher drinking age was transferring deaths from 18-year-olds to 21-year-olds—with a slight increase in the loss of life. This reexamination also reveals how serious flaws in earlier drinking-age studies led to erroneous conclusions—and why the chimerical "16,000 lives saved" by the 21 drinking age, claimed by national officials, are nowhere to be found in real-death statistics.

The first mistake drinking age studies made was to compare death statistics for 18–20-year-olds with those of adults in their early 20s. Since raising the drinking age increases deaths among adults in their early 20s, teenage deaths would appear to decline in comparison. To be valid, the comparison, or "control," group must be unaffected by the factor being examined. That is not true of 21–24 year-olds. Thus, a more appropriate comparison group—in the re-analysis below, ages 25–49, should be substituted.

The second mistake was to analyze only drunken driving crashes, as measured by traffic accidents that occur at night. True, nighttime fatal accidents are several times more likely to involve drinking than daytime ones. But, suppose that barring teenagers from bars resulted in more teenage drinking during daytime hours. Further, suppose that raising the drinking age reduces drunken driving by teens but has no effect, or even increases, teenage deaths from other violent causes often associated with alcohol, such as drownings, falls, suicides, or homicides. The only way to analyze whether, overall, raising the drinking age to 21 is a good idea or not is to examine all forms of teenage deaths which are related to drinking compared to similar deaths among adults who are too old to be affected by changes in the drinking age—that is, those over age 25.

Using this method, let us examine the starkest comparison possible. Consider the modern sequence of teenage drinking laws:

- In 1968-71, New York and Louisiana allowed liquor, and nine other states permitted beer drinking by teens. A couple of small states had drinking ages of 19 or 20. All others had drinking ages of 21.

- In the early 1970s, 24 states reduced their drinking ages, usually to 18.

- When the dust settled, by the 1974–78 period, 28 states allowed their 18-year-olds to drink beer, and most hard liquor. In 12 states, the drinking age remained 21. The remainder had drinking ages of 19 or 20.

- From 1978 to 1989, all states raised their legal drinking ages to 21.

- By 1990–94, the drinking age was 21 in all states, which meant that none allowed 18–20-year-olds to drink lawfully.

This massive enfranchisement followed by massive disenfranchisement of some five million young people ages 18–20 should have marked effects on behavior. Since a large share of violent deaths—accidents, suicides, and homicides—involve alcohol, this has been the most studied effect.

Studied how? While the public image has been one of masses of sotted youth causing artery-spurting motorway crashes and other carnage, in fact the effects turned out to be so subtle that intricate computer studies were required to find it.

What happened was most mysterious. The biggest effect of mass-legalized followed by zero-tolerance-outlawed teen drinking was that not much happened. The effect of lower drinking is to raise (slightly) the rate of violent deaths among teens ages 16–18 while reducing them among adults ages 21–24. Nineteen- and 20-year-olds are not much affected, since they drink as they wish under either scheme (Table 5).

The larger point is that no one cares. The purpose of the NHTSA's "16,000 lives saved" was to generate a sound-bite number that could be endlessly recycled in the press whenever legal drinking ages arise. Obsession with teenage drinking is a key factor in denying the adult problem, which in turn is crucial to maintaining lenient standards for adult alcohol use. The same adult society which demands "zero tolerance" for teenage drinking allows grownups to drive while severely drunk.

Table 5

The 21 drinking age: slightly fewer deaths among 16–18 year-olds, slightly more among 20-agers

Net rate of violent deaths

	Age 16–18	19–20	21–23
1971–74: drinking ages reduced from 21 to 18/19			
Change in death rates, 1975–78 vs. 1968–71	+3.1%	+4.7%	-1.7%
1978–89: drinking ages raised from 18/19 to 21			
Change in death rates, 1990–95 vs. 1975–78	-1.2%	+1.0%	+5.2%

Note: Violent deaths are those from motor vehicle accidents, other accidents, suicide, homicide, and deaths undetermined as to intent. From 1971 to 1974, states lowered drinking ages, usually from 21 to 18. From 1975 to 1990, states raised drinking ages to 21. Compared are the 1968–71, 1975–78, and 1990–95 periods, when drinking ages were stable. The 27 states which lowered, then raised, their drinking ages are compared to the 12 states which maintained drinking ages of 21 for the entire 1968–95 period. For both sets of states, drivers ages 25–49 are used as a control group to factor out other influences, such as changes in state drunk driving or other safety laws aimed at all age groups so as to isolate the effects of drinking age changes aimed only at youths. The "net rate" thus refers to the rate of violent deaths among the affected age groups versus those ages 25–49 for states which reduced their drinking ages from 1971 to 1974 and then raised them from 1979 to 1989, versus the same net rates for states which maintained constant drinking ages of 21 throughout the period.

Sources: National Center for Health Statistics, U.S. Mortality Detail File (annual, 1968–95); U.S. Bureau of the Census, census and intercensal estimates of populations by state and age (annual); Fatal Accident Reporting System, Traffic Fatality Data 1975–94.

Lenient American laws permit adults to drive while twice as drunk (blood alcohol contents of 0.08 to 0.10 percent) as those of other Western nations (typically 0.05 percent). In March 1998, the president and Senate endorsed legislation to pressure states to toughen the legal drunk driving limit to 0.08 blood alcohol percent.[19] The logic: drunken adult drivers with blood alcohol saturations below the lax legal limit murder some 3,000 people every year. That's twice as many as are killed by juveniles with guns.

But at the urging of the alcohol and tavern lobbies, the Republican House jettisoned the measure on April Fool's Eve. The bill wound up only suggesting that states enact the change. Even a primitive attempt to bring the U.S. into mainstream Western standards by demanding minimal responsibility from adult drinkers proved too much for the Republican paragons of virtue and zero-tolerance drug punishment. Nor did the liberals and cultural leftists obsessed with alcohol ads and teenage drinking rally to a bill asking modest life-saving restraint among grownup drinkers. America continues to have virtually no constituency for effective European alcohol control, which focuses on preventing damage from alcohol abuse, not chasing around "underage" drinkers.

The American notion that bad adult behavior is tolerable so long as parents and police enforce absolute purity on adolescents goes with today's epidemic of bad adult behavior and the denial thereof. It is a relatively new attitude, one not found (at least, not so openly celebrated) in past decades. Reviews of surveys reveal that contrary to the repeated modern hype that "children are drinking at younger and younger ages," American teenagers began drinking in the 1950s and '60s[20] at about the same ages (12) and drank as much as teens do today.[21] But authorities in past decades had a much more integrated view of teenage and adult drinking. They noted that kids tended to drink in the same way as adults;[22] hard-drinking youths tended to come from families with heavy-boozing parents.[23]

Viewed benignly, perhaps absolutist "zero tolerance" standards applied to teenage behaviors stem from a genuine concern about the dangers of alcohol and a protective concern for youths. But if that is the case, it is curious that the media and authorities shrug off adult drinking that endangers and kills even more young people.

All Fatalities Are Not Created Equal

The Los Angeles press and alcohol program officials endlessly headlined, analyzed, featured, re-headlined, re-analyzed, and re-featured a 1995 desert rollover in which a drunken Orange County 17-year-old driver killed four classmates. Television documentaries, conferences on "teenage drinking," newsmagazine features..."The Accident" as it came to be called, still generates front-page commentary.[24] It doesn't occur to commentators that if such events were common among teenagers, they wouldn't have to keep citing the same three-year-old accident over and over.

More telling, in the months surrounding the above teen tragedy, three drunken adult drivers caused smashups in Orange and adjacent Riverside counties that killed 18 people, including 10 children and teens. A 35-year-old driver killed a family of eight; a 53-year-old driver killed a family of six; a 56-year-old driver killed four. These are not isolated instances. Eight major drunken driving crashes killing 14 young people ages 10 to 20 were reported in the Los Angeles and Orange County press, according to my cataloguing of the first six months of 1997 *Los Angeles Times* articles which concern youth. The drunken drivers at fault in these accidents that killed youths were as follows: two aged 17, and one each aged 22, 30, 35, 46, 49, and 56.

Reaction to adult booze bloodbaths was entirely different. Most were out of the papers in a day or two. There was no mass-assignment of "collective guilt" to the entire adult age group, no demands for mass restrictions on adult driving or adult drinking. Even though the bloodiest hours for drunken wrecks are right after taverns' weekend closing times, the sheriff did not propose to post plainclothes "cops in bars" to prevent intoxicated adults from driving to match his much-touted "cops in shops" program aimed at stopping teens from buying hooch. No demands that lawmakers enforce a zero-tolerance standard on adult drinking and driving "to save lives," as is applied to teens.

Two-Fisted Hypocrisy

A couple of years ago, Hugh Johnson, author of the bestselling *The World Atlas of Wine* and *Encyclopedia of Wine*, issued a "deadly serious message" at a symposium in Chicago. It is time, he told a ritzy dinner, that Americans get realistic and start exposing their kids to alcohol at a young age in order to "demystify" it.

Fortunately, Knight-Ridder reporter Christopher Cook was covering the event:

> The audience, all people in the wine trade and wine lovers, went dead silent. Johnson might as well have suggested that incest be legalized.[25]

This tongue-clucking shock by wine-pushers themselves, no doubt indulging in their own product at the "gala dinner," speaks volumes as to why Americans of all ages display the worst alcohol problems of any Western nation.

British, Italian, and Spanish teens drink much more freely than American teens. French youths can buy alcohol at 14, Germans at 16.[26] According to American experts, adolescents given free access to booze should be inebriated killers. Yet European teens display far fewer drinking problems than American teens and American adults. Continued Cook:

> In Europe, where most alcohol is incorporated with food and children generally get the two together as soon as they can sit at the table, the teen use of alcohol is vastly different...
>
> I grew up in a household of seven children in the south of France. Red wine was served at dinner every night. Our places at the table were marked by how deep the red wine in the glass was.
>
> As the oldest, I was allowed one full-strength glass of wine with dinner once I was 9 years old.
>
> For the younger kids, the glass was cut more and more with water, so that the 4-year-old got a glass of one-quarter wine, three-quarters water.

> In my teens, I never saw much attraction to getting drunk. It never
> really made much sense.

Indeed, Cook first encountered drunkenness among Americans.

In working in drug and alcohol and various youth programs during the 1980s, I saw far too much of America's bitter attack on "teenage drinking" in order to excuse lax standards for grownups. Those who insisted on zero-tolerance for teenage alcohol use, including all manner of policings and punishments, usually were not prohibitionists. They were comprised of individuals whose politics were quite liberal as a rule and who were frequently seen in bars.

In an egregious example of alcohol irresponsibility, one youth program had held a fundraiser at which free champagne led to mass adult drunkenness. As the event's "designated driver," I soberly beheld some of the community's leading lights well lit, some falling into the pool, getting sick, lying passed out on tables, insisting on driving themselves, the whole edifying trip. This occurred in front of the program's kids ages 11–15 who volunteered to wait tables and many of whom, it turned out, were simultaneously getting in the same smashed "adult" condition. This youth program's board responded to the problem not by instituting strict alcohol controls to prevent drunkenness (patron drunkenness, in fact, was used to lubricate fund raising), but by banning youths from future fundraising events.

Americans' lenience even toward extreme cases of adult over-drinking is constantly illustrated. For example, at a posh 1998 New Year's Eve fundraiser for Chicago's "world class" Field Museum of Natural History, 1,300 "society folk" who paid from $125 to $2,500 per ticket "to dine and dance with royalty" rioted after downing too much booze, the *Chicago Tribune* reported. The reasons? Not enough bartenders. Not enough free drinks. Mistaken beliefs by partiers that all would personally get to hang out with Chicago Bulls star Dennis Rodman. Not enough hors d'oeuvres. A band didn't show. Chicago's grownup elite consoled itself with hootch. "People were throwing up all over the place," said one. Rowdy behavior was rampant, including injuries and broken bones. "Partygoers stormed into the check room." Fights ensued, then police responded. Imagine the extreme, zero-tolerance "personal responsibility" reactions such a scene would have attracted if it involved teenagers. All Chicago's upscale-drunk riot caused was an embarrassing newspaper story (which largely blamed "understaffed" promoters, not violent Arthurs) and a distinguished museum whose "reputation was bruised."[27]

In another example, I watched a local high school administration and school board lecture high school seniors to abstain from drinking alcohol, with 90-day suspensions for drinking even "one drop," because seniors are "role models" for younger students. Having sent the message, administrators and board members retired to a nearby restaurant, ordered stiff drinks, and got bombed and boisterous in front of the junior high kids who worked in the kitchen. I could see why the town needed 17-year-olds to be role models for children.

These attitudes were by no means monolithic. The town's chief drug/alcohol counselor, a serene recovering alcoholic, had a radar for abuse but was tolerant of alcohol use by persons regardless of age. Many parents worked out ways for their kids to learn to drink in reasonably safe settings without stirring up the booze gestapo. But I learned important lessons. Those who are most frantic about any use of alcohol by adolescents have intimidated an entire society. Often this faction issues stridently puritanical assertions about drinking at the same time it tolerates, even promotes, irresponsible use of alcohol. That dangerous contradiction is maintained by strict silence and denial of real drinking practices.

Working with troubled families, and in drug and alcohol programs, I had plenty of occasion to go with youths and parents to Alcoholics Anonymous and Alateen meetings. It seemed to me that larger society's attitude toward teenage drinking resembled what AA calls a "dry drunk." A dry drunk rigidly and angrily condemns other people's drinking, even the tiniest amount, to cover up his own vulnerability to drunken relapse. Bizarre as it may seem, the most rabid anger was hurled not at drunkenness, but at any notion of responsible use of intoxicants—especially by teenagers, the age group in the best position to use alcohol in moderation at a stage of life when they are most able to learn restraint. It seemed to threaten the very adulthood of many grownups that a youth could handle alcohol as or more responsibly than they could. It is an attitude amply modeled in the rightist war against drugs and the leftist war against "underaged drinking."

Having decreed a not-one-drop prohibitionist standard on adolescents, dry-drunk logic then attempts to make teenage drinking as dangerous as possible. For example, parents who supervise parties where teenagers drink, or teenagers who serve as sober designated drivers for other youths, can be prosecuted and severely punished under state and local laws and school policies. Taxi drivers who provide "home free" rides to adult drunks ban teenagers from using their service. Schools which teach, or even discuss, responsible and moderate use of alcohol with students, as opposed to a strict absolute abstinence message, risk loss of federal funds provided for drug education. Despite exhaustive efforts to prevent teenagers from drinking, more than half the high school seniors and one-fourth of the eighth graders drink once a month or more, much the same as adults. Further, as the National Youth Rights Association points out, it would be unrealistic to expect them not to in a country "where drinking is considered an important part of everything from New Year's Eve to summer baseball."[28]

American adults seem to strenuously resist the idea that access to alcohol should be regulated according to individual ability to handle it, not prohibited or enfranchised en masse based on age alone. Any argument against teenage drinking can be made with equal force against adult drinking. Perhaps the wine industry's "silent shock" at the idea of any teenage imbibance was not puritanism. More likely, the wine sellers' reps were petrified at the potential threat to one of their biggest advertising points: drinking is an ADULT habit.

It is my hope that drug and alcohol reformers will stop exploiting the age issue and stop evading the addiction issue. Drinking ages and legal minimum ages in marijuana liberalization schemes are unwise for exactly the reason they are politically popular: they are lenient toward adult intoxicant abuse even as they severely criminalize the slightest teenage use. For the same reason, I hope that schemes to legalize marijuana for adults do not succeed. Age-based measures reinforce perpetuation of the dangerous American hypocrisy toward mood-altering substances.

There is no evidence that drugs and alcohol are any more dangerous for adolescents than for grownups. In societies in which adult drinking is moderate, adolescent drinking tends to be occasional and moderate. Children learn about drinking
from their parents, and children of alcoholics are many times more prone to abuse of
alcohol than average.[29]

The safest alcohol and drug control measures would permit use by those whose
patronage does not represent a hazard to society and crack down much more strongly than at present on those whose addiction and hazardous practices are a menace.
The most useful transitional reform is to legalize beer and wine purchase by
teenagers, including a return to the "3.2 bars" (which refers to the alcohol content
of beer) present in 10 states for decades prior to Congressionally mandated youth-
Prohibition in the 1980s, which statistics clearly show were not associated with
increased fatality. In fact, the traditional "3.2" states (Colorado, District of
Columbia, Kansas, Mississippi, North Carolina, Ohio, Oklahoma, South Carolina,
South Dakota, and Wisconsin) experienced sharply increased teenage deaths when
forced to raise their drinking ages to 21 in the late 1980s. Since Congress's mandate
for the 21 drinking age contains numerous loopholes—it does not apply to private
locations, and it requires that either sale of alcohol to or purchase of alcohol by persons under 21 (but not necessarily both) be prohibited, to cite two—states have
considerable room to experiment with more reasonable approaches than no-no-
no.[30]

Drinking age reform should be coupled with tougher European-style drunken
driving standards and licensing provisions restricting convicted alcohol abusers of
all ages from alcohol use. Absent proven hazard, decisions regarding drinking and
drugs should be for teens to make with their families, not police wielding arbitrary,
over-21-versus-under-21 laws.

Mass prohibition of teenagers is harmful. Mass enfranchisement of adults is
even more so. These are not a matters of age, but individuality. At present,
America's "double standard" sends a clear message to teens, one we're lucky most of
them are smart enough to reject: the more you drink, the more "adult" you are, and
the more adult you are, the lower the standards of behavior expected.

5 Myth: Teens Are Camel Clones

The degeneration of healthy reform groups once opposed to irresponsible alcohol and tobacco excess into vitriolic anti-youth campaigners corresponds to the declining effectiveness of these movements. In the 1970s and 1980s, groups fighting smoking and drunken driving won legislative victories, tough new laws, tax increases, public awareness, and large reductions in bad behavior. Not incidentally, refreshing questioning of American societal values supporting intoxicated excess and the corporate promotion thereof (in the name of "freedom") blossomed. I participated in anti-drunk-driving and tobacco-tax-raising groups, and it was a heady time. It was short-lived. The temptations of anti-youth sentiment in the 1980s and '90s diverted health campaigns into futile side alleys and provided unwitting relief for the industries they previously fought.

As the success of campaigns against drunken carnage and tobacco addiction mounted in the 1980s, they began to cut into industry profits and the "freedom" of powerful people (such as legislators) to indulge as they pleased. Resistance built. By the late 1980s, campaigns against adult drunkenness and smoking became risky. At this point, reform groups turned their fury on teenagers. Generalized anti-youth feeling and industry self-interest worked to take the focus off adults. In all cases, the switch to an anti-adolescent agenda (emphasizing exemption of even the worst adult alcohol and tobacco abuse in favor of strict focus on stopping all teenage smoking and drinking) won hearty official and industry endorsement. It was popular—and it fit perfectly into industry promotional strategies, as will be seen.

Only two problems intruded. One, age-based restrictions as a substitute for real health policy don't work. Two, in the Clinton era in which health promotion is secondary to exploiting health issues for political gain, it matters less and less whether it works.

Smoking is another sad example of this syndrome. In past decades, anti-smoking groups such as the American Medical Association were dedicated to the radical goal of a smoke-free society. The health coalition that commissioned me to lead a 1990 petition drive to raise Montana's cigarette tax by 25 cents wanted to end smoking, period. The titular head of the national movement was the Reagan administration's Surgeon General C. Everett Koop, who blasted the tobacco industry as "sleazy" and wanted nothing less than making smoking socially unacceptable.*

---

*A note to the smokers'-freedom lobby: "smokers' rights" to me means no more than any other legitimate right: that is, to practice the habit in a manner that does not harm or cost others. The vast majority of smokers, it seemed to me, had made the public practice of their habit unacceptable. Parents and adults knew their secondhand smoke harmed chil-

During the radical anti-smoking movement's heyday, the 1970s and '80s, smoking plummeted among all age groups. Then, in the Clinton presidency, the movement changed. The administration's relentless polling and focus group research (more than done by all previous presidencies combined) revealed that votes could be won from calculated exploitation of health issues. In particular, attitude research showed that while there were political risks in attacking smoking by grownups, an attack on teenage smoking was a guaranteed, risk-free strategy to pitch to key constituencies (i.e., the proverbial "soccer moms").

What has emerged by the mid-'90s is a new "anti-smoking" movement, one more opportunistically positioned to reap grant funding, media accolade, and political reward than to achieving a smoke-free society. Clinton officials berate the industry in public, but in private the goal is no longer eliminating smoking, but negotiating mutual benefit. The campaign has shifted away from attacking smoking as unacceptable and toward attacking teenagers as stupid risk-takers, pressured by evil peers, sheeplike slaves to industry advertising glitz, unworthy to even consider mature, adult pastimes such as...coffin nails and stogies.

Clinton (a cigar smoker) declared: "Adults are capable of deciding whether to smoke or not." He reiterated his acceptance of smoking as a permanent American fixture in his April 4, 1998, radio address on tobacco legislation: "We're not trying to put the tobacco companies out of business. We want to put them out of the business of selling cigarettes to kids." Since teen smoking is connected to whether adults in their lives smoke, Clinton's support of a continued tobacco presence in American adult life automatically supports tobacco use by youths, whatever his rhetoric to the contrary.

The new, politically-created goal, guaranteed to preserve the industry, is the plausible-sounding one of "preventing underage smoking before it starts." But this goal is pointless now that politics dictates that the real basis of teenage smoking— its continued social acceptability, as demonstrated by adult smoking and particularly by smoking parents—will not be confronted. Perhaps it is meant to be pointless.

Only in recent months have health lobbies become concerned that the biggest cheerleader for the get-tough campaign to "prevent smoking by children" is the

---

dren—it was obvious from the visible health effects on kids alone, as will be discussed later— and they didn't seem to care. I only met one adult in 15 years of working with kids who would so much as go outside to light up in order to protect children's health. I saw babies choking in blue-hazed trailers and houses, children with breathing difficulties, teenagers who couldn't compete in sports. I saw families in which buying grownups's smokes came before kids' food. I had been in restaurants, on planes, on trains, in bathrooms, in shared public facilities in which the heavy smoking of a few individuals who accepted no restraint and who made use and enjoyment of public places harder for the elderly, pregnant women, asthmatics—sometimes shutting them outside. Smokers themselves are fully to blame for the sweeping countermovement their indulgence brought down, and I only hope the day will arrive in which smokers are prohibited from forcing their habit on children in homes and other private locales as they are on adults in public ones. Finally, as a beer and wine drinker, I felt strict restrictions on alcohol use to prevent the damage drunkenness causes were fully appropriate, and I lobbied for tougher drunken driving laws and higher taxes on alcohol even though the price of my drink went up as well. The fraction of considerate smokers I knew were in favor of stronger restrictions on tobacco use—in fact, three of our 10 petition coordinators for higher tobacco taxes in Montana were smokers.

tobacco industry. Sounding an early alarm was Stanton Glantz, anti-smoking pio-
neer and America's premier tobacco industry document analyst. From the time an
anonymous Deep Cough in the industry dumped 10,000 pages of secret tobacco documents on his doorstep, the University of California, San Francisco medical professor has survived bitter industry attacks, lawsuits, even legislation designed personally to de-fund him. His 1996 encyclopedia, *The Cigarette Papers*,[1] is the leading compendium of industry marketing strategies.

If anyone knows how tobacco companies peddle, it is Glantz. But his findings
have not pleased anti-smoking activists. In recent journal, op-ed, and news articles,
Glantz has attacked the "kids only" focus of anti-smoking strategy, called the
National Center for Tobacco-Free Kids "a total waste of time," and declared that
the government "got suckered" in its recent out-of-court agreement with tobacco
companies that Congress, in any case, later jettisoned.[2] Glantz's February 1996 editorial in the *American Journal of Public Health* warned that if anti-smoking activists
continue to obsess over teenage smoking while conceding the social acceptability of
smoking by adults, "we will look back on the mid 1990s as a time that the tobacco
industry once again outsmarted the public health community."[3]

What did Glantz find from scrutinizing industry documents and observing its
strategy that led him to strongly criticize health groups' sacrosanct designs to "prevent teenage smoking"? Mainly that the industry was all for it—and had good reason to be. Unlike health lobbies, cigarette companies cannot afford to be in denial
as to why youths smoke. "As the tobacco industry knows well, kids want to be like
adults," Glantz writes, citing a key tobacco marketing document recovered in a
Federal Trade Commission investigation in 1981:

> An attempt to reach the young smokers, starters, should be based, among
> others, on the following major parameters:
>
> • Present the cigarette as one of the few initiations into the adult
>   world.
>
> • Present the cigarette as part of the illicit pleasure category of products
>   and activities.
>
> • In your ads, create a situation taken from the day-to-day life of the
>   young smoker, but in an elegant manner have this situation touch
>   on the basic symbols of the growing-up, maturity process.

The recent exposure of RJ Reynolds' "smoking documents" about marketing to
kids, called "explosive" in the press, were a stale butt after those revealed in *The
Cigarette Papers* and in FTC reports. RJR schemed not how to entice nonsmoking
kids to try cigs, but how to increase their brands' "market share" among teens. As
Mike Salisbury, key designer of the Joe Camel figure, declared, the Joe Camel model
"had to be 25 or older"[4] for exactly that reason. Cigarette marketers wanted smoking (and their brands) portrayed not as juvenile, but firmly linked to the image of
the adult puffers children from high-smoking environments see all around them.

This is a matter of considerable sensitivity among adults of all stripes. Clinton
smokes cigars. Leftists like the *Progressive*'s Will Durst irritably attack the neo-puri-
tans' societal cleansings. Left to right, adults seek the common denominator that
interferes not with mine own profit, politics, or personal nasty-habit ("But I love it,"

Table 1

The demography of teenage smoking:
Where adults use tobacco more, teenagers do, too

1996 tobacco use levels* compared to national average:

Age/group	12–17	18–34	35–older
Male	Above	Above	Above
Female	Below	Below	Below
White	Above	Above	Above
Hispanic	Below	Below	Below
Black	Below	Below	Above
Asian/other	Below	Below	Below
Northeast	Below	Below	Below
North Central	Above	Above	Below
South	Above	Above	Above
West	Below	Below	Below

*Used cigarette or smokeless tobacco within previous month, 1996.

Source: Substance Abuse and Mental Health Services Administration, *National Household Survey on Drug Abuse: Population Estimates 1996.* Tables 14–15.

American leftist emeritus Mark Twain rued). The industry divides, conquers, and passes out the cigs. In the Clinton era, "anti-smoking" lobbies are not like those of the radical '70s and '80s. The new wave is not interested in actually cutting tobacco patronage. They consult pollsters, assemble focus groups, and intensively study only popular topics, which turn out to be (drum roll): Teenage Smoking!

This is a point the health lobbies consistently, and today deliberately, miss: teenagers smoke (or don't) because adults around them smoke (or don't). Joe Camel, the Marlboro Man, and other images have never been shown to induce kids to smoke, only to influence what brands kids who smoke choose. What brands teen smokers pick are of crucial interest to the industry but of little importance to anti-smoking campaigns.

If ads caused kids to smoke, smoking would be more or less evenly distributed among the youth population. After all, every teen is exposed to some part of the $2 billion per year in tobacco advertising. There are three reasons to question the popular notion that adolescents are mere puppets of tobacco ad wizardry.

First, survey data indicate that rates of teenage smoking are not random but highly predictable from smoking rates among adults of their respective communities, races, genders, income levels, and eras (Table 1). When broken down by population group and region, teenage smoking and tobacco use mirrors adult rates. This is true in

Table 2

Smoking declined first among teens, then among adults.
By 1997, declines among age groups was virtually identical...

Smoked in past 30 days:	1974	1997	Change
Age 12–17	25.0%	19.9%	-21%
Age 18–25	48.8	40.6	-17%
Age 26+	39.1	29.1	-25%

Smoke half a pack-plus per day:	1975	1995	
High school seniors	17.9	12.4	-31%

Source: SAMHSA, *National Household Survey* (1974–97), *op cit*, Table 17. Johnston LD et al (1996). *National Survey Results on Drug Use from the Monitoring the Future Study, 1975–1995*, Tables 11, 14.

every case in which teenage rates are compared to those of adults of their group who are ages 18–34 and in eight of 10 cases when compared to adults age 35 and older.

Second, the trends in teenage and adult smoking over time are very similar. Despite industry spending of tens of billions in advertising in the 1970s and 1980s, smoking rates were down by one-fourth among both adolescents and grownups by 1990. There is nothing to keep a kid from taking up the killer weed, this child of two smoking parents can attest, like watching the agonizing, humiliating efforts of a father or uncle trying to quit, or watching emphysema and cancer set in among elders who didn't.

Thus, even though teenagers tend to copy adults around them, given the right health strategies, kids will refuse to take up harmful adult habits. Anti-smoking educational campaigns in the 1970s—which, unlike today's, were not punishing, threatening, condescending, or angry in tone—doubtless contributed to decisions by one-fourth to half of teens who otherwise might have been expected to take up smoking not to. From the first reliable survey in 1974 through the most recent in 1997, smoking declined by almost identical rates among youths and adults (Table 2).

The decline among teenagers had two components. There was a modest decline in youths who experimented with cigarettes. And, of the experimenters, there was a larger decline in the proportion who progressed to smoking half a pack a day or more by senior year of high school.[5] This indicates that those youths who try cigarettes are much less likely to continue their use or to become addicted. By the most comparable measure, smoking half a pack per day or more, today's high school seniors are less than half as likely to smoke as their parents. There is no justification for recent press reports claiming teenagers smoke more than adults.

Smoking among teenagers decreased the most rapidly in the 1970s and early 1980s; adult declines began more slowly in the late 1970s and then accelerated. This resulted from another expected fact: those youths who were ambivalent about smoking, whose environments promoted smoking in a so-so way, were the ones who shunned the habit in the '70s. As those kids aged into adults of the '80s and '90s, adult smoking "declined" as well. However, kids from backgrounds of heavy and/or prevalent smoking by adults often continued to smoke. By 1990, a leveling off in the decline and a slight rebound set in among hard-core smoking populations. Just as youths had shown the largest and earliest decline in the 1970s, youth smoking was the first to level off and rebound in the 1990s.

Putting the information in Tables 1 and 2 together confirms common sense: the current adult smoking level is the biggest influence on the current youth smoking level, the current youth smoking level is the biggest effect on future adult smoking level (that is, the trend), and *the two must be addressed together*. Anti-smoking groups have done exactly the opposite.

The incessant 1990s' claim that "teenage smoking is rising while adult smoking is going down" represents hype by self-interested groups who ignore the lessons of long term trends. Adult and teen patterns may vary over the short term, particularly when youths are the first to respond positively to new health promotions and adults catch up later. But in the long run, they track each other because they are inextricably *dependent upon each other*. After three years of hysteria that teenage smoking was rising, the press reported in 1997, "Adult smoking rises sharply in California."[6]

What is left today are the hard-core puffers. The 1997 National Household Survey on Drug Abuse indicated that one-third of the parent-age adults (around 20 to 50) and one-fifth of the 12–17-year-olds are still hooked in the mid-1990s.[7] The adult smokers and teen smokers tended to be huddled together in low-income, poorly educated sectors, creating dense blue haze under the same roofs. It is a tough population for anti-smoking campaigns to reach, all the more so when their political jockeying yields unreal notions about why kids take up nicotine.

Third, bringing the general trends and levels down to the household level, parents who smoke are three to four times more likely to have teenage kids who smoke than are nonsmoking parents.[8] Though the 1994 Surgeon General's reports buried them, its review of studies of family influences on youth smoking consistently found large effects,[9] especially at the youngest ages. So do more recent studies.

In 10 years of working with low-income families, I had plenty of opportunity to see kids take those first puffs. It wasn't Joe Camel or cowboys, or even peers that enticed them. Kids started smoking right at home, with Mom or Dad or Auntie, alongside Big Bro' and Second Cuz, with a cigarette they were handed by an older family member. Sometimes the grownups would resist a bit, sometimes the kids would "rebel" by choosing a different brand or chewing tobacco like the baseball coach. For kids who had been inhaling adults' tobacco fumes daily and nightly since birth, the transition to active smoking around 11 or 12 was simply grownups' grudging affirmation of entry into the adult world—the Light of Passage.

In 1993, I surveyed 400 Los Angeles middle school students ages 10–15 for a study published in the *Journal of School Health*.[10] I found the unsurprising fact that those whose parents smoked were four times more likely to smoke by age 12 and three times more likely to smoke by age 15 than students whose parents did not smoke. Further, children of smoking parents were more likely to resist anti-smoking messages. Six in 10 youth smokers had parents who smoked—and I neglected to ask about other adult family members.

The 1997 Bogalusa Heart Study of 900 third-through-sixth graders did ask that question. It found that 133 (15 percent) of the kids had tried cigarettes. Of that 133, only five said they did so to be like people in ads, and only nine to be like people on TV. In contrast, 61 tried smoking because an older family member smoked, and nearly all of these had their first cigarette with a family member. Four out of five grade schoolers who sampled cigarettes had close family members who smoked; 60 percent of these were parents and one-fourth were older siblings. Only one-fourth of the smokers had friends who smoked.[11]

The Bogalusa study of younger kids highlights an important issue about "peer pressure," the culprit both the tobacco industry and anti-smoking officials blame for teenage smoking. Full-page industry ads and the 1994 Surgeon General's report both claimed that teens smoke because of evil "peer pressure." This is questionable. A recent research review noted that the popular misconception "is that the more similar teenagers are to their friends, the more they have been pressured to adopt the friends' attitudes or behaviors." However,

> researchers have consistently shown that similarity stems primarily *not* from processes of peer influence but from adolescents' inclinations to choose like-minded peers as friends and the tendency of peer groups to recruit as new members individuals who *already* share the group's normative attitudes and behaviors [emphasis in original].[12]

In fact, "adolescents rarely expected their friends to favor, much less pressure them to begin, cigarette smoking."[13]

At the most influential time, the biggest influences on youth smoking turn out to be Mom, Dad, and family. Most younger smokers, the Bogalusa study found, get their first cigarette from adult family members. The fraction of kids already influenced to smoke at early ages tend to choose peers at later ages who also favored smoking.

The most important implication is that teenage smoking is not rebellious, but *conforming*, behavior. The industry, driven by the practical motives of profit and survival, knows this. Its efforts to market cigarettes as symbols of adulthood, maturity, sophistication, and independence show the industry is well aware that the best strategy is to reinforce the smoking links between adults and kids. The anti-smoking movement, increasingly driven by the needs of the politicians fronting it, engages in strenuous acrobatics to separate teen from adult smokers and to deal only with the former. More than anything else, the industry's greater connection to the reality of why people smoke has enabled it to triumph again and again—including its defeat of the tobacco settlement bill in June 1998.

Tobacco Ads: Create New Teen Smokers or Grab Market Share?

Of all the senseless assertions modern progressive lobbies make about kids, the worst have to be their notions of why kids smoke and drink. Camels, cowboys, and frogs? (If you think about it, it's strange to claim that a jazz-playing cartoon camel, a grizzled real-life Montana cowboy, and now a Red Kamel Lights promo adorned with a Pamela-Lee cyberbabe and the Moslem crescent *all* could be effective images luring teens to smoke.) Granted, it's a fine anti-corporate rallying cry to charge Big Business with "hooking children"—especially industries which most certainly would entice more third graders to smoke and swill if they only knew how.

But as the recently exposed RJR documents indicate, the industry knows its tactics are limited to squabbling over a declining pool of smokers. RJR marketers wrote in memos to company leaders in 1973 and 1974:

> This young adult market, the 14–24 age group…represents tomorrow's cigarette business. As the 14–24 age group matures, they will account for a key share of the total cigarette volume—for at least the next 25 years…
>
> …If our company is to survive and prosper, over the long term, we must get our share of the youth market…the learning smokers.[14]

Another RJR document lamented that Philip Morris's Marlboro was the brand choice of three times more 17-year-old smokers than RJR's Camel, Winston, and Salem. The documents propose strategies to lure "younger smokers" age 14–24 away from Marlboro by correcting the "comparative weakness" RJR brands showed.

Nothing revealed in the confidential RJR documents indicates the company believed advertising would increase teenage smoking. The entire thrust was to entice teen smokers away from competitive brands. The fight, one the industry repeatedly and falsely denied existed, was over a *rapidly declining* teenage market. The role of Joe Camel was to get a few kid to declare "independence" by boldly choosing a different brand than his/her Marlboro-puffing elders. While most kid smokers adopted their parents' brands, around one-fourth mutinied by switching to the dromedary, studies published in the *Journal of the American Medical Association* in December 1991 found.

That's billions more for RJR and billions less for Philip Morris, but who except them cares? The role of health lobbies toward youths in hard-core smoking environs ought to be to encourage the kids to declare independence from bad adult habits by not smoking. There was no evidence that Joe Camel lured more teens to smoke. In the surveys bracketing the camel's advent in 1988, both the Monitoring the Future and the National Household surveys showed declines in teenage smoking rates, particularly among the youngest.[15]

Liberal and leftist media critics depict as unassailable gospel that advertising manipulation of adolescents is the source of teen habits. In progressive mantra, tobacco ads cause kids to smoke; rarely do commentators on the left mention any other causes might exist (see Chapter 8). Yet even authors of studies on the subject did not make that claim until very recently.

In the June 24, 1992, *Journal of the American Medical Association*, the nation's top researchers on cigarette marketing acknowledged they had not documented that "cigarette advertising [has] an independent effect on the initiation of smoking." In June 1996, after two decades of intensive effort, researchers admitted to the *Los Angeles Times* that they still had no evidence that advertising lures teens to light up.

Researchers continue to make energetic efforts to show that kids smoke because of camels, cowboys, and promotional t-shirts. The two most recent, key studies, highlighted in the press even though they contradicted each other on key points, are discussed below. I was contacted by a number of left-leaning folks who argued these studies proved I was wrong in my insistence, in *In These Times*, *The Progressive*, and *Scapegoat Generation* writings, that tobacco promotions do not cause teenage smoking. I asked if any of my critics had actually read these two recent studies or previous ones cited uncritically in leftist publications which normally would be skeptical of medical industry claims. None of the progressive writers had. Here is what these new studies actually said.

In December 1997, a Dartmouth study of 1,200 New England sixth-to-twelfth graders appeared in the *Archives of Pediatric and Adolescent Medicine*. It reported that one-third owned cigarette promotion items (t-shirts, caps, lighters, etc.), and these youths were more likely to smoke than kids who didn't own such items.[16] The study was widely headlined and drew dire comments from the National Center for Tobacco-Free Kids that "stealth advertising" was luring ever-stupid kids to smoke.[17]

It certainly might reveal an industry effort. But when examined, the study actually found that the people kids were most likely to get such items from were their *parents*. Owning cigarette promotion items (CPIs) had no effect on high schoolers' smoking. Only younger kids were reported to be affected, which is the same group that gets most of its cigarettes (as well as cigarette promotion items) at home.

"We are unable to infer a direction between the exposure (ownership of a CPI) and smoking behavior," the authors admitted. In other words, there was no determination of which causes which. Certainly, youths who ride dirt bikes are the most likely to wear motocross t-shirts, but do t-shirts cause kids to ride bikes? It would not be a bit surprising that kids from homes where adults smoke and where adults give kids cigarettes and CPIs would be more likely to smoke and to own such items.

More important, the Dartmouth study found strong links between youth smoking and smoking by their friends and parents. A youth with both friends and parents who smoked was 28 times more likely to smoke than one amid smoke-free humans. That effect dwarfed the one claimed for cigarette promotional items—which, after all, often came from parents and family members.

Consider this powerful parent/peer smoking connection in light of another study, one which received enormous attention because it claimed to be the first to show that tobacco promotion caused teenage smoking. In a February 1998 paper in the *Journal of the American Medical Association*, researchers led by Dr. John Pierce of the University of California, San Diego, reported that tobacco advertising and promotional items influenced about one-sixth of those who turn 17 each year to experiment with cigarettes.[18] They also estimated that 30 percent of those who experiment with cigarettes will become smokers. So the study argued, in effect, that 5 percent of all teenagers become smokers because of tobacco promotions.

That's a big number of smokers—but the study doesn't support it. The study first classified the smoking habits, "susceptibility to smoking," and "receptivity to tobacco promotional activities," of 3,400 youths ages 12–17 in 1993. About half were so categorized as smokers or susceptible in 1993; the other half were "nonsusceptible nonsmokers." Researchers then re-surveyed the same youths (now age 15–20) in 1996.

The study did not ask whether the youths actually smoked on a daily, weekly, or other basis. Instead, it classified them anew in four categories of "progression toward smoking:" (a) non-susceptible non-smokers, (b) susceptible nonsmokers, (c) experimenters (took even a few puffs), and (d) established smokers (smoked more than 100 cigarettes in their life).

Their conclusion: Of the "non-susceptible nonsmokers" in 1993, 29.5 percent had experimented with at least a few puffs by 1996, and 3.6 percent had smoked as many as 100 cigarettes. An additional 16.6 percent were now rated as "susceptible." The experimenters were more likely to have a favorite tobacco ad or a promotional item (34 percent) than those who did not (22 percent).

The study examined youths at the end of their high school careers in 1996, yet 70 percent of this sample had not even tried one puff, and only 4 percent had smoked as many as five packs in their lives! In other words, the sample of teenagers Pierce claims are headed for smoking are really committed *non-smokers*. Further, it would have been useful to know how recently the small amount of smoking found in this group took place. That would ballpark whether the 17-year-old classified as an "established smoker" snarfed two packs before breakfast that morning or was like me—smoked a few packs (but didn't inhale!) around age nine, then quit and became a rabid anti-smoker for life. The authors argued that they were more interested in the entire "smoking uptake process" than in whether the youth actually smoked.

However, since only a minority of these so-labeled susceptible, experimenting, and established youths will ever become addicted smokers, this study's categorization of teenage risk is very broad. Add up its risk categories: half of all students were classed as "progressing" toward smoking in 1993, and half of 1993's nonprogressing half was classified as "progressing" toward smoking by 1996. That means 75 percent of the entire sample of youths were classed as "progressing toward becoming addicted to cigarettes"—triple the number even the highest estimates would find actually smoked.

The biggest, and most revealing, curiosity of the study is its finding that neither parental nor peer smoking "appear(s) to significantly influence which adolescents begin the smoking uptake process." They acknowledge this "is somewhat contradictory to previous studies." That it is—note the huge effect found in the Bogalusa study, and many others. Buried in the appendix of the 1994 Surgeon General's report are citations of more than 40 recent studies which find parental or peer smoking to be significant predictors of adolescent smoking,[19] and this is only a partial listing. Indeed, right down the block, the University of California, San Diego, School of Medicine runs a smoking prevention program which reports that "70 percent of teen smokers report that a family member smokes."[20]

Pierce and colleagues try to reconcile their study's peculiar finding by speculating that "the influences of other smokers in facilitating and encouraging adolescents to smoke may be most apparent after the first experimentation rather than influencing the adolescent to experiment for the first time." This also contradicts many studies, such as the earlier-cited Bogalusa and New England papers, which find high rates of family collaboration in kids' nicotine deflowerings and cigarette paraphernalia acquisition. And it would be tantamount to suggesting that family and other nearby smokers may turn out to be the most important predictors of whether a teenager smokes after all.

I suspect that the Pierce and colleagues' findings contradict those of previous studies because their definitions of teenage "progression" toward smoking are so vague that they wind up including nearly all non-smokers as well. Their data show that in their 1996 sample, 70.5 percent had never even taken so much as one puff on a cigarette, and 96.4 percent had not smoked even as many as 100 cigarettes in their entire lives. This sample averages 17.5 years old. According to smoking doctrine, if they're not addicted to tobacco by that age, they never will be. If these young people the study claimed to be incipient smokers were surveyed a few years hence, virtually none would be smoking then, either.

So this study made no sense. Pierce basically took a group of adolescent *non-smokers*, including all teens who ever ventured near a cigarette (or even thought about it), and redefined them as smokers. Thus, his procedure and definitions do not differentiate between that fraction of youths who will be settling into the hardcore habit and which will chuck the smokes for good, as the large majority of teenagers do. The reason he doesn't find family and peer influences to smoke in this group is because they are, overwhelmingly, present and future nonsmokers.

In that regard, the authors' most obnoxious conclusion is that smoking is caused by teenage irrationality: "Once people are old enough to rationally evaluate the well-known health risks of smoking, they choose not to start smoking." It is important to keep perspective. What Pierce and colleagues find, even accepting the study in its broadest terms and at face value, is that 95 percent of adolescents are *not* influenced by advertising and promotion to become cigarette addicts. Teenagers who smoke are not a commentary on all or even most adolescents, and teenage smoking decisions are not "irrational" given the continued acceptability of smoking among adults around them.

The second question I have is whether these researchers have ever seen the family environments of young people who start to smoke. Both my observations and studies consistently find heavy involvement of family adults in the provision of cigarettes and tobacco promotion items to their children, as well as a great deal of youth smoking in the company of family adults. Pierce's finding of virtually no adult (or peer) involvement in youth smoking should raise red flags as to the validity of his findings.

Studies and researcher attitudes like these hamper realistic smoking prevention. But because they are pleasing to a variety of interests, they are rarely scrutinized. Further, such studies give great sound bite. The Pierce study was one-sentenced in the press as follows: "Young people who own promotional tobacco products such as hats and T-shirts and who recognize tobacco ads are far more likely to become smokers than those who do not."[21]

In their obsession with Joe Camel and Cancer Cowboy, health groups swallowed the industry bait. RJR and Philip grandly put the pair out to pasture after extracting huge concessions that saved the industry's hide in a recent settlement with states. More accurately, many health groups discovered that in the '90s, exploiting the teenage enemy yielded more attention and funding than doing anything that might reduce smoking.

Thus, anti-smoking lobbies began a relentless smear campaign against the very adolescents who showed the largest declines, the lowest smoking rates, and the greatest anti-smoking attitudes of any age group. In journal and liberal periodicals, teenagers were depicted as mass-vulnerable to smoking because of their supposed irrationality, developmental immaturity, craving for popularity, and fixation on colorful images. None of this slander of adolescents made much sense when the solid demographic and family connections of adolescent to adult smoking were analyzed.

In the lament over the post-1992 rise in smoking among teenagers, no one asked whether the sarcastic, openly anti-youth tactics among health groups sabotaged their own effectiveness. Or whether these prejudices might be modified if experts actually spent time with heavy-smoking families to see how kids take up the habit instead of just name-calling adolescents as irrational.

Dousing of the cherished myth that tobacco ads robotize teenagers to smoke (based on misinterpretation of a bad set of studies to begin with) came from an unusual source. USA Today consistently has been one of the worst of the Big Media in yellow-journalism fear-mongering about teens. But in its February 2, 1997, issue, the paper decided to study in-depth "how ad images shape habits."[22] The results of their survey and focus groups with over 500 teenagers were so illuminating that the paper could barely stand to report them.

The progression of USA Today's retreat from popular myths is charted by the succession of headlines over the stories as they progress from front page hype to sober inside-page analysis:

"How ad images shape habits: Ads for adult vices big hit with teens" (front page)

"Curiosity about ads rarely clinches sale" (page 2)

"Do young people fall under the influence? Youths aren't buying the cute and flashy beer images" (page 4B).

The article began with the usual breathiness:

An astonishing 99% of those (teenagers) surveyed knew the Budweiser-croaking amphibians. Frog familiarity breeds affection; some 92% said they liked the frogs. And 98% of those surveyed are familiar with the cigarette-puffing Joe Camel cartoon character.

Had the report stopped there, it would have amounted to the usual superficiality common to the studies criticized earlier: if teens know ads and like ads, therefore they slavishly buy the ads' products. But USA Today impaneled focus groups of teens and found that "conventional wisdom aside, the ads teens like most seem to have only occasional correlation to the tobacco and alcohol products they want." Budweiser was rarely the favorite brand; Joe Camel was ridiculed more than loved; and so on. (Just like the award-winning Jules Feiffer ads for Jax beer in the '60s, loved by consumers but no good at hawking the brew).

When USA Today's numbers were examined, they showed that ads influence brand choice among the fraction of youths who have already decided to smoke. But ads had little impact on the large majority who don't already light up. For example,

60 percent of the smokers said the Marlboro ads made them want to smoke Marlboro more (like adults, for whom Marlboro is by far the most popular brand), but virtually none of the non-smokers did.

Marlboro and Joe Camel ads appealed to only one-fifth of the teens. Adult smoking rates can be used to make demographic predictions of how many teens would smoke without the ads' influence. Answer: one fifth, indicating that the group to whom the ads appealed were already prone to smoking, not hooked by the ads.

Many teens held the same they-are-weak-but-I-am-strong belief about ads' effects that adults believe. Overwhelming margins said the ads didn't make them crave the particular brands being hawked. But 30 to 40 percent thought ads might influence other (particularly younger) kids to indulge.

"Teen views on the marketing of tobacco products and alcoholic beverages was consistently surprising," USA Today found. "...Teens may say they love the frogs, penguins, and other clever images, but they aren't putting their money where their mouths are." If the USA Today study (which went a step beyond and probed teens on their decisions) is flawed, the more simplistic JAMA studies on Camels widely cited by progressive commentators are even more so.

There's one big reason to believe the kids who say teens don't fit the ad automaton mold, however: statistics are on their side. Alcohol abuse, and particularly smoking, are not random events among teens, as would be expected if ubiquitous advertising (seen by 99 percent) were the cause. The demography of teenage smoking (see Table 1) and drinking is very similar to that of adults. The habits kids adopt tend to be those of their parents.

The Disciples of Discipline versus the Lure of "Maturity"

The 1990s preoccupation with tobacco advertising, cigarette sales to kids, and "teen smoking" in general represents a backwards trend. Glantz's American Journal of Public Health analysis charts the retreat from Reagan to Clinton:

> During his tenure, Surgeon General C. Everett Koop transformed the public debate over tobacco use by calling for a smoke-free society by the year 2000. He was the first major public official to articulate clearly the message that smoking need not be a part of American life. The tobacco industry went wild and aggressively attacked Koop, because his message went to the core of the tobacco issue: tobacco use in public was no longer socially acceptable. Today, that message has been eclipsed by a less potent—and probably counterproductive—one: "We don't want kids to smoke."[23]

Because of the adult-teen smoking link, efforts to forcibly prevent children and youths from acquiring tobacco with criminal penalties are pointless: "There is no consistent evidence of a substantial effect on prevalence or consumption of tobacco among kids," Glantz points out.

Indeed, Massachusetts General Hospital researchers conducted a two-year study of 17,000 teenagers in six towns (three where laws against selling tobacco to youths were vigorously enforced and three towns where they were not), published in the New

England Journal of Medicine in October 1997.[24] In the towns where laws were strongly enforced, health departments conducted nearly 1,000 compliance tests (four for every tobacco vendor) and levied fines of up to $200 for violation; none of the three control communities did so. The study found that tobacco sales enforcement does indeed lead to fewer vendors selling to youths. Eighty percent of the stores in the enforcement-happy communities refused to sell tobacco to persons under 18, double the number in the non-compliance towns. Researchers also surveyed 22,000 students in the six cities, 85 percent of those enrolled in school, before and after the strict enforcement began.

Result: even the severest restrictions on tobacco sales to youths "did not alter adolescents' perceived access to tobacco or their smoking." In fact, the three cities which did *not* enforce tobacco sales laws had significantly better results! The rate of teenagers reporting daily smoking fell by 0.4 percent in the non-enforcement towns, but rose 2.5 percent in the get-tough towns. Similar results were reported for current smoking and tobacco experimentation.

The centerpiece of the recent "landmark" Food and Drug Administration rules governing tobacco, requiring photo identification from buyers who appeared to be under age 27, is silly. If inconvenienced by laws, kids get their smokes from grownup habitués. "The smoking habits of children [are] highly correlated with the smoking habits of parents," the Office on Smoking and Health stated in the 1986 Surgeon General's report, back when it was safe to acknowledge the link between adult and youth behaviors.[25]

The worst effect of the anti-teen-smoking crusade has been just this kind of political tail-chasing. Glantz points out that tobacco industry advocates have joined health lobbies to convert effective campaigns against the social acceptability of smoking into a narrow, kids-shouldn't-smoke crusade:

> California's anti-tobacco campaign once focused on discrediting the tobacco industry and educating the public about nicotine addiction and secondhand smoke (messages that appeal to both adults and kids); now it focuses on youth access...Next door in Arizona...the tobacco industry's lawyers and the pro-tobacco members on the [state policy] committee have loudly demanded that the health department strictly limit the program focus to children. Programs with any crossover between kids and adults have been opposed.
>
> In Massachusetts, the tobacco industry raised a huge fuss when the health department mounted an aggressive and effective media campaign and coordinated local programs concentrating on secondhand smoke and denormalization of tobacco use. The department has backed off from the campaign to concentrate on the less controversial issue of youth access.

My view is less charitable still. The committed anti-smoking movement of the past whose main concern was health promotion has been taken over by charlatans whose main goals are personal and political promotion. In an airport layover I catch a news clip of Clinton confidante and retired federal judge Abner Mikva confirming once again that the administration shrank from stepping into the anti-smoking movement until surveys and focus groups convinced the president there were poll points to be gained.[26]

The reversals Glantz lamented accompanied not just industry pressure, but the rise of smoking as a profitable political issue among liberals. Fifty million adult smokers vote. Clinton wanted their votes. Until recently, his regime of loud anti-youth-smoking rhetoric had not taken a single concrete step to reduce smoking. In fact, the industry was latching on to his campaign.

Coincident with the Clinton administration's anti-teen-smoking efforts beginning in 1995, Philip Morris and RJR spent wads of cash running full-page newspaper/magazine ads and poignant radio/television spots declaring that "underage smoking" was wrong. "Only adults should ever face the decision to smoke or not," an RJR Tobacco Company ad in October 1995 declared. The industry ads plagiarized the identical statement by President Clinton two months earlier at a press conference on August 10, 1995: "Adults are capable of making a decision to smoke or not." Industry jubilation was understandable. Here was the president resurrecting smoking as a legitimate habit.

Glantz (and a few health groups, such as the American Heart Association) wanted to know why the administration, Pete Wilson's California governorship, and other supposedly anti-smoking groups were reinforcing the industry line: "we don't want kids to smoke."[27] The real message in that message, Glantz pointed out, was that "if you want to look and act like an adult, do it."

Statistics Up in Smoke

The bizarrities of modern "anti-smoking" campaigns go even further than helping the industry promote smoking as "adult." The newest crusade of anti-smoking groups has been to inflate numbers to make smoking appear normative when in fact it is rejected by the large majority of adolescents. Pierce's study, as noted, classed three-fourths of teenagers as on the highway to hacking. Recent surveys frame questions in ways guaranteed to wildly exaggerate how many teens smoke. Often, the embellished teen *monthly*-smoking numbers are then compared to adult *daily* smoking rates diluted by the inclusion of senior citizens, with the aim of proving the falsehood that "teenagers now smoke more than adults."

"One fourth" and "one-third" are now the working media numbers for teenage smoking—much higher levels than found in more consistent studies. For example, the 1996 National Household Survey reports that 18 percent of 12–17-year-olds smoked at least one cigarette in the previous month—far lower than rates among adults. The 1997 National Longitudinal Study on Adolescent Health found that 3.2 percent of the 7–8th graders and 12.8 percent of the 9–12th graders smoked six or more cigarettes per day.

If reducing smoking is the goal of "anti-smoking" groups (and it is no longer clear that it is), then making teenage smoking appear popular is another truly stupid strategy, one Glantz points out "reinforces a tobacco industry message" that smoking is a normal part of life. Again, he hits the coffin nail on the head:

> One reason that kids start to smoke is the fact that they grossly overestimate smoking prevalence. Ubiquitous tobacco advertising has contributed to this misimpression, but so has anti-tobacco education that says, "resist your peers, don't smoke." The message should be "be like your friends, be a nonsmoker."

But advocating emulating your peers would mean affirming teenagers, not vilifying them as a generation of nicotine zombies. It would mean reversing the imagery of the administration's purported anti-teen-smoking crusade, which to date has been an attack on teenagers, not on smoking. Clearly, anti-smoking groups would rather preserve smoking than treat adolescents as something more than diabolic idiots.

As a result, there is little to morally distinguish an industry which craves profits from an administration and anti-smoking cabal that craves grant bucks and political gain. "This is not about politics. This is not about money. It is about our children," Clinton declared in urging Congress to ratify another round of tobacco populism.[28] Clinton's party coffers swelled with $2 million in tobacco industry donations in the last decade. Make that black coffee, with ashtray.

Smoked

Harsh overstatements? The fate of three studies illuminates the way today's so-called anti-smoking administration and lobbies have backed away from "caring about kids' health" at exactly the point that caring might risk popularity.

While media and official obsessed with studies of tobacco ads and t-shirts—which mistakenly equate recognition and popularity of icons with increases in smoking—other, far more important new studies were ignored. In particular, studies of the health damage to children caused by Moms and Dads who smoke got so-what shrugs from the same anti-smoking lobbies who piously claimed to care about the health of kids.

In July 1997, the University of Wisconsin, Madison, Medical School surveyed 16 years of research and concluded:

> Parental smoking is an important, preventable cause of morbidity and mortality among American children...Involuntary tobacco exposure contributes each year to millions of cases of disease and disability, as well as to thousands of deaths of American children...it results in annual direct medical expenditures of $4.6 billion and loss of life costs of $8.2 billion.[29]

The study estimated that at least 6,200 children die from lung infections and fires and 5.4 million suffer health damage every year from household smoke emitted by their parents. (The study estimates that 40 percent of parents smoke; one-third seems more defensible.) "More young children are killed by parental smoking than by all unintentional injuries combined" from gunshots to car accidents, the study's authors declared.

Likewise, a 1996 University of Massachusetts Medical Center review of more than 100 studies, published in *Pediatrics*, found that "the use of tobacco products by adults has an enormous adverse impact on the health of children"—hundreds of deaths and hundreds of thousands of illnesses and injuries, even by conservative estimate.[30] Tiny, inside page squibs, with no comment by authorities, were all the Big Media ran on the Wisconsin and Massachusetts studies.

In December 1997, the Centers for Disease Control finally broke its Clinton-age silence on the hazards of adult smoking to kids. The CDC released a report conservatively estimating that "15 million (21.9%) children and adolescents aged <18 years were exposed to ETS (environmental tobacco smoke) in homes" due to parents' smoking. "Approximately one third to one-half of adult current cigarette smokers have children residing in their homes," the CDC found, "and in most (>70%) of those homes smoking was permitted in some or all areas of the home."

I suspect the CDC is taking smokers' claims of restraint too seriously. In 15 years of working with teenagers and families, I never saw (and heard of only one) smoker who refrained from smoking around teenagers or children.

The CDC reiterated the following health effects imposed by smokers on kids:

> In 1992, the Environmental Protection Agency classified ETS as a Group A carcinogen known to cause cancer in humans. The primary source of children's exposure to ETS is in the home; children exposed to ETS are at an increased risk for sudden infant death syndrome, acute lower respiratory tract infections, asthma induction and exacerbation, and middle ear effusions.[31]

These are not new findings. In 1992, a research review by the Environmental Protection Agency estimated that smoking by parents causes or aggravates 350,000 to 1.3 million respiratory diseases in young children every year.[32] During the 1980s, reports by Surgeon General Koop and the Office on Smoking and Health regularly pointed out the severe health damage done to children and youths by their parents' smoking. In 1986, the National Research Council urged "eliminating tobacco smoke from the environments of young children."[33] Even after recent studies revealed a tripled rate of asthma among children, that Reagan-era proposal remains far too radical for Clinton-era politics.

Does today's highly politicized anti-smoking establishment give a rip about kids' health? The health lobbies and press, famous for headlining every Joe Camel and teen-smoking salvo, showed less interest in kids damaged and killed by adult smoking during the supposedly "anti-tobacco" Clinton years than during the Bush and Reagan regimes. Clinton and the RJR Tobacco Company locked arms in agreement that adults are capable of maturely deciding whether to smoke.

Unlike Koop, Clinton Surgeon General Joycelyn Elders dodged the adult smoking issue. Her 1994 report, *Preventing Tobacco Use Among Young People,* hyped tobacco ads and "peer pressure" for teen smoking. Advertising was repeatedly implied as a causal factor even though the report admitted there was no evidence. The report buried in back pages research findings such as, "approximately 17 percent of lung cancers among nonsmokers can be attributed to high levels of ETS (environmental tobacco smoke) during childhood and adolescence."[34]

Studies of the effects of environmental tobacco smoke could be exaggerated. Even if so, one could forcefully argue that smokers have no more right to force smoke down the throats of unwilling nonsmokers than drinkers have the right to force booze down the gullets of unwilling non-drinkers. That children are required by law to live with parents or adult caretakers imposes a special state obligation to protect children from bad parental habits.

Health lobbies certainly take passive-smoking research seriously when their own nostrils might risk offense at a posh Massachusetts Avenue watering hole. "Most attention regarding ETS has been focused on harm to adults," the Wisconsin doctors observed, "even though data accumulated during the last 20 years have consistently found a link between ETS and ill effects on the health of children." The Massachusetts researchers reported:

> More than 20 states have enacted laws granting smokers the right to smoke when they are not working. Yet, not a single state has enacted a law recognizing the right of children to remain free from bodily harm as a result of smokers' use of tobacco products. Smoking should be banned wherever children are present.[35]

Smokers and the tobacco industry, following self-interest, would loudly protest any measure to restrict smoking in homes or vehicles merely to protect children. But the silence of anti-smoking groups, which tacitly put the right of adult smokers to practice their addiction conveniently ahead of the health and lives of kids, is unconscionable. It legitimizes smoking even in its most harmful form.

Joseph Banzhaf, leading anti-tobacco crusader with Action on Smoking OR Health, is an example. He drips with contempt for adolescents. Philip Morris has just come out with a gadget through which smokers can puff without generating (much) secondhand smoke. It costs $60 and is widely predicted to be a marketing flop. But CNN tracked down some teenagers to pose attempting to puff through the device. Now Banzhaf's voice intones that teens will take up smoking en masse just so they can sport the clunky, boxlike device from their lips. Because all teenagers are stupid, rich, and "buy hundred-dollar shoes," scoffs Banzhaf, "they'll buy it, they'll buy it."[36]

When the EPA reported back in 1992 that parents' smoking damages kids' health, Banzhaf used the results to push for bans on smoking in workplaces and public buildings where fumes annoy nonsmoking grownups.[37] During the 1990s, anti-smoking groups increasingly have ignored the child health issue and have attenuated themselves by protecting nonsmoking adults. The National Center for Tobacco-Free Kids harps constantly on teenage smoking but only mentions reducing kids' "exposure to second-hand smoke" at the end of its brochure.[38]

Joseph DiFranza, MD, lead author of the Massachusetts study, is a staunch force in the anti-smoking campaign. I've quarreled cordially with him in the past for his advocacy of criminalizing teen smoking but have admired his implacable loathing of the "predatory" tobacco industry. DiFranza's 1991 studies on Joe Camel advertising roused loud cheers from the press and anti-smoking groups even though they showed only that ads might affect brand choice, not teen smoking rates. However, DiFranza's 1996 study on adult smokers and children's health, like that of Wisconsin physicians, aroused virtual silence. Nothing better demonstrates the Clinton-corrupted nature of modern anti-smoking lobbies and their playing of popularity politics with vital health issues.

Second Hand Campaign Contributions

Politicized anti-smoking lobbies have manufactured a melodrama and cast themselves as the heroes, locked in titanic struggle with a fiendishly clever industry for the souls and lungs of youth. Each survey point increase in teenage smoking is proof of industry puppetry in "hooking" stupid kids. Each point down is caused by the patient and conscientious skill of health promoters' reverse manipulations. In reality, the demography of teenage smoking shows this imaginary battle has little to do with why certain teenagers smoke.

What does the tobacco industry fear? Glantz's exhaustive *Cigarette Papers* indicates two prime industry concerns: higher taxes on tobacco, and restrictions on adults' tobacco use based on fears of "passive smoking" damage. Little fear of attempts to reduce teenage smoking are evident; the industry has even joined them "for good reasons," Glantz notes.[39]

Much tougher measures targeting all ages will be necessary to reduce the social acceptability of smoking. Continuous tax increases raising the price of cigarettes by dollars per pack, spaced over time so as not to stimulate bootlegging, are key. Bans on smoking in all enclosed areas where nonsmokers, particularly children, are present. Political parties refusing tobacco donations and pressuring members to refuse tobacco money. Removal of all tobacco advertising and substitution of industry-financed health promotions aimed at adults and youths alike. In short, strong action inconveniencing adults sends the "message" to smokers, especially young ones, that this habit is no longer acceptable to impose on others.

Instead, the theme of modern anti-smoking groups is that teenagers cause responsible grownups trouble. Teenagers smoke to rebel against adults, the CDC's Office on Smoking and Health chief Michael Eriksen said. Right. "Seventy-five percent of teenage smokers come from homes where parents smoke," Eriksen's agency's own excellent *Smoking, Tobacco & Health Factbook* reports. Some rebellion.

Teenagers stupidly get addicted to cigarettes, wrecking well-intentioned health goals, officials say. Former FDA Commissioner David Kessler won headlines branding smoking as a "pediatric disease." Joycelyn Elders' tone leading off the administration's 1994 report, *Preventing Tobacco Use Among Young People*, is petulant, self-righteous, and all too typical of the purported anti-smoking lobbies' attitudes toward adolescents:

> Despite 30 years of decline in overall smoking prevalence, despite widespread dissemination of information about smoking, despite a continuing decline in the social acceptability of smoking, substantial numbers of young men and women begin to smoke and become addicted. These current and future smokers are new recruits in the continuing epidemic of disease, disability, and death attributable to tobacco use. When young people no longer want to smoke, the epidemic itself will die.[40]

Smoking has become so socially unacceptable that Elders's boss merely smokes cigars openly at White House parties. After 30 years, the strategy of health lobbies is to maintain gutless silence while children marinate in adults' tobacco smoke for a dozen years, then express outrage that some youths take up the habit their role models and communities have proffered and their government's politically-compromised subsidies and low taxation make absurdly cheap and legitimate.

Her report holds "young people" absolutely responsible for the smoking "epidemic," yet turns around and holds grown parents and adults blameless for the influences and damage their cigarette habits impose on kids. Her report fails to hold blowhards at both ends of Pennsylvania Avenue responsible for a cowardice so profound that in 1994, federal taxation of cigarettes (a measly 14 percent of retail price) was only one third of what it was in 1950 (40 percent)![41] In short, Elders' attitude, representing the Clinton regime, is impeccable '90s politics: blame kids for massive adult dereliction.

Moreover, if teenagers impose smoking addiction on grownup society, then any sanction (short of ones that might inconvenience the victimized adult smoker) is justified in the name of prevention. In Gothenberg, Nebraska, police employ undercover stings with video cameras to catch teen smokers. North Carolina, tobacco industry whore suprema for decades, now fines teen smokers up to $1,000 (would an inveterate tobaccracy do that if such a strategy really would cut smoking?). In Florida, Minnesota, and Texas, teen smokers can lose their driver's licenses. In Idaho, underage smokers are liable to six months in confinement. Congressional Republicans, too craven to impose even modest tax boosts on cigarettes, now propose legislation to kick kids out of school for up to six months for possessing tobacco. The move to criminalize teen smokers is a national rampage among lawmakers and policy makers who recognize no teenage or child right to be free from being forced to passively breathe adults' fumes.[42]

The crassest youth exploitation came at the 1996 Democratic National Convention. Vice President Al Gore "riveted" delegates with "an achingly personal account of his sister's death from lung cancer" in 1984. Press accounts worshiped his crescendo:

> Tomorrow morning another 13-year-old girl will start smoking…Three thousand young people in America will start smoking tomorrow. One thousand of them will die a death not unlike my sister's. That is why, until I draw my last breath, I will pour my heart and soul into the cause of protecting our children from the dangers of smoking.[43]

Disgusting. Former Democratic Party advisor William Bradley pointed out that in the 1988 presidential primaries, four years after his sister's death, Gore "boasted of being a tobacco farmer and continued to derive substantial personal income and political contributions from the industry into the 1990s."[44]

"Democrats as well as G.O.P. profit from tobacco," the *New York Times* reported a few weeks before Gore's podium pounding. In the last decade, the national Democratic Party collected $2.1 million in donations from tobacco interests. Only months before Gore poured out heart and hot air, Philip Morris poured in nearly half a million dollars to national Democratic Party and campaign committee coffers without a whisper of protest from the White House.[45]

Au contraire. In late July 1996, Clinton offered to let tobacco companies escape tough FDA regulations and the harsher penalties of the tobacco settlement (even including deducting their death/disease settlement costs on their taxes as a normal business expense!) if they would accept "tough rules to curb teen smoking."[46] These "tough rules" were the same kinds of silliness found to be woefully ineffective—age limits on cigarette sales, fiddling with tobacco ad colors and formats, bans on t-shirts, caps, and other sporting promotions, and vending machine restrictions. While Republican challenger Bob Dole represents the old order of tobacco accommodation (take the money, and hell, it ain't that bad for ya), Clinton represents the slick new school: loud anti-industry rhetoric in public, mutually beneficial agreement in the back room filled with you know what.

The fascinating thing about the warehouse of private tobacco documents (33 million pages of documents subpoenaed from companies in state lawsuits, millions more slipped out by insiders) perused by anti-smoking authorities is the complete lack of industry concern about efforts to curb teenage smoking. Behind closed doors, in secret memos, and in private strategy documents, industry moguls express intense fear of tax increases, measures to restrict public and job-related smoking, and health concerns surrounding passive smoking. California, in particular, has been targeted by industry counter-measures, Glantz's analysis revealed. The industry documents are replete with schemes to divert money raised by Proposition 99 (the 1989 cigarette tax increase), to promote the clobbered 1994 industry initiative to overturn Assembly Bill 13 (the law banning workplace smoking), and to beat back local ordinances banning public smoking.[47] Yet in its most private strategizing and candid memos, the industry expresses not a whit of anxiety about the health lobbies' biggest crusade: to stop teenagers from smoking. Nor is there any evidence of an industry strategy, even a surreptitious one, to counter anti-teen smoking campaigns.

Let us look at what the tobacco industry smiled and howled about in its March 1998 full-page ads on the settlement. Philip Morris, R.J. Reynolds, Brown & Williamson, and Lorillard Tobacco Company ringingly endorsed:

- A massive and sustained assault against underaged smoking…
- A multibillion-dollar anti-smoking public education program, including $500 million a year for an independently managed campaign aimed at preventing young people from smoking…
- A ban on outdoor advertising and on the use of cartoon characters or human figures in other advertising.
- A ban on cigarette vending machines.
- Regulation of nicotine and tobacco products by the U.S. Food and Drug Administration, backed by severe penalties for violations…
- [Agreement to] reduce underage tobacco use, while protecting the right of adults to use tobacco.

"Good for all concerned," cigarette sellers puffed amiably in conceding *every demand* of modern anti-smoking lobbies regarding youth smoking.

Now, what did the industry squawk about?

> Some are now calling for immediate and massive increases in excise taxes on tobacco products. These taxes are not only unfair to millions of our customers, but also will have a devastating impact on the hundreds of thousands of people who work in our industry.[48]

Twenty years of public and private industry documents reveal not the slightest fear of crusades (even massive, well-funded, independently-run ones) against teenage smoking. Nor advertising bans. Nor vending machine bans. Nor draconianingly tough age-limit, photo-ID sales laws. But raise the tax and price to penalize adult smokers? The industry goes berserk.

The industry's priority is to protect adult smoking. It knows that if adults smoke, teenagers will smoke.

When the *Los Angeles Times,* whose news stories and editorials have portrayed teenage smoking as caused solely by tobacco ads and teenage stupidity, surveyed an array of experts on the tobacco settlement, it found that "those who study the issue have decidedly mixed views on the role of advertising in luring new smokers."

"Some experts believe advertising has almost no effect," the paper's survey reported. "Even those who believe it does are convinced there are other more significant factors." The danger is that the zeal whipped up in Congress to ban tobacco advertising (the only tobacco industry concession that Congress cannot impose by law) has serious negative tradeoffs:

> So eager are some members of Congress to get the advertising ban that they say they are prepared to give in to the tobacco industry's chief demand: partial immunity from future lawsuits brought by smokers seeking recompense for the damage done by their habit.
>
> But in their zeal for advertising restraints, lawmakers may be exaggerating the effectiveness that Joe Camel, the Marlboro Man and other tobacco promotions have in hooking young people on cigarettes.

Note the paper's assumption that the Republican Congress really wanted to cut smoking, one disproven only a couple of months later when it dumped the proposed settlement.

Clinton's former labor secretary, Robert Reich, seems ready to let the industry off the hook once again for the chimera of cutting teen smoking. He declares that "tobacco companies know more about how to get teenagers to do things (or stop doing things) than almost anyone else." Therefore, if the companies "succeed in reducing teen smoking," they would pay "only a small portion" of their fines and "their yearly liability limit should be lowered."[49] Reich's plan is the ultimate industry delight. For the effort of a few easily manipulable surveys showing reduced teen smoking, the plan would make cigarettes cheaper, which would lead to more smoking by all age groups.

How easily manipulable are surveys? When the National Household Survey, in 1994, started asking subjects with private questionnaires whether they smoked, 20 percent more admitted smoking than when asked face to face. While, on self-reporting surveys, 25 percent fewer Americans say they smoke today than did in 1970, cigarette sales per capita have declined only by 10 percent in that time.[50]

Even the Centers for Disease Control's Eriksen acknowledges that "if you [could do] only one thing to discourage smoking, the best evidence we have is on price increases." Each 10 percent increase in the price of cigarettes leads to a projected 7 percent fewer youths taking up smoking, and also more adults cutting back or quitting.[51] Now that smoking issues are on the block, authorities are right to wonder if the emotional crusade insisting that "ads hook kids" will wind up letting the industry off even bigger hooks.

Canada's experience argues that prices and taxes are paramount. Although tobacco advertising is technically banned in Canada, Canadian youth are exposed to $80 million in tobacco ads and promotions per year as well as the same barrage of tobacco pitches U.S. kids see, especially through the U.S. media widely circulated in the north country. Yet from 1989 to 1995, Statistics Canada reports, there was no increase in smoking by Canadian teens.[52] In what was once a heavy-puffing nation, teenage and adult smoking declined sharply over the last 25 years, slam-dunked in recent years by the $2-per-pack tax increase. Canada's tobacco control efforts continue to be hampered by the smuggling of cheap U.S. cigarettes courtesy of our lax law enforcement and low taxation.

Of course, one way to curb smuggling would have been to raise U.S. tobacco taxes to Canadian levels. In 1996 and 1997, after four years of verbosity, the Clinton administration finally proposed two measures shown to be effective in reducing smoking. The first was belated acceptance of the proposal of the Occupational Health and Safety Administration to ban smoking in most federal buildings. A number of studies have found workplace bans reduce employee smoking by 20 to 25 percent.[53] The second was a plan to raise cigarette prices by boosting tobacco excise taxes $1.10 over five years and extracting $370 billion from tobacco companies as the price of settling government claims. Higher prices have been shown to reduce smoking, particularly by youths.[54]

If taxes and settlement costs raise the price of cigarettes from today's average of $1.90 per pack to $3.00 over the next few years, the United States still would have the cheapest cigarettes of almost any western nation, the Smoking and Health Action Foundation reported.[55] Today, a pack costs $3.00 in Canada, $3.18 in Germany, $3.47 in France, $4.50 in Sweden and Australia, $5.27 in Great Britain, and $7.00 in Norway, with most of the price comprised of taxes. Only a handful of Western nations sell cigarettes cheaper than the U.S. does, or will even after the settlement between the U.S. and big tobacco. An even more astonishing example of the power of the tobacco industry to sidetrack true threats: assuming the Clinton-backed $1.10 per pack tax increase (to $1.34 per pack) wins, federal taxation as a percentage of the price of smokes (40 percent) would be boosted back up to the bold level of that anti-business, anti-smoking time, 1950.

The Kiddie Culture War

But even this modest inconveniencing of adult interests was not to be in 1998. In June, Senate Republicans blocked the tobacco bill following a massive industry public relations campaign against its tax increase and a lackadaisical administration lobbying effort. What goes? Isn't this the age of culture war, absolutist moral edicts, Zero Tolerance for misbehavior? Isn't this the same Congress that sternly mandated that states impose not-one-drop of alcohol standards for teenage drivers and is now frothing for new legislation to demand school expulsion, driver's license suspension, and jail for even the slightest teenage stogie, booze, or weed misdeed?

The reasons for the ashcanning were transparent. Republicans have learned from their stunning defeats at the hands of New Democrats such as Clinton: pious culture wars in the 1980s style of GOP virtuist William Bennett scare Baby Boom voters. Clinton stole the Republicans' high-morals thunder with incessant attacks on the young and the poor. The winning strategy perfected by Clinton is kiddie culture-wars: getting tough on teens. And more important, its other side: going easy on grownups. Now that the Democrats finally proposed a measure that would improve public health, primarily by inflicting higher tobacco taxes on grownups, Republicans saw a chance to steal that constituency back.

Republicans now aim to trump the Democrats in their own suit. You want pure teen bashing? Let the GOP show you how it's done. Stealing pages from Clinton's playbook, Senate Majority Leader Trent Lott (R-Mississippi) lambasted the bill as "big-government, big-tax, big-spending" legislation and announced a new bill that would focus on "the original noble cause of just dealing with teenage smoking and drug abuse."[56] The planned failure of the larger tobacco bill gave all sides center stage for emotional odes to protecting children and restraining teenagers in the modern American moral style of risk-free reverence. For all the industry-slamming indulged in by politicians on both sides, neither party had the ethics to refuse tobacco industry donations to their coffers, which totaled $7 million over the last decade.

Sho'nuff, the Republican sequel featured an absurdly punitive youth-control script mandating that states criminalize teenage smoking, punishable by driver's license suspensions and community service, and launching an "anti-smoking advertising campaign."[57] This measure is certain to be happily endorsed by a tobacco industry which knows it has nothing to fear (in fact, everything to gain) from government crusades against teenage smoking. Further to the industry's liking, higher taxes were dropped. It is likely that product liability caps to protect the industry from large lawsuit payouts will be slipped in soon. Also in the wings is the GOP salvo against teenage marijuana use.

It will be interesting to see how long the public, media, and institutional experts continue the illusion that the capitol charade has anything to do with smoking. Getting tough on unpopular groups is the natural territory of conservatives. Yet the hijacking of public health and safety policy into a get-tough-on-teens electoral strategy has been a major element in Clinton's appeal to traditional suburban constituencies, the so-called "soccer moms." Conclusion: neither party cares about teenage smoking if the addressing thereof would inflict the tiniest carbuncle on its stride to the constituent ribbon. The message both parties compete to champion is that grownups don't have to sacrifice our pleasures merely for the sake of the kids.

Thus, for all its bluster against smoking, political dictates mean the federal government today does less in practical fiscal terms to discourage it than it did half a century ago. If, however, the price of cigarettes eventually rises substantially because of his advocacy, Clinton will deserve credit for cutting smoking. Nothing else he has done has made a dent.

Smooth Customers

As this book goes to press in October of 1998, two new studies of youth smoking have emerged. From 1994–97, the Center for Disease Control surveyed 78,000 Americans over age 12, asking respondents if they had ever smoked on a daily basis and at what age they first tried cigarettes. The CDC claimed that daily smoking by teens rose by 73 percent since 1988, the year Camel introduced Joe.[58]

Table 3

Percent of teens reporting smoking in previous month

	Monitoring the Future 12th graders	National Household age 12–17	Estimated new smokers numbers (000)*	percent of pop 12–17*
1980	30.5%		2,753	10.5%
1985	30.1	29.4%	2,816	11.3
1986	29.6		2,782	10.7
1987	29.4		2,566	9.9
1988	28.7	22.7	2,484	10.7
1989	28.6		2,503	10.0
1990	29.4	22.0	2,645	10.2
1991	28.3	20.9	2,567	10.1
1992	27.8	18.4	2,707	11.1
1993	29.9	18.5	2,897	12.1
1994	31.2	18.9	3,178	13.1
1995	33.5	20.2	3,263	13.9
1996	34.0	18.3		
1997	36.5	19.9		

Sources: Substance Abuse and Mental Health Services Administration (August 1998), Preliminary Results from the 1997 National Household Survey on Drug Abuse; National Institute on Drug Abuse (1997), Monitoring the Future, 1996. Blanks denote years no comparable survey was reported.

*Calculated by SAMHSA (August 1998) from total numbers of new smokers of all ages, and number of new cigarette experimenters aged 12–17 each year as a percent of the population aged 12–17 which had not previously tried cigarettes.

This "retrospective" research, as it is called, asks subjects to recall past events (in this case back to 1965). In addition to the flaws of self-reporting surveys, retrospective studies are hampered by respondents' faulty memories and are usually done only when current information is inadequate. So it is of interest that the CDC's retrospective study contradicts major surveys of teen smoking done each year. These include Monitoring the Future and the National Household Survey, the newest released in August 1998 (Table 3). Yet the CDC made no effort in press statements to explain why its survey reached such radically different results than those of other major government studies.

The Monitoring and Household surveys reach different findings because the former polls only high school seniors while the latter interviews a sample of all youth age 12–17, including those in school and dropouts (the latter have higher rates of smoking).

Not only is there nothing unusual about the year 1988, the following year of 1989 shows a slight drop, precisely at the time Joe's campaign has been around for a while. In fact, the 12–17 population displays lower smoking levels today after nine years' exposure to Joe Camel ads than before his 1988 debut. If anything, 1988 was a year of unusually low numbers of new smokers.

If one were to guess when things started to escalate in terms of smoking initiation or high school seniors' trends, it would be 1992–94. This pattern—a turnaround in youth smoking from a low point in 1992 and a rise thereafter—shows up for smoking daily (as well as at least once in the previous month) among high school seniors, 10th graders, and 8th graders, according to the newest (1997) Monitoring the Future survey posted by the National Institute on Drug Abuse's Home Page.

If we are going to accept simplistic "correlation equals causation" logic (if B occurs after A, then A caused B), then rather than blame Joe, there are better grounds for blaming punitive policies that criminalize youth smoking. The genesis of these policies from anti-tobacco groups coincided with the growth in teen puffing—or, at least, with a growth in teens' tendencies to report more smoking.

The Monitoring and Household surveys reach different findings because the former polls only high school seniors while the latter interviews a sample of all youth age 12–17, including both students and dropouts (the latter have higher rates of smoking). Even so, the findings are contradictory. Why should smoking among 12th graders be rising (up 20 percent in the '90s) while 12–17 year-olds' smoking is stable or declining? Why does the Monitoring poll find eighth graders' tobacco use rising steadily while the Household survey finds flat trends? Even though agencies and the media worship these surveys, they readily discard findings that they don't like, even from the most reputable surveys.

The reason is that political expedience, not reducing smoking, rules the roost. There are dozens of surveys today, enough for the industry and so-called anti-smoking agencies to affirm whatever is needed to keep their common interests safe from attack. And they've succeeded. It's teens, not tobacco moguls and craven policy chiefs, that Congress and the states are threatening to shake down, expel, and jail for taking up a cigarette habit which business and polticians find profitable to the last drag.

6 Myth:
Teen Moms Are
Ruining America

The trumpeting of teenage sex and motherhood as cataclysmic social crises is a tragic case of political exploitation combined with institutional malpractice. A decade before Charles Murray came along with his *Losing Ground* thesis that welfare causes illegitimate births which cause poverty which causes welfare, liberal groups perversely strove to publicize "pregnancy among teenagers as a fundamental cause of poverty."[1] Long before conservative affirmative action opponents of the 1990s began abolishing measures designed to compensate for three centuries of overt racism, 1970s Democrats such as Senators Daniel Patrick Moynihan and Ted Kennedy and former Carter Health Secretary Joseph Califano, Jr. were laying the groundwork with the claim that poverty was caused by sexual irresponsibility, primarily among those of dark pigment.

During the 1970s, Democratic liberals charged that high rates of birth among teenagers were the reason that entire groups, such as blacks, were poor. African and Native Americans had been liberated for almost a whole decade since the 1964 Civil Rights Act—why were they still poor and having so many babies? For the next 20 years, mostly white, affluent, liberal interests blamed the "epidemic of teenage pregnancy." From far right to far left, from the Family Research Council to Planned Parenthood, the basic assumptions about "teenage" sex and fertility were the same. Dumb, promiscuous, immoral (right) and/or dumb, promiscuous, underprogrammed (left) teenage girls were being knocked up by hormonal teenage boys in rising adolescent lustiness.

The difference was that while Ford-era conservatives saw teenage pregnancy as just one component of poor people's misbehavior, liberals saw it as *the* misbehavior. And, while rightists proposed tougher, often compulsory, controls on reproduction by the poor, liberals proposed programs to educate, contracept, and plan. Much of the liberal misportrayal of teenage pregnancy, which reached near-lunatic unreality by the 1990s, resulted from the benign goal of preserving vital health programs in a chilling political climate.

The larger problem that came back to haunt progressive groups was that by inveighing against teenagers having babies, Democrats effectively endorsed the conservative credo that poverty is caused by bad personal behaviors rather than indicting poverty as the major cause of poor health and limited choices. Califano, a tirelessly senseless voice on youth policy for two decades, declared in 1976:

> Teenage pregnancy—the entry into parenthood of individuals who barely are beyond childhood themselves—is one of the most serious and complex problems facing the nation today...The birth of a child can usher in a dismal

future of unemployment, poverty, family breakdown, emotional stress, dependency on public agencies and health problems of mother and child...Scarcely
anyone—liberal or conservative—can read these figures about teenage pregnancy without a sense of shock and melancholy.[2]

The "melancholy" figures Califano distorted showed that teenage birth rates
had been *declining dramatically for two decades*. From 1957 to 1975, birth rates fell by
40 percent among both black and white teens. This plummet had occurred without
any special attention to "teenage pregnancy," a non-issue prior to 1975, which
should give modern moralists pause. Rather, it had accompanied dramatic declines
in poverty among youths and rapidly increasing enrollment of minorities in college
in the wake of Great Society programs and civil rights advances of the Sixties.

Apparently, that progress was resented. Thanks to the meshing of the political needs of New Democrats with Republicans', it quickly reversed in the 1970s,
victim of false claims and abundant moralizing. Sociologists call the creation of
new social crises where none exist "moral entrepreneurship." In this case, 1970s
Democrats (like their 1990s counterparts) were trolling for gut-grabbing morality
issues to bury their unpopular reputation for social reform. The myth of a "teenage
pregnancy epidemic" was great for burnishing the New Democrats' nouveau-puri-
tan image. It was a disaster for American social policy and the young, given what
was actually going on.

The new problem was not wed or unwed teenage motherhood, but the fact
that men of all ages, in sociologist Kristin Luker's words, had "retreated from a commitment to their children, both within and outside marriage."[3] Single parenting had
risen rapidly among teenage and adult mothers, driven by growing divorce and
unwed childbearing. The rise in fathers' default was clearly visible in the mid-1970s,
as were some of its causes. The shutdown of industries in inner cities had left hundreds of thousands of men jobless, devaluing their worth and making them burdens
to families.[4] By 1973, income was reversing among younger workers of all races.
This "Great U-turn" can be seen in the figures in Chapter 9.

Here was an ominous economic drop Democrats traditionally would have
spotlighted. But the social-concern days of the Sixties were done, now a bad memory. Yuppie, pre-tax-revolt voters were in no mood to hear about the job woes of
swarthy 25-year-olds. The loss of five of six presidential elections from 1968
through 1988 molded a New Democratic Party interested in the hot buttons of
profit and morals.

"Teenage Pregnancy" and "Risk": the N-Words of the '90s

Liberal theorists thus constructed an ideology that discarded every fact that got
in the way of the assumption that "teenage pregnancy" was caused by misbehavior
among ignorant, maladjusted adolescents. Using "teenage pregnancy" as a codeword
"permitted people to talk about African Americans and poor women (categories
that often overlapped) without mentioning race or class," Luker pointed out.[5]
Especially in the punishing Clinton era, the liberal insinuation is that minorities are
fine Americans except for their inexplicably fertile and violent teenagers. The
masking of America's new tolerance for racial and socioeconomic inequality behind

the increasing furor directed at "teenage pregnancy" and adolescent "behavior risks" was succinctly skewered by George Curry, publisher of the innovative African-American magazine *Emerge*: " 'at-risk' is the n-word of the '90s."

The New Racism, which we have seen before in the Clinton-era "get tough" criminal justice policies and in the War on Drugs, is the same deployed in selective welfare reform aimed at impoverished mothers. Behind the administration's sunny facade of tolerant (and do-nothing) "conversations about race" and the courting of minority leadership, the New Racism was imprisoning hundreds of thousands more African-American and Latino men and jeopardizing more poor families than the Republicans' stern moral regime (but policy inaction) of the Eighties.

Democrats' rules of covert racism, perfectly comfortable to Republicans once they belatedly got the hang of them, were simple: don't talk race, talk "youth violence;" don't talk race, talk "teenage pregnancy;" don't talk race, talk "adolescent morals, values, and at-risk behavior." When necessary, the egregious behavior of a rich kid (nearly always white) could be played up in the press to obscure who the attack was really against. And, of course, there were plenty of poorer white kids swirling down the drain of 1990s reforms to ensure a supply of gravid white eighth graders to portray as poster-girls in New-Democrat condemnations of "teen pregnancy." The New Racism isn't afraid to toss poorer white youths, and even a few rich ones, overboard in order to profit from a subtle assault on the "illegitimate" and "superpredator" hordes of the mostly dark-skinned "underclass."

It was strange to witness conservatives such as columnist George Will and the American Enterprise Institute's Douglas Besharov decode the truth that Democratic policies were menacing the well-being of African Americans and poor families as never before. It was scary to see Republicans learning from electoral defeats how Clinton's "values" agenda, ripped off from the right, could be recaptured. Family Research Council chief Gary Bauer, a right-wing power supreme and likely presidential candidate, deduced that "Bill Clinton looked more traditional" to fearful voters: "He was talking about school uniforms, curfews, while our guys were talking mostly about balance-sheet issues with green eye shades on."[6]

Two decades of liberal morals ideology and neglect of race-economic issues inevitably led to the brutal reactionary mood of the 1990s, as Clinton and Republicans jockeyed to slam adolescent mothers with vicious punishments. The angry Clinton/right teen-mother blitzkrieg came at exactly the time new research was uncovering crucial facts about what had been called "teenage motherhood," ones that should have been discovered decades earlier. For example, "teenage pregnancy" is highly concentrated among the disadvantaged: six out of seven teen mothers were poor or low income.[7] Another vital fact: most teenage mothers had histories of childhood sexual and physical abuses, many severe.[8] Further, most "teenage births" were fathered by adult men age 20 and older, not by teenage boys.[9] Finally, early motherhood may well be a rational survival response by impoverished young women to their narrow and dangerous predicaments, as it has been for eons throughout the world.[10]

It is hard to imagine a behavior less amenable to influence by a focus on teenage moral choices, particularly those of adolescent girls, alone. Yet that has been exactly the strategy of two decades of policy, whether conservative abstinence

preaching or liberal contraceptive education. Literally no effect from all the hulla-
baloo is visible. Relative to the adult birth rate, America's teenage birth rate stands
at the same level in 1997 that it did in 1930, 1950, 1970, and 1990.

That none of these critical facts received serious attention until the mid-1990s
(most still haven't) is a damning indictment of liberals' exploitation of a social
problem they themselves manufactured. The grievous cost of two decades of myth-
making is evident as liberals now strive to rescue poorer, young mothers from the
Clinton/rightist "welfare reform" napalming.

Ignoring Poverty

"Teenage" sex, pregnancy, and other sexual issues are policy fictions created by
politicians, academics, and politically-attuned moral entrepreneurs. Teenage sexual
behaviors do not exist as distinct entities in real life. Worldwide and throughout
history, they are mirrors of the economic and political status of women. Teenage
sexuality is like that of the adults around them, partly because most teenage babies,
and nearly all teenage HIV infections, are acquired through relations with adult
men.

These individual adult-teen similarities are also society-wide ones. For as far
back in time as figures are available, trends in adolescent births, unwed births, abortion, sexually-transmitted disease, and AIDS have been identical to those among
adults. Whatever causes these sexual outcomes to increase or decrease among
grownups has a similar effect on teens. The long-term trends and local rates of births
among teenage mothers can be predicted with 90 percent precision from corresponding adult birth rates and youth poverty rates. Just as black and Latino adult
women have higher birth rates (and different trends over time) than white women,
so black and Latino teenagers have birth rates three to four times higher than white
teens and display trends resembling those of adults of their respective races.
Contrary to the statements of many liberal commentators, abortion does not
explain the difference between birth rates among white girls and those of color.
Surveys by the Alan Guttmacher Institute find abortion rates four times higher
among black than white teens.[11]

But the powerful have always had trouble comprehending why poor people do
what they do. Health and Human Services Secretary Donna Shalala's moralistic
complaints that teenage mothers cause their own poverty are in keeping with her
upbringing in the rich suburb of Shaker Heights, Ohio.[12] No one in the echelons of
the American Medical Association can comprehend why anyone would have a baby
at 16. Teen mothers did not grow up in the same preppie circumstances as the
politicians and academicians who presumed to lecture or dictate how poor youths
should lead their lives.

The privileged interests who invented, then harshly judged, "teenage pregnancy" got every key fact wrong it was possible to get wrong—that is, the image of
the issue that various teen-sex constituencies required was not the same as the
reality teenagers experienced. The first crucial reality the teen-welfare-mom furor
sidestepped is the fact that most teenage mothers were poor *before* they became
pregnant.

Third World USA

More clear-headed, humanitarian policy might flow out of the White House if officials put aside ideology and just looked out the window. Teen motherhood rates in Washington, D.C., are 17 times higher among blacks than among whites who live a couple of Metro stops away. White D.C. teens have poverty and birth rates lower than The Netherlands'. Black D.C. teens have poverty rates 10 times higher than whites and birth rates like Mali's. Right away, it is clear that this is not a "teenage" phenomenon.

In visiting several dozen American cities to give conference presentations in the past two years, I spent days walking poorer neighborhoods. They varied from pocked, crumbling inner cities everywhere that looked as if they had been strafed by bombers to shattered post-industrial hells like Camden, north Philadelphia, Gary, and East St. Louis that would look better if they were bombed. These neighborhoods, full of boarded buildings and weedy lots, are densely populated with young people. It is profoundly sobering to imagine growing up there realizing that larger society offers little escape.

Rochester, New York, is an archetype of America's declining industrial cities but by no means among the worst. I was asked by the Monroe County Health Department in 1996 to speak on the city's growing teenage birth rate. As in most cities I visited, the abandonment of youth is in the news. Rochester's papers headline a $4 million cut in the local school budget. An editorial points out that segregated housing patterns "leave the poor without realistic choices." "The opportunities for moving out of urban areas like Rochester in the 1950s and 1960s gave families unprecedented chances," *Times-Union* editors lamented. "As the gulf between city and suburb grows wider, it is easier to abandon Rochester and its residents."[13] In 1996, Rochester houses less than one-fourth of Monroe County's 1 million people. But half the county's poorer whites, and 96 percent of the poorer blacks and Latinos, live in the city.

I spent two spring days walking Rochester's formerly prosperous neighborhoods, once well fed by its chief employer, Eastman Kodak, and other topside industries. On North St. Paul sits the 10-story Bausch & Lomb plant, abandoned, windows broken. From the bridge, vacant, silent factories flank the roaring Genesee River. To the right is the Kodak tower, where corporate cutbacks chopped the labor force from 65,000 in past heydays to fewer than 30,000 today.

Rochester's north and westside formerly-working-class neighborhoods are shabby. In another decade they will fall into the bombed-out look of Camden, Baltimore, Richmond, and Philadelphia. It is mostly a white city, one-sixth black. Among black youths, poverty has risen from 31 percent in 1970 to 48 percent today. Among white youth, poverty tripled from 8 percent in 1970 to 22 percent now.

Beginning in 1980, lagging a decade behind the unemployment and poverty caused by industrial abandonment, the unwed birth rate among white teenagers also tripled. Among black youth, unwed births are up 50 percent. More and more, rates among urban whites look like those of blacks. But in Rochester's green, hilly suburbs stretching to Lake Ontario, prosperity is evident. The teenage birth rate, one-fourth the rate of urban whites and one-tenth that of urban blacks, has not risen.

Every region, state, and metropolis of the United States mirrors Rochester's teen-pregnancy microcosm of the world. In the most middle-American city of Des Moines, Iowa, the inner-city African-American population displays teenage birth levels (125 births per 1,000 females age 15–19 per year) like those of Ethiopia. Drive a few miles to affluent west Des Moines and further to the suburbs, and teen birth rates (15 per 1,000) are lower than Norway's. In between, census tracts with teen birth rates like Brazil, the Philippines, Poland, and every other nation can be found.

"To see the relationship between poverty and early childbearing," the Northwest Environment Watch's excellent population study, *Misplaced Blame*, offers, "take a quick tour of the Pacific Northwest:"

> Consider Yakima County, Washington: a great sprawling expanse of orchards, migrant labor camps, and Indian reservations stretching east from the Cascade crest. Yakima County has the highest teen birthrate in the entire bioregion. Of every 1,000 women aged fifteen to nineteen in this county, 113 give birth each year. Yakima County is also the poorest county in the bioregion. Of every 1,000 children living there, 301 belong to families that fall below the federal poverty line.
>
> Now go down to Clackamas County, Oregon. Gleaming new Wilsonville High School in the heart of this suburban Portland county brims with sexually active young men and women, just like all the region's secondary schools. But almost no one at Wilsonville High has a baby; the students go to college instead. At 34 per 1,000, the teen birthrate in Clackamas County is less than a third of the rate in Yakima County.
>
> Last tour stop: the North Shore health district of British Columbia, comprising the city of North Vancouver and neighboring jurisdictions across the Lion's Gate Bridge from Vancouver. The North Shore has the bioregion's lowest poverty rate. It also has the lowest rate of teen parenting. At 5 births per 1,000 young women—one-ninth of the region's average (43 per 1,000)—the North Shore makes Sweden (14 per 1,000) look bad.[14]

Culture or Poverty?

Even the crazy-quilt of racial and ethnic mix of giant California or New York City adds little to the extremes that can be found in any modest-sized city or small state. What California's diversity shows is that race, ethnicity, and age are meaningless when larger economic patterns take hold. Consider how radically different teen birth rates are not just between races, but *within* the same races and ethnicities. It takes a couple of hours to drive from California's wealthy Bay Area coastal counties to its impoverished Central Valley. Teen-birth-wise, it's like traveling from Copenhagen to Calcutta. In migrant-labor dominated Tulare County, one in five black teenagers gives birth each year, among the highest rates on the planet. But in affluent, university-dominated Santa Cruz, the low birth rate among black teens would do even Canada proud.

"Latina teens defy decline in birthrates," the *Los Angeles Times*' front page reads on February 13, 1998. Various experts, including Latinos, blamed "cultural preferences for larger families, the role of the Catholic Church in discouraging contraception and abortion, and economic and educational obstacles that prompt some Latinas to choose early childbearing."

True, as the article notes, Latina birth rates are three to four times higher than those of Euro-whites *on average*. But as Table 1 shows, Euro teen birth rates vary *nine-fold* between the highest and lowest major counties of California. Latina teens in wealthy Marin County, whose poverty rates are below the state average, do not display cultural or religious propensities to have more kids. The poverty rate of Latina teens in Marin County is about the same as for Euro-whites in Kern County—and Latinas' birth rates are a bit lower.

The Northwest Environment Watch report cited earlier is an example of the new thinking on teenage motherhood that is gradually revising 25 years of myths and rising anger. Washington state's Advancing Solutions to Adolescent Pregnancy, in Seattle, is also at the forefront of examining the new issues of poverty, sexual abuse, older male partners, and the images young females (particularly poor ones and abuse victims) receive of their place in society.

Judith Musick, Debra Boyer, and David Fine's pioneering studies of sexual abuse and teenage mothers argued strongly that "prevention" was not the mere technical, contraceptive-abstinence "message" challenge previously assumed. Planned Parenthood of Greater Northern New Jersey, led by director Peggy Brick, pioneered the use of teenage and adult focus groups to design new sexuality education programs which confront adult-teen sexual relationships, an area traditional programs continue to ignore.

Along with Musick's 1993 *Young, Poor, and Pregnant*, the broadest challenge to the conventional conservative/liberal teenage sexuality myth was Berkeley sociologist Kristin Luker's 1997 work, *Dubious Conceptions*. Luker flatly argued that "early childbearing does not make young women poor; poverty makes women bear children at an early age."[16] Class biases had blinded traditional academics to the narrow choices of poorer teenagers. Privileged scholars and officials could not understand why a ghetto or rural youth would have a baby at 16, tossing away her chance at prep school, Harvard, Grande Tour of Europe, and Wall Street brokership. What they don't seem to understand is that for the poorest classes of teens, the chances of succeeding by that route are on par with winning the lottery.

Early motherhood is a survival strategy by young women from indigent, chaotic families which often successfully attracts resources from family, public agencies, and men that would not otherwise have been available. Interestingly, the first long-term study of teenage motherhood, by University of Chicago psychologist Joseph Hotz and colleagues (summarized below) affirmed that decision: teenage mothers were poorer than their non-fruitful peers at first but by their 30s were earning considerably more money.[17]

By 1998, teen pregnancy prevention groups seemed to be splitting. A growing number were holding conferences whose agendas brimmed with items reflecting new lines of thought such as the above. These tended to view "teenage" pregnancy as part of a larger continuum of American economic and sexual inequality. The majority, in contrast, pursued technical agendas that looked the same as they had a

Table 1

Ethiopia to Denmark in one state
Poverty, not race, predicts teen birth rates

California teen birth rate extremes
Highest and lowest for populous* counties by race

	Highest county	Lowest county
White (European)	Kern County	Marin County
teen birth rate/1,000	79	9
teen poverty rate	12.7%	4.0%
is like:	Bulgaria's (rural)	Denmark's
Latino	Fresno County	Marin County
teen birth rate/1,000	137	70
teen poverty rate	39.1%	15.2%
is like:	Guatemala's (rural)	Argentina's
Black	Tulare County	Santa Cruz County
teen birth rate/1,000	195	23
teen poverty rate	41.0%	20.4%
is like:	Mali's	Canada's
Asian	Fresno County	San Luis Obispo County
teen birth rate/1,000	142	12
teen poverty rate	56.4%	3.9%
is like:	Bangladesh's	Finland's
All teens	Tulare County	Marin County
teen birth rate/1,000	106	19
teen poverty rate	31.2%	5.5%
is like:	India's	Norway's

*County population exceeds 200,000.
Source: Bureau of Vital Statistics, California Department of Health Services.

decade or two ago. The latter's focus continued to be techniques for contraceptive education and services, or how to say no, or social costs, or seductive messages in rock'n'roll—that is, the politically safe remedies.

The Role of Sexual Abuse

The role of sexual abuse in teen pregnancy is often ignored because it doesn't fit policy makers' interest in defining the issue in terms of the personal choice and morality of teen girls. Yet sexual abuse certainly is a crucial factor in the lives of young people who endure it. The willingness to confront tough, unsettling issues such as poverty and sexual abuse rather than the easy, satisfying ones of supposed adolescent immorality and ignorance defines a program that sees itself as existing to serve kids rather than kids existing to serve programs.

I worked closely with low-income families for a decade and saw the effects of rape and sexual abuse on adolescent girls. When young females are subjected to terrible violations in their own homes and beds by household males, they quite reasonably become fearful, insecure, confused. Their abuses cause them distress, which for many leads to school failure, alcohol and drug abuse, and thoughts of suicide. They look for escape from their frightening daily lives. They are vulnerable to older males who promise rescue in exchange for that one special favor. Sometimes they pick the right guy, often they do not. Sometimes they have babies young to promote themselves out of an untenable childhood and into an adult status that couldn't possibly be worse.

Judith Musick, of Chicago's An Ounce of Prevention program, compiled interviews with and diaries of hundreds of teenage mothers. Her 1993 study, *Young, Poor, and Pregnant*, details the severe psychological stresses imposed by hostile economics, chaotic families, and sexual pressures from older men. A girl who becomes a mother often spent a harsh childhood "struggling to take care of herself and frequently of others as well, such as younger siblings or older family members lost to drink or drugs:"

> Those who come of age in poverty are given very little margin of error in negotiating the tasks of adolescence...Girls growing up in poverty need to possess not just average but above-average psychological resources and strengths, self-concepts, and competencies.[18]

Musick reported that her organization's study of 445 pregnant and parenting teens found past (and often present) sexual abuse pervasive:

> The preteen girls asked whether it was right to have sex with their fathers, stepfathers, or their mothers' boyfriends. The older girls in the parenting program spoke of having been forced or tricked into sexual relations with fathers, uncles, brothers, older cousins, and grandfathers.
>
> Sixty-one percent of the sample reported having been sexually abused, and 65 percent of these victims reported abuse by more than one perpetrator. For many of the victims, the abuse was an ongoing situation: although one-quarter of the victims stated that the abuser had committed the act only once, 50 percent reported having been abused between two and ten times, and the remaining 25 percent reported being abused more than ten times... The average age of first occurrence was 11.5 years of age.
>
> ...We found that only 18 percent of the abusers were two or fewer years older than the victims, another 18 percent were three to five years older, and 17 percent were six to ten years older. The remaining 46 percent

were more than ten years older than their victims. Very large age differences were especially common among victims abused before the age of 14
years.[19]

A similar Alan Guttmacher Institute finding, issued at the height of the welfare reform debate in 1994, represented a national call to action for health officials
concerned about young people. Of the "sexually active" girls ages 14 and younger,
60 percent said they had been raped. For 43 percent, rape was their only "sexual"
experience. Most of the rapes, the Institute reported, were by "substantially older"
men.[20]

The Clinton White House is infested with liberal scholars and program representatives well aware of the findings by respected organizations such as Guttmacher,
An Ounce of Prevention,[21] Advancing Solutions to Adolescent Pregnancy,[22] and
New Mexico's La Clinica de Familia[23] that most teenage mothers suffered histories
of severe sexual abuse and family violence. Yet Health and Human Services
Secretary Donna Shalala, who takes a "hard line" to punish teenage mothers,[24] has
never issued a major statement on violent and sexual abuses of hundreds of thousands of children by parents and caretakers every year. When asked about the
Guttmacher report that most of what were called "sexually active" girls under age 14
had been raped, mostly by older males,[25] Shalala responded that "children" should
be taught not to have sex.[26] The president, who bitterly complained in top-level
press conferences that teenage mothers impose billions of dollars of "social costs" on
society, displayed zero interest in the rape of junior high girls. Officially, the Centers
for Disease Control maintains that rape and abuse of children and adolescents by
adults don't exist—only violence perpetrated by peers.

Inevitably, when I raise the Guttmacher findings among academics or sexuality experts, someone suggests the girls are lying. The girls had sex, feel guilty, and
want to blame it on the guy, these experts say. It has not been my experience in
working with kids that younger girls are eager to claim histories of rape. Intense
shame and reluctance to reveal such a tragedy are far more common reactions to
childhood violations, a fact Freud observed a century ago[27] that hasn't changed. But
I agree that self-reporting surveys are questionable and hard to interpret. We don't
know what the girls reporting rape mean. The larger point is that these same sexuality experts never seem to question patently idiotic findings from surveys more to
their liking, such as the Kaiser teen sex figures discussed later.

California statistics provide grounds for concern that "abuse," in turn, is a
charge levied more often against impoverished parents. The figures can be read
either way. Blacks constitute 6 percent of the state's population but comprise 18
percent of the child victims and one-fifth of those charged with abusing or neglect-
ing children, the state Legislative Analyst reported.[15] The state's other three major
racial groups are not over-represented when it comes to child victims, but blacks are
greatly overrepresented, and Latinos moderately overrepresented, when it comes to
those charged with perpetrating abuse or neglect. There is a clear implication that
poverty, not bad parenting per se, is a major factor in getting charged with child
neglect. Blacks and Latinos are also under greater scrutiny from social service and
law enforcement agencies than are more affluent whites and Asians.

Ignoring Adult-Teen Sex

That adults have sex and babies with teenagers creates singular problems for "teenage" pregnancy lobbies on all sides. Two-thirds of what we call "teenage" births, and even larger shares of "teenage" STD and AIDS, result from sexual relations between men over age 20 and adolescents. The father of a baby born to a California mother age 17 or younger is more likely to be over 22 (5,625 in 1996) than under 18 (4,513).

The "social costs" of single motherhood, adult as well as teenage, are the result of adult male default. Since the 1950s, men have steadily withdrawn from supporting their children. Divorce and unwed births play equal roles in the increasing impoverishment of single mothers, though only the latter has drawn the wrath of the pundit and politician. Today, in California alone, 3.3 million children are in the state child support enforcement system. Over 1 million are without support orders. Of those with orders, only four in 10 receive any kind of payment.[28]

Charlie Langdon, executive director of Washington state's Advancing Solutions to Adolescent Pregnancy, proposes that in lieu of imprisonment for a statutory rape that results in childbirth, civil judgments assess fathers for half the cost of raising the child over 18 years.[29] Many can pay more. A survey of divorced fathers in Denver found two-thirds spend more on car payments than child support; nearly all were up-to-date in paying for their wheels but more than in half were deadbeat in paying for their kid.[30] On the other hand, it is clear that not all "deadbeat dads" are to blame. Many would support their kids if jobs were available and equitable support orders were implemented. Since five out of six children receiving public assistance are owed child support, reforming welfare and paternity enforcement to address the varied problems of deadbeat and/or unemployed fathers seems a far better reform than continuing to beat up on the mothers.[31]

The "older male" issue is real, not just numerically but in its heightened risks for pregnancy and HIV infection. A 1994 survey of black and Hispanic 14–16-year-old females found that half had partners three or more years older when they lost their virginity. Compared to those with partners within three years of their age, those with older partners were almost a year younger when they first had sex. They were less likely to use condoms. Three times more had been pregnant, and twice as many had a sexually-transmitted disease, though the rate was low (6 percent).[32]

California's Office of Family Planning studied 27,000 adolescent mothers who gave birth during 1993.[33] Half their babies were fathered by men over age 20, and these men averaged 6.4 years older than the mothers. As a rule, the larger the age gap, the more likely both partners were screwed up. Both the men involved with young females and the girls themselves had much lower levels of schooling than their ages would predict—behind even the teenage fathers and their teenage female partners in the study. Older-younger couples were also likely to have more babies and to have been born outside the U.S. Other studies found that compared to teenage fathers, older fathers involved with adolescent mothers tended to have greater problems with drug and alcohol abuse, crime, and school dropout—but also had better jobs and higher incomes.[34]

Young women with older partners were more likely to have been abused or neglected, come from violent homes, and (understandably) suffer low self-esteem and depression. Musick concluded from extensive interviews that sexual abuse and paternal abandonment make young girls much more susceptible to the allure of older partners. The reasons are both psychological and economic:

> What about the characteristics of males who are attracted to much younger (adolescent) females? Are they simply less mature: "My boyfriend is 14 years older than me, but he doesn't act it or look it" [teen mother]. Or are they exploitative, disturbed, or sexually deviant? If so, what does that tell us about the relationships these girls are repeatedly drawn to, and how might these men function as revictimizers?...sexual offenders seem to have special antennae that pick up signals of vulnerability in the girls they select as victims. These girls tend to be needier and more passive, dependent, depressed, and unhappy. They may be more conspicuous to adults interested in molesting them. Could a less severe form of this dynamic be at work when older males prefer to date adolescents, particularly younger adolescents?[35]

The choices of girls in difficult situations may appear crazy to advantaged observers, but they often represent a rational gamble. An older man is much more likely to have the resources to rescue a girl from a dangerous or dead-end life.[36] If he fails, well, life was no picnic before.

In the 1996 presidential campaign, the "predatory older male" got its few minutes of fame. Republican contender Bob Dole briefly tried to make an issue of the "adult male" in teen pregnancy. States beefed up statutory rape laws. The Montel Williams Show called me twice for leads on 40-year-old men who'd fathered babies with sixth graders. I didn't know any.

Orange County would be the place to look. The conservative county has the oldest fathers with teen mothers I've ever encountered. Nearly two-thirds of *junior* high mothers are paired with men too old to be in high school. County social workers found themselves on the national hot seat in September 1996 for facilitating court-approved marriages between adults and teens, including a 20-year-old who fathered a baby with a 13-year-old.

"Love or Abuse?" the press headlined. When the man, the girl, the girl's parents, and all the attorneys and agencies involved were asked, the consensus was that the marriage was a better bet than the girl had before. The man voluntarily married her and took over the role of father. The social workers, court, and district attorney's office all investigated the marriage and declined to take action.[37] Better that the System apply its underfunded, understaffed, and inadequate resources to addressing the 40,000 Orange County parents who beat and neglect their kids, the thousands cooking crystal methamphetamine on the kitchen stove, the 170,000 fathers behind in child support. Perhaps Mr. Twenty and Ms. Thirteen will join that list, but there are too many proven bad parents demanding attention ahead of them.

No matter. In jumped the politicians, sporting nary a clue. A grand jury investigation revved up. Media calls swamped the agency. California Social Services Director Eloise Anderson declared that "we should draw the line so hard in the sand that if anyone steps over it, he gets his foot cut off." *No* girl under age 18 has the cognitive ability to be a spouse or parent, she said.[38]

It occurred to me that so far at least, the adult-teen pair at the eye of this moral-cane had not screwed up their marital life as badly as Anderson had hers. They were married, he had a good job and was buying a house, they were not collecting welfare. Anderson, in contrast, was a single mother who collected Food Stamps after divorcing her child's father in the 1970s.[39] Anderson is now a conservative Republican, harshly judgmental of welfare mothers, directing reforms in Wisconsin and California that made the system far less generous to recipients than it was in her welfare-mom days.

Anderson's larger point is correct, however. As noted, there is extensive sexual abuse, including rape, of younger girls by older men which is not being redressed. Relationships between much-older men and junior high-age girls have sparked legitimate concern. Several studies have found that teenage mothers and so-called "sexually active" young girls are very likely to have been victims of childhood rapes and sexual abuses, perpetrated primarily by older teenage and adult males.[40] These, it seems to me, are the cases to prosecute.

I worked with low-income youths and saw a lot of relationships between younger teen girls and men who were considerably older. They were diverse, which makes it difficult to give a blanket answer when I am asked by the press and program groups what we should do about the "older male" problem. If we draw a "hard line in the sand" as Anderson advises, what should it be? America's birth records are reasonably complete back to 1920 or so and before that are increasingly haphazard back to colonial days. They show that teenagers have always had babies, with adult partners, ones who were generally older in the past than today. Older men knocking up teenagers is as American as...James and Elizabeth Monroe, Theodore and Alice Roosevelt, and Jimmy and Rosalynn. My grandfather, 25, married my grandmother, 16, in Oklahoma in 1912 (no, they were not cousins!), a marriage that lasted seven decades.

Despite recent claims about "predatory older males," most adult-teen relationships appear voluntary. The real issue seems to me the power balance between the partners—the kind of distinction sexual harassment law makes—of which age difference is only a part. Maybe we should trust the opinions of the younger partners more as to whether they were taken advantage of. The alternative is to force hundreds of thousands of unwilling "victims" up on witness stands, where they can be counted upon to appear more collected and mature than the "predators." That alone tells us a lot about the absurdity of over-reliance on age-based laws.

But many interests have staked out large investments in "teenage pregnancy" as a "social problem" which is defined solely by the "teen age" of the mother. For that reason, the routineness of adult-youth sex throws a wrench into everyone's notion of "teenage" pregnancy, AIDS, and motherhood. In most states, an adult deemed old enough to drink whisky and control every aspect of his life may legally have sexual intercourse with a youth the law holds is too immature to even glance at a *Playboy* over a near-beer.

So what do we mean by "teenage" sex? What age are we even talking about? Are 18- and 19-year-olds part of the "epidemic of teen pregnancy," or not? Interests desiring to generate large, scary numbers to provoke attention and funding included 18–19-year-olds in the "one million teen pregnancies" and "half a million teenage births" every year. Then the troublesome problem of older fathers surfaced. Three-fourths of mothers age 18–19 had their babies courtesy of men over age 20. So now it's fashionable to exclude 18- and 19-year-olds and concentrate only on "minor" mothers.

So 18 becomes the sexual Maginot Line. Big problem: 80 percent of minor mothers have partners over age 18. Even more adult-teen sex!

Should we just draw the line at the legal "age of consent," then—16, as most states set it? Ninety percent of the mothers (and a 50 percent of the very small number of fathers!) under age 16 have partners older than 16. The younger the age below which society sternly forbids sexual behavior, the more likely the partners will be older than that age. This is a big problem for the whole political issue of "teenage pregnancy," which is inextricably tied to age-based rigidities. In fact, more problems are created for conventional theories of prevention if, in fact, most adult partners are *not* predators.

However, teenagers can be decreed as adult and child at once, a convoluted 1997 study by Urban Institute (UI) researchers affirmed.[41] The strange logic of this study is worth examining, and not just in terms of its efforts to uphold the contrary notions of traditional program interests to continue heavy focus on the sins of the pregnant teenage female while downplaying those of the adult male who helped get her where she is. It also reveals what slippery concepts "adult" and "teen" have become among groups which use "young age" as a rigid criterion to define and address social problems.

UI argues the "older male" dilemma is "very small." The study begins with a good point: sterner enforcement of existing statutory rape laws will not prevent much teen pregnancy because the laws apply to only a small fraction. Averaging wildly inconsistent felony statutory rape provisions in five large states, the authors calculate that only 8 percent of all births among mothers under age 20 result from prosecutable statutory rape.

California is a case in point. Fifteen thousand new mothers under age 18 every year have partners 20 and older; imagine how many hundreds of thousands more adult-teen liaisons there must be. The state poured $12 million into a new "vertical prosecution" program in 1996. The state's statutory rape arrest volume rose from... 580 in 1995 to 893 in 1996. That's $40,000 per increased arrest. Had the UI authors stopped there, public policy would have gotten a cold slap in the reality.

However, disregarding age limits means abolishing altogether the lucrative issue of "teenage pregnancy," which is, after all, based strictly on age. So UI's authors wound up advancing the contradictory conclusion that while it is not socially acceptable for teenage girls to have babies, it is socially acceptable for adult men to impregnate teenage girls.

The math underlying this conclusion gets a bit mixed up. The UI authors began by defining *all* births to mothers age 15–19 as the scope of the female behavior problem laws and programs were supposed to prevent. All 500,000 per year. However, when it came to defining the scope of the older-male behavior problem, the authors excluded all men, no matter how much older, who fathered babies with (a) 18- and 19-year-old mothers (married or unwed) and (b) minor mothers to whom they were married. That eliminated 400,000 annual births right there. They also excluded all men who fathered babies with (c) unwed minor mothers less than five years younger. Subtract another 50,000 to 60,000. Poof…no more adult male problem.

The authors are emphatic on this point: "Regardless of the mother's age, the pattern of fathers being slightly older than mothers fits squarely within societal norms." "Slightly" means up to five years older. (No, the authors are not from Orange County).

Even after all these exclusions, 40 percent of the unwed births among 15-year-olds and 25 percent among 16–17-year-olds were fathered by men five or more years senior. That alone shows how different the concept of "teenage pregnancy" had become from its portrayal only a few years ago. But compared to *all* 15–19 births (here authors reinserted the 450,000 births to married minors and to 18–19-year-old mothers they had previously excluded), "only 8% of all births to 15–19-year-olds are to unmarried minors with a partner five or more years older." That was the sound-bite number badly misquoted in the *New York Times* and other news media.

More big problems. The UI authors defined adults up to age 22 or so and minor teens as "similar age" peers. But if it is acceptable for 21-year-olds to engage in such profoundly adult behaviors as having sex and babies with 16- and 17-year-olds, why not let minors vote, drink, own guns, have children without stigma, and otherwise exercise full adult rights? If adults and "similar age" youths are peers, for that matter, why make any distinction between adult mothers and minor mothers?

The only way to rescue the conventional concept of "teenage pregnancy" was to impose a new Nineties double standard, one to make the Fifties' look egalitarian. The new version set forth by UI authors goes like this: a teenage mother is judged deviant because deciding to "prematurely engage in childbearing and other adult behaviors" is unacceptably precocious behavior for a minor female. However, her adult impregnator is exonerated as "squarely within society's norms" because sex and reproduction with younger females is socially acceptable behavior for a young adult man.

The UI's contradictory stance applies a strict, age-based "birthday standard" to teenage behaviors and a lenient, flexible, "similar age" standard to adults. This is fully consistent with modern American policy thinking. Adults are entitled to be judged according to the individual merits of our behaviors. However, adolescents may be judged rigidly, sweepingly and without regard to individual differences. America's double standard (which is not shared by nations with more successful social policies) is bad enough, but it seems especially lunatic when applied to an adult and teen sharing the same bed.

The monumentally confused stance toward "teenage" sex is not unique to the Urban Institute authors I pick on. The Supreme Court has endorsed a variety of legal concepts under which adulthood justifies tolerance for immaturity, but juvenility carries an expectation of absolutist, mature rectitude. Smoking, drinking, drug testing, parental consent laws, abrogations of free speech, curfews, and other youth-targeted policies embody similar official oxymorons.

Here are the ages of consent at which adult men up to age 125 can legally have sexual intercourse with teenage females: 18 in 14 states, 17 in five states, 16 in 26 states, 15 in four states, and 14 in two states.[42] Here are the states in which a teenage girl can buy a zero-alcohol near-beer, rent a video in which bare breasts or profanity occurs more than perfunctorily, or purchase a pack of nicotine-free clove cigarettes: zero. If ever an entire nation, beginning with its executives, legislatures, and Supreme Court, should be declared unfit to raise children, it is the United States.

Twisted Stories: Of Vixens and Victims

The suddenness with which teenage "children" can metamorphose into sophisticated manipulators of adult men is illustrated not just by the official contradictions of convenience, but by media and popular views. The most prominent is the early-'90s "Long Island Lolita" case of 17-year-old Amy Fisher's attempted murder of the wife of her 30-year-old lover, Joey Buttafuoco. Throughout the media munching on this menage (the FBI reports 200 "romantic triangles" every year involving real murders that receive no similar coverage), reporters routinely dismissed Fisher's allegations of incest and family abuses. The general portrayal of her community of Merrick, Long Island, was of "Middle American normality" and her family as "adoring and indulgent"—press euphemisms for "upper middle class" or "rich." Whatever the causes, Fisher was clearly a mess with serious emotional troubles manifested by age 16, when Buttafuoco met her and began their sexual relationship with dozens of encounters at motels, her home, and on his boat.

When the affair erupted in the media after Fisher maimed Buttafuoco's wife Mary Jo in a botched shooting, Buttafuoco first admitted, then denied, he had a sexual relationship with the girl. Unlike Fisher's efforts at self-exoneration, which at best were ridiculed as another morally vacuous example of the "abuse excuse," Buttafuoco's contradictory claims of his purity and suffering due to Fisher's fatal attraction were largely accepted in both news and fictionalized depictions. After some motel receipts bearing the Long Island Humbert's signature and some untoward bragging to friends about his trysts with Fisher surfaced, Buttafuoco plea-bargained a confession to one incident of having sex with a minor.

Now the media's position was that it didn't make a bit of difference. What married American man, 1993's television dramatization, "The Crush," suggested, wouldn't take up with swimsuited, sex-dripping Alicia Silverstone, who played the Fisher role (fearsome and age 14, male victim wedded and 28)?[43] Just as they had earlier accepted Buttafuoco's denial of Fisher's now proven assertion that the two had a sexual relationship, so the media uncritically accepted his denial of Fisher's claim that he forced her into prostitution and later encouraged her to kill his wife.

Even in an era in which politicians were in statutory-rape eradication mode, the vixenization of Fisher and victimization of Buttafuoco remained the popular image. In the Arts & Entertainment channel's execrable "The Amy Fisher Story," Buttafuoco was shown as a rightly indignant husband who confessed to statutory rape out of exhaustion with the sensational charges and, in any case, was guilty only of having sacked out with a girl "just days short" of the legal-consent age of 17. Wife

Mary Jo was quoted only as excusing her husband's dalliance because "everyone had sex with Amy Fisher." This appeared to be a reference to Fisher's prostitution service, which had no lack of older male customers willing to pay her hundreds of dollars to have sex after school in Merrick, that model of "Middle American normality."

The show's conclusion was that Buttafuoco was just one of many poor dupes who "paid for their relationships with Fisher."[44] Maybe. But the image isn't consistent with the media's, and official, attitude toward utter immaturity of 16-year-old "children" when it comes to having any adult rights whatsoever such as beer drinking or being out at 11 p.m. on a school night versus the presumed maturity of "responsible" 30-age grownups whose inalienable rights are held to be beyond question.

As with other areas, concern over "protecting teenagers" quickly becomes the element of larger political agendas inimical to young people. Sure, it's fine for grownups to have sex with minor girls even as young as 15, say legislators in 36 states. But she's too immature to get an abortion, say legislators in the 35 states which require parental notification or consent for minor girls' abortions. If a "minor" girl is judged too incompetent to get an abortion, the solution is to manufacture a legal runaround to force her to become a mother. "Parental consent" laws and efforts to punish adults who help minors get abortions are being pushed in 1998 by Republicans with election-year vengeance.

In the August 1997 *American Journal of Public Health*, a well-designed study by Charlotte Ellertson of the Population Council dispelled both liberal and conservative homilies about the effects of parental consent laws on adolescent girls' abortions.[45] The study found that teenage girls are not witless fools. Confronted with a humiliating legal barrier manufactured by adults bent on punishing them, girls seeking abortions travel to other states or avail other alternatives.

Conservatives crow about the reduction in teenage abortions that occurred in states with parental notification/consent laws. But Ellertson found that from available data, "minors who traveled out of state may have accounted for the entire observed decline" in in-state abortions. After Missouri's law took effect, abortions to Missouri minors in neighboring states rose "by over 50 percent."

Contrary to liberal assertions, there is no evidence that such laws making abortion harder to get for teens drive up teenage birth rates. However, they do delay minors' abortions into more hazardous later weeks. As Minnesota and Massachusetts judges, both pro- and anti-abortion, declared with near unanimity in past court cases, parental consent laws are useless. They cause young women trauma and accomplish nothing in the way of family harmony.[46]

Particular cruelty is inflicted on girls in Arkansas, Minnesota, Mississippi, and North Dakota. In these states, even long-gone, brutal, estranged fathers must be located to give consent for the abortions of daughters they haven't seen in years. The 22 states requiring parental consent establish a principle adults refuse to impose on ourselves: that a female, in this case a juvenile, may be forced by third parties to become a mother against her will.

Perhaps the best discussion of the statutory rape dilemma is by Michael Lynch, Washington editor of the libertarian magazine *Reason*. Lynch delineates the issues involved in law enforcement discretion in evaluating which older-younger liaisons to prosecute in order to preserve maximum individual freedom while preventing predation. He points to the troubling tendency among combatants in the teen-sex debate to maintain their political positions by manipulating statistics (often by switching assumptions back and forth) rather than adjusting their stances to what the evolving statistics actually show.[47] That conceptual and statistical manipulation has led to an unrealistic image of teenage sex, which has led to a pack of trouble.

Another, related factor in the accumulation of barbaric policy that surrounds "teenage pregnancy" derives from the unreal thinking of popular, escapist psychologists such as Neil Postman, Bruno Bettelheim, and David Elkind. Works titled, The Disappearance of Childhood, "Letting children be children," and The Hurried Child, exemplify their soothing notions that today's kids "grow up too fast." Media and pubescent biology, said Bettelheim, "help explain why girls and boys are engaging in sex—and consequently are also having children."[48] The problem, the New Escapist School pronounced, was that "children" (meaning ages 1 hour to 19 years) were "incompetent" to handle any kind of freedom.

In this pop-evasion world, represented in the 1990s by blue-ribbon panels such as the Carnegie Council on Adolescent Development and agencies such as the Centers for Disease Control and Prevention, sweeping problems such as child sexual abuse, violent families, and adult-youth sex do not exist. "PhDelusion" results when experts give themselves permission to ignore problems that are crucial to the young people American society seems to dislike. "This argument," child advocate Lucia Hodgson points out,

> has given many cultural pundits the notion that...young people have more to fear from the television than from abusive adults and unjust adult policies. As a result, articles that lament the perceived erosion of childhood innocence do not focus on rape, sexual exploitation, or poverty. Instead, they identify media, "the saturation of American popular culture with sexual messages, themes, images, exhortations," as the true culprit.[49]

The ascendance of PhDelusion's Unreal over Life's Real, as is discussed in Chapter 8, is a major factor in the liberal disarmament and collapse in the face of right-wing cultural attack. As will be discussed at the end of this chapter, it is also an escapism in an era of AIDS that has deadly consequences.

Creating the New Teen-Sex Myth

We might guess that such triflings as crushing poverty, disintegrated families, rape and sexual violence in childhood, and adult sexual pressures might be of importance to the adolescents who experts find so baffling and infuriating. Yet authorities swept aside abundantly evident realities about what we called "teenage sex" in favor of wide-eyed, unquestioning hyping of teenagers' *self-reported* sexual behaviors. If ever a subject were apt to yield socially-acceptable (as opposed to truthful) answers, it would be sexuality.

The 1998 survey of 650 teens ages 13–18 by the Kaiser Family Foundation and YM Magazine provides the latest example of many.[50] Table 2 shows the sexual experience reported by boys and girls in the report.

Table 2

**PhDelusions: Two to five times more boys than girls
have had sex...and with more partners?**

How old were you when you had your first sexual intercourse?

	Boys	Girls
Age 12 or younger	9%	2%
Age 13 or younger	21	8
Age 14 or younger	41	18

How many people have you had sexual intercourse with?

	Boys	Girls
1	40%	54%
2–4	34	37
5 or more	23	9

Source: Kaiser Family Foundation, YM Magazine (1998), *National Survey of Teens*, Tables 26–27.

Now...four times more boys than girls report having had sex at age 12 or younger; 2.5 times more at age 14 or younger. So are a couple of pubescent girls really getting around? Not likely; the *boys* report having had many more different sexual partners. Who, then, are all these boys, particularly junior high ones, having sex *with*? (Were they explicitly told not to count themselves?)

This nonsensical finding gets downright absurd given the fact that many, if not the large majority, of sexually experienced young teenage females have older, not peer, partners. Girls who lose their virginity before age 15 report partners averaging four to six years older as well as a lot of coercion. Ninety percent of the births among girls under age 16 are fathered by males older than that age. Sexually-transmitted disease (including HIV and AIDS) is several times more prevalent among younger teen females than males. In other words, at least for sexual outcomes such as pregnancy and disease, younger girls tend to liaison with older teen and adult males, not boys their own age. How can it be that young boys report having more sex at younger ages with more partners but evidence so few progeny and chancres? Answer: men, from gym class to barroom, often claim achievement beyond that which transpires.

The opposite phenomenon, young boys having sex with older girls and women, appears to be increasing (see later data on marriages). But birth, STD, and marriage figures indicate older-female/younger-male relationships remain extremely rare, especially when the male is a junior high boy. They do not occur in numbers nearly large enough to account for the surplus of sex and partners 12–14-year-old boys claim. For Kaiser's figures to be true, 175,000 boys have had sex by age 12, but fewer than 40,000 girls—and the boys had more partners and the girls had older ones. This kind of scary-sounding impossibility may be fine for Dear Abby columns, but it is crazy to report it uncritically to the media and policy makers.

The failure of the Kaiser survey and those before it to account for male embell-ishment reveals a more profound weakness, one inexcusable given 1998's greater knowledge. The purpose of these surveys is to design, and win political support and funding for, programs to combat teenage pregnancy and sexual disease. Yet seven in 10 births among females ages 13–18 are fathered by men 19 and older. STD and HIV infection patterns likewise show that males beyond high school age are the cul-prits in two-thirds to 90 percent of the cases in girls and the large majority of sexual-ly-transmitted HIV infections in boys. Whether or not adolescent boys and girls have a lot of apparently harmless sex with each other, high school age males and females clearly are *not* sexual peers when it comes to pregnancy and disease—and never have been, anywhere in the world. Kaiser's and other liberal lobbies' assump-tion that they are reinforces the myth of an exclusive world of "teenage sex" in which boys and girls conspire with each other in massive pregnancy and pestilence.

The liberal Sexuality Information and Education Council of the United States (SIECUS) was right in tune with the times. Its 1994 Roper poll of students in grades 9–12 ignored the rape question and just asked if the non-virgins wish they'd waited. Of the 36 percent who had had intercourse, half said they should have wait-ed until they were 17 or so. That study is widely cited even though it lacks some crucial nuances.

For example: 40 percent of the "sexually active" girls ages 15 and younger, and large majorities of the non-virgins 14 and younger, told the Guttmacher survey they had been raped. The Washington state study found that girls with histories of sexual abuse typically had sex earlier in their teen years and were de-virginized by "part-ners" averaging five to six years older. Yet SIECUS director Debra Haffner was quoted as concerned only that, "there's a lot of contradiction between their atti-tudes and what they're doing."[51] She does not address the possibility that what they were doing wasn't done voluntarily or that the contradiction may not be the result of an immature confusion over choices, but the violent crime of rape. In effect, it appears that SIECUS was asking a substantial portion of the students if they wished they hadn't been raped by an older guy.

A 1997 Child Trends report commissioned by the National Campaign to Prevent Teen Pregnancy asked the right questions about voluntary versus involun-tary sexual initiation and came up with an entirely different conclusion than SIECUS's poll. The Child Trends study of 11,000 girls and women found that seven in 10 teenage girls welcomed their first sexual experiences, two thirds of which were with boys near to their age.[52] However, the younger the girl, the greater the age gap between her and her partner, and the more likely the girl was to report the sexual experience as unwanted. Of the small number of girls who lost their virginity before age 13, 22 percent reported the experience as a rape, 49 percent more reported it as unwanted, and most were considerably younger than their rapists/partners. Of the girls who lost their virginity to a boy within two years of their age, three-fourths were happy with the experience, compared to 63 percent of those whose partners were five or more years older.

Another discovery of the study goes against the prevailing attack on youth and speaks well of teen boys: the smaller the age gap, the more likely the couple was to use contraception. Adult men (at least, adult men of the type who devirginize young teens) were less responsible than teenage boys.

Progressives' manufacture and exaggeration of the chimerical notion of "teenage sex" set the stage for an angry conservative counter-reaction. Conservatives logically claimed that liberals' own statements about "rising" and "epidemic" teenage sexual activity, pregnancy, and STD proved the liberal public health, sex education, and contraception agenda had failed disastrously.

Inventing "Social Costs" of Teen Pregnancy

"Logically," writes Hodgson,

> our empathy for the baby born into a difficult life should extend to its young mother, also recently born into the same difficult circumstances. But it doesn't. We want to rescue the baby because we know how unhealthy and damaging those life circumstances are, but we have very little empathy for the young girl or boy who has already been damaged by those same circumstances.[53]

This is the '90s. Humanitarianism is inoperative. As Hodgson elsewhere documents, we aren't concerned about the well being of the "socially costly" baby born to a teen mother either, other than as a symbol of that last word: cost. What 1990s policy makers want scholars to affirm is the following politically useful hypothesis: that procreation by teenagers (mostly black and Latina and nearly all poor) causes their poverty and devours taxpayer money, thereby justifying punitive response.

That is the essence of the "social cost" argument most recently voiced by the Robin Hood Foundation's 1996 and 1997 *Kids Having Kids* reports.[54] Robin Hood is not objective. Its self-description claims the Foundation already knows "the pervasive and damaging impact of adolescent childbearing in the city's very poorest communities." Its report concluded that mothers having babies before age 18 cost taxpayers $6.9 billion per year in direct costs (increased welfare, medical care, tax losses, foster care, and incarceration expenses) and $29 billion per year when all social costs were considered.

The authors begin the report by admitting:

> Teenage parents are disproportionately concentrated in poor, often racially segregated communities characterized by inferior housing, high crime, poor schools, and limited health services. Many of the teens have been victims of physical and/or sexual abuse.

Robin Hood then proceeds to a conclusion that reveals a limited moral horizon in the same way that John DiIulio's "adolescent superpredator" concept does. Both acknowledge that society allows children at high risk to become teenage mothers (or to become superpredators if male) to grow up in horrendous conditions of deprivation and violence. *Neither the august, liberal foundation nor the conservative crime expert consider destitution, poverty, violent abuse, and rape imposed on children to be worthy of a crusade, or even a social-cost analysis, in and of themselves.* Yet both Robin Hood and DiIulio are indignant that the children whose plight was ignored by society then have the gall to turn around and impose "social costs" (welfare payments to females, violent crime by males) on that same society.

Clearly, teenagers who grew up in poverty and abuse did not create these conditions. This delineates the opposite assumptions by Robin Hood and Washington's Advancing Solutions to Adolescent Pregnancy (ASAP). ASAP's philosophy appears in the Northwest Environment Watch's *Misplaced Blame*, quoted at the beginning of this chapter.

Robin Hood's report intimates that teenagers' early motherhood causes the poverty and other adverse conditions of their communities. Robin Hood blames teenage mothers for creating "social costs." In contrast, ASAP argues that conditions of childhood poverty and abuse cause early childbearing as a survival mechanism. ASAP blames larger society for allowing such dismal conditions, which impose personal costs on children and youths. Luker's, Musick's, and my own studies of teenage mothers suggest ASAP's position is not only more humane, but closer to reality.

Even if Robin Hood claims teen mothers cause poverty and bad family life, it can hardly argue that teenage mothers are to blame for the "segregated communities," "inferior housing," "poor schools," and "limited health services" it finds. The Robin Hood panel claimed to control for background factors in order to isolate only those costs that could be attributed to teenage mothers' young age. However, their report shows all that was controlled for were a set of demographic variables—socioeconomic status, education, parents' education, etc.—and these unevenly. There are no controls for personal variables such as histories of sexual abuse or family breakup.

This is a crucial omission for the cost factors Robin Hood is assessing. Sexual abuse is a major risk factor both for early motherhood and for job, school, and childraising difficulties. The Washington study cited above found that "the CPS [child protective services] had contact with children of 21% of the respondents with a history of sexual victimization, compared to 8% of those with no such history."[55] Robin Hood's study winds up tallying the charge for foster care, incarceration, and other abuse-related expenses at around $3 billion annually. The root cause: "nothing except early childbearing itself." Yet it is only fair to blame the "teen age" of the mother for these costs if analysts can show these costs do not accrue when sexually abused adult mothers have children. This Robin Hood does not do.

Whether social cost studies are reliable depends heavily on whether researchers identify and factor out all relevant background influences that might affect whether young age is really the culprit. Academics who study teenage pregnancy have vexing habits of ignoring relevant factors, especially if they are difficult, distressing, or impolitic to study. Worse still, the factors adults have the most trouble facing are often those that affect teen mothers the most. Thus, such "social cost" studies as the 1986 Urban Institute report[56] which compared *straight across* mothers who had babies as teenagers with those who had babies as adults were absurd. Since teen moms were more likely to live in poverty *before* they got pregnant than adult moms, the costs of public support will be higher for teen moms not because they are teens, but because they have always been poorer than the adult group.

The Liberals' Bell Curve

The most troubling aspect of Robin Hood's core assumption is how closely it resembles that of Charles Murray's *The Bell Curve*.[57] Both pick a demographic variable—black race in Murray's treatise, young age in Robin Hood's—and argue that social costs and waste of resources accrue from bad behaviors resulting from the inferior natures of this group. All that would need to be done to convert *Kids Having Kids* arguments into *Bell Curve* arguments would be to invert the former's charts to make mother's race the main variable of interest rather than mother's age.

In and of itself, race is a much more compelling variable in "social costs." For example, a white 13-year-old's baby is less likely to have a low birthweight (10.4 percent) than the baby of a black mother in her 20s (12.5 percent).[58] Even though pregnant blacks were much less likely to smoke (smoking is tied to poor infant health) than pregnant whites, reports the National Center for Health Statistics, "LBW (low birth weight) rates for black births were higher than for white births, regardless of maternal age, marital status, or smoking status."[59] Robin Hood's charts show similarly large racial disparities for nearly all measures. Yet it would be unthinkable for the foundation to issue a report on the social costs of black motherhood.

Once again, the only effect of holding up "teen age" instead of "black, Latino, or Native American race" as the demographic scapegoat is to enable moderates and liberals to support punitive "nonracist" policies which wind up punishing poorer, minority youth the most. The personal-behavior emphasis of Robin Hood, and the embracing of its report by Clinton (in a press conference) and other moderates and liberals, solidified the shift away from the commitment to social responsibility and obligation to reverse the legacies of racism.

Teen Moms: Losers or Winners Economically?

Interestingly, the Robin Hood authors reveal a major reason why poorer teenagers have babies. After unreeling a list of social costs claimed to result from adolescent motherhood, the *Kids Having Kids* authors arrive at a most unusual and overlooked finding:

> Surprisingly, after accounting for differences in background and closely linked factors such as motivation, adolescent mothers earn only slightly less during the first 12 years of parenthood than they would be expected to earn if they delayed childbearing until age 20 or 21. In contrast, over their young adult lives (ages 19 to 30), they work and earn somewhat *more* than do their later childbearing counterparts.
>
> Moreover, although their sources of income differ, adolescent mothers have combined incomes from their own incomes, earnings of spouses, child support, and public assistance comparable to those of older childbearers, after background and closely linked factors are controlled for. During their first 13 years of parenthood, they have income and medical-care assistance valued at just nearly $19,000 annually, compared with just over $20,000 annually for their later-childbearing counterparts. After netting out the effects of background and other factors closely linked to early childbearing, adolescent childbearers fare slightly *better* than later child-bearing counterparts in terms

of their overall economic welfare, having total incomes of nearly $20,000 annually as compared with just over $16,000 for the comparison group [emphasis added].[60]

Wading through the sentence tangle, one finds that when teenage mothers are raising younger children (infancy to 12), they earn about $1,000 less per year than mothers who waited until 21 to have babies. However, after their kids get older, adolescent mothers earn substantially more money than women who waited until age 21 to become moms, the latter of whom are then raising young children.

Light bulb goes on: it is not adolescent motherhood that causes social costs, but *raising young children* regardless of the mother's age. Young children require the mother's constant supervision, restricting her from the work force. What is surprising is that the "young child" penalty for teenage mothers is only $1,000 in lost income per year. The small size of the penalty is due to the fact that teenagers are already paid extremely low wages be they parents or not. Economically, it is the ideal age to be out of the work force.

However, by their late 20s, the children of adolescent mothers are old enough to be left alone, and the mother can work. But women who delay motherhood until 21 or older still have young kids requiring supervision, keeping them out of the workforce into their 30s. The income penalty for mothers who delay childbearing appears more severe. If my math is right, the above figures indicate teenage mothers earn approximately $80,000 more over 20 years than similarly situated poor women who delay motherhood.

Robin Hood's surprising conclusion results from research by University of Chicago public policy professor V. Joseph Hotz and colleagues for the only long-term study of teenage mothers I'm aware of.[61] The results got him banished from cocktail receptions sponsored by Clinton's National Campaign to Prevent Teenage Pregnancy because, the press reported, "neither liberals nor conservatives view Hotz's findings with much relish."[62]

Hotz's exhaustive analysis of former teen mothers and non-mothers tracked over two decades by the National Longitudinal Survey of Youth was published as part of the Robin Hood study. His findings "call into question the view that teenage childbearing is one of the nation's most serious social problems." Over the long term, teenage mothers have no greater odds of failing to graduate from high school, earning less money, or winding up on welfare than similarly situated females who delay motherhood until adult years. One of the most poorly understood facts is how little a high school diploma augments the income of poor women. Census reports show that poverty afflicts 51 percent of black women and 41 percent of Latina women who have high school diplomas. Black and Latina women with college training were just as likely to be poor as whites with only a high school diploma,[63] a matter that returns us to the economic racism the Clinton presidency should be confronting with more than a conversation.

The problem with previous social-cost studies, Hotz found, was "misleading" apples-oranges comparisons. Adolescent mothers grew up in families twice as likely to be headed by single parents and whose incomes were only half those of adult mothers, for example. If we want to know whether adolescent motherhood (as opposed to growing up poor or in chaotic families) causes social costs, then teen mothers must be compared to women as much like them as possible who were not teen mothers. So Hotz compared mothers who had babies at 17 or younger with mothers who had miscarried at age 17 or younger and delayed childbearing until adulthood.

Thus, the study compared about 700 women who had babies before age 18 with 70 women who would have been under-18 mothers except for miscarriage (500 more women who gave birth and 80 who miscarried at age 18–19 were used for confirmation). Data were available for these mothers up to age 34. Hotz found that unlike the comparison groups used in other social cost studies, prior family incomes, single-parent status, and other background factors of the teen mothers and miscarriers were very similar *before* they had babies. For example, women who miscarried as teenagers grew up in families with incomes only slightly higher than those of teenage mothers. The only significant difference was that their median age at first birth was 20, three to four years older than the average age at first birth for adolescent mothers.

There are drawbacks to using miscarriers as a comparison group. For one, women who miscarry may have health problems that reduce their later earnings. The fact that the women who miscarried as teens later bore children mitigates against, but does not entirely eliminate, the health objection. More important, Hotz's results turned out to be so strong ("robust," statisticians call it) that, even using the most conservative assumptions stacked against his thesis, the conclusions remained the same. Overall, Harvard University poverty research specialist Christopher Jencks affirmed, Hotz's research methods are "'way better than anything anyone else has done."[64]

Hotz's findings were groundbreaking as well:

- "Teen mothers are likely to have significantly *higher* levels of income from husbands than if they had delayed childbearing."

- "There is *no* significant causal effect of early childbearing on the probability that teen mothers obtain a high school-level education, if high school diplomas and GED's are taken as equivalent…the labor market returns to the GED are no different from those of a high school diploma for the typical *woman*."

- "At early ages, teen mothers supply significantly fewer hours to the labor market (between 90 and 370 fewer hours per year), while, by their mid-20s and early 30s, these mothers work more (130 to 500 more hours), than if they had delayed their childbearing."

- "The earnings of teen mothers are higher at every age through age 34 than would be the case if these women delayed their childbearing…Teen mothers earn $12,745 per year in 1996 dollars; their earnings would be 35 percent lower, or $8,237 per year, if they delayed their childbearing."

- "Delaying childbirth appears to reduce benefit receipt during the teen years. But it seems to make no difference during the early 20s and actually increase the amount of benefits received at older ages."

Hotz and colleagues thus find few education costs, no higher welfare costs, and considerably higher employment and earnings among women who had babies as adolescents compared to women in an equivalent economic situation who waited until adulthood to become mothers.

But his most surprising conclusions surround how little teenage mothers cost *after the taxes they pay* are subtracted from the welfare payments they receive:

> Each year government spends $11.3 billion (in 1996 dollars) on AFDC, food stamps, Medicaid and other forms of public assistance for women ages 17 through 34 who began motherhood as teens. This expenditure represents 6 percent of the total expenditures on AFDC, food stamps, and Medicaid in the United States in 1993 and amounts to an annual expenditure of $3,596 per woman...They are offset, in part, by the taxes that women who bore their first child as a teenager can be expected to pay. In fact, the total annual public assistance costs of early childbearers, net of the taxes they pay, amounts to a net annual cost, per woman, of $665.

If my math is right, Hotz is calculating that present and former teen mothers pay some $9 billion per year in taxes. The government cost of a teenage mother and children is less than half the cost of the average Social Security household. No wonder Hotz isn't popular.

But even this doesn't tell the real story. The blockbuster:

> Most of this government outlay is not attributable to the failure of teen mothers to delay their childbearing, however. In fact, the total annual expenditures on public assistance would increase slightly, rising by $0.8 billion, if all these women had delayed their first births by over 3 to 4 years. Moreover, the *net* (of taxes) annual outlays by government for cash assistance and in-kind transfers to these women would actually *increase* by 35 percent, or $4.0 billion. This increase in net expenditures associated with delaying childbearing would amount to over $1,200 per mother (emphasis in original throughout).

Teen mothers actually *save* governments $4 billion per year! How can that be?

> That getting teen mothers to delay their childbearing would result in additional costs to taxpayers, rather than savings, is a direct consequence of our finding that teen mothers would earn less over their lifetimes if they were forced to delay their first births. This loss in earnings translates to a reduction in taxes paid by these women and an increase, rather than a decrease, in the net costs to government associated with the postponement of motherhood.

This is certainly an astonishing, and well-grounded, alternative way to look at teenage motherhood: teen moms earn $80,000 more, and save the government $4 billion in costs, in the long term! But it is important to understand what is being said: Hotz does not argue that teen mothers economically benefit society. What he argues is that impoverished girls who have babies as teenagers wind up earning more money, and costing society less money, in the long run than these same girls would if they delayed motherhood until adult years.

This is social science at its finest, refining the issue to its nub: the only way poor women can avoid inflicting "social costs" is to never have babies at all, ever, in their lives. Do liberals' "social cost" arguments, then, mean that poor, mostly non-white, women should *never* have children? That the infants and small children of poor mothers, unlike the elderly and other groups, are deemed uniquely unworthy of public support? If so, why don't liberals just say that?

Hotz also found two negative, long-term consequences of early motherhood. Compared to older mothers, adolescent mothers were likely to spend more of their lives as single mothers. Second, on average they had 12 percent more babies. This suggests the trade-off of teenage motherhood: slightly more kids, considerably higher income during motherhood years, and less partner presence. Depending on the prospective partner, this might not be a bad thing.

Many teen mothers I've interviewed describe their lives prior to motherhood as dangerous and out of control. Childhood abuses had translated into self-destructive behaviors (another sequence too many experts have trouble incorporating into their regression equations). Both psychological research and clinical testing have consistently found that girls' drug and alcohol abuse, criminal behavior, depression and suicidal thoughts, and other dangerous habits decline dramatically upon discovery of their pregnancy.[65] Even though much poorer, teenage mothers are less likely to smoke or drink heavily during pregnancy than adult mothers.[66] This improvement in behavior appears particularly strong in girls who suffered sexual abuse.[67] As Yale Gancherov, former chief social worker at Los Angeles' Florence Crittenton Center for teenage mothers, told me:

> Troubled, abused girls become more centered emotionally when they become mothers. They often gain the attention of professionals and social services. Such girls are more likely to stay in school with a baby than without. Their behavioral health improves.[68]

Their heightened sense of organization and purpose may explain why teen mothers often return to school, work longer hours at jobs, eventually earn more money, and wind up paying almost enough in taxes to reimburse government for earlier welfare payments! This record would seem deserving of greater investment, not the divestiture Clinton/conservatives mandated.

Thus, early motherhood is a survival strategy. Sociologist Luker points out that for poor women in a society that supports neither work nor motherhood, "there is never a 'good' time to have a baby:"

> The birth patterns of poor and affluent women in the United States have begun to bifurcate...Poor women continue the traditional American pattern of early childbearing, because in this way they can become mothers before they enter the paid labor force and while they can make moral claims on kinfolk who will help with the childrearing. Affluent women, on the other hand, tend to wait until they are well established in the labor force before having a child.[69]

In addition, poorer women tend to accumulate health problems in adulthood, making pregnancy riskier than at younger ages. "Given the peculiarities of the American situation, it makes sense for poor women, both black and white, to have babies at an early age," Luker concludes. And those same peculiarities make it impossible for more privileged Americans to understand why on earth poorer teenagers would do that.

Could it be that inner-city adolescents understand their lives and prospects better than the elite academicians who drop in to study (and judge) them? That improved health, mental attitude, and economic futures provide rational reasons for poorer young women to have babies early in life? What emerges from Hotz's study is a troubling picture of the narrow, short-term thinking—not of teenage mothers—but of the social-cost bean-counters who seem unable to comprehend how a decision that would be disastrous for teenagers of the academics' middle and upper social strata may be perfectly reasonable for those from less privileged upbringings.

Because scholars can weigh "social costs" in rarefied think tanks does not mean teenage mothers enjoy such contemplatory vacuums. In a typical example of the latter, scholars for the liberal Child Trends berated teenage mothers for creating "families at high risk of poverty" and urged that "parents, schools, community leaders, and the mass media have to communicate constantly and clearly that it is unwise to have children when you are emotionally and financially unprepared to care for them."[70] Income trends show that the average youth of the 1990s will not earn enough to support a family until age 35 (see Chapter 9). Most of today's blacks and Latinos will *never* be financially able to support children by conventional definitions. Again: if liberals are declaring that poor people, especially minorities, should never have babies, they should state that flatly instead of hiding behind a focus on "teenage mothers."

One Person's 'Social Cost' is Another's 'Health Insurance'

Selective "social cost" obsession is bigotry. The United States spends one-third of its federal budget on the elderly, yet official "social cost" analyses don't evaluate this politically potent group. "No one has ever referred to the epidemic of pregnancy among forty-somethings, but there is one," Luker writes, "and the costs of pregnancy among older women are socially subsidized just as surely as are the costs of births to younger women, though the former are more hidden." High-technology reproduction and birth defects among babies born to older women are staggeringly expensive, "creating their own crisis in the medical system."[71]—which presumably raises the cost of health insurance for the rest of us. Don't expect Robin Hood, the Urban Institute, or this administration to venture anywhere near the "social costs" generated by a constituency that votes or donates to campaigns.

Clinton's ledger politics selectively applied to teenage mothers carries a particular cruelty that defines his presidency even more than those of Republican predecessors. To the president and his liberal Welfare Reform Task Force discussed next, these young women were simply a commodity, routes to enhanced poll standing.

Creating Democratic Family Values

Smugness metamorphosed into righteous anger as the welfare reform debate heated up. The viciousness with which America attacked teenage mothers was orchestrated by President Clinton's Welfare Reform Task Force in 1994 in a crass attempt to create what it called "Democratic Family Values." It is important to review this bit of history in light of the current furor over the September 1998 report by special prosecutor Kenneth Starr of Clinton's lustings with a barely-post-teenage intern.

The Task Force assembled by the president contained knowledgeable and liberal advisors. Its members were well versed in recent studies showing that four-fifths of teenage mothers came from the poorest strata of society, most were black and Latina, most had suffered childhoods of sexual abuse, violence, and disrupted families, and most of their impregnators were considerably older adult men.

Who cared? What attracted the Task Force to the issue was the prospect of a safe group to beat up on in order to grab the high ground on the heretofore Republican issues of welfare reform and morality. The Task Force plan called teenage pregnancy "a bedrock issue of character and personal responsibility" (remember that phrase for the later discussion of Bill and Monica). If teen pregnancy is a bedrock issue, one wonders where, say, the $100 billion savings-and-loan bailout registers on the personal responsibility scale.

The Task Force blamed crime, poverty, drugs, and educational failure on unwed mothers, particularly teenaged ones, and called for a high-profile presidential roadshow to denounce them.[72] The Task Force avoided the issue of divorce, which creates just as much family poverty and even greater likelihood of fathers abandoning kids.[73] Divorce is rampant among the middle and upper class voters the president's salvo was courting, as well as politicians.

Ending Truth as We Know It

"Breathtaking," gushed health secretary Shalala of the welfare reform plan. President Clinton, in his 1994 State of the Union, indignantly lied that America's welfare payments—the most miserly of any Western society—promote more teenage motherhood. He accused young, poor mothers of regarding a child "as meal ticket to a life of indolence at the working nation's expense."[74] Even right-wing sociologist Charles Murray had more integrity, giving up that fiction months earlier.[75]

And for obvious reasons. Family welfare in the form of Aid to Families with Dependent Children (AFDC) and Food Stamps had declined by 30 percent in real value since 1970 (see Chapter 9). Yet the rate of unwed births had risen by 80 percent among both teens and adults. States with stingy AFDC benefits (such as Louisiana, which paid $46 per child per month in 1996) uniformly had rates of teenage motherhood two to four times *higher* than states with relatively generous aid (such as Minnesota, $162). Clinton's own teen pregnancy chieftain, Dr. Henry Foster, fessed up in November 1996 that welfare does not promote teen births.[76] By that time, of course, the administration had milked all the poll points it could from "ending welfare as we know it."

Clinton's jousting with Republicans to exploit America's poorest and most unfortunate young women for political lucre drew only sporadic liberal challenge to its fundamental assumptions. Instead, prurience seemed the main focus. Liberals were rightly annoyed over Clinton's prudish firing of Surgeon General Joycelyn Elders for murmuring that masturbation might reduce teenage sex. Elders' remark did not merit firing, but it deserved no defense. It was little more than a pointless aside. Like Shalala, Elders seemed unable to find her sharp tongue for frank discussions of the real issues in high birth rates among poorer teens and their mostly-adult partners.

Even the bipartisan, professional moralists of the 1990s, dubbed "Virtuecrats" by the press, ducked the larger morality issue. Asked directly by *U.S. News & World Report* reporter David Whitman, America's top teen-chastity sermonizers such as William Bennett and the Family Life Council's Gary Bauer refused to comment on adults having sex outside of marriage. Clinton's former teen-pregnancy point man, William Galston (whose junior-high abstinence promotions displayed breathtaking disregard for the fact that 90 percent of the births among junior high girls are fathered by older teens and adults) confessed that discussing adult sexual irresponsibility is "inconvenient." Indeed it would be around Pennsylvania Avenue, as events were quickly to prove.

First Magnitude Starrs

Contrast the lives of poorer, inner-city girls with the lurid sexcapades of middle-aged Clinton White House chieftains and their $200 hookers, payoffs to mistresses to conceal abortions, destructive extramarital affairs denied and then red-facedly confessed by officials as the press closed in. Common decency would seem to dictate that they at least refrain from denigrating the morality of young people in far more trying circumstances, from pushing policies to force abused young women in front of judges or back into dangerous families.

Clinton has profited politically from ruthless pumping of "family values," "zero tolerance," "personal responsibility," and other moralistic absolutisms that have made life immeasurably harsher for indigent teens, welfare mothers, public housing occupants, and other powerless groups. Given that recent history, it was astounding how many liberals rushed to defend the Philanderer in Chief while dodging the class and power issues once vital to their ethos. Conservatives were right in their outrage at the double standard liberals applied to Clinton and reactionary Supreme Court nominee Clarence Thomas, though conservatives indulged the opposite hypocrisy. Had Thomas engaged in sex with a 21-year-old intern at the agency he chiefed, liberals would have complained that was sexual harassment by the very power-imbalance definition of the term. So what if Monica "consented"? Aren't 21-year-olds considered too immature to be able to rent cars? Mere fledglings only scant months past the age Clinton himself terms "children"? Hardly past the day of sufficient judgment to order an Apple Beer? Of that notorious 15–24 age group branded "high risk" by Clinton's own officials, who gained much press mileage deploring the grave dangers of their supposed sexual promiscuity (White House AIDS agents blame teens and young adults for propelling the epidemic); mental instability (the CDC constantly hypes their purportedly rising suicide); and criminality (administration crime experts automatically equate 15–24 agers with mindless violence)? How could the president sexually consort with a "high-risk young person" barely older than daughter Chelsea, of whom the First Parents were so marmishly protective?

Houston to Clinton apologists: this is the *Commander in Chief of the World's Leading Meganuke Colossus* indulging sexual relations with a *novice intern whose long-term Washington career is subject to his authoritative whim*. It isn't the 30-year age difference between the Oval Office carnalogists (Bill's and Monica's high-risk propensities seem a match), but the huge power imbalance that should trigger violent reaction. Yet, other than ridiculing Lewinsky for ditzheaded homewrecking and the president for handing the right a charged issue, where were the feminists who rightly rallied around Anita Hill? Wrote *Ms.* magazine contributing editor Adele Stan:

> ...I'm expected to condemn the president for his callousness toward women and then qualify it with some tortured explanation of how the Monica mess differs from sexual harassment. But I don't care what the president did to Lewinsky or what she did to him. I've dealt with my share of cads and, at best, that's what the man is. What I care about is what Clinton did to me and my colleagues in the trenches. He sold us out for a romp with a randy young woman who had little to lose.[77]

The "tortured explanation" would be that Hill rejected Clarence Thomas's alleged advances while "randy" Monica solicited Bill's. But feminists excused the warm notes, offers of airport rides, and other cordialities Hill displayed toward Thomas after the traumatic harassment occurred because of power imbalance: Thomas was a key player in Hill's career. The power men in high places hold over female subordinates, particularly younger ones, transforms into personal sexual privilege and "callousness" toward women, an issue feminists "in the trenches" used to recognize.

Feminists knew Clinton was a "cad" by his own admission before major women's groups helped elevate him to power in the 1992 and 1996 elections; on what grounds do they complain now that they've found out he's *really* a cad? Stan presents no evidence of knowing how much Lewinsky had to lose (that Lewinsky was "young" seems to inspire not added sympathy for her, but added anger at her). Nor does she draw a connection between the callousness in Clinton's private behavior and the exploitativeness of his public policies toward young people. Only a few, such as columnists Norman Solomon and Barbara Ehrenreich, seemed to recall the president's coldness in blaming young, poor women for undermining American morality and his stern demands that they adhere to sexual "abstinence" and "personal responsibility."[78]

This is a president who has pushed strict "zero tolerance" for dozens of misbehaviors and backed this moral austerity with punishments. In February 1994, to klieg lights and rolling cameras, Clinton delivered a chastity sermon to impoverished black Anacostia, D.C., eighth graders. A few months before finally admitting his affair with Gennifer Flowers, the president insisted that federally-funded sex education emphasize that absolute abstinence from sex outside of marriage "is the expected standard" of American behavior.[79] At the time he was unburdening these pieties, Clinton was being unabstinent with an apparently confused junior employee of age to be a sister of the kids he was lecturing on chastity. More shocking still, a large majority of American adults—including family-values conservatives and sexual correctness-sensitive liberals—seem to agree the president's sexing up an intern he supervised was (in Clinton's words) "nobody's business but ours."[80]

Apologists might argue that unwed teenage pregnancy entails social costs but high-level grownups' philandering doesn't. A highly inconsistent stance on all counts. A majority of teenage mothers do not receive welfare, and those who do sop up a lot less than other groups whose slurping at the public saltlick isn't questioned. Ah, but that's not the point, the bipartisan virtuists, beginning with the president's own welfare reformers, declare: the issue is unwed teenage mothers' *immorality*, the insidiously bad *values* they represent and pass on to their children, their debasing of America's "bedrock" of "character and personal responsibility." That is why the rhetorical, educational, and moral exhortations for extra-marital sexual abstinence are angrily aimed at all youths.

In fact, by the lights of the moral purists themselves, it's all the same. True, most adultery does not lead to social costs either. But adultery is the leading cause of divorce, which is every bit as large a contributor to single parenthood and welfare costs that unwed motherhood is—and besides, it's *immoral*. The height of high-level immorality is imbued in the practically limitless demands from adults, particularly powerful ones, that the young and powerless observe standards that the older and the powerful themselves cannot or will not meet. Let us at least be honest about what such "values" really value.

Yes, Franklin Roosevelt was a fine president, and John Kennedy no worse a one in his brief tenure, for their adulteries. But this defense of Clinton's compulsive philandering misses yet another vital point: Roosevelt and Kennedy did not build their political careers and public policies by whipping up punishing anger at the sexual morality and personal behaviors of impoverished, stigmatized groups. Roosevelt's moral castigations were directed at the greed of the rich and corporate, not the sexual sins of the sharecropper or depression-camp youth.

Just who ignited this 1980s and '90s fervor for absolutist righteousness, this Big Daddy prying into the private sexuality of teen mothers and welfare moms, unannounced searches of public housing, forced drug-testing of students, as legitimate government business? The same pants-down politicians who now indignantly and/or contritely (depending on the latest handler poll) claim the right to privacy and understanding for behavior standards far below those of the people they were vilifying.

From the very Washington from whence emanated a fiery "zero tolerance" only months before emerged a whiny September refrain: "it's our personal business," "oral sex is not sex," "lying about adultery is not lying," and "judge not." Clearly, minimum morality is not a standard Clinton or Gingrich expect of their own behavior, nor that of their staff, nor colleagues. White House staff tested positive for drug use and kept their jobs. Clinton even invited former aide Dick Morris back from $200-whore disgrace in January 1998 to help fix the president's P.R. problem. Morris promptly went on national radio to insinuate the president womanizes because the First Lady preferred women, too.[81] Then the president admitted, under duress, that he had previously lied when he denied two extramarital affairs.

If they were teenagers caught in like wantoness at school, Clinton and aides likely would suffer expulsion, strict curfews, and constant supervision. (Teenagers working as pages in Washington get sent home for such conduct, unless it's with a congressman). It is just another bitter '90s irony that on the day Monica Lewinsky testified about her presidential zipper games, the ACLU sued the Covington, Kentucky, school district for expelling two teens from the National Honor Society because they had become mothers. In Los Angeles, black-yuppie columnist Karen Grigsby Bates piously lauded the Tournament of Roses' decision to bar two black teenage mothers (even though good students and parents) from participation in its Rose Court on the bizarre "underlying philosophical" grounds that girls who visibly violated the "presumption of virginity" should have "the wonders and pleasures of other experiences" such as parade participation "closed" to them.[82] Would Bates deny such larger-life opportunities to celebrities and leading politicians who had extramarital sex or cheated on their spouses? (Of course not. The Rose Parade would be three minutes long.)

There was something about the Starr report, with its grave tones of impeachment followed by augustly footnoted, leadenly graphic detailings of what seemed to be utter erogenous idiocy by America's Most Admired in the Hallowed Office where the once-solemn Hot Line and Nuclear Button now took on risque parody, that caused Americans across the spectrum to unhinge. The White House's "scorched earth" strategy in the wake of excruciatingly embarrassing Oval Office conduct exposed by Starr and trumpeted by Republicans was to clandestinely alert the press to like indiscretions by his chief GOP accusers. The initial salvo revealed an impressive arsenal.

Representative Dan Burton (R-Indiana), powerful House committee leader and brander of the president as a "scumbag," took the first hit. He angrily admitted, just before *Vanity Fair* was set to expose it, fathering a boy, now 15, during an extramarital affair in the 1980s. Burton's cruel immorality in refusing to acknowledge fatherhood of a living, breathing child because of danger to his political career pales beside Bill and Monica's silly-sex, yet the family-values conservatives rallied to Burton's defense. The next to take incoming was House powerhouse and arch-abortion foe Henry Hyde (R-Illinois). Hyde, under threat of exposure, confessed to an extra-marital affair in the '60s, which he whimpered was a "youthful indiscretion" (he was 40 years old!). In any case, Hyde's Capitol Hill displays none of the sweet Sixties indulgence for indiscretions among today's youth, such as the teen mothers in Covington or Los Angeles, that it demands for its own. Far-right Representative Helen Chenoweth (R-Idaho) caught the next flak and confessed to violating the Commandments, just before an *Idaho Statesman* tell-all.

Similarly, when the morality-shouting House Republican 1994 freshmen were caught in embarrassing extra-marital diddlings and divorces their first year in Washington, top House leaders indignantly complained about press attention and blamed the problem on fast-paced social life in the capital.[83] When justifying their own, Republicans see no irony in blaming sexual irresponsibility on social conditions. Conservatives and religious rightists split hairs, refined situation ethics, and indulged moral relativism to defend their own white-haired libertines—no more right-is-right, sin-is-sin from their pulpits.

If I got to make the rule on press prying into public figures' private lives, it would be this: the figure sets the standard. If a politician focuses on statesmanlike issues as Roosevelt and Kennedy did and refrains from self-righteous sex-and-sin preachings, leave his/her private sex life alone. But if the politician makes political hay and public policy trumpeting personal morals and family values, his/her own private moral behaviors become legitimate targets of scrutiny. In that case, the press does a public service by publicly revealing how that politician's own "private" conduct stacks up against the standards he/she would harness government authority to impose on others. And not just politicians. In my ideal world, Karen Grigsby Bates, the Rose Court's officials, the Covington School District trustees, and every other punishing moralist would have their sex lives investigated, subject to barrings from their public positions if improprieties were unearthed.

The reason is a very practical one: the unrealism and unfairness in the zeal among the powerful for forcing ridiculously punitive "zero tolerance" standards on the powerless is exposed when the powerful are held accountable to those same standards—in which case, human frailties and imperfections in behavior are found to be the rule across the spectrum. If it takes "scorched earth" to shut Dan Burton up about "illegitimacy," Henry Hyde about "unchastity," and Bill Clinton about "family values," then wheel out the flamethrower.

Still, the earth was merely singed a bit—no explicit Starr-hot details on how conservatives do sex with their mistresses. "Crybabies," columnist Robert Scheer ridiculed Republican protests over fully justifiable prying into politicians' private lives in a prying climate politicians themselves had created. The virtuous Anteaters were getting their own taste of the Long Tongue. Hilariously, *Orange County Weekly* cybercolumnist Wyn Hilty pointed out, had the courts not overturned the Republican's austere 1997 Communications Decency Act, the Grand Old Party "smutmongers" could never have posted the salacious Starr diggings for all to behold. On the other side, the same Clinton who pushed V-chips so parents could "protect kids" from the sleazy pop media now found media descriptions of his own behavior had become the main sleaze parents wanted to protect their kids from. The ugliness should not be forgotten: the Clinton and GOP miscreants now asserting their right to enjoy public tolerance displayed no such tolerance toward the welfare-reform victims trapped in the hotspot of their searing moralistic magnifying glasses only months earlier.

Behind the whole dismal leadership scandal lay a press and public displaying, by their own language and values, just how we got to the point of presidential cigar games and leather-thong pizza slicings posted on the internet. Even in this quintessentially "adult" scandal involving sex, power, perjury, and job tradeoffs, pundits could find no words except those they normally used to demean the young. In face-off columns, former Democratic leader Bill Press compared women who accuse the president to "teenage groupies, trying to score big time," while conservative columnist George Will branded Clinton "a developmentally arrested adolescent."[84] Careful, gentlemen: are your sexual rectitude papers in order?

The sleaze and cruelty of Clinton's political policies (see Alexander Cockburn's and Ken Silverstein's more detailed documentation, *Washington Babylon*[85]) are reflective of a moral checkeredness his own supporters don't deny. The same voters who gave him a solid 1996 election victory and whooped 70 percent support for him in the 1998 travails rated the Clinton's ethics and honesty lower than any recent president other than Nixon; most rated the credibility of an unknown White House aide over that of the Oval Office chief.[86] The American people gave rising, ringing votes of confidence for the president during the sex scandals even though "large majorities say they do not believe the president has high moral standards." Why? Because a booming economy is putting money in their pockets.[87] Wrote public opinion analyst William Schneider:

> In polling this year, 60% of Americans say they do not consider Clinton honest and trustworthy. A majority thinks he sets a poor moral example. Don't those views have any consequences? Maybe not, as long as the economy stays good.[88]

So much for grownups' stern "moral values" sermons. Kids, it's all about money.

Meanwhile, polls indicated the American public's biggest concern was whining that their 11-year-olds could read the raunch their president was up to in the Oval Office. Immediately, the press and pop-psychologists erupted with advice on how to explain to your toddler that the esteemed imperials we, yes we, installed in the highest positions of power are ethically challenged self-destructive sex-lunatics. A marvel it is that any kid can manage to grow up in a society whose adults harbor such insanely weird priorities. *Tikkun* magazine editor Michael Lerner probably had the best idea: a national Day of Atonement to reverse America's greed and selfish values of which Clinton's were only the chief[89] (and hey! Yom Kippur's at hand!).

The lesson of the scandal for kids was that as a culture, American adults do not perceive moral standards relative to perceived notions of right and wrong, but rather of power and powerlessness. Those at the bottom—youths and the poor—are expected to adhere to rigid standards of absolute purity and are punished severely for even slight transgression. For those at the top, the adult and powerful, moral standards are lenient, considered important only if other matters (such as the economy) are going wrong. The public condemns intern Monica far more harshly (75-80 percent lashing) in the scandal than the president, evidently because sexual variety and forgiveness for trespass are the right of powerful men such as the president but not of mere weaklings like 21-year-old interns.

Kids were beamed that message loud and clear, both from Democrats and most of the public who indulged Clinton's egregiosities and from Republicans and conservatives who condemned the president but found expedient ways to forgive the sinners in their own midst. As with American attitudes toward drugs, alcohol, guns, and violence, these morals-of-convenience explain a great deal about why the United States is a more dangerous society for young and old alike than similar nations whose adults are more grounded. As in the attack on teenage mothers, reactions to the White House scandals show how easily the powerful blame the powerless even for problems the powerful themselves caused.

Let Us Bray

Only faint liberal criticism greeted the administration's bipartisan National Campaign to Prevent Teen Pregnancy's slam of teenage mothers as "a plague on the nation"[90] and its absurdly-titled May 1997 report, "Whatever Happened to Childhood?"[91] that harks back to halcyon days that never were. What will it take to get elite panels to realize that the childhoods of poorer, particularly minority, youth in the U.S. have *never* been like those of mostly privileged, white-collar panelists?

The National Campaign's report states that teen pregnancy trends result from trends in rates of teenage sexual activity and contraception use combined with trends in the size and racial/ethnic composition of the teenage population. It mentions that most fathers in "adolescent" births are adults, then dedicates exactly one sentence in five pages of recommendations to targeting "men and boys." It re-recommends the litany of contraception/abstinence programming it admits have not worked.

A rundown: the report concedes the impact of sex education is "modest." Further, "there does not currently exist any credible scientific research demonstrating" that abstinence-only programs "actually delayed the onset of sexual intercourse or reduced any other measure of sexual activity." Community family planning programs "have produced mixed results." Comprehensive and intensive programs are "expensive" and "hard to sustain financially." "Community innovation" is needed. More media, official, parental, and celebrity "messages" to teens, unspecified "national leadership," and less squabbling are championed. Thus, the best thinking of the Clinton administration consists of rehashing meaningless non-causes, disgorging pointless platitudes, and recommending that locals fashion miraculous new "solutions" without spending money or straying beyond the assumptions of the old, failed approaches.

The emptiness of the National Campaign's ideas results from its assiduous constraint by 1990s political ground rules for reports on youth (see Chapter 7). These tacitly state that (a) social conditions are off the table, (b) adult behaviors are off the table, and (c) more government spending is off the table. Thus, the report is compelled to ignore the solid fact that today, as in other societies and past eras, how many teenagers get pregnant and give birth continues to depend on only two factors:

(a) The RATE of teenage births is a function of the youth poverty rate;

(b) The TREND in teenage births, both wed and unwed, is a function of the trend in births among adults around them.

Teenage birth rates for any race, any year, urban or suburban, can be predicted within 5 percent accuracy if the youth poverty rate and the adult birth rate are known (see Figure 1). This suggests that we are wasting considerable time attempting to "prevent" teenagers from having babies without addressing the two factors which so precisely predict it. For example, improving economic prospects and family planning programs directed at all ages appear to prevent unwanted pregnancies; those focused only on teenagers over the last quarter century show no discernible effect.

The National Campaign report begins with the standard lament that U.S. teen pregnancy rates are much higher than Europe's, then fails to mention the single biggest difference between U.S. and European teens: poverty levels. Still, at one point, the report starts to ask the right question:

> We also need to recognize that, especially for those at highest risk, reducing teen pregnancy often requires that better, more attractive options be on hand. In a community characterized by poor schools, insufficient adult atten-

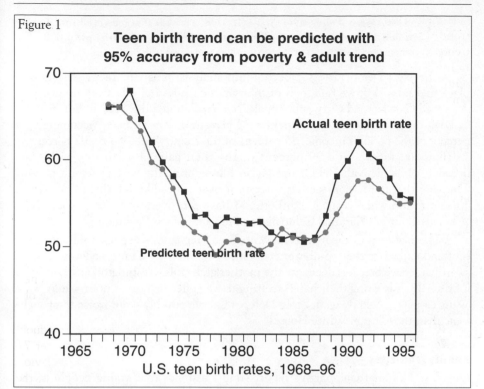

Figure 1

Teen birth trend can be predicted with 95% accuracy from poverty & adult trend

Actual teen birth rate

Predicted teen birth rate

U.S. teen birth rates, 1968–96

tion and guidance, limited jobs, and few recreational opportunities, early pregnancy and childbearing can sometimes seem the most appealing life course available. Babies, after all, can bring purpose and joy to life, even in the most stressful circumstances, and early family formation is sometimes a more reasonable choice than it seems. We need to give teens ample reasons not to become pregnant or cause a pregnancy by pointing them toward a better future.

The Campaign then proposes exactly nothing to improve poor schools, limited jobs, and bleak futures. In an incredible statement, its report concludes:

> Much concern has been voiced about this nation's lagging rate of economic growth and widening income disparities. But too little attention has been paid to the way in which children's very early family environments affect both trends or to the difficulties and expense of helping children overcome early disadvantages...Until more is done to ensure that as many children as possible begin life with parents who are ready to nurture and care for them, progress on those other fronts will be difficult at best—and perhaps impossible.

Teenagers wrecked America's economy! What teenagers? The National Campaign tells us exactly who's to blame for America's compromised "future competitiveness and social cohesiveness:"

> Birth rates are higher among African-American and Hispanic teens than among white teens. In 1994, the birth rate for Hispanic teens was 108 births

and for African-American teens was 105 births per 1,000 women aged 15–19. For non-Hispanic whites, the birth rate for 1994 was 40 births per 1,000 women age 15–19.

The New Democratic socioeconomic analysis: pregnant teenagers (mostly black and brown) drove hundreds of thousands of industrial jobs from inner cities, destroyed Camden and Gary and Appalachia, precipitated the $100 billion Savings & Loan debacle, and forced the richest 20 percent of Americans to accumulate 56 percent of the nation's income, 85 percent of the country's net worth, 92 percent of its financial wealth, and 99 percent of the total gain in wealth over the last decade.[92] Was the National Campaign on Pluto during the welfare reform tumult? Claiming that the nation seethes with furor over trifles like job flight and wealth concentration while teenage motherhood has been overlooked? Ask yourselves: Where is Clinton's National Campaign to Prevent Tycoon Pyramiding?

The National Campaign to Prevent Teen Pregnancy's explicit findings represent and exonerate the top-drawer economic elitism of the Clinton administration: swarthy teenage breeders decimate the motherland while Washington and corporate CEOs helplessly wring their hands (setting down coffee first, so as not to stain West Wing carpet). Could Reagan, Bush, Dole, or Quayle possibly spout worse Limbaugh-logic than the Clinton White House?

Family Valueless

The National Campaign's report simply assumes that young people are to blame for the formation of unstable, high-risk families and should be discouraged from marital liaison. Traditional wisdom is that teenagers suffer relationships that are short, brutish, and mean. Commentators denigrate teen marriages as the epitome of a losing proposition and decree that kids should wait until after 20, after 25, even after 30 to marry and/or have kids.

Once again, the truth is related to socioeconomics, not young age, and is not of the apocalyptic sort that commentators attach. Teen marriages are indeed unstable, but adult marriages are not Gibraltarlike either. National Center for Health Statistics' "Marriage and Divorce" tabulations report detailed statistics on some 2 million marriages and 500,000 divorces every year from the marriage and divorce registration states.[93] A particularly surprising revelation is that teen marriages which end in divorce lasted much longer than similarly failed adult marriages. The 1995 divorce figures showed that on average, teen marriages endured 11 years from I-do to big yellow taxi, compared to just six years for marriages among 30-agers.

Maybe those who get married as teenagers stick it out for more years of hollering and dish-throwing because those who marry young got the idea from their folks that warfare is what marriage is all about. However, this persistence is offset by the higher proportion of teen marriages that go on the rocks. Using the average length of marriages by age to calculate the divorce rates for past marriages, a chart can be set up which predicts the odds of teen and adult marriages winding up in divorce within one, five, 10, 25, or whatever number of years one wants to examine. I compared the numbers of divorces in 1995 by length of marriage and age of betrothed at time of marriage to the numbers of prior marriages by age for each year from 1970 through 1995. Brides and grooms had to be tabulated separately because, in standard adult-teen pattern, most teens of *both sexes* marry partners over 20.

About two-thirds of marriages involving a teen partner are splitsville within 20 years, which means they're fine as personal growth experiences but bad for raising kids. But so are 50 percent of 20-age marriages and 40 percent of 30-and 40-age marriages. Teen marriages fall disastrously short of death-do-us-part, but it's a lousy record all around. All in all, teenage marriages are as stable as those of blacks as a group, suggesting once again that poverty is a major family destabilizer.

If it makes its sarcastic critics feel better, (a) the teenage marriage always was a rarity and misnomer, and (b) its '90s version is headed the way of the spotted owl. In 1965, 220,000 teens married other teens; in 1980, 160,000; in 1995, 56,000. Not only did the numbers fall sharply, the percentage of teenage marriages that hitched a teen bride to a teen groom was 33 percent in 1965, 30 percent in 1980, and 25 percent in 1995. The increasing tendency to marry older partners was evident both for teenage brides (66 percent married men over age 20 in 1965, 73 percent in 1995) and, in an interesting development, even more so for teen grooms (10 percent married women over age 20 in 1965, tripling to 28 percent in 1995!). In accelerating trends, today's teens of both sexes are marrying less often and marrying older partners. That, too, could be a reflection of growing youth poverty, which renders teen-teen liaison less economically viable than adult-teen marriages.

Unfortunately, facts don't seem to slow down rampant adult sarcasm about teenage marriage or induce sober reflection on the instability of adult liaisons. The statistics above indicate that four-fifths of children under 18 affected by divorce had parents who married when both were 20 or older.

If American adults insist on raising one-fourth of our kids in abject poverty while enriching older age groups and the wealthy, if we continue to tolerate high rates of sexual irresponsibility among adults from the Potomac to the local 'hood, if we continue to indulge groundless prejudices against young people instead of facing uncomfortable facts, we will continue to have high rates of teenagers having babies—mostly with adult partners. And worse sexual consequences as well.

Aquarian AIDS

AIDS used to be a "gay disease." However, the proportion of new HIV infections diagnosed in 1996 and 1997 show the share attributed to gay men has dropped to less than half. HIV infection patterns reveal its true nature as a disease of poverty, the abuse of women and young men, and related tragedies of runaways, prostitution, and "survival sex." The latter involves trading sex for money, protection, food, shelter, or drugs, or to avoid violence—thinly negotiated rape.

Among adolescents, the roots of HIV are sexual abuse and household violence, homelessness, minority status, economic need, and sex with older males. "The trend in Los Angeles has been part of a national pattern that has seen an explosion in homeless women and families in cities large and small," the *Times* reported on July 28, 1998. "A 1997 survey of 29 cities, including Los Angeles, by the U.S. Conference of Mayors found that families are the fastest growing segment of the homeless population, accounting for 36 percent nationwide." The reasons? Job loss, lack of affordable housing, drug abuse and emotional instability among parents, and the disappearance of social services that used to cushion the effects of the above.[94] Growing thousands of families can no longer find even temporary food stamps or housing in the face of joblessness—which was the predictable result of Clinton's welfare reforms.

Given that history, emotional alarms about "adolescents and AIDS" emanating from the Clinton regime bear dreary resemblance to those surrounding youth crime and drugs. Wild exaggerations of numbers. Dire fabrications of trends. Absolution of his own anti-youth policies in exacerbating the poverty and homelessness of young people. Claims that the whole problem is teenage ignorance, attitude, and "high-risk behavior." Sanitized assertions designed to make the teen/AIDS issue exploitable by a variety of interests purely as a programming challenge.[95]

Consistently, Center for Disease Control reports present "adolescent HIV/AIDS" simply as the result of "teenagers...engaging in behaviors that may put them at risk."[96] "Three terms the CDC can't spell are 'child abuse,' 'sexual abuse,' and 'rape,' " a veteran Los Angeles prevention official told me "you didn't hear me say."

The White House Office of National AIDS Policy's 1996 report claimed that "one in four new infections in the United States (occur) among people under the age of 20." A large exaggeration, arrived at by assuming that all HIV infections diagnosed in persons under age 25 were contracted before age 20, then rounding up radically.

Of the newest HIV infections in the 18 months ending June 30, 1997, 18 percent were in persons ages 13 to 24. HIV can be diagnosed as rapidly as six months, and is typically discovered within three to five years after infection. Thus, many of these cases would have been contracted in the 20s. The figures indicate that fewer than one in six HIV infections is acquired in teen years.

Teenagers are *not* the age group most likely to acquire HIV infection. Adults in their 20s and 30s are far more at risk, while adults in their 40s have HIV contraction rates nearly as high as teens age 15–19. If socioeconomic status is controlled to neutralize the higher numbers of youth in poverty, teen age is associated with lower risk of acquiring HIV than adult status up to age 60.

Teenagers do *not* have the fastest-rising rates of HIV infection. They have one of the *lowest* rates of increase. AIDS has a seven- to 10-year incubation period after HIV infection, but conservatively, let us assume that *every* AIDS case diagnosed before age 30 resulted from HIV contracted during teenage years. From 1988 through June 1997, the rate of HIV infection among teens (as measured by AIDS diagnoses among persons ages 13–29) rose by 76 percent. This compares to a 91 percent rise among persons who contracted HIV in their 20s (diagnosed as AIDS in their 30s) and more than 100 percent increase among adults over age 30 (diagnosed after age 40).

So, despite the dangers imposed on them by adults, teenagers are not uniquely at risk. Further, their risk is shared—literally—with adults. There is no such thing as "adolescent AIDS (or HIV)." In no sense is the teenage aspect of this deadly disease

Table 3

**Teen infecting each other? Male and female teenage
HIV infection trends go in radically different directions...**

Proportion of total HIV/AIDS* cases by sex and time period:

	Teenage male infections as a percent of all male infections	Teenage female infections as a percent of all female infections	All teenage infections as a percent of all infections
AIDS cases diagnosed through 1992	18.7%	24.6%	19.4%
AIDS cases diagnosed through 1997	16.9	22.8	17.9
New HIV diagnoses, 1997	15.7	25.7	16.8

...as the most recent HIV infections clearly show

The "leading edge": newest (1997) HIV diagnoses, projected national rate per 100,000 population by age at which disease was ACQUIRED*

Age	Total	Male	Female
<13	0.6	0.5	0.7
13–19	5.5	4.7	6.4
20–29	13.7	18.8	8.5
30–39	11.4	16.0	6.7
40–49	5.5	8.3	2.8
50–59	2.3	3.8	1.0
60+	0.3	0.5	0.2
Total	5.8	7.8	3.9

*All AIDS diagnosed at age 13–29 and HIV infections diagnosed at ages 13–24 are assumed to have been acquired during teenage years. AIDS diagnosed through 1992 was probably contracted during the early and mid-1980s; AIDS diagnosed through 1997 was probably acquired in the mid-1980s to early 1990s; HIV diagnosed in 1997 was probably contracted in the mid-1990s. HIV rates are from 30 reporting states.

Source: Centers for Disease Control and Prevention (1998). *HIV/AIDS Surveillance Report* (semiannual).

different or separate from its adult pattern except that adolescents are somewhat less at risk and experience lower rates of increase than do grownups.

HIV infection among teenagers nearly always results from adult-teen sex. If teenagers were spreading AIDS among each other, as the White House report claims, we would expect to see similar trends among teenage males and females. That is far from the case (Table 3).

Table 4

**AIDS increasingly is a disease of poverty,
which means nonwhites and women**

Percent of cases:	Whites	Blacks	Hispanics	Females	Females <20
AIDS through 1985	60.0%	24.3%	13.3%	6.4%	2.2%
AIDS in 1990–93	48.9	34.3	14.4	13.6	3.4
AIDS in 1994–96	40.6	40.2	16.9	18.5	4.2
AIDS in 1997	33.5	44.5	20.5	21.8	4.5
New HIV infections, 1997	*	*	*	30.6	7.3

*New HIV infections in 1997 are from 30 reporting states, which allows accurate estimation by age and gender but not by race, since these states are not racially representative of the nation. Cases for females <20 are AIDS cases diagnosed in females under age 30 and HIV cases diagnosed in females under age 25.
Source: Centers for Disease Control and Prevention, *HIV/AIDS Surveillance*.

The trends in teenage male and female infection are in opposite directions. As we move forward in time to the present, the proportion of male HIV infections contracted by teenagers drops dramatically while the female share has stayed the same. For the 8,000 newest HIV infections diagnosed in 1997—the "leading edge," showing the epidemic's shape into the near future—teenage boys display less risk of being infected than adult men up to age 50! This pattern could only indicate an astonishingly effective disease control regimen among young gay men. But teenage females occupy a large, slightly increased share of female infections. Note that the same pattern is occurring for nonwhite race (Table 4).

The news for young, impoverished women gets worse as the leading edge of the disease is examined. In 1997, 440 of the 533 heterosexually-transmitted AIDS cases diagnosed in persons under age 25 (83 percent) were females. More tellingly, 381 of the 445 *new*, heterosexually-infected HIV patients (86 percent) in 1997 were females—as were 89 percent of those under age 20. Of the male, under-25 HIV cases for which the cause of infection was known, only 8 percent were from heterosexual intercourse—compared to 86 percent of females. Homosexual relations are the cause of four-fifths of the teen male infections. In 1997, males and females under age 25 had virtually equal HIV rates.

These radically opposite teenage male-female trends, and the huge surplus of heterosexual cases in young females, are not the pattern of teenagers spreading HIV by sex with *each other*. Even the most politically-blinded AIDS scholars ought to be able to figure this out. This is a pattern of adult men infecting greater numbers of teenage females—and younger males as well, though in lower numbers.

The circumstances under which those infections occur are well documented. Even among low-income teenagers, such as the 270,000 Job Corps applicants[97] and 150,000 clients of public clinics[98] tested, HIV and AIDS are practically non-existent among non-promiscuous heterosexuals who do not inject drugs—that is, 85 percent of the teenage sample. However, infection rates are as high as one in six

Table 5

**White teens now have lower HIV risk
than black and Latino *senior citizens***

The newest AIDS cases, diagnosed in the last half of 1997,
per 100,000 population by age at which infection ACQUIRED*

Age	New male HIV infections			New female HIV infections		
---	White	Black	Latino	White	Black	Latino
<13	0.3	3.8	1.8	0.2	4.8	1.9
13–19	15.9	93.0	53.9	3.8	56.6	20.2
20–29	48.0	304.6	175.5	6.4	112.2	46.6
30–39	32.7	306.5	153.1	3.7	92.0	35.7
40–49	16.2	156.5	88.0	1.7	33.3	20.4
50+	3.0	43.3	26.2	0.3	9.2	7.6
Total	17.5	122.0	66.8	2.3	45.6	18.2

*AIDS diagnosis assumed to occur 7–10 years after infection. Those cases listed as having been acquired at age 13–19, for example, would be diagnosed at age 20–29, etc.

Source: Centers for Disease Control and Prevention (1998). *HIV/AIDS Surveillance Report* (semiannual).

among teenage runaways and prostitutes. This is where the "teenage epidemic" dwells. These clearly evident facts are met with silence by officials charged with controlling it.

The newest patterns by race in the AIDS epidemic are revealed in the 30,000 new AIDS infections diagnosed in 1997. (HIV figures are adequate to calculate rates by age but unreliable by race, since only 30 states report HIV infections, and these erratically.) The 1997 figures continue to show that AIDS is a disease of poverty. A 1995 article in *Science* reported that black men were four times more likely to be infected than Euro-white men, and black women were 17 times more likely to be infected than Euro-white women. Hispanics and other nonwhites were in between.[99]

While the White House fixates on winning votes by scaring the parents of suburban teenagers, the ravaging of poorer inner-citians has accelerated (Tables 4 and 5). Rates of infection among black men have increased to seven times higher, and among black women to 20 *times higher*, than among Euro-whites. Black teenage males display much higher risk than white males but lower rates than black adult males up to age 50. Black teenage females are 15 times more at risk than white teenage females but less at risk than black adult women up to age 40. Latinos have AIDS rates three to four times higher for males, and five to 12 times higher for females, than do Euro-whites. This is an infection pattern that almost perfectly traces the poverty rates by race and age—but not gender. For the young, females are more at risk; for the old, males.

As in nearly all of American social and medical science's prejudices regarding "teenage risk," statistics from other Western societies demolish them. In Canada, persons under age 30 accounted for one-fifth of the nation's 9,400 AIDS diagnoses (again, indicating HIV infection during teen or young adult years) prior to 1993. By 1996–97, Canada's under-30 AIDS toll had declined dramatically to just 12 percent of 900 cases.[100] Canada, unlike the U.S., does not raise huge proportions of its young in poverty, forcing legions into dangerous sexual enterprises to survive. Canada, unlike the U.S., does provide its poorer citizens free health care.

None of these patterns seems to matter to the procession of White House, CDC, and expert panels. They continue to recycle the same report that they have for 10 years. HIV is just a gay and/or teenage behavior crisis. Get more programs into high schools and communities and prevention messages into the media. Not one of the 1996 White House Office of National AIDS Policy report's 11 recommended steps and strategies addressed the issues of runaways, prostitution, poverty, rape, or sexual abuse. If a deadly epidemic can't force health authorities to dismantle the unreal image of "teenage sex" and AIDS they have constructed, what will it take?

Fertile Politics

A striking image from the magnificent 1997 movie, *The Ice Storm*: 1970s suburban parents lounge giggling in living-room languor, passing joints and wine and plotting sex partying; the camera pans upward to the skylight, where kids are plastered like insects, observing the strange phenomenon called modern adulthood. If 45-year-old parents have sex with their friends' 20-year-old kids in random-exchange car-key parties, can 14-year-olds declare open season on fifth graders? Mom shoplifts (ineptly) to regain the wildness she sees in her adolescent daughter but gains only a humiliating arrest; the daughter fumbles (ineptly) with sex to challenge adult corruption but winds up imitating it instead.

The notion that youth and adult behaviors could in any way be linked is bizarrely denied in the White House spin that accompanies release of annual National Center for Health Statistics birth figures. Teen birth rates are down in the mid-1990s; births among blacks under age 30 are at their lowest levels since the 1950s. Washington interests break both arms to grab credit for "getting the message through" to fertile teenagers. Health Secretary Shalala congratulated the "strategy of parents, community leaders, religious leaders and schools all sending the same consistent message" for reducing the teen birth rate by 12 percent from 1991 through 1996.[101]

Washington, schools, parents, preachers, and community leaders deserve no credit. Adult birth rates are also down, by an equal amount since 1991. The most telling measure of what is going on among teenagers is the ratio of the birth rate among females age 15–19 to that of females age 20–44. It was 0.73 during the 1950s, 0.70 in 1960s, 0.78 in the 1970s, 0.76 in the 1980s, and 0.86 in the 1990s. That is, the era of most intensive prevention effort coincided with an unexpected rise in teen birth rates relative to those of adults, probably due to growing youth poverty in the post-1970 period.

Musick points out the consensus of researchers that teenage pregnancy prevention programs "have failed," a point confirmed by researcher Douglas Kirby of the National Campaign to Prevent Teen Pregnancy.[102] A major reason for the failure is continuing refusal to face that fact that the vast majority of teenage mothers have babies not because of bad values, ignorance of sex, or ineptness with contraception, but because they want their babies, Musick states from her extensive interviews with teens. Given the intense pressures on young women in impoverished environments, she marvels repeatedly, "it is remarkable that rates of adolescent childbearing are not even higher."[103]

For now, the prevailing policy stance wallows in 1970s and '80s retro ignorance of convenience: teenage mothers are stupid, and they're stupid because they're teenagers. The worst example of the traditional-program smugness is "Baby Think It Over," a thoroughly demeaning scheme in which schoolgirls are forced to lug around squalling dolls to "disrupt their sleep schedule and social life." This purports to "help our youth wake up to the hard realities of teen parenting." Ads with a shrieking-brat logo (one which communicates nothing so much as a hostility to babies) show a miserable white girl blankly cradling a "Caucasian infant simulator" doll.[104] Most of the teen mothers I interviewed over the years not only did not miss their former "social lives," they had more childhood experience caring for younger brothers and sisters and other extended-family infants than any dozen privileged academics. "Baby Think It Over" illustrates the wrongheaded notion of "teen" pregnancy as an affliction of teenagers rather than of conditions.

Still, the new directions in the "teenage pregnancy" debate provide hope. For the first time, the refreshing question is being asked as to whether authorities have been shortsighted, arrogant, and even exploitative in presuming to dictate whether poorer inner-city teenagers should become mothers. The issue is not how teenage mothers damage society, but the other way around.

7 Myth: Teens Are Reckless, Suicidal, and "At Risk"

If I had to pick the weirdest, most blatant, most obtuse pack of lies top authorities tell about adolescents, it would be the unanimous insistence that California teenage suicide is skyrocketing. This decade-long saga evidences a broad swath of expertdom so blinded by its own prejudices and programmatic self-interest that it no longer cares what is really going on, even with a deadly issue. It is the quintessential example of the way many modern services once set up to serve young people have devolved into viewing young people as in their service.

The California myth holds lessons for the similarly questionable claim that teenage suicide in the United States has mushroomed. When teenage suicide untruths are unraveled, a major set of falsehoods about the mental health and self-destructive behavior of young people is shattered along with them. A whole new set of questions is raised about why the myths of rampant teenage self-destruction were created, and for whose benefit.

In past decades, California had a high suicide rate among all age groups, as symbolized by its legend of starlets leaping off the Hollywood Sign, Marilyn Monroe's demise from barbiturates, and Golden Gate plunges. As a result, the state's universities and institutions house some of the world's leading authorities on suicide. Statistics on California suicide over the last three decades (shown for teenagers in Table 1) are detailed, readily available on diskette or in any middle-sized library, and take minimal time to assemble. There is little excuse, then, for misrepresentation.

Note from Table 1 that the trend is completely misrepresented. For California teen deaths ruled as suicides, the most recent three years (1994–96) represent the lowest three since the late 1960s. For those mysterious kinds of deaths many experts feel harbor hidden suicides (drug overdoses, falls, drownings, hangings and suffocations, self-inflicted gunshot wounds or cutting), the most recent years may be the safest in state history. Take your pick—the 1994–96 period represents by far the lowest three years for teenage self-dispatch in at least 35 years.

And yet, with unanimity, the state's leading authorities insist into the mid-1990s that California teen suicide and self-destructive deaths are skyrocketing. Logically, California teen suicide should be rising. With divorce, abuse, poverty, no future, Governor Wilson, Democrats, bad radio, and having to listen to experts relentlessly malign their morals and mental health, modern California kids should be offing themselves in record droves. Our self destruction is not rubbing off on '90s kids.

Table 1

In 1996, California teenage suicides and self-destructive accidents reached their lowest point in 30 years.

	Deaths from Suicides	Accidents*	Total	Pop 10–19 (million)	Suicide rate	Total rate
1965	100	176	276	3,215	3.1	8.6
	134	204	338	3,366	4.0	10.0
	161	257	418	3,445	4.7	12.1
	140	345	485	3,552	3.9	13.7
	223	451	674	3,654	6.1	18.4
1970	241	440	681	3,781	6.4	18.0
	240	417	657	3,827	6.3	17.2
	260	352	612	3,859	6.7	15.9
	223	417	640	3,891	5.7	16.4
	211	399	610	3,929	5.4	15.5
1975	200	334	534	3,970	5.0	13.5
	195	323	518	3,957	4.9	13.1
	262	310	572	3,919	6.7	14.6
	192	302	494	3,878	5.0	12.7
	206	264	470	3,843	5.4	12.2
1980	208	239	447	3,948	5.3	11.3
	210	226	436	3,997	5.3	10.9
	179	187	366	4,026	4.4	9.1
	204	210	414	4,027	5.1	10.3
	183	205	388	4,001	4.6	9.7
1985	216	153	369	3,993	5.4	9.2
	214	207	421	3,996	5.4	10.5
	193	138	331	4,012	4.8	8.3
	228	170	398	4,030	5.7	9.9
	234	147	381	4,047	5.8	9.4
1990	220	162	382	4,082	5.4	9.4
	223	161	384	4,103	5.4	9.4
	194	167	361	4,167	4.7	8.7
	229	160	389	4,243	5.4	9.2
	192	156	348	4,350	4.4	8.0
1995	215	151	366	4,472	4.8	8.2
	207	141	348	4,601	4.5	7.6

*Accidents, mostly self-inflicted, most likely to be suicides. Included are accidental deaths from poisonings (including drug overdoses), firearms, hangings and suffocations, drownings, knives/razors, and falls, and deaths undetermined whether accidentally or purposely inflicted. Rates are per 100,000 population age 10–19.
Source: California Vital Statistics Bureau, Department of Health Services.

The saga of expert distortion of California teen suicide is not Homeric. Back in the halcyon days of the Sixties, experts did tell the truth. Teen suicide had risen sharply in California; UCLA suicidologist Robert Litman reported in 1973. As with adults, barbiturates were the big culprit. In 1970, the era of pot and acid, the big drug killer of California teens and young adults was…Mama's little helper. In 1996, California teenage suicides and self-destructive accidents reached their lowest point in 30 years.

Litman examined hospital records of 1,100 Los Angeles child and teen drug overdoses classified as "accidents." He reported that one-fourth were suicide attempts, another 48 percent were "suicidal gestures," and only 13 percent were "drug trips" which took a bad detour:

> Between 1960 and 1970, the suicide rate for men in their 20s doubled and that of teen-aged boys tripled, Litman said…The suicide rate of women in their 20s more than quadrupled…and that of girls in their teens rose eight times…
>
> "It is estimated that there are more than 100,000 self-poisonings each year in this country involving children between 6 and 17," Litman said.[1]

Unlike modern foolishness regarding teenage suicide, Litman's 1970s analysis displayed solid grounding in reality:

> "It has been found that 34% of the children came from broken homes, and a history of significant emotional stress at the time of poisoning was obtained from 43% of those 6 to 10 years old and from 78% of those over 10."
>
> …Litman said that suicide is still a fact for a comparatively few, especially children. He said suicide prevention as a social movement is part of the general effort to balance increasing social isolation and alienation that accompanies urbanization, automation and excessive mobility.

This is the classic "anomie" theory of suicide derived from pioneering 19th century studies by French sociologist Emile Durkheim. Suicide rises, Durkheim found, in societies in which norms are in rapid flux, people are mobile, and many individuals are ungrounded. Not a bad description of California in the Sixties. Check the suicide and self-destruction deaths among California teens of my generation (1968–73) shown in Table 1. In that five-year period, 3,200 teens died.

California officials told the truth about teenage suicide in the early 1970s—it was rising. For the next decade or so, they continued to tell the truth.

Alarmed by alarms from national authorities of a "tripling" in teen suicide rates, the California Senate Select Committee on Children and Youth held hearings in 1981. Kay Moser, chief of the California Center for Health Statistics, had a surprise for the committee chaired by Senator Robert Presley:

> MS. MOSER: During the 1970s, suicide rates have increased in the United States while they have decreased in California…In the United States suicide rates have increased 35.6% for teenagers 15 to 19, while they have decreased by 30% in California. This is a tremendous shift from the increase we had from 1960 to 1970, but beginning in 1970 they are starting to come back down again.
>
> SENATOR PRESLEY: …Why is that? Does anybody give you any ideas as to why that is?

MS. MOSER: No.

SENATOR PRESLEY: ...I guess the surprising thing—most of the information has been that [teen] suicide were increasing. I find this rather encouraging that they are decreasing. Maybe we better just not do anything.[2]

The record showed that the state's top suicide experts attended the hearing. Presumably, they heard Moser's testimony and viewed her detailed exhibits on the state's large, decade-long decline in teen suicide. Presumably, scholars were familiar with tables in the appendix of the U.S. Centers for Disease Control's 1986 *Youth Suicide Surveillance* that clearly showed a major drop in California teen suicide, though the report's authors failed to point it out.

Presumably, scholars rushed out to discover why California teens were defying the national trend in hopes of learning more about what deters suicide. Uh, no. No journal articles, no conferences, no press.

Far be it from me to suggest that one big reason behind the lack of professional enthusiasm for the good news was that the psychiatric hospital industry had vastly overbuilt hospitals in a 1970s orgy sparked by tax breaks. Now the industry was busy filling empty beds with teenage patients. From the 1970s to the 1980s, adolescent commitments to psychiatric care quadrupled. Hospital recruitment of young patients relied heavily on hyping the suicidal-teen angle, including frightening ads showing teenagers with guns to their heads and parents weeping over graves.[3]

In 1988, an American Psychological Association task force reported that teenagers were vastly over-committed to hospitals under vague diagnoses in order to enhance the profits of a financially troubled psychiatric hospitals. A California study, in particular, found that teenagers with health insurance were held in treatment twice as long as uninsured youths. Yet diagnosable mental illnesses such as schizophrenia and manic depression (and outcomes such as suicide and self destruction) had not risen among teens in recent decades. Therefore, a variety of insurance industry, professional, and National Institute of Mental Health researchers concluded, hospital profiteering, not a rise in teenage mental problems, were prompting commitments of rising numbers of youths.[4]

The teen suicide decline had nothing to do with the increased psychiatric commitments. The decline began years before the mass commitment era. Suicide among California black youth declined as much as it did for whites even though black youth were less likely to have access to and be committed to psychiatric hospitals. States in which teens were treated in droves (such as Minnesota, where laws required insurance to pay for commitments) displayed no better suicide statistics than states which left kids alone.

By the mid-1980s, California figures showed teen suicide had fallen to its lowest level since 1968. No one noticed, and experts kept ringing alarm bells. In 1987, the California Department of Education assembled leading experts and held hearings around the state. On page 1, their report, *Suicide Prevention Program for California Public Schools*, stated: "Teenage suicide has risen dramatically in recent years."[5]

Bizarre.

By 1996, California teenage suicide and self destruction stood at its lowest level in at least 35 years. The plummet in California teen drug deaths, in particular, was beyond belief. In 1970, 250 overdosed. In 1996, 35.

Los Angeles County's record was miraculous: 129 teen drug deaths in 1970 had dropped to nine by 1996. In the entire year of 1994, in a county of nine million people and dangerous drugs abundant, not one teenager died of an accidental drug overdose.

Overall, Los Angeles County teen suicide had dropped by 50 percent, to its lowest rate in four decades. But it was not zero. In May 1996, two San Pedro, California, girls jumped off a cliff. The Big Media flocked. Said the experts to *Time* magazine: "Suicide rates are rising steadily for teenagers." No Ph.D. cliché about adolescents escaped mention in *Time*'s frantic article on the "psychiatric disaster." Teens are depressed, teens are suicidal, teens have no concept of death, it shouted.[6] Other local experts blamed "increasing drug abuse" for the "rise" in teenagers killing themselves. By the way, paying shrinks more money will solve the problem.

If experts and the media were trying to promote more teen suicide by depicting it as normal, they would have done exactly what they did. In fact, adolescents are uniquely invulnerable to taking their own lives. Teenage rates are considerably below those of adults. In 1995, national suicide rates per 100,000 population were as follows: age 10–14, 1.8; 15–19, 10.4; 20–49, 15.4; 50 and older, 15.9.

The Death of Statistics

The Big Media and the experts who lie to it are one kind of modern adolescent affliction. Another is professionals who lie to each other. In late 1997, I reviewed a grant proposal by the California Family Health Council, which contained a report by Planned Parenthood. They stated:

> An increasing number of adolescents engage in risky behavior that threaten their current and future health...Recent years have seen an increase in the number of attempted and completed suicides among adolescents.[7]

Never since the Fabulous Fifties, and probably since the Gold Rush, had California teenagers been LESS self-destructive than they were in 1996 (re-refer to Table 1). Yet not one in this state of tens of thousands of mental health scholars had the honesty to step forward to say just that.

The conclusion to this strange trip was the *Los Angeles Times* front-page splash on teenage suicide in May 1997. Big Media, Professional Authority, and Program Interest collaborated on a portrayal of L.A. youth suicide that can only be described as pathological prevarication.

The *Times* contacted me early for information. I sent them reams of data showing major declines in youth suicide, especially in Los Angeles—ages 5–9, 10–14 and 15–19, going back decades. Even larger declines in child and teenage self-destructive deaths were evident. Reporter Sonia Nazario thanked me profusely but was clearly dissatisfied. She kept asking for data on child suicide (a couple of kids under age 12 kill themselves in California every year, making trends impossible to establish) or "suicide attempts" to demonstrate that youth suicide was up—as she told me every expert insisted it was.

Nazario's story was six months in the making. It appeared on the front page on Sunday, March 9, 1997, headlined, "Children who kill themselves: A grim trend." The lead-in: "As young as 10, they see life clouded in pain. More are seeking—and too often finding—a way to end it."

The story began with the suicides of three kids, ages 10, 11, and 13. "Kids this young didn't used to kill themselves in America," it announced.

The earliest national record I had was from 1908. It showed 15 suicides among age 10–14 in an era in which death registration was far less systematic and covered only half of a nation with much smaller population.

More dire assertions by doctors from the University of California, Los Angeles, followed: "Children too young to get their learner's permits increasingly are thinking about ending their lives." (Famed Stanford University child psychologist Lewis Terman wrote in 1913: "In these days, children leave their marbles and tops to commit suicide, tired of life almost before they have tasted it.")[8]

"It's really scary," Mark D'Antonio, director of inpatient adolescent services at the University of California at Los Angeles's Neuropsychiatric Institute, said to the *Times* in 1997 of the "numbers of children" who kill and injure themselves deliberately today. "I didn't see this 10 to 12 years ago."

"Ten to 12 years ago" would be the mid-1980s. State vital statistics show that in the 1983–86 period, there were 16 suicides among Los Angeles 10–13 year-olds, including two seven-year-olds and one nine-year-old. In 1996, in a much larger child population, there were 15 suicides, none under age 10. But panic was the object, not perspective. The paper's lengthy feature was filled with gut-wrenching hysteria.

Finally, in the second part of her series, in the 58th paragraph at the bottom of page 12, reporter Nazario finally got around to the unmentionable truth:

> In Los Angeles...between 1970 and 1994...the teenage suicide rate dropped from nearly triple the national average to 28% below it.

That is an incredible decline. In plain English, L.A.'s child and teenage suicide levels had dropped by half in the last quarter century. But that detail was not raised to point out that kids were *less* self-destructive, or examine why. Rather, it was brought up to hype the schools' suicide prevention programs, which first appeared in 1987.[9] But L.A. teen suicide had been declining for 15 years before that.

Those sincerely interested in suicide prevention would be eager to analyze the California and Los Angeles surprises. A few were, especially members of California's small, volunteer suicide prevention programs and veterans who toiled in the old L.A. Suicide Prevention Network, such as consulting psychiatrist Norman Tabachnick.

But no one in California's huge mental health, medical, or academic establishment evinced any curiosity. Most interests seemed openly resentful of the findings and implied that they risked funding cuts if word got out that teen suicide was not, in fact, rocketing upward. When I raised California's teen suicide and drug death decline at an august panel at the November 1997 State of the World Forum in San Francisco, a roomful of experts sat in indifferent silence and quickly changed the subject. No one's program needs could benefit from this information; hence, it didn't exist. This was a forum in which world luminaries modestly had pledged themselves to usher in a dramatic "paradigm shift" in attitudes about youth.

California's teen suicide scare remains one of the most systematic special-interest falsifications I have been acquainted with. When I unrolled the Sunday *Times* containing Nazario's article, I finally resigned myself to the fact that the problem with public mistruths spread about American teenagers was not faulty information, confusion, or good faith errors. It was reckless distortion by powerful interests allied against an unpopular minority group, just as has occurred throughout history.

Lying up teen suicide

Experts' difficulty telling the truth is not confined to California. Here is what the American Association of Suicidology, an august association of Ph.Ds and professionals, told the media in 1997 about teenage suicide:

> Suicide has become a serious public health problem for young people...
> - Between the years 1980–1992, a total of 67,369 people under the age of 25 committed suicide, accounting for 16.4% of all suicides.
> - Suicides account for 1.4% of all deaths in the USA annually, but they constitute 14% of all deaths each month among 15- to 24-year-olds.
> - Black males (ages 15–19) have shown the largest increase in suicide rates among adolescents: 165% since 1980.
> - Up to 60% of high school students report having suicidal thoughts.[10]

The above statements carry such misleading implications that no reputable college introductory research course would accept them if made by a struggling freshman.

Note first of all that "under the age of 25" does not equal "teenager." Teenagers (persons ages 13–19) account for fewer than 7 percent of all suicides, a rate far below that of adults of all ages.

Note, second, that the reason suicides account for a higher proportion of deaths among "15- to 24-year-olds" is *not* because that age group is more suicidal than older ones—which is what the Association is insinuating. It is because younger people don't die from cancer, heart disease, or other diseases of old age. So even if the suicide rate is lower in the younger age group, it can still account for a greater percentage of deaths.

Note, third, what is left out of the statement about black males. In the most recent year tabulated, 1995, 197 black teenage males out of a population of two million committed suicide—a rate far below that of the old white men who form academic panels.[11] Black teen males were less at risk of self-destructive death in 1995 than in 1980 or earlier years. The biggest thing that has changed, I and other authors documented in articles[12] published in the American Association of Suicidology journal, *Suicide & Life-Threatening Behavior*, is that teenage deaths (particularly those of minorities) are far more likely to be investigated and certified as suicides rather than as "accidents" than in the past.

The statement, "up to 60% of high school students report having suicidal thoughts" would be unworthy of *National Enquirer*. "Up to 100 percent" of adult human beings have suicidal thoughts. Who of post-pubertal cognitive development has not thought of suicide, however fleetingly? Although several studies have shown that youths with histories of sexual abuse are several times more likely to seriously consider or attempt suicide than non-abused youths,[13] health officials and programs never talk about this.[14]

What the experts are saying is that 60,000 of every 100,000 high school students report having thoughts about suicide. Yet records show that 30 in 100,000 commit suicide during their entire four years in high school. Clearly, it is extremely rare for thought to translate into action. As a group, teenagers are by far the least suicidal of any age group except children and infants. The very infrequent teenage suicide is an unquestioned tragedy. That is why experts owe the subject serious scrutiny, not generalized frenzy.

In fact, teenagers experience no higher levels of mental disturbance than adults do, comprehensive textbook and literature reviews show.[15] But as funding tightens, as competition increases, groups are pushed to ever more drastic claims about all types of teenage malaise in order to get attention. The original motive might have been benign: to maintain services in a time of conservative cutbacks. But the exaggeration now has gone beyond all reason. It is damaging to young people and disastrous for effective policy.

Just as one well-intentioned fib often requires a second, worse lie to cover up, the expert-fabricated epidemic of teenage misbehavior required an expert-fabricated teenage psychology to explain. Whether the issue was crime, violence, drugs, alcohol, smoking, depression, suicide, or any other behavior, institutional interests were locked into one, unvarying statement about adolescents: they're worse than ever.

The danger in this demonization of young people was that some might ask who is to blame for breeding all these terrible teenagers. Rotten parents? Ineffective programs? Sick societal values? That threat was swept aside by the resurrection of 19th century myths about supposedly innate teenage biological and psychological defects. Raging hormones. Delusions of invulnerability. Innate risk-taking. Mindless defiance and rebellion. The same things experts used to say about minorities.

Acquitting bad parents

Some explanation had to be found for all this purportedly bad behavior. Enter the pop experts—those selected by political and media imperatives, not by careful research and objective theorizing. These political imperatives and the select authorities who uphold them account for the colossal errors in presenting teenage issues.

In the 1980s, the rising numbers of unstable parents demanded theories tailored to excuse adult deficiency and transfer blame to "natural" teenage barbarity. Obligingly, authorities resurrected long-debunked notions of "adolescent rebellion," "teenage storm and stress," and youthful delusions of immortality. These early-century theories of the innate crises and dark evils lurking in teenhood were fashioned by psychiatrist G. Stanley Hall, whose personal life was revealed to be more of a basket case than those of the adolescents he bemoaned. Hall's 1904 treatise likened the

innate defects of nonwhite race and young age in his terming of nonwhites as "adolescent races."[16] Notions of faulty adolescent biology, like that of race and sex, have
since been disproved by research and practical experience.

Rotten parents of the 1980s and '90s also spawned a vast and growing legion of
treatment, programming, behavior education, and other services designed to manage pathologies those rotten-parent supremos, *Toughlove*'s Phyllis and David York,
insisted were plaguing all modern youth. Every teenager in all "geographical, social,
and economic backgrounds" is "satanic," the Yorks railed.[17] Even drug reformer Dan
Baum reinforced the sullen door-slamming mallrat image:

> Parents and teenagers always fight; the power struggle between them is one of
> the great conflicts in American life. Acting combative, secretive, and thorough-
> ly unpleasant is how teenagers carve out their new, proto-adult identities.[18]

This stereotype has no more validity than characterizing black men as shuffling,
eye-rolling watermelon thieves. Neither study nor family observations support
Toughlove's insistence that family conflict is inevitable or always the fault of stoned,
rotten youths when it does occur.

Parent-teen conflict is far less pervasive and destructive than, say, spouse-
spouse conflict, which ends half of all marriages and ensures that more than half of
today's children and youths will spend part or all of their growings-up in one-parent
families. In the majority of families in which teenagers and parents fight occasionally, and in the fraction in which they fight chronically, the teenager is not always at
fault, as rotten parents and programs assume. Nor is the parent always at fault.

Though no generalization applies to every case, the overwhelming rule in the
dozens of families I worked with was that the parents had the kids they had raised.
For every sullen teenager, there was a moody parent. Serene kids tended to go with
serene parents; messed-up kids tended to have more messed-up parents. Teenagers
were not any more "combative, secretive, or thoroughly unpleasant" than adults.
Conflicts between parents and teens, as between spouses or any individuals in prox-
imity, were expressions of individuals, not generic adolescent rebellion or generic
parental repression.

Most parents and adolescents got along fine. When they didn't, a lot of the
problem was parents getting payback for their own miscreancy. Parents would put
their kids through constant marital strife and bitter divorce, then complain their
kids were "acting out." One mother, who had three divorces and a series of live-in
boyfriends her kids hated (for good reason), told me she was furious at her daughters' bad taste in boyfriends. Parents would broadcast that their kids were the worst
creatures in the world, then express indignance that their kids thought their parents
were the stupidest persons in the world. The ultimate shamelessness was the parent
who went public. Hauling the brats onto Sally Jesse, disgorging a *Newsweek* "My
Turn," or writing a book like *Toughlove* won applause from people who never
stopped to ponder what kind of parent would do that.

The quality of parent-adolescent relationship, in short, reflected a personal
interaction and family history that detached adult society of the 1980s and '90s was
in no mood to bother with. The interests of parents, programs, and politics demand-

ed that widespread teenage rebellion against wise parental values must be seen as the menace to family and republic alike. So, in the 1980s long-discredited, unreconstructed Hallist theory was resurrected just about every time the media and pop-experts took up the topic of terrible teen torturing pacific parent.

What does research show?

The problem is not that myth-making is replete in the giant body of research literature about teenagers. In fact, the more rigorous scholars engage in a good deal of head-shaking at how solid, consistent findings are contradicted by popular images in the press and by the excitable authorities reporters quote.

"Few ideas in adolescent psychology are as accepted by *researchers* with such unanimity as the notion that parent-adolescent relations basically are not stressful," the *Journal of Early Adolescence* reported in summary articles in 1983 and 1988 (emphasis original).[19] In a 1992 review of 150 studies in the *Journal of the American Academy of Child and Adolescent Psychiatry*, psychiatrist Daniel Offer and psychologist Kimberly Schonert-Reichl lamented that so many ignore research findings and "continue to believe many of the myths about adolescence."[20]

"The 'typical' adolescent is assumed to be out of control, in constant conflict with his or her family, and incapable of rational thought," the authors wrote. This belief is based on misleading studies of "the clinical experiences of psychiatrists and psychoanalysts working with emotionally disturbed youth." Studies by Offer and others of thousands of typical youths consistently found that 85 percent of teenagers were healthy and confident, 90 percent were concerned with the future, and 90 percent held attitudes and values similar to those of their parents.[21]

The 1995 *Monitoring the Future* survey asked 2,600 high school seniors to rate "the way you get along with your parents." Seventy percent were favorable, including one in four who said "completely satisfied." Fifteen percent were neutral, 11 percent were negative—and only 4 percent "completely dissatisfied." (Spouses should rate each other so positively). Ask to rate themselves, three-fourths of the teens had a good self-image (28 percent thought themselves damn near perfect), 16 percent were neutral, and 11 percent unfavorable.[22]

This result is consistent with polls as well. The April 1998 *New York Times*/CBS News poll of 1,000 youths ages 13–17 (supposedly the most rebellious age) found 97 percent got along with their parents—51 percent "very well" and 46 percent "fairly well."[23] It is doubtful that any other kind of family relationship would produce such a positive response. Naturally, the press, given a generally upbeat poll of teens, accentuated the negative. The *Times*' story's lead sentence, on page 1, read: "They carry beepers, prefer permanent tattoos to body piercing and are as likely to take lessons in shooting guns as they are to play musical instruments." That is, the Everyteen is a Gothic dope-gunner. The poll actually found that 18 percent carry pagers, 5 percent have tattoos, 4 percent have body piercings, and 31 percent took shooting lessons at some time in their lives—hardly strange, since the poll found 38 percent of their parents owned guns.

Offer's research review also dismantled Hall's unscientific 1904 fable of "raging hormones" addling teenage behavior:

Pubertal hormones frequently have been portrayed as the impetus for adolescent turmoil, and relatedly, moodiness and emotionality. Current research findings, however, contradict this relationship between puberty and disturbance, and instead suggest that the effects of pubertal hormones are neither potent nor pervasive.[24]

It is amazing the routineness with which "raging hormones" are cited as disrupting teenage equanimity, especially by those of political correctness who would bristle at any intimation that hormones addle women's behaviors.

In a review in *Psychology Today*, psychologist Joseph Adelson reported a strong consensus among researchers against the "stubborn, fixed set of falsehoods" that teenagers generally are impulsive, disturbed, or in rebellion against parental values.[25] Some of the most bizarre myths about adolescent irrationality and incompetence were popularized by pop psychologists such as David Elkind from anecdotes about disturbed youth in treatment. This is like creating a theory of typical womanhood from studying the multiple personalities of Sybil (who, to take this analogy to its logical end, turned out to be a clinician-invented hoax).

But the avalanche and consistency of research findings generally affirming adolescents did not meet the needs of 1990s politics. Academic resurrection of false stereotype that all teenagers are innately barbaric had three major purposes. It exonerated the misbehaviors of disarrayed parents. It fed clients into, and excused the failures of, ineffective programs. And it advanced the political interests of the Reagan era.

As Baum pointed out, if all teenagers were crazy, and if teenage craziness went with (and proved) drug use, ergo all teenagers used drugs. Industries and political careers were built on transferring the deficiencies of rotten parents to their kids, a share of whom were rotten as well. The most skilled exploiters of 1980s and '90s family upheavals, Democrats such as Bill Clinton and California Lieutenant-Waffler Gray Davis, won high offices in Republican climes by exempting adults from the moral crusade and pitting "we parents and our values" against "those teenagers and youth culture." For the fraction of parents who were rotten, the teenage enemy would be their own progeny, justifiably imprisoned or committed. For the majority of parents possessed of well-functioning kids, the enemy was other people's fearsome spawn, out to corrupt, spread drugs, and kill.

Psychologists Arthur Horne and Thomas Sayger published the first comprehensive study of "conduct disorder" and "oppositional defiant disorder," the two most common clinical terms for "rotten kids." They found that kids clinically diagnosed with these maladies "could not be differentiated from nonclinic children based on their behaviors, but…90 percent of the clinic children and 90 percent of the nonclinic children could be correctly classified on the basis of *the negativism and commanding behavior of the parent*"[26] (emphasis mine). The importance of this insight goes beyond simply blaming the parents, who often had pressures of their own, for screwed-up kids. It pointed to the paramount influence of environment on adolescent behavior.

When I took the worst kids in the programs I worked in camping or let them stay at my house for days or even weeks, the usual (not universal, but usual) result was model behavior. The same teenagers locked in battle with their parents over washing dishes or mowing the lawn at home would get up at 7 a.m. to toil at hard labor day after day during summers in the wilderness with the Youth Conservation Corps. YCC, and the conservation corps movement in general, was one of the few environments I've encountered in which youthful energy and temperament were admired, and kids inevitably responded to it with good attitude and work.

Conversely, youths sent to treatment (and prison) often returned home angry, feeling blamed for their family's problems and ready to sink back into the worst of their previous environments. The reason mass interventions of the 1980s and '90s did little to produce better kids was because they did almost nothing to produce better conditions. After the 30 days of insurance-funded treatment was up, the kid went back home to the negative parent. Thus, the programmatic approach evolved into little more than a blame-fixing endeavor, one reflecting the growing frustration of grownup society that its kids insisted on acting like grownups. And once blame was fixed, another set of interests was ready to cash in on what to do with the mobs of little satans.

Privatizing the War Against Adolescents

As states have grown alarmed about the cost of imprisonment, state-run treatment, and foster care, private interests have stepped in, *Youth Today* reported in May 1998.[27] The entry of private, for-profit interests into youth imprisonment and treatment have mushroomed at a 45 percent *annual* growth rate over the last decade into a $25 billion per year industry. One, Res-Care, Inc., a Kentucky-based "entrant into the at-risk field" (as Wall Street puts it), generated $300 million in revenues in 1997 and added $95 million in acquisitions in just the first three months of 1998. The chain employs 15,000 and cares for 17,000 clients. Securities analysts estimate "very conservatively" that tougher anti-drug and juvenile justice laws will double the teenage lockup and non-residential-treatment population from 103,000 in 1995 to 200,000 by 2004.

The high cost of caging prisoners and treating clients is the big reason states want to privatize and private interests want to economize. Earl Dunlap, of the National Juvenile Detention Association, argues that only a tiny fraction of juvenile offenders (about one-fourth of one percent) require incarceration and intensive supervision to protect public safety, while others are best treated in smaller residential settings and local community programs. But, *Youth Today* reported,

> Such an approach flies in the face of the economies of scale on which private operators depend. They usually prefer 500-bed or more facilities that they can build in out-of-the-way sites where land and construction costs are low, and unions are weak or non-existent.
>
> ...Some authorities estimate that over 20 years, a prison bed can cost about $1.25 million to maintain. If treatment and rehabilitation costs are added, the amount could come to between $1.4 million and $1.6 million. For-profit companies believe they can turn a profit on those kind of numbers. Since they must shave costs to make money, they generally set out to hire fewer employees and pay less in wages and benefits than state, federal or non-profit operations.

In the 1970s, sociologist Robert Chauncey documented how fledgling federal drug and alcohol abuse agencies fabricated a "teenage drinking" crisis to win attention and funding.[28] In the 1980s, as discussed earlier in this chapter, the financially struggling psychiatric hospital industry whipped up a profitable "teen suicide" scare to fill empty beds. It is easy to predict that the 1990s expanding "at-risk" industry's interest in mass referrals, cost-cutting, and warehousing in out-of-the-way facilities will predominate over community and individualized youth treatment. Note that at the investment costs projected above, each treatment center bed would have to generate $200 per day in revenue (that is, perpetually full capacity, no uninsured or poor kids admitted) just to break even.

The sinister implications are legion. First, to survive, private youth-management industries will require constant media and promotional barrages of frightening news about teen suicide, addiction, violence, and other perils. Good news about teens will represent a direct threat to its profits and will be vigorously suppressed. Second, the industry will make money from each new, get-tough measure lawmakers and policy makers enact to corral more kids. Its lobbyists can be expected to join the clamor for criminalizing and medicalizing ever broader categories of teenage behavior. Third, as with past efforts, the incongruity between the recruit-clients/reduce-costs needs of treatment interests versus those of their clients will ensure a large abrogation of teenage rights and little treatment benefit—management as opposed to genuine therapy. Fourth, as they have with each moral panic in the past, academia and the news media can be counted on to cooperate in uncritically hyping whatever inflammatory anti-teen terror promotions and miraculous troubled- youth "cures" private interests need publicized.

Justifying academic bigotry

In 1994, I investigated adult stereotypes of teenagers in a study of University of Oklahoma School of Public Health graduate students and University of California, Santa Cruz, undergraduates. The study was great fun. Thanks to help from the University of Oklahoma public health professors, the return rate on written surveys exceeded 90 percent. That turned out to be modest compared to the response at the idyllic, redwooded Santa Cruz campus. It was true! The Sixties lived! Every single one of the solicited 88 students, a preponderance tie-dyed, flowered, or at least mellow, agreed to fill out the lengthy survey as I sipped espresso and kicked back on the deck of the national-parklike Redwood Building. A more enjoyable research project I've never had.

The results were most dispiriting.

Young-leftward politics produced no more benign view of teenagers than over-30 conservative synapse. Two-thirds of the wonderfully laid-back Santa Cruz undergrads, average age 23, rated themselves as liberal or radical, double the number of also pleasant, straightlaced Oklahoma grads (average age 34). Seven times more Oklahoma grads rated themselves as "conservative." Yet Santa Cruz bolsheviks and Oklahoma Main Streeters were equally likely to agree with false negative stereotypes of teenage suicide, drug abuse, and sexuality. (Female Santa Cruz undergrads guessed correctly, or knew, that most "teenage" births are fathered by men over age 20.)

One point of my study involved asking whether an unplanned pregnancy among three couples—both partners age 24, male 24 with female 17, and both partners age 17—would be the result of immaturity or just bad luck. Both liberal and conservative students consistently decreed that the teenage couple was victim of its own childishness, while the older couple was more likely to have suffered from mere bad luck that "could happen to anyone." Younger, liberal students were likely to assign more guilt to the 17-year-old female when paired with the 24-year-old male, though women students of all ages were rough on the older male.[29]

University of Oklahoma Health Sciences professors Robert Hill and J. Dennis Fortenberry explored attitudes toward adolescents among a variety of groups.[30] "Adults perceive adolescents in largely negative ways, and these negative images are consistent among a wide social spectrum," they found. Of the 800 people surveyed, 54 percent had negative views, 31 percent gave neutral answers, and just 15 percent were positive. Interestingly, groups containing large numbers of young adults, such as medical students and college undergraduates, were the most negative. This may reflect the rising disparagement of young people in recent decades. The most positive views were found among vocational-technical institute managers and economic development officials. In the middle were Southern Baptist church members and union members.

Overt prejudice against adolescents seems more general and widespread among adults of all political persuasions than prejudice against other groups in society. Offer and Adelson note that popular myths about teenagers shift radically depending on "the sociocultural climate in which adolescents are being perceived." Academics who analyze the sources of prejudice have found that even the most educated are, after all, members of their society.

Bigotry against teenagers is pervasive among modern professionals. Offer's 1981 study found that mental health and other professionals predicted that adolescents would rate themselves three to four times more neurotic than real teenagers rated themselves on standard psychological tests![31] I used his design in my 1994 study, with identical results.

"Even though adolescence is a relatively stable and harmonious period, no more characterized by psychiatric disorder than other developmental periods, health professionals tend to endorse the storm and stress view of adolescence," concluded a review by psychologists and educators led by Stanford University's Christy Buchanan. "...Medical personnel also believe adolescent problems are more attributable to 'developmental stage' than problems of other age groups."[32] The tendency to blame the problems of persons in one group on their internal weaknesses in ways not applied to persons in other groups defines bigotry.

Similarly, Hill and Fortenberry found that "a new language about adolescence was heard during the decade of the eighties" among professionals:

> Phrases such as "high risk youth" were used to describe the excess rates of sexually transmitted diseases, pregnancy, substance use, suicide, and accidental death among the heterogeneous groups between ages 12 and 21. Subsequently, a largely unsubstantiated theoretical position explains excess adolescent morbidity and mortality by "risk taking"...It now seems that con-

ditions associated with excess rates among adolescents (high risk) are due to a propensity inherent to adolescence (risk-taking), so that adolescence itself becomes a "risk factor," and thus a disease.

A political bonus of making adolescence itself a disease was that true (but impolitic) risk factors such as "racism, the juvenalization of poverty, underemployment, inadequate education, and declining per-capita resources for dependent children and youth" could be swept aside. Thus, scientists' invention of adolescent "risk taking" meshed perfectly with 1980s and '90s political movements to cut welfare, taxes, and schools, emphasize "personal responsibility" over negative conditions, and reduce investment in youths. As Hill and Fortenberry pointed out, once the true risk factors inherent in conditions, and the tendencies to pathology found among all age groups, are subtracted, "adolescence is neither a disease nor an epidemic."[33]

Why are teenagers the subject of more negative prejudice today than in the past? University of Wisconsin-Madison human development professor Robert Enright and colleagues conducted a fascinating survey of research articles on teenagers by leading authorities published in psychological and educational journals.[34] Enright's main finding:

> Whether youth will be portrayed as competent to assume adult roles, or as psychologically incapacitated to warrant their exclusion from adult roles, will depend largely on the labor and economic requirements of the society in which they live.
>
> Theorists view the adolescent very differently in wartime than in economic depressions…When youths' labor was needed, they were viewed as quite capable and adultlike.
>
> When youth were not needed in the work force, they were viewed as more immature and slow to develop by psychological theorists.

I took the last finding personally. When I arrived in adolescence in the 1960s, society was busy awarding youths all kinds of voting, drinking, and other adult rights. The reason: 18- and 19-year-olds were being shipped to Vietnam in record hundreds of thousands, the youngest soldiery in U.S. history. In quaint Pentagon terminology, half the 55,000 U.S. Vietnam War dead had reached an "attained age" of only 20 or younger. Adult society decreed us as adults because it wanted to keep its aging hide out of a miserable jungle war.

Enright's study concluded:

> There is strong correspondence between the ideas of adolescent psychology and the legislation passed by the U.S. Congress…One cannot retreat from the implication that such theories mask an ideological purpose…What are our current ideological stereotypes of youth and what societal/economic conditions are we trying to aid by holding such views?

Economic forces, natural prejudices, and other adult self-interests appear to be major reasons why today, few in institutions, public agencies, or the media seem to care whether what they say about teenagers is true, fair, or contributes to the well being of young people. If a theory or program doesn't work, it's much easier to blame the "inherent" flaws of the subjects than to re-examine strategy and prejudices.

After a 21-year-old drug seller infected nine teenage girls and adult women ages 13–24 with the AIDS virus in Chautauqua County, New York, in late 1997, local assistant schools superintendent James Coffman feared his school sex education curriculum might be in line for criticism. So he blamed innate teenage idiocy: "Young people in general, they feel they're invincible. They could have all the education in the world, but they all feel it doesn't affect them."[35]

Further investigation showed the AIDS-infected man had sexual relations not just with teens, but with dozens of women of all ages. As mentioned previously, Judith Musick pointed out, "sexual offenders seem to have special antennae that pick up signals of vulnerability in girls they select as victims:" girls who tend to be "needier and more passive, dependent, depressed, and unhappy."[36] Several of the infected girls appeared on a daytime talk show and indeed revealed histories of sexual abuse. These were callously dismissed by the host and ridiculed by the audience.[37] One would expect that a school AIDS expert such as Coffman would know that youths who contract HIV are not typical of "all…young people." The ignored lesson, crucial to effective programming, might have been that a few hours' instruction can't be expected to reverse a childhood of violation.

More reprobation targeting the infected teenage girls came from pundits. "Maybe it's my Christian view, but I don't believe that 15-year-olds having sex is healthy, normal, or acceptable," wrote columnist Sandra Smokes in USA Today, a typical view.[38] Smokes did not condemn sex by unmarried 21-year-olds, though equally un-Biblical.

University of Pennsylvania education professor (and teen pregnancy "social cost" analyst) Rebecca Maynard, miffed at the failure of an initiative she championed to prevent second births among inner city teenage mothers, lashed out at their natural foolishness. "Adolescents, regardless of income or social class, are risk takers," she said. "They are impulsive. They feel invincible and they fail to plan ahead."[39] Maynard failed to mention that teenage and adult sexual behaviors, including rates of pregnancy, abortion, and sexually transmitted disease, show identical patterns over as many decades as we have statistics.[40] This is partly because adults have sex with teenagers, among the many realities teenagers face that experts don't.

Nor do apostles of the newer theories, such as evolutionary psychology, display improvement. The 19-year-old English nanny convicted of killing an infant led to a denigration of all teenage girls by Vassar College psychologist Debra Zeifman.[41] Evolutionary psychology predicts that teenage females will not value children as much as older mothers, as proven by "the plethora of data on the inferior care provided by teenage mothers," Zeifman wrote. But, taken this literally, evolutionary psychology's theories about humans' drive to promote their own genetic survival also would predict that no adult male should be allowed to care for a child other than his own, and no member of one race should care for a child of another race. Zeifman applies the theory selectively to teenagers in ways that would be considered racist or sexist if applied to other groups. She does not suggest that the individual characteristics of the caretaker, not some presumed mass (and very small) statistical tendencies which may be due to socioeconomic differences, should be the defining factor. Zeifman presents no information to contradict the evidence that the killing of infants by young au pairs is very rare. A peculiar exercise in prejudicial non-science.

Table 2

Contrary to claims, teen seat belt use similar to adults'

Percent of fatalities who used seat belt (vehicle)
or helmet (bicycle, motorcycle), California, 1996

Age	Fatalities	Used belt/helmet
0–4	188	27%
5–15	476	25
16–19	1,016	40
20–29	2,381	39
30–39	1,746	47
40–49	1,168	42
50–59	727	48
60+	1,727	54
Total	9,585	43

California Highway Patrol (1994–96). *Annual Report of Fatal and Injury Motor Vehicle Traffic Collisions.* Sacramento: Department of Justice, Table 4G.

Taking Risks

More expert youth-bashing followed a 1996 survey of seat-belt use. The National Highway Traffic Safety Administration reported that males under 25 were the least likely to buckle up. So, to an even greater extent, were males and blacks of all ages. Ignoring the latter, traffic psychologists (the report called them) launched into the standard clichés about young age: "disdain for societal values," "establish a personal identity," "affirm independence from parents," "air of infallibility and invulnerability," "an inability to come to grips with their own mortality," etc.[42]

No one considered whether older drivers might be exaggerating their self-reported seat-belt use. Table 2 shows seat belt and helmet usage by age for the 9,600 California traffic fatalities over the 1994–96 period. The real-death figures indicate that teenagers are slightly less likely than older drivers to use seat belts. The difference does not seem cataclysmic enough to warrant scripting an entire psychodrama. Nor did the experts do their expert duty to consider other alternatives, such as the fact that young ages harbor a higher proportion of males (riskier at every age than women) and poorer groups (riskier than richer ones) for the lower buckle-up rate. In any case, teens are about the same as 20-agers, the age group we trust to raise infants, and 40-somethings, that high-risk Baby Boom set again.

When scientists compare the attitudes and behaviors of teenagers toward risk to those of the adults around them, they find that teens and adults are astonishingly alike. The notion that adolescents "take more risks than adults do" is "a myth," health psychologist Nancy Adler and colleagues recently reported in the *American Psychological Association Monitor.*[43]

In an exhaustive review of 100 studies, published in *American Psychologist*, Carnegie Mellon University scientists found that adults harbor more delusions of invulnerability than do adolescents.[44] Their study found that teenagers (average age 15) assessed personal risks similar to their parents (average age 43). There are only "small differences in the cognitive decision-making processes of adolescents and adults," they concluded.

Offer, widely considered the nation's leading authority on adolescent psychology, studied 30,000 teenagers and adults over three decades. Writing in the *Journal of the American Medical Association*, Offer reported that when it comes to drugs, sex, smoking, drinking, and other behaviors, "decision making for teenagers is no different than decision making for adults."[45] The average 16-year-old and average grownup are quite similar in mental development, Offer concluded.

The danger of indulging prejudice against teenagers, the Carnegie Mellon scientists reported, means "misdiagnosing the sources of their risk behaviors, denying them deserved freedoms, and failing to provided needed assistance." In a direct swipe against both Clinton and other "protectors" of youthful morals from all manner of imagined evils, researchers declared:

> Unsubstantiated claims about the incompetence of adolescents tilt the balance toward...paternalism. They threaten to disenfranchise and stigmatize adolescents. They encourage denying teens the right to govern their own actions, as well as viewing them as a social problem rather than a resource. They interfere with the experimentation that is part of the business of adolescence. They make teens rather than society responsible for teens' problems. They place adults in the flattering position of knowing what is right. It might be constructive to study the cognitive and motivational factors that promote this harsh view of adolescents.[46]

If studied, we might find that paternalism, stigmatization, disenfranchisement, interference, blaming the young, and flattering the old is the *purpose* of today's widespread academic malpractice against teenagers.

Risk Taking on the Brain

Put these practical findings in the context of the newest "scientific" claim to have found the biological basis for why, in the words of McLean Psychiatric Hospital neuropsychologist Deborah Yurgen-Todd, teenagers "may not appreciate the consequences of their behavior." Using brain imaging studies, Yurgen-Todd reported that adolescents respond to emotional situations more with the brain's amygdala, and adults more with the frontal lobe. Because the amygdala evolved before the frontal lobe, Yurgen-Todd argued that "adolescents are more prone to react with gut instinct when they process emotions, but that as they mature into early adulthood, they are more able to temper their instinctive gut reaction response with rational reasoned response."[47]

As in the cases of past scientists who believed that women were less intelligent and rational than men and explained this "fact" by noting women's smaller brain size, biological claims about adolescents begin with researcher bias. Yurgen-Todd makes it clear she believes teenagers engage in riskier, less rational behavior than adults do; therefore, instinctive ("gut") response must be riskier than "rational" response. Now, reverse the assumption: suppose bio-researchers were trying to explain why teenagers actually engage in less risky behavior than grownups?

Despite possessing at least three major risk factors—inexperience, lower socioeconomic status, and a higher proportion of males—teenagers display more moderate behaviors than adults with respect to drug and alcohol use, suicide, most types of accidents, and other risks that most involve personal choices. In that case, Yurgen-Todd's findings would explain why: confronted with a risky situation, teenagers rely on the amygdala—a complex, older part of the human brain whose responses are thought to be more instinctual. Yet the amygdala is not the cerebrum's savage dynamo (the "id," in psychoanalytic terms), but the opposite. In fact, a noted text on brain functions reports researchers' consensus that the amygdala's role is to *moderate* the "spontaneity of aggressive behavior" found in the hypothalamus.[48]

So teenagers, who lack experience in figuring out what is going on, are wired to exercise more caution in unfamiliar situations. That would be a logical survival mechanism, and the amygdala is all about promoting survival through regulating the rashness of the hot-blooded hypothalamus. In a pinch, it operates independently of the individual to promote prudence—irrational prudence, in some cases. But children who run from garter snakes live longer than ones who try to play with cobras. In contrast, adults may be more at risk due to our illusory overconfidence that our reason can assess dangers and tell us how to beat them. This is because "rational" thought is controlled by the individual and allows information to be slanted to favor the desired conclusion.

In a way, this counter-hypothesis fits my experience with teenagers in wilderness programs. Youths were typically very cautious in the woods, downright petrified at night in bear country. An outhouse trip involved the entire crew. Adults, including me, were bolder because I rationally knew the perils of the wilderness were vastly overstated—that is, the slavering grizzly approaching me on the dark path represented a remote statistical rarity. The teenage strategy was, of course, safer in yielding more survivors per million outhouse trips.

Take a more practical mystery, the greater teenage moderation with alcohol puzzled over in chapter 5. A male individual has a few drinks, probably a somewhat more likely occurrence for a 17-year-old than a 40-year-old. The hypothalamus's id-like urgings are intensifying: "drive! kill! mate! maraud, invincible road-warrior!" The amygdala's job is to promote survival: "slow down, man (dude), you're not in such hot shape. Sack out there on the couch until the walls stay put." The frontal lobe's task is to rationally assess: "if you drive, you could kill someone or get a costly, embarrassing DUI arrest…but if you take back streets and drive really slow, the odds are just about 100 percent that you'll get home okay without meeting a cop or telephone pole; nothing bad happened when you did this before." We could easily find that the 17-year-old's fear-based caution would lead to less, and the 40-year-old's rational (mis)calculation of the odds would lead to more, drunken driving. That would lead to the higher statistics for adult drunken driving, drunken pedestrianship, and other booze-involved mishaps that we saw in Chapter 4.

A similar anomaly Yurgen-Todd's findings might explain is the low rate of teen suicide. Suicide is now thought to relate closely to an individual's hopelessness, a cognitive state arrived at by a process of reason. If emotional responses are handled by the reasoning part of the brain, some individuals will deduce that their lives are hopeless and suicide is a solution. If the amygdala is in charge, the organism's "instinctive" need to survive is the chief concern. That would explain the almost complete absence of suicide among children and its rarity among teenagers compared to adults.

The Splat Factor

On the other hand, adolescents seem to lack fears that might seem rational to adults, such as fear of heights. Teenagers in wilderness programs seem much more fearless than grownups about climbing trees and rocks or working high up on building projects. On the Youth Conservation Corps' annual climb up the back side of Yosemite's Half Dome, I watched in terror as teenagers with backpacks nonchalantly clambered up the sheer cables overhanging a half-mile drop, hanging on with one hand as they talked, even scrambling outside the cables to pass slow-moving climbers (such as me, the Splat potential upper in my rational mind). Once atop Half Dome, many would sit legs dangling over the edge of the 3,000 foot cliff face (the one postcards show), even sleeping in hollows next to the abyss. Had I known about the adolescent amygdala then, I would have wondered what planet it had disappeared to.

Viewing the teenage attitude toward heights, one would expect a huge death toll from the Splat. In fact, teenagers almost never die from falling off things. Of the 1,100 Californians who died from falls in 1996, 14 were teenagers. Turns out that heights are not all that dangerous. Three-fourths of falling deaths are among those over age 50. Since the amygdala seems to function like a catalog of human risk informed by hundreds of thousands of years of experience, it does not uniformly promote caution—as researchers studying this complex brain region have found. If we think again in the evolutionary terms, a fear of heights would not contribute to survival. Human hunting, escape from danger, and other tasks required the ability to scale without panic. In a situation in which climbing is necessary, panic itself is the biggest danger.

We might expect, then, that younger humans' lower risks of death by suicide, falls, intoxication, and other dangers that have been around for thousands of years would reflect natural biological adjustment. We would also expect that the young would be more in danger from recent developments, such as motor vehicles and guns, that human brains have not had time to catalog and whose control improves with experience. Yurgen-Todd's preliminary findings would indicate not viewing teenagers as some kind of alien risk machines, but ones whose instinctive reactions provide greater safety in certain circumstances and whose inexperience exposes them to greater perils in others.

The above re-interpretation reflects my own bias, of course. I would argue it better fits the known facts of risk outcome according to the type of risk involved. For certain risks, teenagers may behave more prudently. The point is, the spin a researcher begins with determines how the researcher will interpret findings. Because social scientists are products of the adult society that cares for and feeds them, researchers uncannily wind up supporting popular prejudices.

Other than ignoring alternative interpretations, biological determinists are known for ignoring practical evidence. European, Canadian, and Japanese teens do not display the risky behaviors that Americans' innate-flaw theories predict. Nor do most American teens. When American teens display the consequences of risky behavior, in the vast majority of cases an adult collaborator (or exploiter) is also involved. How does Yurgen-Todd's notion of the "tempering" of brain development in "early adulthood," for example, explain the fact that most "teen pregnancies" are fathered by adults, or most murdered teens are killed by adults? Joint adult-teen sex, violence, crime, drinking, smoking, and drug taking is a fact of life that it is high time erudite researchers began studying seriously.

GIGO

By the late 1980s, kid-fixing industries assembled to service chaotic families had allied with crime, health, and drug-war establishments in an anti-youth mission. Codifications of this alliance emerged with regularity from expert-political panels in the form of a litter of blue-ribbon reports, all adhering to 1990s standard-issue format. Four are reviewed below.

The reason for the dreary sameness was that panels, by their political attunement, unquestioningly accepted the ground rules of the 1990s. These involved scrambles by the interests represented to (a) grab credit for every good trend, (b) deny blame for any bad trend, and (c) avoid offending any powerful constituency, such as business, politicians, taxpayers, or Baby Boom voters.

The "rules of the '90s" teen-report went like this: no proposals could require "more taxes," "bigger government," scrutiny of adult behaviors from Oval Office to boardroom to living room, or serious challenges to conventional youth-fixing doctrine. Such reports must be adult-friendly cover to cover—no child abuse, no drunken parents, no lamenting the lack of good jobs, no advocacy for more government resources, no undue grownup sacrifice beyond "volunteer," is permitted. Government is limited to dissemination of "messages," easing private and volunteer work, and policing kids. The role of business is to make voluntary donations and lend expertise to worthy programs. Evaluation of program interests must propose slight permutations of more of the same, synchronized by vaguely-recycled "community coordination" schemes. The role of parents is micro-monitoring of youths and referral to programs at the hint of aberrance. The role of the media is to purify its fare during kiddie hours and pitch in to spread "healthy messages." At all times, an "us-adults-versus-those-kids" image, not an integrated view, must be maintained. In short, no groundbreaking 1960s Kerner Commission or National Commission on Marihuana and Drug Abuse surprises are desired in the '90s.

Still quoted today is the October 1995 Carnegie Corporation study on adolescents, *Great Transitions*.[49] Like the 1987 *Risking the Future* study of teenage pregnancy, the 1990 *Code Blue* report on teenage health, the 1996 White House National Office of AIDS Policy report on teenage AIDS, and the 1997 National Longitudinal Study of Youth report, the Carnegie study demonstrates how modern panels of experts wind up retreating into the same platitudes social critic Paul Goodman ridiculed as hackneyed 40 years ago. I pick on the Carnegie study not because it is worse than the others (the worst is probably Child Trends' 1994 *Running in Place*), but because it continues to guide policy. The Carnegie Council on Adolescent Development includes such luminaries as Michael Dukakis, Daniel Inouye, James Jeffords, Nancy Kassebaum, and Ted Koppel.

Its report is vintage '90s standard-issue. Examples abound. Though today's parents are a dozen times more at risk of drug abuse than their adolescent children, the 1990s ground rule is that drugs may be discussed only as a teenage issue. Thus, Carnegie's 135-page report, which claims to address the "underlying factors that contribute to problem behaviors," devotes one sentence to parents' drug and alcohol addictions.

Every year, more than 350,000 children and youths are substantiated victims of violent or sexual abuses inflicted by parents, a toll hospital emergency room surveys indicate has risen sharply. But the '90s rule is that violence may only be talked about as an item perpetrated by youth. The Carnegie report dedicates two sentences to child abuse.

Some four million youths ages 10–14 live in poverty, half of these in destitute households with incomes of less than $8,000 per year. The Carnegie report dedicates two sentences and one chart to poverty.

So together, parents' addictions, abusiveness, and family poverty occupy perhaps one-fourth of one page. What do the other 134 3/4 pages cover? Mostly a breathless roster of adolescent misbehaviors caused by purported adolescent attitude and developmental deficiencies in this so-dangerous modern age. The report begins with an incredible assertion:

> Barely out of childhood, young people ages ten to fourteen are today experiencing more freedom, autonomy, and choice than ever at a time when they still need special nurturing, protection, and guidance. Without the sustained involvement of parents and other adults in safeguarding their welfare, young adolescents are at risk of harming themselves and others...threats to their well-being [include] AIDS and easy access to lethal weapons and drugs that were all but unknown to their parents and grandparents.

Lethal "drugs" and "lethal weapons" were "all but unknown to their parents"? Did I read that correctly?

The parents of most young adolescents would have came of age in the early and mid-1970s. In 1975, 4,000 teenagers died from drugs or guns—and that was by no means the worst year of the '70s. Lethal drugs and weapons were well known to the parents of today's kids. The acquaintance is more than a passing one today. As pointed out in previous chapters, Baby Boom youths suffered death rates from drugs such as heroin and barbiturates double to triple that of today's young people. And while it's true that AIDS was unknown in the childhoods of today's parents and grandparents, half a million in these older generations contracted the disease in adulthood.

The Carnegie report's illusory juxtaposition of robust adult health and dissolute teenage hazard is all too common to centrist and liberal organizations. Healthy adults and innocent parents, they say, just don't understand the unheard-of dangers today's world poses to kids—and today's kids pose to the world.

Table 3

Contrary to experts' hype, younger teens safer
from violent death now than at any time in last 50 years

Rate of violent death per 100,000 population age 10–14

	Self-inflicted*	Homicide	All other*	Total
1950	15.0	0.6	8.0	23.6
1955	13.7	0.5	7.4	21.6
1960	12.3	0.5	7.2	20.0
1965	10.7	0.7	8.2	19.6
1970	11.7	1.2	9.6	22.5
1975	11.4	1.2	8.4	21.0
1980	8.2	1.4	8.1	17.7
1985	7.7	1.5	7.4	16.6
1990	6.4	2.1	6.4	14.9
1995	6.3	2.3	6.4	14.4

*Self-inflicted deaths include suicide and drug deaths, gun deaths, falls, drownings, hangings/suffocation, and other mostly self-inflicted causes. All other include car wrecks, plane crashes, and similar mishaps that don't involve self-infliction.

Source: National Center for Health Statistics (1950–92), *Vital Statistics of the United States*, Mortality; and U.S. Mortality Detail File (1993–95).

In fact, the age group their report picks, 10–14, displays very low risk, including a death rate that has declined by a staggering 39 percent since 1950 and 28 percent since 1960 (Table 3). The biggest decline in deaths among 10–14-year-olds are those likely to result from bad behaviors (drugs, guns, drownings, falls, hangings, etc., whether ruled suicide or accident). What might be called "society-inflicted" deaths—traffic wrecks, plane crashes, etc.—are down, but not as much. That the latter type of accidental death has not declined as much as suicide/self-inflicted types indicates that better behavior, not just better safety technology and medical attention, is a big reason for the death decline.

Homicide, a very rare fate for this age group, rose. However, this does not signal a behavior problem of young adolescents so much as older groups. Most murders of 10–14-year-olds are inflicted by older teens or adults (often their parents), not by peers. Due largely to better behavior, then, today's 10–14-year-olds don't die nearly as much as those of the past four decades. In fact, the fatality decline has been steady since 1970. Conversely, due largely to the slightly more homicidal behavior of older teens and adults, 10–14-year-olds are slightly more at risk of being murdered—about 1 in 60,000, greater odds than in 1960.

In total contravention to these facts, Carnegie's report depicts today's kids as afflicted with monumental death crises:

> The continuing decline in the health status of American adolescents is deeply disturbing. Since 1960, the burden of adolescent illness has shifted from the traditional causes of disease toward the "new morbidities" associated with health-damaging behaviors, such as depression, suicide, alcohol, tobacco and drug use, sexually transmitted diseases, including HIV/AIDS, and gun-related homicides...
>
> The vulnerability of young adolescents to health and educational risks is far greater than most people are aware of, and the casualties are mounting.

This statement shows how free modern experts feel to fabricate complete nonsense about young people. In fact, adolescent health and behavior are improving, not declining. In 1995, there were two million more 10–14-year-olds than in 1960. Yet there were 4,000 fewer deaths, including 600 fewer violent deaths, among age 10–14 in 1994 than in 1960—a mortality decline of 42 percent!

In 1960, students missed an average of 5.3 school days due to illness, disability, or injury. In 1994, 4.5 days. Given the higher proportion of students with disabilities who attend public school today instead of being warehoused as in the past, this is an impressive improvement. In any case, the same pattern occurred among adults: 5.2 work days missed per worker per year in 1994, compared to 5.6 in 1960.[50]

Death, injury, illness, and disability should just about sum up "health status." Even by their own year of comparison, 1960, Carnegie's portrait of grimly declining teenage health is erroneous on every count. So are its panicky claims.

That "injury and violence have now replaced illness as the leading causes of death for adolescents" has been true since the mid-1950s. It does not mean teenagers suffer rising rates of violent death (to repeat: violent death rates among 10–14-year-olds have fallen by 28 percent since 1960). Rather, it results from reduction in the large number of deaths formerly caused by infectious disease. It means that many fewer teens die from influenza, polio, and tuberculosis today than in the past. It means that many fewer teens than adults die from cancer and heart disease. Blind pollyannas like me might claim these developments are highly positive ones for young people, not a reason to panic.

Nevertheless, there have been negative health developments among adolescents in the last 25 years. These have occurred, overwhelmingly, among stressed and impoverished populations. As detailed elswhere in this book, they are:

- AIDS, which wasn't recognized until 1980 and which has risen in identical manner among adults;

- Unwed births, which have risen in equal fashion among adults;

- Arrest for homicide and robbery, which was accompanied by an even larger increase in adult domestic violence and felony assault; and

- Firearms death, which was accompanied by a unique rise in adult drug deaths.

There is a complex, interrelated, and revealing pattern of youth and adult risk behavior which has not been analyzed in terms of designing effective prevention response. Carnegie dodges the intermixing of teenage and adult risk. Instead, the

Table 4

Gun deaths track socioeconomic status:
Black teens very high risk, White teens safer than the elderly

U.S. firearms deaths per 100,000 population by age an race, 1995

	White-Euro	Hispanic	Black	Asian/NA	Total
0–9	0.4	0.6	1.1	0.1	0.5
10–14	2.4	4.5	6.5	3.0	3.4
15–19	11.8	38.1	69.5	18.4	24.4
20–24	15.6	41.5	88.5	17.4	29.7
25–29	14.0	27.3	62.6	12.5	22.3
30–34	13.3	19.6	43.0	10.9	17.9
35–39	12.2	15.1	29.3	7.8	14.7
40–44	12.4	14.1	22.8	6.5	13.8
45–49	11.3	10.9	18.7	6.3	12.1
50+	13.3	5.6	12.0	4.4	12.7

Source: National Center for Health Statistics. U.S. Mortality Detail File, 1995; Bureau of the Census, Statistical Abstract of the United States 1997.

report drums on the notion that "grim statistics about the health of adolescents are a continual reminder of the potentially tragic consequences of choices at this age."

Incredible. According to the U.S. Department of Justice, 90 percent of the murder victims under age 12 and half the victims ages 12–14 are murdered by adults, and most violent crimes against youths are committed by adults, not other youths.[51] Most sex before age 15 consists of rape by substantially older men.[52] The most severe drug, alcohol, and cigarette damage to young adolescents is inflicted by their parents' addictions, not the behaviors of youths or their peers.

For example, teenage firearms deaths are a reflection of similar gunnings among grownups (Table 4). Note the enormous differences in gun deaths by race, which reflect income level. Age 10–14 is not particularly high risk for any race or ethnicity. If "teen age" were the main cause of firearms risk, Euro-white teens would not be less at risk than Hispanics over 40, blacks of any age, or white adults up to age 45.

Most murdered and injured 10–14-year-olds appear to be victims of domestic assaults. This, as noted, relates closely to the fact that one-fifth of kids are raised in homes in which parents abuse drugs and alcohol. This fact is a taboo topic among modern panel reports on "teenage risk."

Bound by '90s rules not to discuss adult-imposed behaviors or social conditions, Carnegie repeats the "innate" theory of teenage risk: kids have too much freedom, kids hurt themselves, kids hurt others. Younger teenagers are naturally dangerous and vulnerable. Listen to the dangerous voices of the "youth culture" that speak to them:

> Today, information conveyed to adolescents comes largely from the media and peers. Much of it is incorrect or misleading or embodies values that are inimical to young people's self-image and health...
>
> Many parents see their teenagers drifting into an amorphous, risky peer milieu, popularly termed "the youth culture." This culture is heavily material-istic and derived mainly from the adult world and the commercial media. It has its own cultural heroes, made up of rock and film stars and prominent athletes, and its own preoccupations—cars, clothes, being part of the crowd, being physically attractive. As a result, adolescents spend little time with their families. With more money of their own, whether from earnings, an allowance, or illegal activity, adolescents do not need to go home even for dinner; they can buy their meals at a fast-food place.
>
> Often parents become perplexed, even angry, as they feel their authority weakened and their values challenged.

Escapism incarnate. Consistent research findings showing the powerful paral-lels between the values and behaviors of adolescents and those of their parents are brushed aside by Carnegie's experts. This is because a more troubling reality is sug-gested: American adults, including parents, are perplexed and angry not because young people are challenging adult values, but because many young people are *embracing* adult values. Materialism. Preoccupation with appearance. Clothes and fashion. Attention to cultural heroes. Popularity. Teenage expenditures today ($105 billion in 1996), though arousing much tongue-clucking, comprises about the same proportion of consumer spending (2 percent) as it did 40 years ago.[53] Could *People*, *Cosmopolitan*, *Rolling Stone*, major newspapers and broadcast networks, the "adult world" in general, persist if they defied the values of American grownups? What kind of crazy culture becomes enraged when its kids copy its ethos?

But frontal challenges to unhealthy societal values, adopted by parent and kid alike, are not permitted in Carnegie's format. Its panel of experts reduces teenage problems to bad teenage choices influenced by bad youth culture. In fact, they insinuate, adults should blame adolescents for taking up "damaging patterns of behavior," since bad adult health is the result of "a time bomb set in youth." Yet they assume that parents' and adults' behaviors have no influence on the way kids act.

In the end, the issue boils down to the privileges of power. The glitterati of Carnegie and others enjoy the luxury to dismiss rape, violence, unhealthy conduct, murder, and dubious cultural values inflicted on youths by their parents and other adults as too messy, too impolitic to consider even in concept. If only adolescents had the same privilege to avoid bad adult values and behavior in the realities of their own homes and communities.

The second report examined here, the National Longitudinal Study on Adolescent Health, summarized in the September 10, 1997, *Journal of the American Medical Association*,[54] also rigidly observes '90s doctrine. Adult behavior is off the table. The challenge is invoking stepped-up adult supervision to prevent teenage "access" to parents' cigarettes, alcohol, drugs, and guns.

The study found that teenagers living in homes where these items were present were more likely to use them than teenagers living in homes where the items were absent. This is not a particularly profound conclusion. If a home harbors cigarettes, booze, dope, or gats, it is likely that parents use these items, which is the true source of enhanced teenage risk.

What the study finds, without going there, is that teenage and adult behaviors are closely connected. Of the 11,500 teens in grades seven through 12 surveyed, 26 percent reported being "current smokers" (whatever that means). In addition, 31 percent reported cigarettes were present in their homes. Deduction: these household adults, mostly the parents, smoke. Guess whether the study found students more likely to smoke if their parents smoked. Now repeat the exercise for marijuana and alcohol.

Similarly, 3.6 percent reported a suicide attempt in the previous year. Students also reported that an identical 3.6 percent of their parents had attempted suicide in that time. Guess whether the students of suicidal parents were more likely to be suicidal themselves.

If you nodded "yes" quatrice, you have arrived at the study's conclusion. It is not stated in those terms, of course:

> If homes provide a venue in which adolescents have easy access to guns, alcohol, tobacco, and illicit substances, adolescents are more likely to have an increased risk of suicidality, involvement in interpersonal violence, and substance use.

Chips off the old block.

But, just like previous studies, the National Longitudinal study avoids the most obvious conclusion that parents' behavior influences youths' behavior. Instead, it speculates that the problem with kids today must be...

> ...the increasing scarcity of time that parents have for their children, driven largely by workforce pressures. Compared with 1960, children in the United States have lost, on average, 10 to 12 hours per week of parental time. The present study confirms the importance of time availability of parents for their children (and) the monitoring function.

And, like other studies, this one downplays economic issues. In a particularly meaningless dismissal-by-anecdote, the study declares that there are teenagers (who they call "children") who are "relatively advantaged, socially and economically" but who "sustain significant morbidity as a consequence of their behaviors." Yes, as Table 3 indicates, the gun death rate among older white teens (more advantaged on average than blacks) is not zero. It is merely 84 *percent lower* than that of black teens—despite the considerably greater "availability" of guns in the homes of whites than of blacks.

I wrote to the National Longitudinal study's chief author, Dr. Michael Resnick of the University of Minnesota's Adolescent Health Program, to ask if it was really the study's contention that mere teenage "access" to temptation was more important than the behaviors and modeling of parents. He responded cordially that this was not the authors' intention. So perhaps the follow-up study of parents will redress the artificial disconnection between youth and adult behaviors recent studies assume.

As reluctant as the Carnegie and National Longitudinal studies are to venture anywhere near the real causes of youth malaise, the third study analyzed, Child Trends' 1994 *Running in Place*, takes the ricecake for flatly denying these causes exist.[55] The Child Trends report begins promisingly with a discussion of rising family poverty, which it calls the "first challenge" to family stability. However, poverty and family diseconomics are cited as reasons for excusing *parents*, both at the policy and family levels, from responsibility for what is portrayed as epidemic teenage misbehavior. The study's chief challenges are "combating negative peer influences" and "maintaining parental control as children grow older." Indeed, ALL teenage problems are depicted as caused by "negative peer influences" and "the mass media and popular entertainment industry."

What emerges is a neo-Puritan view of children as innately evil. The Child Trends study's method is to ask parents how they want their kids to behave. Perfectly, the parents say. Only 2 percent say that it is all right for youths to smoke, only 4 percent for youths to drink. However, 45 and 44 percent of youths think their peers think it's all right for them to smoke or drink, respectively. Therefore, Child Trends finds, the whole problem is "encouragement of smoking and drinking by peers." The arena where peers corrupt each other is the public school, where much dispensation of booze and cigarettes is darkly claimed (but never shown) to occur.

As a "stupid Ph.D. trick," this rivals anything Joseph Califano's wildly inflated, have-you-ever-known-anyone-who-ever-ever drug surveys described in Chapter 3 have disseminated. Child Trends does not ask how many youth are exposed to a fog of parents' smoking at home. They do not ask how many kids are given cigarettes and/or cigarette gear by their parents. They do not ask how many parents drink, how many drink abusively, or speculate on what effects parental behaviors might have on their kids. No questions about parents' violence or drug addictions.

Other studies have asked these questions (see Chapters 1–6). The consensus is that parents' behaviors and family influences are the most powerful predictors of youth behaviors, strongly influencing even what "peers" youths later choose to "influence" them. But like the Public Agenda survey discussed in Chapter 10, Child Trends simply asks adults to kick back and moralize. The answers are predictable. I can't believe such reports could be written by anyone who has actually seen and worked with the families where "at risk" youths dwell.

Child Trends' main prevention strategy seems to be to "reduce the formation of families at high risk of poverty" by exhorting poor people, particularly poor young people ("who are emotionally and financially unprepared"), not to have babies. This disapproval is to be communicated through "messages" in the media and by parents and community leaders. The second conclusion is for parents, schools, and society to control teenagers better.

The notion of reversing the public disinvestment in, and private abandonment of, 16 million poor children is downplayed in a series of some-say-this, some-say-that ambivalence. "Although these steps will not create jobs where none exist" and "narrow considerations" dominate political allocation of public resources, the Child Trends authors conclude in a '90s non sequitur, "...our future as a nation depends on how well future generations are raised."

Thus, good jobs and public support for young people apparently play only marginal roles in "our future as a nation," or even "how young people are raised." The challenge is halting bad behaviors of poor people and teenagers. The above are not conservative organizations. Carnegie and Child Trends, in particular, are on the liberal side of the spectrum.

In institutional research on adolescence, "risk" and "teen age" are defined as synonymous terms. In the last of the major research reports examined here, Research Triangle Institute authors released a computer-assisted survey of 1,700 teen males ages 15–19 which claimed that risk to adolescent boys may be "worse than anyone thought."[56] The study, published in the May 8, 1998, issue of *Science*, claimed that when young men were allowed to respond to questions on a laptop computer, they reported far more risky behaviors than when they answered the same questions on paper. For example, 7.9 percent reported carrying a gun in the previous month on paper, but 12.4 percent when asked by computer. While only 3.3 percent said on standard surveys that they used crack or cocaine within the previous year, 6.0 percent told the computer they did.

The study failed to compare computer-reported teenage risks with actual outcome measures. The paradox of "teenage risk" quickly becomes apparent: the more prevalent surveys make the risky behavior (such as carrying guns) appear, the safer risky teenage behavior must be, given the low number of outcomes (such as gun deaths and injuries) (Table 5).

Notice that if these survey findings are correct, a risk-taking youth age 15–19 would have to carry a gun every month for 300 years before it would be statistically likely to cause a death of any kind. A teen boy could use cocaine or crack for nearly a millennium before suffering even odds of fatality. Even under the most pessimistic assumptions, it would take at least 300 years for a teen male who does drugs with needles, or who has sex with IV drug users, to get AIDS. Note that these odds apply only to the fraction of teens who engage in the specified high-risk behaviors; the risks of these mishaps to teen boys in general is microscopic.

We can only conclude two things: either the survey technique radically overstates the numbers of teenage boys who engage in such risky behaviors, or such "risky" behaviors as carrying guns, using cocaine, or injecting drugs are not really dangerous for teenage males. Perhaps a certain small number of survey respondents like to play with laptop computers. For example, although the survey breathlessly reported that "computer respondents were nearly 14 times as likely to report sex with an injection drug user," that result occurred because just 20 boys out of 1,670 surveyed answered "yes."

Conversely, it is unlikely that the vital statistics used to estimate deaths, injuries, and infections would much underreport teen casualties since there are only so many bodies to account for. Teen males age 15–19 account for 11 percent of the nation's gun deaths, 1 percent of its cocaine/crack deaths and hospitalizations, and 10 percent of its AIDS infections from injecting drugs (even assuming all AIDS cases diagnosed before age 30 were contracted at age 15–19). So whether or not such deaths, injuries, and disease are significantly underreported, which is unlikely, the adult risk is much higher than the teenage risk.

Table 5

**If so many teen boys engage in risky behavior,
how come so few get injured or die?**

	Number of boys reporting behavior	Odds that the risk-taker will cause	
		Injury	Death
Carried gun in past month	1.2 million	1 in 60 years	1 in 300 years
Used crack/cocaine in last year	570,000	1 in 30 years	1 in 950 years
			Contract HIV/AIDS
Had sex with someone who shoots drugs	130,000		
			1 in 300 years
Ever taken street drugs with a needle	500,000		

Note: Deaths from firearms include all suicides, accidents, homicides, and undetermined deaths. Cocaine deaths include overdoses and other cocaine-related deaths. Cocaine injuries include hospital emergency treatments. AIDS infections include those diagnosed before age 30 and infected by injecting drug use or sex with persons who inject drugs, based on 5-year totals through June 1997.

Sources: Risky behaviors are from Turner et al, *Science* (May 8, 1998). Outcomes are from National Center for Health Statistics, Mortality Detail File (1994); SAMHSA, Drug Abuse Warning Network (1994, 1995); Centers for Disease Control, *HIV/AIDS Surveillance* (1997).

Oddly enough, the conclusion we would draw from surveys claiming to show high levels of "risky" teenage conduct is that we should leave teens alone. Apparently, they can do dangerous things and not suffer. Given the limited resources available to public health agencies, chasing around hordes of teenagers who supposedly "take risks" is an inefficient strategy given that very few are hurting themselves or others. Better to apply scarce resources to the fraction of a fraction who engage in frequent, sustained, or multiple risky behaviors.

Carnegie's panel, Califano, and similar interests clamor for more "research" on adolescence, the time of life they single out as responsible for lifelong and society-wide calamities. Califano has made a career out of absurdly deceptive "surveys" which seek to resurrect G. Stanley Hall's myth of adolescence as a secretive, subterranean subversion of the squeaky-clean grownup world. But there is an avalanche of research on adolescence readily available. The kid-fixing lobbies just don't like what it shows. The Carnegie and Child Trends reports systematically ignore decades of solid research showing teenagers closely reflect the values and behaviors of adults around them, are not seduced into anti-social amoralities by the imagined depravities of "youth culture," and are not dangerous to themselves or to others. What requires new research is the danger posed by modern middle-aged detachment and scapegoating, and how the worst crazies keep winding up in positions of institutional and media prominence.

Laundering the Dogma

When one surveys the wasteland of august reports on teenagers over the last decade, a single glaring reason for their gross inaccuracies and embellishments becomes clear. A set of axioms about modern teenage behavior—of the type Adelson dubbed a "stubborn, fixed set of falsehoods"—have been created and, no matter how wrong, are endlessly circulated and have acquired false citation pedigrees. By this, I mean a kind of myth-laundering in which re-citation by various authors obscures where these assertions came from in the first place. They plague every report on teenagers at every point that secondary (someone else's) statements, rather than information taken directly from original sources (such as raw figures) are used.

The National Research Council's careful 1993 study of teenage environmental conditions, *Losing Generations*, is a fine example of good research that was ignored because it violated a crucial 1990s rule (don't discuss poverty, poor schools, or other adult-imposed risks). But even it goes astray when it relies on orthodox, "fixed falsehoods." The most typical example, and one widely cited in study after study: "More than 5,000 adolescents kill themselves each year," so that teen suicide rates are "now second only to those for people over age 65."[57] As pointed out, the true number of adolescent (age 19 and younger) suicides is about 2,000 per year, and teens have the lowest rates of suicide of any age group (other than children) by a considerable margin. The NRC's chapter cites dozens of reputable sources and itself was assembled by a distinguished academic panel. How can so many august reports be making so many faulty declarations—and recommending flawed policy based on those faulty declarations—that are not even in the right galaxy? The reason seems to be that no one is checking common assertions about teenagers against the original source data on which they are supposed to be (but are not) based.

And so blue-ribbon panels of the '90s discharge the same report with the same conclusion: more "adult supervision" (Carnegie), more parental "monitoring" (National Longitudinal Study), more "contact with adults" instead of "the negative influence of peers" (Child Trends). Round and round the expert panels go, and all they come up with is findings like the following:

> The most common popular, and mayoral, prescription for delinquency is "more parental supervision."

wrote Paul Goodman in *Growing Up Absurd*—in 1956. Only Goodman added:

> An important condition for the troubles of growing up is the troubles between the parents at home, brutal quarrels and drunkenness, coldness, one or the other or both parents getting away as often as possible and being withdrawn while present, and marriages breaking up…"More parental supervision" [in] the usual circumstances would likely *increase* the tension and trouble, but be that as it may the question is how? how to have reasonable supervision when the marriages themselves are no good? [emphasis original].[58]

Now, why is it that a social critic from dim Eisenhower America speaks with more clear-headed realism to the youth plight of the 1990s than our own leading scholars impaneled by esteemed institutes? "I do not think the public spokesmen are serious," Goodman said in his time, perfectly applicable today.

Growing Up Absurd—The Sequel

There is no sign that the destructive kidxploitation trend will abate any time soon. Wilder begets wilder is the rule. The latest all-the-rage reincarnation of teenage-rebellion is textbook writer Judith Rich Harris's theory that parents have nothing whatever to do with how their kids turn out—all youth behavior can be explained by genetics and peer influence. Harris, written up enthusiastically in *The New Yorker* for her "bold" and "startling new theory"[59] and given a prestigious award by the American Psychological Association, offers an emancipation proclamation for parents whose kids get in the way of personal self-fulfillment. When a theory achieves sudden popularity, count on it to neatly justify what contemporary grownups want to do anyway.

Harris's Group Socialization theory is largely pointless if taken at face value and dangerously fanatic when overstated. "Do parents have any important long-term effects on the development of their child's personality?" she begins her award-winning paper in the July 1995 *Psychological Review*.[60] "...The answer is no." Harris argues that "the aspects that are not likely to be important at all" in how the kid turns out are "almost all of the factors previously associated with the term *environment*, and associated even more closely with the term *nurture*."

That flushes all of them, all right. Irrelevant not only are "the parents' personalities or philosophies of child rearing," but even their physical "presence or absence in the home." It makes *no* difference whether parents spend happy days with their kids in warm quality time, utterly ignore them in alcoholic stupor, or lock them in crackhouse toilets—provided, she acknowledges in a final parenthetical comment, they don't "inflict grievous injury." With respect to the last, Harris implies that most violent abuses of children are "child-driven"—that is, obnoxious children with bad genes provoke parents (who share those bad genes) to pound them. As a general rule, that is an unconvincing notion, especially with respect to sexual abuse, which Harris does not mention.

Ultimately, Harris's theory is founded in standard adult bigotry against adolescents and equally unthinking exoneration of grownups. The battlescape is "*teenagers versus adults*," she announces (emphasis hers):

> Delinquent acts during adolescence are extremely common, even among individuals who were well-behaved children and who will become law-abiding adults... Adolescents are not aspiring to adult status—they are *contrasting* themselves with adults. They adopt characteristic modes of clothing, hairstyles, speech, and behavior so that, even though they are now the same size as adults, no one will have any trouble telling them apart. If they truly aspired to adult status they would not be spraying graffiti on overpasses, going for joyrides in cars they do not own, or shoplifting nail polish from drug stores. They would be doing boring adult things, like figuring out their income tax or doing their laundry (emphasis hers).[61]

Harris's characterization of delinquent teenagers subverting law-abiding adults, published in an august journal and lauded by Ph.D.s of consummate largeness, is virtually identical in scientific rigor and objectivity to that of Warren Beatty's fine movie *Bullworth*. In the movie, Beatty's senator-parody drunkenly tells a black audience they will never gain The Man's respect so long as they slouch around on doorsteps swilling malt liquor, chomping chicken wings, and cheering for a washed-up full-back turned slasher.

But Harris's superficial stereotyping is not satire or facetious quip. It constitutes her Big Evidence that teenagers are not adults-in-progress, but rebels against adults, a recycling of Hall's century-old prejudices of adolescent defiance. This is the revelation she describes "as if a light had gone on in the sky." It forms the heart of her leading-edge theory of child development, certified legit by the A.P.A. itself.

So, tiresomely, it has to be pointed out that even in big cities, the vast majority of "them" do not spraypaint overpasses (else every interchange in the nation would look like Graffiti Bridge); FBI figures show that even by the most wildly exaggerated calculation, fewer than 10 percent of "them" will steal a car any time in adolescence; and however unknowably widespread "their" nail-polish filching is, similar adult delinquencies (ie, theft from employers) are every bit as common. Even Harris's examples are ironic: public name recognition, car ownership and driving, and glamor are valued adult prerogatives which most adolescents are denied, and so some acquire them illicitly.

Harris's Saul-like enlightenment that adolescents don't want to be like adults so much as they want to be like other adolescents is a pointless tautology: acting like other adolescents means acting like adults. It isn't that peers matter more than parents or vice-versa; it's that peers and parents are members of the same culture to begin with. In real life, "youth culture" is interconnected with "adult culture" at all levels, the most influential "peers" of children and teens often *are* adults, and adult culture includes and influences parents whose behaviors help form the culture. Harris admits that "culture is transmitted from the parents' peer group (and from other cultural sources) to the children's peer group," but she winds up arguing that children, and particularly adolescents, reject large chunks of adult culture and substitute their own "innovations."

This is clearly not true as a rule. Amid the stacks of findings Harris ignores are those showing adolescents' values and behaviors, both statistically and by survey, closely track those of adults around them, particularly their parents. But, as with many popular theories, Harris's overstatement seems to result from a personal issue. Her real daughter turned out to be a perfect, quiet, scholarly youth ("very much like me and Charlie," her husband, she said), while her adopted daughter was wild. While Harris understandably seems to want to take credit for her influencing her good daughter, she blames her bad kid's badness on genetics. (Alternatively, it's also possible that Harris treated her biological daughter better than her adopted one.) But if parents truly have no influence, parents can't take credit for model children, either. It must have been her wonderful peers that made her real daughter turn out great.

In a backwards affirmation of Harris's youth "innovation" point, there are generational (that is, generalized peer) effects evident in certain behaviors such as youths' lower rates of drug abuse and declining rates of criminality compared to their parents. There may be healthy peer (and peer-adult) innovations, but why they are prevailing instead of more negative adult influences has not been studied. Rarely do popular scientists raise the issue of differences between teenage and adult attitudes or behaviors for the purpose of investigating why youths are acting more positively. Nor is another of Harris's positive points, that children and teenagers are not fragile wisps irrevocably damaged by any and every malign influence, likely to be accepted nearly as much as her more pro-zeitgeist findings.

Understanding is the First Casualty of Hype

Many groups of benign intent exaggerate youth malaise out of understandable belief that in the Nineties Chill, only the services shouting the loudest and staving off the direst threats will get funding and attention. Further, a good case can be made that greater services are needed, targeted primarily at parents in difficulty.

But the real problem requiring louder liberal dissent is the anti-youth and anti-poor Chill among policy makers and the public itself. Slandering teenagers to promote more programs is not only grossly unfair, it quickly evolves into liberal groups' placing of self promotion ahead of their original service goals. And the bill has come due.

In February 1998, the Harvard School of Public Health released a poll of American adults about the health issues facing children and youths.[62] Drugs was the number one problem cited. A distant second was crime.

Poverty, child abuse, day care, affordable health care, and injuries did not even attract 1 percent of the respondents. The only disease to make the list was AIDS, cited by 1 percent.

The deterioration in public knowledge and caring about the real hazards that injure and kill kids reflects the evasions and bamboozling of Clinton-era interests. Where 28 percent cited child abuse as a major problem in the 1986 poll, practically no one did in 1996.

Harvard professor of health policy and poll director Robert Blendon said he was "staggered" by the results. Ruby Hearn, senior vice president of the Robert Wood Johnson Foundation, which funded the poll, expressed concern about the narrowness of the public fears of drugs. The fact that 11 million children lack health insurance ought to be the biggest public concern, she and Blendon said. Experts' bafflement is more baffling than the public's blindness. Do academics honestly have no clue as to how American citizens could arrive at the idea that drugs and crime are the biggest menaces facing kids?

The public has been fed a five-year banquet of hype, escapism, and moral condemnations of young people by their most esteemed academic and official colleagues. And professionals are shocked that the public now thinks the whole juvenile health problem boils down to bad morals?

The Robert Wood Johnson Foundation funded the Child Trends study, which claimed youth culture, and its drugs and anti-social values, was the big danger. Why wouldn't the public now copy what the experts have been telling them: kids' behaviors are mere moral failings needing stern correction?

Liberal groups have scuttled their own agenda. If Blendon, Hearn, and others want to know why "poverty, day care, health insurance" are "off the radar screen," why the "family values agenda has caught on with public more than the health care agenda," they should read the preachments of their own colleagues. *They* don't talk about real youth problems. How would they expect the public to grasp them?

The well of panic has been drawn from once too often. Now, predictably, an angry public and policy arena is sabotaging their priorities. Kids are paying the price.

Erudite institutions and blue-ribbon panels are supposed to function on a higher plane than *National Enquirer* editors. They shouldn't be afraid to present new information and ask bold questions. The boldest is: why are young people behaving better, displaying fewer health and behavior risks, and enrolled in school in higher proportions than ever before in a world of greater poverty, deteriorating schools, and unstable, hostile grownups? What can we do to build on positive trends? Might good policy result from allocating youth and young families a fairer share of society's resources?

For the chapter ends as it began, with a baffling number. From 1985 to 1996, the rate of violent deaths among California's two million white teenagers declined by a flabbergasting 43 percent. In 1985, 891 white teens died from violent causes; in 1996, 503. That during a period in which the white teen population grew by 50,000. White teenage murders, down 5 percent. Firearms deaths down 30 percent. Suicides, down 36 percent. Traffic fatalities, down 54 percent. Drug deaths down 61 percent.

That's right: in a dangerous state and decade thought to have brought unheard-of perils to the young, a white kid today is only half as likely to die from a violent cause as a white kid of the mid-'80s. More limited national figures showed the same—white youth are safer than ever from violent death.

Yet this fatality plummet spanned a decade of nonstop yowling by hordes of experts and programmers, from school counselors to impaneled erudites, that youth demise was everywhere, the same among rich, poor, white, dark, suburb, inner city and hamlet, just one undifferentiated mass of X-generated young carnage. Consult your paper, *Mother Jones*, *Rolling Stone*, blue-ribbon report, William Bennett cultural indicator and Bill Bradley lifestyle danger (talk about undifferentiated), and there it is: grownups barking madly that kid wipeout from Paterson to penthouse has never been worse.

California white teen deaths cut in half in a decade. Although statistics by race are hard to come by before 1985, it appears from aggregated death stats that if 1996 were compared to 1975 instead, the decline among whites would be even larger. Now, why on earth would no one want to talk about that?

Consider the moral dilemma on race for that most moralistic administration's Initiative on Race: death rates among black and Native youths stayed about the same, and they rose considerably among Asian and Latino youths. (As with crime, Asian rates rose from a very low base and still remain the lowest of any group). And the issue goes beyond race. California whites are among the nation's most affluent. In Oklahoma, my home state, where poverty rates among whites are double those of California, trends among white youth are less optimistic. Among Oklahoma white

Table 6

**Life, death, and poverty risks by race,
California of the '90s**

Annual violent deaths per 100,000 population age 10–19 by race, 1985–96

	White	Latino	Black	Asian	Native
Violent death	37.6	44.6	77.8	27.5	42.2
Accident	26.5	20.6	22.2	15.0	26.4
Suicide	6.9	3.6	4.5	4.0	7.2
Murder	4.2	20.4	51.1	8.5	8.6
Change in violent death rate, 1985–96	-43.5%	+25.9%	-3.6%	+29.5%	-1.6%

Annual births/1,000 females ages 10–19, by race, 1995

	White	Latino	Black	Asian	Native
Births	16.8	60.3	47.2	15.1	36.7
Poverty rate 1990	8.1%	26.1%	28.6%	19.5%	23.9%

Source: California Vital Statistics Bureau. Microcomputer Injury Surveillance System (MISS, annual, 1985–96). Births by race, age, marital status, county (annual). Sacramento: Department of Health Services. Bureau of the Census (1990). *Social and Economic Characteristics*, California.

youth, violent crime has risen, violent deaths have not fallen, and rural birth rates rival those of blacks. Is, then, the false claim that all youth are "at risk" simply a cover-up for the failure of official health and social policies to address the risks of poorer youths?

Of course, authorities need face no such dilemmas. Until some powerful interest forces them out of their game plan, authorities can continue to snarf credit where they wish, dodge blame where they wish, battle Eastasia or Eurasia as they please. When it comes to rolling over and waving grant-stuffed paws in the air, America's academic and institutional authorities offer almost no check on politicos' ever-wilder craziness and lies. That leaves the media to lead us to sanity.

8 Myth: The Media Tell the Truth about Youth

There it is, right on schedule, at two to three per week. Today's (February 19, 1998) installment in the endless teens-gone-to-hell series is right on the *Los Angeles Times'* front page. It concerns the worst possible topic: "States put brakes on teen drivers."

Driving is the one behavior adults can lord over teens, though not as much as we do. For just plain, sober traffic wrecks, California Highway Patrol reports variously show that teen 16–19 have death and injury rates:

- higher than any other age group (if figured "per mile driven" or "per driver"),
- lower than age 20–34 (if figured "per person"),
- lower than age 20–39 (if figured in gross numbers of fatal and injury crashes), and
- lower than age 20–44 (if figured in gross numbers of fatal crashes).

Teenaged drivers don't account for a lot of wrecks or deaths: 10 percent of the injury crashes and 9 percent of traffic fatalities in California in 1996. That's a lot for a population that comprises only 4 percent of licensed drivers—2.5 times what one would expect. However, as noted, a staggering share of California's traffic deaths and injuries are caused by unlicensed drivers. Since we can't know how many of each age group actually drives or the total miles they drive, and since traffic casualties include pedestrians and cyclists, "per person," which includes the entire population, would seem a better measure. In that light, teens are about as bad as drivers in their 20s.

The most excruciating part of media stories such as the *Times'*, whose morning issue I eye gloomily, is reading the pathological lies told by authorities. When experts and the media intersect on the subject of teenagers, almost any idiocy is possible. *L.A. Times* science editor K.C. Cole, for example, soberly cited scientist Hal Lewis (author of *Technological Risks*) that "most auto fatalities involve drunken teenage boys" while "middle-aged business men and women...are not high risk drivers."[1] In fact, drinking teenage male drivers cause fewer than 2 percent of traffic deaths. A 45-year-old is more likely to cause a drunken traffic death than a 17-year-old. The difference between "2 percent" and "most" would seem to me noteworthy, especially for that technical elite of journalists known as science editors, but my protest letter to Cole failed to win response or correction.

So I open the *Times* braced to wince at expert pontificating on that "teenagers think they're immortal...," the implied denials that adults are every bit as risky customers. The usual junk.

I am pleasantly surprised. Reporter Mark Fritz's story has a subtler message. The new "brakes on teen drivers" are not occurring in response to a youthful highway bloodbath. Like adult deaths, teen fatalities are down 20 percent in the last eight years. As with teenage drug, alcohol, pregnancy, and crime problems, the fervor for greater shacklings on teenage drivers comes years after sharp decline had set in on its own.

Instead of indulging the typical media formula of showcasing the scariest quotes, Fritz's story pokes holes in authorities' statements, wryly making many of them sound ludicrous:

> "Kids are driving faster, and the result has been more serious accidents, more fatal accidents," said Jeff Siegel, a Concord (New Hampshire) High adminis- trator in charge of driver education. "Well, I don't know if kids are driving faster. I do know there is more traffic on the road."

Siegel, the type of hands-on expert source the media lionizes, ashcanned in sen- tence two his dire apocalism of sentence one. I constantly clamor for reporters to check dire claims such as "more serious accidents, more fatal accidents" against real, easily available data. Fritz, for one, does this and nails the cluelessness:

> Yet according to federal highway statistics, the number of fatalities in which a teen was driving dropped from 38 in 1987 in New Hampshire to 18 in 1996. In fact, the number of traffic fatalities for teens nationwide fell from 9,356 in 1976 to 5,779 two years ago.

So we have a new story: what's driving the anti-teen-driving frenzy? The wave of new restrictions is rooted in "the attitudes of today's parents, the baby boomers whose children are finally coming of age in an era that just seems more dangerous," Fritz notes. Why does it seem more dangerous? Because the Baby Boomers them- selves had, and have, so many problems that are off limits for media discussion—and because the media hypes dangers to youth all out of proportion to reality.

Today's kids would have to drive gonzo to kill as many as their parents did. Teenage and adult motorway fatality peaked in 1969 at a level 1.7 times that of the mid-1990s. "I don't think most of them would be real eager to see their children do some of the things that they did as children," Patricia Waller of the University of Michigan's Transportation Research Institute said. In 1969, 9,600 teens 15–19 died in vehicle wrecks. This compares to about 5,500 deaths in a slightly smaller teen population of 1996. Once again, today's kids are punished because many Baby Boomers are afraid of themselves.

For that reason, it may not be a good idea for states to require that parents drive with their teenagers for longer probationary periods. "A lot of parents don't drive that well," Waller pointed out. Catch-22: a University of Michigan study found that "the best predictor of a student's driving record was his or her father's record." Leadfoot Dad is likely to mentor pedal-metal junior.

Whether rational or not, various interests, beginning with the news media, are ever-willing to exploit adult fears. "Every time a carload of youngsters cracks up…a television news helicopter hovers overhead, bringing scary footage back to high- strung parents," Fritz writes. Politics and media coverage "leaves a lingering feeling that the highways are littered with dead teenagers."

So do the experts. In a squabble on National Public Radio over restrictions on teenage drivers, I hear Susan Ferguson, research director for the Insurance Institute for Highway Safety, declare that 16-year-olds are the only age to show an increase in drivers involved in fatal traffic crashes over the last 20 years.[2] I have the California Highway Patrol figures in front of me. I tell her and the NPR audience that traffic deaths among the state's 16-year-olds have dropped precipitously over the last two decades, from an average of 130 per year in the mid-'70s to 80 in the mid-'90s even as the teen population grew. When I get home, I look up the national figures. Compared to the first five years of driver statistics available (1975–79), the most recent five years (1991–95) show declines in 16-year-olds killed in traffic crashes (down 25 percent), involved as drivers in deadly wrecks (down 17 percent), and killed as passengers (down 23 percent).[3] So Ferguson's statement is not particularly accurate, though selective choice of years (say, the safest year of the '70s versus the worst year of the '90s) to be compared could make it technically right. When it comes to elderly drivers, Ferguson applies kinder, gentler standards to make them appear safer than they are, as noted below.

And once again, California statistics reveal a larger drop in teenage risk than in other states. The declines among 16-year-olds from the 1970s to the mid-1990s is a whopping 36 percent for traffic deaths, 41 percent for driver involvements in deadly wrecks, and 16 percent in passenger demise. This huge gain in 16-year-old safety predates the restrictions proposed by Ferguson and is almost identical to that of older drivers. None of this was mentioned in the legislative debate. Nor was another crucial fact: a large majority of 16-year-olds killed in traffic mishaps are passengers (and, to a much lesser extent, bicyclists or pedestrians), not drivers. Of the 79 California 16-year-olds killed in motorway accidents in 1996, only 26 were drivers.

For drunk-driving fatalities, California's 1996 figures are more dramatic: only four of the 23 deaths among 16-year-olds were drivers. That is, the number of 16-year-olds killed at the wheel is low and declining, but these savings are negated by an increase in the number killed as passengers. Here we go again: traffic deaths, like pregnancy, like drug and alcohol use, like smoking, like homicide, are age-integrated—teen statistics parallel those of their elders. So...if we want to save 16-year-old lives, restricting older drivers is just as essential as clamping down on 16-year-olds.

As I find out in the NPR squabble, never mind...the crusade to "save kids' lives" seems to apply only when other teens are the killers. It evaporates quickly once restrictions on adult behavior are suggested.

Later on, a caller asks Ferguson if more restrictions shouldn't be put on elderly drivers, as the Insurance Institute has proposed for teens. Ferguson replies that the elderly are a safe bunch. Again, when I get home, I look up the hard numbers. In terms of drivers getting into deadly wrecks, teens dropped from 9,700 in 1975 to 6,800 in 1996, a rate decline of 25 percent, the same as young and middle-aged drivers. However, drivers over age 65 were in 3,700 fatal traffic crashes in 1975 and 6,500 in 1996, a per-person rate 13 percent *higher* than two decades ago. True, those ages 65 to 110 still are a little less likely to die in traffic crashes than older teenagers are, but those odds have risen sharply.

Ferguson has it exactly backwards: teens show large drops in highway carnage while seniors' traffic safety improvements lag behind the national trend. It is baffling that an agency with "highway safety" in its title is not concerned about the growing toll among older drivers.

The reason, most likely, is politics and profit. Whipping teen drivers creates a popular image. Insurance companies drastically overcharge teenage drivers in ways they don't other "high risk" drivers in more powerful constituencies, such as men. Car manufacturers have even used the fear to sell heavier, more expensive cars to elders. In the January 1998 *Sunset* magazine, an ad shows a pile of teenage driver's licenses and the statement: "They're coming. Be prepared...Over 11,000 new drivers every day. Kids who were riding bikes or skateboards yesterday. That's why you need a Chevy Lumina..." (An equally appropriate ad for the bikers and skateboarders might go: "They're coming. They kill more people on the roads than teenagers do. Thousands of elderly driving bigger, heavier cars...")

Corrupting or Framing?

This book cites the media as major influences on Americans, yet it denies that the media influence adolescent behavior. How can both be true?

The distinction involves two types of media influence progressive critics have delineated: the media as corrupter of public morals, and the media as framer of public debate. Of these, the media's power to frame the debate—in this case, by presenting a systematically false image of teenagers—is far more powerful and far worse than its ability to corrupt. After working with children, adolescents, and their families for a dozen years and studying patterns of youth and adult behavior, detailed in earlier chapters, I'm doubtful that the media corrupt innocent, jello-brained kids. Parents may not like it that their kids are learning American values, all the worse that these expose the parents' (unadmitted) values as well.

For example, progressive media critic Norman Solomon aptly criticizes the new *Teen People* as "colorful. Stylish. And disturbing."[4] *Teen People* is a shallow, conforming publication concerned with good looks, fashionable clothes, celebrity lifestyle, glamor-anorexic body images, and self-worth proven by lavish consumption. Solomon reminds us where we've seen this before: "*People* magazine now has a clone." That is, *People*-junior hawks the same rotten values to kids that *People*-senior peddles to grownups. Which are, by virtue of adults' endorsement of the magazine to the tune of 3.5 million copies sold per week, the values of grownups—unless media critics want to argue that adults are mere media puppets as they insinuate teens are. So *Teen People* stands accused of socializing kids into Adult *People* culture.

What is needed is a long-overdue reevaluation of the last two decades' incredible leap in grownups' acquisitiveness—not finger-pointing at the tube, screen, and billboard. Leftist Bennettism, clucking its tongue over commercial media seducing children and teenagers into sinful alien values, is one of the most discouraging developments of the '90s. "American society," writes Henry Giroux, "increasingly produces and spreads through the media a hyped-up rhetoric of moral panic about the state of youth culture,"[5] and the left is leading the shriek.

Leftist philosopher Richard Rorty's newest critique of 20th century leftist thought, *Achieving Our Country*, laments that much of the post-Vietnam cultural left has forsaken protesting growing economic inequality in its preoccupation with the "theoretical hallucinations" and "ubiquitous specters" of the right's pop culture Satans.[6] "The cultural left thinks more about stigma than about money," he argues. Given that the Clinton/right considers welfare reform a morality fable, it is not clear where cultural parts from class. But something is badly amiss when liberals and leftists write a dozen pages about the likes of MTV and Joe Camel for every paragraph about youth poverty and half-sentence about child abuse.

The Media and Democracy Congress's 1997 *We the Media* guide contains much valuable information on the increasingly concentrated Media-Industrial complex: corporations buying into and consolidating networks to create mega-outlets which restrict information disseminated to the public to favor established interests.[7] It shows how cigarette and booze advertising dollars restrict magazine coverage of legal-drug abuse. It exposes how business domination and kowtowing to official agendas slant media coverage. Especially in a cogent satire by Kim Deterline of "We Interrupt This Message," it documents the manner in which the mainstream press "frames the debate" by confining and distorting issues such as welfare reform—just as French sociologist Pierre Bourdieu argued that the television owners' relentless drive for higher ratings and more ad dollars imposes a uniform, "invisible censorship" on public debate as effectively as any government Ministry of Truth could.[8] It includes favorable quotations on myths about youth from my research. It contains a fine brief by Julie Winokur pointing out that "youth (who have become synonymous with drugs, promiscuity, and violence)" are "typically scapegoated by the press" in "biased coverage." On the whole, a book well worth perusing.

But again and again, the predominant portrayal in *We the Media* engages the same scapegoating and dysymbolizing of young people as values-challenged violent drug/alcohol/nicotine addicts. And it exonerates adults as morally concerned, well-behaved parents alarmed at the media "selling vice" to their kids. The guide includes the breathless assertions of a plethora of liberal groups. Examples:

- Most kids watch adult TV, including nighttime soaps heavy on sex and violence. In the 1994–1995 season nine out of the top 10 shows watched by kids ages 6 to 11 ran in primetime (Children Now).

- The average American child will witness 8,000 murders on TV by the time he or she is 12. He or she will see 20,000 commercials a year and have viewed over 20,000 acts of violence by the time of high school graduation (Center for Media and Public Affairs).

- Percentage of Americans who believe TV violence encourages real-life violence: 79 (TV-Free America).

- A 1994 *Newsweek* poll found that 67 percent of those asked blamed TV and other popular entertainment for the country's moral crisis (Children Now).

I do see sin on TV, make no mistake. On just one evening, March 3, 1998, trapped in the hotel room of a Nevada casino (downstairs, thousands of middle-agers smoked, drank, and gambled away a Tuesday night) where I was addressing a juvenile justice conference, I saw corrupting '70s sitcom on "Nick at Night." Jack Klugman drinks beer for breakfast in "The Odd Couple." Mary Tyler Moore pours wine on "The Dick Van Dyke Show." Mary progresses to dishing out brandy to a man she's brought to her apartment on "The Mary Tyler Moore Show." The Newharts down wine and talk of getting drunk on the new "Newhart." On the old (Suzanne Pleshette) show, Newhart talks about a whisky chain-letter joke. Lucille Ball is blind drunk in a promo for "I Love Lucy." In "Rhoda," the boyfriend is at her place for breakfast—implying he spent the night! No wonder Baby Boomers, growing up with the booze-soaked boob tube, are a rotten generation.

Fun aside, kids have real problems. As pointed out in Chapter 1, 2,000 to 3,000 kids are killed and half a million are injured in violent assaults inflicted by their parents or caretakers every year. Households contribute by far the largest share of hospital emergency treatments for violence, the Bureau of Justice Statistics reported last year. Some 130,000 kids were confirmed victims of sexual abuse in 1995—no doubt an underreported number. If media causes real-life violence, it is the grownups whose exposure to "heavy sex and violence" we should worry about.

The liberal claim in *We the Media* that the media seduces the young to violate our values is stated flatly:

> Far from a passive mirror of society, it [advertising] is an effective medium of influence and persuasion, both a creator and perpetuator of the dominant attitudes, values, and ideology of the culture, the social norms, and the myths by which most people govern their behavior...Targeting the young, advertisers are aware of their ability to create a kind of national peer pressure that erodes individual as well as community values and standards. They do not hesitate to take advantage of the insecurities and anxieties of young people, usually in the guise of offering solutions: a cigarette provides a symbol of independence; designer jeans or sneakers convey status; the right perfume or beer resolves doubts about femininity or masculinity (Jean Kilbourne, media critic).

Made in the name of taking advertising to task, this is a damaging anti-youth assertion. It is contradictory, claiming that advertising creates and perpetuates "dominant attitudes," "community values," and "social norms" at the same time it beguiles the young to violate "community values and standards." Which is it?

As detailed in Chapter 7 and contrary to Kilbourne, repeated studies have found that while grownups, including professionals, massively overstate anxieties they imagine the young must suffer, young people are no more insecure or anxious than older people. Rather, the same studies find that the values—and habits, such as smoking and drinking—of young people mirror those of their parents and parent culture.[9] If ads are the seducers, they seduce old and young alike. And especially the media itself. The *New England Journal of Medicine* reported from a study of 99 magazines in 1992 that those running tobacco ads contain a lot fewer articles on the hazards of smoking than magazines that refuse the ads.[10]

Grownups' intense fear expressed on behalf of youths' supposed anxieties about good looks and sexuality masks an even worse Baby Boom insecurity. Pharmaceutical companies developed dozens of new drugs for 1990s middle-aged adults designed solely to counteract the natural effects of aging. The new anti-baldness drug Propecia is expected to generate $300 million in sales in 1998. Viagra, a

new drug to counteract sexual decline connected with getting old, goes for $10 a
pill, with 36,000 prescriptions written its first week on the market, 113,000 its second, and $4 billion in sales anticipated annually.[11] New diet pills are being market-
ed to thin the explosion in obesity among Baby Boomers, who for all our talk about
fitness are getting fatter far faster than our kids (see below).

Age-reversing drugs are only a part of the graying generation's good-looks
obsession. Half a million cosmetic surgeries are performed every year to alter natural
appearances, at least two-thirds of which are to erase the natural effects of aging. Of
these, 100,000 reform breasts, 120,000 remove fat, and 250,000 alter facial (including hair) features.[12] The biggest clients for cosmetic surgery are adults in the 30–50
age range; teens comprise only 3 percent. This suggests that teenagers may form the
American ideal for appearance, which may be one reason that adults resent young
people and transfer our own insecurities (founded in the wrongheaded belief that
aged features are ugly) to them. "I have always believed that part of the underlying
dislike that Americans have towards their young is due to the tremendous fear they
have of getting old," psychiatrist and student of adolescence Daniel Offer
observed.[13]

Nevertheless, Kilbourne and many others of leftward stripe let adults, adult
values, and adults' dislike of teenagers off the hook. Instead, We the Media's authors
assign the combination of weak kids and evil Madison Avenue blame for America's
worst behavior problems:

> Seagram's announced plans to air its liquor ads on TV after 9 PM, but at that
> hour in New York and Los Angeles, the largest media markets in the country,
> 16 percent of the audience, or more than two million people, are under 17
> (Center on Alcohol Advertising).

Scarier still, the Center fails to mention, 84 percent viewing the liquor ads are over 18,
an age group that accounts for 97 percent of alcohol-related traffic crashes and deaths.
Seventeen-year-olds are only one-third as dangerous with booze as 35-year-olds.

> Between 1991 and 1994, the prevalence of smoking among eighth graders
> rose 30 percent—a time that coincides with the controversial "Joe Camel"
> advertising campaign.

Fifteen to 25 million kids grow up in homes where parents smoke, seriously
damaging the health of young people and tripling the odds they will smoke. Smoking
among adult women of parent age (especially those ages 25–44) rose sharply in the
early 1990s, pre-dating the teenage rise, the Centers for Disease Control found.[14]
Interestingly, studies found that Camel smoking among adult women rose coincident
with Joe Camel's campaign,[15] yet commentators have yet to note this.

We the Media goes out of its way to deny the staggering teenage poverty rate.
Instead, it favorably quotes the New York Times' Christina Ferrari about the
"increase in teenagers' disposable income" and their supposedly selfish consumption:
"Teenagers have a lot of money...and the only people they have to spend it on is
themselves." Baloney. Teenagers account for a whopping 2 percent of the nation's
$5 trillion in annual consumer spending, and most of what they spend is on family
necessities. In contrast, adults wager five times more in gambling amusement than

teenagers spend on *everything*. These perspectives should tell us whose materialistic values are really driving the acquisitive, brand-name-obsessed market.

Ironically, the leftist media watchdog *Extra!* criticized reporters Bob McNamara and Bob Goldberg of "CBS Evening News" for hawking exactly the myth that American kids suffer from "affluenza" (too much money). CBS, *Extra!* noted, failed to mention that "the U.S. has the highest rate of child poverty in the industrial world."[16] Like CBS, *We the Media* illustrates how the urge to moralize quickly leads progressive authors to ignore, even deny, the role of poverty and family disintegration as well:

> The truth is, young people grow up in a world today that is dramatically new and different—and dangerous.
>
> Much of what they learn is brought to them by corporate sponsors who care little for their interests beyond what they consume.
>
> ...The hip-hop culture that [gangsta rapper Tupac] Shakur helped shape was once a relatively sober, drug-free culture. It was mainly marketing—not family disintegration—that made it synonymous with malt liquor and violence. And parents couldn't even monitor what was going on because the targeting was so narrow, so precise, that few adults were exposed to it.
>
> ...After decades of drinking and drugging less than their white cohorts, alcohol use among African-American youth rose dramatically in the 1990s (Makani Themba, Praxis Project).

Fact: the world of black people is not dramatically more dangerous than in the past. Older folks may remember past eras as poor but peaceable, times of strict discipline and parental control. A recent article on the recollections of Los Angeles' "Eastside boys" asserted that "there was no crime" in black neighborhoods during the Great Depression.[17]

And yet, this is utter delusion. During 1930–36, the murder rate among California blacks (120 per 100,000 population) was twice as high as in 1990–96 (55 per 100,000). In the '90s, 80 percent of black murders were by guns; in the 1930s, 85 percent of a larger number of black murders were by guns. Nationally, as well, rates of homicide among blacks (and whites) were considerably higher during the Depression, and slightly higher during the early 1970s, than during the 1990s (Table 1). Since crimes against nonwhites were not investigated as seriously in the 1930s and 1950s as today, the murder rate in those decades likely was higher than reported. Incomplete 1930s crime reports, cited in Chapter 1, show that urban rates of other types of violent crime were higher than those of the 1990s as well.

Fact: violent gang conflict has occurred for decades. Even for the times remembered as the most pacific, veteran gang researcher Malcolm Klein points out, the "West Side Story" image that gang conflict was just rumbles and occasional switchbladings was a myth:

> In the gang world of the 1950s and 1960s...people did get hurt; people did get killed...Drive-by shootings were not uncommon, even though today's police and writers believe that drive-bys are a new feature of gang life. I have three taped interviews with gang members in the mid-1960s. All three describe drive-by shootings in a matter-of-fact way, a part of gang life.[18]

Table 1

The 1990s are dangerous? Black (and White)
murder rates were higher in the past generations

Homicide deaths among African Americans, by era:

	Murders	Population*	Annual rate*
1930–35	36,000	12.0	50.1
1950–55	25,000	16.0	26.0
1970–75	60,000	23.6	42.4
1990–95	74,000	31.6	39.0

*Black population in millions. Rate is annual murders/100,000 population.
Sources: National Center for Health Statistics, *Vital Statistics of the United States*; Bureau of the Census, *Mortality Statistics*.

The media's framing is a key factor in the how the public perceives crime. Violence in prior eras may have generated less attention because TV wasn't around to beam killings all over the region and nation into every household nightly.

Fact: the world of black teenagers in particular is not more dangerous. The murder rate among black youths was higher in 1980, when hip-hop was flourishing in peace and love, than it is today. During the 1990s, when hip-hop and gangsta rap was selling rising millions of recordings, the murder rate among black teenagers in Los Angeles (home to Tupac, and to gangsta what New Orleans is to Dixieland) *plummeted* as never before. Black teen homicide arrests fell from 149 in 1990 to 35 in 1997. Latino teen murder dropped from 196 to 80. Among whites, from 11 to three.

"Rap's influence is so pervasive that it has emerged as the first musical style to truly rival rock'n'roll as the primary music choice for American youth culture," the *L.A. Times* Sunday "Calendar" magazine reported in July 1998. "It's already battled rock to a standstill on MTV…and it's virtually no contest on the sales charts, where rap albums and singles regularly clog the national Top 10 lists. The most popular new albums have continued Tupac's thuggish persona." Half of all rap music is purchased by youths under age 18, and two-thirds by whites.[19] So…if teenage violent crime and homicide *declined dramatically as rap ascended*, shouldn't those who insist pop culture drives youth behavior be lauding the gangstas as good influences?

I don't think media influences are a pivotal factor on youth behavior, but if I did, I'd be obliged to praise rapsters for the fact that drug and alcohol abuse is relatively rare among black youths. The National Household Survey reported that only 6 percent of black youths ages 12–17 drank an alcoholic beverage more often than once a month in 1996, half the rate among whites. *Monitoring the Future* reported that in the previous year, 70 percent of black high school seniors did not get drunk at all and 87 percent did not get drunk more than twice (again, half the drinking rate among white teens).

But drug and alcohol addiction are devastating black adults. There were 100,000 hospital emergency trips and 2,500 deaths from drugs among urban blacks over age 25 in 1995—compared to 20 drug deaths among urban black youths. Two-thirds of black children grow up in single-parent families. One in nine lives with neither parent. Nearly five million black children live in poverty. If malt liquor ads are the problem, they are ruining adults more than kids.

Listening to group counseling sessions for California black teenagers imprisoned for violent crimes reveals universal histories of violent abuses at home—ones kids themselves, ironically, are reluctant to blame for their current problems. Shakur is an example. His mother was a crack addict who put him on the street. Yet he wrote fervent odes to her ("Dear Mama," *Me Against the World*) at the same time he coined the "thug life" ("the hatred you give little infants fucks everyone") acronym to arraign larger society's war against young black people.

It is time for adults, black and white, to cut out the denial: the finger-pointing, the superior "values" claims, the incessant moralizing. I hear stronger values in Shakur's lyrics—especially his last albums, which articulate the sorrow and bitter self-deprecation grown out of ghetto entrapment—than I do in the whip-'em and lock-'em-up righteousness of the elders. Shakur's music is far from an advertisement for thug life. "Look what hell made," he declared of his gangsta career, urging kids not to follow his example "to an early grave:"

> No mother no father see this nigga's all alone
> Old timers my role models in the war zone
> Raised with this game 'til it's a part of me
> It ain't hard to see the future's looking dim
> I'm trying to make a profit out of living in this sin…
> I'm a witness to homicide drive-bys takin' lives little kids die
> Broken-hearted as I gaze at the chalk line gettin' high
> I wanna change but ain't no future right for me.[20]

In the attack on Shakur and the presumed culture of gangsta rap, many liberals joined former civil rights activist and now right-wing Bill Bennett sidekick C. Dolores Tucker. Tucker is an addled case. On C-Span's coverage of Congressional hearings on pop culture and the suicide of a North Dakota teenager never even alleged to have heard a Tupac lyric, Tucker is churning out fulminations like (to borrow from Hunter Thompson) three iguanas on a feeding frenzy. She is beyond reason. Her arch enemy, Tupac Shakur and his Death Row claque, causes all teenage malaise from death to drugs.

Tucker has been busy on the lecture circuit with Bennett, denouncing rap and rock music as corrupting fragile kids. Actually, the fragile one turned out to be Tucker. She sued Tupac Shakur's estate for $10 million, claiming that she hadn't been able to have sex with her husband for two years after Shakur made derogatory references to her on his 1995 album, *All Eyez on Me*.[21]

The only song on that album that references Tucker is, "Wonder Why We Call U Bytch." My hair-filled ear's translation and the lyric transcripts posted under the Hiphopstore index on the internet agree. The song is an explanation as to why rappers call certain women ho's and bitches, but it does not so label Tucker or threaten her. It seems to me (and may be generally thought) to exemplify a major irony. The song decries young black prostitutes who, abused by men in childhood and adolescence, now cynically exploit their sexuality to escape the ghetto. The result is not the easy life, but early death from AIDS. In a brutal line, Shakur declares:

> I loved you like a sister
> But you died too quick
> And that's why we called you "bitch."

Shakur's other music makes it clear he also considers himself a kind of whore born of racism and violence, sardonically parlaying his ghetto talents into riches. ("If this rappin' bring me money/Then I'm rappin' till I'm paid.") He was aware that he, too, would "die too quick." The song is one of those who-is-this-really-about conundrums, and it ends with a cynical footnote to his virtuist critic:

> Dear Ms. C. Delores Tucker
> Keep stressin' me
> Fuckin' with a motherfuckin' mind
> I figured you wanted to know, you know
> Why we call them ho's, "bitches"
> And maybe this might help you understand
> It ain't personal
> It's strictly business, baby
> Strick-lee business.

All right, so Shakur considers the whole bitch matter, including his squabble with Tucker, strictly business. That could be argued, but the point is: these are the lines that caused C. Dolores to cut off the hubby for two years? Tucker is lionized by the media and Congress as a hero, the black woman righteously warring against evil music to save a generation of warped children. Turns out there's no evidence that rap, gangsta or otherwise, corrupts kids—but for the sake of her husband, C. Dolores Tucker should be kept away from it.

Left Bennettism and Caffeine Fiends

This seems to me the danger sign: when a campaign demanding more corporate or government responsibility veers into blaming teenagers for harboring vulnerability (biological, moral, developmental) to bad behavior and defying their parents' healthy values. To establish such a premise, liberal groups sink into repeating debunked stereotypes and falsehoods that teenagers are acting particularly badly and that adults must rescue them from their corrupters—advertisers, pop culture, their own young dumbness. At this point, left meets Bennettism in a we-versus-them mode of self-congratulatory "values" and panaceas emphasizing greater controls over what the young hear, read, and view. This kind of thinking has thrown anti-smoking, anti-alcohol-abuse, and media responsibility movements off track.

Illustration of these two kinds of thinking—one which deftly pinpoints the real corporate dereliction on one hand, versus one which indulges a raft of over-statement demeaning young people on the other—appeared side by side in Fairness and Accuracy in Reporting's May/June 1997 *Extra!* The articles, by Vassar College sociologist William Hoynes and Johns Hopkins media studies teacher Mark Crispin Miller, concern the very worthwhile campaign by the Center for Commercial-Free Public Education's "Unplug" against Channel One.

Channel One contracts with schools to provide educational television to public school classrooms. The channel's eight minutes of daily fare include news and feature programming plus two minutes of commercials. Why would companies pay Channel One $200,000 for a 30-second spot to advertise to teenagers during school days? Because, Channel One's 1997 pitch to corporate sponsors declares:

> Advertisers who target teens know they watch an average of 10 hours less television a week than other groups. Channel One doesn't just deliver teen viewers—it delivers the hardest to reach teen viewers.

Contrary to stereotype, adolescents are not compulsive vidiots. Neilsen Media Research's May 1997 survey found that teens age 12–17 average only an hour and a half per day watching TV, 40 percent less than adults.[22] Thus, the industry needs other ways to reach teens who watch little or no TV on their own time. Channel One promises to do this through the schools, which have the power to force students to watch "educational TV."

There are eight million students in Channel One's 12,000 contractee public schools, mainly in less affluent districts which receive equipment and free programming from Channel One. Unplug, a coalition of students, parents, and media monitors, challenged the commercialization of the public schools represented by Channel One. Disturbingly, a campaign which began positively by affirming student rights not to be force-fed advertising in public schools (and the sort of "educational TV" agreeable to corporate sponsors) shows signs of becoming yet another movement which promotes a negative view of youth stupidity and censorship to protect them.

Hoynes' study succinctly captures the wrong being perpetrated: "In essence, schools deliver a highly sought teen audience to Channel One, which sells the attention of captive teens to youth-oriented marketers."[23] His analysis of three dozen Channel One broadcasts aired in 1995–96 reaches intriguingly mixed conclusions. He finds that Channel One does not attempt to indoctrinate with a heavy-handed pro-business message. Rather, the channel simply confines the news to a safe official framework. Coverage of domestic issues allotted politicians 86 percent, men 93 percent, and whites 97 percent of the air time, for example. Even worse was the morality fable communicated to teenagers:

> While reporting on teen-oriented social issues had the most depth and was often the most nuanced, these reports generally employed an underlying theme that recast these social issues as morality tales. While reports on teen pregnancy, parenting, drinking, and crime imply that there are broader social questions at stake, the stories suggest, often quite directly, that the

fundamental issues are about individual moral choices. For example, a report on teenage mothers closed with an explicit call for teen abstinence from sexual activity. And reports on pregnant teens and teenagers in prison suggested that teens are responsible for their own poor choices and the resulting consequences.

Channel One relentlessly avoids discussions of the historical and social contexts of race and inequality, Hoynes found. "Economic questions—particularly about poverty, jobs, and education...are almost entirely absent."

Thus, Channel One reinforces political convention and a moral framework that sidesteps social context. Then, it insinuates that "bad" individual indulgences cause dope addiction or imprisonment, while "good" indulgences are those suggested by the commercials. That is, the programs encourage teens not to identify with those portrayed as drinking, using drugs, or having sex at the same time ads encourage teens to indulge in commercially approved pleasures, healthy or not.

This dichotomy encompasses an important, unspoken American adult value: that one's own unhealthy self-indulgence is perfectly acceptable so long as one verbally embraces high moral standards and stridently condemns unhealthy behaviors by others, preferably unpopular others. The presentation of this value in classroom sanctity affirms its stamp of social approval. While "all commercial media have the same underlying goal," Hoynes sums up, "Channel One makes use of classroom time and needs to be evaluated for its educational value, not simply its popularity or profitability."

Where Hoynes upholds teenagers' agency and argues for better information to strengthen it, Miller denies young people agency. Like Hoynes', Miller's article connects Channel One's messages to those of the larger mainstream media.[24] But Miller goes beyond the youth rights issue to argue that Channel One's worst sin is calculating commercial pitches to take advantage of adolescent weaknesses. What weaknesses? The usual set of grownup bigotries.

Miller asks readers to sympathetically "imagine, or remember" being a teenager "with your mind rebelling and your hormones raging." Adolescents, he declares, "generally feel bad enough about themselves." Miller's evocation of the all-purpose teenager, whose generic experience any adult can call up from mind or memory, de-individualizes adolescents into a faceless mass characterized by vulnerability. As discussed previously, teenagers suffer no more from raging hormones, rebellious minds, or negative self image than adults do. Had Miller characterized blacks as generic clones or women as in hormonal turmoil, his stereotyping would have been vigorously challenged.

Having asserted that teenagers are uniquely ripe for commercial plucking, Miller (without presenting a shred of evidence) pins a host of teenage social ills on Channel-One style imagery:

> Channel One continually assures its audience, through the commercials, that it's really cool to be an idiot. This is partly the result of the great corporate interest—prevalent throughout the entertainment industries—in exploiting the inevitable rebelliousness of adolescent boys. Whether on Channel One or regular TV, the ads aimed at that uneasy group appeal to a defiant boorish-

ness that, in the real world, routinely lands a lot of young men in jail, and that the movie studios and video-game manufacturers endlessly glamorize in works like Happy Gilmore, Ace Ventura 2: When Nature Calls and Down Periscope ("See it and Win!"), Virtual Boy, Donkey Kong 2 and Killer Instinct ("PLAY IT LOUD!"), among many others advertised on Channel One.

Miller goes on to blame Channel One's ads for compelling drug use among "children" (the '90s term for adolescents) and causing "emotional disorder among teenagers." Miller's thinking represents the same vulnerability to popular image and convention that he attributes to the teens puppeteered by Channel One. It rests in the left's utter failure to challenge modern media/corporate/political myths about teenagers. In truth, there is no research evidence that adolescent boys are uneasier or more rebellious than older males. Studies consistently have shown that 80 to 90 percent of teenagers are confident and share their parents' values. "Defiant boorishness" is a demeaning generalization to do William Bennett proud. It overlooks the fact that over-30 males show the biggest increase in "boorishness" and that among the young, poorer nonwhite men are the most likely by a wide margin to wind up in jail.

The Unplug campaign and other leftists endorse many of these anti-youth images. Unplug promotes recent books by the University of Missouri's Roy Fox and by Children First that claim that the "corporate product world" aims "to separate children from their parents in order to sell and sell to them directly and through you."

Fox contends that Channel One "commercials control kids" by "harvesting minds."[25] Fox's finding resulted from written questionnaires and focus groups with 200 rural Missouri students, most in ninth grade. The results are interesting in terms of how youths view commercials (in varied ways), but Fox admits he does not investigate such crucial consumer influences as "recommendations from friends" and "personal needs and tastes."

Fox reports that 40–50 percent of students "bought a specific product because of a specific commercial" within "several days." My reaction was: then 50–60 percent didn't? The channel advertises some of America's most popular products, from Pepsi to Snicker's to Nike. Think about the poll questions asked teenagers and what the answers would reveal if you were surveyed. If Fox goes to a restaurant, attends a movie, or gets a haircut after seeing an ad, has his mind been "conditioned," "controlled" and "harvested"? If, as Fox suggests, "brand loyalty is established at an early age," giving advertisers incentive to target youths, what does that tell us about adults? Are grownups of such robotized mentality that we cannot make different choices later in life than we made in adolescence—i.e., to change from costly Marlboro cigarettes (the most advertised and most popular among adults as well as teens) to some cheaper brand?

Fox obediently accepts negative myths of adolescents, including their supposed "downright insecure and fearful" identities, rebelliousness, vulnerability to conformity, and possession of "vast 'disposable incomes.' " As with most media critics, he cannot admit that any youth behavior is getting better; because commercial media manipulation is getting more intense, then everything teenage must always be getting worse (i.e., he repeats the falsehood that teens' liquor consumption is increasing when it is declining rapidly). His conclusions are quite emotional: "When kids buy things they see on commercials, they pay with more than just dollars and cents. They pay with their minds, hearts, bodies, and spirits." He talks of "reclaiming them" from being "systematically conditioned to be consumers" by advertising whose "values" he sees in conflict with those of "what parents and teachers want." He proposes, as many liberals do, media literacy, or "mediacy," programs for schools—and proposes an excellent curriculum structure for evaluating commercial messages in his conclusion.

Media literacy is reasonable, but it doesn't get at the real problem. What is really required is reevaluation of the far larger effect on youths of growing up in a product-driven society whose adults, including parents and teachers, spend $5 trillion per year on personal consumption, including $100 billion on alcohol and tobacco, $40 billion on jewelry, $45 billion on sports supplies, and $90 billion on video and audio products (including 600 million "adult movie" rentals). American adults spend three times more ($300 billion per year) on clothes and accessories than on their own education.[26] American adults gamble half a trillion dollars per year, an amount equal to the total national, state, and local spending on all primary, secondary, and higher education.[27] Where's the liberal tongue-clucking on that "moral barometer"?

The problem with analyses such as those by Fox, Miller, Children First, Ferrari, and We the Media is that they encourage the distancing of adults' from youths' values, blame media for the latter, and hamper sober examination of adult values. None argue that adults should examine our own values and consumption. They do not compare teenage consumption to adult spending, nor to any notion of normal spending, but to an apparent standard of zero consumption. Any independent purchasing, just like the tiniest sip of beer, by a teenager is declared sinful, violating adult norms and menacing parental control.

Left to right, pop culture and "youth culture" critics play up their own morality tales of personal misbehavior—anecdotal, exaggerated, fabricated—without providing larger social context beyond what Miller calls "loutish" media images. This is the same limited horizon Hoynes' more sober analysis rightly attributes to Channel One. Thus, the implications of Miller's left-wing analysis wind up the same as Channel One's moral fables and Bennett's right-wing doctrine: teenagers (equals "children") should receive only wholesome messages. Bad messages should be censored from kids' purviews. Teenagers are too vulnerable to negotiate any hint of untowardness, such as Skittles commercials, "Do the Dew," and Donkey Kong. This, in fact, is exactly what Miller argues.

A March 1998 study linking childhood obesity to television watching by children is the latest to fuel calls for more restrictions. The study found that 43 percent of African-American, 30 percent of Latino, and 20 percent of Euro-white children watch four or more hours of TV per day. Children who watched that much TV had 20 percent more body fat than low-viewing kids. Immediately the experts, such as sociologist Steven Gortmaker of the Harvard School of Public Health, blamed TV-watching for child obesity and demanded more controls. Forgotten is that correlation does not equal causation; it may be that other causes underlie both chunkiness and channel-surfing.[28]

TV could be the cause, but it's a weightier issue than that. Waistbands among American adults of all ages, particularly older and nonwhite ones, have ballooned more than they have among children. Today, among adults ages 20–74, 35 percent of whites, 42 percent of blacks, and 42 percent of Latinos are overweight, up one-fourth since the early 1980s. The proportion of teens ages 6–17 who are overweight: 11 percent for whites, 15 percent for blacks, and 15 percent for Latinos—a much slimmer percentage than that of adults of their races/ethnicities. Teens are the least likely to be overweight of any age group.[29] (Maybe that *is* because they watch the least TV!)

Growing rotundity is an American health threat to all ages. Its expansion occurred among all age groups simultaneously, suggesting common origin. If TV viewing is indeed the cause and restrictions are the answer, they should apply to all ages. It is unreasonable to demand that kids act better than their role models.

Obesity's opposite, anorexia and bulimia, are similarly blamed by media critics on cultural and media influences. The argument is an appealing one. The main sufferers from eating/starvation disorders are adolescent and young adult white females; the diseases rarely strikes women over age 25 or men. Incidence of anorexia and bulimia have increased in the past three decades. These afflictions involve obsession with body image and thinness—exactly the ideals promoted by the fashion industry. Thus, progressive media critics pin full blame for starvation disorders in young women on culture and fashion messages.

As plausible as this sounds, medical research has had great difficulty establishing it as more than speculative theory. "Fashion magazines and the like, with their depictions of the ideal woman as malnourished in appearance, undoubtedly exacerbate" women's dissatisfaction with body image, but that "hardly seems a complete explanation" for anorexia and bulimia, an extensive review of research concludes.[30] The greatest research-established commonality in anorexics and bulimics is family problems: over-controlling, over-protective, but emotionally absent parents who deny daughters the chance to develop as individuals.[31]

Starvation disorders may be rooted in recent decades' greater family breakup, parental abandonment, and the rise in arbitrary youth-control mechanisms that deny individuality, more than in fashion advertising per se. The emphasis on thinness in the American media is not new. An excellent compilation of pop-media images of adolescents in the 1930s, '40s, and '50s, *Teenage Confidential*, reveals pathologically thin nubiles in astonishing quantity, yet starvation disorders were rare in these decades.[32] A more complete explanation may be that modern teenage children of the growing ranks of problem adults are displaying behavior disorders, and opportunistic corporate promotions have arisen to suggest how that disorder should be expressed. A great deal more nuanced and sophisticated examination than simply calling young people weak and stupid is badly needed.

But to the cultural left, the symptoms of socioeconomic and family attrition against the young are bigger news than the attrition itself. An April 1998 *Nation* cover story, "Generation Wired," elevates the sins of corporate opportunism over those of societal oppression of youths in warning of "kids' newest drug of choice: caffeine:"

> The marketing strategy behind the new high-caffeine products is ingeniously suited to a generation confronting more family instability and a less secure job future, and dogged by stress and powerlessness.[33]

So kids are slamming The Dew, and teenagers (the article declares in tones Christian Temperance Unioners once applied of toddlers crawling whisky-soaked saloon floors) are sighted in...Starbucks. Medical experts (a profession whose dope addiction rate is many times worse than the general population's[34]) state that kids don't need another drug, given all today's stresses. It is implied that kids didn't used to drink coffee, that teenagers are simply manipulees of Madison Avenue caffiends, and that modern parents are blissfully unaware of their kids' caffeine inhalation. The insinuation is that ad-driven adolescents are driving increased soft drink consumption (in fact, soda swilling among all ages has doubled in the last two decades to over 50 gallons per person—two cans a day for each American ages five to 65). While teens consume more soft drinks, adults consume more coffee.

Caffeine in quantity has bad health effects, but this is elevating symptom above cause...WHO is causing that family instability, that poor job market, that disempowerment stressing today's kids? When is the matter of addicted parents abusing kids and busting up families going to be a regular progressive cover story? The cultural left seems far less concerned about kids' distress than the fact that corporate pleasure-dispensers might make a buck off it. Instead of oblique references to the real stresses kids face, the big emphasis seems to be compiling a growing list of products and activities whose consumption by young people should be severely regulated or forbidden—including television, movies, internet sites, advertising, coffee, soft drinks, sugar, alcohol, tobacco, and consumer spending. This crusade employs puritan tones, but it is not puritan. No criticism is directed at adult indulgence, even overindulgence, of the above products, except as the future consequence of adolescent excess.

Children and youth have an across-the-board right not to be made into negative symbols for larger social problems—especially not under the false banner of "protecting" them. Further, adults have a duty to take responsibility for adult misbehaviors and to quit blaming them on young people.

Cyberjake

The newest media debaucher is the Internet, which has stirred up a frenzy going light years beyond even TV violence. The visceral fear whipped up over imagined cyberduction of young minds and bodies by witches lurking in the dark woods of the Web has spawned a lockout and filtering industry whose sales will soon hit $75 million per year.[35] So blocked, filtered, and locked out is school Internet access that "the internet is now a useless tool for us," said one Los Angeles art teacher whose class can't even call up basic portfolios. Frustrated when its sweeping Communications Decency Act (and its $250,000 fines for transmitting even mild untowardness where minors might call it up) was struck down by the Supreme

Court in 1997, Congress (the Starr-report dispensers) now wants to use federal funds to force even more school censorship such as mandatory library blockers. An absurdly broad set of filtering systems ban student access from CNN, *USA Today*, scholarship information, and the Middlesex, Connecticut, website (zipped out of teenage purview because it contained That Word).

What is it that American adults are so petrified of? Yes, schools and businesses have an interest in keeping students and employees on task rather than browsing sports or porn sites, but that (as in any other kind of sluffing) is the job of supervision, not hysterically sweeping technical censorship. Two concerns drive what can only be called a national terror: pedophiles luring children via Internet contact, and corruption of youths through exposure to hard-core pornography or other untoward material.

The actual extent of abduction and molestation of young internetters via candyman.con appears minuscule. In 1995, the National Center for Missing and Exploited Children reported "ten or twelve" cases per year. The total to date is about 135—each of which seems to have been the subject of a "frightening new trend" news splash. Like school gunplay, Internet abduction "grabs headlines because it's so rare," criminologist Gregg McCrary of California's Threat Assessment Group said.[36] It's rare because the vast majority of kids are normal and have no interest in perverted new friends. Statistically, youths are far safer in front of an unregulated screen than with their parents, priest, or scout leader.

"Child sex cases over the Web are soaring, police say," the *LA Times* story headlined in July 1998. "There's been an explosion of these crimes," a police spokesman said. "Young people have been enticed to leave their homes," Police Chief Bernard Parks declared, arguing for more parental supervision. "In the first six months of this year, the LAPD has filed twice as many criminal Internet-related child exploitation cases as it did for all of last year," the story said, referring both to pedophile contacts with children and child pornography distribution. How many cases would that be? Sixteen, compared to eight in 1997.[37] Los Angeles is a city of 3.7 million people. There are several dozen child sexual abuse and exploitation cases involving parental offenders reported in the city every day.

So the physical threat posed by the Internet is much smaller than children face in dozens of unregulated areas of everyday life. What about spiritual corruption? True, the Internet makes explicitly violent, sexual, and demented material available to anyone who can click through a simple search. It seems that parents concerned about surfing by very young children could be served by filtering software even if it is overly censorious, on the grounds that six-year-olds probably aren't interested in the Middlesex, Connecticut, website anyway. Or setting the PC in the middle of the family room. For teenagers, I think the issue is the same as for adults: the large majority find Net wierdness amusing, briefly interesting, or disgusting, a small fraction are deeply affected. We think that the damage done to already off-kilter minds by cranium-spurting video-game gunning and Nazi child porn is obvious, but real-life killers who claim pop culture made 'em do it turn out to have unexpected media influences. Is there anyway for society to forestall a Charles Manson who hears murderous cryptics in Beatles songs about a roller coaster ride, an Arizona man who thought the Irish anthem-rock band U2 prompted him to shotgun a young actress with whom he was obsessed, or a teenager who hears suicidal cues from an Ozzy Ozbourne song warning about the dangers of alcoholism?

All I can say is that I worked a lot with kids for years and, while I met many whose misdeeds related to difficult family lives, I never met one whose bad behavior could be attributed to the media. (I am sure they exist, but they must be both rare and swayed by unpredictable influences.) Statistics also do not support the notion that the Net is sweeping youth to savagery. The 1990s period during which Internet access has exploded in American homes does not seem to coincide with any tangibly bad effects. Just the opposite. Among juveniles, rape and other sex offenses declined since 1990. In computer-infested California, juvenile sex offense rates fell by 25 percent from 1990 to 1997. Birth rates are down. Teenage murder's down. Suicide's down. Drunk driving's down. Drug abuse is down (among kids, not grownups). Binge drinking is down. Violent crime's down. Property crime's down. Misdemeanors are down. Car wrecks are down. Drownings are down. In 1997, California's juvenile rate of rape arrest reached its lowest level in 30 years, well below the rate of 1967. School attendance is up. SAT scores are up. No evidence of mass kiddie seduction to the Dark Side. Don't laugh—these are all the bad things that are supposed to go up when kids are exposed to some new kind of source of carnality. Imagine the histrionics if trends had gone the other way.

But because America's cyberphobia isn't really concerned with the welfare of kids, no one cares which way kid-trends actually go. Among leading scholar and tennis-shoed fanatic alike, youth "trends" are custom-manufactured to fit any argument. A nation which shrugs at 130,000 real, confirmed cases of sexual abuse of children by parents and caretakers every year is gripped in fear of a teenager witnessing sex steam on the monitor. Studies of teenagers' exposure to pornography find the same as for any other medium—the vast majority are unaffected even by hardcore stuff, and those who are have serious disturbances that pre-date the first porn sighting. The same is true of adults. And what are we to do about that messy reality that no matter what age limit is set for legal porn access, virtually all the pregnancies, sexual disease, and homicide among those younger than that age are caused by persons over that age?

As Jon Katz points out, mediaphobia left to right is "not concerned about real problems, but [is] an anxiety disorder, an increasingly irrational spiral of often unwarranted fears:"

> The Mediaphobe is frightened and angry. His fear transcends traditional social, cultural and political boundaries. You almost have to admire the unity fear can generate: Civil rights activists join forces with right-wing politicians; ex-hippies take up arms alongside Christian evangelists; a liberal boomer president stands shoulder to shoulder with his conservative challengers. A nation bitterly divided on an array of issues from gun control to Medicaid can unite on this: New media, popular culture, modern information technology—all of it endangers our young, corrodes our civic sphere, decivilizes us all.[38]

Katz rightly sees smug arrogance in the crusade to curb and censor. "Left to yourselves," he imagines the "superior culture" warrior telling the unwashed parent, "you'll read and watch moronic and pointless things and your children will go straight to screen hell." Worse, Big Media self-interest is threatened, which may explain the breathless hype of the terrors of unregulated cyberspace, its porn sites, its ultra-rare child seductions:

> For much of this century, news has been controlled by a handful of newspapers, newsmagazines and, more recently, broadcast networks...That has changed, suddenly and radically...[with] the Internet...there is more freedom of the press than journalists conceive of in their worst nightmares.

Katz expresses refreshing confidence in the ability of his 15-year-old daughter to negotiate the corruptions, charlatanisms, and boundless information and communication opportunities the Internet offers. I have full confidence in the youths I worked with, even the miscreants, to do the same, without lockouts and cluckings. The worse horror is that once more, adults have found a way to evade the overdue look at our own values.

There is something bizarre about how many aging sinners feel compelled to manufacture moral panics about teenagers. The Internet-censoring crusade is led by Gary Hart concubine Donna Rice. The execrable movie *Kids*, whose director, ex-violent-con Larry Clark, filmed his obsession of savagely lusty adolescence ("fucking in the backseat. Gangbangs...a little rape," he fantasized to one interviewer),[39] was loudly applauded as "realism" by the '90s kid-hating zeitgeist. Clinton and Gingrich exonerate their philandering by demanding teenage purity. Etc.

I admit bitterness. I was a volunteer appointee to Montana's Children's Trust Fund Board from 1989 to 1992, including one year as president. With the board, I lobbied the legislature and solicited private funds to prevent real child abuse. The response was a lot of sympathy and little money. Our budget, funded mainly by a voluntary state income tax checkoff, hung at about $50,000 per year, which wasn't enough (went our worn joke) to send every abused kid flowers. Yet sky-is-falling pop culture and Internet phobes can win sweepingly repressive legislation from Congress and legislatures in Pearl Harbor crisis mode. All state Children's Trust Fund budgets put together wouldn't approach that paid-for Internet and TV lockout software. Congress wanted to fine persons who provided Playboy to minors via the Internet up to $250,000. I couldn't even win a minor amendment to child pornography legislation assessing offenders $500 to pay for victims' mental health assessment.

With apologies to those few who've warred against both real and virtual child abuse, I do not believe the larger Internet-lockout campaign is sincerely aimed at protecting children. As with anti-drugs, -teen drinking, -TV-violence, and -pop culture hysteria, the purpose is to allow adults to take strident, risk-free moral stances while denying the realities of bad grownup values and conduct. The '90s-morality campaign is not puritanical. It seeks to preserve and reserve Internet porn (like alcohol, TV violence, consumption-promoting ads, and all manner of pop culture depravity) for adults—which is essentially what the Supreme Court ruling striking down the Communications Decency Act mandated. Since adults create their culture's values and behavior standards, the '90s-morality campaign is not about changing national values. It is about *not* changing them.

The real travesty is that the media and officials cooperate to limit and distort public information in order to achieve mutually beneficial goals, and this does affect public perception and values. Adolescents are victimized by bad public information. The media's damage to kids lies not in enticing them to vice, but in spreading lies about them. When the left demonizes kids, even and especially in the name of protecting them from evil corporate forces, it upholds the larger media lie.

Framing Youth

The systematic maligning of teenagers by the media has aroused progressive criticism. The March/April 1994 issue of *Extra!*, by Fairness and Accuracy in Reporting (FAIR), was dedicated to exposing the media scare campaign against youth. Progressive media critics Robin Templeton, Meda Chesney-Lind, Laura Flanders, and Janine Jackson have regularly examined press distortions of youth violence and teenage women's issues. Jon Katz's *Virtuous Reality* vigorously debunks the populist crusade to portray the Internet as deleting child morals. Various groups, such as Chicago's unfortunately-disbanded Youth Vision, have fought the print and airwave demonization of kids. This, it seems to me, is where the action is.

In 1995, Youth Vision held focus groups with 80 Chicago adults to explore the sources of adult hostility toward youths. Hostility there was. Adults overwhelmingly cited "gangs, drugs, sex, and a general feeling that youth are out of control," youth have no respect for adults (who did kids learn that from?), and teens in groups look threatening. Particularly negative attitudes were expressed toward urban black and Latino kids. "While some respondents attributed their negative perceptions of youth to personal experiences, most said that media (especially TV news) played a vital role in informing their opinions," Youth Vision found.[40]

As part of a class in survey work led by U.C. Irvine professor Mark Baldassare, a local consultant firm assembled similar focus groups of a couple of dozen Orange County citizens. Old, young, white, black, Latino, Asian, and affable, ready to unburden their opinions. My job was to inquire about citizen attitude on violent crime to shape questions for the 1997 Orange County Survey.

I asked them: How much of Orange County's violent crime do you think is caused by youths under the age of 18? The assembled bit into that one like pit bulls into a kitten. "Forty percent," guessed the 19-year-old student on my right. "Hell, 80 at least," the white-shocked senior next to her spat. I repeated "under age 18" at every chance. Estimates averaged 65 percent. These folks were rabid as no other topic had gotten them. "Why, you've got eight- and nine-year-olds out in our neighborhoods in Westminster with machine guns," an elderly black woman snapped to affirmative nods. "They're killing people."

Law enforcement reports show that youths under age 18 account for fewer than 13 percent of violent crime arrests and 10 percent of violent crime in the county. In a county of 2.6 million people, just 26 juveniles were arrested for murder in 1995, 11 in 1996, and 14 in 1997. No child under age 12 had been arrested for murder in the county in decades, if ever. Where was this well-educated group chosen to represent an affluent, low-crime county getting such wildly distorted ideas about youth violence?

Clue: when I asked, only one of the 12 had been personally victimized by a youth in any way. The victimization: the 19-year-old's white boyfriend, sitting in his car, was asked by a menacing Latino kid if he was "looking" at him. The boyfriend said uh, negatory. End of incident.

Was it just my imagination, or was violent crime by youths being drastically overplayed in the press? I stacked all 365 issues of the Orange County edition of the *Los Angeles Times*, local edition of the nation's fourth largest newspaper, in my living room throughout 1997. I and volunteers at the Los Angeles National Conference for Communities and Justice (formerly of Christians and Jews) clipped all stories, no matter how small, on violence, other crime, drugs, sex and pregnancy, and media issues regardless of age, and all other stories in any way concerning youths.

This being L.A., clippings from the paper's first six months yielded nearly 500 stories on violent crime. Of these, 200 stories covered 118 murder cases (the Oklahoma City bombing, Ennis Cosby's slaying, and the North Hollywood bank robbery generated a number of stories each). In addition, there were 62 stories which concerned L.A.-area violent crime as a public issue.

We classified murder stories as "youth" if they explicitly cited the age of the arrestee as under 18 or (if no age was cited) used "gang" or "youth gang" descriptions without mentioning adults. A homicide story was classed as "adult" if the offender age provided was over 18, or (if no age was specified) the story concerned domestic violence or child abuse. Table 2 shows how youth violence was depicted in the newspaper versus its reality from law enforcement records for 1995–96.

Law enforcement reports show that youths under age 18 comprise 16 percent of the murder arrestees and commit 9 percent of the county's murders. But in the largest newspaper, youths account for 24 percent of the murder arrestees reported and 17 percent of the stories on murder incidents. The bottom line: compared to adult murderers, youth murderers are three times more likely to have their deeds reported in the press.

Could this surplus be because youth violence is more heinous and injures or kills more victims? Just the opposite. Both law enforcement records and news stories show the average adult murderer killed 1.5 times more victims than the average youth murderer. Thus youths were over-represented in news stories even though they committed lesser offenses.

But the *Times'* over-reporting of youth incidents of *individual* murder incidents paled in comparison to reporting of youth violence as a *public issue* (Table 3). Public issue stories were classified as "youth" if they dealt only with youth, juvenile, or youth gang issues, and as "adult" if they concerned only adult crime issues such as domestic violence, child abuse, or Megan's Law (registering sex offenders). The controversy over Megan's Law generated nearly all the "adult crime" issue stories.

By the most conservative measure, media reporting on youth murder and violence as a policy issue was *triple* what youths' contribution to violence arrests would warrant, *five times* more than youths' contribution to the volume of homicide merited, and *nine times* more than adult violence as an issue. Compared to coverage of adult violence as a public issue, youth violence was reported as public issue 18 times more than the youth contribution to the murder toll would warrant. Indeed, youths accounted for 16 percent of murder arrests and 9 percent of homicides, but

Table 2

The *Times'* stories overplay youth murder
and underplay adult murder

Youth murder arrests and victims as a percent of total murders:	Arrestees	Victims
As portrayed in news stories	23.9%	16.9%
As shown in police reports	15.8%	9.1%
Adult murder arrests and victims as a percent of total murders:		
As portrayed in news stories	72.3%	68.6%
As shown in police reports	84.2%	90.9%
Ratio of murder stories to real murders:		
Youth	2.84	1.75
Adults	0.90	0.86
Odds, youth vs adult	3.2	2.0
Total stories	155	172

Source: author's/National Conference's study of *Los Angeles Times* stories, 6 months, 1997.

48 percent of the stories on violence as a public issue (64 percent where an age group is specified).

Adding national crime and violence stories yielded the same picture. The press overplays youth violence three to 20 times more than youths' contribution to the murder arrest and volume would predict.

Could this be because youth violence had risen dramatically in the Los Angeles area? No. Teen violent crime rose less than adult violent crime over the last 10 to 20 years and had been declining for six years. Were teens accounting for a terrible murder toll, then? No. The juvenile homicide rate had plummeted by 75 percent over the previous seven years, the largest decline of any group. Was it because crime reports were just too hard for the average news reporters to read? No. The *Times* and rival *Orange County Register* repeatedly presented detailed, front-page charts carefully selecting certain measures of youth crime to "demonstrate" an increase, showing that reporters understood the state Department of Justice's clear and readable figures.

I invite readers to compare the press coverage given youth-perpetrated crimes with that given similar or worse adult-perpetrated crimes in their own communities. *Times* reports were typical of the print media nationally and mild compared to the broadcast news. A 1997 study by the Berkeley Media Studies Group found two-

Table 3		
Times **stories on violence as a public issue overplay "youth violence" even more drastically**		
	Los Angeles Area	National
Youth violence	48.4%	43.9%
Adult violence	27.4	17.1
Violence, age not specified	24.2	39.0
Percent of violence stories on youth:		
- versus youth arrestees	3.1	2.9
- versus youth murders	5.3	5.0
- versus adult arrestees	9.5	14.4
- versus adult murders	17.6	26.7
Total issue stories	62	41

Source: author's/National Conference's study of *Los Angeles Times* stories, 6 months, 1997.

thirds of the news reports on violence on California's major television stations involved youths or young adults.[41] In a standard example, Cox Communications incessantly broadcast a 1996 documentary, "Lost Future," on the locally infamous 1993 San Clemente paint-roller murder. This killing resulted after a highly disputed beach confrontation in which a Latino youth threw a sharpened paint roller which, in what authorities called a "freak accident," killed a white youth. By the time the case got to trial, the six Latino youths in the altercation had been branded "gang members" and were convicted of manslaughter and second-degree murder.

Cox's documentary went for emotional blood. It claimed that 78 Orange County youths were murdered by other youths in 1993—which works out to one every four and a half days. It ended with a faces-in-the-clouds scene of pictures of several of the murdered "children." "The fact is, kids are killing kids," video producer Phil Martin of Charter Communications told the *Times Orange County*,[42] which repeated the video's figure without checking it.

A simple call to the state Department of Health Services would have shown that a total of thirty-nine Orange County kids ages zero to eighteen were murdered in 1993 by assailants of all ages. State crime figures show that around three-fourths of murdered children and youths are killed by adults, not other "kids." Thus the Cox video's claim was at a bare minimum double, and probably five to 10 times, the true total. Even after I and editors for the alternative paper, *Orange County Weekly*, reported on the impossibility of the documentary's figures—to say nothing of its inflammatory nature in a county undergoing difficult racial transition—Cox continued to run it without correction.

The demonization of youth has become a deadly issue. A 1996 RAND Institute survey found respondents estimating that kids accounted for half the violent crime in America, with one-fourth fearful that a violent kid had their number.[43] A September 1994 Gallup Poll found an angry public convinced that youths commit three times more violent crime than they do, contributing to majority public support for executing juveniles.[44] Chesney-Lind's 1997 study[45] found that while the rate of Hawai'i youths arrested for serious offenses continued its decline begun in the previous decade, and gang activity in Hawai'i showed little change from 1992 to 1996, the press's reporting on "youth crime" and "gangs" jumped 10-fold in the last four years.

These findings should have brought winces of shame to editors at *Time*, *Newsweek*, CNN, ABC, CBS, NBC, the *Los Angeles Times*, *New York Times*, *Washington Post*, *People*, and other mass implements of instruction—the same way students' low test scores shame local schools. But media's only reform was to step up the frantic campaign to depict all youth—a group which accounts for 13 percent of violent offenses and 8 percent of murders—as savage slaughterers of American life.

Dissin'

The June 23, 1997, cover of *People* Magazine blared, "Heartbreaking Crimes: KIDS Without a Conscience?" High-school yearbook photos of four white and one black youth adorned. Inside, we learned that "in the last decade, the number of murders committed by teenagers leaped from roughly 1,000 a year to nearly 4,000:"

> Worrisome as that trend may be, a fleeting glance at recent headlines—announcing that, in Texas, a teenage couple, formerly students at U.S. military academies, will soon stand trial for the carefully plotted murder of a girl who interrupted the smooth course of their love affair or that, in New Jersey, an 18-year-old high school senior delivered a baby while attending her prom, left the infant in the trash, and returned to the dance—suggests some teens these days are also committing crimes of incomprehensible callousness.

The article illustrated to perfection the new media youth-crime scam:

- Statistics of the 1980s and early '90s homicide increase among nonwhite, inner-city youths are used to provide a scary "numbers" backdrop.

- Anecdotes ("a fleeting glance at recent headlines") of wealthier, mostly white youth killings are used to provide the gore-streaked "human face" and to dismiss the notion that socioeconomic conditions could have anything to do with the greater numbers of murders shown by statistics.

- Exaggerations are employed at every juncture, usually so wild that they add up to outright lying.

People's statistics, presented in large headlines, were meticulously inflated. According to FBI statistics on murder clearances, juveniles accounted for an average of 1,300 murder arrests and 1,000 murders every year in the early 1980s.[46] In the peak year of 1994, juveniles accounted for 3,200 murder arrests and 2,500 murders—nowhere near "nearly 4,000." In 1996, juveniles accounted for 2,400 murder arrests and 1,700 murders, half the number *People* reported as the current level. The rate of juvenile homicide commission in 1996 was about 33 percent above the 1980 level and 65 percent above the 1985 level—far below the four-fold "leap" implied by the magazine. This is noted because *People*'s reporters-without-a-conscience would have to have been intimately familiar with the numbers in order to distort them in this fashion.

Next came the designated moral heavy hitter, New York psychologist Michael Shulman, to discount poverty, broken homes, and physical, psychological, and sexual abuse as "hollow" explanations for such crimes. *People* assured us he was right, as proven by the "variety of backgrounds" of the nine alleged killers ages 15 to 19 they squibbed.

True, in its December 15, 1997, issue, *People* ran an 11-page feature on the "national nightmare" of child abuse.[47] "The reality of child abuse is more disturbing than even the most lurid headlines," it wrote. Instead of detailing the effect of abuse on kids, the feature focused on the heroism of the social workers who investigate it. While all economic backgrounds experience child abuse, it is most prevalent among the poor and unemployed, the story said. There were no sweeping statements implying that "parents these days" increasingly were "without a conscience" and guilty of "incomprehensible callousness."

However, when teenagers were the subject, the magazine's message was that all kids everywhere were killer Chuckies. Eight of the nine cases *People* selected involved upscale kids (seven whites and one Latino). One was an inner-city black. The events spanned a seven-month period from November 1996 to June 1997 and locales 3,000 miles apart, from Southern California to northwestern Washington to New York City. Although the article was titled "WHY Are Kids Killing?" only two of the nine were juveniles. Given seven months, an entire nation, and 25 million subjects to extract a few grisly killings from, *People* could have depicted any group in society as steely-eyed maniacs.

"Teens these days...committing crimes of incomprehensible callousness," *People*'s shrieker, is a shopworn media rerun. For example, *Newsweek*'s cover story of September 6, 1954, "Our Vicious Young Hoodlums," deplored "the national teenage problem," an "orgy of crime...shocking...growing more and more common every year." The article pictured four white youths ages 15 to 18 who admitted horsewhipping and setting fire to New York parkgoers, killing two "slowly and painfully." Their leader called the murders "my supreme adventure." Another teen gunman was quoted declaring, "I just get a kick out of it when I see blood running." The reporters roamed the nation, citing teen shootings, beatings, and rapes by punks as young as 10 from Gardena, California, to Atlanta and New York, just the worst of the million kids "in trouble with the police every year." *Newsweek*'s language of panic about all teens, blaming television and "salacious, sadistic" pop culture ("horror comics" in this case), and sweeping aside of factors like poverty and violent homes, was identical to the format of *People*'s and those of other media of the 1990s. As with "kids and heroin," some editor should copyright the formula to cash in on the next round.

In May 1997, there was a gun carnage with all the elements of national media and politician fodder (except one).[48] Media lure Number One: Affluent, Pastoral

White Setting Where Things Like This Do Not Happen. It occurred in the wealthy, suburban towns of Ojai and Simi Valley, California, the latter of which had been cited by crime officials as the safest city in the nation. Media lure Two: Copious Blood, Child Bodies, and Tears. It involved public gun slaughters that killed seven people, including three children, their mother, and another mother in front her screaming three-year-old son. Media lure Three: Shocking New Trend. It involved separate killing sprees five days apart which were so brutal that veteran police officers and paramedics required counseling.

It got zero national attention and only one regional analysis. Why? The gunners were ages 43 and 44, not 13 and 14. Contrast this with CNN's continuous, on-the-scene coverage of the Springfield, Oregon, school cafeteria shootings by a 15-year-old, which killed four—two students and his parents. For days, CNN headlined the Oregon shootings. But the network's March 25 news analysis gave a totally different picture, indicated by its title: "School shootings have a high profile but occur infrequently." Question for CNN: who's giving what the news analysis called "rare" school shootings such a high profile? The "media paradox:" could the *infrequency* of school massacres be the *reason* for their high profile? Could the relative *commonality* of adult rage killings and murders of kids be the reason the media treats them nonchalantly?

One of *People*'s cover-storied "kids without a conscience," Jeremy Strohmeyer, illustrates the media stampede not just to feature "killer honor students," but obfuscate even the most obvious facts that get in the way of insinuating that every American kid is a millimeter from mayhem. Strohmeyer, a Long Beach 18-year-old, was charged with (and later admitted) sexually assaulting and brutally suffocating seven-year-old Sherrice Iverson in a Las Vegas casino bathroom in May 1997. Topping the media parade was the *Los Angeles Times*' Sunday, July 19, 1998, front-page spread, which continued through three full inside pages.[49] It detailed his good student record which evaporated in an apparently baffling attraction to the "darker world" of drugs, alcohol, pornography, and violence. 'Way 'way down in the story we read in a couple of brief sentences that Strohmeyer's biological father was a chronic prison inmate serving lengthy terms for felony drug offenses. His biological mother was an addict, diagnosed as schizophrenic, unable to care for herself, and confined to a psychiatric hospital. His brother, like Jeremy taken from his parents and sent to a foster home, also displayed emotional troubles.

We might start with the working hypothesis that Strohmeyer's "fractured life" might have roots in mental illness (schizophrenia literally means "fractured brain") and addiction. But the newspaper story preferred to depict his obsession with booze and cyberporn as typical, inexplicable adolescent rebellion which the everyparent's honor student might choose next. Another advantage of the Strohmeyer story was that *People* and other mainstream media got to express concern about the death of a black child murdered by a white teenager that they never would have expressed if she had been killed by a black youth or (especially) by an adult. It is difficult to imagine the *Times* expending the same journalistic energy it does exhaustively profiling the region's handful of white teenage killers on the scores of black or Latino youths accused of homicide every year, who usually merit but a paragraph or two.

In fact, the media is missing a huge story. Strohmeyer was one of just five white Los Angeles/Long Beach youths arrested for murder in 1997 in neighbor cities housing four million people, the newest Criminal Justice Statistics Center printout showed. Of California's 1.5 million white teens, only 27 were arrested for homicide in 1997. In sprawling Los Angeles, just one—ONE—white teenager was arrested for rape. Just 42 for burglary—fewer than one a week. Felony offenses by white L.A. kids were down 10 percent in 1997 compared to 1996. None of this made a shred of conventional sense, especially since there was yet another leap in felony offenses by white adults—led by white adults in Los Angeles.

Strohmeyer's brutality deserved attention, but it also deserved perspective. The media does not dwell in similar fashion on the far more numerous crop of murderous-adult stories such as the following: "Prosecutors filed murder charges against a 34-year-old woman for allegedly suffocating her four young daughters and trying to cover up the killings by setting her house on fire."[50] The *Times* stories on the murders of these children, ages five, seven, 11 and 12, in the mountain suburb of Santa Clarita appeared just a few days before the mammoth Strohmeyer spread. It occupied but a few, below-the-fold inches.

And that was whopping compared to the second-section, inner-page bit three weeks earlier on June 25, headlined, "Mission Viejo mom held in son's death." Consider the press pandemonium that would erupt if (say) a 15-year-old boy in Mission Viejo, California, a wealthy Orange County enclave, murdered an infant. Now, consider the press treatment of the following:

> An Orange County woman was arrested on suspicion of aggravated murder in the death of her 17-month-old son. Alexander Sohel Kashefi suffered wounds to his stomach, most likely caused by a sharp instrument, police said. The boy's mother, Marieluise Kashefi, 36, of Mission Viejo was held without bail.[51]

Front page? Major feature? CNN continuous coverage, Oval Office lamentation? Dream on. No one important saw a single poll point, newspaper sale, rating, or grant-whoring advantage to be gained by publicizing the demise of Alexander Sohel. You just read two-thirds of the story, a fingernail squib at the bottom of page A18 of the *Times Orange County*, the *local* paper.

Also scant was the press mention of a 42-year-old Watts father who killed his wife and daughter a few days later. When a 40-year-old South Bay, California, father massacred his three kids, ages four, 10, and 13, and wife with a .357 magnum handgun on August 4, it finally caught the *Times*' notice (in a bottom-of-page-three story) that these "rampages" in which "entire families have been wiped out" appeared to be a rising pattern.[52] In just 10 weeks, southern California alone had seen more kids killed in family violence than in 10 months of school murders nationwide.

What charlatanism America's "caring about children" turns out to be when the circumstances of a kid-killing event aren't suitable for political exploitation. No wonder the public thinks teenagers are rampaging while grownups are meek and mild—the press is presenting a systematically false image. When the nation and our leaders are as horrified by the Simi Valleys, Daly Citys, South Bays, Santa Claritas, and Westons—where a total of 18 kids were murdered by parents in multiple slayings in the last year—as we are about the Pearls, Paducahs, Edinboros, Jonesboros, and Springfields, we can claim that our concern is really about kids.

The society-wide indifference to injury and death inflicted on children in domestic violence lends support to Lucia Hodgson's view that Americans see children as akin to the property of their parents.[53] When a child dies, the parents understandably are viewed as the victims, receiving an outpouring of sympathy after such tragedies as the Jonesboro killings or stranger abduction-murders such as that of Polly Klaas. But when parents kill their children, there is rarely any similar public or presidential attention since the child, being property, is not afforded independent sympathy or concern. Even the rare exceptions, such as the media attention focused on Union, South Carolina, mother Susan Smith's drowning of her small children in 1995, resulted from Smith's initial claim that her kids were abducted by a black gunman—again, the suburban parent's nightmare.

Teenagers are chosen for media stigma because they are the officially-designated scapegoat of the '90s, and media conformity is sadly predictable. (Even sadder, *People*'s statistical shenanigans were no worse than those perpetrated by top crime scholars and agency officials). The question is why the magazine—like the press in general—increasingly chooses mostly affluent, white kids rather than inner-city dark ones to illustrate their "killer kid" splashes.

An answer to that question can be found in the September 4, 1997, and October 1, 1998, *Rolling Stones*.[54] The former issue featured yet another installment in its long-running series on Upscale Suburban Teen Devil-Cult Cheerleader Stone-Killer Slut Posses. In a decently-premised piece on four affluent Agoura Hills, California, boys given life sentences for a freak pocket-knife stabbing murder, crime specialist Randall Sullivan disgorged the obligatory '90s "family values" sermonette on today's youth generation gone to hell:

> Most adults couldn't quite comprehend that their teenage children lived in a community where almost everybody was in trouble with the law at one time or another, where "good kids" were largely a figment of their parents' imagination.
>
> A cultural climate that fostered freedom from inhibition also had produced a kind of generational disorientation. Did somebody out there believe these kids were watching *Pulp Fiction* 10, 15, 20 times to be instructed or uplifted? It had to mean something that during the 1995–96 academic year, teenagers profiled by the annual edition of *Who's Who Among American High School Students* had for the first time in the publication's history listed "decline of moral values" as their chief concern.

Quickie reminder: this is *Rolling Stone*, the journal of pop culture record, sower of the "cultural climate of freedom from inhibition," moralizing about teenagers watching *Pulp Fiction*? The magazine that recently featured a star-studded tribute to Alan Ginsburg, the beat poet who proudly had sex with juvenile boys? The magazine that effuses a tolerant drug-sex hipness amid a torrent of tobacco, booze, and high-fashion ads? Whose cover was graced by the stars of the selfsame pulp movie hits, with the likes of Janet Jackson, Winona Ryder, and Jennifer Aniston nude or semi-nude? Whose corporate attitude that women are the subtraction of their clothes was reflected in editor Robert Love's comment after Wal-Mart (that arbiter of family morals, which gladly purveys cigarettes and raunchy blood-dripping pop-novels), Kmart, Target, Stop & Shop, and other chains refused to stock the magazine's August 1998 "hot issue" issue flaunting a model au naturel: "This was a strategic idea of pushing the envelope" to boost flagging newsstand sales?[55] Whose ad and article images are fully consistent with the magazine's own 1988 poll showed its unrepentant Baby-Boom readership rife with extramarital sex, drugs, abortion, and drunken driving?[56]

Let us tour a recent *Rolling Stone* at random (Issue 792, August 6, 1998). The inside cover is graced with a full two-page ad showing a guy wearing Ralph Lauren Polo Jeans pushing a boat in a reedy marsh. Next is another full two-page ad showing a purple rabbit's foot and promoting Winston "straight up" cigarettes. The fifth and sixth pages are yet another two-pager showing four clothed women laughing at three butt-naked streaking men carrying Abercrombie & Fitch boxers. Yet another double-spread advertises the movie *Lolita* for Showtime, showing crimson-lips and captioned "No Limits." (Finally, on page 15, we get to see the table of contents.) Next is a two-page orgy-scene warning, "Viewer discretion advised: Unassigned Seating, Male Cellulite, Condiment Abuse," all on behalf of Camel Lights. Then, after letters to the editor, there is a full page ad for Smirnoff vodka. Two pages out of 20 have anything other than ads, a ratio that diminishes only a bit further on. There is a big Kool insert in which the cigarette company hawks its search for new bands. A multi-racial Tommy perfume ad follows. Next is an ad for MTV depicting cloven, barely-tethered mammaries, no caption. Ralph Lauren is back a few pages later, with a football hunk displaying Chaps. Merit cigarettes check in with a full-pager promising free gifts. A *Rolling Stone* insert advertises itself via model in tiny pink crotch frill, arms crossed over bare breasts ("Special Double Issue"). This common theme continues in the full-page "got milk?" promo, which features a sultry oscura's jutting, laced accoutrements and the caption, "revealing outfits and the undead. What else can't young guys get enough of? Calcium." Virginia Slims promises more gifts in another full page "light up the night" display, featuring a "hot nights lighter" and "unexpected evening bag." A two-page caricature of Keyshawn Johnson sporting Mr. T countenance sells "Voooooosh!!" Adidas. Bacardi chips in with a full page showing a couple of hefty drinks surrounding a blue-eyed dreadlocked bongo player: "deadlines by day, Bacardi by night." A guy suspended upside down pushes underwear: "I love hanging fruit." Lucky Strike gets its page, showing white toughoids leering from a fire escape. Red Kamel Lites dedicates its page to a Pamela Anderson futurism, whose flourishing exhale just happens to thrust out the red pack angling from the netherwear. (Nicorette and the American Cancer Society also bought a page, listing sexless points for quitting.) Geoffrey Moore briefs and Captain Morgan Rum are the unlikely team on another full page. Marlboro captures the back cover with a blurred image of the Cowboy (didn't he get retired?). This is a thin issue, partly because the fashion section promulgating thousand-dollar duds is not scheduled. In 90 pages, 43 are completely ads, 11 are partly so, and there are six commercial inserts totaling 14 pages (and the magazine still costs three bucks!). With a few lightweight exceptions, none gives readers any intellectual reason to smoke, drink, drive, or don their products other than you-are-what-you-consume slogans and imaging. One would guess that *Rolling Stone* editors and advertisers, if there is a difference, consider their readers to be as abysmally shallow as Channel One advertisers consider schoolkids. Would that political writer and corporate-power critic William Greider train his fine analytical scope on the deterioration of his own magazine.

The point I make is not to raise counter-priggishness (I'm an admirer of Howl poet Ginsburg, and I don't care if *RS* peddles its "hot issue" at Chuck E Cheese). Rather, how on earth could this mindless-ad-stuffed, pop culture-lionizing Voice of the Baby Boom wax in indignant prudery over the morals of kids?

And wax they do. Here is *Rolling Stone* founder and publisher Jann Wenner, pitching his May 1998 ABC special, "Where It's At," on "youth culture" (whatever that is), featuring over-30 rock stars lecturing teenagers on morals.[57] Age is the font of sensible attitude, Wenner backpats his generation. Thirty-three-year-old actress Rosie Perez's acumen ("You don't *have* to have sex. Why don't they tell *that* to young people?") is contrasted with that of a tequila-smashed 20-year-old who doesn't care about condoms. (The only time I saw Rosie perform, she told big-boob jokes.) "Youth plus alcohol doesn't equal wisdom," Wenner adds, as usual failing to mention that his own wizened age (52) is more dangerous with a drink than high school juniors, or that his own magazine rakes in jillions from pages of 86-proof advertising behind covers of semi-nude starlets. "Rosie has been around longer, she is more experienced, more thoughtful," Wenner declared, as if her and his witless clichés about teenage sex and drinking evidenced thought. It is exactly the Wenner-style exploitation of purity-for-image and T&A-for-profit that the next generation would serve us all by rejecting.

And why the sermonette from Randall Sullivan about a few suburban stoners with curfew violations and a pop-movie habit? Why, Nineties parents just don't understand "the way the world had changed," Sullivan's article on the Agoura Hills killing prissed. Changed? Why, yes it had. As noted, today's L.A. suburban kids are 40 PERCENT LESS drug- and arrest-prone than their parents were as kids in the 1970s. Agoura Hills police records show that out of 2,500 youths ages 10–17, just 72 were arrested in 1995 for any kind of offense.[58] This hardly adds up to a generation in mass wastage.

And no, it doesn't have to mean anything that a group of students hand-picked by an elite "Who's Who" panel declared (like adults have in *every* pontification on the subject I've found back to Greek poet Hesiod's in 700 BC) that moral values today are going to hell. Had Sullivan done some homework, he would have found many more meaningful superlatives to characterize the modern generation, as have been listed throughout this book.

What Sullivan and those who intimate that "today's kids" violate adult sensibilities can't seem to comprehend is the way the grownup world has changed. It is adult violence and drug abuse that has skyrocketed. Even Sullivan's innocent Agoura Hills parents who just "couldn't comprehend" today's teenage evil turn out to be mass-divorced customers who berated their kids as "fucking nothings" and "little bastards" and busted their noses.

The larger point of the *Rolling Stone* piece was to express outrage at the "lynching" meted out to a small clique of suburban wastoids whose bleary clubhouse fist-fight climaxed in a tragic freak-death. The deceased happened to be a cop's son. Three teens were sentenced to life in prison without parole and the fourth, 15 at the time of the crime, to 25-years-to-life. Sentencing Judge Mira handed out his own sermon:

> I believe that on this tragic day [that the defendants] formed their own gang. The genesis of this group was in their lifestyle, their aimlessness, their purposelessness. They didn't take their education seriously; they rejected their families' values. They adopted a we-do-whatever-feels-good-for-us attitude. That is classic hedonism.

Isn't this only slightly stronger than Sullivan's own condemnation? Is it so incomprehensible that an ambitious, at-loose-ends judge would hand out the sternest medicine? To deter an entire generation that everyone seems to agree is in utter dissolution, right in the vital coccyx of suburbia? The reason Judge Mira tossed the book at them is the same reason *Rolling Stone* covered the story—these are *our* kids who must be put away to protect *us*.

Sullivan's us-versus-them moralizing adds to the very climate of adult anger and repression against all adolescents that produced the harsh life-sentences he deplores. Though demurring that the four youths were made "victims of our political times," Sullivan's article explicitly endorsed the damaging, larger view that today's kids really are "fucking nothings."

Drive-By Journalism

Even given my complete disillusion with a magazine I used to admire and subscribe to, I was unprepared for Sullivan's diatribe against young people in his two-part series, "Death in the Schoolyard," in the September 17 and October 1, 1998, issues of *Rolling Stone*. Inside yet more busty covers (Janet Jackson's sprawling set hawking the mag again), Sullivan flatly blamed the entire younger generation mesmerized by violent television for the five school recent shootings, most explicitly the Springfield, Oregon, school cafeteria slaughter. There was no pretense at fact or fairness, not a shred of honest introspection, in Sullivan's lie-upon-lie attack on the supposed mass violence and immorality of middle-class youth and accolades to smug grownups.

Continuing Sullivan's long-standing preoccupation, a few Extreme White Youth were commodified as horror-entertainment for hip readers in the same manner as a Freddy Krueger or Gothic pop star. His specialty has been profiling weird, vanishingly uncommon atrocities by the upscale Caucasian young, beginning with what his editors lauded as "*River's Edge* theory of reporting" on a cheerleader murdered by a pampered Orinda, California, high schooler in 1984. Wrong. The fine Tim Hunter film, *The River's Edge*, was incisive because it depicted confused youths, paralyzed when harsh dilemmas intrude, as junior permutations of the equally clue-challenged grownups around them. In contrast, Sullivan's journalism is dedicated to enshrining *Rolling Stone*'s yuppie readers as exemplary, too-generous adults menaced by "our children…the most damaged and disturbed generation the country has ever produced."

Instead of doing the homework necessary to select and report on cases that illuminate real national trends, Sullivan and similar glam-journalists gravitate toward rare, high-profile incidents whose larger significance, minimal in reality, is manufactured by the reporter. Because school killings are extremely unusual and by no means increasing, and because youth murders of any kind come decades apart in places like Agoura Hills, Orinda, or Springfield, their prominence stems from the ephemeral agendas of powerful interest groups which, in turn, govern the priorities of *Rolling Stone*, Sullivan, and other mainstream reporters.

Sullivan's "evidence" for youth apocalypse consisted of ascribing profound insight to the hackneyed complaints of grownups fulsome in praise for themselves and contempt for kids: 90 percent of kids in my day were good, 90 percent of kids today are bad; the whole problem is just "the way kids today are acting;" modern middle-class youth are "spoiled, nasty, misbehaving, and off-the-wall bad," etc. etc. This is the same kind of perpetual youth-bashing found just about word for word in any era.

I (don't) hate to break this to Oregon native Sullivan and his angelic adult quotees, but the murder rate among white teenagers (the only race of youth Sullivan cares about) in Oregon was exactly the same in the 1970s and 1980s as it is in the 1990s—as is true of other states whose populations are dominated by Euro-whites. (Murders among nonwhite Oregon teens quadrupled during that period, but are still rare.) Further, given his claims that self-destructive behaviors have risen among teens, the death-record shows that his own Oregon Boomer adolescents of the '70s sported violent fatality rates 40 percent higher than teens of the '90s—figures similar to those nationwide. To wit: in teenage populations identical in size (220,000), 498 Oregon teens died by violent means in 1974–75, compared to 359 in 1994–95. These facts took about 10 minutes to retrieve from standard mortality data bases,[59] an endeavor that doesn't seem too much to expect from the crackerjack crime expert, editors, and fact-checkers for a national magazine, circulation 1.3 million.

But clearly, Sullivan and his editors don't care. They are not interested in reality or introspection or insight about their own generation, but in self-justification. They care about homicide only when it affects their own comfortable society. They are thoroughly desensitized to the thousands of kids killed by parents—an event the Bureau of Justice Statistics' *Murder in Families* reports is six times more likely than the rare cases of kids killing parents. *Rolling Stone*'s hysterical slashings emerged at the crucial point of congressional consideration of legislation mandating that all youths 13 and older be tried in adult courts at the federal level and offering millions of dollars to bribe states to do likewise. Once again: these are the *liberals*, more vicious than Rush Limbaugh when it comes to youth, doing the worst damage.

Sullivan's aggressive anger at teenagers, and *Rolling Stone*'s editors' judgment to run such a biased piece in today's punitive anti-youth climate, is deeply disturbing evidence of their own ethical vacuity. At one point, Sullivan berates several Springfield students who, understandably guarded in answering a stranger's questions about their school's nationally spotlighted tragedy, offend his moral nostrils because they seem insufficiently full of hatred toward the killer. This condemnation from a writer who, privileged to express his views in one of America's most prominent forums, has never so much as admitted the violence and disarray in his own parental generation. Is Sullivan outraged by 30- and 40-age adults who gun down their families, duct-tape their daughters' faces, feed their infant to rats?

He dismisses in brief sentences the fact that the student gunman had been prescribed Prozac for depression, a drug strongly linked to suicidal and violent behavior in certain individuals.[60] He claims that youths are increasingly "desensitized" and "numb" to violence, as if a stranger breezing into this or that bloody suburb of the day and breezing out after a few interviews could possibly make such a slapdash judgment about youths everywhere, or even there. Nothing is allowed to interfere with Sullivan's pop-illogic that if the Springfield cafeteria killer can be proven an average, all-American kid, then *any* average, all-American kid can be a mass slayer, and, by extension, *all* average, all-American kids are murderous.

Sullivan also dismisses poverty and family abuses and instead blames TV violence as "the most corrosive of all factors" in causing violent teens. Sullivan spends a page touting the loony theory of West Point psychology professor Dave Grossman that "television is a greater factor in this increased degree of violence than all other factors combined." For starters, it would be tough to explain the black youth homicide rate, 10 to 40 times higher (depending on time and place) than that of whites, by TV puppetry. But Sullivan's writings betray not a shred of concern about black or poor kids or kids who grow up in violent, abusive households.

"It isn't the glassy-eyed, stone-hearted products of abuse and neglect who most frighten and outrage adults these days," he writes, "but rather the middle-class kids." Sullivan, whose reporting along with that of most of the rest of the mainstream media has systematically misled the public for a decade and a half about America's real youth-crime issues, now cites the fears of a misled public as vindicating his reporting. Sullivan's piece came the same month that new figures in California (the quintessentially TV-saturated state) showed the rate of serious, felony (and also misdemeanor) crime by youths in 1997 dropped to its lowest point since the first statistics were assembled 25 years ago, including an astonishing 56 percent drop in teen homicides since 1990. With regard to the middle- and upper-class kids Sullivan disparaged, the murder rate by California's white youth now stands at *less than half* its 1975 level; white teens today are less likely to commit murder than teenagers in Canada; and white students reported less violence in school to *Monitoring the Future*'s latest, 1996 survey than to its first survey in 1976.

In short, if Sullivan and other pop-media luminaries aspired to a higher goal than journalistic sycophancy, they might raise a fascinating counterpoint: kids are *better* behaved today than in the last generation, and they watch a lot *less* TV! 'Tis true: Neilsen Media Research surveys show the average 12–17 year-old two decades ago watched TV more than 20 hours per week; the average teen of the mid-1990s, about 12 hours.[61]

Virtually every relevant measure (all selectively excluded from *Rolling Stone*'s and other media hatchet jobs) shows kids today are much better behaved than their Baby Boom detractors were as kids in the 1970s and are as adults in the 1990s, yet the attack on the next generation by ill-motivated grownups only gets more frenzied with every passing month. In truth, it is the moral emptiness of the *Rolling Stone* editors, the Sullivans, and similarly enlightened scribes who, indifferent to the economic thrashings and family beatings millions of youth suffer, instead quest for self-flattery embodied in lambasting the latest, all-the-rage Melrose Place gunner.

Set-Up

The extremes to which the mainstream media can go to turn even the worst adult egregiosities into a mere teenage attitude problem were exemplified (among many examples) by the *Los Angeles Times*' Sunday, April 5, 1998, front-page profile on "Chad MacDonald's Short, Tragic Life." Here was a story to upset anyone's notion of the new age-obsessed politics.

The battered, strangled, slashed body of Chad MacDonald, age 17, was found in a Los Angeles alley in March 1998. Arrested in the murder of the white, suburban Yorba Linda teenager were three sinister-pictured south-L.A. Latinos, ages 28, 21, and 19. MacDonald, it turned out, had been a civilian informant the Brea, California, Police Department wired to gather information on a local methamphetamine drug ring.

Can you see where this is leading? Guess again.

Here was a story ripe for press and politician feast to (a) condemn the threat of Latino "gang violence" to suburban life, as they had in the San Clemente "paint roller" murder, (b) condemn methamphetamine rings and their mostly-white over-30 customers also menacing the suburbs, and (c) condemn police for employing juvenile informants in deadly work. Coverage and editorial indeed started out focusing on the last, but it quickly changed to suit the larger media agenda: All-American Whiteboy from Fine Family who, inexplicably, has A Dark Secret Life.

The real "mystery," the *Times* profile of Chad MacDonald headlined (and Brea police quotes heavily bolstered), was "why he became involved with drugs at all." Why, the front-page story led off, MacDonald, a "handsome one-time Little Leaguer...appeared to be that most typical of suburban youths, a likable jock who cherished his ride—a white 1991 Nissan pickup truck." But his life was "a net of deceit." He ferried crystal meth with selfsame "prized truck." He was a "juvenile police snitch." He "cut deals to save his own skin." He took drugs. He "lied to his mother."

Offhand, down in the inside pages, the feature briefly squeezed out a couple of trifling clues why MacDonald might get involved with drugs. Call them (a) "genetic" and/or (b) "environmental." A month before Chad's first birthday, his father was killed in a drunken driving crash that severely disabled his mother. His mother, described by her brother as "not a well person," then married a man with severe alcohol and cocaine habits. This created much household volatility, including stepfather exposing small kids to drugs, chaos, divorce, and restraining orders during Chad's most formative years. Ponder, Watson, yet another enigma of this most peculiar clime: how clearly the media scribes see yet how puzzlingly they profess willful blindness to how young Chad could have iced himself with narcotic.

The article transmogrified Brea police into pillars of blue-eyed innocence. When MacDonald offered to cooperate after a drug bust, police wired him to make an undercover sting. Mom signed the permission slip. Cops, who denied they did anything to place the lad in danger, raided the house two days after MacDonald's buy but found no drugs. Cynics would say such a police strategy might as well have emblazoned MacDonald's picture with "Narc!" badge on a billboard.

Brea police also denied they ever intended to further exploit a young arrestee with what the chief sadly called "a deep involvement with drugs." After Chad's first buy failed to yield arrests, police merely hauled MacDonald into court and threatened prosecution, declaring in court papers that the youth "owes them one more bust" as a condition of dismissing drug charges.[62] A couple of days later, his family's lawyer said, MacDonald was confronted by the angry woman who sold him the methamphetamine in the police setup and surmised that the cops' appearance at her door two days later had something to do with it. The woman identified him as a "narc" to gun-toting "gang members." MacDonald fled town and hid out in a motel in south L.A. His girlfriend was kidnapped, beaten, raped, shot, and left for dead. Chad's battered body was found a few days later.

In the final *Times* profile, the grownups bailed ignominiously. The police emerged as makers of a few small mistakes that understandably go with doing a tough job by the book. Mom (who had not even reported her son missing) ran a family full of "loving and closeness" who gave the son "lectures about saying no to drugs." The meth dealers remained faceless, like stirred-up rattlesnakes. No, the paper said, "the mystery of Chad MacDonald lies not in his death, but in his life, and why he stepped so willingly and fully into the world of drugs."

Psychotic. This is a media, and police, that piously label 17-year-olds "children" and "protectively" declare them incompetent to buy clove cigarettes or hit the library after curfew. Yet real grownups, as in suburban parents who raise youngsters in years of drunkeness, addiction, turmoil, and probably worse (the real mystery of the suburbs) were sanitized as model family folks victimized by their son's "secret life." (Had the press wanted to portray the secret life of methamphetamine addiction accurately, it would have landed on the parent end. Seventy percent of California's 117 meth deaths in 1996 were Euro-white and over age 25. Teens under age 20 accounted for just one of L.A. and Orange counties' 32 fatalities.)

The cops, whose pressuring of what they knew was a troubled youth and whose clumsy tactics set up their own informant's tortured execution, were depicted as sadder, wiser victims of double-agent Chad as well. Thus, the only person the story, the police, and headlines held 100 percent culpable was: "MacDonald, trapped in lies," "MacDonald, life cut short by drugs."

The media had warped a most unlikely story into its favorite '90s motif: suburban kid, great family, All-American Little Leaguer, Nissan truck, yet gone to hell by his own evil adolescent hand. Millions of them, everywhere.

And it's not just bad boys, either.

Slasher Sluts

A continuing '90s media potboiler is the "new" violent girl. In truth, juvenile girls commit so little violence that media sensationalizing of "violent girls," nearly always in tones of shock at their violations of traditional feminine passivity, belongs in this chapter on the media more than in one on crime.

Traditional sex-role stereotypes, taboo for all but Old Testament rightists to raise for adult women today, have resurfaced in mainstream condemnations of teenage girls who cross the line. As with the first wave, the "second wave of the liberation hypothesis" launched by the media hints that too much freedom leads '90s girls to crime just as it did '70s women, Hawai'i sociologist Meda Chesney-Lind's 1996 study of girl-gangs found.[63] Chesney-Lind cited a 1992 CBS program, "Girls in the Hood," in which the opening voice-over declared:

> Some of the politicians like to call this The Year of the Woman. The women
> you are about to meet probably aren't what they had in mind. These women
> are active, they're independent, and they're exercising power in a field domi-
> nated by men…street gangs.

Killer-chick stories spread in the media with peer-pressure, everyone's-doing-it rage, what Chesney-Lind termed "pack journalism." Waves of big stories washed not only *Newsweek* and CBS, but the *Wall Street Journal, Washington Post, New York Times, Los Angeles Times, Philadelphia Inquirer, San Francisco Examiner*, NBC, everyone else with ink or a camera, and, of course, talk shows. All upheld the lofty journalistic ethics to which youth have become entitled.

Single incidents became trends. An unspecified few razor-wielders revealed a generation of distaff cutters. "Some girls now carry guns," *Newsweek* said. "Others hide razor blades in their mouths." Yes, and "some" superlative newsmagazine writers crave being whipped naked by dominatrixes on crack howling the Song of Solomon.

Absorb the professional objectivity of the lead paragraph of *L.A. Times'* writer Elizabeth Mehren's "Girl Trouble" series' concluding installment:

> Thirteen-year-old girls steal cars. Fourteen-year-old girls stab each other with
> screwdrivers. Fifteen-year-olds fight with their hands until one ends up in a
> coma, all because she slept with the other's boyfriend.[64]

Those who doubt that youths are routinely demonized in the mainstream media are invited to insert "black people" or "gays," or even "illegal immigrants," where Mehren uses "— year-old girls." The result would be rightly condemned in outraged tones as racist and phobic. Why, then, is it acceptable to demonize young people?

Mehren's five-part multi-page series on what she grossly misnamed "equal-opportunity badness" was both journalistic overkill and revealing in its adult bias. There are 300,000 girls ages 13–17 in L.A. County. In 1996, L.A. girls under age 18 accounted for five murder and 864 violent felony arrests. That is, juvenile girls comprised a terrifying one-half of 1 percent of the county's 1,042 murder and 1.7 percent of its 50,173 violent felony arrests.[65] Almost any adult age group of equivalent population—including adult women in their 20s, 30s, and 40s—account for more violent crime, as well as bigger increases over the last decade, than that. For both juveniles and adults, males had violence arrest rates eight to 30 times higher than females, nowhere near "equal opportunity."

The adult prejudices were even worse. Mehren freely admitted that a large majority of girl criminals have histories of sexual abuse, rape, and family violence.

Mehren even quoted one expert's apt comment that, "girls are tougher because they have to be." But while Mehren spent a dozen full newspaper pages on the minuscule issue of juvenile-girl "badness," she and the media in general did not see the far larger epidemic of violence *against* girls as worthy of any similar top-news billing. No six-part, or even one-part, feature series on abuses of girls by fathers, uncles, family members, male authorities. The only violence against girls the media seemed interested in was an occasional story on date rape, and then only by peer boys.

Chesney-Lind found that the media and authorities routinely engaged in "demonization of young girls," especially those of color, for presumed violations of female non-aggressive norms. But few showed interest in these girls' "bleak and harsh present" which included "high levels of sexual and physical abuse."[66] In a society with even minimal affinity for young people, the features could have carried the opposite message: how astonishingly non-violent teenage females are given the brutality so many absorb.

Demons in the Cyberforest

The bizarre philosophy that comes out of cultural left/right thinking in this most Scientific of Ages is reversion to Puritan devil theory. Devils are making our kids rebel against our values and sink into misbehaviors unheard-of among clean-living grownups. Devils on television. Devils in rock and rap music. Devils on Channel One. Devils in pop culture. Devils in video games. Devils in cyberspace. Devil peers. Conspiring to corrupt the weak and willing teenage mind, velcro for devil messages but Teflon for saintly ones.

The cultural left's descent into fascination with fictional images parallels its retreat from the Real. A beating, a rape, grinding poverty, warring parents, drugged and drunken family members, are Real. All kids see violent media, but three L.A. zip codes have more youth murders than 40 California counties with 10 million people. All kids see tobacco ads, but children of smoking, low-income, high school-educated parents are a dozen times more likely to smoke than children of nonsmoking, high income college-educated parents. Obsession with media's and pop culture's effects on kids is the way unhealthy, Real adult behavior and values have been denied. Real affects kids more than Unreal.

Media framing, not seducing, is the Real. *Truths to Tell*, a fine 1996 report by Florida's Poynter Institute for Media Studies to the American Society of Newspaper Editors, concerns youth patronage of mainstream dailies.[67] This is a subject that has to do with their future profits, so editors wanted the truth. The Poynter study found that teenagers "do not find themselves in the newspapers they read:"

> They see themselves generally presented as problems in need of solutions,
> part of the "blight" of violence and poverty, and broken bits of a system in
> need of being fixed. "Crusades" that center on children and youth invariably
> portray them in stories with predictable plots: individual boy or girl "escapes"
> the problems of family or neighborhood by moving out or away or is "saved"
> by adult authority who intervenes to protect the adolescent from a "destruc-
> tive" environment.

"They want to see and hear far less of what one observer called 'bad boys and invisible girls.' " Likewise, in a 1994 poll of 850 youths ages 11–16 by Children Now,

> Nearly three-fourths of the African-American children and about two-thirds of the Latino children said the only time members of their group were portrayed in the news was in connection with crime, violence or drugs...66% of the girls polled said they felt angry after watching, reading, or listening to the news, compared to 46% of the boys.[68]

Isn't it time for both the mainstream media and its liberal/left critics to call a halt to their stereotype of youth as a blight, broken bits in need of fixing, waifs saved by adult crusades, corrupted bad boys and brainwashed passive girls (except the ones with razor blades in their mouths)?

The Poynter survey of teens found,

> Many carry heavy doubts about their futures, and yet moments of optimism come through often enough. They flock with their friends to films of violence and listen to lyrics that seem to adults to inspire them to higher risks, flagrant disregard for civil behavior, and an irreverence for life. Yet, they vehemently claim that they make decisions independent of entertainment influences, and they want adults and local news media to give them credit as positive resources in their communities.

"The youth reader looks for action, familiarity, affirmation," the report summarizes. "The youth reader finds victimization, criminalization, exclusion." From mainstream media and media critic alike.

9 Myth: Young People Are Not Oppressed

Today, for the first time in the history of the United States, the younger generation is growing up not just poorer, but much poorer, than its elders.[1] This oppressive development is caused by concentrating wealth and public-private collaboration to cut off the pathways young people traditionally used to escape poverty. This attrition against young people is capped by a smugly self-centered debate over Social Security and other senior welfare programs, in which defenders of the status quo squabble with conservative "reformers" over various schemes to rip off the young and poor.

Generation war, endangering the futures of millions of young, is a profoundly serious reality. This is not the mythical "generation war" claimed by rightist lobbies for privatizing Social Security such as Third Millennium, which argue that the young will mutiny against subsidizing a mushrooming senior benefit system whose reality they believe is akin to flying saucers. So far, no youth antagonism against elder welfare is in evidence. Rather, the real generation war is in the other direction: a 25-year, increasingly larcenous alliance of aging voters with wealthy interests against the job, education, and public service needs of poorer, generally younger people. The war against the young is fought under the flags of tax revolt, business efficiency, cutting big government, and promoting personal responsibility.

Middle-aged and elder Americans embrace these new, austere values in conveniently belated and selective ways. The conservative homily that Baby Boomers and elders pulled ourselves up by our bootstraps is nostalgic hokum. Americans over age 40 were subsidized by some of the most generous social programs government has ever funded. In their 1930s youths, today's seniors gained handsomely from a Rooseveltian budget that spent hundreds of billions (in 1998-equivalent dollars) on public employment and education grant programs for the young. In the 1950s, today's aging collected hundreds of billions more through the GI Bill's direct education, housing, business, and other subsidies.

In the 1960s, generous Great Society education, jobs, and welfare initiatives, which paid double in public assistance what today's programs do, yanked millions of Baby Boomers out of poverty. Still more hundreds of billions of taxpayer aid to schools and universities made the Baby Boom America's apex of affluence.

Tax-subsidized all their lives, the fortunes of middle-aged householders have never been sunnier. Three-fourths boast home ownership, triple the rate among householders under age 30. Median household incomes of those ages 45–64 top $50,000 per year.[2] The average senior household owns $100,000 in assets (including a home only a small fraction of today's young can aspire to buy), a dozen times more than 30-year-old householders. Some increase in wealth with age is to be expected, but today's 12-fold imbalance is not only far out of proportion to the past gap between young and old, it is a major threat to the financial stability of young families. This is especially true because wealth, or net worth, is "a better indicator of long-run economic security" than income, economist Edward Wolff points out. Those senior apologists who ludicrously claim home ownership doesn't enhance wealth should ponder the concepts of "rent," not to say "homelessness."

How did today's middle-aged and older Americans repay the enormous public generosity of their elders? By voting with increasing fervor from the mid-1970s on for candidates and measures to slash taxes, rip school and university spending, reward the propertied and corporate, and pound the poor and young. As middle-aged and elder poverty fell, child and young-family poverty, which had declined from the 1950s to the mid-1970s, reversed and skyrocketed.

In 1960, American children were 1.4 times more likely to live in poverty than American adults 18 and older. Reforms of the '60s reduced that ratio to 1.3 by 1970. Since 1970, the ratio of children in poverty to adults in poverty has exploded, reaching a record 2.0 by the mid-90s.[3]

As generational historians William Strauss and Neil Howe wrote:

> During the 13er ["Generation X"] childhood era, America has substantially shifted the federal fiscal burden from the old to the young. Since 1972, older generations have deferred paying for some $2 trillion in current consumption through additional U.S. Treasury debt—a policy five times more expensive (in lifetime interest costs) for the average 15-year-old than for the average 65-year-old. Federal tax policy has shifted in the same direction. In 1990, according to the House Ways and Means Committee, a young 13er couple with one worker, a baby, and $30,000 in wage income had to pay five times as much ($5,055 in taxes) as the typical retired G.I. [senior generation] couple with the same income from public and private pensions ($1,073 in taxes).[4]

In the mid-1990s, a stronger economy produced a balanced budget, which may signal an end to the runaway deficit spending of the Reagan-Bush era and further additions to the federal debt—or it may persist only so long as the temporary economic boom. The tax gap between young and old has persisted, however. Including the FICA tax, the same committee reported in 1992, the younger couple's tax burden in the example above was eight times that of the elderly couple's with the same income.

Old Left to New Right, the debate over governmental responsibility to young versus old occurs on radically different planes. A few weeks after President Clinton signed the bipartisan 1996 "Personal Responsibility Act" dismantling and dispersing the $20 billion federal income support program for the young and poor, an automatic cost-of-living increase added $10 billion to the $250 billion Social Security program benefiting the elderly without a whisper of dissent from either party.

Add to this a much larger problem: the rapid decline in income among younger and poorer workers over the last 20 to 25 years. Since 1975, as real median household incomes of middle-agers rose to nearly $60,000 per year, real median incomes of workers under age 25 fell by 19 percent and of age 25–34 fell by 2 percent. (I use median income to reflect the typical income of an age group because it avoids the skew caused in measuring the average by a few Bill-Gates-bracket incomes that mean income reflects.) The "Great U-turn" in the fortunes of the young—the loss of both public and private resources as the middle-aged and elders have become richer in ways that will prevent the next generation from accumulating similar wealth by the time they reach the same stages of their lives—is the signature of the generation war.

Protecting the growing economic privilege of older Americans goes a long way toward explaining why officials, special interest groups, and the media spread negative, inflammatory falsehoods about young people—and why the adult public is so receptive to them. The economic figures in this chapter, more than anything else, explain why we are hearing such strident moralism and angry condemnation by American adults directed at American children and teens. An aging generation abandoning its kids on this scale can be expected to justify itself with massive calumnies to match.

Social Security debaters seem not to perceive, or care, that income patterns have radically changed. Coming generations will not just be poorer, but much poorer, than the elders they are asked to subsidize—largely because today's elders and middle-agers are systematically abandoning their commitments to the young.

Urban historian Mike Davis pointed out that while the city of Los Angeles invested $2 billion financing corporate towers in the wealthy downtown and Wilshire districts,

> factory closings in the early 1980s…shuttered ten of the twelve largest non-aerospace plants in Southern California and displaced 75,000 blue-collar workers, erased the ephemeral gains won by blue-collar blacks between 1965 and 1975.
> …This deterioration in the labor-market position of young black men is a major reason why the counter-economy of drug dealing and youth crime has burgeoned. But it is not the whole story. Correlated to the economic peripheralization of working-class blacks has been the dramatic juvenation of poverty amongst all inner-city ethnic groups. Statewide, the percentage of children in poverty has doubled (from 11 percent to 23 percent) over the last generation. In Los Angeles County during the 1980s, a chilling 40 percent of children either lived below, or hovered just above, the official poverty line. The poorest areas of the County, moreover, are inevitably the youngest: of sixty-six census tracts (in 1980) with median family incomes of under $10,000, over 70 percent had a median age of only 20–24 (the rest, 25–29).[5]

Get a job, aging America of the '90s tells the poor. In 1995, the federal government spent just $7 billion for job training, one-third of the per-capita amounts spent in the 1970s and early 1980s (1995 dollars).[6] One more federal subsidy poorer Baby Boomers sopped up that are now denied to today's poor. However, 1990s polls show aging Boomers loudly demanding that welfare recipients go to work.

Mid-1990s economic figures indicate no one explanation is definitive in America's growing wealth and income divisions. For example, today's poorest class of young (those under 18) suffer poverty levels (20.5 percent in 1996) triple those of the richest age group (45–54, 7.6 percent). The median household income of adults ages 45–54 ($57,161) is triple that of age 18–24 ($19,937 in 1996), compared to a gap of only 50 percent in 1965. So a strong case can be made for a widening "generation war" that transcends race alone.

However, the race gap is also substantial. In 1996, the median income of Euro-white families ($47,100 in 1996) was nearly double that of black and Latino households $26,500). There is a growing segment of upper-middle-income (median household incomes exceeding $50,000 per year in 1996) minorities who are better off than poorer whites.

A "class gap" is the most definitive, since it simply takes the poor of all ages and races and compares them to the rich (see below). However, because the poor are overwhelmingly young and predominantly nonwhite and the wealthy overwhelmingly middle-aged and white, class is in most respects derivative of color and young age. Further, the class pattern is more complex than in the past. America's large upper-middle-class is expanding, and its richest fifth exploding, in terms of wealth accumulation while lower income groups are static or becoming poorer. As discussed next, the most serious problem is rapidly concentrating wealth, followed by the increasingly repressive attitudes of generally older upper-middle income groups toward poorer and generally younger groups.

Corporate Attack

How did poorer youths traditionally escape poverty? First, by higher education. Second, by industrial career. Third, by public investment supplementing opportunity. All three of these pathways are being cut off.

That today's young should be much poorer than their elders defies demographic logic. Traditionally, economics professor Richard Easterlin pointed out in his definitive 1980 work, *Birth and Fortune*, it's great to be a smaller generation following a larger generation—the "baby busters" following the "baby boomers" in this case. The scarcer baby-busters of Generation X should enjoy less crowded schools and "an improvement in the labor market for young adults" in the 1980s and '90s, he predicted, with "earnings and employment prospects improving and their income increasing relative to older persons."[7]

With the benefit of a dozen more years' evidence that exactly the opposite was occurring, psychiatrist Daniel Offer and epidemiologist Paul Holinger's 1994 analysis refined Easterlin's sunny demographic forecasts.[8] Baby Boomers did indeed emerge in a time of crowded schools and flooded job markets in the 1950s and Sixties. But by middle age in the 1980s and '90s, Boomers were flexing their hefty political and management muscle to their advantage over the smaller, younger set. A large and growing class of middling-affluent to very wealthy middle-agers sprouted, along with a much smaller class of fabulously rich whose wealth ballooned as never before. The economic self-interests of aging American increasingly rested in divestiture, not support, of the younger generation.

The philosophy underlying the rise of the middle-aged and elderly as privileged classes, authorized both to accumulate private largess and receive public support as "entitlements" which are denied to younger groups, is a recent development. The growing age-split in the allocation of both private and public wealth to older groups is one of the clearest trends in America's generational division. Prior to 1970, equality was the rule. Since 1970, the Great Public-Private U-turn has devastated younger groups while continuing to enrich older ones.

Astonishingly, until 1970, a 25-year-old earned a salary only slightly lower than a 45-year-old, and the public welfare system was equally supportive of young and old.[9] Because of the greater equity of the public-private resource allocation system, including low-cost higher education, the typical young American of 1970 grabbed the bottom rung of middle-class status (earnings double those of poverty threshold) by age 22 and climbed rapidly thereafter.

The violence to America's young and poor by the business and corporate establishment has been severe. Those senior advocates who argue (in their own self interest, incidentally) that there is no generation war, that all we are seeing is traditional race/class division, are a quarter century behind the times.

Figures 1 through 4 depict the age and generational split in private income occurring within each race and ethnic group. From 1975 to 1996, real incomes for families headed by persons under age 25 fell by 8 percent among whites, 23 percent among Latinos, and 32 percent among blacks. Yet for families headed by persons over age 45, median incomes rose by 21 percent for blacks and whites and by 5 percent for Latinos during the same period. WITHIN each gender, race, and ethnicity, youths suffer poverty levels 1.6 to 2 times higher than those over age 40.[10]

At every turn, Howe and Strauss point out in *13th Gen: Abort, Retry, Ignore, Fail?*, "the workplace is rigged against" younger ages:

> Nothing exemplifies this age-graded inequality more than the two-tier wage ladder. In the 1980s, battered by foreign rivals, many a Fortune 500 company negotiated a union contract that protected elders while making the new hires bear the full burden of market competition. Entirely new wage-and-benefit ladders were established, the new ones lower than the old ones at every pay step. These two-tier contracts "grandfathered in" older workers at noncompetitive higher wage and benefit levels—and "grandsonned out" all new young hires.

This might be called "two-tiered villainy" as well: the Villain (big V) corporate downsizers who dictated reduced jobs/job quality to employees, and the senior employees who accepted terms that preserved as much of the smaller pie as they could rescue for themselves even at the expense of younger workers to follow. The same elders-profit-youngsters-pay philosophy—this time initiated by upper-middle, not by the super-rich, groups—was incorporated in Proposition 13's discriminatory property tax scheme, discussed later.

Thus, the victims of the 1990s new Depression, whose graduating classes "face the most difficult job search since the Great Depression:"

> During the Bush years, most of today's 40 million 13ers (Xers) living on their own hit their first recession. And behold: This was the only cyclical downturn ever recorded in which all the net job loss landed on the under-30 age bracket. Not on Boomer post-yuppies, not on Silent [age 55–75] prime-of-lifers, certainly not on GI [over 75] retirees. Subtract 13ers from the employment tally, and presto: No recession![11]

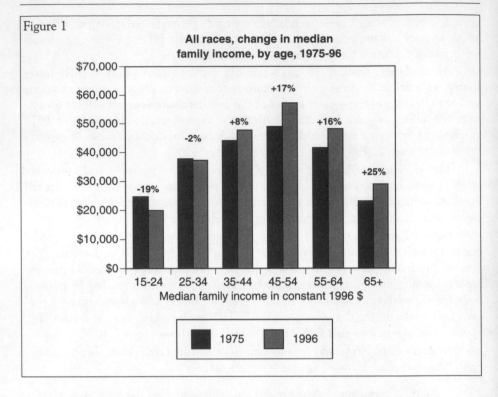

Figure 1

All races, change in median family income, by age, 1975-96

Median family income in constant 1996 $

1975   1996

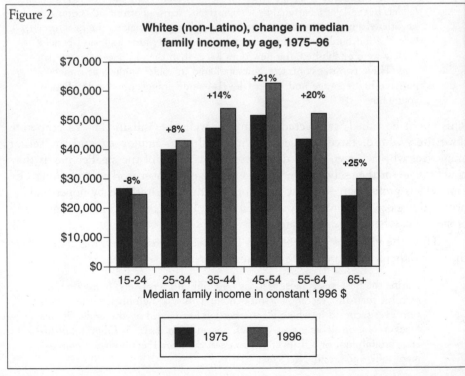

Figure 2

Whites (non-Latino), change in median family income, by age, 1975–96

Median family income in constant 1996 $

1975   1996

Figure 3

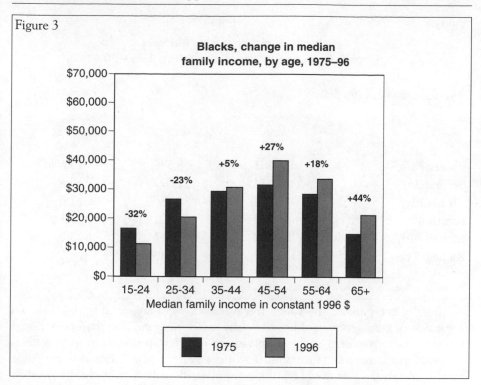

Blacks, change in median family income, by age, 1975–96

Median family income in constant 1996 $

Legend: 1975 (black), 1996 (gray)

Figure 4

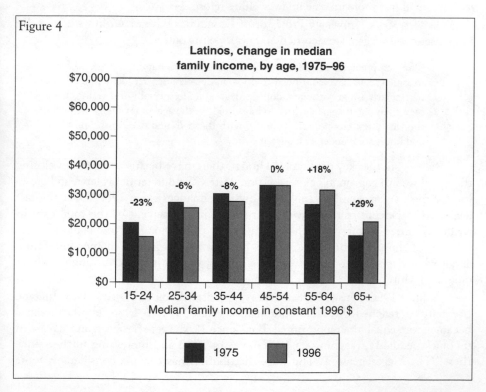

Latinos, change in median family income, by age, 1975–96

Median family income in constant 1996 $

Legend: 1975 (black), 1996 (gray)

Table 1

Rich getting richer as never before:
Growth in income by population fifths, 1980–96

Average income, 1996 dollars

	1980	1996	Change
Poorest fifth	$ 8,301	$ 8,596	+3.6%
Second fifth	20,034	21,097	+5.3
Third fifth	32,974	35,486	+7.6
Fourth fifth	48,551	54,922	+13.1
Richest fifth	85,279	115,514	+35.5
Richest 5 percent	122,359	201,220	+64.5

Source: U.S. Bureau of the Census, Department of Commerce.

By virtually every index, the young (regardless of race) are sinking while the old (regardless of race) are rising. Just as wealthy minorities suffer less than poorer ones from racism, so wealthier young people suffer less than poorer ones from generationism. But the oppression remains. It will get worse, former Clinton welfare aide Peter Edelman pointed out: 11 million families (8 million with children), most working, will lose more income under welfare reform.[12]

As New York University Professor of Economics Edward Wolff's study of the immense spending gap between rich and poor points out:

> One key predictor for differences in wealth among families is age...Upper income groups have continued to do well, decade after decade, while others, particularly those without a college degree, and especially the young, have seen their real income decline...Households in the age group 45–69 are by far the wealthiest group in our country, with those 70 and over in second place and households under 45 a distant third.[13]

Race is another key predictor: "Though there have been some gains in closing the racial wealth gap among better-off nonwhites, the differential is large and growing for the median family." Table 1 shows the changes since 1980. Over the last decade, 133 percent of the growth in income and 99 percent of the total gain in wealth occurred among the richest fifth of the population.[14] (How could a single fraction of the population receive 133 percent of the growth in income? Think about what happened to the lower fifths.) Thus, wealth is concentrating rapidly in older and whiter hands.

A June 1996 Census Bureau report, "A Brief Look at Postwar U.S. Income Inequality," reached the same conclusion. From 1947 to 1968, family incomes became more equal, the report noted. But "since 1968, there has been an increase in income inequality, reaching its 1947 level in 1982 and increasing further since then." The biggest reason: "The wage distribution has become considerably more unequal."[15] That is, the last two decades of political leadership have aided and abetted the rapid concentration of wealth—a process which has accelerated under Democrat Clinton—bad for poor people but a boon to those giving and receiving at White House coffees.

It's no mystery why so many young teeter on the brink of penury. Two-thirds of workers under age 30 earn incomes below even threadbare middle-class status ($24,000 per year for a family of three).[16] While the average young male of 1970 attained lower-middle-class income by age 22, young men of the 1990s will not reach it until age 35. In the past two decades, real median incomes rose sharply among the richest fifth of the population but declined among the poorest two-fifths. Age was the key divider: real income declined by 29 percent for workers under age 30 but rose by an identical amount for those over 45. A similar pattern is evident for home ownership trends.

Scarier still, struggling Generation X-ers today are well off compared to the generation following them who are now in elementary and high school. The poverty rate among youth today is 50 percent higher than the declining rate among youth of 1970. Half the new jobs created during the 1980s and '90s pay below poverty-level wages. Where college tuition and house payments consumed 5 percent and 15 percent, respectively, of young-family median incomes during the postwar years, today the share paid for college has quadrupled and for homes has tripled.

Today, 40-agers collect triple (and rising) the income of 20-agers. The median net worth of households headed by persons over age 65 exceeds $100,000, 10 times that of householders ages 18–35. No comparable figures can be found for the 1960s and '70s, but home ownership provides a rough index of the changes. In 1970, one-fourth of 15–24-year-olds and 55 percent of 25–34-year-olds owned their homes; today, those numbers have dropped to 15 percent and 40 percent, respectively. In contrast, the proportion of home ownership among those over age 50 has risen from around 70 percent in 1970 to 80 percent today. Clearly, the "income gap," the "wealth gap," and the "poverty gap" between young and old have widened from fissures in the previous generation to chasms today. That some of the latter will be bequeathed is of little use to young families, since middle age is typically the time when inheritances are received.

As Canadian social scientists Anton Allahar and James Cote point out in their excellent 1994 work, *Generation on Hold:*[17]

> The least desirable jobs go to those with the least power in society. While the dimensions of power have long been thought of along the lines of race, gender, and class, what these data indicate is that age, or more specifically youth, is an increasingly important component of power and therefore economic and social franchise. It is also the case that once a job becomes predominantly associated with low-status individuals, the pay drops along with the benefits and job security. Businesses and corporations have both contributed to and capitalized on the diminishing social status of young people by restructuring jobs and reducing salaries...[to] below minimum wage, part-time, with few benefits and little opportunity for career advancement.

That, and a government laissez-faire that would make President Herbert Hoover look activist, has produced the yawning age-wage canyons shown in the figures. In the last period of wealth concentration, the Great Depression, government led by Roosevelt stepped in—inadequately, critics argue, but at least actively. Corporate taxes were raised and public works and education programs benefiting millions of young unemployed were funded at today's equivalent of tens of billions in tax dollars per year. A generation worked and schooled its way out of violence and chaos. Exactly the opposite of the message Clinton's Volunteer Summit and its "no big government" delivered to poorer young people of the '90s.

"It is part and parcel of the discrimination against youths that these [business] practices are seen to be normal and fair," Allahar and Cote continue, "even by many of those who say they speak for equal opportunities for all groups in society." Who decided this extreme and growing maldistribution? These Canadian authors push on to a key generation-war point:

> While businesses and corporations benefit from the disenfranchisement of youth, the above data suggest that older age groups also benefit at the expense of their younger colleagues. Notwithstanding unemployment and underemployment problems that all age groups face, persons aged 35 and over are more likely to be established in careers and naturally presume that they are entitled to more pay, benefits, and security. Because more older people are in positions of influence, they can establish how much they are financially rewarded for their labor and how much, or little, others are rewarded. They appear to have been giving themselves an increasing share of the pie, and their juniors a decreasing share, thereby taking advantage of the latter group's vulnerability.

This process is analogous to that of race or sex. No one argues that every white male is rich or every nonwhite or female poor. But the white male dominance of economic decision making has produced undeniable economic privileges for white men. In the case of age, the situation is less an issue of 100 percent equity. One would expect some economic advancement with age, along with greater tax and economic burdens. But when elders allocate a huge share of private resources to their corner, and cut their economic burdens (primarily taxes), the generation war suddenly looms as the most powerful political force legitimizing widening race and class division.

Princeton University researchers found that growth in elder populations has increased national income inequality.[18] More troubling, aging Baby Boomers present problems not just in numbers, but in lifestyles:

> Social Security and employer-provided pension plans provide substantial incentive to leave the labor force early...The American population is aging rapidly and individuals are living longer. Yet Americans are saving less and older workers are leaving the labor force at younger and younger ages.[19]

Early retirement traditionally benefited younger workers by opening up senior job slots. This is less true today, in a downsizing economy in which senior jobs are eliminated with their holders' departures. Early retirement also reduces the income

Table 2

U.S. has lowest tax rate, highest child poverty rate, of any affluent nation

Tax revenues as percentage of gross domestic product, and child poverty rate

	1970	1980	1991	Child poverty rate*
France	35.1%	41.7%	43.6%	6.5%
Italy	26.1	30.2	42.4	9.6
Germany	32.9	38.2	39.6	6.8
Canada	31.3	31.6	36.5	13.5
United Kingdom	36.9	35.3	35.2	9.9
Japan	19.7	25.4	29.4	*
United States	29.2	29.3	29.4	21.5

*Percentage of persons under age 18 living in poverty as calculated on uniform international basis by Luxembourg Income Study, 1995. Japan is not comparable because employers are expected to provide many of the health, education, and other welfare benefits for employees that are provided by public assistance in other nations.

Sources: Organization for Economic Cooperation and Development, *Revenue Statistics of OECD Member Countries* (annual); Luxembourg Income Study (1995).

of older workers, exacerbated by their increasing failure to set aside retirement savings from typically high middle-aged incomes. Early retirement forced by employers (usually in exchange for compensation) is likely to increase in the future as a direct consequence of the greater salaries and benefits earned by middle-agers today, especially for those jobs which can be filled by a younger worker at a fraction of the cost. The two-tiered contract, in short, may come back to haunt its older beneficiaries.

These developments foretell a large crop of retiring Baby Boomers who have spent their substantial earnings during middle age and face retirement with the prospects of drastically diminished lifestyle. Powerful political pressures from the enormous Baby Boom generation to soak younger workers to pay for more senior benefits would result not just from larger numbers of longer-lived elders, but poorer economic planning by the soon-to-be retired. The power of Baby Boom seniors due to their larger numbers and wealthier status will be immensely greater than that of today's elderly. If Boomers continue their self-centered ways, they will concentrate wealth even more heavily in their corner—a prospect that has not yet shown up in calculations of senior benefit costs.

Modern anti-government and anti-tax revolts were not instigated by declining wealth or burdensome taxation. The most recent international comparison shows U.S. taxpayers are the lightest-taxed of any industrial nation except for Japan (where corporations shoulder most welfare provision) and, except for the United Kingdom, show the least increase in recent decades (Table 2).

The United States' low tax level results from failure over the last 25 years to tax increasingly concentrated wealth and the cuts in taxes upper-middle-income property owners voted themselves in 1970s and 1980s tax revolts. Notice that most

Figure 5

1970's "Great U-Turn"
Older getting richer, young poorer

other Western nations, especially corporate-friendly Japan, sharply increased their taxes through progressive revenue systems as national wealth boomed. Not coincidentally, the U.S. also has the West's highest child poverty rate.

There was certainly no economic need for older Americans to cut their taxes and support for kids and young families in the 1970s and '80s. The younger generation (the smaller "baby busters") imposed a lower burden for schools and other tax-supported services on its elders in the 1970s and '80s than giant Baby Boom generation did on its parents and grandparents. There was no fiscal squeeze to explain the unprecedented and growing selfishness of the old—just the opposite. The pyramiding of private wealth in older and richer hands has accompanied allocation of more public resources for aging Americans at the expense of the young as well.

Public Attack

Figure 5 shows the "Great U-Turn" in public welfare flowing to the young. Its pattern is similar to that of private income. Until around 1970, young and old received equal entitlement. After 1970, the old have mopped up as the young have been mopped. The identical public-private reversal argues strongly that these are the result of a massive, generational attitude change—disownment of the young by the old.

It may seem puzzling that of the two stages of life during which individuals are unable to earn enough to support themselves, childhood and old age, the United States, unlike other industrial nations, chose to universally entitle only the latter to income support and medical benefit. If the reasons were Americans' allegedly fierce individualism and respect for family autonomy, neither young nor old would be seen as deserving of public subsidy. Adult children would be expected to support their aged parents just as adult parents were seen as obligated to support their young children. Or, like European nations, we could have viewed both young and old as entitled to support.

Interestingly, as Figure 1 illustrates, the U.S. seemed to be moving toward the both-deserving social philosophy in the postwar period. The number of families entitled to Aid to Families with Dependent Children expanded rapidly, and payments per family were as generous as those received by seniors.

In 1945, 700,000 children received AFDC; in 1970, seven million. The average family benefit rose from $50 per month to nearly $200. Child beneficiaries rose six times faster than the child population, and benefits grew at a clip 75 percent faster than the rate of inflation.[20] Both increased nearly as fast during the Truman and Eisenhower years as in the Great Society social program expansion, indicating a bipartisan evolution toward a more generous stance toward poorer children.

Due to young families' rapid postwar wage and public assistance growth, the percentage of children in poverty dipped from around one-third in the 1950s to less than 15 percent in the early '70s. Social Security payments rose in like fashion to a like level, around $200 per family, in 1970. That year, the total numbers receiving AFDC, including parents, was 10 million, nearly as many as receiving Social Security (10 million retired workers and spouses plus three million deceased workers' survivors).

Then the 1970s arrived and the age split suddenly appeared. In a startling irony, the same year, 1972, that the Democratic Congress and Nixon White House indexed Social Security benefits to rise automatically with inflation, AFDC payments started to fall. Clearly, this was not an anti-social-spending clime per se, else Social Security would have faced cuts along with young-family benefits. It is likely that the growing power of senior lobbies, especially the American Association of Retired Persons, had something to do with winning greater senior subsidies.

The reasons for the post-1970 split—the attitude that elders are entitled but children are undeserving—seem to me not very edifying. The first, I think, is fear of racial change. Old-age welfare overwhelmingly benefitted whites (90 percent of those over 65 in 1970 were Euro-white), the patriarchs and matriarchs of a noble American past. In contrast, child and young-family welfare recipients were in large and growing percentage (60 percent by 1970) black, Native, and Latino, harbingers of the uncertain future that post-Sixties white Americans were dimly beginning to fear.

Second, when social cohesiveness begins to fray, self-interest gains strength. Since all of us are getting older, not younger, aid to the old is a future benefit aging Americans can anticipate receiving; aid to kids is one we no longer need.

Third, there also seemed a generalized anger at youths, possibly provoked by perceived excesses of Sixties radicals—ironically, the Baby Boom kids. In California, a statewide university bond issue lost for the first time ever in 1968 and the first university tuitions were imposed in 1969, largely as punishment for student radicalism. This indicates some antagonism against white kids as well. Finally, increasingly concentrated wealth after 1970 contributed to business relocation, job loss, citizens' increased hoarding mentality reflected in tax revolts and opposition to social programs, and exacerbation of racial, age, and economic class divisions.

Thus, the increasing concentration of wealth in the hands of older and whiter Americans is occurring at the very time that the younger population is becoming more racially and ethnically diverse. Open expressions of racism have become impolitic. Therefore, a new and acceptable way allows for older, wealthier Americans to express fear of the diverse society the younger generation foretells. As Stanford journalism professor Dale Maharidge charts in *The Coming White Minority*, fear of racial transition strains California's growing economic faultlines even in a time when most white residents genuinely do not consider themselves racist.[21]

Los Angeles and California, in particular, are "not merely being polarized between rich and poor, but more specifically between old rich and young poor," urban historian Mike Davis observed: "California as a whole is an incipient gerontocracy, and any post-Blade-Runner dystopia must take account of the explosive fusion of class, ethnic and generational contradictions."[22] Explosive is right. The 1998 census estimate shows that two-thirds of Californians over age 40 are Euro-white, but 60 percent of Californians under age 20 are black, Latino, Asian, and Native.

University of California at Berkeley researchers charted a half-century decline in voter support for school bond issues.[23] In the 1950s, they found, California school bonds typically passed in all 58 counties with percentages averaging 70 percent. By the 1980s, that proportion had fallen to 60 percent. In the 1990s, votes for school bonds averaged just 50 percent. In 1994, a statewide school bond issue was defeated, losing in all but 12 counties.

The seminal event of generational abandonment was California's Proposition 13, an unparalleled elder/corporate divestiture of social responsibility. The genesis of Prop-13's 1978 electoral triumph was a 1974 ruling by the California Supreme Court requiring that local school funding be equalized regardless of how rich or poor each school district was. Jonathan Kozol points out in *Savage Inequalities*:

> Baldwin Park, a low-income city near Los Angeles, was spending $595 for each student while Beverly Hills was able to spend $1,244, even though the latter district had a tax rate less than half that of the former. Similar inequities were noted elsewhere in the state.[24]

The Court ordered equalized funding of schools, enacted by law in 1977. That meant Beverly Hills 90210 property taxes would flow from an even state funding spigot to ghetto Compton 90221 schools. What followed, Maharidge writes, was a white riot at the polls. The effects were summarized by Kozol:

As soon as Californians understood the implications of the plan—namely, that funding for most of their schools would henceforth be equal—a conservative revolt surged through the state. The outcome of this surge, the first of many tax revolts across the nation in the next ten years, was a referendum that applied a "cap" on taxing and effectively restricted funding for all districts. Proposition 13, as the tax cap would be known...was described succinctly by a California legislator: "This is the revenge of wealth against the poor. 'If the schools must actually be equal,' they are saying, 'then we'll undercut them all.' "

Proposition 13 won with 59 percent of the vote in 1978. Its biggest pushers were senior citizens, who whooped two-thirds approval—the same elderly collecting generous Social Security and Medicare welfare checks funded by the same young whose kids they were divesting. The second biggest champions were middle-agers, California's extraordinarily wealthy elite.

A major irony: the executives of dominant corporations *opposed* the initiative, fearing its impact on public services, even though they would rake in the biggest windfalls. Southern California Edison's property tax bill plummeted by $54 million, and Pacific telephone companies' by $130 million, per year.

Passage of the referendum locked in inequality. Homeowners—certain homeowners—also benefited. Those who owned property in 1978 saw their taxes capped at 1 percent of assessed value. Property may only be reassessed when it changes hands. No matter how much inflation rages, property taxes may not increase more than 2 percent in any year. Most new taxes require two-thirds' approval from voters, meaning a minority may block them. In California of 1998 (average house valuation, $200,000), one-fourth to one-third of houses are still assessed at absurdly low 1975 values (average valuation, less than $50,000). So a house owned by a longer-term owner and taxed at $500 per year sits next to an identical house owned by a newer, usually younger, resident whose taxes top $2,000.

Proposition 13 represented a war by the Established against the New on multiple fronts. Those who, in 1998, bought their property two decades ago and still occupy it are predominantly over 50 years old. They benefited from low pre-1975 housing prices, from the huge increases in their property's values in the 1970s and 1980s, and subsequent larcenous rents landlords now gouge as the result of runaway housing-cost inflation. At the same time, their taxes are assiduously capped at low rates by Proposition 13. New housing buyers (the young and the immigrant) are not protected by Proposition 13 and are assessed at higher rates. Not all young face this problem, of course, since homeowners can bequeath their property to their children without suffering reassessment and higher taxes. Thus, propertied Californians of 1978 committed robbery against the future, cutting off the access of younger, more recently arrived, and poorer groups to property ownership in order to vote the elder and richer, and their kin, comfort.

These were the grownups whose own wealth, in large part, derived from massively tax-funded public spending, high quality public schools, and practically free universities. It isn't just pot and free love that modern American adults indulged in themselves and would now deny their kids, but money and education as well. "Today," Kozol writes in *Savage Inequalities*:

Figure 6

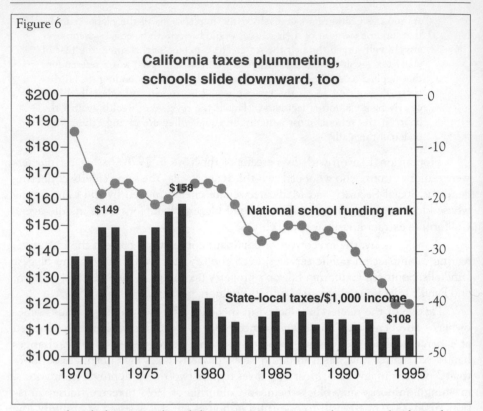

California taxes plummeting, schools slide downward, too

though the state ranks eighth in per capita income in the nation, the share of its income that goes to public education is a meager 3.8 percent—placing California forty-sixth among the 50 states. Its average class size is the largest in the nation.

After Prop 13, affluent Californians sent their kids to private schools or set up private foundations to pour money into their already sumptuous public schools. Irvine, for example, is among the state's wealthiest cities (despite my presence here) even by Orange County gold coast standards. Average annual family incomes top $80,000. "The need for private funding to support public education has never been more critical," said a brochure mailed to district residents by the Irvine Company in late May 1998. Quoth the president of the Irvine Public Schools Foundation:

> State funding has change dramatically over the past 10 years. Per student expenditures in California are well below the national average, local taxes pay only a fraction of the school costs, and lottery funds provide less than two percent of our school district's budget.

This is not a lobbying effort by the giant firm to raise property taxes to fund California's public schools. This is strictly to boost the local well-to-do. The private foundation set up to supplement Irvine public schools "raised $1.1 million to help fund projects like the district's computer technology learning centers, summer school, after-class educational enrichment, science little league, teacher grants, a

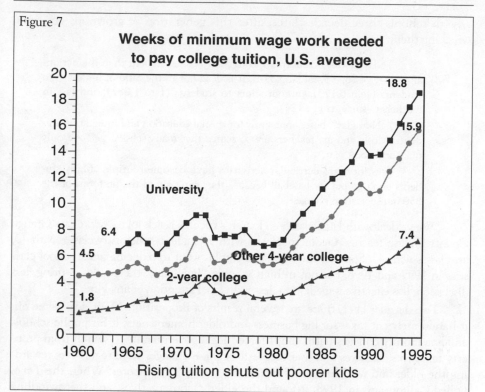

Figure 7

**Weeks of minimum wage work needed
to pay college tuition, U.S. average**

Rising tuition shuts out poorer kids

students' honors concert and much more."[25] Recent pledges include $3.3 million put up by the Irvine Company, Standard Pacific, and other corporations. Doubtless, these extras helped Irvine's University High School to place first in the state in SAT scores—1208, well above state norm (1002) and much above scores in the poorer, mostly-Latino city of Santa Ana (847) next door.

The private-public schools' fortunes in richer districts contrasted sharply with declines in poorer ones. In the California tax revolts of which Prop 13 was the coup, increasingly wealthy California adults cut their tax burdens by one-fourth (Figure 6). Public elementary and high schools dropped from the fifth best-funded in the nation in 1965 to 37th in 1998. University tuition jumped from a nominal $200 per year in 1967 to over $4,000 by 1997—a rise triple that of inflation (Figure 7).

A May 1998 *Los Angeles Times* special supplement, "Why Our Schools Are Failing," contrasted California schools of 1965...

> Field trips were plentiful. Schools taught art and music along with the three Rs. High schools ran up to seven periods a day.
>
> Band instruments, athletic uniforms, and bus transportation to and from school were free...Funding wasn't a constant worry. In 1964, California ranked fifth in per-pupil spending. And there was the Master Plan for Higher Education, defining the mission of the three systems—U.C., Cal State, and the community colleges—that made California the first state to guarantee every high school graduate a place in college.

...with schools three decades later, after this generation of grownups got done wrecking them:

> Today (1998), California spends $911 less per student than the national average of $6,495, ranking 37th. It is dead last in the ratio of librarians to students (1 in 6,179), in counselors to students (1 to 1,082), and last in teachers to students (1 to 24).
>
> ...Nowadays, buses are mainly for special education and integration students. Music and art teachers are so scarce that many schools get one only once or twice a year.
>
> Fees for extra-curricular activities have become routine...Many students don't go out for baseball because they can't afford the uniforms or the $50 transportation charge.[26]

"We've dealt with large classes so long it's become a sick joke," wrote one Orange County English teacher. Geometry classes with 37 students, chemistry classes with 40, art classes with 45. Some of the new state surplus went to reducing grade school class sizes in 1997 and 1998, but not in high schools. "Inevitably, there is less writing, less discussion, less effective remediation, less individual attention of any kind."[27]

Two decades later, there are several results of Proposition 13 all sides agree on: it handsomely cut taxes for big business and older homeowners, it hit public schools and community colleges hard, and it forced local governments to switch from property taxes to sales taxes and user fees. All of these changes were regressive, rewarding the older and wealthier and hurting the younger and poorer. When the *Times* polled Californians in 1998, it found the elderly, conservatives, and the dwindling share of middle-class homeowners still overwhelmingly favoring Proposition 13 despite the clear damage to schools and institutions needed by the young.[28]

Nationally as well, schools serving poorer children are consistently underfunded. In 1991, the National Research Council reported in *Losing Generations*, the nation's 47 largest school districts spent an average of 7 percent less than suburban school districts when revenues and expenditures were considered:

> Although an average of $873 per pupil funding gap may not appear significant, in an average class of 25 students, the difference is $21,825—enough to employ a teacher's aide, pay higher salaries, offer special instructional assistance, or improve dilapidated classrooms. Difference in funding of this magnitude could make a clear qualitative difference in the total educational experience.[29]

We are accustomed to thinking of "social costs" only as something selected, unpopular subgroups (such as teenage mothers) impose on established society. Reverse the perspective and observe the huge social costs imposed on younger students by the tax cuts that California's elders voted for themselves. For California's five million elementary and secondary school students, the social costs of Proposition 13 and related tax cuts can be assessed two ways. The per-student gap of $900 between the national average in spending for schools and what California spends adds up to $5 billion—annually! But it gets worse: if California had maintained its standing as the fifth highest school spender in the nation, it would have to spend $10 billion per year more than it does today.

Educational Feudalism: College Student as Serf

Of far more importance to aging taxpayers is how spending an average of $1 million less per urban school (of 1,200 students) enhances our total yuppificational experience. Property tax cuts which overwhelmingly favor the affluent propertied and give special breaks to seniors force today's young to bear tens of billions in education costs Baby Boomers never shouldered—the staggering "intergenerational shift in responsibility for funding" the American Council on Education deplored.[30] This attrition compounds with corporate downsizing and deterioration in job quality to relentlessly punish young workers. Historians James Rawls and Walton Bean reported that in 1991, architects of California's Master Plan for Higher Education warned that funding cuts were breaking its covenant to provide college spaces for all high school graduates:

> Like every other segment of public education, the community colleges' basic problem was lack of money...Lacking sufficient funds to hire additional teachers, the community colleges canceled more than 5,000 classes in 1991. The colleges were placed in the ironic position of canceling classes just as demand for classes was at an all-time high.
>
> Similar pressures affected the multicampus California State University (C.S.U.) system. Budget deficits and soaring enrollments eroded the system's ability to fulfill its obligation under the Master Plan to admit the top one-third of the state's graduating high school seniors...funding for the C.S.U. system was cut drastically. As a result, 1,000 full-time faculty were laid off in 1991, and nearly 4,000 classes were eliminated...Students also faced stiff increases in tuition, even as the number of available classes declined. The sharp increases in fees forced many students to drop out and discouraged others, particularly minority and low-income students from applying...[threatening] de facto educational, economic and social apartheid.
>
> ...Tuition at the University of California dramatically increased in the early 1990s...In 1991, the enrollment of black, Hispanic, and Native American freshmen at the University of California dropped more than 12 percent, the first decline in a quarter of a century.[31]

"At San Diego State University," wrote Robert Rheinhold, "where 550 part-time instructors have been let go and 662 classes canceled,"

> more than 1,300 students got none of their requested courses when the semester began. Some have perfected the process known as "crashing," by which they attend classes to which they have not been assigned and beg overloaded professors to admit them. And many are "freeway flying," madly dashing by car between the campuses and various junior colleges trying to gain the credits they need to graduate.[32]

I have worked for four years as a University of California, Irvine, teaching assistant for mammoth classes (200 to 500 students taught by one professor). These are repeatedly "crashed" by masses of frantic undergraduates, some of whom attend the entire term in hopes of getting admitted. I have also seen the rise of a second student-unfriendly development: grant-grubbing administrative pressure. Tax-defunded campuses understandably are turning to corporate and institutional fun-

ders for support. UCI's quest to enter the prestigious Top 50 institutional grant-fun-
dees requires that faculty pursue independent funding more vigorously and "attune
ourselves to them [the funding agencies and their agendas]" because "doing so will
be our route to the top ranks of research universities," then-Chancellor Laurel
Wilkening candidly announced in 1994.[33]

Putting aside how fine-attuning might affect academic freedom, the most
salient result is that undergraduates see less and less of professors and more and more
of graduate teaching assistants like me. While it has been broadening for me to
learn how to explain to 80 students in my Environmental Analysis discussion group
how the net energy of stream flow accumulates in a river's middle phase, freshwater
biology is a long turnpike away from anything I know about.

TAs delight in accusing lecture-only professors of laziness and student neglect,
but the real problem is that the Ph.D.s are busy hunting and fulfilling grants. In
April 1998, the Carnegie Foundation for the Advancement of Teaching pointed
out that the move to "research universities" means that "senior professors, when
they teach undergraduates, tend to teach majors in advanced courses." Freshmen in
particular get screwed: bleacher seats in packed classes in which individual attention requires sustained student aggressiveness. Handing out and collecting 500 tests
under moderate security procedures can take half the test period, indicative of how
crowd control increasingly detracts from teaching time. Even in the relatively privileged senior writing seminar—a state-required course in which individual attention
and paper commentary is paramount—one professor and five TAs work with 200
students per quarter. Accepting that universities aren't going to get any more tax
dough from states, Carnegie recommends that faculty teach by involving undergrads
more in grant research.[34]

Pay more tuition, sardine more in classes, serve the monied more, emerge deep
in debt—the recipe for the new, indentured student serf. Where prior to 1970 (that
year again), a youth of modest means would have had to work full time only four
weeks at prevailing minimum wage to fund a full year's tuition at the University of
California, by the mid-1990s it would take six months' minimum-wage work.
Increases for the state and junior college systems (essentially free prior to 1970)
were equally staggering. This "disaffirmative action" caused minority student enroll-
ments to drop dramatically, long before the anti-climactic repeal of affirmative
action through Proposition 209 in 1996.

The social cost of Proposition 13 and other elder tax cuts to state university
and college students is approximately $2 billion per year. For a four-year undergrad-
uate program, the average U.C. student pays $10,000 more, and the state university
student pays $5,000 more, in tuition (in constant, inflation-adjusted 1998 dollars)
than their forbearers did 30 years earlier.

Student borrowing and debt has skyrocketed. The average undergraduate now
racks up $10,000 to $20,000 in student loan debts by graduation day. Today's political leaders seem to see nothing wrong with this. California's Republican governor,
gubernatorial candidates, and lawmakers wanted to spend the $4.4 billion 1998
state budget surplus to buy car owners' votes by repealing the vehicle registration
tax. A compromise with Democrat legislators split the surplus between schools, welfare benefits, and reduced vehicle taxes.

Table 3				
California higher education costs shift from older taxpayers to younger students				
Annual resident tuition	Actual tuition 1968–69	Inflation-adjusted tuition 1998–99	Actual tution 1998–99	Excess
UC system	$331	$1,720	$4,022	+$2,300
State universities	108	560	1,868	+1,310
Community/junior colleges	0	0	360	+360

Sources: *Governor's Budget* (1998, 1967), Office of the Governor, Sacramento; California Postsecondary Education Commission (1997), *Fiscal Profiles*, Sacramento. "Inflation-adjusted tuition" is calculated from the Higher Education Price Index in Research Associates of Washington (annual), *Inflation Measures for Schools, Colleges, and Libraries*, Washington, DC. Inflation alone indicates a 1998 tuition 5.2 times that of 1968's in unadjusted dollars; California's real tuitions rose 12-fold to 17-fold over that time.

In Washington, Congress wrangles over how much profit lenders should collect at student expense. Analyses by the U.S. Treasury Department and Congressional Budget Office found that despite the fact that student loans are federally guaranteed against lender loss and should command lower interest rates, banks providing student loans earn an average rate of return almost twice that of lenders in other banking sectors. Minor relief was approved by Congress and the White House in October 1998, expanding grants and reducing interest payments enough to save the average student borrower about $700 on a $14,000 loan.

Notice of that modest good news was immediately buried by a new College Board study showing public university tuitions rose from 1997–98 to 1998–99 at double the rate of inflation, crowning a decade of the '90s in which tuitions rose 50 percent while family incomes went up only 1.5 percent. Lack of "state support" is the reason for the tuition hikes, Lawrence Gladieux of the College Board declared. Attending a public, four-year university now costs about one-fifth of a middle-income, and two-thirds of a low-income, family's earnings.[35]

"Today's college students are saddled by debt that would have financed a small house in their parents' college days," *Los Angeles Times* editors observed.[36] Added the American Council on Education's David Merkowitz: "We've broken the historical promise we've had in higher education: that the current generation will help pay for the education of the next generation." Unlike their parents, today's students "begin their careers in debt."

Welfare Attack

Time, Newsweek, National Review, the *New York Times*, and other established media headline a Social Security and Medicare "crisis" and propose drastic reforms. Counter-spreads in *In These Times, Mother Jones, Monthly Review, Rolling Stone*, and *Extra!* identify a "Wall Street conspiracy" to panic lawmakers into gutting senior benefits through cuts and privatization. Because the debate is confined to only what is good for middle- and upper-income elders and various economic elites, it swirls only around how to keep the money flowing.

Three serious intergenerational issues are ignored by all sides in the senior welfare debate:

- The deeply regressive wage and payroll tax used to fund Social Security and Medicare. A minimum wage income is taxed at a rate dozens of times higher than a penthouse income because the earnings which are taxable are capped (at $68,000 in 1997), meaning the wealthy pay less.

- The trickle-down nature of senior benefit disbursement. Social Security pays twice as much to the rich as to the poor because payments are based on earnings during working years. Even after spending one-fourth of the entire federal budget to support the elderly, the United States still has three million elderly in poverty.

- The political split caused by providing guaranteed ("entitled") welfare to the old while denying it to younger groups. The effect is to turn seniors against welfare for the young and poor.

Instead, self-serving clichés abound. Social Security, backers say, "is America's only popular and viable social insurance system." Of course it's popular. It serves the two most powerful political constituencies—middle-agers and the elderly—who collect and anticipate collecting it. Of course it works. Social Security spends $240 billion per year to supplement the incomes of 30 million retiree beneficiaries, an average of $8,000 each.[37] Of course it's viable. It spends one-fourth of the entire federal budget on a heavy-voting elderly constituency that comprises only 13 percent of the population. It penalizes the retired poor, provides modest supplements to the masses in the middle, and rewards the wealthy. How could such a scheme not be popular?

To illustrate the contradictions of age-discriminatory welfare designs, imagine that a think tank designed a new scheme to reduce child poverty:

> Each American worker and Social Security and pension recipient would be taxed 13 percent of his or her wages and each employer 13 percent of payroll to fund it—except that all income over $70,000 per year (and its payroll), as well as all investment income, would be exempt from the tax. The $600 billion collected every year would be distributed to the families of all 70 million children and youths under age 18. Rich families would receive two to three times more in benefits than poor families. A Scarsdale family with two kids would receive about $30,000 in income support per year, while a South Bronx mother with two kids would get $13,000. Analysis would show that eight million children would remain in poverty and two million workers and elders would join them in penury solely due to the income lost by paying the tax. Even though blacks would transfer income to whites, its backers would defend the plan as "progressive" because it would transfer money from single men to poorer single mothers.

How would liberals and leftists react to this hypothetical scheme? We can't know for sure, because no one has proposed anything so preposterous as a child-welfare plan modeled on Social Security's. But I suspect (and hope) the response would be fierce opposition. I predict that reaction because of the above scheme's deeply regressive taxation and trickle-down disbursement and the left's oft-articulated principle: reducing poverty among one group should entail redistribution of income from the rich, not the impoverishment of other groups of modest means. That is why leftists rightly deride any notion that money should be taken from senior benefits and redirected to help poor children.[38]

When it comes to funding senior welfare, however, aging progressives abandon that principle. They are perfectly willing to acquiesce in a scheme which takes money from poorer children to pay benefits even to well-to-do seniors. Social Security funding levies a deeply regressive tax on workers. It taxes 7.65 percent to 15.3 percent of the incomes of those making minimum wage, but less than 1 percent of the incomes of those making $1 million or more per year. It distributes its benefits in such a top-heavy fashion that even after doling $240 billion in Social Security and $150 billion in Medicare in 1997, 3.3 million seniors remained in poverty.

The wage tax used to fund Social Security exacerbates the drastic divisions in wealth. The Social Security (called Old Age Survivors and Disability Insurance, or OASDI) tax takes 6.20 percent of covered wages on incomes up to $68,100 (in 1997). The Medicare (Health Insurance) tax takes another 1.45 percent on incomes, regardless of size. The same proportions are deducted from employer payroll. Thus, a single parent supporting two kids on $15,000 per year by patching together a couple of 25-hour-per-week no-benefit Macwage jobs ponies up 7.65 percent of her earnings ($1,150, enough to pay the year's utility bill) in payroll taxes to support the elderly. A penthouse CEO reporting $1 million in annual income pays just 2 percent of income—less than one-third as much by proportion. The Congressional Budget Office calculates that the poorest fifth of Americans pay two to three times' greater share of their income for Social Security than does the richest 1 percent. Americans with below-average incomes pay more in Social Security taxes than they do in income taxes.[39]

The FICA (that is, the combined OASDI and Health Insurance) tax alone pushes the families of 850,000 children below federal poverty guidelines.[40] If older and richer Americans were paying their fair share to raise children and young families out of poverty, this burden might be equitable. But senior welfare, funded many times more generously, was vastly more effective in reducing poverty among the old than family benefits were in reducing child poverty even before AFDC's denouement.

Of particular concern should be results from a 1998 study by Columbia University's National Center for Children in Poverty.[41] It found that a booming economy and welfare reform had led to 6.7 million Americans leaving welfare rolls to take jobs. But whether parents were on welfare or working, their kids continued to languish in poverty. While 55 percent of poor kids had working parents in 1993, today 63 percent do. In sum: "the 1996 federal welfare reform law has contributed to the child poverty rate." As parents take low-wage no-benefit jobs because of welfare cutoff, their poverty is worsened. Deductions for senior benefits diminish their small paychecks.

For the low-income self-employed, like myself, the bite is large: On an adjusted gross income of $23,000 last year, I paid $1,250 in taxes to support the elderly. Of

---

Table 4

Social Security payments shortchange the poor

Monthly Social Security benefit, 1997

Income prior to retirement	Individual
Low (average $12,000)	$566
Middle (average $26,700)	$933
High (average $65,400)	$1,326
Average (all retirees)	$750

Source: Social Security Administration (August 1997). U.S. Department of Health and Human Services.

---

course, at age 48, I'm delighted to do so, since I occupy a generation set to receive much more in benefits from elder welfare than we paid into it.

Bush administration economic advisors once argued that the regressive Social Security program is progressive because it is less wealth-concentrating than America's grossly top-heavy private income structure. Truly a Republican notion of "progressive." A real-world analysis by RAND found that Social Security is progressive only because it channels money from men to longer-lived, generally poorer women. But Social Security is deeply regressive in all other respects, particularly in its transfer of "between $2,000 and $21,000" per-capita from blacks to whites.[42] The reason is that blacks live, on average, six years less than whites do (if calculated from age 18) and two years less (if calculated from age 65), meaning that they pay into the system but live fewer years after retirement to collect senior benefits. RAND also exposed the demeaning claim made by Social Security advocates that the program is redistributive because it replaces a higher proportion of the income of the poor than the rich elderly. "As a group, blacks may earn a better return on their contributions than whites *because* of their lower average incomes," RAND found, not because Social Security is progressive.

While liberals shy away from discussing race and class, conservatives use it to promote privatization to minorities: Wrote Texas state demographer Steve Murdock: "The population will be one in which an increasing number of elderly Anglos may be dependent on young minority populations."[43] This is the kind of fact progressives should be citing to demand strong public reforms to Social Security, rather than allowing conservatives such as the Heritage Foundation to use it in arguments to privatize the program.

Progressives also have not confronted Social Security-enforced elder poverty. Social Security benefits are based on income before retirement and indulge richer seniors twice as much as poorer ones (Table 4), guaranteeing the U.S. the highest senior poverty level (10.5 percent) of any Western nation.

As Randy Albelda and Nancy Folbre of the Center for Population Economics point out in *The War on the Poor*:

> The benefits of Social Security are unevenly distributed...Elderly women and people of color remain particularly vulnerable to poverty...28 percent of African Americans and 21 percent of Latinos over age 65 were poor, compared to 11 percent of whites.[44]

Today, 30 percent of black and Latina women over age 65 live in poverty, six times the rate of Euro-white men. Folbre in particular has been vilified by liberal senior advocates for suggesting greater means-testing of senior benefits; those advocates should disclose what their plan is for relieving senior penury.

Although depicted as senior bonanzas, Social Security and Medicare also represent subsidies to the middle-aged. In the past, 40–60-agers footed much of the care of aging parents, a reasonable burden since middle age, after kids leave home, combines highest income with lowest liability. However, the rising FICA tax increasingly roped younger workers into helping the middle-aged support the elderly. In 1995, workers under age 35, most also supporting children on median household incomes averaging under $30,000, funneled $65 billion from thin paychecks into senior assistance.

Thus, the young help to shoulder what was once a middle-aged and senior burden. Today, middle age (when most incomes top $50,000) has become a time of high income and low liability. As will be seen, Baby Boomers are using their immense voting and economic power to augment both trends in their favor in ways no previous generation appears to have done.

Generational oppression is a recent development. Until the 1970's "Great U-turn" in the fortunes of America's young, government funded the young and old equally—as did the private sector. Only in the last 25 years has senior welfare, along with the private income structure, come to symbolize the greater value an aging society places on old than on young. The old are guaranteed a huge chunk of public resources, indexed to inflation and cushioned against economic downturns, while the young are not. While 30 million elderly received $240 billion in popular, publicly-funded income support in 1997 (up $10 billion from the previous year), 40 million poor parents and children received an angrily begrudged $40 billion or so in income and food support—down from previous years and headed for more cuts.

Virulent charges of corrupt morals and values have been directed at young, poor parents. But there is no values issue. Just as adults were and are seen as obligated to support their kids, so adults of the past were seen as obligated to support their aging parents. As American government has taken over the latter burden to guarantee security to the aged, but not the former, age-based double standards have become rampant. There are four times more poor children than poor elders, yet the entire $20 billion per year spent on the late, berated Aid to Families with Dependent Children (AFDC) program would have funded just four weeks of Social Security payouts. As elder benefits rose, welfare reforms shredded the frayed federal entitlement net for impoverished youth and young families and cast it to the ill wills of 50 states.

Leftist senior advocates such as Dean Baker assail such comparisons as "granny bashing" that pits victims against one another under the false flag of "generation war" when the real enemy is the wealthy. Problem is, granny has been doing some bashing of her own in an unholy "generation war" alliance with the wealthy for 20 years. Similarly, progressives such as Hans Reimer and Christopher Cuomo indignantly decry the corporate sponsorship of groups promoting "the right's imaginary rift between young and old," such as "Generation X" lobbies Lead or Leave and Americans for Generational Equity.[45] But they dispense no like fury against the growing legions of seniors whose votes to dismember schools, family welfare, and taxes create genuine generational rifts and massively benefit super-wealthy interests.

Senior advocates condemn means-testing (that is, providing higher benefits to the needy) of Social Security because of Americans' hostility toward "welfare handouts" to the poor. They point out, correctly, that the coalitions guarding liberal social insurance in Canada and Europe include a broad base of beneficiaries—the poor and middle-class students, workers, elders, and civil servants united in defense of their unified entitlement system. But the larger logic of their argument eludes progressive senior advocates: if U.S. seniors are guaranteed their own separate entitlements, they will oppose benefits for other deserving groups. Contrary to the Concord Coalition's Peter Peterson (who calls Social Security a "Ponzi scheme"), it was not a "mistake" that Social Security benefits were indexed to rise with inflation in 1972,[46] but that AFDC and other welfare benefits were not. And contrary to Peterson and leftist Social Security defenders alike, the real issue is not Social Security and Medicare's *fiscal impact*, but their *political effect* in buying off a potentially powerful senior constituency which might otherwise champion genuine social reform.

This split was and is predictable from the history of child versus senior welfare systems. University of Wisconsin labor lawyer and teacher Katherine Sciacchitano pointed out that extensive sex-discrimination concepts underlie such "male-worker benefit" programs as Social Security and Unemployment Insurance versus such "female dependency" programs as Aid to Families with Dependent Children (AFDC):

> Dating from the New Deal, this system has helped maintain divisions between women, African Americans and the labor movement, and has fostered liberal economic and social policies as impoverished as welfare recipients. New Deal programs such as old-age and unemployment insurance assumed breadwinners were men, and aimed at reducing poverty by ensuring the stability and adequacy of a "family wage." With benefits pegged to earnings, these programs favored white male wage-earners and were never considered welfare. By contrast, as Linda Gordon explained in *Pitied But Not Entitled*, Aid to Dependent Children, the precursor of AFDC, was intended not to lower poverty rates, but to enable widows, and to a lesser extent divorced mothers, to stay home with children. This is one reason that welfare has never reduced poverty among children to the extent Social Security has among the elderly.[47]

Leftist senior advocates perpetuate that debilitating division today when they indignantly distance the superior "right" of elders to "entitlements" from the "charity" and "welfare" doled to younger and poorer classes. They insist that elder "entitlements" should be kept safely above the messy "welfare" debate. Senior advocate John Hess is typical in his opposition to taxing benefits received by affluent elders because this would amount to "means testing," which would turn Social Security into welfare and subject it to the neglect and hostility that is now ruining the welfare system. The beauty of Social Security from the beginning is that it is not welfare, not charity, but a right—an entitlement, if you wish—designed to guarantee everyone a degree of security and dignity in old age or disability.[48]

This sounds good, but it gets the matter backwards and leads to wrongheaded divisiveness. Sciacchitano is more on the mark: in truth, Social Security is admiringly *called* an "entitlement," a "right," not because of its design; it is designed and denoted as it is because the groups it subsidizes (originally retired men, and now 30 million senior beneficiaries plus 50 million middle-agers relieved of supporting aged parents) are powerful constituencies. Powerful groups are seen as deserving, and the design of their subsidy reflects the entitlement, dignity and security that goes with power.

Conversely, the words "welfare" and "charity" do not describe lesser or different types of subsidies than the word "entitlement" does; the former terms have acquired derogatory status because they denote subsidies to powerless groups (poorer, mostly single mothers and children). Powerless groups are seen as undeserving, and given aid only grudgingly, by definition.

Social Security, more correctly, is an entitlement for the better-off and semi-entitlement for the poor. It only guarantees security and dignity to higher income seniors who receive its higher benefits; for low-income seniors, it only makes continued poverty more bearable. That is better than nothing, but in terms of guaranteeing freedom from poverty, Social Security is not universal. Like America's public welfare system in general, it serves its richer recipients well and its poorer ones less so.

The absoluteness of Hess's position regarding means-testing leads to an absurd extreme whose general principle would threaten all redistributive measures. He and other senior advocates oppose higher taxes *even on the benefits received by the wealthiest seniors*—which (they fail to mention) are double to triple those received by poorer ones in the first place—as just another form of means-testing. Hess calls "increasing taxation of the benefits of the affluent...a mistake" even though "a large majority of the elderly would not be affected"—and even though the wealthy would still take home much higher Social Security income than the indigent even after higher taxation.

This is nuts. Progressively taxing the benefits of rich seniors reduces the *reverse*-means-testing ("reverse means-testing" means paying the rich *more* than the poor) of Social Security benefits, not imposing means-testing! Coalitions are built from meeting the interests of the "large majority," not by rewarding the opulent fraction. But Social Security backers have gone the other way. They now defend the use of a regressive tax imposed on workers to support a reverse-means-tested benefits system, both of which are intended to bribe wealthy interests into leaving Social Security alone. By that principle, would they support a high defense budget in order to maintain the jobs of low-level defense workers? The $65 billion annual home mortgage interest deduction, half of which goes to subsidize homeowners with incomes exceeding $100,000, in order to free up more money for the rich to hire low-income chambermaids? If seniors can avoid tough political battles by giving breaks to the monied, shouldn't other worthy interests be able to do so as well?

"Beauty" is not exactly the right word for the multiple regressiveness that is Social Security. In the larger sense, preserving Social Security's retrograde popularity means the redistributive battle must be fought more vigorously elsewhere. If the income or property tax structure is made more progressive to compensate for Social Security's regressiveness, then taxes become more vulnerable to Proposition 13-style revolt by wealthier interests.

Leftists who angrily oppose Peterson's proposal to means-test Social Security and other federal benefits remain silent as to how America's 3.3 million impoverished seniors (including 600,000 in utter destitution) should be supplemented. Under the status quo progressives support so rigidly, Ross Perot's benefits must be sugared with two dollars for every dollar more to help the poor. That guarantees that poor seniors stay poor.

It is interesting how the phrase "means testing"—which originally meant fulfilling the Marxist concept of "from each according to his ability, to each according to his need"—has become the vilest of obscenities among liberal and leftist Social Security backers. The reasoning is sound in a narrow sense: Americans excluded from a means-tested Social Security system would oppose it. As Peterson's proposal to expand Supplemental Security Income (S.S.I.) benefits for poorer seniors showed, means-testing is politically faulty. In 1996, S.S.I. was carved on the welfare-reform chopping block precisely because it was vilified as means-tested "welfare." S.S.I., critics charged, was being sopped up by disabled children. Under tightened eligibility requirements, 100,000 to 200,000 handicapped children will be knocked off the rolls even though they would be considered disabled if adults, particularly ones with multiple impairments.[49]

There seems to be a tacit terminology agreement among Social Security debaters: neither critic Peter Peterson nor the leftists such as Hess who criticize his criticism call Social Security "welfare." Social Security is welfare, if "welfare" is taken at its literal meaning: a public subsidy. The average senior collects three times more in Social Security and Medicare benefits than paid in taxes. Either the public assistance young and old receive is welfare, or both are entitlements. To falsely claim and avail a distinction between "welfare," "charity," "entitlement," and "right" when the recipients all are deserving has the effect of splitting vital constituencies.

That leftists adamantly differentiate senior "entitlements" from child "welfare" illustrates how America's divided child and senior welfare programs' built-in iniquities based on sex, race, and class continue to provoke conflict between normally allied groups. This is now occurring. Californians over age 65 were the staunchest supporters of a 1992 Republican initiative to slash young-family benefits by up to 25 percent, an atrocity even the corporate media pointed out would devastate poor children.[50] California seniors lined up by landslide margins behind measures to shear school and university funding, cut tax burdens by a fourth, kick children of illegal immigrants out of school, abolish affirmative action, restrict labor (particularly teachers' unions') participation in political campaigns, and eliminate bilingual education.[51]

In 1992, for one example of many, California Governor Pete Wilson (Republican) proposed Proposition 165, a vicious welfare dismantlement ballot issue that would have cut benefits for poorer, young families by up to one-fourth. The press prominently pointed out that two-thirds of the victims of the issue's cuts would have been children. Proposition 165 failed narrowly. A *Times* Poll of 1,100 voters showed the split:

> People over age 65 favored it, but voters in their 20s were opposed. Affluent people supported it, but those on low incomes objected. Anglos leaned in favor, but minorities were against.[52]

In all cases, seniors' support for reactionary issues was the largest of any age group, more solidly aligned with wealthy, white, and Republican voting patterns even than rightist middle-agers. While seniors are more likely to be white (and therefore more in opposition to liberal policies), they are also more likely to be female (women favor liberal social policies more than men). Even when demographics is considered, seniors were still 20 to 30 percent more likely to vote for reactionary measures than their race, gender, and income would predict. This indicates that another factor is at work splitting seniors from compassionate social policies for others of the type they themselves avail.

Progressive advocates for seniors exemplify the generation split even as they deny it exists. Social Security defenders inadvertently raise a poignant point regarding intergenerational attitudes. They point to the fact that even a 1996 poll by Third Millennium (a conservative group lobbying to privatize senior benefits) showed that "nearly nine in ten young people said the elderly are getting 'about' or 'less than' their fair share" of public benefits. "That," wrote Hans Reimer of the 2030 Center, a Washington young-person's group which backs the elder welfare status quo, "should settle the generation conflict question once and for all."[53]

Yes, there is no evidence that young people favor slashing senior benefits. But Reimer and senior advocates who deny there is a generation war should look in the other direction. The old are now society's most reactionary group. This is something of a shock to me. In 1968, when I campaigned for Gene McCarthy in Wisconsin and Oklahoma, and in later utility reform, environmental, and social issue campaigns, "the elderly on fixed incomes" were a key constituency we targeted. The old used to be a constituency distinctly open to progressive ideas. No more.

The pattern of seniors slamming the younger generation's interests has become fixed in concrete in modern California voting, showing up on education, tax, and social issues most vividly. The fact that young people are not retaliating is discussed in the last chapter as hopeful evidence of the greater maturity today's youth display compared to lost and avaricious grownups.

Ripoff A versus Ripoff B

As usual in the generation war, it's the expediency of the left versus the even more devastating plots of the right. Currently, a well-funded coalition of bankers and brokerage interests champ to privatize and profitize Social Security through various mechanisms, some endorsed by White House advisers.[54] Privatization would be a disaster for younger workers, even by the lights of its own backers.

Time, Newsweek, and *National Review* (all of whom championed welfare cuts for the young and poor) headlined various "reforms" touted as necessary to save senior welfare from a projected crisis. The crisis is said to consist of a rapidly growing elder population whose numbers will strain the resources of the smaller, working-age population whose payroll taxes support it. The reforms to meet this "crisis," as proposed by a recent federal task force and supported by conservative and many mainstream interests, consist of various schemes to turn elder welfare over to private management.

Money taken out of Social Security and invested would come out of current system revenues. Higher wage and payroll taxes would be needed to pay current retirees while the invested funds racked up interest. The transition costs and brokerage costs would total tens of billions of dollars per year and would be paid by—you guessed it, younger workers. The Cato Institute, a conservative thinktank and leading advocate of privatization, estimates transition costs at up to $7 trillion over the next 75 years. A long and painful phase-in indeed. So privatization schemes anticipate raising the wage and payroll tax immediately by 1.6 percent to 2 percent—for up to 70 years.[55]

Social Security's fiscal "crisis" posed by conservatives is manufactured, no more true today than when Republican anti-Roosevelt warhorse Alf Landon declared the system "unworkable" in 1936. Senior welfare added up to $400 billion in 1997, providing 30 million senior citizens an average of $12,000 in income and medical benefits each, hardly extravagant. Nor is its future in jeopardy, other than from political dereliction: abolish the upper-income cap on Social Security taxes, and/or restore corporate taxation to pre-1980s levels, and the funding shortfall vanishes.

Both sides of the Social Security debate are wrong, and the wrongness betrays how smug and insular gerocentric politics has become. In fact, there is a crisis in Social Security and elder welfare funding. It has nothing to do with how much money is going into Social Security, and nothing to do with how much welfare senior citizens pocket. The crisis in elder welfare is the way in which its taxes and benefits are structured—and who benefits and loses from preserving its backwards system. Just as redistributing Social Security away from older people is not the way to aid America's increasingly destitute young families and children, maintaining Social Security's ripoff of the young and poor is also indefensible. If America is to build a young-old constituency to challenge pyramiding wealth, it must come from recognition that political expediency in defense of a deeply flawed status quo is the best friend of corporate hegemony.

Where, then, is the crunch coming in elder welfare funding? In my view, apologists for the present system have made a major mistake in calculating future Social Security tax collections from the nation's predicted growth in *total* income. Total income is not what is taxed to fund Social Security—only payroll income under a rather low ceiling ($68,000 in 1997, indexed to rise with inflation).

Senior advocates such as economist Dean Baker correctly point out that under reasonably foreseeable inflation and growth projections, gross taxable wages will be available to fund Social Security in the future. Not considered, however, is the pyramiding maldistribution of income growth. The only sector to experience any significant income growth in recent decades has been the richest fifth of the population—

those whose annual incomes exceed $70,000. This is exactly the group whose incomes are largely exempt from Social Security taxation because of the $68,000 ceiling. Thus, a growing share of America's income is not taxed to fund Social Security. That means lower income groups must take on an increasing share. That means a higher payroll tax on lower real incomes.

In 1996, the richest fifth of the population averaged over $110,000 in annual household income. An average of $40,000 of their income was exempt from Social Security taxation. Among the richest 5 percent, an average of two-thirds of income is exempt. In contrast, all covered income of the bottom four-fifths of the population was subject to taxation. The ceiling on Social Security taxability means the richest receive huge and growing breaks. That four-fifths of the nation's richest householders are over age 40, and four-fifths are white, completes the crushing age/race iniquity of the elder welfare state: the senior and middle-aged groups who most benefit from having younger workers help pay for senior welfare are exactly the ones who pay lower shares of their incomes to fund it.

By rough calculation, it appears that 20 to 25 percent, and rising, of the nation's total income is exempt from Social Security taxation because it is derived from investments or accrues to incomes in excess of the first $68,000. If all income was taxed just at the same rate as the first $68,000—that is, a flat tax on all income—the Old Age Survivors and Disability Insurance (OASDI) tax could be lowered sharply, returning tens of billions of dollars every year to poorer and middle-income workers and reducing child and young-family poverty. If the OASDI tax was made progressive, taxing higher incomes at higher rates than lower ones, then we would be taking aim at true wealth redistribution.

Finally, if the benefits schedules were equalized, some three million seniors could be lifted out of poverty. If each retiree was paid $750 per month, all seniors would live on annual incomes of at least $9,000, $1,500 above poverty level for a family of one in 1998, without increasing Social Security taxes or disbursements.

Have progressives proposed these two elemental reforms—lifting the OASDI tax ceiling in order to tax upper-income earnings, and equalizing disbursements to eliminate senior poverty? Only sporadically and quietly, if at all. Progressive senior advocates have not advocated (and in some instances, have opposed) taxing the rich in order to increase benefits to lower and middle income seniors. Such reform would hardly produce means-testing. But it would make the wealthy mad. Imagine if you earn $10 million per year and suddenly saw your OASDI tax bill rise from $4,000 to $620,000. Scrutiny of recent leftist writings on elder welfare reveals virtual silence on these two fundamental class issues (which even Peterson discusses).

Left Business Observer editor Douglas Henwood, in a rare instance of broaching the subject, suggested meeting any shortfall by taxing wealthier and investment income—along with "modest and temporary increases in the social security tax."[56] In contrast, raising the disastrously regressive wage and payroll tax is mentioned casually and routinely by leftists. Incredibly, so-called progressive senior advocates, fixated on maintaining elder benefits, not only dismiss the generational thrashings but acquiesce in worsening them.

Writes Economic Policy Institute economist Dean Baker in *In These Times*: "As far as Social Security is concerned, the latest trustees' report shows that the fund could be kept solvent for 75 years with a tax increase equal to 2.2 percent of the covered payroll."[57] Max Richtman, president of the National Committee to Preserve Social Security, which claims to represent 5.5 million people, endorses the oppressive current scheme: "Congress throughout Social Security's 60-year history has periodically adjusted revenues and benefits to keep the system solvent and up to date with changing demographics, and it can do so again."[58] The traditional means of adjustment Richtman cites, and to which he suggests no alternative, has been raising the wage and payroll tax. The bite taken out of wages and payroll to fund Social Security and (after 1965) Medicare has rocketed from 1.5 percent in 1950 to 4.8 percent in 1970 to 7.65 percent today—rising five times faster than wages have risen. Currently, Social Security's actuaries estimate a 4.7 percent increase in payroll taxes would be necessary to put the system on permanently sound footing.[59] As the middle-aged and old pay less and less to support the young, they demand more and more support from the young.

Richtman, Baker, Henwood, and other senior welfare defenders accept this tax iniquity without protest. The 2.2 percent hike envisioned as "an option" by Baker would take $300 more from a $15,000 annual paycheck of a mother supporting two kids, boosting her contribution to senior welfare to nearly $1,500. This in a time in which California's Children Now reported that:

> In 1997, the state's total economy surpassed one trillion dollars for the first time—an economic output equal to the entire continent of South America. Yet, many families with children are not sharing in the new wealth. Of California's 9.5 million children, fully one-quarter live in poverty (an annual income of $15,600 or less for a family of four). Nearly another quarter of children (46% total) live in families with incomes low enough to qualify for subsidized school meals ($29,000 or less annually for a family of four).[60]

Yet senior advocates calling themselves "liberal" and "progressive" not only acquiesce in ripping 7.65 percent out of the incomes of such poor families with children, they seriously consider raising that tax—to fund seniors whose average wealth exceeds $100,000. The wealth-protecting positions of leftist senior advocates are unconscionable, part of the callous indifference interests across the spectrum display toward young. The wage and payroll tax should not be part of progressive Social Security defense or reform. It should be decreased for poorer and younger groups and raised for older and richer ones. Wolff's proposed wealth tax is a model, one which would redistribute wealth and "shift the burden away from young households onto elderly ones."[61]

In response to administration and conservative proposals to "reform" (that is, privatize and reduce) America's elder welfare and medical programs, Social Security and Medicare, progressive groups have accepted the terms of a conventional debate that places political popularity ahead of generational and fiscal fairness. As a result, elder welfare represents a profound, and profoundly unnecessary, threat to the present and future well-being of poorer children and young families. Further, by rigidly defending a large, severely regressive tax on earnings in a time of rapid wealth concentration and reverse-means-testing of benefits in a time of entrenched poverty, leftists and moderates are promoting an unnecessary crisis in Social Security funding that Wall Street is set to exploit.

At all levels—public, private, family—today's middle-aged and elderly are providing less aid to the young than past generations provided to us while shoveling unprecedented debts and expenses onto coming generations. The crisis in Social Security is not in the future, but right now. The threats senior entitlement schemes pose to younger generations are serious and deserve more than curt dismissals. There are legitimate concerns about Social Security that do not stem from corporate chicanery.

Re-establishing the Shared Fate

In fairness, it's not just the young and poor that today's senior advocates brush aside. Hess and colleagues offer no plan to supplement the impoverished of their own cohort, either, even though he acknowledges that "one out of eight old Americans is classified as living below the poverty level."[62] Yet I can find no proposal, either current or long-range, among leftist seniors to relieve elder poverty. They seem to cite it solely as proof that elders are not getting fat off senior welfare, which is part of their larger argument for preserving a Social Security status quo that leaves so many elders poor.

I repeatedly stated (in five places in *Scapegoat Generation*[63]) that I do not advocate cutting or reducing senior welfare, because the problem is not with its cost. Nor is the solution to re-mold senior assistance into a charity serving only the poor and therefore vulnerable to attack. Rather, the problem is the deeply inequitable nature of the senior welfare system, the increasing damage and difficulty its regressive taxation will impose on poorer workers in an economy of concentrating wealth, and the political damage caused by the selfish indifference to younger generations guaranteed welfare has engendered in seniors and their advocates—including ones normally of progressive stripe.

Cuts in senior welfare would devastate low-income elderly. Why should a book concerned with youths spend more pages discussing the plight of poorer senior citizens than their own progressive advocates do? Because voting patterns indicate that poor elders are resisting measures to disown poorer kids and seem to identify with them. Poorer seniors show that class identification triumphs over age and racial division. Even in California, one-third of grayhairs continue to prove themselves staunch friends of the young.

And well poorer seniors should identify with poorer kids (who probably are their grandkids!). The biggest danger to Social Security comes not from Wall Street schemes to privatize it per se, but from the same kind of alliance of large numbers of upper-middle-income elders and the super-rich that has blasted schools and other public services. Check the demographics as projected by the Census Bureau: the senior population, 34 million in 1998, will grow slowly in numbers, wealth, and political influence until 2010 or so. In the following two decades, the elder population will explode: 60 million over age 65 by the year 2025. Not only will the numbers be large, but unprecedented Baby Boom wealth will multiply their political power beyond their huge numbers.

It is ludicrous to think this superannuated political colossus is going to be victimized against its will. What happens to senior welfare will be exactly what senior lobbies want to happen. The most likely scenario, viewing Baby Boom sentiments to date, is that lower-income elderly will be at risk of divestiture regardless of whether dominant lobbies opt for private, public, or (most likely) publicly-guaranteed privately-profitable schemes. Poorer seniors, already treated shabbily by Social Security's hierarchical benefit schedule, may get the same shaft in the 2010s that poorer kids got in the '90s. Today's natural alliance between indigent elder and younger has the potential to coalesce into a common defense.

That is why it is crucial that progressive groups emphasize the vital, generation-unifying economic case: senior welfare is funded pay-as-you-go by younger workers, who depend on high quality education and living-wage jobs. Seniors are not detached but have a powerful personal stake (even if the better-off among them feel no moral one) in the fortunes of the young. Today's generation can win lower taxes and higher benefits for itself only once, at the expense of future young and old.

Virtually any progressive reform will diminish support for Social Security among the affluent, but with the advantage of molding a larger coalition of low- and middle-income interests invested in the shared risks and benefits of a truly universal scheme. That is the real battlefield. Success for the poor of all ages requires a broadening of the narrow sightlines that characterize today's profound abandonment of coming generations by a smug, detached, and self-centered aging America.

10 Myth: Teens Are in "Moral Meltdown"

America of the Millennium seems to have no place for young people. Increasingly, teenagers are banished from public places by daytime and nighttime curfews and from private locales by commercial policies, age limits, and prohibitive admission prices. There are fewer places where they can gather at their own behest without harsh policings. They are subject to ceaseless attack from the White House to the local press as destroyers of schools, streets, communities, civilization itself. A single bad incident, an isolated miscreancy, among thousands or millions of youth is held up as proving mass evil at the same time worse, more widespread misbehaviors by adults are excused as unimportant. Behind this moralistic attack, and a key element of it, lies the backdrop of an elder generation which cares little about the education, job, or future well-being of its own youth.

Given the worsening social environments of young people, it would seem logical to characterize them as unhappy and negative. Henry Giroux argues at the beginning of *Channel Surfing* that "despair, exemplified by the death of Kurt Cobain (and more recently, Tupac Amaru Shakur)…is developing among large segments of young people." Cobain, lead singer for the popular grunge band Nirvana, committed suicide in 1994; gangsta-rapper emeritus Shakur was murdered in 1996, apparently by rivals.

"Youth no longer appear to inspire adults" to create a better future, Giroux laments:

> The new economic and social conditions that youth face today…suggest a qualitatively different attitude on the part of many adults toward youth—one that indicates that the young have become our lowest national priority. Put bluntly, American society at present exudes both a deep-rooted hostility and a chilling indifference toward youth, reinforcing the dismal conditions under which young people increasingly are living…Many youth not only are situated beyond the margins of acceptable society, but also are seen as irrelevant to the way in which society unfolds.[1]

Yet, however despairing we think they should be, kids do not really seem to be so. Harvard University Afro-American Studies professor Cornel West (who co-authored *The War Against Parents* with economist and parent advocate Sylvia Hewlett),[2] reacted with puzzlement to a 1998 Children Now survey of teenage attitudes:

> I would have thought they'd be more disillusioned, more cynical, more despairing. Yet their optimism is staggering. They must draw on sources of resilience I can't imagine. Maybe my own 44 years have led me to a certain darkness.[3]

"Fortunately," Giroux concludes, "there is always an indeterminacy in youth, a vibrancy that seems to exceed the limits adults place on them; this is what makes youth appear dangerous and at the same time provides the ground for prophetic action."

For the truth is that today's teenagers are not more despairing, suicidal, drug-abusing, pregnant, or criminal than Baby Boom youths were. Against all conventionally calculated odds, they are much less so. Consider California '90s kids compared to their parents as '70s kids: teenage suicide and self-destructive behavior, down 50 percent; crime, down 40 percent; drug abuse, down 90 percent. School attendance and graduation rates rising when they should be plummeting. In 1997, higher proportions of a considerably poorer and more diverse high school senior class took Scholastic Aptitude Test and American College Testing exams than in 1975. When adjusted for new scales, scores appeared slightly better in 1997—a little lower for verbal, quite a bit higher for math. Not a generation of talkers.

Nor is there much evidence of general despair. Despite terrific efforts of the press to negativize youths and their responses to surveys, young people seem astonishingly, almost overbearingly, self-confident and optimistic. We should be wildly celebrating the new generation.

In the weird Nineties, it could be exactly *because* kids are acting better and are not indulging self-pitying whining and finger-pointing at others that fills Baby Boomers (who tend to all the latter) with an envy expressed as hatred and contempt. Our attitude is summed up by Howe and Strauss:

> Boomers in the media waste no occasion to describe how superior they are to the pile of demographic junk they see in their rearview mirrors. They persist in heaping insult on injury, hyperinflating their already huge collective egos with every tidbit that documents the alleged stupidity and vacuity of the young.[4]

Demonization of modern youth, writes State University of New York education professor Sue Books, is "the Faustian bargain that allows the society to 'buy' a pleasing picture of itself at the cost of young people who, by contrast, become crime bombs, broodmares, terrorists, and predators."[5]

To return to the question raised in chapter 9, why was 1970 a turning point, and why are youth now the target of attack? This remains a difficult question to answer or, more correctly, to untangle the many possible answers to. I believe the driving factor is that the 1970s and afterward represent the period in which the traditional majority, Euro-whites, began to realize that the U.S. will in the near future (estimated at year 2050 or earlier) become a nation of no racial majority. This all-minority future is portended by the younger generation and is particularly visible in urban states.

The result is a tendency on the part of the elder, wealthier, and white to disown, hoard, and escape. This generational abandonment results from the belief that the chief threat to our society is that the young, particularly the young and dark, will bring it down through "youth violence," "gangs," "teenage pregnancy," and "drugs." We are looking in the wrong direction. The obsession over "youth problems" diverts attention from the worst threats menacing national well-being: the disastrous accumulation of resources in the hands of giant, footloose enterprises whose interests diverge sharply from those of the American people, and the deterioration in adult attitudes and behaviors.

Former Nixon polling consultant Kevin Phillips formulates an angrier rallying cry against the anti-future alliance built by the post-1980 New Democrats and Republicans than most liberal luminaries:

> The deficit is to be eliminated by the year 2002—but not by any shared sacrifice. Even as the poor, elderly, and students must prepare to give up hundreds of billions of dollars in federal-program support from now until 2002, tax preferences—mostly for corporations and the richest 25 percent of American families—are scheduled to grow by about a third and to total about $3.5 trillion over the next seven years. Packaged as "deficit reduction," this has become one of the decade's biggest ripoffs.[6]

But, were it just a matter of the super-rich gobbling up the future while Americans pointlessly beat up their kids, this book would have a simple ending: get ready for the inevitable Great Depression II or similar cataclysm sufficient to bring down the New World Order. What is weird, and complicates the problem greatly, is the second major threat: the way a large chunk of the Baby Boom generation fell apart from drug abuse and individual disarray in the 1980s and 1990s at the same time larger economic forces were choking jobs from the inner cities and cutting off the pathways out of poverty for poorer young.

Is it just a miserable coincidence that the personal and family chaos of aging Baby Boomers created fear of "out of control" youth in general (not just poorer kids, but many middle-class and affluent Baby Boomers' own as well) at the very time business and government leaders were cooperating to eliminate younger workers' prospects by downsizing, two-tiering, and moving jobs overseas? Are the private attack and the public attack on youth cited in Chapter 9 an accidental convergence? This intersection of the economic agendas of the rich coinciding with the personal disorder of the middle and upper-middle classes would account for the virulence and irrationality of the assault on the younger generation, its quick embracing by long-antennaed New Democrats, its timing in the post-1970 period, and the fact that it is not confined to simple race or class division. Of course, this coincidence may not be one; wealth concentration and Baby Boomer disarray may be closely connected, though how is not immediately evident. As a generation, middle-agers are not suffering economically.

What is clear is that wealth concentration and job elimination were at the core of the third major trend: the cyclical increase in gangs, gang violence, homicide, and early childbearing among inner-city youth and young adults in the late 1970s and 1980s. Of the three trends, this one was fingered by national chieftains as the main (if not sole) cause of the nation's malaise. This was a diversion, because the increase in difficulties among youth of color clearly was a reaction to the disappearance of work and the rise of survival-oriented urban "frontier economies" such as gangs and drug enterprises.

In late 1997, an exhaustive, five-year study of 1,700 gang killings in Los Angeles, undertaken by a team of researchers led by major Los Angeles universities and medical schools, found that demographic factors (such as the presence of young men or single mothers in neighborhoods) paled in significance to unemployment and depressed earnings as a cause of gang violence. Neighborhoods with the highest unemployment rates had murder rates 15 times those of highest employment, and "gang homicides in the city were almost entirely confined to communities where the per capita income was $25,000 a year or less during the five-year study period." In fact, unemployment and low income were such powerful factors, dwarfing the other six factors studied, that the study pronounced gang killings entirely socioeconomic in cause.[7]

These findings, like William Julius Wilson's, predict that negative behaviors among inner-city youth (and poorer rural youth) driven by adaption to surviving bleak urban conditions will take care of themselves when those conditions improve, opportunities expand, and avenues to meaningful participation in larger society clear. The unexpected, rapid abatement of violence in America's inner cities in the mid-1990s appears to signal that conflicts of the 1980s are being sorted out and paths are opening up outside of traditional education-economic channels.

America's challenge, then, involves three primary trends (concentrating wealth, racial transition, and deteriorating grownup behavior), a fourth trend derivative of the first (unemployment and gang/violence cycles among young inner city dwellers), and a fifth trend derivative of the second and third (colder government and institutional policy which is both repressive and ineffective). The defense of pyramiding wealth and excusing of government failings demanded a scapegoat to divert public attention. The rising disarray among Baby Boomers and the darkening in youths' skin color marked "out of control" youth—*all* youth—as that scapegoat. Although occasional conspiracy can be glimpsed (i.e., the cynical decisions of Clinton's welfare reform and teen-pregnancy advisers to blame poorer mothers for national economic problems), a convergence of interests seems to have designated youth as the new scapegoat almost by default.

Whose Future?

As pointed out in Chapter 9, the fact that seniors but not children are seen as meriting entitlement to public aid relates to the fact that the old-aged represent the *future* of every *individual*. In contrast, children and adolescents represent the *future* of *society*, but the *past* of every adult *individual*. When society's cohesion weakens as the United States' now is, individuals tend to guard individual futures more than society's future.

In an increasingly diverse, economically split society, American adults' penchant for moralistic stereotyping represents a direct threat to the future of a cohesive society. When polled as to why poor people are poor, William Julius Wilson points out, nine in 10 Americans blame the lack of effort, morals, and abilities of the poor, while two-thirds of Europeans cite social injustice, bad luck, or changes in labor policies.[20]

Since Europeans blame the economic system rather than individuals for poverty, they recognize "social rights"—the right of each citizen to a fair share of national resources sufficient to allow a reasonably comfortable life according to the nation's standards. Thus, Europeans support through employer taxation a broad-based social welfare system guaranteeing income, housing, necessities, health care, and schooling that prevents nearly all poverty and prevents accumulation of wealth more effectively than in the United States. In addition, European nations provide more generous means-tested welfare to specifically needy groups such as the indigent disabled, low-income elderly, and one-parent families. Child poverty rates in Western Europe, even though none of its countries enjoys per capita national wealth as high as America's, range from one-half to one-tenth that of the U.S.[21]

Are Europeans simply more moral and humane than Americans, particularly when it comes to preventing poverty among children? The answer is more complex than that. Part of the difference in attitude may stem from the apparently widespread unawareness among Americans that government policies, such as the manipulation of interest rates by the Federal Reserve Board to control inflation, purposely prevent full employment. Europeans, in contrast, may better understand their governments' policies of preserving good-paying jobs at the cost of high numbers of unemployed whose sacrifices entitle them to public support.

In turn, this public understanding may relate back to the greater cohesiveness of other Western nations. Why do people in European countries see their fate as a shared one between citizens and across generations than as an individual one? Once again, I think diversity is the key. As noted in the introduction, European nations (and Canadians, Australians, and New Zealanders, who support similarly generous welfare systems) are monocultural, monoracial, and (usually) monoreligious. The most diverse European nation, United Kingdom, is less than 3 percent non-British in racial origin. Citizenship standards for nearly all nations maintain the racial monochrome. Simply put, in Europe, the parents look like the children.

The U.S. seems to have had much greater difficulty coalescing as a society. This may be due to any number of factors: our frontier heritage which, until recent decades, allowed the disgruntled and poor an outlet to escape (as opposed to reforming) established society; the fact that Americans have not, since 1812, had to unite to defend our soil against foreign invaders. But the most important factor today, I argue, is the United States' great and growing racial/ethnic diversity. In urban America, the parents do not look like the children.

Racial diversity presents Americans with more difficulties in seeing "other people" as entitled to social rights simply because they are American citizens. Worse, America's difficulty in coalescing as a society has fostered greater tolerance for anti-social acts and a greater reluctance to deputize government, in the name of protecting the collective interest, to confront them. In fact, the U.S.'s worst anti-social trend is the government-corporate collaboration to concentrate wealth.

Studies indicate that the American public links poverty not just to innate flaws in individuals, but to race. As William Julius Wilson notes:

> A recent [1990] study of attitudes toward poverty among white middle-class Americans revealed that the image of unmarried black women with babies evoked strong negative responses when the race of the person in poverty was considered. Young black women were more likely to be held responsible for their plight and much less worthy of government support than single white welfare mothers.[22]

Studies by University of California, Los Angeles, public policy professor Frank Gilliam found a similar link for race and crime. Gilliam found that when subjects were presented with photos of the same individual criminal, "morphed" by computer coloring to appear white or black but with no other change in features, the public attributed more negative tendencies to the "black" criminal. This racial effect was most pronounced among subjects who rated themselves as liberals.[23]

Today, nonwhite race, impoverished status, and criminal tendencies are associated in the public mind. Add to this image the American belief that poverty goes with inferior personal qualities—that economic poverty is the consequence of moral poverty—and a unified, as yet unspoken conclusion emerges: the young, and the nonwhite, are justly poor and undeserving of public aid because they are inferior to the old, and to the white.

Here, then, is another clue as to why youth have become the new scapegoat. *Directly* stating that the increasing number of nonwhites is the cause of rising poverty, unwed births, and crime is politically taboo and, I think, genuinely abhorrent to most people today—especially to liberals. To preserve what social psychologists call "cognitive consistency" (in this case, consistency between what one really believes and what one feels one should believe or has to believe to maintain social acceptability), an alternative is sought that reconciles the conflict. That alternative has been to displace onto youth the fears which stem from racial prejudice. Thus, white teenagers as well as teenagers of color became the proxies for public anxiety. This would also explain why liberals, the most conflicted on race in Gilliam's research, seem to be the ones who scapegoat youth the most vigorously.

America of 1998 is not the America the older generation wanted to bequeath, though the real reasons for the disillusion are both difficult and impolitic to state openly. Which, to make the next leap, is why we are hearing so much about "morals" and "values" today.

Nuclear Nonfamily

According to a June 1997 poll by Public Agenda, Inc., American adults believe that teens are in "moral meltdown."[8] More than that: adults harbored "stunning hostility" against teenagers and children as young as five.

Although Public Agenda praised the grownups as self-evidently insightful, the sentiments were about as original as adulthood itself. In 700 BC, the Greek poet Hesiod proclaimed "no hope for the future of our people if they are to be dependent upon the frivolous youth of today, for certainly all youth are reckless beyond words, exceeding wise and impatient of restraint." In 1700, American Increase Mather declared that "if the body of the present generation be compared with what was here forty years ago, what a sad degeneracy is evident." Mark Twain's youth cohort of 1850 was derided by elder erudite George Templeton Strong as "so much gross dissipation redeemed by so little culture."[9] In 1935, scholars declared the younger "generation, numbering in the millions, has gone so far in decay that it acts without thought of social responsibility" and "is even now rotting before our eyes."[10] Etc.

In 1997, Public Agenda announced—as if this was something profoundly new and startling—that two-thirds of Americans thought "kids these days" were " 'rude,' 'irresponsible,' and 'wild,' " and portend a bleak future.

Neither pollsters nor the media betrayed an inkling that the poll could be viewed in reverse: as an ugly self-portrait of adults' prejudices. Public Agenda's authors, and the media, immediately issued yet another edition of false, out-of-context statistics and anecdotes about the "morally unfathomable"[11] acts of today's young people.

Even taken at face value, the poll's results represent a comedy of elders directing bile at the younger generation *they themselves raised.* Like the mother who accuses her offspring of being SOBs, the image of a nation's grownups accusing the kids it reared of being in "moral meltdown" would seem comical.

But it's funnier than that. The parents polled by Public Agenda thought their own kids were fine. But only one in five thought other parents set good enough personal examples to be proper role models for their kids. That is, two-thirds of adults judged kids as rotten, but four-fifths thought parents were rotten. Parents who insisted their own kids were upstanding while other parents' kids were hoodlums did not comprehend that they were the ones being accused of raising brats by other parents who felt their own children were angels. No, indeed; a large majority of parents indignantly complained that a large majority of parents resented being told that their kids were hooligans. To top off the circus, six in 10 adults thought the next generation would be worse—as if it possibly could be.

The Public Agenda poll's largest irony was that teenagers surveyed did not volley back their elders' hostility. Teens did not view grownups with one-size-fits-all negativity. Four out of five trusted their parents; 70 percent had favorable views of other adults. Teens' willingness to judge adults as individuals, mostly good and a few bad, contrasted sharply with the blanket bigotry against adolescents expressed by two-thirds of the alleged grownups. Public Agenda's explanation for this surprise displayed yet more senescent sullenness:

> Although it is obvious that most youngsters do not have routinely antagonistic relationships with adults—nor are they particularly dissatisfied with the major features of their lives—it is important to reiterate that *the public's fundamental concerns about young people center not on their day-to-day happiness, but on the quality of the moral guidance they receive.* In fact, it is not unlikely that some adults interviewed for this project might think many youngsters would be better off if they occasionally had a few antagonistic encounters with adults telling them to behave themselves (emphasis original).

Despite our best efforts, kids today just refuse to be miserable. Maybe if adults kick them around even more, they'll sadden up.

Today's grownups and our "morals" are depressing, even when handled kindly by worshipful fans. Boston University political science professor and "silent majority" hagio-chronicler Alan Wolfe surveyed 200 American adults in eight communities in what he termed the "Middle Class Morality Project."[12] They averaged 50 years old, seven in 10 were white, and their mean annual household income was $70,000. Nearly 40 percent took in more than $75,000. That would seem upper-middle class.

Wolfe's results, glowingly reported, provide a dismal view of conventional narrowness. In a dozen pages on kids and morality, there was only one positive statement about the younger generation (which the author called "refreshing"). Seven in eight adults said kids are "harder to raise" today. They blamed "the forces of modern life" arrayed against their "middle class values," which hampered parents' efforts "to protect kids from their own temptations." Asked to name the worst problems facing teenagers, 37 percent said drugs, 22 percent said crime and violence, 10 percent said sex and pregnancy, and 9 percent said peer pressure.

No one mentioned violent homes, parents' drug/alcohol abuse, or poverty. In fact, "a surprisingly large number of middle Americans believe that one of the problems facing children is *too much* money" (emphasis Wolfe's). Respondents thought kids "have too much" and "hard times strengthen character." They were "unambiguously upset about the number of options their kids have," the "cravings of their children for material things," and the way "the glitz and the hard sell of TV" and "the glitter to attractions of expensive goods will always win out over the seemingly old-fashioned values of parents."

Since Wolfe interviewed his subjects in their homes, it is more than a little strange that he failed to point out some contradiction between these parents' "old-fashioned" rhetoric of self-denial and their manifestly lavish consumerism. Remember that these respondents average $70,000 in annual income. Orange County, California, is the fourth richest county in the nation's 12th richest state. Its median household income is about $50,000 per year. So the folks Wolfe interviewed would be upscale even here. I have plenty of occasion to gaze upon Orange County neighborhoods. I do not see the householders in this most flag-waving of counties suffering hard times and embracing stern personal privation to strengthen their character. I see multiple vehicles in driveways of well-appointed condos and ranch houses. Boats. RV's. Often several. Swimming pools. When allowed inside on rare occasion, I see expensive home entertainment centers, appliances, and furnishings. No shortage of material things.

Generational historians Strauss and Howe's incisive *Generations* hints at the true nature of the new Baby Boom Puritanism. Aging Boomers, they write, "look upon themselves as 'growing up' to a new sense of responsibility and self denial," imposing strict moral standards on themselves and their peers in a "purgative" vision that "denial, even pain will be necessary today to achieve righteousness tomorrow."[13] Yet Baby Boomers "who preach honesty and sacrifice" nonetheless "remain personally self-indulgent" and "consume heavily while pretending otherwise."[14] Baby Boomers believe in self-denial and purgative cleansing, right on, but we have no intention of experiencing this self-sacrifice *ourselves*. We had the vision, someone else can have the pain.

Wolfe's sample, like Public Agenda's, thinks its own kids are okay but most other kids are bad. They also think most other parents are doing a bad job. These are the attitudes that disunite society, that pass Proposition 13, that build prisons, that hide behind gates, that abandon other people's kids as too far gone.

Author Osha Gray Davidson's review of Wolfe's *One Nation, After All* expresses a fine from-the-left critique.[15] The polled affluent are "complacent, morally smug." Wolfe's "smiley-face" portrayal is a cover-up for the bleak mindset he transcribes. She notes the narrow suspicions of the medium-affluent of all races against gays, non-Christians, women working, the poor. Diversity is viewed suspiciously. People who are not like us are threatening. "Over the years, concerns for larger social issues have given way to safety and economic security," Los Angeles supervisor Zev Yaroslavsky reports on why his solidly liberal Westside district now votes for crime-busting Republicans.[16]

Most people of progressive mentality would emphatically reject these prejudicial middle-American attitudes regarding race, religion, sexual orientation, class, and working wives. But when the subject is teenagers, it is troubling how many adult attitudes in liberal and leftist volumes such as *We the Media* resemble those of middle-rightist volumes such as *One Nation, After All.*

For examples, former U.S. Senator Bill Bradley, now with "CBS News," leads the Advertising Council's new initiative "to improve the lives of youth"—volunteerism. Bradley is probably the most prominent liberal politician. He acknowledges the high poverty rate among America's children is "shocking." But when it comes time to fix blame, he exonerates adults from responsibility for the "children's crisis." Instead, Bradley pins it squarely on young people: "We are in danger of losing a generation of young people to a self-indulgent, self-destructive lifestyle."[17]

In a vicious set of articles titled, "Why Kids are Ruining America" in the liberal magazine *George*, preppie novelist Bret Easton Ellis (who thinks his own "occasional drug use or driving while intoxicated" were just part of growing up rich in the Eighties) disgorges lurid ludicrousness about teenage crime, dope, and cultural gaucheries which amount to little more than an extension of his fiction:

> Teens are running roughshod over this country—murdering, raping, gambling away the nation's future—and we have the bills for counseling and prison to prove it. Sure, not all kids are bad—but collectively, they're getting worse. Why should we blame ourselves?
>
> ...When I was a teenager, in the early '80s, I felt I was growing up in a fairly sinister period...[but] things have changed drastically in the last 20 years, to the point where one can really only chuckle in grim disbelief. Cheating on exams? Smoking cigarettes? Shoplifting? You wish. Murder, rape, robbery, vandalism: the overwhelming majority of these crimes are committed by people under 25, and the rate is escalating rapidly.[18]

Eighties kids are sighing with "back in my day..." nostalgia? It may be hard for Ellis to accept that when he "was a teenager in Los Angeles in the early 1980s," rates of the crimes he pins on kids today—"murder, rape, robbery, vandalism"—were much *higher* among teens than they are in the mid-1990s. This is especially true among the L.A. white teenagers, his own caste: 110 arrests for murder, 198 for rape, 1,707 for robbery, and 2,615 for vandalism in 1980–84 (the five years of the "early '80s"), versus 55 arrests for murder, 68 for rape, 1,176 for robbery, and 2,898 for vandalism in 1992–96 (the five most recent years when Ellis wrote his piece). The three violent crimes are much rarer, and only vandalism is slightly more prevalent, among today's teens. Cheating on exams is hard to measure, but smoking cigarettes and shoplifting are also much less popular among today's kids than those of the early 1980s. Note that these comparisons, the ones Ellis himself cites, demolish his entire thesis.

George is published by Joseph Kennedy Jr. It's been a long intergenerational slide—not among American youth, but in the Kennedys. Imagine the devolution from a president who championed young people as America's greatest strength in 1961 to a Kennedy Jr. who vilifies them as America's greatest ruination in 1996.

Not Just Baby Boomers

Failure to recognize generational strength also plagues *Revolution X* by Rob Nelson and John Cowan. In their "Lead or Leave" Website's "100 Harshest Facts about our Future," these Generation Xers correctly cite tough economic statistics ("from 1929 to 1933, real income fell by 25 percent; for couples with kids in our generation, it's dropped 30 percent"). They then follow with what sounds like the logical behavior consequences: "Since the first members of our generation were born (1961), America has experienced a 560 percent increase in violent crime, a 400 percent increase in births to unwed mothers, a tripling in teenage suicide, and a drop of almost 80 points in SAT scores." The cited source is William Bennett's phony "Index of Leading Cultural Indicators." While the economic reversals are real, most of the above cultural denouements are statistical falsehoods. Former Education Secretary Bennett surely is aware that the "drop" in SAT scores resulted from expansion of the test's administration in the 1960s beyond the most elite students during the Baby Boom's growing up, not Generation X's. Bennett's other numbers are equally dubious, as noted in previous chapters, raising a moral question about lying.

Nor is it always adult complainers; teens are often negative about their peers. At the North Central California 4-H conference in Sacramento, I made my spiel that youths, even though abandoned, were acting much better than California elders have a right to expect. The multi-color youth panel chosen to respond was having none of it. Most hailed from an organization called Promoting Our Future, or something like that.

They announced that none of the panelists do drugs, but all their friends/peers were stoned slackers. (Shades of the adults polled by Califano who have all these doper "friends.") I've given up trying to figure out how millions of the angelic youth-panelists' "peers" can be snarfing bad drugs and not winding up in hospitals or morgues.

Everything about youth, the youth panel said, is execrable. (Shades of parents polled by Public Agenda who think most other parents are rotten). When I say more kids are enrolled in school than ever before, they almost spit: "Sure, more kids want to go to school and get other kids into drugs and drag them down like them," one says. Another panelist recited a Partnership for a Drug-Free America press release verbatim to claim that adults just don't understand how terrible their children are. He wound up declaring that marijuana sold for $40 per pound in his school. Derisive laughter erupted as respectable-looking 4-H adults amusedly asked for the names of these cut-rate pot dealers. Evaluations later showed the adult audience didn't buy the youth panel pessimism.

Which also points to the fact that a large segment of American adults don't think kids are stupidly dangerous. The Public Agenda poll found 37 percent of adults defying the vitriol barrage and predicting that today's kids will make the world a better place. Every once in a while I read refreshing commentary such as the following, written by Raymond Garcia of Anderson Valley, California:

> The privileged Baby Boomer generation is determined to deny their young the opportunities they were afforded as they shift the social investment that hasn't been gutted by tax cuts to police state expansion...The elimination of school arts programs and extracurricular activities is a shameful example of this.[19]

Montana and California 4-H (county organizations traditionally associated with state fairs and rural normalcies) have grown indignant about the trashing of youth. In Bozeman, Montana, local skateboarders were unable to win approval for use of city recreation facilities, even though the city government accommodated other sports, including an MX bike park. Liability was the excuse but legitimacy was the issue—skateboarders were not associated with a recognized ("adult") organization. Kirk Astroth, youth specialist with Montana 4-H, saw the controversy in the newspaper and invited the teen skateboarders to affiliate.

So, "Montana is the only 4-H with a skateboarder chapter," Astroth told me. "At the first meeting, 200 kids showed up." Some had piercings, tattoos, gothic attire. They readily joined an organization known for middle-American kids who raise prize steers and angora rabbits. The upshot—in an era in which many cities are banning public skateboarding—Bozeman anoints half-pipes (skateboard ramps) as legitimate sport. Because 4-H insists on an educational result, the local youth produced a manual on skateboarding techniques and history.

The fact that there is a solid contingent of adults who are concerned about adults' deteriorating support for the young and, conversely, youths who make no excuses for their own predicaments also are hopeful counter-signs that the generation war may abate. Peer-blaming youth panels aside, there is something to be said for ending the Baby Boom ethic that the ills of American society are always the fault of someone else—pop culture, the media, rap music, peer pressure, on and on.

Most black gang members I interviewed in prison or studying at jobsites tell me they don't blame their parents. "Hey, my mom ain't why I got in to trouble. I blame me," an 18-year-old former Oklahoma City gang member told me at his new job in film production. It is a sentiment I hear often from young people. "You can blame your parents, you can blame your teachers, you can blame so-si-ya-tee, for all your problems, and how does that make you any better?" one of the 4-H teen panelists in Sacramento demanded.

Rather than taking solace from such comments, grownups should be mortified. If the dreary Starr-Clinton squabble and the public response to it holds any larger lesson, it is the appalling degree to which Baby Boomers refuse to hold themselves or their leaders to any kind of standards. In refreshing contrast, the younger generation evidences reluctance to counter-blame the old and a willingness to accept the personal responsibility the aging virtuists only preach about. That would be a welcome practicality...but I still hope there's some searing intergenerational criticism from the younger end to light our middle-aged path to enlightenment.

Fortunately, nobody at the 4-H conference in Sacramento asked me to articulate these muddled thoughts. A black San Francisco kid boiled out of the audience and grabbed the microphone. "The problem is not that kids are smoking *weed*," he glared at the youth panelists. "The problem is that you"—he glared at the adult audience—"aren't providing *opportunity*." His lecture inspired a quiet Latina family-planning volunteer on the youth panel to agree: "We hear so much bad stuff about ourselves that we can't even imagine there could be anything positive," she brooded.

Getting Schooled

"We have traced the root cause of our social ills, and we have found it literally inside the amoral character of our teenagers," writes Lucia Hodgson in *Raised in Captivity*. Now our task "as a society" is "building prison cells for all the children we plan to fail."[24]

As this book goes to press, Washington unveils its latest dismality in the form of the White House Conference on School Safety, scheduled just 19 vote-shopping days before the 1998 elections so that politicians and academics can deplore "youth violence" and push for (in the administration's initial press release) "school uniforms, tough truancy laws, community-based curfews, and zero tolerance for guns." The Bureau of Justice Statistics and Department of Education prepared a statistical analysis for the *Annual Report on School Safety: 1998* and the conference's edification. It contains bad news for the anti-school hysterics: the schools attended by some 50 million kids are incredibly safe.

Only 10 percent of schools reported any serious violent incident in the 1996–97 school year, 47 percent only minor incidents, and 43 percent reported no incidents of violence (either serious or minor). Nor is violence rising: "the percentage of 12th graders injured in violence at school has not changed over the 20-year [1976–96] period," and threats of injury showed only "a very slight overall upward trend" over the last two decades, the report said. Most astonishing of all, just seven-tenths of 1 percent of all murders and suicides involving students occur at school, a locale at which youths spend more than one-fifth of their total waking hours (assuming they're awake at school).[25]

A glance back to the school violence section in Chapter 1 shows this information has been available for several years, which means that experts and officials should have quashed the terror over school safety stemming from last year's isolated shootings from the beginning. The findings of the new report called into question why a conference on school safety was being held at all. If 99.3 percent of youths' violent deaths occur at other locales, especially homes and workplaces, why not focus on those institutions?

Schools are vilified as violent because they are dominated by youths; homes, workplaces, and government are excused from responsibility because they are dominated by adults. A case in point is Atlantic City, New Jersey's, Go-Directly-to-Jail conduit, a.k.a. Albany Avenue School. In 1998, it won unwelcome national news attention for being "a leading example of the problem of violence in American schools":

> ...more than 700 suspensions, 68 arrests and two knifings since September. Students have attacked each other and their teachers. Other students have set fires. Many have vandalized and roamed the halls, banging on lockers and classroom doors, yelling. Stairwells, bathrooms and the basement have served as venues for sexual encounters.[26]

Count on the media and experts to fix blame:

> Nationally, every hour "40 teachers are physically attacked, 900 teachers are threatened with bodily harm and 2,000 students are physically attacked by other students," says Stephen Wallis, an administrator at a public high school in the Washington-Baltimore area and co-author of a 1997 study of crime, poverty and family structures in America.

A footnote '90s academician Wallis fails to provide: there are 50 million-plus students in American primary and secondary schools every day. At the end of the story, readers get a second opinion about what might be wrong at Albany Avenue School:

> ...ceiling panels are missing, exposing electrical wires. Other ceilings are collapsing. Paint is peeling. One classroom reeks from trash being stored beneath it. Sections of the building are condemned. The school does not have a playground...The school [was] closed four years ago for safety reasons...

...and re-opened in September 1997 without renovation. Then it was crammed with every middle-schooler in the city, double the number it was designed for.

Buried at the story's end is 13-year-old Steven Yarleque's insight that kids are "prisoners" in the school, "locked up...like we are some kind of criminals." The school bureaucracy, a beleaguered teacher added, "decided to throw 2,000 kids in the trash"—in the nation's third richest state.

New Jersey, to reiterate from the introduction, has an average household income of $70,000, making even upscale California look a bit rumpled. But the dismal refrain is the same, Garden State to Golden. Eighty percent of New Jersey's over-40 population is Euro-white. Ninety percent of Atlantic City's 8,000 children are black or Latino. Half live in poverty. In one crumbled set of neighborhoods, 800 of 1,300 children are poor. Surrounding the shabby retro-resort of the '90s are wealthy hinterlands, nearly all white. Atlantic City's Monopoly-famed streets wink from the spas luxuriating in Pacific Avenue and Boardwalk glitterdom as thousands of its kids stagnate a short roll of the dice away on Mediterranean Avenue, mortgaged.

Students at Atlantic City's Albany School must be getting an education about their times and town, the model for America's most subversive popular board game. Inventor Charles Darrow designed Monopoly for Parker Brothers gamesters to reflect the economic striations of 1933. Acquire both water and power utilities, boost rates to 10 times the dice roll. Own all four railroads, gouge eight times the fare. "Take a Walk on the Boardwalk," a winner if unowned for players with $400 in loose change, the hell card if it sited the monopolist's hotel. In the losing endgame facing a phalanx of opponent's green and red lodgings, it was a relief to sit out two turns In Jail.

Today, Atlantic City's middle-schoolkids are viciously warehoused by the thousands in a rickety hellhole collapsing on their heads. In the state Bill Bradley represented in the Senate for 18 years, Atlantic City's middle-schoolers are getting schooled in Advanced American Abandonment 301. The press titled the story, "a textbook case in student violence." A textbook case of adult, of generational, violence against the future would be a more accurate description.

The radical, often race-based disparities in school funding publicized by Jonathan Kozol's *Savage Inequalities* go to the heart of whether the United States will survive as a coherent, governable society. Kozol's interviews with inner-city youths show they are keenly aware of the unequal start in life they are getting from a society that demands so much personal responsibility from them. The public schools knit America's fabric. Our uniquely democratic goal of universal education and equality through schooling is crucial to the survival of a diverse society.

The tragedies of Atlantic City's, Camden's, New York's, Rochester's, Los Angeles', and urban America's minority-dominated public schools go beyond defunding and neglect. What purpose do these schools now exist to accomplish?

Public and vocational schools are designed to provide pathways out of poverty for yesterday's economy of job promotion and rising income. This unskilled industrial and skilled-trade economy, tied to factories, largely is gone from urban centers. The poorer kids of the future will be employed in service jobs which are sporadic, temporary, advancement-doubtful and benefit-free. Youths can be trained quickly on site to feed paper into Kinkos copiers, sweep casinos after Baby Boomer mobs have gambled away the day's junk bond dividends, drive lift-vans transporting the ambulatory geriatric millions, and assemble cybercomponents in globetrotting maquiladores relocatable as border politics demand.

The schools and economies of the past at least promised—and grudgingly delivered—some upward mobility to the poor. But that process reversed in 1970. Today's and tomorrow's economy, welcomed by New Democrats, Republicans, and global business interests as "Third Way politics" ("creating opportunities, not guaranteeing outcomes") appears explicitly geared to managing an employment structure that promises little career opportunity (in fact, not even basic job stability) for most of its young employees. Meanwhile, as recent Federal Reserve System bailouts of gargantuan market miscalculations by shadowy brokers and their mega-bank clients show, outcomes remain "guaranteed" for big financiers—at least, until the 1929-caliber Big Mistake is made.

The message from today's U.S. government, as opposed to the Labor or Social Democratic governments of Europe or the U.S. government of Roosevelt's time, is that it will not flex one bejeweled pinkie to interrupt to process of concentrating wealth or the global mobility of jobs. But free enterprise means free enterprise. Inner-city entrepreneurs (like their Western frontier counterparts of the 19th century) are giving established interests a big dose of it. Choke off advancement through the legitimate paths of school and career, and gangs arise to provide alternative paths.

A major irony is that the drug woes of the Baby Boomers have underwritten many an inner-city fortune in cocaine and heroin. The profit-sharing for 18-year-old clockers far beats what they'd earn flipping hamburgers. The risk of arrest or drive-by beats the risk of layoff from legitimate, mind-congealing no-wage goodbye jobs. Spraypainting freeway walls and abandoned factories beats sitting around chugging Hennessey on doorsteps working up a bad case of lack of self-efficacy.

The current education system, dwelling on divergent test scores riven by unequal preparation, advances the rift. The much-deplored comparisons of U.S. school products with those of other Western nations is absurd, debunkers have found. An analysis of the latest by Massachusetts Institute of Technology consultant David Friedman:

> The high performing U.S. talent pool was larger than the combined total of several of its competitors. The real problem wasn't a lack of cutting-edge skills, but America's deeply disturbing, class-based division between high and low performers.
>
> ...In today's America, wealthy, socially advantaged children outperform just about everyone else in the world. Poorer rural and urban students from broken homes rank dead last. Class appears far more important than ethnicity. A 1992 study showed that while U.S. Asians score the highest of all groups on global math tests, wealthy black students outperform them, even though overall African-American test scores are low.
>
> ...One of the nation's most cherished beliefs is that the poor can educate themselves out of poverty. But if economic well-being and social stability are prerequisites for academic success, the chance of such self-generated upward mobility is remote.[27]

And this returns to the question that seems uniquely suited to public schools, one bandied for decades: in a changing, diverse nation in which the old industrial-school training model is passe, what could schools be? What role can they play? If schools do not step into the void between poor young and rich old, there seems no other connective institution that can. Society will split, gated communities uphill, gated prisons down—the enclave/chaos future imagined by the science fiction writers and novelist Octavia Butler. Continues Friedman:

> Although nativists have long fought against educating immigrants, in a striking new development, they are being joined by a growing number of once socially liberal aging baby boomers who are enamored of the lifestyles of a Sweden or Norway. The explosion of private schools amid politically liberal urban communities, the growth of homogeneous white-flight cities in outlying areas and the anti-immigrant backlash now roiling the Sierra Club are all symptoms of this emerging reality.
>
> As newly disaffected elites create privileged communities in America, their politics has become increasingly intolerant of change. Industrial development, for example, is already a target. To the extent public education attracts aspiring classes that impinge on elite lifestyles, it, too, will likely come under attack. This conflict will add a new, potentially explosive dimension to what is already a contentious debate about public schools.

Norway's folk are 96 percent Nordic and 88 percent of the same Lutheran religion. Sweden's populace is 92 percent Swedish/Finnish and 94 percent Lutheran.

European monocultures can afford homogeneous class-based lifestyles because homogeneity applies to the entire cultural fabric (a few faraway Lapps excepted). Canada, the most diverse of our Western compadres, is 88 percent European white and, even so, is bitterly torn between French and Brit.

The U.S. is 36 percent "minority;" California of 1998, 48 percent, set in perfectly scripted drama to become all-minority just as the new millennium arrives. No religion commands even one-fourth of us. We cannot survive enclavism.

Whatever happens, the schools will be in the middle of it. During the 1990s, a record 96 percent of the nation's 14–17-year-olds are enrolled—up from 94 percent in the 1970s and 87 percent in the Fifties. The National Center for Education Statistics reports the most kids in school in 1997 (52 million) ever and "forecasts record levels of public school enrollment during the late 1990s."[28] Defying expectations, Generation Y is enrolled in school in record-high proportions; dropout rates are down among all ethnic groups.

One Good Idea, Two Bad Ones

The idealistic framework for a unitary American society was outlined by John Kenneth Galbraith in *The Affluent Society* in 1958 and requires little updating:

> To eliminate poverty efficiently we should invest more than proportionately in the children of the poor community. It is there that high-quality schools, strong health services, special provision for nutrition and recreation are most needed to compensate for the very low investment which families are able to make in their own offspring. The effect of education and related investment in individuals is to enable them either to contend more effectively with their environment, or to escape it and take up life elsewhere on more or less equal terms with others.[29]

Even a pessimistic 1998 *Los Angeles Times* special supplement ("Why Our Schools Are Failing") found that amid the state's deteriorating public school system, student initiative was at an all-time high. A higher percentage of students were enrolled in school, taking harder college preparatory classes, and applying to college than ever before. But students were being dragged down primarily by lack of funding; the nation's most crowded classrooms; the most poorly-staffed libraries, counseling offices, and administrations; and the failure of schools to provide rigorous enough classwork to qualify for university admission.

Does money well spent make a difference in the performance of poorer students? In the late 1980s, the Los Angeles Unified School District implemented its Ten Schools Program, which provided $1 million more per year to each of 10 schools whose students were all black or Latino and had the district's lowest test scores. The additional money funded smaller classes, higher staff quality, intensive reading programs, and full-time nurses (as opposed to nurse staffing only once a week, the district norm).

The spending was hardly lavish. It brought the 10 schools up to $5,097 per pupil in 1995–96, above the abysmal average of L.A. schools in general ($4,297) but far below the U.S. average ($6,200). Yet the improvements were dramatic.

Comparing 1991–94 with 1987–90, reading scores at the 10 targeted schools jumped at all grade levels—up 50 percent among first graders and 24 percent among fifth graders. This occurred even though the Latino student population, many of whom entered with limited English proficiency, increased dramatically during the period. Math scores rose above the 50th percentile. The targeted schools' scores in 1995–96 were much higher than those in neighboring, similarly indigent schools.[30]

Imagine what even the national-average investment in L.A. students might accomplish. But the bad attitudes of the older generation, which dumped the world's finest public school system in the trash to save a few bucks on property taxes, are beyond belief. "The *Times* Poll found that almost two-thirds of Californians believe that raising academic standards, rather than increased funding, is the best way to improve schools," the paper reported.[31] Would these adults apply the expectation of higher quality for less outlay to their own lives and businesses?

Given the large increases in youth poverty, rising numbers of recent-immigrant students for whom English proficiency is marginal, and higher proportions of students taking college entrance exams, it is encouraging that California verbal and reading test scores declined only slightly (math scores have risen) in the last 25 years. While English as a Second Language (ESL) students are portrayed as a liability, particularly in the acrimonious wedge battle over bilingual education whipped up by 1998's Proposition 227, the state's bank of languages could better be seen as a crucial asset in the new global economy.

The per-pupil amount of money spent on public schools has risen slightly faster than the rate of inflation in this century. However, in the last two decades, most of this increase has been absorbed meeting new requirements to educate students (such as the physically, psychologically, or mentally impaired, now termed "special education" students) that in the past were not in school. These are good trends contributing to America's long term goal of universal education, which in turn recognizes that students who do not fit in to traditional school settings are highly educable. But the increases in school funding to meet broader education goals should not be interpreted to mean that more money is being spent to school mainstream students.

Two threats have emerged to universal education, both surfing the false popular image of violent, drug-stuffed public schools. The first is the voucher system, which allows parents to retain tax money otherwise spent on public schools for use in sending their children to private schools.*

Voucher advocates cite Milwaukee, Wisconsin, schools as their crown jewel. The 100,000-student system is 70 percent African American. Its public schools had a 50 percent dropout rate, and most of its teachers said they would not send their own kids to the schools in which they taught. In stepped the Milwaukee Choice Program in 1990. Parents received $3,000 per child in voucher funds, equal to what the city paid to educate each public school student. The vouchers could be applied toward tuition at private schools. The private schools were not required to accept

---

*The following discussion of vouchers is based on information provided by Robin Templeton, who works with San Francisco's incarcerated youth and helps produce their newspaper, *The Beat Within*.

special education students. They were not even required to stay open if not profitable. So the ultimate result of this voucher plan, at best, would have been the enrollment of more middle-class students (that is, those whose family incomes plus $3,000 vouchers would enable parents to pay private tuition) in private schools at the expense of a defunded public school system serving the poorest and special education students.

However, the experiment had worse results than that. A four-year evaluation by John Witte of the University of Wisconsin, Madison, found the Milwaukee Choice Program didn't even improve performance of the students the private schools did accept. Reading and math scores were highly erratic, allowing voucher advocates to pick and choose what years and schools they would cite, which is where the cheering for the Milwaukee experiment derived from. Witte's more comprehensive evaluation found that "there is no systematic evidence that choice (privately-schooled) students do either better or worse than MPS (Milwaukee Public School) students once we have controlled for race, gender, income, grade and prior achievement." One private school closed down, costing its students a year of schooling. The unreliability of private schools and bungling of the school bureaucracy were to blame.

The failure of a voucher system, even citing the district most touted by its backers, is predictable from the limited scopes of private schools. Establishing a dual school system which entails shifting significant numbers of students from public to private schools will result in large increases in per-pupil costs in both systems. More spending on education is exactly what the '90s is not about.

In that light, the second, more pervasive threat to America's long-term goal of universal and equitable education is likely to be paramount. That is California's post-Proposition 13 landscape of fund-starved public schools in poorer districts versus public schools in richer districts, such as those in opulent Irvine or Corona del Mar, California, supplemented with millions of dollars in funding from local foundations. California voucher initiatives, soundly beaten in the legislature and at the polls, do not enjoy support even from mainstream Republicans because the "public-private" school system effectively accomplishes their backers' goals. That goal is a school system resegregated along community lines, which usually means economic class.

In pursuit of that goal, the strategy of the stratifiers is to freeze or reduce funding for poorer schools while raising support for richer ones. This goal, no matter how pushed, represents the front-line of enclave society. It is the harbinger of a future in which America's educational system will be formally applied to keeping poor people poor and preventing upward mobility—a process already well advanced due to the collapse of the industrial economy and distress of central cities. It can be reversed by intensified funding commitments to public schools with the goal of applying lessons learned from experiments which took the best features of private schools and applied them to public ones.

The education performance and other behaviors of Generation Y suggest kids today are doing astoundingly well due to their own initiative and are uniquely amenable to imaginative educational and social experiments. Yet, the 1998 budget resolution approved by the Republican-controlled House of Representatives pushed $13.8 billion in education funding cuts over the next five years, all to finance tax reduction.

Excuse Me for Existing

"It comes as a great shock," wrote James Baldwin (America's most enduring idealist) three decades ago, to discover at a young age "that the flag to which you have pledged allegiance, along with everybody else, has not pledged allegiance to you."[32]

The disinvestment in youth by government, education, and private economic sectors is accompanied by a movement literally to banish youth from public space. "Releasing itself from its obligations to youth," writes Henry Giroux in *Channel Surfing*, "the American public continuously enacts punishment-driven policies to regulate and contain youth within a variety of social spheres."[33] The disinheritance and banishment of youth shows the extent to which this adult generation increasingly reserves to itself society's resources, even extending to public space—raising yet again a profoundly moral question of social sharing (that skill we're supposed to learn in kindergarten).

The thrust of '90s policy and institutional reports is the ceaseless surveillance of adolescents. President Clinton already backs year-round schools combined with daytime and nighttime curfews (if anyone needs constant chaperoning, it's him). Bills in several legislatures would give shopping malls the right to ban youths under age 17 unless accompanied by adults. The coalescing policy goal is to sharply curtail teenagers' freedom in public, replaced by 'round-the-clock supervision schemes in which the youth would be delivered from parent to school to after-school program to parent. During periods at home, reports by the Carnegie Corporation, the Centers for Disease Control, Child Trends, and other institutions recommend parents should be present to constantly "monitor" their teenagers. Police scrutiny, drug testing, institutional confinement, and even electronic spying are increasingly available to erase any hint of independence from growing up.

"Boomer (parents) are more inclined to establish firm rules, reinforced by adult supervision and careful attention to any transgressions" by kids, generational historians William Strauss and Neil Howe note.[34] Mark Fritz's perceptive piece in the *Los Angeles Times* points out that recent, strenuous crusades to restrict teenage driving stem from "other reasons" than fear of accidents (which are declining). "Parents today seem eager to micromanage their children's lives," he sums up his interviews.[35]

But there is nothing to stop parents from micromanaging to their hearts' content without a raft of new laws. Parents bent on getting all over their kids' lives would not demand rigid rules imposed from the outside. Curfews telling their kids what minute to be home, driving and drinking ages establishing exactly what birthday their kids many indulge, school uniform codes telling kids what they must wear, and no-muss no-fuss drug test kits evidence a parent generation that wants their children micromanaged by government and professional authorities. Widespread support for legally enforced, absolutist wholesomeness betrays large segment of parents who have tasks other than childraising to attend, such as dealing with their own head trips.

The commonly held misperception is that Baby Boomers lived through a wild youth and now have settled into sedate, stern middle age. Wrong. The doubly dangerous problem for today's young is that Boomers' worst drug, alcohol, crime, and marital disarray crises are right now. They have worsened with each decade. Baby Boom 40-agers of the 1990s have worse drug problems than they did as 30-agers, which in turn were worse than they were as 1970s 20-agers and much worse than in their Sixties' teenhoods. Heroin and cocaine death and injury are spreading into heretofore unheard of old-age groups.

Just as two decades of sustained public and private disinvestment of youth led to claims that "kids today" morally deserve their poverty, and the post-1970 deterioration in family stability and parental behavior led to insistence that youths need tougher controls, so the sustained reduction in public space for youths in the 1970s and '80s *preceded* the 1990s "discovery" that teenagers have no call to be outdoors on their own anyway. In post-Proposition 13 Los Angeles's growing population, chronicles Mike Davis,

> public amenities are radically shrinking, parks are becoming derelict and beaches more segregated, libraries and playgrounds are closing, youth congregations of ordinary kinds are banned, and the streets are becoming more desolate and dangerous...in the massive privatization of public space and the subsidization of new, racist enclaves.[36]

As the flight from Los Angeles and other major cities expands past the suburbs to exurbs farther away, higher up, and on less buildable land, Davis writes, protecting the "luxury enclaves and gated hilltop suburbs" such as Malibu and Laguna Hills from fires, floods, mudslides and other natural disasters "is becoming one of the state's major social expenditures, although—unlike welfare and immigration—it is almost never debated."[37]

If youths increasingly have no right to be in public, investment in public facilities for young people can be cut still further. University of California, San Diego, communications professor Susan Davis's 1997 study found that "in poor neighborhoods, there has been an absolute decline in recreational space for children" accompanied by

> the expansion of corporate influence over space, and especially public space. In the case of spaces for children and teens, corporate America has generally been supportive of the cost-shifting from school districts to individual families at the same time that particular companies in the entertainment and retail parts of the economy have moved into the provision of entirely new or formerly state-funded services.[38]

In affluent areas, privately franchised "chains of playgrounds and activity centers combined with retail shopping" and "newly invigorated video arcades and virtual reality palaces" are replacing parks and public facilities. "Discovery Zones" for children and "Nightzones" for older youths, which involve pay-to-play recreational theme parks usually attached to shopping centers, promise to be the "paid-for community center" of the future, Discovery Zone's CEO predicts—what Susan Davis calls "branded space."

Other recreation providers, such as DisneyQuest, Gameworks, and Sagacities, plan affluence-serving high-tech entertainment centers and arcades "tailored to regional specialty malls, redeveloped downtowns, and mega-tourist destinations like

Orlando and Las Vegas." At the same time older arcades are being driven out of business, Susan Davis writes,

> the mall masters are explicit that they are not interested in the old-fashioned audience—the teenage boys without dates or steady jobs. Price and location function as ways to keep teenagers out, as efficiently as the formal screening of customers on the basis of clothes and appearance.

Disney admits to such screening. No doubt, however, the youth-banishing malls and high-tech arcades would be happy to take a chance on teenagers harboring charge cards.

The driving force behind the defunding of public facilities and removal of public space for youths, and now the moves to banish young people from public itself, is "fear," both Davises independently agree. "Fear of the dangerous streets, fear of unsupervised youth, fear of youth of color…the city itself," concludes Susan Davis, creates the market for corporate-designed settings based on "exclusionary practices" and providing "few unstructured spaces" for growing up. Thus the tub-thumping of agencies and institutions to convince parents that all adolescents harbor debauched "secret lives" of pure risk which must be stamped out via full-time adult supervision and control, which a myriad of for-profit interests just happened to be geared up to provide.

For youth of lesser means or those for whom home is a difficult place to be, and those who stubbornly assume the right to congregate in public, the policy just seems to be banishment. For example, "ravers" represent a large and growing youth movement to create a space for growing up. Raves usually consist of relatively cheap, outdoor, all-night parties involving disco-style musical presentations and other entertainment. Organized by DJs, artists, and promoters in their teens or 20s, they draw a few hundred to tens of thousands of youths. Like Woodstock, that vital growing-up landmark for Baby Boomers, many take place in rural settings. The patrons typically are mostly-parentless youth of more modest means who want to congregate and dance at entry prices under $30.

With utterly dismal predictability, police and the mainstream media have butchered raving, inflating isolated or fabricated incidents to connect it to drugged youth gone wild. In Orlando, Florida, sheriff's deputies subjected 17,000 ravers to strip searches; in San Bernardino, California, to dispersal with tear gas and rubber bullets.[39]

Use of marijuana and psychedelic drugs appears to be fairly widespread at raves, though not as prevalent as at, say, Woodstock. And like Woodstock, "there is absolutely no violence at raves," rave promoter Susan Mainzer told me. "In fact, rave culture stands against the macho mosh-pit mentality of corporate 'alternative' rock." (Mosh-pits are standing-room areas directly in front of the stage at live concerts, where tumultuous dancing, crowd-surfing, and proudly acquired injuries therefrom occur). Raves display more of a family-like atmosphere unique to parentless youths that mitigate against violence and problems with drug abuse, Mainzer said.

Imagine if the press and police subjected routine adult entertainments—such as tavern drinking, casino gambling, dance clubs, beer-soaked sports events, or booze-drenched high-class extravaganzas like the Chicago's Field Museum of

Natural History fundraiser-riot described in Chapter 4—to bans, strip-searches, and violent dispersals. After all, the most dangerous hours by far for thousands of intoxication-related deaths every year are 7 pm to 3 am, when half of all drunk driving fatalities occur, overwhelmingly involving grownup drinkers. If youths should stay home after dark for public safety reasons, why not adults?

McGruff with Love Beads

As the newer statistics of the late 1990s unfold, they demonstrate the irrationality of adult fears and futility of repressive panaceas. California's astonishing crime decline among youths of all colors over the last 25 years was discussed in Chapter 1. New York provides an equally surprising picture.

New York's Division of Criminal Justice Services' newest figures on murder by race and ethnicity report that the state's white teens showed no rise in homicide over the last two decades and consistently have murder rates lower than Canadian teens' low level.[40] As in California, New York's black and Latino youths show huge swings in homicide, with a high peak in the early 1990s and then a sharp decline (down 47 percent for Latinos and 57 percent for blacks from 1990 to 1996).

Together, California and New York account for nearly one-fourth of the nation's murders. Similar to California's pattern, New York's black teens suffered murder arrest rates 20 times higher, and Latino teens nine times higher, than white teens in the 1990s. Conversely, in two of America's most murder-prone, gun-filled urban states, white kids are safer from murder than Canada's! It is hard to imagine a greater testament to the role of economic conditions in spawning cycles of violence.

Police and many top officials claim the reduction in youth crime is not due to improved teenage attitude and behavior, but more policing. The media and politicians troop from Boston to San Jose to New York to Dallas in praise of cops who fumigate their mean streets of teenagers via curfews, petty drug and booze busts, and anti-truancy crackdowns. Yet they have failed to similarly exalt San Francisco, an odd oversight given that that city shows in many ways the most remarkable crime decline of all.

From the body-bag gang days of the early '90s to the most recent months available (1997, and 1998 through August), San Francisco boasts a 43 percent decline in violent crime. Its teen murder toll dropped from an average of 20 per year during the 1990–93 period (including a record 34 in 1993) to one in 1997 and zero in the first eight months of 1998.[41] Only 55 students were expelled from its schools in 1997–98, just two for carrying guns (both unloaded).[42] Teen drug deaths and suicides in the most recent year tabulated (1996): zero and zero. All are the most impressive figures of any big city in the state.

How did San Francisco—a packed burg of 50,000 teenagers, a heavy gang presence, a poverty rate among black youth the most shameful (40 percent) of any large California city—do it? Better to ask what the city didn't do.

San Francisco didn't impose a youth curfew (dumped by police in 1992, rejected by voters in 1995). It didn't adopt school uniforms or metal detectors. Countering the national stampede, it sharply reduced marijuana possession busts. It resisted the trend to try more youths as adults. It rarely invoked Three Strikes' harsh sentencing guidelines for repeat felons. It didn't impose status, truancy, or other roundup-kids laws to ban youths from public. It didn't enforce anti-gang injunctions. In short, San Francisco did *nothing* right, according to 1990s tough-on-crime dogma.

Contrast San Francisco's record with the clampdown of California's biggest cities in enforcing busting-kids-because-they're-kids laws (curfew and other status crimes such as truancy and loitering, and minor marijuana possession) in 1997: Los Angeles, 13,533 arrests; San Diego, 2,038; San Jose, 1,082—and San Francisco, 98. The average youth is 20 times more likely to be arrested under juvey-roundup laws in L.A., San Diego, and San Jose than in San Francisco.

Now, the change in violent crime from the early '90s to the most recent months of 1997–98: Los Angeles, down 40 percent; San Diego, down 35 percent; San Jose, up 2 percent—and San Francisco, down 43 percent. What about youth homicide, the scourge of the early '90s that ignited the corral-kids mentality to begin with? Down an average of 65 percent in L.A., San Diego, and San Jose—and down 80 percent in San Francisco.

San Francisco police were not shy about felony arrests: 2,000 youths and 24,000 adults in 1997. Perhaps its spectacular crime plunge, particularly among youth, points the way to an radical new morality: if kids do something really bad, bust them; if they're not doing anything wrong, leave them alone.

The Generational Effect

We have arrived at the question as to why the younger generation is doing so much better than it should be. Even raising the question may seem dangerous, since it would appear to affirm that it's okay to subject kids to rising poverty, economic attrition, and irresponsible adults. They'll be fine anyway, 's good for 'em.

Raised amid a crazy grownup culture that rebukes the morals of five-year-olds, hallucinates that kids are too rich, and rues that teenagers don't enjoy enough antagonistic encounters with their betters, we should hope today's young don't copy "the quality of the moral guidance" recommended by Public Agenda. Modern adults' indulgence of negative stereotypes are maladaptive to a future in which diversity will be the rule.

A more questioning academia and media would have jumped on this point already. We need more analytical rebukes to the popular hysteria of the child-saving and child-condemning lobbies. More of the likes of *U.S. News & World Report* writer David Whitman, who took on Hillary Clinton's standard claim in *It Takes a Village* that the laundry-list of terrors afflicting teenagers "are not new, but in our generation have skyrocketed." Baloney, said Whitman's detailed 1997 analysis: "Far from skyrocketing, some of the social maladies the first lady ticks off have actually diminished." In fact, he concludes after reviewing the status of health, drugs, drinking, and morality, "teens aren't all that troubled."[43]

Well, why aren't they? What could be behind the surprisingly good behavior and attitudes of today's young people, an improvement that began with the younger Generation Xers of the late 1970s and has now expanded apace in the teens of Generation Y? Conventional theory is no help. So let us end by exploring the unconventional future this country faces at the hands of today's kids.

Historians Strauss and Howe, arguing against simplistic "linear" forecasts of the future (that is, that present trends will always persist), point out that 500 years of American generations fall into four basic types that succeed each other in repeating cycles. Innocuous intervening generations such as the 1930s "Silent (Lost)" and 1970s "Thirteenth (X)" are holding actions. They "react" and "adapt" to the turbulent activist cohorts surrounding them. Idealistic generations such as the Baby Boom accomplish wondrous innovations in youth but devolve into moralistic repression in old age that often becomes self-indulgently dangerous enough to provoke a national crisis.

Strauss and Howe postulate that the early-century "Missionary" generation was like the Baby Boomers. In a familiar-sounding sequence, the Missionary generation imposed Prohibition on the nation but wasn't about to bring down Carry Nation's hatchet on its own drinking, irresponsible financial practices, and the disastrous accumulation of wealth—ushering in the Great Depression and a period of exceptional violence. In contrast, America's real builders are the "civic" generations of sacrifice and duty (whose indiscretions were mostly overlooked) such as the "G.I." generation of Kennedy, Johnson, Nixon, Carter, Reagan, Bush, ones which repair the damage done by superannuated moralists and then create bland new conventionalities for the next generation of young idealists to challenge.

Strauss and Howe set today's generation lineup as follows: the dying, over-75 civic "G.I." (World War II) generation; the amiable, adaptive "Silent" (or "postwar") generation ages 55–75; the idealistic Sixties Baby Boom 40–55-agers now taking the whips and reins; the confused and demoralized Thirteeners (Generation X) of 20–40-agers currently being crushed by the giant Boom mob; and the new Millennial generation (what I call Generation Y) in infancy, elementary, and high school.

Millennials, Strauss and Howe postulate, are of the civic type. "Cute. Cheerful. Scoutlike. Wanted."[44] Contradicting elder pessimism, they predict America "is going to love these kids." I think they are overexuberant, but right.

Their thesis would be strengthened considerably if not for a tendency in their works (Generations; 13th Gen: Abort, Ignore, Retry, Fail?; and The Fourth Turning[45]) to accept culturally popular but grievously false negativisms, particularly phony statistics, about young people as evidence of youth distress rather than blatant prevarication by the aging. I think these will be recognized as such once the surprisingly good behavior of America's young people finally becomes too compelling for the graying virtuists to lie about any longer.

The Millennials' leading edge, ages 12 to 17, does indeed appear civic. They are not shooting people, not abusing drugs, not much troubled by booze, not self-destructing. Their pregnancy rate in 1995, the Alan Guttmacher Institute reports, is the lowest since 1975, despite much higher youth poverty levels today that would normally predict higher birth and abortion rates.[46] Although health officials are trying to take credit for "getting the message through," the fact that the same message accompanied rising teen birth rates in the 1980s indicates a generational, not governmental, success.

So far, the young are not retaliating with hostility toward grownups. They seem to harbor no desire to chop Social Security or publicly blame their parents. Like the "G.I.'s" of Kennedy vintage, they are not puritans. Unlike the Baby Boomers, they are not overdoing the vices. The new generation doesn't even like to burn things. California arson reports dropped by 50 percent from the mid-70s to the mid-90s, even with L.A.'s 1992 urban flambeaux. The new generation seems to have learned from the mistakes of its parent generation—puritanism and its vicious judgments are not the answer, but neither is unrestrained excess, and the two combined (as in the present era) are deadly to society.

So maybe this poverty-stricken, multi-hued new generation has broad enough shoulders to shrug off the punishment its elders needlessly inflict and to get about building a new multicultural society outside the gates. History, the enduring cynic, suggests the young adopt the attitude of the old. Still, while opinion polls (always suspect) indicate that youths share their parents' views on most issues and are not always more liberal when they disagree, race seems to be an exception. For example, the April 1998 *New York Times*/CBS News Poll found 60 percent of teens ages 13–17 believed that blacks, discriminated against in the past, should be given preference in the workplace and in college admissions, double the percentage of adults who held this view.[47]

"Today's youth culture is marked by a diversity that goes beyond tolerance," writes *New York Times* popular culture critic and author Ann Powers in the paper's April 1998 supplement, "Teens." "All of the youngsters who spoke about their relationships for this article said they had dated interracially."

> "Their world is getting more raceless," said Susan Kaplow, the development director for Alloy, a popular catalogue and Web site that features a rainbow coalition of fashion models. "Kids don't think black and white."
>
> ...As their parents turn inward concentrating on personal fulfillment and making more money, young people are coming up with their own social vision. "The Baby-Boom psyche is focused on the development of the self, whereas young people are preoccupied with multicultural diversity and globalism," said Donna Gaines, a sociologist of youth who teaches at Columbia and is the author of "Teen-Age Wasteland: Suburbia's Dead-End Kids." But these positive trends are often ignored. "We're busy with our inner-life project," Ms. Gaines said. "We don't have time for them."[48]

Which would explain why Baby Boomers want police, institutions, and government to micromanage their kids.

"From dating and marriage to language, film, music, and literature, never has America seen a generation with so much racial and ethnic crossover," Howe and Strauss write. Noting that "the over-30 crowd cares more about what gets said than what gets done" about racism, today's young are well aware they "are the generation that must be most burdened with the social remedy."[49] The president's transparent Initiative on Race, winding up its national "conversation" with a bland report recommending more talk, is a case in point.

Yet at the same time, a fraction of the new generation engages in rare but growing numbers of hate crimes—violence or vandalism against people of color, gays, or minority religions. Most individual hate crimes for which arrests result appear to be committed by white teens and young adults, though organized attacks are usually connected to adult-run groups such as the Klan or Aryan Nations. The exceptional brutality of most hate crimes and evidence that they do not stem from any provocation or societal threat (a Native American man savagely beaten in Huntington Beach, California, or a gay Wyoming man tied to a fence and bashed in the skull with a gun butt) argue that these are not generalized responses to white fear of minority ascendance, but individual viciousness. The best evidence for the above assertion is that hate crimes are extremely rare.

Bizarrely, once again, the mainstream media and institutions seem determined to ignore the broader, healthy trends and to portray pathological savagery as normative to teens. The Scared Straight! program—a hate crime in its own right in its forcing of juveniles (usually ones who have no criminal records) to screaming, swaggering inmates threatening them with rape and mayhem in prison if they turn delinquent—twists the fact that a little more than half of all hate crimes are committed by persons under 21 into the reverse-implication that most teenagers are potential bigots and require anti-racism straight-scaring. Newsweek, reporting on the shooting of a Mauritanian immigrant by racist Skinheads in Denver, depicted the assailant's family as nice, liberal, religious folks and asked, "is anyone's kid safe" from being "thoroughly seduced by hate"?[50] (Yes, 99.99-plus percent are, as can be calculated from comparing even the highest estimates of hate crimes and groups to the total population of youths. Is any mainstream reporter or program safe from being thoroughly seduced by histrionic idiocy when adolescents are the subject?)

Even among Skinheads, racism is not the rule. A movement called Sharp's (Skinheads Against Racial Prejudice) Gang emerged to counter the culture's violent-bigot image. A good part of Sharp's image-recasting consists of inflicting poundings on racist Skinheads.[51] Sharp's and Scared Straight! seem like a natural alliance: profitable programming, narrowly identified target population, persuasive (though as yet poorly evaluated) attitude adjustment techniques.

A more telling message was sent on March 28, 1998, when The President's Initiative on Race collected four dozen young people for a panel at the Children Defense Fund's conference in a grotto of the cavernous Los Angeles Convention Center. For the finale, the moderator asked the youths to say to the cameras the most important thing they'd want the president to know about race—in unison. The Initiative's promos drooled for a knockout video image ornamented with multicolored young faces, mouths open in an earnest chorus of heartfelt racial sentiments to their commander in chief...without anyone able to understand a word they were saying.

The young panelists caught the drift and collectively balked. They soberly passed the microphone from one to another for individual expressions. For the Native American youths, it was the only chance they had to speak. "We are silenced in our own land," one said. The moderator asked them three more times to make their statements in chorused babble, without success.

One answer to otherwise inexplicable generational improvement, then, is normal idealism coupled with a kind of moral rebellion that surfaces in unexpected ways, such as was fomented by the youth-and-race panel above. Another occurred on June 13, 1998, when high school students in Springfield, Oregon, delivered a stunning statement to the nation, the older generation, and its bullying president: quit exploiting young people's tragedies for cheap personal and political profit.

As Springfield adults lined the streets to welcome the president to their town in the wake of a gun massacre by a 15-year-old in their high school cafeteria the previous month, students stayed away in droves from Clinton's gymnasium speech. The gym "was half full although all of the school's 1,400 students had been invited," CNN reported.[52]

Imagine yourself as a high schooler, as I was when President Kennedy came to southeastern Oklahoma in 1963 to dedicate a recreation area. Kennedy aficionado (as I was then) or Baptist Nixonite who equated Camelot with Vatican infidels annexing the White House, no matter. You show up by the tens of thousand—especially the young.

So the Springfield student boycott of Clinton was remarkable. "I don't feel like he really came for us," 18-year-old Aubra Lewellen said. "We're tired of hearing about it," said Luke Jiminez, 17. "We want to move on." Fortunately for a chagrined White House, the protective press dropped the profoundly moral message students were sending by their boycott—perhaps because the media is equally implicated in viciously attacking young people under the rubric of caring.

Two Futures

The previous "civic generation," the G.I.s, came of age during the Great Depression. Negativism about youths was rampant then as well, which seems standard procedure when adults have wrecked the country. True, suicides and homicides peaked during the early 1930s at levels higher than today, but then (as today) teenagers accounted for only a small percentage. Nevertheless, the 1930s press and expertdom pulsated with bad news about youths. Reports from Army and National Youth Commission tests claiming that half to three-fourths of the young men were physically or mentally debilitated. Kids couldn't read, kids carried guns, kids were in drugged and sexual torpor, leading journalists and social scientists declared.[53] The "rotting" younger cohort would end American society within the next generation. All that is said today by Carnegie and Public Agenda and Clinton youth bashers was said then, just as vehemently.

Like today, bad conditions imposed on youth were the foundation of anti-youth pronouncements by authorities and the media. *The Soil Soldiers*, educator Leslie Lacy's fine book on the Civilian Conservation Corps, reports "the depressing condition of the nation's youth" in 1932 and their growing realization that "capitalism was not working for their generation:"

> More than half of them lived in the slums and congested parts of cities, and many belonged to families...forced on the public dole. In this situation, many abandoned their homes only to discover that there were no greener pastures. Resentful and turning hostile to the economic and social system, numbers of them turned to gangsterism and crime. Losing confidence in themselves over their inability to find work, and beaten down at an age when they should have normally been starting in life...many of the youth had already shown signs that they were permanently alienated from the values of the dominant middle-class culture.[54]

Sounds familiar. President Franklin Roosevelt could have cited any number of spectacular crimes of his time (such as *Reefer Madness*'s famous drug-crazed Florida teen who murdered his family) to blame the nation's woes on the young and called a Hoover-style Volunteer Summit at which those very capitalists and politicians could deny responsibility and lecture youths on moral values—the stance Clinton takes. Instead, FDR, declaring the young justified in their disillusion "with a society that hurts so many of them," called on them to rally against "the forces of organized greed."[55] He boosted corporate, excise, and income taxes, dedicating one-fifth of the strained federal budget to new employment and education programs for young people. Two million youths ages 17 to 25 were employed in 3,500 camps by the Civilian Conservation Corps, which spent approximately $10 billion per year in 1998-equivalent dollars from 1933 to 1938.

In contrast, Job Corps and Summer Youth Employment programs of the 1990s spend less than $2 billion per year to employ a youth population half and again larger than 1932's. I had the rare privilege to work three summers in Olympic, Yellowstone, and Yosemite national parks as a crew leader for crews of youths ages 15 to 18 employed by today's tiny Youth Conservation Corps. Signature CC sweat labor— tree-planting, revegetation, bridge building, miles of litter pickup, acres of painting, campground maintenance, fisheries restoration, erosion control, fencing, long hikes uphill both ways with heavy packs to work projects—changed little in six decades.

Day after day, kids in my crews got up at 6 a.m. to make breakfast and ready the camp for work, then put in a hard eight hours of labor, then stayed up until midnight playing and talking, then spent weekends hiking the backcountry even in heavy rain. I could find no evidence that today's young people were any less willing to work hard (or any less creative in their endless complaints about working hard) than the young of 1933. It is striking how similar the organization, projects, work attitudes, poetry and humor, and every other aspect of the modern YCC's were like those in the old CCC's, vivified in Leslie's chronicle.

An anonymous 1930s corpsmember's "CCC's Soliloquy" Leslie reprints ("Whether 'tis tougher on the mind to suffer/The slams and sarcasms of outrageous foresters...to freeze or sweat in this dreary camp") is strikingly similar in spirit to "YCC Camp Blues," a groaned 1980s dirge ("Leader leader can't you see/Make my feet swell and bleed/Make me walk ten miles a day..."). "The louder we complained, the harder we worked," a grizzled old CC graduate told me. "It's when I stop bitching you better worry about me," a 15-year-old on my Yosemite crew grinned when I threatened to throw her over Vernal Falls if I heard one more adolescent complaint about trail maintenance drudgery.

The genius of the CCC in saving 1930s America was its connective function. It linked disaffected youths to the larger society of the day through job training, wages, and education—the last technical, through camp libraries, literacy classes, and schooling, supplemented with vouchers to fund college and vocational training. It brought youths of different backgrounds and classes (but not races) together in common work projects. It was a product of its special time.

Designing a year 2000 version requires thinking about what such a program would link today's poorer youth to and to whose benefit. Labor-intensive construction, maintenance, and restoration of public works is what CCs do best. A large-scale YCC program would alleviate unemployment and underemployment among the young, accomplish crucial upgrading of America's deteriorating public lands and infrastructure, and provide earned educational opportunities. Today's tiny YCC summer program's total costs are about $5,000 per enrollee and return about $7,500 per enrollee in appraised work value.[56] A summer YCC program employing two million youths plus a year-round program employing half a million young adults would cost around $20 billion (equivalent to the latest B-1 bomber phase) and return a net gain in work value instead of a crash-happy warplane. So cost is not really the issue.

But what skills would be imparted? Can the young fit into today's downsized, stratified, global economy? The use of young crews to maintain public facilities and lands in exchange for wages and vouchers for higher education meets a number of national needs—in a country willing to make any investment in youth at all. Clinton's tiny Americorps program, viciously attacked by Republicans, represented the right general spirit but wrong in many particulars. Inner city junior drug cops are not the ideal.

If government, education, and private-sector commitments to youth opportunity are not forthcoming, there are other private entrepreneurs ready to absorb the disaffected. Chief is the new urban phenomenon represented by Los Angeles's 18th Street Gang, the largest in the world, so mammoth that several dozen subgangs have arisen just to fight over its leftovers. Police are scared not just because Dieciocho's size far outstrips even the Bloods and Crips, but because it is "the gang of the 21st century" employing "equal opportunity recruiting":

> Although primarily Latino, 18th Street has broken with gang tradition, opening its ranks to comers of all races from many working-class neighborhoods* in a calculated move to boost its numbers...blacks, Samoans, Middle Easterners, and whites.
> "If you think 10 or 15 years from now...it ain't gonna be no brown this, black that," says one gang leader. "It'll be about who's got the numbers."[57]

Like other enterprise gangs, 18th Street is run by a collection of older adults ("veteranos") who "remain in the shadows" while "youngsters are recruited to bolster the gang's numbers and carry out its criminal activity." The employment of teenagers and young adults as entry-level street-and-gun enforcers goes a long way toward explaining why a dozen L.A. zip codes (combined population 300,000) have more murders among black and Latino youths than among youths of all races in the entire states of Wisconsin, Minnesota, Iowa, the Dakotas, Nebraska, Idaho, Wyoming, and Montana (population 18 million) put together. It also explains why homicide can decline so rapidly when gangs sort out differences. And it explains why popular youth-control measures haven't and won't work.

What is bizarre is how closely 18th Street's global structure—dealing directly with Mexican and Colombian drug cartels, renting street corners to drug franchisees, enforcing its interests with a philanthropic hand here and ruthless cruelty there, and mushrooming interstate and international reach—is like the corporate structure that abandoned inner-city Los Angeles and America in the first place.

---

*Make that "former working-class neighborhoods."—author

When the old industry leaves and established government and business default in whiny moralizing and self-justification, then the rise of new industries such as 18th Street are predicted by capitalism's most fundamental theories of entrepreneurship. Where traditional corporatism founded in elitist enclavism profits from isolating poorer groups, the new enterprises recruiting from a growing, multicultural future profit by openness and integration.

Downtown, the winner is obvious. The chief U.S. attorney in charge of gang prosecution admits law enforcement cannot control the "many-headed hydra." Each Proposition 13, president pontificating at flag-bedecked volunteer summit, get-tough curfew, employment cutback, welfare reform, and prison salvo might just as well be termed an "18th Street recruitment initiative."

So let us hope for the passing of the bad attitudes of aging America. In October 1998, as this book goes to press, institutions continue in destructive frenzy. An absurd survey by the Josephson Institute for Ethics deplores that 70 percent of teens reported cheating on a test, 92 percent reported lying to parents, half reported stealing something, etc.[58] The Institute's press release did not disclose what percentage of its own Esteemed Ethicists ever lied, cheated, or purloined. A let-them-eat-cake sermon by National Campaign to Prevent Teen Pregnancy president Isabel Sawhill, posted on the Brookings Institution's website (repeat: these are the *liberals*), dismisses joblessness, youth poverty, bad schools, and rotten adult behaviors; blames poverty on teen pregnancy (particularly by African Americans); and blames teen pregnancy on the fact that "women became more liberated," "sexual mores changed dramatically," and "shotgun marriages" declined in the 1970s.[59] Ironically, these moral/ethical furors were summed up in the imbroglio of the commander in chief (whose administration was approved by 60-plus percent of adult America) captured on newsfilm departing for a family retreat to explain his indignant, finger-jabbing lying about his Oval-Office sexual mores to all 270 million of us, including the First Lady and Daughter. Let us leave them behind with the vision of teenager Chelsea, striving to prevent a White House shotgun divorce, bravely smiling for the cameras, the only bonafide grownup (and victim) in the picture.

What We Have Is Not a Failure to Communicate

"Warning! Attempts to ram gates will result in severe damage to vehicles and persons!" apprises a sign above the truculent spear-jutting portals to a ridgeline community above Monterey. Downstate, Coto de Caza, Southern California's Finest Private Residential Community, advertises the genteel, walled life: "Custom homesites along the 18th fairway," its ad in the Sunday *L.A. Times* boasts, where parents can rediscover "peace of mind, raising children behind the gates." No celebration of multicultural diversity welcome here. All two dozen Coto denizens pictured are European-white, though one of the kids might be Japanese. "Well-being" is promised "from the low $200,000s." Twenty-five minutes via private San Joaquin tollway to John Wayne Airport and quick getaway.[60]

This is the future America's elder, richer half seems to envision for itself and its descendants. Fractured, gated, unshared. The leaders and media voices of the older generation wearily exhort that young people go home, go to jail, just go away.

Let us hope that the evidence from statistics and images is more than idealizing: that the emerging generation really does harbor healthier, more integrative attitudes to counter America's selfish, centrifugal drift.

It certainly seethes with ideas. One bring-us-together plan is suggested by graffitist William Upski Wimsatt in *Bomb* (mass-spraypaint) *the Suburbs*:

> You want attention for bombing? You want fame? You want adventure? Bomb the suburbs…The farther away and richer, the better. That way, they'll know they can't escape from the city they left behind.

In free time between targeted enamelings: "Overcoming isolation and broken homes by creating a family out of friends."[61]

The parentless of the new generation seems good at creating families: gangs, YCC crews, tagger crews, raves, zines, posses, runaway squats, skateboarders, gothics, too many groupings to keep track of, most disapproved (and many injunctioned) by authority. The grownup generation that increasingly fails to provide traditional families futilely attempts to suppress youths' efforts to form new ones around common interests and challenges.

"My art represents the other side of the guns and the bars and the handcuffs," wrote an imprisoned 16-year-old San Francisco girl:

> My art represents the child of my imagination. It represents my creative side, my side of hope and my side of fantasies, on the other side of the depression, the anger, the hate, and the lust that fill our veins with greed, infidelity, and self- and co-destruction. This shows the dreams that died along with the childhoods we never lived. Our imaginations live in suspended animation as we hustle, rob, and slang to make bread and break bread on things superficial and materialistic. These things of fiction show my love for things unseen and unreal. In this world, people have looked for an escape; search within your imagination.[62]

At San Francisco's 1998 Youth & Media exhibition, I marvel again at the enormous and ever-changing gamut of thousands of youth-run publications such as *The Beat Within* (prison), *Youth Outlook, Brat, Freedom Voice, New Moon, Tennis and Violins, Suburbia.* "Give me any topic, and I can name at least 2 zines that deal with it," the gay editor of the last writes, announcing her retirement at age 16 after four years of editing her own ("I'm getting old and jaded"). Scores more are listed: *AUTOreverse, Crackwhore, It Came from the Eighties, Lab Rat, Los Olvidados, Office Supply Youth, Puberty Strike, What He Did, You Might As Well Live.* There is more confession than an Oprahthon, but to chosen, sympathetic peers rather than blood-howling studio audiences. The cavernous Embarcadero warehouse echoes with the din of so many forms of adolescent expression that I wonder how anyone can find this generation enigmatic.

On an empty desert highway, I encounter another mysterious, no less energetic youthful display. I am driving back to Los Angeles from a Laughlin, Nevada, talk to the California Juvenile Officers' Convention on the positive developments among California youth.

Laughlin was a corner of hell. Sprung up on the Colorado River 25 miles north of Needles, it sports booming casinos in a high-rise strip more impressive than the downtowns of many big cities. Even on a Tuesday night, its slot machine and gambling arenas are stuffed with thousands, 98 percent white, 98 percent over age 40, smoking like fiends, drinking bourbon in plastic cupholders, all bathed in neon glare and a weird, ringy-dingy musical sheen from the simultaneous machinations of hordes of gaming devices.

This must be where a huge chunk of Middle America hangs out, in between moralizing to pollsters. Unlike Atlantic City's casinos, Laughlin's are not flanked by a decaying, ex-working-class slum but by a barren condominium sprawl which erupted in the last decade in the stark basin-and-range landscape.

Driving back, I exit from I-40 to Old Route 66, a sentimental umbilical cord from my Okie upbringing to Los Angeles adolescence back in the Summer of Love. The springtime desert is vast, enchanting, and silent. A car passes every half hour, headlights lit in Mojave custom. An occasional empty building appears, abandoned when the interstate shifted the main route north.

Suddenly I screech to a stop and pitch into the gravel turnaround in front of a vacant cement edifice, past function unclear. The building is awash in graffiti. Not Jane (heart) John, but tagger crew stuff. Three-letter scrawls, even some colorful, mathematically-dimensioned wildstyle.

This is 250 miles, a hard five-hour drive, from Los Angeles or Vegas. It's 50 miles from Needles (population 6,000), 120 miles from Barstow (population 22,000). Halfway between Essex (nothing) and Amboy (even less). Nothing here but sand and sage and querulous crows.

Yet many someones came out here to spend hours spraypainting a building only Snoopy's brother Spike will see, tagging desert signs lackadaisically just to maintain presence. An '80s song by the Australian aboriginal-rock band Midnight Oil[63] eerily fits the scene:

> Spraycan information
> Covers the lonely station
> Checkpoint for the state of the nation.

Raised by adults who forced it to grow up quickly and then punished it for growing up quickly, Generation Y stakes out extremes in every direction. Just as many Chelseas had to be the grownups in their families early in their own growings-up, so many young people must be the grownups for society early in their generation's life. Rising to that challenge may be the reason that the extreme chosen by the vast majority of today's youth is goodness— not just better attitudes and behaviors than we have a right to expect, but an optimism and responsibility that leave elders' empty moralisms in the dust. The attack on youth is a national pathology, unwarranted by fact, smokescreen for the failure of adulthood and its leadership to confront larger predicaments. No rescue by the monied, governing, institutional, or otherwise privileged is in sight. It's up to the energy and inventiveness of the younger generation to pull the gated minds of millennium America toward acceptance of diversity, community, and fairness, and I hope they have as much fun as I did in my adolescence achieving what we Sixties kids only imagined.

Notes

Introduction:
Myth: Today's Youth Are
America's Worst Generation Ever

1   Wilson WJ (1996). *When Work Disappears: The World of the New Urban Poor*. New York: Vintage Books, pp 29–30.

2   Shapiro RJ (1994, January). *Cut-and-Invest to Compete and Win: A Budget Strategy for American Growth*. Washington, DC: Progressive Policy Institute, p 4. See also Hage D, Black RF (1995, 10 April). America's other welfare state; Getting business off the dole. *US News & World Report*, pp 34–38.

3   Albelda R et al (1996). *The War on the Poor*. New York: Center for Population Economics, p 39.

4   Kozol J (1991). *Savage Inequalities: Children in America's Schools*. New York: Crown Publishers, pp 137–156, 236.

5   Shogren E (1997, 28 April). Clinton sounds call for citizens to volunteer. *Los Angeles Times*, pp A1, A8.

6   Goodman P (1956). *Growing Up Absurd: Problems of Youth in the Organized Society*. New York: Vintage Books, pp 42–44.

7   Maharidge D (1996). *The Coming White Minority: California's Eruptions and the Nation's Future*. New York: Times Books, p 293.

8   Kozol J (1995). *Amazing Grace: The Lives of Children and the Conscience of a Nation*. New York: Crown Publishers, p 230.

9   Howe N, Strauss B (1993). *13th Gen: Abort, Retry, Ignore, Fail?* New York: Vintage Books, pp 17 (quoted), 18–28.

10 Blumstein A (1995, August). Violence by young people: Why the deadly nexus? *National Institute of Justice Journal*, p 3.

11 Children Now (1998). *A Different World: Children's Perceptions of Race and Class in the Media*. Oakland, CA: Children Now.

12 Males M (1998, 29 April). Five myths about teenagers and why adults believe them. *The New York Times*, Special Section, Adolescents.

13 Bureau of the Census (1997). *Statistical Abstract of the United States 1996*. Washington: U.S. Department of Commerce, Table 23.

14 Maharidge D (1996), *op cit*, pp 11, 129.

15 See Chester L, Hodgson G, Page B (1969). *An American Melodrama*. New York: Viking Press, pp 307–13; Williams TH (1969). *Huey Long*. New York: Alfred A. Knopf, Inc.

16 Shrag P (1998). *Paradise Lost: California's Experience, America's Future*. The New Press.

17 Presiding Justice (Gardner). *In re Ronald S. California Court of Appeals*, Fourth District. 69 Cal.App.3d 866, 138 Cal.Rprtr. 387.

18 Davis A, in Males M (1989, 18 October). Youth crime is tied to earlier abuse. *Bozeman Daily Chronicle*, p 3.

19 Office of Juvenile Justice and Delinquency Prevention (1996). *Juvenile Offenders and Victims: A National Report*. Washington, DC: U.S. Department of Justice, p 144.

20 See discussion and references in Males M (1996). *The Scapegoat Generation: America's War on Adolescents*. Monroe, ME: Common Courage Press, pp 242–53.

21 Kearns R (1998, May). Finding profit in at-risk kids. *Youth Today*, pp 1, 10–11.

22 Baum D (1996). *Smoke and Mirrors: The War on Drugs and the Politics of Failure*. Boston: Little Brown, p 155.

23 Kozol (1995), *op cit*, p 107.

24 Rorty R (1998). *Achieving Our Country: Leftist Thought in Twentieth-Century America*. London: Harvard University Press, pp 14, 86.

25 Males M (1992, September). Top 10 school problems are myths. *Phi Delta Kappan*, p 54.

26 Cockburn A, Silverstein K (1996). *Washington Babylon*. London: Verso, p viii.

27 Pinkerton JP (1998, 13 August). Clinton turns 180 degrees away from Clintoncare. *Los Angeles Times*, p B9.

28 Rhule P, Soriano CG (1998, 1–3 May). Teens tackle their identity crisis. *USA Weekend*, pp 6–18.

29 Califano JA Jr (1995, 16 September). Adult smoking victims all started young. *New York Times*, p A14.

30 Rosenblatt RA, and AP (1998, 31 May). Clinton sees no need for school prayer measure. Drugs behind youth crimes, senator says. *Los Angeles Times*, p A4.

31 Ivins M (1995, 27 March). Illegitimacy ratio—another idiotic GOP policy. *Liberal Opinion Week*, p 4.

32 Wiscombe J (1998, 18 January). I don't do therapy. *Los Angeles Times Magazine*, p 12.

33 Mitchell JL (1998, 31 May). Larry knows best. *Los Angeles Times Magazine*, p 15.

34 Young CM (1997, 18 September). Geraldo Rivera. *Rolling Stone*, 769, pp 118–19.

35 Derber C (1996). *The Wilding of America: How Greed and Violence Are Eroding Our Nation's Character*. New York: St. Martin's Press.

36 Children Now (1998). *Report Card 1997: Spotlight on California's counties*. Oakland, CA: Children Now, p 5.

37 Davis M (1990). *City of Quartz: Excavating the Future in Los Angeles*. New York: Vintage Books, p 223.

38 Docuyanan F (1998, March). *The heavens, the lake, the river, and the pit: Graffiti and the politics of space in urban Los Angeles*. Irvine, CA: University of California, summary of poster presentation to the Environmental Research Design Association, St. Louis, MO.

39 Davis M. How Eden lost its garden, cited in Docuyanan (1998), *op cit*.

40 Wilson WJ (1996), *op cit*, pp 73–78.

41 Wimsatt WU (1994, October). *Bomb the Suburbs*. Chicago: The Subway and Elevated Press Co, p 66.

42 Docuyanan F (1998, 4 February). *Inscribing at the Crossroads of Culture and Crime: A Study of Urban Graffiti Writers in Southern California.* Irvine, CA, University of California, School of Social Ecology: Dissertation Proposal, Literature Review, p 33.

43 Males M (1994, 7 July). In defense of graffiti: There's worse ugliness than tagging. *Coast Weekly* (Monterey-Seaside, CA), p 8.

44 Appel C (1994, 28 July). Letters. *Coast Weekly.*

45 Thompson AC (1998, 11 March). The writing on the wall. A nighttime bicycle tour of S.F.'s graffiti galleries. *Bay Guardian*, pp 24–27.

46 Rodriguez LJ (1993). *La Vida Loca: Gang Days in L.A.* New York: Simon & Schuster, p 250. English title: *Always Running.*

Chapter 1: Myth: Teens Are Violent Thugs

1 Levine B (1995, 6 September). A new wave of mayhem. *Los Angeles Times*, pp E1, E4.

2 Vanzi M (1997, 11 April). Speaker open to executing 13-year-olds. *Los Angeles Times*, pp A3, A19.

3 *Time* (1996, 15 January), Now for the bad news... p 52.

4 Wilson JQ (1975). *Thinking About Crime.* New York: Basic Books, p 18.

5 Bennett WJ, DiIulio JJ Jr, Walters JP (1996). *Body Count.* New York: Simon & Schuster, jacket.

6 Dailey D (1998, 9 August). The unthinkable for kids. *Los Angeles Times Book Review*, p 7.

7 Gould SJ (1981). *The Mismeasure of Man.* New York: W.W. Norton & Co.

8 Fanon F (1963). *The Wretched of the Earth.* New York: Grove Press, pp 297, 300.

9 Rodriguez R (1996, 21 January). The coming mayhem. *The Los Angeles Times*, pp M1, M6.

10 Fanon (1963), *op cit*, p 298.

11 Kantrowitz B (1996). Youths are increasingly violent. In Bender D. and Leone B. (editors). *Violence: Opposing Viewpoints.* San Diego, CA: Greenhaven Press, p. 50.

12 Zoglin R et al (1996, 15 January). Now for the bad news: A teenage time bomb. *Time*, p 52.

13 Easton NJ (1995, 2 May). The crime doctor is in. *The Los Angeles Times*, pp E1, E7.

14 Gould SJ (1981). *The Mismeasure of Man.* New York: W.W. Norton & Co.

15 Davis M (1993). Who killed Los Angeles? Part Two: The verdict is given. *New Left Review*, 199, pp 29–54. Quoted is p 46.

16 Statistics Canada (1998, 2 July). Homicide Survey. Firearms: Canada/United States comparison. Website posting.

17 Hanlon M (1998, 2 August). Squeegees: Rebels without a cause. *Toronto Star*, p A3.

18 Kozol J (1995). *Amazing Grace.* New York: Crown Publishers, p 143.

19 Bennett WJ et al (1996), *op cit*, p 41.

20 McDonnell PJ (1997, 7 June). Theory on age and crime disputed. *Los Angeles Times*, pp A26–A27.

21 Butterfield F (1997, 12 October). Property crimes steadily decline, led by burglary. *New York Times*, p 1.

22 Wilson JQ (1975), *op cit*, p 20.

23 Wilson JQ (1975), *op cit*, pp 17–18.

24 Wilson JQ (1975), *op cit*, p 11.

25 Bender D, Leone B, eds. (1997). *Juvenile Crime.* San Diego: Greenhaven Press, pp 92–93; *Time* (1996, 15 January), *op cit.*

26 DiIulio JJ Jr (1995, 16 December). Moral poverty. *Chicago Tribune.*

27 Editors (1997, September–October). Unconditional love. *Sojourners*, pp 16, 19.

28 Hodgson L (1997). *Raised in Captivity: Why Does America Fail Its Children?* St. Paul, MN: Graywolf Press, p 144.

29 Wilson JQ, editor (1983). *Crime and Public Policy.* San Francisco: ICS Press, pp 19–20.

30 Davis M (1990). *City of Quartz: Excavating the Future in Los Angeles.* New York: Vintage Books, pp 272–73, 277.

31 Snyder HN et al (1996, February). *Juvenile Offenders and Victims: 1996 Update on Violence.* Washington, DC: Office of Juvenile Justice and Delinquency Prevention, p 1.

32 U.S. Advisory Board on Child Abuse and Neglect (1995 April). *A Nation's Shame: Fatal Child Abuse and Neglect in the United States.* Washington: U.S. Congress.

33 American Humane Association (1989). In Bureau of the Census (1992). *Statistical Abstract of the United States 1992.* Washington, DC, U.S. Department of Commerce, Table 301; Vanzi M (1996, 6 January). State leads U.S. in child abuse but fails to address problem, study says. *Los Angeles Times*, p A31.

34 Sickmund M (1996, Summer). 3 in 10 juveniles who killed had an adult accomplice. *National Conference of Juvenile and Family Court Judges*, p 15.

35 Klein MW (1995). *The American Street Gang: Its Nature, Prevalence, and Control.* New York: Oxford University Press, p 21.

36 Klein MW (1995). *op cit*, pp 104–05.

37 Grad S (1998, 24 January). More kids and adults in gangs, study shows. *Los Angeles Times*, pp B1, B5.

38 Braun S, Moehringer JR (1998, 25 March). 5 shot dead at school in Arkansas; 2 boys held. *Los Angeles Times*, pp A1, A10,

39 Associated Press (1998, 25 March). Mother accused of suffocating her 3 children in S.F. suburb. *Los Angeles Times*, p A19.

40 Associated Press (1998, 15 June). Parents accused of dismembering 16-month-old. Chicago.

41 Hodgson L (1997), *op cit*, p 68.

42 Young D, Grove J (1997, 10 December). Murder. *LEO*, p 7.

43 Bureau of Justice Statistics (1997, August). Violence-related injuries treated in hospital emergency departments. Washington, DC: U.S. Department of Justice, NCJ156921.

44 Dodge KA, Bates JE, Pettit G (1990, 21 December). Mechanisms in the cycle of violence. *Science*, 250, pp 1578–1683.

45 National Center on Child Abuse and Neglect.

National Child Abuse and Neglect Data System. In Bureau of the Census (1997). *Statistical Abstract of the United States 1997.* Washington: U.S. Department of Commerce. Table 352.

46 Widom CS (1989, April). The cycle of violence. *Science,* 244, pp 301–308.

47 Legislative Analyst's Office (1996, January). *Child Abuse and Neglect in California,* Part I. Sacramento: California State Legislature, p 1. See web posting.

48 Murphy K (1998, 23 April). Student's home yields cache of weapons. *Los Angeles Times,* p A1.

49 Taken from *Los Angeles Times* (Orange County edition) reports (1997, December 19, 20, and 1998, April 23, 26, May 20, 23, August 5, 11). Outside of a small circle of friends, taken from *Phil Ochs, RIP.*

50 Slater E (1998, 5 September). Prosecutors drop murder case against boys, 7 and 8. *Los Angeles Times,* p A40.

51 Chen E (1998, 22 May). Clinton asks for crusade against juvenile violence. *Los Angeles Times,* p A4.

52 Alberto A *et al* (1992, 24 September). Effect of the Gulf War on infant and child mortality in Iraq. *New England Journal of Medicine,* 327, pp 931–36.

53 U.S. Information Agency (1998, 3 March). Clinton says UN resolution sends clear message to Iraq. Washington, DC: USIA. Reuters (1998, 4 February). Yeltsin: Clinton's Iraq actions could lead to world war. Moscow.

54 Associated Press (1997, 7 December). Shootings a 'wake-up call,' Clinton says. Washington.

55 Lacey M (1998, 21 July). Clinton to hold forum on school safety. *Los Angeles Times,* p A10.

56 Yagemann S (1997, 4 August). 90% of "187" is based on schoolteachers' reality. *Los Angeles Times,* p F5.

57 Will GF (1997, 10 August). "187" opens a window on the dark side. *Los Angeles Times,* p M5.

58 Cohan L (1997, 25 August). Facing what's really going on in the schools. *Los Angeles Times,* p F5.

59 CNN (1998, 22 March).

60 California Department of Education (1998). California safe schools assessment, 1996–97. Web posting.

61 Kachur SP *et al* (1996, 12 June). School-associated violent deaths in the United States, 1992 to 1994. *Journal of the American Medical Association,* 275, pp 1729–33. Quoted is p 1733.

62 Lewin T (1998, 20 March). Study finds no rise in school crime. *New York Times.* Associated Press (1998, 20 March). Serious crime plagues 20% of U.S. schools. Washington.

63 Wilke A (1998, 27 March). School violence hysteria. Progressive Sociologists Network, posting, wilkeas@mail.auburn.edu.

64 Warchol G (1998, July). *Workplace Violence,* 1992–96. NCJ 168634. Rockville, MD: Bureau of Justice Statistics. Quoted is p 5.

65 Maguire K, Pastore AL (1997). *Sourcebook of Criminal Justice Statistics.* Washington, DC: U.S. Department of Justice, Table 3.38.

66 Bruan, Moehringer (1998), *op cit,* p A10.

67 Books S (1996, Fall). Stigmatization, scapegoating, and other discursive dangers in the lives of children and young people. *Proteus,* 13, p 13.

68 Elam S *et al* (1995). The 26th annual Phi Delta Kappa/Gallup Poll of the public's attitudes toward public schools. *Phi Delta Kappan,* 76, pp 41–56.

69 Woo E, Colvin RE (1998, 17 May). Why our schools are failing. *Los Angeles Times,* special report, section S.

70 Center for Media and Public Affairs (1996, July/August). Network news in the Nineties: The Top Ten topics and trends of the decade. *Media Monitor.*

71 Baker DP, Hsu SS (1998, 16 June). Two are shot at school in Richmond. *Washington Post,* pp A1, A16.

72 Donohue E, Schiraldi V, Ziedenberg J (1998, July). *School house hype: School shootings and the real risk kids face in America.* Washington, DC: Justice Policy Institute, p 21.

73 Criminal Justice Statistics Center (1977–96). Criminal Justice Profiles, Statewide. Sacramento, CA: Department of Justice.

74 Fellmeth RC (1998, 26 July). The 'crackdown on youth crime.' *Orange County Register,* Commentary, p 4.

75 Data Analysis Unit (1998, 28 July). New admissions to prison, 1997. Sacramento: Department of Corrections.

76 California Criminal Justice Statistics Center (1998). California Criminal Justice Profile 1997, Statewide. Sacramento: Department of Justice.

77 DiIulio JJ Jr (16 December 1995), *op cit.*

78 FBI (1998, 17 May). FBI reports less crime in U.S. for sixth straight year. Web posting. McDonnell PJ (1997, 7 June), *op cit.*

Chapter 2: Myth: Teens Need More Policing

1 Safe City/Safe Campus Program (1995). City of Monrovia, California.

2 Riccardi N (1997, 5 June). Small-town success. *Los Angeles Times,* p B14–15.

3 Enemy Alien Curfew Friday (1942, 24 March). *San Francisco News,* United Press International.

4 Richter P, Saar M (1996, 23 July). Anti-truancy law hailed by Clinton. Some students laud ordinance, others scoff. *Los Angeles Times,* pp A3, 14, 16.

5 *Harrahill et al vs Santoro and the City of Monrovia.* Case No. BC 170089, Superior Court, County of Los Angeles, 1997.

6 Johnson R, Monrovia Police Department, deposition in *Harrahill vs Santoro,* 8 January 1998.

7 Wilgoren J, Fiore F (1997, 2 December). Curfews cited for drop in juvenile crime rate. *Los Angeles Times,* pp A1, A26, A27.

8 Los Angeles Police Department (1998). Enhanced curfew enforcement effort. January and July.

9 Office of Juvenile Justice and Deliquency Prevention (1996, April). Curfew: An Answer to Juvenile Delinquency and Victimization? *Juvenile Justice Bulletin.* Washington, DC: U.S. Department of Justice.

10 Dolan M (1997). State high court allows injunctions to restrict gangs. *Los Angeles Times,* pp A1, A22, A34.

11 Lamb D (1997, 8 April). New approach stifles Boston's gang troubles. *Los Angeles Times*, pp A1, A18.

12 Males M, Macallair D (1998, September). The impact of juvenile curfew laws in California. *Western Criminology Review*, in press.

13 Marks R (1998, 16 July). Pros, cons of curfew debated. *Charleston Times*, pp 1A, 11A.

14 U.S. Supreme Court (1989). *Stanford v Kentucky*. 492 US 361.

15 Coalition for Juvenile Justice (1995). In Bender D, Leone B (1997). *Juvenile Crime: Opposing Viewpoints*. San Diego, CA: Greenhaven Press, p 185.

16 UN Convention on the Rights of the Child (1991, January). Melton GB (1993). In *The Rights of Children*. Greeley, CO: University of Northern Colorado, pp 6–20.

17 Ndiaye BW, in Turner C (1998, 4 April). UN study assails U.S. executions as biased. *Los Angeles Times*, pp A1, A8.

18 U.S. Supreme Court (1989), *Stanford v Kentucky*, *op cit*, dissenting opinion.

19 Cockburn A, Silverstein K (1996). *Washington Babylon*. London: Verso Press, p 288.

20 For summary and analysis, see, Editorial (1998, May). Better dead than S.10. *Youth Today*, p 2.

21 See review by Quadrel MJ, Fischhoff, Davis W (1993, February). Adolescent (in)vulnerability. *American Psychologist*, 48, pp 102–116.

22 Berk LE (1991). *Child Development* 2 ed. Boston: Allyn & Bacon, pp 238–41, 484–85.

23 Weithorn LA, Campbell SB (1982). The competency of children and adolescents to make informed treatment decisions. *Child Development*, 53, pp 1589–98.

24 Campos P (1998, 1 June). When a lemon drop equals a kilo of cocaine. *Los Angeles Times*, p B9.

25 Butts JA, Snyder HN (1997, September). The youngest delinquents: Offenders under age 15. *OJJDP Juvenile Justice Bulletin*, OCJ 165256, p 11.

26 Johnson K (1996, 13 December). Study eases fear of teen crime wave. *USA Today*, pp 1A, 4A.

27 Klein M (1995). *The American Street Gang: Its Nature, Prevalence, and Control*. New York: Vintage, p 165.

28 Davis M (1993). Who killed Los Angeles? Part Two: The verdict is given. *New Left Review*, 199, pp 29–54. Quoted is p 34.

29 Wilson P (1998, 3 February). Fact sheet: Stopping juvenile and gang crime. Sacramento: Office of the Governor.

30 Federal Bureau of Investigation (1997). *Uniform Crime Reports for the United States*, 1996. Washington: U.S. Department of Justice, Table 28.

31 Bureau of Justice Statistics (1996). *Criminal Victimization in the United States*, 1994. Washington: U.S. Department of Justice, Table 39.

32 See Blumstein A, in Wilson JQ, Petersilia J, editors (1995). *Crime*. San Francisco: Institute for Contemporary Studies, p 413–16.

33 Campaign for an Effective Crime Policy. What every policymaker should know about imprisonment and the crime rate. Washington, DC, pp 1, 9.

34 Ryan M (1998, 28 April). Before teenagers become criminals. *Parade Magazine*, p 16.

35 FBI (1996), *op cit*, Tables 28, 38.

36 Humes E (1996). *No Matter How Loud I Shout: A Year in the Life of Juvenile Court*. New York: Simon & Schuster, pp 34, 47, 261, 384.

37 California Task Force to Review Juvenile Crime and the Juvenile Justice Response (1996). *Final Report*. Sacramento and Riverside. pp 63, 80.

38 Letters (1998, 15 February). *Los Angeles Times Magazine*, p 8.

39 Education Fund to End Handgun Violence (1993). *Kids and Guns: A National Disgrace*. Washington, DC. Reprinted in Bender D, Leone B (1997). *op cit*, p 93.

40 Press release (1998, 25 March). In wake of Arkansas killings, new study finds juvenile homicides dropping. Washington, DC: Justice Policy Institute.

41 Goodstein L, Connelly M (1998, 30 April). Teen-age poll finds support for tradition. *New York Times*, pp A1, A18.

42 Emergency Preparedness and Injury Control (EPIC) Branch (1996). *Homicides: Californians under Age 18*. Sacramento: California Department of Health Services, Tables A2, B3, B4.

43 Edelman MW (1998, 28 March). Address to 25th annual conference, Children's Defense Fund. Los Angeles, CA.

44 Klein (1995), *op cit*, p 172.

45 Klein (1995), *op cit*, pp 138, 156, 234.

Chapter 3: Myth: Teens Are Druggie Wastoids

1 Davis M (1990). *City of Quartz: Excavating the Future in Los Angeles*. New York: Vintage Books, p 287.

2 Articles from the Springfield, Ohio, *News-Sun*, April 1996, provided by Gregg Fry, Springfield, Ohio, letter to *Progressive*.

3 Drug sniffing dogs kept on duty in schools. *Los Angeles Times* (1995, 15 June), p B3.

4 U.S. Supreme Court (1995, 29 June). *Vernonia School District v Acton*, 94-590. Also Savage DG (1995, 29 March). Justices consider school drug tests. *Los Angeles Times*, p A17.

5 Baum D (1996). *Smoke and Mirrors: The War on Drugs and the Politics of Failure*. Boston: Little Brown and Co., pp 206–07.

6 Savage DG (1997, 11 November). Supreme Court upholds students' strip searches. *Los Angeles Times*, p A33.

7 Substance Abuse and Mental Health Services Administration (1997, July). Drug Abuse Warning Network Annual Medical Examiner Data 1995. Rockville, MD: U.S. Department of Health and Human Services, p 11.

8 Fulwood S (1996, 20 October). Clinton says teens should pass drug test to get license. *Los Angeles Times*, pp A1, A33.

9 Gauck J (1997, September/October). Surveys shed light on inconsistencies of Drug War. *Youth*

Today, p 27.

10 Ferrell D (1996, 16 December). Scientists unlocking secrets of marijuana's effects. *Los Angeles Times*, pp A1, A20.

11 Goldberg C (1996, 21 August). Survey reports more drug use by teenagers. *New York Times*, p A8.

12 Nelson J (1996, 10 September). Teens, parents tolerating drug use, poll finds. *Los Angeles Times*, pp A1, A33.

13 Purer product, cheaper price: Smokable heroin floods U.S. (1997, 31 December). Boston: Reuters.

14 Morain D (1998, 21 January). Lt. Gov. Davis urges random drug tests in state's public schools. *Los Angeles Times*, pp A3, A17.

15 Nazario S (1997, 16–17 November). Orphans of addiction. *Los Angeles Times*, p A1 ff.

16 Substance Abuse and Mental Health Services Administration (1996, August). Historical Estimates from the Drug Abuse Warning Network. Rockville, MD: U.S. Department of Health and Human Services, pp 39–42.

17 Substance Abuse and Mental Health Services Administration (1997, July). Mid-year Preliminary Estimates from the 1996 Drug Abuse Warning Network. Rockville, MD: U.S. Department of Health and Human Services, pp 42–53.

18 Vital Statistics Section (1970–97). Vital Statistics of California (annual) and California Mortality Detail File (electronic). Sacramento: Department of Health Services.

19 Substance Abuse and Mental Health Services Administration (1995, January). Overview of the National Drug Treatment Unit Survey (NDATUS): 1992 and 1980–1992. Rockville, MD: U.S. Department of Health and Human Services, p 17.

20 McCaffrey B (1997, June). Teens, drugs and the media. PSAY Network, pp 1–2.

21 Substance Abuse and Mental Health Services Administration (1996, August). Preliminary Estimates from the 1995 National Household Survey on Drug Abuse. Rockville, MD: U.S. Department of Health and Human Services, p 31.

22 See cost estimates in Zimring FE, Hawkins G (1995). The Search for Rational Drug Control. Cambridge, UK: Cambridge University Press, p 42.

23 SAMSHA (1996, August), *op cit.*

24 SAMHSA (1996, August), *op cit.*

25 SAMSHA (1993). Annual Emergency Department Data. Rockville, MD: U.S. Department of Health and Human Services, p 34.

26 Rx for kids, teens key to boost of antidepressants, stimulants. American Medical Association News (1998, 23 February), p 12.

27 Breggin PR, Breggin GR (1998). *The War against Children of Color: Psychiatry Targets Inner-City Youth.* Monroe, ME: Common Courage Press, p 103.

28 SAMHSA (1997), *Annual Emergency Department Data, op cit*, Tables 2.06, 2.09.

29 Fulcher R (1996, 18 January). Bitter bong water: How the times they have a changed. Redondo Beach: *Easy Reader*, pp 12, 14.

30 Substance Abuse and Mental Health Services Administration (1997). National Household Survey on Drug Abuse: Population Estimates 1996. Rockville, MD: U.S. Department of Health and Human Services.

31 Gauck J (1997, September/October). Surveys shed light on inconsistencies of Drug War. *Youth Today*, p 27.

32 Jackson RL (1998, 15 February). Gingrich blasts Clinton's anti-drug plan. *Los Angeles Times*, p A29.

33 Nelson J (1996, 10 September). Teens, parents tolerating drug use, poll finds. *Los Angeles Times*, pp A1, A13.

34 Ostrow RJ (1998, 13 April). Parents underrate children's exposure to drugs. *Los Angeles Times*, p A14.

35 Whitmire R (1994, 13 December). Drug abuse rises among U.S. teens. Washington, DC: Gannett News Service.

36 Duncan DF, Nicholson T (1997). Dutch drug policy: A model for America? *Journal of Health & Social Policy*, 8, pp 1–15.

37 World Health Organization (1982–97). World Health Statistics Annual, 1980–95. Causes of death by sex and age. Geneva.

38 Editors (1995, 11 November). Deglamorising cannabis. *The Lancet*, 346, p 1241.

39 Kleber HD (1995, 23/30 December). Decriminalisation of cannabis. *The Lancet*, 346, p 1708.

40 World Health Organization (1997). *World Health Statistics Annual 1996.* Geneva: United Nations, Table 2B.

41 Reinarman C (1997). The drug policy debate in Europe: The case of *Califano vs The Netherlands*. *International Journal of Drug Policy*, 3. Web posting.

42 Zimring, Harris (1993), *op cit*, pp 6–7, 179–80.

43 Baum, *op cit*, p 222.

44 FBI, *Uniform Crime Reports 1996*, p 282.

45 Cunningham JK *et al* (1997). Heroin/Opioid-Related Hospital Admissions: Trends and Regional Variations in California (1986–1995). Irvine, CA: Public Statistics Institute, pp 22–23.

46 Cunningham JK *et al* (1996). Cocaine-Related Hospital Admissions: Trends and Regional Variations in California (1985–94). Irvine, CA: Public Statistics Institute, pp 18–19.

47 Baum, *op cit*, pp 33.

48 *Ibid*, pp 26–27.

49 *Ibid*, p 39.

50 National Commission on Marihuana and Drug Abuse (1973). *Drug Use in America: Problem in Perspective.* Second Report. Washington, DC: US Government Printing Office, pp 43–90.

51 Newcomb MD, Bentler PM (1988). Impact of adolescent drug use and social support on problems of young adults: A longitudinal study. *Journal of Abnormal Psychology*, 97, pp 64–75.

52 Shedler J, Block J (1990, May). Adolescent drug use and psychological health: A longitudinal inquiry. *American Psychologist*, 45, pp 612–630.

53 Zimmer L, Morgan JP (1997). *Marijuana Myths, Marijuana Facts.* New York: The Lindesmith Center, p 4.

54 Unselling heroin (1996, 30 July). *Los Angeles*

Times, p E1.

55 Baum, *op cit*, p 297.

56 Cooke J (1980, 28 September). Jimmy's world. *Washington Post*, p 1. Baum, *op cit*, pp 132–34.

57 Katz J (1997, 30 November). Old enemy stalks kids of privilege. *Los Angeles Times*, pp A1, A28.

58 Klaidman D, Leland J, Schoemer K (1996, 26 August). Rockers, models, and the new allure of heroin. The fear of heroin is shooting up. The politics of drugs: Back to war. *Newsweek*, pp 50–58.

59 Bass D (1997, 14 August). Poll finds sharp rise in drug use among youngsters. *Los Angeles Times*, A4.

60 Baum (1996), *op cit*, p 297.

61 Neergaard L (1995, 7 July). Marijuana use sends teens to hospital emergency rooms. Washington: Associated Press.

62 SAMSHA (1993), *op cit*, pp 32, 34, 50.

63 Marin Institute (1997, February). *Backgrounder*.

64 Musto DF (1991, July). Opium, cocaine and marijuana in American history. *Scientific American*, 265, pp 40–47.

65 Nelson J (1996), *op cit*.

66 Bailey E (1996, 16 September). Initiative on marijuana use pits unlikely opponents. *Los Angeles Times*, pp A1, A18.

67 See Baum, *op cit*, pp 281–82.

68 Baum D (1996), *op cit*, p 27.

69 *Time* (1996, 9 December). p 31.

70 Woldt BD (1996). Precursors, mediators and problem drinking: Path analytic models for men and women. *Journal of Drug Education*, 26, pp 1–12.

71 Lardner G (1998, 27 April). Drug abuse common link of jail inmates, study finds. *Los Angeles Times*, p A4.

72 Legislative Analyst's Office (1996, January). *Child Abuse and Neglect in California*, Part I. Sacramento: California State Legislature, p 9. See web posting.

73 Baum D (1996), *op cit*, p 263.

74 Hamilton N (1997, 10 November). Child welfare and substance abuse: Bridging the gap. *Children's Services Report*, 1, p 5.

75 Weber T (1998, 22 May). Dependency Court: Lives in balance. *Los Angeles Times*, pp A1, A30.

76 Weikel D (1997, 24 April). A grueling waiting game for addicts seeking help. *Los Angeles Times*, pp A1, A34–35.

77 Ostrow RJ (1993, 20 October). War on drugs shifting its focus to hard-core addicts. *Los Angeles Times*, p A26.

78 Ostrow RJ (1995, 15 December). GOP cuts hurt war on drugs, White House official says. *Los Angeles Times*, p A31.

79 Nazario S (1998, 16 May). 2 'orphans of addiction' in foster care. *Los Angeles Times*, pp A10–11.

80 Ellis V (1996, 29 December). Alcoholics, drug addicts to lose aid. *Los Angeles Times*, pp A1, A37.

81 McCoy AW, in Kutler SI, ed. (1996). *Encyclopedia of the Vietnam War*. New York: Charles Scribner's Sons, pp 178–82. Quoted is p 180.

82 Reifman A, Windle M (1996). Vietnam combat exposure and recent drug use: A national study.

Journal of Traumatic Stress, 9, pp 557–568.

83 Jackson RL (1998), *op cit*.

84 Associated Press (1998, 5 August). House leaders squash drug test idea. Washington, DC.

85 Sobieraj S (1998, 9 July). Federal anti-drug ads to be launched. Atlanta: Associated Press.

86 Riley JK *et al* (1998, July). *1997 Annual Report on Adult and Juvenile Arrestees*. NCJ 171672. Rockville, MD: National Institute of Justice.

87 Chen E (1998, 12 July). Meth use on rise in West as cocaine rates fall. *Los Angeles Times*, pp A1, A24.

88 Howe N, Strauss B (1993). *13th Gen: Abort, Retry, Ignore, Fail?* New York: Vintage Books, p 29.

89 Docuyanan F, Males M (1995, 8–14 December). Look who's dying. *Orange County Weekly*, pp 14–17).

90 Buckley WF (1983, 29 April). Commentary. *National Review*, p 495. Quoted in *Drug Sense Weekly* (Mark Greer, ed) (1998, 12 March).

91 Cimons M (1997, 31 December). Emergency room visits by drug addicts decline. *Los Angeles Times*, pp A3, A15.

92 Reuters (1998, 14 and 17 July). Amsterdam.

93 Kalish CB (1988, May). International crime rates. NCJ-110776. Rockville, MD: Bureau of Justice Statistics, special report.

94 Simons M (1998, 17 July). U.S. drug chief sees how Dutch manage liberal drug program. *New York Times*, website. Grunwald M (1998, 21 July). Drug chief mitigates slap at Dutch. *Washington Post*, p A2.

95 McCaffrey BR (1998, 27 July). Legalization would be the wrong direction. *Los Angeles Times*, p B7.

96 Reinarman (1997), *op cit*, p 2.

97 See Johnston *et al* (1996), *op cit*.

98 Scheer R (1998, 21 July). The drug war can't abide honest stats. *Los Angeles Times*, p B7.

Chapter 4: Myth: Teens Are Drunken Killers

1 Communications Works (1997, February). Issues we urge ABC to address. Letter. San Francisco.

2 Media and Policy Analysis Center (1994, February). *Backgrounder*. San Rafael, CA: Marin Institute for the Prevention of Alcohol and Other Drug Problems, p 2.

3 Substance Abuse and Mental Health Services Administration (1997, May). *Drug Abuse Warning Network Annual Medical Examiner Data 1995*. Rockville, MD: U.S. Department of Health and Human Services, Table 2.07.

4 Marin Institute for the Prevention of Alcohol and Other Drug Problems (1994, February). *Backgrounder*. San Rafael, CA.

5 Wechsler H *et al* (1994, 7 December). Health and behavioral consequences of binge drinking in college. *Journal of the American Medical Association*, 272, pp 1672–77.

6 Hodgson L (1997). *Raised in Captivity: Why Does America Fail Its Children?* St. Paul, MN: Graywolf Press, p 233.

7 Loveline (1998, 23 February). Burbank: KROQ-FM

radio.

8 National Highway Traffic Safety Administration (1997). Overview: Traffic Safety Facts 1996. Washington DC: U.S. Department of Transportation.

9 American Medical Association (1998). We've got a drinking problem: Youth and alcohol. Chicago, IL.

10 Zimring FE, Hawkins G (1995). *The Search for Rational Drug Control*. New York: Cambridge University Press, p 102.

11 Hazleton L (1997, 16 October). Fear is increasing on the roads, but that may not be a bad thing. *New York Times*, Special Section: Cars, p 2.

12 Johnston LD, Bachman JG, O'Malley PM (1997). *Questionnaire Responses from the Nation's High School Seniors to the Monitoring the Future Survey*. Ann Arbor, MI: University of Michigan, Institute for Social Research, p 46.

13 Substance Abuse and Mental Health Services Administration (SAMHSA). *National Household Survey on Drug Abuse: Population Estimates 1996*. Rockville, MD: U.S. Department of Health and Human Services, Table 13A.

14 Johnston LD (1997), *op cit*, p 49.

15 Mehren E (1997, 4 October). Spate of drinking deaths casts a pall over campuses. *Los Angeles Times*, pp A1, A13.

16 Johnston *et al* (1997), *op cit*, p 51.

17 National Highway Traffic Safety Administration (1997), *op cit*, p 2.

18 Asch PT, Levy DT (1987). Does the minimum drinking age affect traffic fatalities? *Journal of Policy Analysis and Management*, 6, pp 180–192.

19 Chen E (1998, 5 March). Senate presses states for tough drunk-driving standard. *Los Angeles Times*, p A14.

20 Blane H, Hewitt L (1977). *Alcohol and Youth—An Analysis of the Literature, 1960–1975*. NTIS #PB-268-698. Washington, DC: National Institute on Alcohol Abuse and Alcoholism.

21 SAMHSA (1996), *op cit*, Tables 13A, 22A.

22 Maddox GL (1964). Adolescents and alcohol. In McCarthy RG (ed). *Alcohol Education for Classroom and Community*. New York: McGraw-Hill, pp 35–37.

23 Lomask M (1954, March). First report on high school drinking. *Better Homes & Gardens*, pp 72–75, 139–142.

24 "The Accident:" Why? *Los Angeles Times Magazine*, (1996, 28 July).

25 Cook C (1994, 17 November). Author says giving children a little wine would help demystify use of alcohol. Chicago: Knight-Ridder News Service.

26 Paxman JM, Zuckerman RJ (1987). *Laws and Policies Affecting Adolescent Health*. Geneva: World Health Organization, p 155.

27 Ryan N, Kennedy S (1998, 3 January). Bones are rattled at Field as Rodman bash gets unruly. *Chicago Tribune*, pp 1, 6.

28 Walcoff M (1998). NYRA position paper: The drinking age. National Youth Rights Association, inter-

net posting.

29 Zucker R (1997). Paper to American Psychological Association, Annual Meeting, Los Angeles. Ann Arbor: University of Michigan, Alcohol Research Center. Rubenstein C (1997, 29 August). In comes parenthood, out goes drinking. *Oregonian*, pp C1, C10.

30 Department of Transportation (1986, 26 March). National Minimum Drinking Age. *Federal Register*, 51:58, pp 10376–81.

Chapter 5: Myth: Teens Are Camel Clones

1 Glantz SA *et al* (1996). *The Cigarette Papers*. Berkeley: University of California Press.

2 Glantz SA (1997, 23 June). What deal? We got suckered. *Los Angeles Times*, p B7.

3 Glantz SA (1996, February). Editorial: Preventing tobacco use—the youth access trap. *American Journal of Public Health*, 86, pp 156–157.

4 Dubin Z (1996, 1 October). Joe Camel an adults-only party animal, creator says. *Los Angeles Times*, pp A1, A12.

5 Johnston LD, O'Malley PM, Bachman JG (1997). *National Survey Results on Drug Use from the Monitoring the Future Study, 1975–1996*. Washington, DC: National Institute on Drug Abuse.

6 Morain D (1997, 26 March). Adult smoking rises sharply in California. *Los Angeles Times*, pp A1, A22–23.

7 Substance Abuse and Mental Health Services Administration. National Household Survey on Drug Abuse: Population Estimates 1996. Rockville, MD: Department of Health and Human Services, Table 14A.

8 Males M (1995). The influence of parental smoking on youth smoking: Is the recent downplaying justified? *Journal of School Health*, 65, pp 228–231.

9 Office on Smoking and Health (1994). Preventing Tobacco Use among Young People: A Report of the Surgeon General. Washington, DC; U.S. Department of Health and Human Services, pp 6–10, 28, 129–130.

10 Males M (1995), *op cit*.

11 Greenlund KJ *et al* (1997, August). Cigarette smoking attitudes and first use among third- through sixth-grade students: The Bogalusa Heart Study. *American Journal of Public Health*, 87, pp 1345–1348.

12 Brown BB. Peer groups and peer cultures. In Feldman SS, Elliott GR (1990). *At the Threshold: The Developing Adolescent*. Cambridge, MA: Harvard University Press, p 191.

13 Savin-Williams RC, Berndt TJ (1990), *ibid*, p 297.

14 Weinstein H (1998, 15 January). RJ Reynolds targeted youths, records show. *Los Angeles Times*, pp A1, A12, A14.

15 SAMHSA (1985–90), Johnston (1987–90), *op cit*.

16 Sargent JD *et al* (1997, December). Cigarette promotion items in public schools. *Archives of Pediatric and Adolescent Development*, 151, pp 1189–1196.

17 Monmaney T (1997, 15 December). Study links ciga-

rette gear, youth smoking. *Los Angeles Times*, pp A1, A26–27.

18 Pierce JP *et al* (1998, 18 February). Tobacco industry promotion of cigarettes and adolescent smoking. *Journal of the American Medical Association*, 279, pp 511–515.

19 Office on Smoking and Health (1994), *op cit*, p 130.

20 Doheny K (1998, 6 April). Science starting to tackle teen smoking. *Los Angeles Times*, p S11.

21 Rubin AJ (1998, 2 March). Tobacco ad curbs may be illegal, memo says. *Los Angeles Times*, p A14.

22 Horovitz B, Wells M (1997, 2 February). Ads for adult vices big hit with teens. *USA Today*, pp 1, 2, 4B, 5B.

23 Glantz SA (1996, February), *op cit*, p 156.

24 Rigotti NA, DiFranza JR *et al* (1997, 9 October). The effect of enforcing tobacco-sales laws on adolescents' access to tobacco and smoking behavior. *New England Journal of Medicine*, 337, pp 1044–51. For commentary on this study, see Haney DQ (9 October 1997). Surprise findings see health cost rise for nonsmokers. Boston: Associated Press.

25 Office on Smoking and Health (1986), *op cit*, p 91.

26 Fornier R (1995, 11 August). Analysis: Clinton hopes for political windfall. Washington, DC: Associated Press.

27 American Heart Association newspaper ad, 30 May 1996.

28 Associated Press (1998, 18 January). Clinton urges Congress to join anti-tobacco battle. *Los Angeles Times*, p A30.

29 Aligne CA, Stoddard JJ (1997, July). Tobacco and children: An economic evaluation of the effects of parental smoking. *Archives of Pediatric and Adolescent Medicine*, 151, pp 648–53.

30 DiFranza JR, Lew RA (1996, April). Morbidity and mortality in children associated with the use of tobacco products by other people. *Pediatrics*, 97, pp 560–568.

31 Centers for Disease Control and Prevention (1997, 17 December). State-specific prevalence of cigarette smoking among adults, and children's and adolescents' exposure to environmental tobacco smoke—United States, 1996. *Journal of the American Medical Association*, 278, pp 2056–2057.

32 U.S. Office of Health and Environmental Assessment (1992, December). *Respiratory Health Effects of Passive Smoking. Lung Cancer and Other Disorders*. Washington, DC: U.S. Environmental Protection Agency, p 1–1.

33 National Research Council (1986). Environmental Tobacco Smoke: Measuring Exposures and Assessing Health Effects. Washington, DC: National Academy Press, p 216.

34 Office on Smoking and Health (1994), *op cit*, p 28.

35 DiFranza and Lew (1996), *op cit*, p. 566.

36 CNN (1997, October 23).

37 Associated Press (1992, 18 June). Study: Secondhand smoke poses severe risks to children. Washington, DC.

38 National Center for Tobacco-Free Kids (1998). Tobacco Kills brochure.

39 Glantz (1996), *The Cigarette Papers*, pp 248–49, 392–93.

40 Elders J, in Office on Smoking and Health (1994), *op cit*, p iii.

41 Indiana Prevention Resource Center (1998). Tax burden on tobacco: U.S. historical data, 1955 to 1997. Internet posting.

42 Herbert B (1997, 12 December). Burning tobacco's victims. *New York Times*.

43 Fritz S, Richter P (29 August 1996). Poignant Gore tale stirs party; Clinton nominated to 2nd term. *Los Angeles Times*, pp A1, A21.

44 Bradley W (9 October 1996). A reality check on Al Gore. *Los Angeles Times*, p B9.

45 Fritsch J (1996, 6 July). Democrats as well as GOP profit from tobacco. *New York Times*, pp 1, 8.

46 Stolberg S, Richter P (1996, 28 July). Compromise on tobacco hinted. *Los Angeles Times*, p A18.

47 Levin M, Morain D (1998, 11 July). Memos afford inside look at California's tobacco war. *Los Angeles Times*, pp A1, A30.

48 Philip Morris *et al* (1998, 11 March). The tobacco settlement: What's in it for you? What's in it for us? Advertisement in the *Los Angeles Times* and other major papers.

49 Reich RB (1998, 10 April). Make tobacco firms cut teen smoking. *Los Angeles Times*, p B9.

50 Bureau of the Census (1996). Statistical Abstract of the United States 1995. Washington, DC: U.S. Department of Commerce, Tables 217, 1262.

51 Rubin AJ (1998, 19 March). Tobacco ads' impact debatable, except to some lawmakers. *Los Angeles Times*, p A5.

52 Canadian Dimensions (1998). Smokers by sex and age group. Statistics Canada, internet posting.

53 Glantz (1996, February), *op cit*, p 157.

54 Moon RW, Males MA, Nelson DE (1993). The 1990 Montana (United States) initiative to increase cigarette taxes: Lessons for other states and localities. *Journal of Public Health Policy*, 14, pp 19–33.

55 Levin M (1997, 13 September). The price of a puff. *Los Angeles Times*, pp D1, D9.

56 Rubin AJ (1998, June 18). Republicans in Senate kill tobacco bill. *Los Angeles Times*, pp A1, A29.

57 Rubin AJ (1998, 26 June). Kids targeted in GOP tobacco bill. *Los Angeles Times*, p A16.

58 Associated Press (1998, 9 October). Daily smoking by teens has risen sharply. *Washington Post*, p A3.

Chapter 6: Myth: Teen Moms Are Ruining America

1 Luker K (1996). *Dubious Conceptions: The Politics of Teenage Pregnancy*. Cambridge: Harvard University Press, p 73.

2 Luker (1996), *op cit*, p 73.

3 Luker (1996), *op cit*, p 256.

4 Luker (1996), *op cit*, p 174.

5 Luker (1996), *op cit*, p 86.

6 Barabak M (1998, 13 September). Gary Bauer: A virtue vulture circles as the president's woes mount.

Los Angeles Times, p M3.

7 Alan Guttmacher Institute (1994). *Sex and America's Teenagers*. New York: AGI, p 70.

8 Boyer D, Fine D (1992). Sexual abuse as a factor in adolescent pregnancy and child maltreatment. *Family Planning Perspectives*, 24, pp 4–11, 19.

9 Males M, Chew KSY (1996, April). The ages of fathers in California adolescent births, 1993. *American Journal of Public Health*, 86, pp 565–568.

10 Luker (1996), *op cit*, p 170.

11 Guttmacher and National Center for Health Statistics, Pregnancies by Outcome, Age of Woman, and Race, in Bureau of the Census (1998). *Statistical Abstract of the United States 1997*. Washington DC: U.S. Department of Commerce.

12 Brownstein R, Lauter D (1993, 12 December). Clinton aides find welfare vow easier said than done. *Los Angeles Times*, pp A1, A18.

13 *Rochester Democrat and Chronicle* (1996, 2 May), p 1; *Rochester Times-Union* (1996, 1 May), p 8A.

14 Durning AT, Crowther CD (1997). *Misplaced Blame: The Real Roots of Population Growth*. Seattle: Northwest Environment Watch, p 32.

15 Legislative Analyst's Office (1996, January). Child Abuse and Neglect in California, Part I. Sacramento, CA: California State Legislature, p 5. See web posting.

16 Luker K (1996). *Dubious Conceptions: The Politics of Teenage Pregnancy*. Cambridge: Harvard University Press, p 192.

17 Hotz VJ, McElroy SW, Sanders SG (1995, March). *The Costs and Consequences of Teenage Childbearing for Mothers*. Chicago: Irving B. Harris Graduate School of Public Policy Studies, University of Chicago.

18 Musick (1993), *op cit*, p 43.

19 Musick JS (1993). *Young, Poor, and Pregnant: The Psychology of Teenage Motherhood*. New Haven, CT: Yale University Press, pp 87–88.

20 Alan Guttmacher Institute (1994), *op cit*, pp 28, 73.

21 Gershenson HP, Musick J *et al* (1989). The prevalence of coercive sexual experiences among teenage mothers. *Journal of Interpersonal Violence*, 4, pp 204–19.

22 Boyer & Fine (1992), *op cit*.

23 Herrera R, Tafoya N (1995, 17 November). Teen sex—who's got the power? Workshop at National Organization on Adolescent Pregnancy, Parenting, and Prevention, Phoenix, AZ. Las Cruces, NM: La Clinica de Familia Community Health Centers.

24 Whitman D, Cooper M (1994, 20 July). The end of welfare—sort of. *US News & World Report*, pp 28–37.

25 Alan Guttmacher Institute (1994), *op cit*, pp 28, 73.

26 Vobejda B (1997, 7 June). Teens improve on prevention of pregnancy. *Washington Post*, pp A1, A9.

27 Freud S (1896, 21 April). The aetiology of hysteria. Translated by Masson JM (1985). *The Assault on Truth*. New York: Penguin Books, Appendix B.

28 Children Now (1995). *California: The State of Our Children 1995*. Oakland, CA, p 20.

29 Durning and Crowther (1997), *op cit.*, pp 34–35.

30 Albelda R *et al* (1996). *The War on the Poor*. New York: Center for Population Economics, p 50.

31 See Ash DO (1997). *Face to Face with Fathers: A Report on Low-Income Fathers and Their Experience with Child Support Enforcement*. Chicago: Center on Fathers, Families and Public Policy.

32 Miller KS, Clark LF, Moore JS (1997, September/October). Sexual initiation with older male partners and subsequent HIV risk behavior among female adolescents. *Family Planning Perspectives*, 29, pp 212–214.

33 Taylor D, Chavez G, Chabra A, Boggess J (1997, February). Risk factors for adult paternity in births to adolescents. *Obstetrics & Gynecology*, 89, pp 199–205.

34 Lamb M, Elster AB, Tavare J (1986). Behavioral profiles of adolescent mothers and partners with varying intracouple age differences. *Journal of Adolescent Research*, 1, pp 399–408.

35 Musick (1993), *op cit*, p 89 (quoted); pp 44–47, 84–99.

36 Elstein SG, Davis N (1997, October). *Sexual Relationships between Adult Males and Young Teen Girls: Exploring the Legal and Social Response*. Washington, DC: American Bar Association, pp 6–7.

37 Lait M, Romney L (1996, 1 September). Agency helps some girls wed men who impregnated them. She's 13, he's 20; Is it love or abuse? *Los Angeles Times*, pp A1, A34, A36.

38 Lait M (1996, 11 September). Teen-adult weddings draw more criticism. *Los Angeles Times*, pp A1, A11.

39 Smith L (1997). Queen of responsibility. *Los Angeles Times*, pp E1, E4.

40 Elstein SG, Davis N (1997, October). *Sexual Relationships Between Adult Males and Young Teen Girls: Exploring the Legal and Social Issues*. Washington, DC: American Bar Association, pp 2–5.

41 Lindberg LD, Sonenstein FL, Ku L, Martinez G (1997, May/June). Age differences between minors who give birth and their adult partners. *Family Planning Perspectives*, 29, pp 61–66.

42 Donovan P (1997, January/February). Can statutory rape laws be effective in preventing adolescent pregnancy? *Family Planning Perspectives*, 29, p 31.

43 Hodgson L (1997), *op cit*, pp 125–30.

44 Curtis B (aired 16 July, 1998). The Amy Fisher Story. Arts & Entertainment channel.

45 Ellertson C (1997, August). Mandatory parental involvement in minors' abortions: Effects of the laws in Minnesota, Missouri, and Indiana. *American Journal of Public Health*, 87, pp 1367–1374.

46 Donovan P (1983). Judging teenagers: How minors fare when they seek court-authorized abortions. *Family Planning Perspectives*, 15, pp 259–267.

47 Lynch M (1998, Summer). Enforcing "statutory rape"? *The Public Interest*, 132, pp 3–16.

48 See discussion in Hodgson L (1997). *Raised in Captivity: Why Does America Fail Its Children?* St. Paul, MN: Graywolf Press, pp 118–19.

49 Hodgson L (1997), *op cit.*

50 Kaiser Family Foundation, YM Magazine (1998). *National Survey of Teens: Teens Talk about Dating, Intimacy, and Their Sexual Experiences*. Menlo Park, CA: Kaiser.

51 Goldberg H (1994, 18 May). Students report regret about sexual activity. New York: Associated Press.

52 Moore KA, Driscoll A, Child Trends (1997). *Partners, Predators, Peers, Protectors: Males and Teen Pregnancy.* Washington, DC: National Campaign to Prevent Teen Pregnancy.

53 Hodgson L (1997). *Raised in Captivity: Why Does America Fail Its Children?* St. Paul, MN: Graywolf Press, p 196.

54 Maynard RA ed. (1997). *Kids Having Kids: Economic Costs and Social Consequences of Teen Pregnancy.* Washington, DC: Urban Institute Press. Quoted is p 309; (1996). *Kids Having Kids: A Robin Hood Foundation Special Report on the Costs of Adolescent Childbearing.* New York: Robin Hood Foundation (summary report).

55 Boyer, Fine (1992), *op cit*, p 10.

56 Burt MR (1986, September/October). Estimating the public costs of teenage childbearing. *Family Planning Perspectives*, 18, pp 221–226.

57 Herrnstein RJ, Murray C (1994). *The Bell Curve.* New York: The Free Press.

58 Ventura SJ et al (1995, 21 September). *Advance Report of Final Natality Statistics, 1993.* Atlanta, GA: Centers for Disease Control, Table 44.

59 Ventura SJ (1995). *Births to Unmarried Mothers: United States, 1980–92.* Series 21, #53. Hyattsville, MD: National Center for Health Statistics, p 22.

60 *Ibid*, pp 11–12.

61 Hotz VJ, McElroy SW, Sanders SG (1997). The impacts of teenage childbearing on the mothers and the consequences of those impacts for government. In Maynard RA (1997), *op cit*, pp 55–94. Quoted are pp 71, 74, 77, 81 83, 85.

62 Cooper RT (1997, 24 May). Contrary take on teen pregnancy. *Los Angeles Times*, pp A1, A22–23.

63 Albelda R et al (1996). *The War on the Poor.* New York: Center for Population Economics, p 69.

64 Cooper RT (1997), *op cit*, p A22.

65 Stiffman AR et al (1990). Pregnancies, childrearing, and mental health problems in adolescents. *Youth & Society*, 21, pp 483–495.

66 Ventura SJ et al (1995), *op cit.*, Tables 28, 32.

67 Bayatpour M et al (1992). Physical and sexual abuse as predictors of substance use and suicide among pregnant teenagers. *Journal of Adolescent Health*, 13, pp 128–132.

68 Males M (1994, July). In defense of teenage mothers. *Progressive*, p 23.

69 Luker (1996), *op cit*, p 170.

70 Zill N, Nord CW (1994). *Running in Place.* New York: Child Trends, Inc., pp 82–83.

71 Luker (1996), *op cit*, p 171.

72 DeParle J (1994, 22 March). Clinton target: Teenage pregnancy. *New York Times*, p 11.

73 Luker K (1997), *op cit*, p 40.

74 Woodman S (1995, May). How teen pregnancy has become a political football. *Ms.*, p 92.

75 Murray C (1994, Spring). Does welfare bring more babies? *The Public Interest*, pp 20, 23.

76 Foster H (1996, 4 November). Committing to a future for our teens. Syracuse, NY: Keynote address to the Central New York Council on Adolescent Pregnancy.

77 Stan AM (1998, 11 October). Have we sold out feminists, or forgotten how to call a jerk a jerk? *Los Angeles Times*, p M5.

78 Solomon N (1998, 18 March). Sex-scandal coverage evades Clinton contradictions. Washington: Creator's Syndicate. Ehrenreich B, quoted.

79 Healy M (1997, 1 March). Clinton frees $250 million for sex abstinence teaching. *Los Angeles Times*, p A13.

80 Shogren E, Ostrow RJ (1998, 18 April). Clinton admits to deception. He calls relationship with Lewinsky "wrong." *Los Angeles Times*, p A1.

81 "A *Times* Staff Writer" (1998, 28 January). Morris' talk about Clinton's sex lives stuns White House. *Los Angeles Times*, p A15.

82 Bates KG (1998, 4 October). Choices and consequences. *Los Angeles Times*, p M5.

83 Ciabbatari J (1998, 4 January). Is Newt's Congress failing at marriage? *Parade Magazine*, p 16.

84 Press B. (1998, 17 March) Widow's tale is last straw for Clinton. Will G. The charge of recklessness sticks at last. *Los Angeles Times*, p B7.

85 Cockburn A, Silverstein K (1996). *Washington Babylon.* London: Verso, pp 249–301.

86 Shogan R (1998, 24 January). Doubts about Clinton's personal integrity reach critical mass. *Los Angeles Times*, p A25.

87 Peterson J, Shogren E (1998, 18 March). Public split on whether to believe Willey, Clinton. *Los Angeles Times*, pp A1, A10.

88 Schneider W (1998, 5 April). Private matters, public affairs. *Los Angeles Times*, p M3.

89 Lerner M (1998, 25 September). A day of atonement for the market-induced ethos of selfishness. *Los Angeles Times*, p B9.

90 *Youth Today* (1997, June–July). Unwed teen moms called "plague on the nation." p 41.

91 National Campaign to Prevent Teen Pregnancy (May 1997). *Whatever Happened to Childhood? The Problem of Teen Pregnancy in the United States.* Washington, DC. Quoted are pp 11–13, 16.

92 Wolff EN (1995). *Top Heavy: The Increasing Inequality of Wealth in America and What Can Be Done About It.* New York: New Press, pp 67–69.

93 National Center for Health Statistics (1997). Marriage and Divorce Statistics 1989–1995 (CD-ROM). Also, *Marriage and Divorce* (years 1988 and before). Volume III. *Vital Statistics of the United States.* Washington, DC: U.S. Department of Health and Human Services, Tables 2-25, 2-46.

94 Rivera C (1998, 28 July). Area's changing face: More women and children living on LA's skid row. *Los Angeles Times*, pp A3, A15.

95 White House Office of National AIDS Policy (1996, 5 March). *Teenagers and AIDS.* Washington, DC: White House.

96 Centers for Disease Control and Prevention (1994, December). Facts about Adolescents and HIV/AIDS. Atlanta: CDCP, p 2.

97 Conway GA et al (1993, 9 June). Trends in HIV

prevalence among disadvantaged youth. *Journal of the American Medical Association*, 269, pp 2887–2889.

98 Wendell DA *et al* (1992, January). Youth at risk: Sex, drugs, and human immunodeficiency virus. *American Journal of Diseases of Children*, 146, pp 76–81.

99 Rosenberg P (1995, 24 November). Reports. *Science*, 270, 1372.

100 Statistics Canada (1998). Canada HIV and AIDS statistics by age and sex. Internet posting.

101 Associated Press (1998, 1 May). Teen birth rates drop across the nation, analysis finds. Washington, DC.

102 Kirby D (1997). *No Easy Answers: Research Findings on Programs to Reduce Teen Pregnancy*. Washington DC: National Campaign to Prevent Teen Pregnancy.

103 Musick (1993), *op cit*, pp 13, 14, 109.

104 Baby Think It Over, ad, *Youth Today* (1998, May), p 7.

Chapter 7: Myth: Teens Are Reckless, Suicidal, and "At Risk"

1 Getze G (1972, 14 April). Many child poisonings not accidents, psychiatrist says. *Los Angeles Times*, pp II-1, II-8.

2 Select Committee on Children and Youth (1981, 16 October). *Youth suicide*. Public Hearings. Sacramento, CA: California State Senate, pp 123, 126.

3 See report of Select Committee on Children, Youth and Families (1985, 6 June). Emerging Trends in Mental Health Care for Adolescents. Washington, DC: U.S. House of Representatives, 99th Congress. Also, discussion and references in Males M (1996). *The Scapegoat Generation: America's War on Adolescents*. Monroe, ME: Common Courage Press, pp 243–53.

4 *Ibid.*

5 School Climate Unit (1987). Suicide Prevention Program for California Public Schools. Sacramento, CA: California Department of Education, p 1.

6 Gleick E (1996, 22 July). Suicide's shadow. *Time*, pp 39–42.

7 Planned Parenthood, and Adolescent Wellness Task Force (1997, 25 September). *The Role of Adolescent Health Care in the California Children's Health Program*. Los Angeles: California Family Health Council.

8 Terman L (1913, January). The tragedies of childhood. *The Forum*, 49, pp 41–47.

9 Nazario S (1997, 9–10 March). Children who kill themselves; A grim trend. Schools struggle to teach lessons in life and death. *Los Angeles Times*, pp A1 ff.

10 Henry T (1997, 3 February). A CD-Rom to 'save lives.' *USA Today*, p 4D.

11 Males M (1991, Fall). Teen suicide and changing cause-of-death certification, 1953-1987. *Suicide & Life-Threatening Behavior*, 21, pp 245–259.

12 Gist R, Welch QB (1989). Certification change versus actual behavior change in teenage suicide rates, 1955–1979. *Suicide & Life-Threatening Behavior*, 19, pp 277–287.

13 Bayatpour M *et al* (1992). Physical and sexual abuse as predictors of substance use and suicide among pregnant teenagers. *Journal of Adolescent Health*, 13, pp 128–132.

14 Shogren E (1993, 20 October). Survey of top students reveals sex assaults, suicide attempts. *Los Angeles Times*, p A22.

15 Berk L (1991). *Child Development*. Boston: Allyn & Bacon, p 445.

16 Hall GS (1904). *Adolescence: Its Psychology and Its Relation to Physiology, Anthropology, Sociology, Sex, Crime, Religion, and Education*. New York: D. Appleton, p xiv.

17 York P, York D, Wachtel T (1982). *Toughlove*. New York: Doubleday.

18 Baum (1996), *op cit*, p 155.

19 Holmbeck GN, Hill JP (1988). Storm and Stress beliefs about adolescence: Prevalence, self-reported antecedents, and effects of an undergraduate course. *Journal of Youth and Adolescence*, 17, pp 285–306.

20 Offer D, Schonert-Reichl KA (1992). Debunking the myths of adolescence: Findings from recent research. *Journal of the American Academy of Child & Adolescent Psychiatry*, 31, pp 1003–1014.

21 Offer (1981), *op cit*, pp 2–4, 63, 65; Offer (1987), *op cit*, p 3408.

22 Johnston LD *et al* (1997). *Questionnaire Responses from High School Seniors. Monitoring the Future Survey*. Ann Arbor, MI: University of Michigan, Institute for Social Research, p 8.

23 Goodstein L, Connelly M (1998, 30 April). Teen-age poll finds support for tradition. *New York Times*, pp A1, A18.

24 Offer, Schonert-Reichl (1992), *op cit*, p 1004.

25 Adelson J (1979, February). Adolescence and the generalization gap. *Psychology Today*, 12, pp 33–34, 37.

26 Horne AM, Sayger TV (1990). *Treating Conduct and Oppositional Defiant Disorders in Children*. New York: Pergamon Press, p 34.

27 Kearns R (1998, May). Finding profit in at-risk kids. *Youth Today*, pp 1, 10–11.

28 Chauncey RL (1980, Winter). New careers for moral entrepreneurs: Teenage drinking. *Journal of Drug Issues*, 22, pp 45–70.

29 Males M (1994, May). *The roles of knowledgeability, political inclination, and neuroticism in mediating graduate and undergraduate students' attitudes toward adolescents*. Thesis, available from author.

30 Hill RF, Fortenberry JD (1992). Adolescence as a culture-bound syndrome. *Social Science & Medicine*, 35, pp 73–80. Quoted is p 75.

31 Offer D, Ostrov E, Howard KI (1981). The mental health professional's view concept of the normal adolescent. *AMA Archives of General Psychiatry*, 38, pp 149–153.

32 Buchanan CM *et al* (1990). Parents' and teachers' beliefs about adolescents: Effects of sex and experience. *Journal of Youth and Adolescence*, 19, pp 363–94.

33 Hill, Fortenberry (1992), *op cit*, p 78.

34 Enright RD *et al* (1987). Do economic conditions influence how theorists view adolescents? *Journal of*

Youth and Adolescence, 16, pp 541–59.

35   Lauter D (1997, 28 October). Man infects 9 with AIDS virus in semirural N.Y. *Los Angeles Times*, pp A1, A15.

36   Musick JS (1993). *Young, Poor, and Pregnant: The Psychology of Teenage Motherhood*. New Haven, CT: Yale University Press, p 89.

37   Discussed by Dr. Drew Pinsky on "Loveline" (1997, 3 November). Los Angeles: KROQ-FM radio. "Loveline" was not the show where the girls appeared.

38   Smokes S (1997, November 7). *USA Today*, p. 25A.

39   Roan S (1995, 11 July). Having the first baby doesn't stop the cycle. *Los Angeles Times*, p E6.

40   Males M (1998, February). Adult partners and adult contexts of "teenage sex." *Education and Urban Society*, 30, pp 189–206.

41   Zeifman D (1997, 7 November). Who's minding the baby? *Los Angeles Times*, p B9.

42   Nauss DW (1997, 4 December). Seat belts often take a back seat. *Los Angeles Times*, pp A1, A36, A37.

43   Adler N (1993, April). Sense of invulnerability doesn't drive teen risks. *APA Monitor*, p 15.

44   Quadrel MJ, Fischhoff B, Davis W (1993, February). Adolescent (in)vulnerability. *American Psychologist*, 48, pp 102–116.

45   Offer D (1987, 26 June). In defense of adolescents. *Journal of the American Medical Association*, 257, pp 3407–08.

46   Jacobs *et al* (1993), *op cit*, p. 114.

47   Yurgen-Todd's statements are reported in Hotz RL (1998, 25 June). Rebels with a cause. *Los Angeles Times*, p B2.

48   Petri HL (1990). *Motivation: Theory, Research, and Applications*, 3rd edition. Belmont, CA: Wadsworth Publishing, p 122.

49   Carnegie Council on Adolescent Development (1995). *Great Transitions: Preparing Adolescents for a New Century*. New York: Carnegie Corporation. Quoted are pp 9, 24, 29–30, 63, 91, 100.

50   Bureau of the Census (1996). Statistical Abstract of the United States 1995. Washington, DC: U.S. Department of Commerce, Table 204.

51   Office of Juvenile Justice and Delinquency Prevention (1995, 1996). Juvenile Offenders and Victims: A National Report, and 1996 Update on Violence. Washington, DC: U.S. Department of Justice, p 1 (1996) and p 29 (1995).

52   Alan Guttmacher Institute (1994), *op cit*.

53   Teens are spending more, saving little (1997, 21 September). *Parade Magazine*, p 14. Our good teenagers (1959, 23 November). *Newsweek*, p 62.

54   Resnick MD *et al* (1997, 10 September). Protecting adolescents from harm: Findings from the National Longitudinal Study on Adolescent Health. *Journal of the American Medical Association*, 278, pp 823–832. Quotes are from pp 823, 831.

55   Zill N, Nord CW (1994). *Running in Place: How American Families Are Faring in a Changing Economy and an Individualistic Society*. Washington, DC: Child Trends, Inc. Quotes are from pp 1–2, 31, 82–83.

56   Turner CF (1998, 8 May). Speaking more freely about risky behaviors. *Science*.

57   National Research Council (1993). *Losing Generations: Adolescents in High-Risk Settings*. Washington, DC: National Academy Press, p 84.

58   Goodman P (1956). *Growing Up Absurd*. New York: Vintage Books, p 119.

59   Gladwell M (1998, 17 August). Do parents matter? *New Yorker*, pp 54–64.

60   Harris JR (1995, July). Where is the child's environment? A Group Socialization theory of development. *Psychological Review* 102, pp 458–89.

61   *Ibid*, p 471.

62   Colburn D (1998, 21 February). Kid's health care fares poorly in poll. *Los Angeles Times*, p S8.

Chapter 8: Myth: The Media Tell the Truth about Youth

1   Cole KC (1997, 3 April). What's the price of a life? Society hazards a guess. *Los Angeles Times*, p B2.

2   Talk of the Nation (1998, 3 August). Washington DC: National Public Radio.

3   Fatal Accident Reporting System (1998). Traffic Safety CD-ROM. BTS-CD-10. Washington, DC: U.S. Department of Transportation. Driver and person files.

4   Solomon N (1998, 8 January). "Teen People" and the souls of young folks. Creators Syndicate.

5   Giroux HA (1997). *Channel Surfing: Race Talk and the Destruction of Today's Youth*. New York: St. Martin's Press, p 2.

6   Rorty R (1998). *Achieving Our Country: Leftist Thought in Twentieth-Century America*. Cambridge, MA: Harvard University Press, pp 94–95.

7   Hazen D, Winokur J editors (1997). *We the Media: A Citizens' Guide to Fighting for Media Democracy*. New York: New Press. Quoted are pp 42, 51, 64, 88–89, 94, 97–98.

8   Bourdieu P (1998). *On Television*. New York: The New Press (English translation).

9   See findings and references in Offer D, Schonert-Reichl KA (1992). Debunking the myths of adolescence: Findings from recent research. *Journal of the American Academy of Child & Adolescent Psychiatry*, 31, pp 1003–14.

10   Warner KE *et al* (1992, 30 January). Cigarette advertising and magazine coverage of the hazards of smoking. *New England Journal of Medicine*, 326, pp 305–09.

11   Hotz RL (1998, 4 May). Boomers firing magic bullets at signs of aging. *Los Angeles Times*, pp A1, A28–29.

12   My calculations from American Society of Plastic Surgeons Internet postings.

13   Offer D (1996, 17 July). Letter to author. Chicago: Northwestern University Medical School, Department of Psychiatry and Behavioral Sciences.

14   Centers for Disease Control (1994, 4 November). Cigarette smoking among women of reproductive age—United States, 1987–1992. *Morbidity and Mortality Weekly Report*, pp 789–91.

15   Pierce JP (1991, 11 December). Does tobacco advertising target young people to start smoking? *Journal of the American Medical Association*, 266, pp 3154–58.

16 Spoiled rotten kids (1995, December). *Extra! Update*, p 3.

17 The Eastside boys (1997, July 20). *Los Angeles Times Magazine*.

18 Klein M (1995). *The American Street Gang*. New York: Oxford, p 69.32 Zimring FE, Hawkins G (1992). *The Search for Rational Drug Control*. Cambridge, UK: Cambridge University Press, p 102.

19 Weingarten M (1998, 26 July). Large and in charge. *Los Angeles Times Calendar*, pp 8–9.

20 Shakur T (1995, 1996). *Shorty wanna be a thug. All Eyez on Me. So many tears. Me Against the World*. Deathrow, Interscope Records.

21 Hendrickson M (1997, 18 September). Grapevine. *Rolling Stone* 769, p 38.

22 *World Alamanac and Book of Facts* 1998, p 260.

23 Hoynes W (1997, May/June). News for a captive audience. *Extra!*, pp 11–17. Quoted are pp 11, 15, 17.

24 Miller MC (1997, May/June). How to be stupid: The lessons of Channel One. *Extra!*, pp 18–23. Quoted are pp 18, 20, 21, 22, 23.

25 Fox RF (1996). *Harvesting Minds: How TV Commercials Control Kids*. Westport, CN: Praeger. Quoted are pp 80, 128, 145–46, 154, 155, 164.

26 Bureau of the Census (1998). *Statistical Abstract of the United States*. Washington, DC: U.S. Department of Commerce.

27 National Center for Education Statistics (1997). *Digest of Education Statistics 1997*. Washington, DC: U.S. Department of Education, p 3.

28 Monmaney T (1998, 25 March). Study links TV viewing, obesity in children. *Los Angeles Times*, pp A1, A19.

29 National Center for Health Statistics (1997). *Health United States 96–97*. Hyattsville, MD: U.S. Department of Health and Human Services, tables 72, 73.

30 Carson RC, Butcher JN (1992). *Abnormal Psychology and Modern Life*, 9th ed. New York: HarperCollins Publishers, pp 242–48. Quoted is p 245.

31 *Ibid*, p 243. See also Berk LE (1991), *op cit*, pp 184–85.

32 Barson M, Heller S (1998). *Teenage Confidential*. San Francisco: Chronicle Books.

33 Cordes H (1998, 27 April). Generation wired. *The Nation*, p 12.

34 Zimring FE, Hawkins G (1992) *The Search for Rational Drug Control*. Cambridge, UK: Cambridge University Press, p 102.

35 Huffstutter P (1998, 30 March). Censors and sensibility. *Los Angeles Times*, pp D1, D8.

36 Katz J (1997). *Virtuous reality: How America surrendered discussion of moral values to opportunists, nitwits and blockheads like William Bennett*. New York: Random House, pp 82–84.

37 *Los Angeles Times* (1998, 23 July). Child sex cases over the Web are soaring, police say. p A10.

38 Katz (1997), *op cit*, p xiv, xvi–ii, xix, xx.

39 Giroux H (1997), *op cit*, pp 56–57.

40 Youth Vision (1995). *Adult attitudes toward youth: Chicago area adults' perceptions of youth 10 to 18*. Chicago: Youth Vision.

41 Dorfman L, Woodruff K, Chavez V, Wallack L (1997, August). Youth and violence on local television news in California. *American Journal of Public Health*, 87, pp. 1311–16.

42 Epstein B (1996, 2 November). Gang killing leads to "Lost Future." *Los Angeles Times*, p F2.

43 Rosin H (1997, 2 June). Tupac is everywhere. *New York Magazine*, pp 17–18.

44 Moore DW (1994, September). Majority advocate death penalty for teenage killers. *Gallup Poll Monthly*, pp 2–4.

45 Perrone PA, Chesney-Lind M (1997, draft). *Media presentations of juvenile crime in Hawaii, 1987–1996: Wild in the streets?* Social Justice, in press.

46 FBI (1997). *Uniform Crime Reports for the United States*. Washington, DC: U.S. Department of Justice, Tables 1, 28.

47 Hewitt B *et al* (1997, 15 December). A day in the life. *People*, pp 48–58.

48 Hadly S (1997, 6 July). String of slayings unnerves safest urban county in the West. *Los Angeles Times*, pp A3, A10.

49 Zamichow N (1998, 19 July). The fractured life of Jeremy Strohmeyer. *Los Angeles Times*, pp A1, A24–26.

50 Willon P (1998, 7 July). Mother charged with murder in 4 girls' deaths. *Los Angeles Times*, pp A3, A24.

51 Associated Press (1998, 25 June). Mission Viejo mom held in son's death. *Los Angeles Times*, p A18.

52 Abrahamson A, Martin H (1998, 5 August). Father of 3 kills estranged wife, children, himself. *Los Angeles Times*, pp A3, A20.

53 See Hodgson L (1997). *Raised in Captivity: Why Does America Fail Its Children?* St. Paul, MN: Graywolf Press, pp 40–41.

54 Sullivan R (1997, 4 September). Lynching in Malibu. *Rolling Stone*, pp 45–62, 78–82. Quoted are pp 58–59, 81.

55 Colford PD (1998, 4 August). Retailers rebuff cover girl in the buff. *Los Angeles Times*, p E2.

56 Scheff D (1988, 5 May). Sex, drugs & rock'n'roll. *Rolling Stone*, p 57.

57 *Parade* (1998, 3 May). TV special explores sex, music and the generation gap, p 14.

58 National Center for Health Statistics (1997). *U.S. Mortality Detail File, 1994–95* (latest available) compared to 1974–75. Calculated are homicides by white race/ethnicity and for all races, ages 12–19, for Oregon, the 19 states with 90 percent-plus Euro-white ethnicity, and all states. Washington, DC: U.S. Department of Health and Human Services.

59 Breggin PR, Breggin GR (1998). *The War Against Children of Color*. Monroe, ME: Common Courage Press. (1994). *Talking Back to Prozac*. New York: St. Martin's Press.

60 Neilsen Media Research (1997, May). *The World Almanac and Book of Facts 1998*. Mahwah, NJ: World Almanac Books, p 260.

61 Criminal Justice Statistics Center (1996). *California Criminal Justice Profile 1995, Los Angeles County*. Sacramento, CA: Department of Justice.

62 Hayes B, Martelle S (1998, 2 April). Files detail

teen's work for Brea police. *Los Angeles Times*, pp A1, A10–11.

63 Chesney-Lind M, Shelden RG, Joe KA (1986). Girls, delinquency, and gang membership. *In Gangs in America* (2nd edition). Thousand Oaks, CA: Sage Inc. p 186.

64 Mehren E (1996, 5 September). Mixed messages. Girl trouble: America's overlooked crime problem. *Los Angeles Times*, p E1.

65 Criminal Justice Statistics Center (1996 update). *California Criminal Justice Profile, Los Angeles County*. Sacramento: Department of Justice.

66 Chesney-Lind *et al* (1996), *op cit*, pp 201, 203, 204.

67 Heath SB, DeWitt S (1996). *Truths to Tell: Youth and Newspaper Reading*. St. Petersburg, FL: Poynter Institute for Media Studies. Quoted are pp 8, 9, 10, 11.

68 Paddock RC (1994, 1 March). Children say media give negative view of youth. *Los Angeles Times*, pp A1, A19.

Chapter 9: Myth: Young People Are Not Oppressed

1   Strauss W, Howe N (1991). *Generations: The History of America's Future, 1584 to 2069*. New York: Quill, pp 325–27.

2   Bureau of the Census (1996). *Statistical Abstract of the United States 1995*. Washington, DC: U.S. Department of Commerce, table 1228; Money Income in the United States 1996, table 4.

3   Bureau of the Census (1996). *Poverty in the United States 1995*. P60/194. Washington: U.S. Department of Commerce, Table C-2.

4   Strauss, Howe (1991), *op cit*, p 327.

5   Davis M (1990). *City of Quartz: Excavating the Future in Los Angeles*. New York: Vintage Books, pp 304–06.

6   Albelda R *et al* (1996). *The War on the Poor*. New York: Center for Population Economics, p 68; Census Bureau (1996). *Statistical Abstract of the United States 1995*. Washington, DC: U.S. Department of Commerce, table 522.

7   Easterlin RA (1980). *Birth and Fortune: The Impact of Numbers on Personal Welfare*. New York: Basic Books, p 134.

8   Holinger PC, Offer D, *et al* (1994). *Suicide and Homicide among Adolescents*. New York: Guilford Press, p 80.

9   Snyder TD, Shafer LL (1996). *Youth Indicators*. NCES 96-027. Washington, DC: U.S. Department of Education, Table 22.

10 Bureau of the Census (1996). *Money Income in the United States 1995*. P60/193. Washington: U.S. Department of Commerce, Table 1 and previous annual, 1975–94.

11 Howe N, Strauss W (1993). *13th Gen: Abort, Retry, Ignore, Fail?* pp 99, 113.

12 Edelman, P (1997, March). The worst thing Bill Clinton has done. *Atlantic*, pp 43–58.

13 Wolff EN (1995). *Top Heavy: The Increasing Inequality of Wealth in America and What Can Be Done About It*. New York: New Press, pp 1, 15, 17.

14 Wolff (1995), *op cit*, p 69.

15 Weinberg DH (1996, June). *A brief look at postwar U.S. income inequality*. Current Population Reports P60/191. Washington, DC: U.S. Department of Commerce, pp 1, 3.

16 Duncan GJ *et al* (1996, November). Economic mobility of young workers in the 1970s and 1980s. *Demography*, pp 497–509.

17 Allahar AL, Cote JE (1994). *Generation on Hold: Coming of Age in the Late Twentieth Century*. Toronto: Stoddart Publishing Co. Quoted is pp 66–67.

18 Deaton AS, Paxson CH (1997) The effects of economic and population growth on national saving and inequality. *Demography*, 34, pp 97–114.

19 Wise DA (1997). Retirement against the demographic trend: More older people living longer, working less, and saving less. *Demography* 34, pp 83–95.

20 Bureau of the Census (1975). *Historical Statistics of the United States: Colonial Times to 1970*. Washington, U.S. Department of Commerce, p 356.

21 Maharidge D (1996). *The Coming White Minority: California's Eruptions and the Nation's Future*. New York: Times Books, Random House.

22 Davis M (1988). Beyond "Blade Runner:" Urban core control, the ecology of fear. Westfield, NJ: *Open Magazine* pamphlet series, p 15.

23 Jones MWM (1995, 3 April). Voting for local school taxes in California: How much do demographic variables such as race and age matter? San Francisco: Paper presented to the Population Association of America annual meeting, p 7.

24 Kozol J (1991). *Savage Inequalities: Children in America's Schools*. New York: Crown Publishers, pp 220–21.

25 Irvine Company (1998, May). The story behind Irvine's excellent schools. Planning Ahead. Brochure mailed to district residents.

26 Woo E, Colvin RL (1998, 17 May). Why our schools are failing. *Los Angeles Times*, special report, p S7.

27 Barron C (1998, 5 October), In class, 45's a crowd. *Los Angeles Times*, p B2.

28 Simon S (1998, 26 May). 20 years later, Prop. 13 still has big impact. *Los Angeles Times*, pp A1, A12–13.

29 National Research Council (1993). *Losing Generations: Adolescents in High-Risk Settings*. Washington, DC: National Academy Press, p 106.

30 Council on Education (1995, January). *Investing in American Higher Education: An Argument for Restructuring*. New York: CAE, p 13.

31 Rawls JJ, Bean W (1993). *California: An Interpretive History* (sixth edition). New York: McGraw-Hill, Inc., pp 500–01.

32 Howe, Strauss (1993), *op cit*, p 77.

33 Binder A (1994, 9 October). UCI policy for future should not hinge on research dollars. *Los Angeles Times*, p B9.

34 Kenny SS *et al* (1998). *Reinventing Undergraduate Education: A Blueprint for America's Research Universities*. Carnegie Foundation for the Advancement of Teaching. Online at www.sunysb.edu/boyerreport.

35 College Board, in CNN (1998, 7 October). College

cost increases outpace inflation. CNN web posting.

36 Cooper RT (1998, 7 May). Clinton, Congress clash on student loan issue. *Los Angeles Times*, pp A30–31. Editorial (1998, 5 June). New approach to student loans. *Los Angeles Times*, p B10.

37 A summary of the most recent figures on social spending can be found in Bureau of the Census (1997). *Statistical Abstract of the United States 1997*. Washington, DC: U.S. Department of Commerce, pp 116–17, 372–88.

38 See, for example, Special issue: Ageism on the agenda (1997 March/April). *Extra!*

39 Pine A (1998, 30 April). Are Americans overtaxed? *Los Angeles Times*, p A5.

40 Bureau of the Census (1997). *Measuring the Effects of Benefits and Taxes 1996*. Washington, DC: U.S. Department of Commerce.

41 Healy M (1998, 13 March). Study says poverty persists for kids of working poor. *Los Angeles Times*, p A21.

42 RAND (1995–96, Winter). Social Security reform: Touching the rail. *Research Review*, 19, p 3.

43 Rosenblatt RK (1998, 25 March). Latinos key to Social Security. *Los Angeles Times*, p A21.

44 Albelda R, Folbre N (1996). *The War on the Poor*. New York: Center for Population Economics, p 29.

45 Reimer H, Cuomo C (1997, April). The generation gambit. *Extra!*, p 14.

46 Peterson PG (1993). *Facing Up: How to Rescue the Economy from Crushing Debt and Restore the American Dream*. New York: Simon & Schuster, pp 84, 237.

47 Sciacchitano K (1997, 3 February). Divide and conquer. *In These Times*, pp 21–23.

48 Hess JL (1993). Clinton taking scalpel to the wrong patient. *New York Observer*.

49 Edelman P (1997), *op cit*, p 48.

50 *Times* Poll. A look at the electorate (1994, 11 November). *Los Angeles Times*, p A5.

51 Profile of the electorate (1998, 4 June). *Los Angles Times*, p A34.

52 Skelton G (1992, 27 October). Times Poll: Voters evenly split over proposal to cut welfare. *Los Angeles Times*, pp A1, A18.

53 Reimer H, Cuomo C (1997, March/April). The generation gambit: The Right's imaginary rift between young and old. *Extra!*, p 15.

54 Dreyfuss R (1996, November/December). The end of Social Security as we know it. *Mother Jones*, pp 50–58. Peterson J, McManus D (1997, 27 December). White House split over fixing Social Security plan. *Los Angeles Times*, pp A1, A17.

55 Dreyfuss (1996), *op cit*.

56 Henwood D (1997, March/April). Bogus crisis, bogus solution. *Extra!*, p 6.

57 Baker D (1996, 23 December). Granny-bashing. *In These Times*, pp 32–35.

58 Richtman M (1998, February). Let's preserve Social Security. *Solidarity* (United Auto Workers International Union), p 24.

59 Kotlikoff LJ, Sachs JD (1998, 5 April). Fix Social Security for good. *Los Angeles Times*, p M5.

60 Children Now (1998). *Report Card 1997: Spotlight on California's counties*. Oakland, CA: Children Now, p 5.

61 Wolff (1995), *op cit*, p 46.

62 Hess JL (1991). Finding gold in gray hair. *Extra!* Reprint supplied by author.

63 My previous book, *The Scapegoat Generation* (Common Courage Press, 1996), argues in four different places against cutting Social Security or Medicare. Samples:

It is not the cost of the old, but the politics of the old, that is the problem (p. 280).

If distributed equitably, spending one-third of the federal budget on the care of Americans over age 65 would be a fine idea. These grayed citizens have worked all of their lives and deserve some payback, one which would be easier to bear if the federal penchant for Aid to Perpetually Dependent Corporations (APDC) and Defense Industry Subsidy Stamps (DISS) weren't so potent acronyms for congressional protection. The problem is not caused by senior welfare per se, which (if made more progressive) would be a model for family assistance programs. The problem is that today's seniors are not responding to the unprecedented security they are receiving at public expense with a like attitude of beneficence toward the young and poor, but with hostility and contempt (p. 40).

The purpose of this comparison is not to begrudge the large majority of the elderly their modest subsidies—not if the large majority of the elderly whose own well-being is tied to welfare would forcefully inform politicians terrorized by elder voting power that the government better not begrudge poor children their more modest subsidies, either. Let's not try to argue that 70-year-olds deserve welfare but seven-year-olds born to dark-hued young moms deserve to go hungry in the streets (p. 83).

The problem is not the amount of money seniors receive from public coffers, even though senior welfare is so maldistributed that 12 percent of the nation's seniors (the highest rate in the industrial world) remain in poverty even after Social Security, Medicare, and the myriad of tax breaks are figured in. The problem is the hostile attitudes today's seniors display toward extending the generous welfare they receive to younger families and children (p. 37).

Chapter 10: Myth: Teens Are in "Moral Meltdown"

1 Giroux HA (1997). *Channel Surfing: Race Talk and the Destruction of Today's Youth*. New York: St. Martin's Press, pp 16, 37, 86.

2 Hewlett SA, West C (1998). *The War Against Parents: What We Can Do for America's Beleaguered Moms and Dads*. Boston: Houghton Mifflin.

3 West C (1998, 7 May). Keynote. A different world: Media images of race and class. Los Angeles: Children Now's Fifth Annual Children and the

Media Conference. Oakland, CA: Children Now.

4   Howe and Strauss (1993). *13th Gen: Abort, Ignore, Retry, Fail?* pp 42–43.

5   Books S (1996, Fall). Stigmatization, scapegoating, and other discursive dangers in the lives of children and young people. *Proteus*, 13, p 14.

6   Phillips K (1995, 29 October). On a collision course. *Los Angeles Times*, p M6.

7   Kyriacou DN (1997, 28 October). Presentation to California Wellness Foundation lecture series, University of California, Los Angeles. See also Krikorian G (1997, 28 October). Joblessness is principal cause of gang epidemic, L.A. study says. *Los Angeles Times*, p A12.

8   Farkas S, Johnson J (1997). *Kids These Days: What Americans Really Think about the Next Generation.* New York: Public Agenda Foundation.

9   Howe and Strauss (1993), *op cit*, p 213.

10 See for examples Marcosson IF (1936, September). Our muddled youth. *American Magazine*, pp 24–25, 109–12. Leighton GR, Hellman R (1935, August). Half-slave, half-free: Unemployment, the depression, and American young people. *Harper's Magazine*, pp 343–53.

11 Applebome P (1996, 26 June). Children score low in adults' esteem, a study finds. *New York Times*.

12 Wolfe A (1997). *One Nation, After All: What Middle-Class Americans Really Think About: God, Country, Family, Poverty, Racism, Welfare, Homosexuality, Immigration, The Left, The Right and Each Other.* New York: Viking. Davidson OG (1998, 8 March), pp 116–32, 288–89.

13 Strauss and Howe (1991). *Generations: The History of America's Future, 1584 to 2069.* New York: William Morrow, pp 312, 314.

14 Strauss W, Howe N (1997). *The Fourth Turning.* New York: Broadway Books, p 231.

15 Davidson OG (1998, 8 March). Middle-Class muddle. *Los Angeles Times Book Review*, p 5.

16 A Westside story for the '90s (1997, 12 December). *Los Angeles Times*, p A48.

17 Bradley B (1997, 3 August). Help America's children. *Parade Magazine*, pp 4–5.

18 Ellis BE, Rossi M, Bernstein J (1996, June/July). *George*, pp 96–102.

19 Garcia R (1997, 17 September). Why are we so afraid of our children? Anderson Valley (California) *Advertiser*, p 7. Cited by Davis, S. (1997).

20 Wilson WJ (1996). *When Work Disappears: The World of the New Urban Poor.* New York: Vintage Books, pp 159–60.

21 See Palmer JL, Smeeding T, Torrey BB (1988). *The Vulnerable.* Washington, DC: Urban Institute Press.

22 Wilson WJ (1996), *op cit*, p 162.

23 Gilliam F (1998, 7 May). Panelist, "From the newsroom to the living room: How media influence public policies concerning children." Presentation to Fifth Annual Children and the Media Conference, Los Angeles. Oakland, CA: Children Now.

24 Hodgson L (1997). *Raised in Captivity: Why Does America Fail Its Children?* St. Paul, MN: Graywolf Press, pp 138, 241.

25 Bureau of Justice Statistics (1998, 15 October). *Fact Sheet: Joint Justice Department and Education Department report shows most crime against students occurs away from schools.* Washington, DC: Bureau of Justice Statistics, press release.

26 Meyer L (1998, 23 March). A textbook case of student violence. *Los Angeles Times*, p A5.

27 Friedman D (1998, 15 March). How smart are Americans? *Los Angeles Times*, pp M1, M6.

28 National Center for Education Statistics (1997). *Digest of Education Statistics 1997.* Washington, DC: U.S. Department of Education, p 3 and Table 6. Children Now (1997). Report Card: Spotlight on California Counties. Oakland, CA: Children Now, p 15.

29 Galbraith JK (1958). *The Affluent Society.* New York: Mentor, p 256.

30 Pyle A, Smith D (1998, 19 May). Not good enough. *Los Angeles Times*, p R2.

31 Woo E, Colvin RL (1998, 17 May). Why our schools are failing. *Los Angeles Times*, pp S7–8.

32 Baldwin J (1965, 17 February). The American Dream is at the expense of the American Negro. *New York Times Magazine*, p 32.

33 Giroux (1997), *op cit*, p 2.

34 Strauss W, Howe N (1991), *op cit*, pp 340–41.

35 Fritz M (1998, 19 February). States put brakes on teenage drivers. *Los Angeles Times*, p A1.

36 Davis M (1990). *City of Quartz: Excavating the Future in Los Angeles.* New York: Vintage Books, p 227.

37 Davis M (1998). *Ecology of Fear: Los Angeles and the Imagination of Disaster.* Metropolitan Books. See Hines TS (1998, 16 August). The eve of destruction. *Los Angeles Times Book Review*, p 3.

38 Davis SG (1997). Space Jam: Family values in the entertainment city. Paper presented at the American Studies Annual Meeting, Washington, DC. University of California, San Diego.

39 Mainzer S (1998, 8 October). Raving is not a crime. Press release, Zen Muzik/Intersound, Los Angeles.

40 Voegler K (1998, 14 October). Juvenile arrests (under 18), New York State, 1980 through 1989 and 1990 through 1996. By race and ethnicity. Albany: Division of Criminal Justice Services.

41 Criminal Justice Statistics Center (1990–97). *California Criminal Justice Profiles, San Francisco County.* Sacramento: Department of Justice.

42 San Francisco School District (1998, 31 August). Take issue. Bay TV.

43 Whitman D (1997, 5 May). The youth "crisis." *U.S. News & World Report*, pp 24–27.

44 Strauss W, Howe N (1991), *op cit*, p 335.

45 Strauss W, Howe N (1997), *op cit*.

46 Alan Guttmacher Institute (1998, 15 October). Teen pregnancy rates at lowest level in 20 years. New York: press statement.

47 Goodstein L, Connelly M (1998, 30 April). Teen-age poll finds support for tradition. *New York Times*, p A18.

48 Powers A (1998, 29 April). Who are these people, anyway? *New York Times*, p 8.

49 Howe, Strauss (1993), *op cit*, p 137, 143, 144.

50 Murr A (1997, 1 December). Didn't seem like much. *Newsweek*, p 37.

51 See Finnegan W (1997, 1 December). The unwanted. *The New Yorker*, pp 60 ff.

52 CNN (1998, 13 June). Clinton visits Oregon school hit by May shooting. Springfield, OR; Associated Press (CNN web posting).

53 Marcosson (1936, September), *op cit*; Leighton and Hellman (1935), *op cit*.

54 Lacy LA (1976). *The Soil Soldiers: The Civilian Conservation Corps in the Great Depression*. Radnor, PA: Chilton Book Co., pp 19–20.

55 Roosevelt FD (1936, 13 April). Address to Young Democrats. Baltimore, MD. *Vital Speeches of the Day* (1936, 20 April), p 442.

56 Males M (1985, January–February). Youth Conservation Corps: What is this thing called WORK? *Montana Magazine*, pp 59–63.

57 Connell R, Lopez RJ (1996, 17 November). An inside look at 18th Street's menace. *Los Angeles Times*, pp A1, A36–37, A39.

58 Thomas, K (1998, 19 October). Teen ethics: more cheating and lying. *USA Today*, p D1.

59 Sawhill IV (1998, October). Teen pregnancy prevention: Welfare reform's missing component. Policy Brief #38, National Campaign to Prevent Teen Pregnancy. Brookings Institutions website.

60 COTO. *Los Angeles Times* advertising supplement, periodically, 1996–98.

61 Wimsatt WU (1994). *Bomb the Suburbs*. Seattle: Subway and Elevated Press Co., pp 99, 110.

62 Provided by Robin Templeton, *The Beat Within*, San Francisco.

63 Midnight Oil (1985). Sleep. *Red Sails in the Sunset*. New York: CBS Records.

Index

About the Author

Mike Males, once expelled from the second grade, is now a doctoral candidate in social ecology at the University of California, Irvine. He serves on the California Wellness Foundation Adolescent Health Advisory Board, and has written extensively on youth and social issues in publications such as *The New York Times*, *The Lancet*, *Phi Delta Kappan* and *In These Times*. His first book, *The Scapegoat Generation*, was hailed by Alexander Cockburn as "excellent...Buy Males's great book."

FOR MORE GREAT BOOKS AND INFORMATION

Award-Winning Common Courage Press has been publishing exposés and authors on the front lines since 1991. Authors include

- Louise Armstrong
- Judi Bari
- Peter Breggin
- Joanna Cagan
- Noam Chomsky
- Neil deMause
- Laura Flanders
- Jennifer Harbury

- Jeffrey Moussaieff Masson
- Margaret Randall
- John Ross
- Ken Silverstein
- Norman Solomon
- Cornel West
- Howard Zinn
- and many others

Also available: the dynamite **The Real Stories Series** of small books from **Odonian Press** including titles from Noam Chomsky and Gore Vidal.

FOR BULK DISCOUNTS CALL 800-497-3207

For catalogs and updates, call 800-497-3207.
Email us at **orders-info@commoncouragepress.com**.
Send us your email address if you want news about forthcoming books sent
    directly to you.

Write us at
Common Courage Press
Box 702
Monroe, ME 04951
Or visit our website at **www.commoncouragepress.com**.

CALL FOR MANUSCRIPTS

We are always looking for new manuscripts and ideas for books. Please don't hesitate to put us in touch with potential authors, or to give us ideas for books you'd like to read.

CALL FOR RESUMES

We are a hard-charging publishing house hacking away at injustice and propaganda by turning pens into political swords. We're not always hiring, but we're always on the lookout for those who share and can further our mission. If this sounds like it may be for you, please mail a resume and cover letter. Or **fax 207-525-3068**. Please do not call regarding employment possibilities; we might be deluged.